MW00574477

Teacher's Edition

by
Robert H. Marshall
Donald H. Jacobs

AGS Publishing
Circle Pines, Minnesota 55014-1796
800-328-2560
www.agsnet.com

About the Authors

Robert H. Marshall, M.Ed., teaches high school physics and algebra for the Baltimore School for the Arts. He is coauthor of several AGS textbooks including *Earth Science, General Science,* and *Matter, Motion, and Machines.*

Donald H. Jacobs, M.Ed., taught mathematics for many years in the Baltimore City Public Schools. He is currently with the Upton Home and Hospital School Program in the technology department. Other AGS textbooks that he has coauthored include *Basic Math Skills, Life Skills Math,* and *General Science.*

Photo and illustration credits for this textbook can be found on page 398.

The publisher wishes to thank the following consultants and educators for their helpful comments during the review process for *Physical Science.* Their assistance has been invaluable.

Rebecca Abreu, Science Teacher, Timber Creek High School, Orlando, FL; **Bonnie Buratti,** Research Astronomer, Jet Propulsion Laboratory, California Institute of Technology, Pasadena, CA; **Barbara Cassius,** Science Resource Teacher, Hoover High School, San Diego, CA; **Norman Gelfand,** Physicist, Fermi National Accelerator Laboratory (Fermilab), Batavia, IL; **Brian P. Johnson,** Science Teacher, Centennial High School, Centerville, MN; **Gary A. Mansergh,** Ed.D., Inquiry-Science Coach, Professional Development Center for Academic Excellence, St. Paul, MN; **Thomas E. Rock,** Teacher, John Marshall High School, San Antonio, TX; **Lorraine S. Taylor,** Ph.D., Professor of Special Education, State University of New York at New Paltz, New Paltz, NY; **Katherine L. Turley,** Specific Learning Disabilities Teacher/Ex. Ed. Curriculum Leader, Timber Creek High School, Orlando, FL; **Dr. Alex Vera,** Science Teacher, Templeton Secondary School, Vancouver, BC, Canada

Editorial services provided by Creative Services Associates, Inc.

Publisher's Project Staff

Vice President, Product Development: Kathleen T. Williams, Ph.D., NCSP; Associate Director, Product Development: Teri Mathews; Senior Editor: Julie Maas; Development Assistant: Bev Johnson; Senior Designer/Illustrator: Diane McCarty; Creative Services Manager: Nancy Condon; Project Coordinator/Designer: Laura Henrichsen; Desktop Production Artist: Peggy Vlahos; Purchasing Agent: Mary Kaye Kuzma; Senior Marketing Manager/Secondary Curriculum: Brian Holl

© 2004 AGS Publishing
4201 Woodland Road
Circle Pines, MN 55014-1796
800-328-2560 • www.agsnet.com

AGS Publishing is a trademark and trade name of American Guidance Service, Inc.

Printed in the United States of America

ISBN 0-7854-3625-1

Product Number 93922

A 0 9 8 7 6 5

Contents

Physical Science

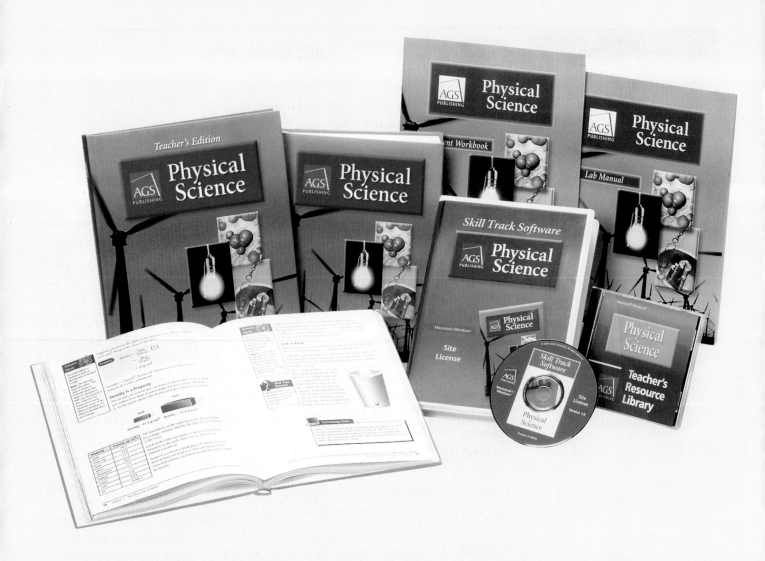

Physical Science is designed to help students and young adults learn the properties of matter, elements, compounds, electricity, sound and light, and more. Written to meet national standards, it offers students who read below grade level the opportunity to practice working with data and sharpen their abilities to infer, classify, and theorize. Throughout the text, comprehension is enhanced through the use of simple sentence structure and low-level vocabulary.

The textbook's short, concise lessons hold students' interest. Clearly stated objectives given at the beginning of each lesson outline what students will learn in the lesson. Examples and illustrations aid in students' understanding of the content presented. Lesson Reviews and Chapter Reviews offer some open-ended questions to encourage students to use critical thinking skills. Hands-on Investigations and Science in Your Life activities lead students to apply the skills they are learning to everyday life. Full-color photographs and illustrations add interest and appeal as students learn key physical science concepts.

Skill Track Software The Skill Track software program allows students using AGS Publishing textbooks to be assessed for mastery of each chapter and lesson of the textbook. Students access the software on an individual basis and are assessed with multiple choice items.

Students can enter the program through two paths:

Lesson
Six items assess mastery of each lesson.

Chapter
Two parallel forms of chapter assessments are provided to determine chapter mastery. The two forms are equal in length and cover the same concepts with different items. The number of items in each chapter assessment varies by chapter, as the items are drawn from content of each lesson in the textbook.

The program includes high-interest graphics to accompany the items. Students are allowed to retake the chapter or lesson assessments over again at the instructor's discretion. The instructor has the ability to run and print out a variety of reports to track students' progress.

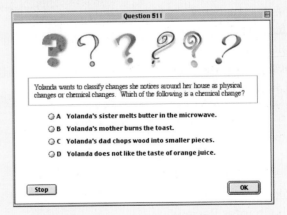

Student Text Highlights

◆ Each lesson is clearly labeled to help students focus on the skill or concept to be learned.

◆ Vocabulary terms are bold-faced and then defined in the margin and in the Glossary.

◆ Notes in the margin reinforce lesson content.

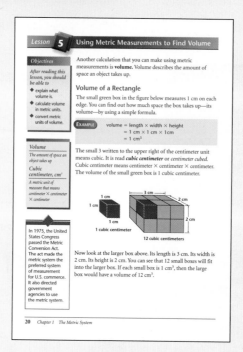

Lesson 5 Using Metric Measurements to Find Volume

Objectives

After reading this lesson, you should be able to
◆ explain what volume is.
◆ calculate volume in metric units.
◆ convert metric units of volume.

Volume
The amount of space an object takes up

Cubic centimeter, cm³
A metric unit of measure that means centimeter × centimeter × centimeter

Another calculation that you can make using metric measurements is **volume.** Volume describes the amount of space an object takes up.

Volume of a Rectangle

The small green box in the figure below measures 1 cm on each edge. You can find out how much space the box takes up—its volume—by using a simple formula.

EXAMPLE volume = length × width × height
= 1 cm × 1 cm × 1cm
= 1 cm³

The small 3 written to the upper right of the centimeter unit means cubic. It is read *cubic centimeter* or *centimeter cubed.* Cubic centimeter means centimeter × centimeter × centimeter. The volume of the small green box is 1 cubic centimeter.

1 cm — 1 cm — 1 cm
1 cubic centimeter

3 cm — 2 cm — 2 cm
12 cubic centimeters

In 1975, the United States Congress passed the Metric Conversion Act. The act made the metric system the preferred system of measurement for U.S. commerce. It also directed government agencies to use the metric system.

Now look at the larger box above. Its length is 3 cm. Its width is 2 cm. Its height is 2 cm. You can see that 12 small boxes will fit into the larger box. If each small box is 1 cm³, then the large box would have a volume of 12 cm³.

20   Chapter 1   The Metric System

Volume

The amount of space an object takes up

Cubic centimeter, cm³

A metric unit of measure that means centimeter × centimeter × centimeter

Science and technology are not the same thing. Science is a study of the world in which we live. Technology uses science to create tools and techniques that solve practical problems.

◆ Goals for Learning at the beginning of each chapter identify learner outcomes.

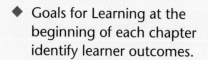

Goals for Learning

◆ To explain what matter and energy are

◆ To tell why measurement is important

◆ To use the basic metric units of length, volume, and mass

◆ To explain the meaning of prefixes used with metric units of measurements

◆ To calculate area and volume, using metric units

◆ To convert metric units

◆ Chapter Reviews allow students and teachers to check for skill mastery. Multiple-choice items are provided for practice in taking standardized tests.

◆ Test-Taking Tips at the end of each Chapter Review help reduce test anxiety and improve test scores.

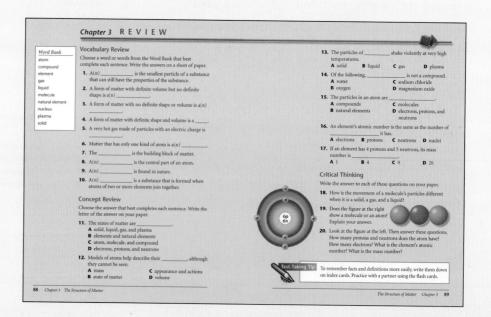

Chapter 3 REVIEW

Vocabulary Review

Word Bank
atom
compound
element
gas
liquid
molecule
natural element
nucleus
plasma
solid

Choose a word or words from the Word Bank that best complete each sentence. Write the answers on a sheet of paper.

1. A(n) _____ is the smallest particle of a substance that can still have the properties of the substance.

2. A form of matter with definite volume but no definite shape is a(n) _____.

3. A form of matter with no definite shape or volume is a(n) _____.

4. A form of matter with definite shape and volume is a _____.

5. A very hot gas made of particles with an electric charge is _____.

6. Matter that has only one kind of atom is a(n) _____.

7. The _____ is the building block of matter.

8. A(n) _____ is the central part of an atom.

9. A(n) _____ is found in nature.

10. A(n) _____ is a substance that is formed when atoms of two or more elements join together.

Concept Review

Choose the answer that best completes each sentence. Write the letter of the answer on your paper.

11. The states of matter are _____.
A solid, liquid, gas, and plasma
B elements and natural elements
C atom, molecule, and compound
D electrons, protons, and neutrons

12. Models of atoms help describe their _____, although they cannot be seen.
A mass
B state of matter
C appearance and actions
D volume

13. The particles of _____ shake violently at very high temperatures.
A solid   B liquid   C gas   D plasma

14. Of the following, _____ is not a compound.
A water   C sodium chloride
B oxygen   D magnesium oxide

15. The particles in an atom are _____.
A compounds   C molecules
B natural elements D electrons, protons, and neutrons

16. An element's atomic number is the same as the number of _____ it has.
A electrons   B protons   C neutrons   D nuclei

17. If an element has 4 protons and 5 neutrons, its mass number is _____.
A 1   B 4   C 9   D 20

Critical Thinking

Write the answer to each of these questions on your paper.

18. How is the movement of a molecule's particles different when it is a solid, a gas, and a liquid?

19. Does the figure at the right show a molecule or an atom? Explain your answer.

20. Look at the figure at the left. Then answer these questions. How many protons and neutrons does the atom have? How many electrons? What is the element's atomic number? What is the mass number?

Test-Taking Tip To remember facts and definitions more easily, write them down on index cards. Practice with a partner using the flash cards.

88   Chapter 3   The Structure of Matter

The Structure of Matter   Chapter 3   89

Technology Note

The scanning electron microscope, or SEM, uses electron beams to look at very small items. The SEM makes a sharply detailed, 3–D picture. An SEM picture can show an item up to 200,000 times bigger than it is. The item is magnified so much that you can see molecules.

Achievements in Science

The Metric System

The metric system is the first standardized system of measurement based on the decimal. Before the metric system, units of length, area, and weight varied from country to country. Ways of measuring were sometimes different even within a country. England had three different systems. In order to trade goods fairly, merchants and tradesmen needed a uniform system. Scientists needed a way to exchange information.

In France, the idea of the metric system first was suggested around 1670. No action was taken, however, for more than 100 years. In the 1790s, the French Academy of Sciences proposed a new system of measurement. The revolutionary assembly adopted the metric system in 1795.

At first, the people of France had a hard tim[e]   m. For a time in the early 1800s, France went back to the old   837, the metric system became the rule in France. Soon oth   e world began using the metric system.

Did You Know?

Hydrogen and helium are the two lightest elements. They exist in great quantities in the universe. Stars are composed mostly of these two elements.

Science Myth

Gases do not have mass.

Fact: A gas is one of the four states of matter. All matter has mass, even if we cannot see the matter.

Science in Your Life

How do different heating systems work?

How can you control the temperature of your home? The chart describes some types of heating systems. People use these types of heating systems to keep their homes at a comfortable temperature.

Heating Systems		
Type of System	Description	How Heat Travels
Hot water 	A furnace heats the water. A pump circulates the water through pipes to a radiator in each room.	Convection and radiation circulate heat throughout the room.
Steam	A boiler sends steam to pipes. Steam forces the heat through the pipes to radiators in each room.	Radiation and convection circulate heat throughout the room.
Forced air	Air is heated by a furnace. It is then pumped into rooms through vents at the floor of each room.	Forced convection circulates heat throughout the room.
Passive solar	The sun[ ]a large [ ]heat up [ ]Heat rad[ ]from the[ ]convecti[ ]	
Radiant electric	Electric [ ]in baseb[ ]ceilings.	

1. Which heating systems heat a
2. Which heating systems provid
3. Which type of heating system Explain your answer.
4. Which types of heating system Explain your answer.

Science at Work

Food Technologist

Food technologists study the nature of foods. They experiment with new ingredients and new ways to use ingredients. Food technologists develop ways to process and to improve the quality of foods. They also test samples to make sure foods meet food laws and standards. Most often, food technologists work in a laboratory, often set up like a kitchen.

Most food technologists have a four-year degree in food science, biochemistry, or chemistry. To do research, an advanced degree is required.

Food technologists are creative. They have curiosity and good instincts about food. They also must be able to carry out tests and to work well under pressure.

3-2 INVESTIGATION

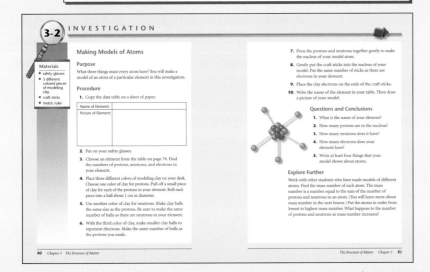

Materials
- safety glasses
- 3 different colored pieces of modeling clay
- craft sticks
- metric ruler

Making Models of Atoms

Purpose

What three things must every atom have? You will make a model of an atom of a particular element in this investigation.

Procedure

1. Copy the data table on a sheet of paper.

Name of Element:
Picture of Element:

2. Put on your safety glasses.
3. Choose an element from the table on page 78. Find the numbers of protons, neutrons, and electrons in your element.
4. Place three different colors of modeling clay on your desk. Choose one color of clay for protons. Pull off a small piece of clay for each of the protons in your element. Roll each piece into a ball about 1 cm in diameter.
5. Use another color of clay for neutrons. Make clay balls the same size as the protons. Be sure to make the same number of balls as there are neutrons in your element.
6. With the third color of clay, make smaller clay balls to represent electrons. Make the same number of balls as the protons you made.

7. Press the protons and neutrons together gently to make the nucleus of your model atom.
8. Gently put the craft sticks into the nucleus of your model. Put the same number of sticks as there are electrons in your element.
9. Place the clay electrons on the ends of the craft sticks.
10. Write the name of the element in your table. Then draw a picture of your model.

Questions and Conclusions

1. What is the name of your element?
2. How many protons are in the nucleus?
3. How many neutrons does it have?
4. How many electrons does your element have?
5. Write at least four things that your model shows about atoms.

Explore Further

Work with other students who have made models of different atoms. Find the mass number of each atom. The mass number is a number equal to the sum of the number of protons and neutrons in an atom. (You will learn more about mass number in the next lesson.) Put the atoms in order from lowest to highest mass number. What happens to the number of protons and neutrons as mass number increases?

◆ Many features reinforce and extend student learning beyond the lesson content.

◆ Achievements in Science offers information about historic science-related events, achievements, or discoveries.

◆ Science in Your Life helps students relate chapter content to everyday life.

◆ Science at Work provides some examples of science careers.

◆ Investigation activities give students hands-on practice with chapter concepts. Students use critical thinking skills to complete each investigation.

Teacher's Edition Highlights

The comprehensive, wraparound Teacher's Edition provides instructional strategies at point of use. Everything from preparation guidelines to teaching tips and strategies are included in an easy-to-use format. Activities are featured at point of use for teacher convenience.

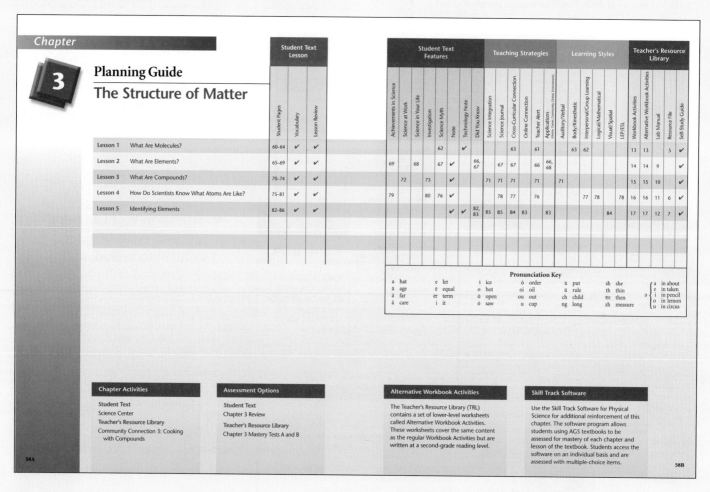

Chapter 3 — Planning Guide: The Structure of Matter

Lesson	Title	Student Pages	Vocabulary	Lesson Review	Achievements in Science	Science at Work	Science in Your Life	Investigation	Science Myth	Note	Technology Note	Did You Know	Science Integration	Science Journal	Cross-Curricular Connection	Online Connection	Teacher Alert	Applications	Auditory/Verbal	Body/Kinesthetic	Interpersonal/Group Learning	Logical/Mathematical	Visual/Spatial	LEP/ESL	Workbook Activities	Alternative Workbook Activities	Lab Manual	Resource File	Self-Study Guide
Lesson 1	What Are Molecules?	60–64	✔	✔						62	✔				63		61				63	62			13	13		5	✔
Lesson 2	What Are Elements?	65–69	✔	✔	69			68	67	✔		66, 67		67	67		66	66, 68							14	14	9		✔
Lesson 3	What Are Compounds?	70–74	✔	✔			72		73	✔			71	71	71		71	71							15	15	10		✔
Lesson 4	How Do Scientists Know What Atoms Are Like?	75–81	✔	✔	79				80	76	✔			78	77		76				77	78		78	16	16	11	6	✔
Lesson 5	Identifying Elements	82–86	✔	✔							✔	✔	82, 83	85	85	84	83	83					84		17	17	12	7	✔

Pronunciation Key

a hat	e let	i ice	ȯ order	u̇ put	sh she	ə { a in about
ā age	ē equal	o hot	oi oil	ü rule	th thin	e in taken
ä far	ėr term	ō open	ou out	ch child	ᴛʜ then	i in pencil
â care	i it	ȯ saw	u cup	ng long	zh measure	o in lemon / u in circus

Chapter Activities
Student Text
Science Center
Teacher's Resource Library
Community Connection 3: Cooking with Compounds

Assessment Options
Student Text
Chapter 3 Review
Teacher's Resource Library
Chapter 3 Mastery Tests A and B

Alternative Workbook Activities
The Teacher's Resource Library (TRL) contains a set of lower-level worksheets called Alternative Workbook Activities. These worksheets cover the same content as the regular Workbook Activities but are written at a second-grade reading level.

Skill Track Software
Use the Skill Track Software for Physical Science for additional reinforcement of this chapter. The software program allows students using AGS textbooks to be assessed for mastery of each chapter and lesson of the textbook. Students access the software on an individual basis and are assessed with multiple-choice items.

58A   58B

Chapter Planning Guides

◆ The Planning Guide saves valuable preparation time by organizing all materials for each chapter.

◆ A complete listing of lessons allows you to preview each chapter quickly.

◆ Assessment options are highlighted for easy reference. Options include:
   Lesson Reviews
   Chapter Reviews
   Chapter Mastery Tests, Forms A and B
   Midterm and Final Tests

◆ Page numbers of Student Text and Teacher's Edition features help customize lesson plans to your students.

◆ Many teaching strategies and learning styles are listed to support students with diverse needs.

◆ All activities in the Teacher's Resource Library are listed.

◆ A Pronunciation Key is provided to help you as you work with students to pronounce difficult words correctly.

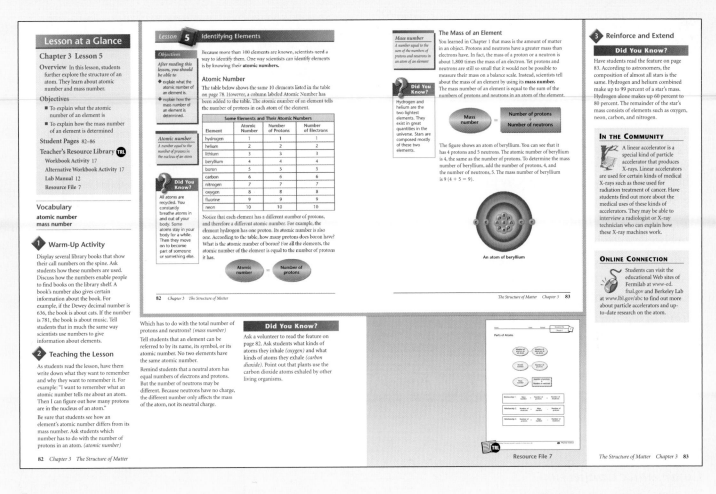

Lessons

- Quick overviews of chapters and lessons save planning time.

- Lesson objectives are listed for easy reference.

- Page references are provided for convenience.

- Easy-to-follow lesson plans in three steps save time: Warm-Up Activity, Teaching the Lesson, and Reinforce and Extend.

- Teacher Alerts highlight content that may need further explanation.

- Science Journal activities give students an opportunity to write about science.

- Cross-Curricular activities tie science to a variety of curriculum areas.

- Applications: Five areas of application—At Home, Career Connection, Global Connection, In the Community, and In the Environment—help students relate science to the world outside the classroom. Applications motivate students and make learning relevant.

- The Portfolio Assessment, which appears at the end of each lesson, lists items the student has completed for that lesson.

- Online Connections list relevant Web sites.

- Learning Styles provide teaching strategies to help meet the needs of students with diverse ways of learning. Modalities include Auditory/Verbal, Visual/Spatial, Body/Kinesthetic, Logical/Mathematical, and Interpersonal/Group Learning. Additional teaching activities are provided for LEP/ESL students.

- Answers for all activities in the Student Text appear in the Teacher's Edition. Answers for the Teacher's Resource Library, Student Workbook, and Lab Manual appear at the back of this Teacher's Edition and on the TRL CD-ROM.

- Worksheet, Workbook, Lab Manual, and Test pages from the Teacher's Resource Library are shown at point of use in reduced form.

TRL All of the activities you'll need to reinforce and extend the text are conveniently located on the AGS Publishing Teacher's Resource Library (TRL) CD-ROM. All of the reproducible activities pictured in the Teacher's Edition are ready to select, view, and print. You can also preview other materials by linking directly to the AGS Publishing Web site.

Workbook Activities
Workbook Activities are available to reinforce and extend skills from each lesson of the textbook. A bound workbook format is also available.

Alternative Activities
These activities cover the same content as the Workbook Activities but are written at a second-grade reading level.

Lab Manual
These activities build critical thinking and teamwork skills. A bound format is also available.

Community Connection
Relevant activities help students extend their knowledge to the real world and reinforce concepts covered in class.

Resource File
These reference sheets on lesson content are tools for student study as well as teaching aids.

Self-Study Guide
An assignment guide provides the student with an outline for working through the text independently. The guide provides teachers with the flexibility for individualized instruction or independent study.

Mastery Tests
Chapter, Midterm, and Final Mastery Tests are convenient assessment options.

Answer Key
All answers to reproducible activities are included in the TRL and in the Teacher's Edition.

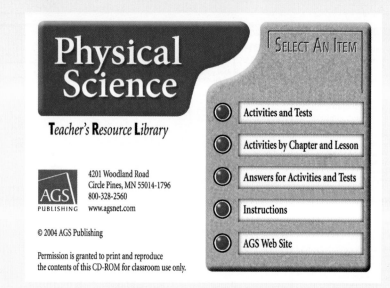

Physical Science
Teacher's Resource Library

SELECT AN ITEM
- Activities and Tests
- Activities by Chapter and Lesson
- Answers for Activities and Tests
- Instructions
- AGS Web Site

AGS PUBLISHING
4201 Woodland Road
Circle Pines, MN 55014-1796
800-328-2560
www.agsnet.com

© 2004 AGS Publishing

Permission is granted to print and reproduce the contents of this CD-ROM for classroom use only.

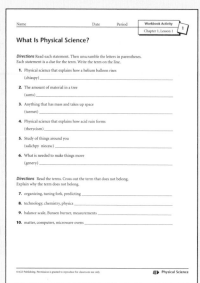

Workbook Activities

Lab Manual

Community Connections

Mastery Tests

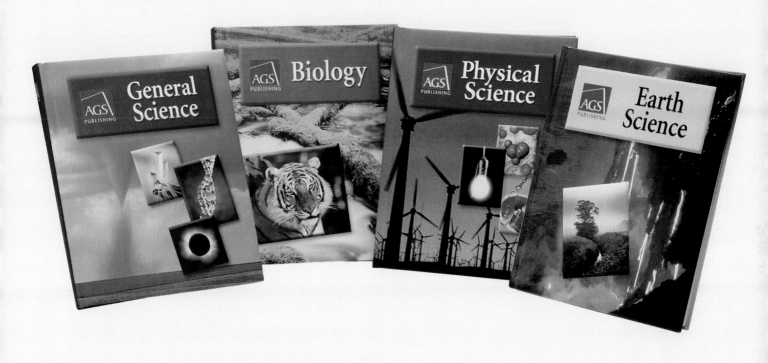

Enhance your science program with AGS Publishing textbooks—an easy, effective way to teach students the practical skills they need. Each AGS Publishing textbook meets your science curriculum needs. These exciting, full-color books use student-friendly text and real-world examples to show students the relevance of science in their daily lives. Each presents a comprehensive coverage of skills and concepts. The short, concise lessons will motivate even your most reluctant students. With readabilities of all the texts below fourth-grade reading level, your students can concentrate on learning the content. AGS Publishing is committed to making learning accessible to all students.

Correlation of Physical Science to the National Science Education Standards

STANDARD A Science as Inquiry

As a result of activities in grades 5–12, all students should develop:

Physical Science

◆ Abilities necessary to do scientific inquiry

Pages xvi–xvii, 1, 4–29, 31–55, 72–74, 80–81, 91–113, 121–40, 143–44, 153–54, 157–69, 174–91, 193, 199–200, 206–10, 216–17, 220–28, 247–48, 260–61, 275, 278–79, 281–82, 287–88, 299–300, 325–27, 333–34, 338–39, 354–55, 367–68, 380–81

◆ Understandings about scientific inquiry

Pages xvi–xvii, 3, 5, 8, 13–14, 18–19, 33, 35–36, 41, 51, 53–54, 64, 73–74, 80–81, 95–96, 111–12, 121–22, 143–44, 153–54, 167–68, 183, 185–86, 193, 199–200, 212, 216–17, 221, 225, 227–28, 247–48, 259, 260–61, 286, 287–88, 298, 299–300, 320, 327, 333–34, 338–39, 354–355, 362, 364, 367–68, 380–81

STANDARD B Physical Science

As a result of activities in grades 5–12, all students should develop an understanding of:

Physical Science

◆ Structure of atoms

Pages 59–61, 65–67, 69–70, 72, 75–89, 91, 97–104, 117, 123–28, 242–43, 310, 356–358

◆ Structure and properties of matter

Pages 31–54, 59–89, 97–113, 117–45, 149–71, 244–46, 280–81, 378–79

◆ Chemical reactions

Pages 117–22, 138–45, 149–69, 244–46, 281, 372–77

◆ Motions and forces

Pages 173–201, 205–10, 218–28, 235, 262–264, 309–45, 347–71

◆ Transfer of energy

Pages 8, 10, 173–78, 192–95, 205–07, 211–35, 240–49, 260–67, 271–307, 309–45, 347–71

◆ Conservation of energy and increase in disorder

Pages 173–75, 182–86, 192–95, 211–17, 239–55, 262–67, 271–307, 309–45, 347–77

◆ Interactions of energy and matter

Pages 262–66, 271–307, 360–69, 372–77

STANDARD E Science and Technology

As a result of activities in grades 5–12, all students should develop:

Physical Science

◆ Abilities of technological design

The ability to address this objective is available on the following pages: 13–14, 18–19, 35–36, 53–54, 73–74, 80–81, 95–96, 111–12, 121–22, 143–44, 153–54, 167–68, 185–86, 199–200, 216–17, 227–28, 247–48, 260–61, 287–88, 299–300, 333–34, 338–39, 354–55, 367–68.

◆ Understandings about science and technology

Pages 3, 5, 8, 12, 23, 33, 40, 41, 48, 51, 64, 69, 79, 85, 98, 105, 109, 120, 140, 142, 155, 159, 162, 166, 183, 191, 193, 198, 212, 221, 223, 226, 243, 255, 259, 279, 286, 293, 298, 313, 320, 324, 327, 350, 362, 364, 366

STANDARD F   Science in Personal and Social Perspectives

As a result of activities in grades 5–12, all students should develop an understanding of:

Physical Science

◆ Personal and community health

Pages 372–77

◆ Population growth

This objective falls outside the scope of AGS Physical Science.

◆ Natural resources

Pages 348–49, 352–53, 356–57, 366, 372–77

◆ Environmental quality

Pages 372–77

◆ Natural and human-induced hazards

Page 141

◆ Science and technology in local, national, and global challenges

Pages 3, 5, 8, 33, 41, 51, 64, 85, 98, 109, 140, 155, 162, 183, 193, 212, 221, 255, 259, 286, 298, 320, 327, 362, 364

STANDARD G   History and Nature of Science

As a result of activities in grades 5–12, all students should develop an understanding of:

Physical Science

◆ Science as a human endeavor

Pages xvi–xvii, 1–5, 8, 12, 16–17, 23, 33, 34, 40, 41, 42, 51, 52, 64, 85, 94, 97, 105, 109, 120, 128, 141, 142, 159, 163, 166, 187–88, 191–95, 198, 208, 213–17, 223–26, 243, 246, 266, 279, 284–85, 292, 293, 304, 313, 319, 324–26, 350, 359, 366

◆ Nature of science

Pages xvi–xvii, 13–14, 18–19, 35–36, 53–54, 73–74, 80–81, 95–96, 111–12, 121–22, 143–44, 153–54, 167–68, 185–86, 199–200, 216–17, 227–28, 247–48, 260–61, 287–88, 299–300, 333–34, 338–39, 354–55, 367–68

◆ Nature of scientific knowledge

Pages xvi–xvii, 13–14, 18–19, 35–36, 53–54, 73–74, 80–81, 95–96, 111–12, 121–22, 143–44, 153–54, 167–68, 185–86, 199–200, 216–17, 227–28, 247–48, 260–61, 287–88, 299–300, 333–34, 338–39, 354–55, 367–68

◆ History of science

Pages 3, 5, 6, 8, 10, 12, 17, 20, 23, 33, 34, 40, 41, 48, 51, 52, 64, 69, 71, 72, 77, 79, 82–83, 85, 94, 97, 98, 105, 109, 120, 128, 129, 139–40, 141, 142, 150–52, 155–56, 159, 162, 163, 164, 166, 183, 191, 193, 195, 198, 208, 212, 221, 223, 226, 243, 246, 255, 259, 266, 279, 286, 293, 298, 304, 313, 319, 320, 324, 327, 350, 359, 362, 364, 366

◆ Historical perspectives

Pages 3, 5, 6, 8, 10, 12, 20, 23, 33, 37, 40, 41, 48, 52, 64, 69, 71, 76–85, 98, 105, 109, 120, 140, 142, 155, 159, 162, 166, 183, 191, 193, 212, 221, 223, 226, 243, 255, 259, 279, 286, 293, 298, 313, 320, 324, 327, 350, 362, 364, 366

Skills Chart

Physical Science

CHAPTER

Science Content

	1	2	3	4	5	6	7	8	9	10	11	12
Chemical Reactions					5	6			9	10		
Conservation of Energy							7	8	9	10	11	12
History and Nature of Science	1	2	3	4	5	6	7	8	9	10	11	12
Inquiry and Investigation	1	2	3	4	5	6	7	8	9	10	11	12
Interactions of Energy and Matter	1								9	10		12
Motions and Forces							7	8	9		11	12
Science and Technology	1	2	3	4	5	6	7	8	9	10	11	12
Science in Personal and Social Perspectives	1	2	3	4	5	6	7	8	9	10	11	12
Structure and Properties of Matter		2	3	4	5	6			9	10		12
Structure of Atoms			3	4	5				9		11	12
Transfer of Energy	1						7	8	9	10	11	

Process Skills

	1	2	3	4	5	6	7	8	9	10	11	12
Balancing Equations					5	6						
Calculating Area	1											
Calculating Density		2										
Calculating Speed							7					
Calculating Volume	1	2										
Calculating Work and Power								8				
Collecting Information	1	2	3	4	5	6	7	8	9	10	11	12
Communicating	1	2	3	4	5	6	7	8	9	10	11	12
Creating Charts, Graphs, Tables, or Diagrams	1	2	3	4	5	6	7	8	9	10	11	12
Describing	1	2	3	4	5	6	7	8	9	10	11	12
Determining Direction							7			10	11	12
Determining Mass	1	2					7					
Determining Weight		2										
Following Written Directions	1	2	3	4	5	6	7	8	9	10	11	12
Identifying and/or Controlling Variables	1	2	3	4	5	6	7	8	9	10	11	12
Making and/or Using Models			3	4	5	6	7	8		10	11	
Measuring	1	2	3	4	5	6	7	8	9	10	11	12
Observing	1	2	3	4	5	6	7	8	9	10	11	12

	1	2	3	4	5	6	7	8	9	10	11	12
Performing Experiments	1	2	3	4	5	6	7	8	9	10	11	12
Reading Charts, Graphs, Tables, or Diagrams	1	2	3	4	5	6	7	8	9	10	11	12
Recording Data	1	2	3	4	5	6	7	8	9	10	11	12
Using Customary Measurements	1	2					7		9			
Using Formulas	1	2	3	4	5	6	7	8	9	10	11	12
Using Metric Measurements	1	2	3	4	5	6	7	8	9	10	11	12
Using Science Lab Equipment	1	2	3	4	5	6	7	8	9	10	11	12
Working with Numbers	1	2	3	4	5	6	7	8	9	10	11	12
Writing About Science	1	2	3	4	5	6	7	8	9	10	11	12

Thinking Skills

	1	2	3	4	5	6	7	8	9	10	11	12
Applying Information	1	2	3	4	5	6	7	8	9	10	11	12
Classifying and Categorizing	1	2	3	4	5	6	7	8	9	10	11	12
Comparing and Contrasting	1	2	3	4	5	6	7	8	9	10	11	12
Drawing Conclusions	1	2	3	4	5	6	7	8	9	10	11	12
Explaining Ideas and Concepts	1	2	3	4	5	6	7	8	9	10	11	12
Formulating Questions	1	2	3	4	5	6	7	8	9	10	11	12
Identifying and Solving Problems	1	2	3	4	5	6	7	8	9	10	11	12
Identifying Similarities and Differences	1	2	3	4	5	6	7	8	9	10	11	12
Identifying Terms and Symbols	1	2	3	4	5	6	7	8	9	10	11	12
Interpreting Data	1	2	3	4	5	6	7	8	9	10	11	12
Interpreting Visuals	1	2	3	4	5	6	7	8	9	10	11	12
Learning Science Vocabulary	1	2	3	4	5	6	7	8	9	10	11	12
Making Decisions	1	2	3	4	5	6	7	8	9	10	11	12
Making Inferences	1	2	3	4	5	6	7	8	9	10	11	12
Organizing Information	1	2	3	4	5	6	7	8	9	10	11	12
Predicting Outcomes	1	2	3	4	5	6	7	8	9	10	11	12
Recalling Facts	1	2	3	4	5	6	7	8	9	10	11	12
Recognizing Main Ideas	1	2	3	4	5	6	7	8	9	10	11	12
Recognizing Patterns	1	2	3	4	5	6	7	8	9	10	11	12
Recognizing Relationships	1	2	3	4	5	6	7	8	9	10	11	12
Understanding Concepts	1	2	3	4	5	6	7	8	9	10	11	12

Learning Styles

The learning style activities in the *Physical Science* Teacher's Edition provide activities to help students with special needs understand the lesson. These activities focus on the following learning styles: Visual/Spatial, Auditory/Verbal, Body/Kinesthetic, Logical/Mathematical, Interpersonal/Group Learning, LEP/ESL. These styles reflect Howard Gardner's theory of multiple intelligences. The writing activities suggested in this student text are appropriate for students who fit Gardner's description of Verbal/Linguistic Intelligence. The activities are designed to help teachers capitalize on students' individual strengths and dominant learning styles. The activities reinforce the lesson by teaching or expanding upon the content in a different way.

Following are examples of activities featured in the *Physical Science* Teacher's Edition:

Auditory/Verbal

Students benefit from having someone read the text aloud or listening to the text on audiocassette. Musical activities appropriate for the lesson may help auditory learners.

LEARNING STYLES

Auditory/Verbal
Ask students to look at the table on page 71. Have them complete this statement for each compound in the table: I know that *(name of compound)* is a compound because it is made of more than one kind of atom. These atoms are *(names of elements)*.

LEP/ESL

Students benefit from activities that promote English language acquisition and interaction with English-speaking peers.

LEARNING STYLES

LEP/ESL
Many students with limited English proficiency may have grown up using the metric system rather than the customary system. Provide these students with the opportunity to teach the class about the system. They can demonstrate the use of metric measuring tools and relate their own experiences with the metric system of measurement.

Logical/Mathematical

Students learn by using logical/mathematical thinking in relation to the lesson content.

LEARNING STYLES

Logical/Mathematical
Instruct students to construct a concept map, relating atom, nucleus, proton, neutron, and electron. Have them expand the diagram to include more information about these terms. For example, students could add to the proton branch descriptions such as "positively charged."

Interpersonal/Group Learning

Learners benefit from working with at least one other person on activities that involve a process and an end product.

LEARNING STYLES

Interpersonal/Group Learning
Instruct students to hold tightly onto both hands of a partner and try to move around. Compare this behavior to that of the molecules in a solid—they do not move easily. Next, tell students to hold only one hand of their partner and try to move around. Compare this behavior to that of the molecules in a liquid, which can move about more easily than the ones in a solid. Finally, have students place their hands near their partners without touching. Have students move around. Explain that molecules in a gas can easily move.

Visual/Spatial

Students benefit from seeing illustrations or demonstrations beyond what is in the text.

LEARNING STYLES

Visual/Spatial
Students will benefit from repeated performance of the measuring activities described in the lesson. Provide a number of containers with water and small objects for which students should find the volume by displacement, using a graduated cylinder and the procedure described in the lesson. Remind students that the graduated cylinder must contain enough water to completely cover the object when it is added.

Body/Kinesthetic

Learners benefit from activities that include physical movement or tactile experiences.

LEARNING STYLES

Body/Kinesthetic
Obtain small swatches of different types of fabrics. Assign partners and explain that one student is to give the other student pieces of material and record the findings. Have students shut their eyes and determine the properties of texture and odor. Then have them open their eyes to determine shininess and color.

by
Robert H. Marshall

Donald H. Jacobs

AGS Publishing
Circle Pines, Minnesota 55014-1796
800-328-2560

About the Authors

Robert H. Marshall, M.Ed., teaches high school physics and algebra for the Baltimore School for the Arts. He is coauthor of several AGS textbooks including *Earth Science, General Science,* and *Matter, Motion, and Machines.*

Donald H. Jacobs, M.Ed., taught mathematics for many years in the Baltimore City Public Schools. He is currently with the Upton Home and Hospital School Program in the technology department. Other AGS textbooks that he has coauthored include *Basic Math Skills, Life Skills Math,* and *General Science.*

Photo credits for this textbook can be found on page 398.

The publisher wishes to thank the following consultants and educators for their helpful comments during the review process for *Physical Science.* Their assistance has been invaluable.

Rebecca Abreu, Science Teacher, Timber Creek High School, Orlando, FL; **Bonnie Buratti,** Research Astronomer, Jet Propulsion Laboratory, California Institute of Technology, Pasadena, CA; **Barbara Cassius,** Science Resource Teacher, Hoover High School, San Diego, CA; **Norman Gelfand,** Physicist, Fermi National Accelerator Laboratory (Fermilab), Batavia, IL; **Brian P. Johnson,** Science Teacher, Centennial High School, Centerville, MN; **Gary A. Mansergh,** Ed.D., Inquiry-Science Coach, Professional Development Center for Academic Excellence, St. Paul, MN; **Thomas E. Rock,** Teacher, John Marshall High School, San Antonio, TX; **Lorraine S. Taylor,** Ph.D., Professor of Special Education, State University of New York at New Paltz, New Paltz, NY; **Katherine L. Turley,** Specific Learning Disabilities Teacher/Ex. Ed. Curriculum Leader, Timber Creek High School, Orlando, FL; **Dr. Alex Vera,** Science Teacher, Templeton Secondary School, Vancouver, BC, Canada

Editorial services provided by General Learning Communications.

Publisher's Project Staff

Vice President, Product Development: Kathleen T. Williams, Ph.D., NCSP; Associate Director, Product Development: Teri Mathews; Senior Editor: Julie Maas; Development Assistant: Bev Johnson; Senior Designer/Illustrator: Diane McCarty; Creative Services Manager: Nancy Condon; Project Coordinator/Designer: Laura Henrichsen; Purchasing Agent: Mary Kaye Kuzma; Senior Marketing Manager/Secondary Curriculum: Brian Holl

Printed in the United States of America
ISBN 0-7854-3624-3
Product Number 93920
A 0 9 8 7

Contents

How to Use This Book: A Study Guide

Overview This section may be used to introduce the study of physical science, to preview the book's features, and to review effective study skills.

Objectives
- To introduce the study of physical science
- To preview the student textbook
- To review study skills

Student Pages x–xv

Teacher's Resource Library
How to Use This Book 1–7

Introduction to the Book

Have volunteers read aloud the three paragraphs of the introduction. Discuss with students why studying science and developing scientific skills are important.

How to Study

Read aloud each bulleted statement, pausing to discuss with students why the suggestion is a part of good study habits. Distribute copies of the How to Use This Book 1, "Study Habits Survey," to students. Read the directions together and then have students complete the survey. After they have scored their surveys, ask them to make a list of the study habits they plan to improve. After three or four weeks, have students complete the survey again to see if they have improved their study habits. Encourage them to keep and review the survey every month or so to see whether they are maintaining and improving their study habits.

To help students organize their time and work in an easy-to-read format, have them fill out How to Use This Book 2, "Weekly Schedule." Encourage them to keep the schedule in a notebook or folder where they can refer to it easily. Suggest that they review the schedule periodically and update it as necessary.

Give students an opportunity to become familiar with the textbook features and the chapter and lesson organization and

How to Use This Book: A Study Guide

Welcome to *Physical Science.* Science touches our lives every day, no matter where we are—at home, at school, or at work. This book covers the area of physical science. It also focuses on science skills that scientists use. These skills include asking questions, making predictions, designing experiments or procedures, collecting and organizing information, calculating data, making decisions, drawing conclusions, and exploring more options. You probably already use these skills every day. You ask questions to find answers. You gather information and organize it. You use that information to make all sorts of decisions. In this book, you will have opportunities to use and practice all of these skills.

As you read this book, notice how each lesson is organized. Information is presented in a straightforward manner. Examples, tables, illustrations, and photos help clarify concepts. Read the information carefully. If you have trouble with a lesson, try reading it again.

It is important that you understand how to use this book before you start to read it. It is also important to know how to be successful in this course. Information in this first section of the book can help you achieve these things.

How to Study

These tips can help you study more effectively.
- Plan a regular time to study.
- Choose a quiet desk or table where you will not be distracted. Find a spot that has good lighting.
- Gather all the books, pencils, paper, and other equipment you will need to complete your assignments.
- Decide on a goal. For example: "I will finish reading and taking notes on Chapter 1, Lesson 1, by 8:00."
- Take a five- to ten-minute break every hour to stay alert.
- If you start to feel sleepy, take a break and get some fresh air.

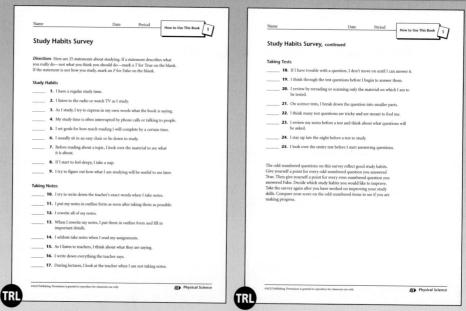

How to Use This Book 1, pages 1 and 2

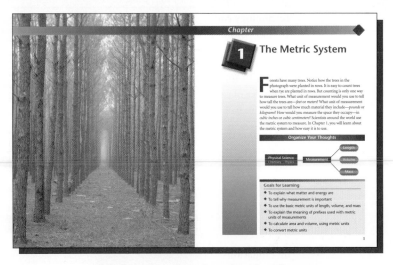

Before Beginning Each Chapter

◆ Read the chapter title and study the photograph. What does the photo tell you about the chapter title?

◆ Read the opening paragraphs.

◆ Study the Goals for Learning. The Chapter Review and tests will ask questions related to these goals.

◆ Look at the Chapter Review. The questions cover the most important information in the chapter.

Note These Features

Note
Points of interest or additional information that relates to the lesson

Did You Know?
Facts that add details to lesson content or present an interesting or unusual application of lesson content

Science Myth
Common science misconceptions followed by the correct information

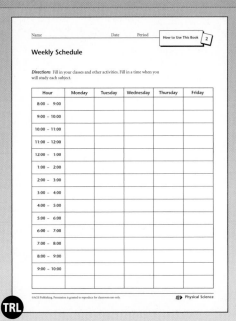

structure of *Physical Science.* List the following text features on the board: Table of Contents, Chapter Opener, Lesson, Lesson Review, Investigation, Chapter Summary, Chapter Review, Appendix A: Alternative Energy Sources, Appendix B: The Periodic Table of Elements, Appendix C: Measurement and Conversion Factors, Appendix D: Decimal, Percent, and Fraction Conversions, Glossary, Index.

Have students skim their textbooks to find these features. You may wish to remind students that they can use the Table of Contents to help identify and locate major features in the text. They can also use the Index to identify specific topics and the text pages on which they are discussed. Ask volunteers to call out a feature or topic and its page reference from the Table of Contents or Index. Have other students check to see that the specific features or topics do appear on the pages cited.

Before Beginning Each Chapter

When students begin their study of Chapter 1, you may wish to have them read aloud and follow each of the bulleted suggestions on page xi. Actually trying the suggestions will help students understand what they are supposed to do and recognize how useful the suggestions are when previewing a chapter. At the beginning of other chapters, refer students to page xi and encourage them to follow the suggestions. You may wish to continue to do this as a class each time or allow students to work independently.

In addition to the suggestions on page xi, the Teacher's Edition text for each Chapter Opener offers teaching suggestions for introducing the chapter. The text also includes a list of Teacher's Resource Library materials for the chapter.

Chapter Openers organize information in easy-to-read formats. Have a volunteer find and read the Chapter 1 title on page 1. Read aloud the second bulleted statement on page xi and have a volunteer read aloud the opening paragraphs of the chapter. Discuss the topics that students will study in the chapter. Have students examine the Organize Your Thoughts chart. It provides an overview of chapter content. Then have volunteers take turns reading

aloud the Chapter 1 Goals for Learning. Discuss with students why knowing these goals can help them when they are studying the chapter. Finally, have students skim the Chapter Summary to identify important information and vocabulary presented in the chapter. Have students turn to the Chapter Review and explain that it provides an opportunity to determine how well they have understood the chapter content.

Note These Features

Use the information on pages xi and xii to identify features included in each chapter. As a class locate examples of these features in Chapter 1. Read the examples and discuss their purpose.

Before Beginning Each Lesson

With students, read through the information in "Before Beginning Each Lesson" on page xii. Then assign each of the six lessons in Chapter 1 to a small group of students. Have them restate the lesson title in the form of a statement or a question and make a list of features in their lesson. After their survey of the lesson, they should be prepared to report to the class on their findings.

Technology Note

Technology information that relates to the lesson or chapter

Science in Your Life

Examples of science in real life

Achievements in Science

Historical scientific discoveries, events, and achievements

Science at Work

Careers in science

Investigation

Experiments that give practice with chapter concepts

Before Beginning Each Lesson

Read the lesson title and restate it in the form of a question.

For example, write:
Why use metric measurements to find area?

Look over the entire lesson, noting the following:
◆ bold words
◆ text organization
◆ notes in the margins
◆ photos and illustrations
◆ lesson review questions

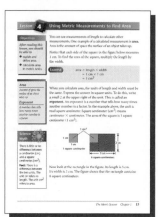

As You Read the Lesson

◆ Read the lesson title.
◆ Read the subheads and paragraphs that follow.
◆ Read the content in the Examples.
◆ Before moving on to the next lesson, see if you understand the concepts you read. If you do not understand the concepts, reread the lesson. If you are still unsure, ask for help.
◆ Practice what you have learned by completing the Lesson Review.

Using the Bold Words

Bold type

Words seen for the first time will appear in bold type

Glossary

Words listed in this column are also found in the glossary

Knowing the meaning of all the boxed vocabulary words in the left column will help you understand what you read.

These words are in **bold type** the first time they appear in the text. They are often defined in the paragraph.

> **Physical science** is the study of matter and energy.

All of the words in the left column are also defined in the **glossary**.

> **Physical science** (fiz′ə kəl sī′əns) the study of matter and energy (p. 2)

Word Study Tips

◆ Start a vocabulary file with index cards to use for review.
◆ Write one term on the front of each card. Write the chapter number, lesson number, and definition on the back.
◆ You can use these cards as flash cards by yourself or with a study partner to test your knowledge.

Physical Science

The study of matter and energy
Chapter 1, Lesson 1

As You Read the Lesson

Read aloud the statements in the section "As You Read the Lesson" on page xiii. Have students preview lessons in Chapter 1 and note lesson titles and subheads. Remind students as they study each lesson to follow this study approach.

Using the Bold Words

Read aloud the information on page xiii. Make sure students understand what the term *bold* means. Explain to students that the words in bold are important vocabulary terms. Then ask them to look at the boxed words on page 2. Have a volunteer read the boxed term *physical science* and then find and read the sentence in the text in which that word appears in bold type. Have another volunteer read the definition of the word in the box.

Point out that boxed words may appear on other pages in a lesson besides the first page. Have students turn to page 3 and look at the boxed words on that page. Explain that these words appear in a box here because they are used in the text on this page. Have volunteers find and read the sentences in the text in which the vocabulary words are used. Have students turn to the Glossary at the back of the book and read the definitions of the vocabulary words on page 3.

Word Study Tips

Have a volunteer read aloud the word study tips on page xiii. You may wish to demonstrate how to make a vocabulary card by filling out an index card for the term *physical science* and its definition (page 2).

Distribute copies of How to Use This Book 3, "Word Study," to students. Suggest that as they read, students write unfamiliar words, their page numbers, and their definitions on the sheet. Point out that having such a list will be very useful for reviewing vocabulary before taking a test. Point out that students can use words they listed on How to Use This Book 3 to make their vocabulary card file.

Using the Summaries

Have students turn to page 27 and examine the Chapter 1 Summary. Emphasize that Chapter Summaries identify the main ideas of the chapter. Suggest that students can use the summary to focus their study of the chapter content. They might write each main idea in a notebook and add a few details that reinforce it. These notes will make a useful study tool.

Using the Reviews

Have students turn to page 5 and examine the Lesson 1 Review for Chapter 1. Emphasize that Lesson Reviews provide opportunities for students to focus on important content and skills developed in the lesson. Then have students turn to pages 28 and 29. Point out that the Chapter Review is intended to help them focus on and review the key terms, content information, and skills presented in the chapter before they are tested on the material. Suggest that they complete the review after they have studied their notes, vocabulary lists, and worksheets.

Preparing for Tests

Encourage students to offer their opinions about tests and their ideas on test-taking strategies. What do they do to study for a test? List their comments on the board. Then read the set of bulleted statements on page xiv. Add these suggestions to the list on the board if they are not already there.

Discuss why each suggestion can help students when they are taking a test. Lead students to recognize that these suggestions, along with the Test-Taking Tips in their textbooks, can help them improve their test-taking skills.

Have students turn to the Chapter Review at the end of any chapter in the textbook and find the Test-Taking Tip. Ask several volunteers to read aloud the tips they find in the Chapter Reviews. Discuss how using the tips can help students study and take tests more effectively.

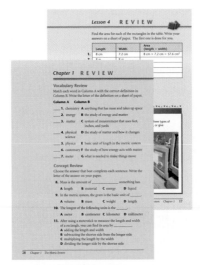

Using the Summaries

◆ Read each Chapter Summary to be sure you understand the chapter's main ideas.

◆ Make up a sample test of items you think may be on the test. You may want to do this with a classmate and share your questions.

◆ Read the vocabulary words in the Science Words box.

◆ Review your notes and test yourself on vocabulary words and key ideas.

◆ Practice writing about some of the main ideas from the chapter.

Using the Reviews

◆ Answer the questions in the Lesson Reviews.

◆ In the Chapter Reviews, answer the questions about vocabulary under the Vocabulary Review. Study the words and definitions. Say them aloud to help you remember them.

◆ Answer the questions under the Concept Review and Critical Thinking sections of the Chapter Reviews.

◆ Review the Test-Taking Tips.

Preparing for Tests

◆ Complete the Lesson Reviews and Chapter Reviews.

◆ Complete the Investigations.

◆ Review your answers to Lesson Reviews, Investigations, and Chapter Reviews.

◆ Test yourself on vocabulary words and key ideas.

◆ Use graphic organizers as study tools.

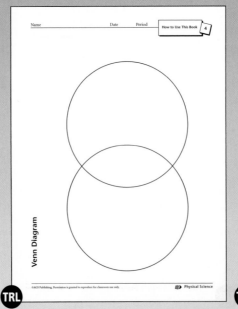

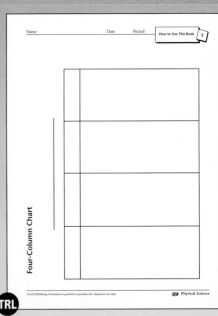

How to Use This Book 4 and 5

Using Graphic Organizers

A graphic organizer is a visual representation of information. It can help you see how ideas are related to each other. A graphic organizer can help you study for a test or organize information before you write. Here are some examples.

Venn Diagram

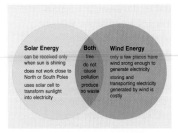

A Venn diagram can help you compare and contrast two things. For example, this diagram compares and contrasts solar energy and wind energy. The characteristics of solar energy are listed in the left circle. The characteristics of wind energy are listed in the right circle. The characteristics that both have are listed in the intersection of the circles.

Column Chart

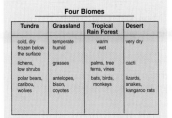

Column charts can help you organize information into groups, or categories. Grouping things in this format helps make the information easier to understand and remember. For example, this four-column chart groups information about each of the four biomes. A column chart can be divided into any number of columns or rows. The chart can be as simple as a two-column list of words or as complex as a multiple-column, multiple-row table of data.

Network Tree

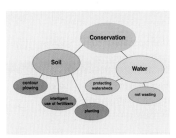

A network tree organizer shows how ideas are connected to one another. Network trees can help you identify main ideas or concepts linked to related ideas. For example, this network tree identifies concepts linked to the concept of conservation. You can also use network trees to rank ideas from most important to least important.

Using Graphic Organizers

Explain to students that graphic organizers provide ways of visually organizing information to make it easier to understand and remember. Emphasize that there are many different kinds of graphic organizers including column charts, Venn diagrams, network trees, and word webs. Encourage students to look at the Organize Your Thoughts chart at the beginning of each chapter. Discuss how these graphic organizers provide a preview of the chapter content.

Tell students that they can use a variety of organizers to record information for a variety of purposes. For example, a Venn diagram is useful for comparing and contrasting information. Draw a Venn diagram on the board. Show students how to use the diagram to compare and contrast two items, such as a ball and a globe. Discuss how the diagram clearly shows the similarities and differences between the two items.

Display other organizers, such as a cause and effect chart, spider map, and two-column chart. Ask volunteers to suggest ways that these organizers can be used to record information. Then encourage students to record information on graphic organizers and use them as study tools.

Have students refer back to the pages in this section, "How to Use This Book," as often as they wish while using this textbook.

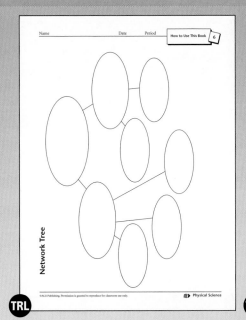

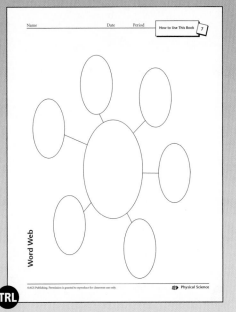

The Nature of Science

Write the word *science* on the board. Ask students what the word *science* brings to mind when they hear it. Record their ideas on the board. Guide the discussion to focus on the major areas of science, such as physical, earth, and life sciences; the achievements students credit to science; scientific investigations; and the kinds of information scientists need to do their work.

Following the discussion have students read the first paragraph on page xvi. Help them conclude that science has played an important role in the development of their way of life. From the time they wake up until the time they fall asleep, they benefit from scientific knowledge and discoveries.

Read and discuss the remaining paragraphs that focus on the scientific method. Emphasize the flexibility of the method and how the steps can be reordered or eliminated depending on the circumstances of the investigation. Discuss how the method can be cyclical. Results can lead to new questions and revised hypotheses and new or refined investigations. Explain that keeping accurate records of an investigation is an extremely important step because the data is used to support conclusions and verify results.

The Nature of Science

Science is an organized body of knowledge about the natural world. It encompasses everything from atoms to rocks to human health. Scientific knowledge is important because it solves problems, improves everyday life, and uncovers new opportunities. For example, scientists develop vaccines and antibiotics to prevent and cure diseases. Scientific knowledge helps farmers grow better and more crops. Science is behind the electricity we depend on every day. And science has launched space exploration, which continues to offer new opportunities.

Scientists use a logical process to explore the world and collect information. It is called the scientific method, and it includes specific steps. Scientists follow these steps or variations of these steps to test whether a possible answer to their question is correct.

1. Ask a question.
2. State a hypothesis, or make a prediction, about the answer.
3. Design an experiment, or procedure, to test the hypothesis.
4. Perform the experiment and gather information.
5. Analyze the data and organize the results.
6. State a conclusion based on the results, existing knowledge, and logic. Determine whether the results support the hypothesis.
7. Communicate the results and the conclusion.

As a scientist researches a question, he or she may do these steps in a different order or may even skip some steps. The scientific method requires many skills: predicting, observing, organizing, classifying, modeling, measuring, inferring, analyzing, and communicating.

Communication is an important part of the scientific method. Scientists all over the world share their findings with other scientists. They publish information about their experiments in journals and discuss them at meetings. A scientist may try another scientist's experiment or change it in some way. If many scientists get the same results from an experiment, then the results are repeatable and considered reliable.

Sometimes the results of an experiment do not support its hypothesis. Unexpected observations can lead to new, more interesting questions. For example, penicillin was discovered accidentally in 1928. Alexander Fleming observed that mold had contaminated one of his bacteria cultures. He noticed that the mold had stopped the growth of the bacterium. Since the mold was from the penicillium family, he named it penicillin. A decade later, researchers found a way to isolate the active ingredient. Since then, penicillin has been used to fight bacteria and save people's lives.

Once in a while, scientists discover something that dramatically changes our world, like penicillin. But, more often, scientific knowledge grows and changes a little at a time.

What scientists learn is applied to problems and challenges that affect people's lives. This leads to the development of practical tools and techniques. Tools help scientists accurately observe and measure things in the natural world. A new tool often provides data that an older tool could not. For example, computers help scientists analyze data more quickly and accurately than ever before. Our science knowledge grows as more advanced tools and technology make new discoveries possible.

Scientists use theories to explain their observations and data. A theory is a possible explanation for a set of data. A theory is not a fact. It is an idea. Theories are tested by more experiments. Theories may be confirmed, changed, or sometimes tossed out. For example, in 1808, John Dalton published a book describing his theory of atoms. His theory stated that atoms are solid spheres without internal structures. By the early 1900s, however, new tools allowed Ernest Rutherford to show that atoms are mostly empty space. He said that an atom consists of a tightly packed nucleus with electrons whizzing around it. This theory of the atom is still accepted today.

Theories that have stood many years of testing often become scientific laws. The law of gravity is one example. Scientists assume many basic laws of nature.

In this book, you will learn about physical science. You will use scientific skills to solve problems and answer questions. You will follow some of the steps in the scientific method. And you will discover how important physical science is to your life.

Display a variety of tools that students will use in their own scientific investigations. Identify each tool and its purpose. Discuss the proper care of the tools and the need to follow safety precautions when performing investigations. You may wish to help students develop a list of safety rules to follow. They can make a poster outlining the rules for display in the classroom.

Tell students that through the investigations in *Physical Science*, they have the opportunity to perform as scientists. Remind them to use the opportunity to follow the scientific method and develop the skills that will enhance their study and understanding of science.

Planning Guide
The Metric System

	Student Pages	Vocabulary	Lesson Review
Lesson 1 What Is Physical Science?	2–5	✔	✔
Lesson 2 Why Scientists Measure	6–8	✔	✔
Lesson 3 Using Metric Units to Measure Length	9–14	✔	✔
Lesson 4 Using Metric Measurements to Find Area	15–19	✔	✔
Lesson 5 Using Metric Measurements to Find Volume	20–23	✔	✔
Lesson 6 Using Metric Units to Measure Mass	24–26	✔	✔

Chapter Activities

Student Text
Science Center
Teacher's Resource Library
Community Connection 1: Competing
in World Markets

Assessment Options

Student Text
Chapter 1 Review

Teacher's Resource Library
Chapter 1 Mastery Tests A and B

	Student Text Features								Teaching Strategies						Learning Styles						Teacher's Resource Library				
Achievements in Science	Science at Work	Science in Your Life	Investigation	Science Myth	Note	Technology Note	Did You Know	Science Integration	Science Journal	Cross-Curricular Connection	Online Connection	Teacher Alert	Applications (Home, Career, Community, Global, Environment)	Auditory/Verbal	Body/Kinesthetic	Interpersonal/Group Learning	Logical/Mathematical	Visual/Spatial	LEP/ESL	Workbook Activities	Alternative Workbook Activities	Lab Manual	Resource File	Self-Study Guide
					✔	✔		4	3	4			4				3			1	1	1	1	✔
				7		✔	6	8		7	8				7					2	2			✔
12		13			✔		10, 11		11	11						10			10	3	3	2		✔
	17	16	18	15						16			16	16						4	4	3		✔
23				21	✔					22		21, 23	21, 22					21		5	5	4	2	✔
								25	25	25	25							25		6	6			✔

Pronunciation Key

a	hat	e	let	ī	ice	ô	order	ù	put	sh	she	a in about
ā	age	ē	equal	o	hot	oi	oil	ü	rule	th	thin	e in taken
ä	far	ėr	term	ō	open	ou	out	ch	child	ᴛʜ	then	ə { i in pencil
â	care	i	it	ò	saw	u	cup	ng	long	zh	measure	o in lemon
												u in circus

Alternative Workbook Activities

The Teacher's Resource Library (TRL) contains a set of lower-level worksheets called Alternative Workbook Activities. These worksheets cover the same content as the regular Workbook Activities but are written at a second-grade reading level.

Skill Track Software

Use the Skill Track Software for Physical Science for additional reinforcement of this chapter. The software program allows students using AGS textbooks to be assessed for mastery of each chapter and lesson of the textbook. Students access the software on an individual basis and are assessed with multiple-choice items.

Skill Track Software
for Physical Science

Teacher's Resource Library TRL

Workbook Activities 1–6

Alternative Workbook Activities
1–6

Lab Manual 1–4

Community Connection 1

Resource File 1–2

Chapter 1 Self-Study Guide

Chapter 1 Mastery Tests A and B

(Answer Keys for the Teacher's
Resource Library begin on page 402
of the Teacher's Edition. The
Materials List for the Lab Manual
activities begins on page 419.)

Science Center

Have students cut out pictures of everyday
objects from magazines and newspapers.
These pictures could depict people,
animals, cars, radios, or quantities of
liquid. As each picture is placed on display,
have students decide what properties of
the object they might wish to measure. For
example, they might want to know the
length and width of a sofa, the weight of a
dog, or the amount of juice in a glass.

Write their suggestions under each picture.
Give each student one or more cutout. As
they go through the chapter, students
should choose the most appropriate
metric unit for measuring the objects
pictured in their cutouts. For example,
meters might be best for measuring a sofa
while centimeters might be best for
measuring a small personal CD player.

Community Connection 1

Chapter

1 The Metric System

Forests have many trees. Notice how the trees in the photograph were planted in rows. It is easy to count trees when they are planted in rows. But counting is only one way to measure trees. What unit of measurement would you use to tell how tall the trees are—*feet* or *meters*? What unit of measurement would you use to tell how much material they include—*pounds* or *kilograms*? How would you measure the space they occupy—in *cubic inches* or *cubic centimeters*? Scientists around the world use the metric system to measure. In Chapter 1, you will learn about the metric system and how easy it is to use.

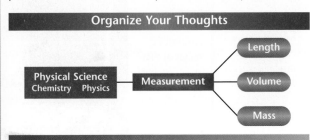

Organize Your Thoughts

Physical Science
Chemistry Physics → Measurement → Length / Volume / Mass

Goals for Learning

◆ To explain what matter and energy are
◆ To tell why measurement is important
◆ To use the basic metric units of length, volume, and mass
◆ To explain the meaning of prefixes used with metric units of measurements
◆ To calculate area and volume, using metric units
◆ To convert metric units

1

Introducing the Chapter

Use the photograph to introduce the idea of measurement and the metric system that scientists use. Write the words *Metric System* on chart paper and draw a three-column chart with headings *What I Know, What I Want to Know,* and *What I Learned*. Ask students to write as many statements as possible in the first two columns—what they know and what they want to know. Display the chart in the classroom. As they work through Chapter 1, have students check off statements on the chart that are verified by the text. Have them write brief explanatory statements on index cards as they find answers to topics they want to know about. Display the index cards next to the chart, with lengths of strings connecting the explanations to the original statement. After students have completed the chapter, have them fill in the *What I Learned* column of the chart.

Notes and Technology Notes

Ask volunteers to read the notes that appear in the margins throughout the chapter. Then discuss them with the class.

TEACHER'S RESOURCE

The AGS Teaching Strategies in Science Transparencies may be used with this chapter. The transparencies add an interactive dimension to expand and enhance the *Physical Science* program content.

CAREER INTEREST INVENTORY

The AGS Harrington-O'Shea Career Decision-Making System-Revised (CDM) may be used with this chapter. Students can use the CDM to explore their interests and identify careers. The CDM defines career areas that are indicated by students' responses on the inventory.

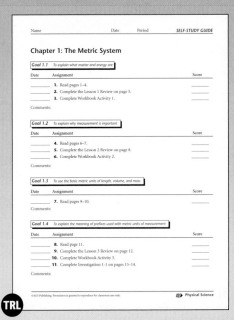

Chapter 1 Self-Study Guide

The Metric System Chapter 1 **1**

Lesson at a Glance

Chapter 1 Lesson 1

Overview This lesson introduces students to the study of physical science. Students learn that physical science is the study of matter and energy. They also learn what skills physical scientists use.

Objectives
- To explain and define physical science
- To explain matter
- To name two areas of physical science
- To describe some tools of physical scientists

Student Pages 2–5

Teacher's Resource Library

Workbook Activity 1

Alternative Workbook Activity 1

Lab Manual 1

Resource File 1

Vocabulary

chemistry	physical science
mass	physics
matter	

Science Background

The difference between matter and energy is straightforward. Matter has mass and takes up space while energy has no mass and takes up no space. Energy will do work. For example, it can heat water or run machines. Chemistry is the area of physical science concerned with the properties of matter and how matter changes from one chemical form to another. For example, specialists in chemistry may study how steel and oxygen change to iron oxide, or rust. Physics deals with how matter and energy are related. For example, physicists might study how satellites stay in orbit.

 Warm-Up Activity

Have students look at the objects on page 4 of the Student Edition. Ask them to identify each tool and what it does or measures.

Objectives

After reading this lesson, you should be able to
- explain and define physical science.
- explain matter.
- name two areas of physical science.
- describe some tools of physical scientists.

Physical science
The study of matter and energy

Matter
Anything that has mass and takes up space

Mass
The amount of material an object has

Have you ever wondered how a camera or a computer works? Do you listen to music on the radio or a boombox? Do you know how the sound is produced? Have you ever noticed that your body seems to weigh less in water? Do you know why?

All of these questions—and many more—can be answered by studying **physical science.** Physical science is the study of the things around you. It deals with **matter** and energy. Matter is anything that has mass and takes up space.

The Study of Matter and Energy

Look around you. What do you have in common with all the objects you see—your desk, the floor, the air? At first, you might think you have very little in common with these objects. But, in fact, all of them—including you—are made of matter. Other examples of matter appear in the photograph.

All matter has **mass**. Mass is the amount of material that an object has. All of the objects in the photo have mass. The cat has more mass than the potted plant.

What do all these objects have in common?

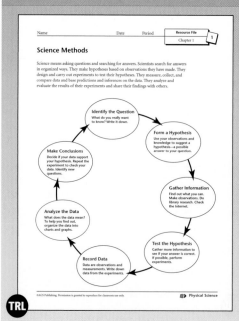

Resource File 1

Energy is different from matter. You cannot hold energy or measure it with a ruler. Energy is needed to make things move. You use it to move your body. A car uses energy to move, too. You will learn more about energy in Chapter 8.

Two Areas of Physical Science

Physical science can be divided into two areas. One area is **chemistry.** Chemistry is the study of matter and how it changes. Chemistry can explain how a cake rises or how acid rain forms. Chemistry is also the study of how matter can be made into new materials. By studying chemistry, scientists have made new medicines, food, clothing, fragrances, and soaps. They have even made artificial skin and bones for people.

A second area of physical science is **physics.** Physics is the study of energy and how it acts with matter. Physics can explain why helium balloons rise or how lasers work. Scientists studying physics have developed television, cellular phones, stereo systems, computers, space satellites, microwave ovens, and jet airplanes.

Computers and cell phones are among the many products physical scientists have developed.

Then ask students to write a short fictional story in which someone uses several of the tools.

 Teaching the Lesson

There are three parts to Lesson 1. Have students find two topic sentences for each part. The topic sentences they choose should represent important ideas. Alternatively, they can write their own topic sentences from the ideas presented. Ask students to read their sentences aloud.

Tell students that in the United States people use two systems of measurement—the customary system and the metric system. Ask students to identify places where they have seen metric measurements. Then organize students into teams. Tell the teams that they are in charge of developing a new product or structure. They might be asked to build a new racing car, a computer, a road under the ocean, or a space station. Ask students to list the reasons why exact measurements are crucial to their project. Students should also consider the problems that might result from inexact measurements.

 Reinforce and Extend

The Tools of Physical Scientists

Physical scientists—and all scientists—use many different skills. The skills they use include observing, classifying, measuring, organizing, inferring, predicting, modeling, analyzing, and communicating. Scientists need to be curious. They need to ask questions such as "Why does sugar dissolve in water when sand does not?" Scientists want to know how and why things are the way they are.

Scientists answer their questions by doing experiments. You will also do experiments to answer questions. In this book, these experiments are called Investigations.

Scientists have to know how to use scientific tools. In the figure below, you can see some of the tools scientists use. You will use many of these tools as you do the Investigations.

Scientists also need to know how to make measurements. Measurements are an important part of the information scientists gather. In the following lessons, you will learn how to measure like a scientist.

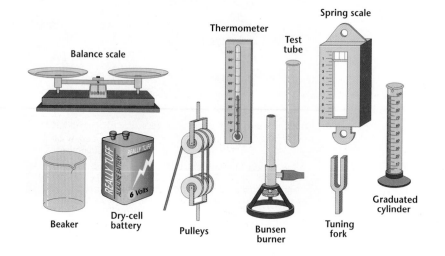

Lesson 1   R E V I E W

Write your answers to these questions in complete sentences on a sheet of paper.

1. What is physical science?

2. What are two examples of matter?

3. What are two areas of physical science?

4. What kinds of things do scientists in each area study?

5. What are three tools that scientists use to do experiments?

6. List three skills that scientists use.

7. How do scientists answer questions?

8. What is matter?

9. What area of physical science would be involved in the search for a cure for the common cold?

10. Name three tools that scientists could use to measure liquids.

Technology Note

In the 1960s, the U.S. government created what we now call the Internet. The Internet was designed to maintain government communications in case of a national emergency. In 1990, the World Wide Web portion of the Internet was born. The WWW was invented to meet the needs of some particle physicists located around the world. These scientists were looking for a faster, more effective way to communicate and share ideas. Though it was originally designed as a collaboration tool for scientists in the high-energy physics community, the Web is now available to everyone.

The Metric System   Chapter 1   5

Lesson 1 Review Answers

1. Physical science is the study of matter and energy. 2. Answers might include a desk and the floor. 3. Chemistry and physics are two areas of physical science. 4. Scientists concerned with chemistry study matter and how it changes. Physicists study how energy acts upon matter. 5. Answers will vary. Possible answers: balance scale, beaker, battery, pulley, thermometer, test tube, Bunsen burner, tuning fork, spring scale, graduated cylinder 6. Answers will vary. Possible answers: observing, classifying, measuring, organizing, inferring, predicting, modeling, analyzing, communicating. 7. Scientists answer questions by doing experiments. 8. Matter is anything that has mass and takes up space. 9. Chemistry is the area of physical science that would be involved in the search for a cure for the common cold. 10. Scientists could use a beaker, a test tube, and a graduated cylinder to measure liquids.

Portfolio Assessment

Sample items include:
- Story from Warm-Up Activity
- Topic sentences from Teaching the Lesson
- Lesson 1 Review answers

Lab Manual Page (bottom left)

Name _____ Date _____ Period _____ **Lab Manual, Page 1** Chapter 1 **1**

Safety in the Classroom

Purpose Why is it important to know where safety equipment is located in your classroom? You will identify and locate the safety equipment in your classroom.

Materials meterstick
metric ruler
colored pencil

Procedure

1. With a partner, draw a floor diagram of your classroom. Use the grid on the next page to make your diagram. Draw your diagram as close to the actual scale as possible. Include the location of desks, windows, doors, cabinets, and other large items.

2. Survey your classroom for safety equipment, such as fire extinguishers and safety glasses. On your diagram, mark the location of the safety equipment. Use a different symbol for each piece of equipment. In one corner of your diagram, make a key for the symbols you use.

3. Locate the electrical outlets in the classroom. On your diagram, use a symbol to mark the location of each outlet. Include the symbol in the key.

4. If your classroom has gas outlets, use a symbol to mark these on the diagram. Include the symbol in the key.

5. Mark the location of your workstation. Use a colored pencil to map out the quickest and safest exit route in case of an emergency.

Questions and Conclusions

1. Suppose the exit route you marked becomes blocked. What other route might you take?

2. What safety equipment is available in your classroom? What additional equipment would you like in your classroom?

Explore Further

Make a copy of the grid on the next page and use it to make a similar diagram of your home. Share your information about safety equipment and emergency exits with family members.

Publishing. Permission is granted to reproduce for classroom use only.   ● Physical Science

Lab Manual 1, pages 1–2

Workbook Activity Page (bottom right)

Name _____ Date _____ Period _____ **Workbook Activity** Chapter 1, Lesson 1 **1**

What Is Physical Science?

Directions Read each statement. Then unscramble the letters in parentheses. Each statement is a clue for the term. Write the term on the line.

1. Physical science that explains how a helium balloon rises
(chisspy) _____

2. The amount of material in a tree
(sams) _____

3. Anything that has mass and takes up space
(tarmet) _____

4. Physical science that explains how acid rain forms
(therycism) _____

5. Study of things around you
(salichpy niecesc) _____

6. What is needed to make things move
(genery) _____

Directions Read the terms. Cross out the term that does not belong. Explain why the term does not belong.

7. organizing, tuning fork, predicting _____

8. technology, chemistry, physics _____

9. balance scale, Bunsen burner, measurements _____

10. matter, computers, microwave ovens _____

Publishing. Permission is granted to reproduce for classroom use only.   ● Physical Science

Workbook Activity 1

Chapter 1 Lesson 2

Overview In this lesson, students explore the importance of measurement as part of a scientific investigation. Students also are introduced to the metric system of measurement.

Objectives

- To explain why measurements are important
- To explain the importance of using units that are the same for everyone
- To identify two systems of measurement

Student Pages 6–8

Teacher's Resource Library **TRL**

Workbook Activity 2

Alternative Workbook Activity 2

Vocabulary

customary
metric system
unit

Science Background

Scientists use measurements to gather objective data. In this way, scientists can compare the results of experiments from around the world. Through measurement, a scientist can also determine how something changes over time. For example, scientists have investigated changes in the ozone layer by taking measurements from year to year. The scientists compare the production of CFCs, the chemical that destroys ozone, with the depletion of ozone in the upper atmosphere. The data convinced them that CFCs were destroying the ozone layer. Scientists use many measuring tools, such as graduated cylinders, that are similar to those used in a school lab.

1 Warm-Up Activity

Use a clean overhead transparency. Have each student put a thumbprint on the transparency. All prints should point in the same direction. Use ground graphite (pencil lead) and an art brush to dust each print.

Be careful not to leave extra fingerprints. Project the transparency and call attention to the different thumb sizes. Ask students what might happen if everyone used his or her own thumb for measuring.

2 Teaching the Lesson

Write the vocabulary words from Lesson 1 on the board. Have students discuss the meaning of each word. Write the vocabulary words from Lesson 2 next to the Lesson 1 words. Have students discuss the meanings. Ask students to write a sentence with at least one word from each lesson.

Make photocopies of the overhead transparency used in the Warm-Up Activity. With the copier set on dark, the

thumbprints should show up on the copies. As a class, select one thumbprint to be used as a standard. Divide the class into teams and give each team a copy of the thumbprints. Ask the teams to determine how the sizes of the other prints relate to the standard print. How much bigger or smaller are they? As a class, discuss and compare the findings of the teams.

Did You Know?

Ask a volunteer to read the feature on page 6. Point out to students that carob is an evergreen tree that produces carob beans in pods. Today the carob bean is often used as a substitute for chocolate.

Objectives

After reading this lesson, you should be able to

- explain why measurements are important.
- explain the importance of using units that are the same for everyone.
- identify two systems of measurement.

Unit
A known amount used for measuring

Did You Know?

In ancient times, the Arabs used carob beans as a standard to measure small amounts. Carob beans are very consistent in size. They usually weigh the same no matter when or where they were grown.

Look at the poles in the photo. Which one is the tallest? Use a ruler to measure each one.

Are the poles the same height?

Though some look taller than others, in reality the poles are the same height. Measurements are important because we cannot always trust observations made with our eyes. Measurements help us gather exact information. Exact measurements are especially important to a scientist.

Units of Measurement

When you measured the poles in the photo above, you probably measured with a ruler marked in inches. You compared the length of the pole to a known measurement, the inch. A known amount in measurement, such as the inch, is called a **unit.** Other units you might be familiar with are the yard, mile, minute, and day.

Customary
Ordinary

Metric system
System of measurement used by scientists

If you had lived thousands of years ago, you most likely would have used units of measurement that were based on the length of certain parts of your body.

For example, Egyptians used the cubit to measure length. A cubit was the distance from the elbow to the tip of the middle finger. The Romans used the width of their thumb to measure length. This unit of measurement was called an uncia.

Compare the widths of the thumbs of each person in your classroom. Do you think they are all the same? Probably not. So you can see why using units of measurement based on body parts does not work very well. The exact length of an uncia or a cubit could vary from person to person.

In order for a unit of measurement to be useful, it has to be the same for everybody. When one scientist tells another scientist that something is a certain length, that measurement should mean the same thing to both of them.

Systems of Measurement

You probably measure in units based on the **customary** system. Some customary units for measuring length are the inch, foot, yard, and mile. Customary units also can be used to measure time, weight, and other amounts.

In the customary system of measurement, it is difficult to convert one unit to another because the units are very different. The units of measure also are not clearly related to each other.

Scientists and most other people throughout the world use a different system of measurement. They use the **metric system.** Metric units are the most common units of measurement in the world. The metric system is simpler to use and easier to remember than the customary system. You will use the metric system in this book. You will find conversion information about some metric and customary measurements in Appendix C on pages 380–381.

*The Metric System   Chapter 1   **7***

 Reinforce and Extend

LEARNING STYLES

Body/Kinesthetic
Identify the lengths of uncias (thumb widths) and cubits (distance from the elbow to the tip of the middle finger). Then organize students into small groups. Have each group devise two ways to measure the number of uncias in a cubit. Students might go thumb over thumb all the way down the arm from the elbow to the fingertip to determine the number. They might draw a line that is the length of a cubit on paper. They then could measure the line with the thumb. They might measure the thumb and the elbow-to-fingertip distance with a ruler. They then could divide the cubit measurement by the uncia measurement. Have groups report their findings to the class. Are there differences among the data? What might explain the differences?

Science Myth

Ask volunteers to read the myth and fact portions of the Science Myth on page 7. Explain to students that any measurement system that uses standardized units can provide accurate measurements. You may wish to display a ruler with measurements shown in inches, centimeters, and picas to measure the length of an object. Use it to demonstrate that measurements can be made accurately using the varying units of measure.

CROSS-CURRICULAR CONNECTION

 Drama
Have students develop a skit about using units, such as the uncia, as standards of measurement. Students might write a creative dialogue that might take place between people with unique ideas for units of measurement. Students might dramatize why people need a standard unit or what could happen when one cubit doesn't equal another.

*The Metric System   Chapter 1   **7***

Lesson 2 Review Answers

1. We can't always trust observations we make with our eyes. Measurements help us gather exact information. 2. It creates a standard unit of measure that is always the same. If each person used his or her own unit of measurement, the measurement would not be clearly understood by everyone else. 3. Some common units in the customary system are the inch, foot, yard, and mile. 4. Scientists use the metric system. 5. You would measure your finger in centimeters. 6. There are 12 inches in one foot. 7. There are 3 feet in one yard. 8. There are 60 minutes in one hour. 9. There are 60 seconds in one minute. 10. There are 3,600 seconds in one hour.

SCIENCE INTEGRATION

Biology
Ask students to use an almanac to find information about the world's largest and smallest marine and land animals. Have them make a chart showing the animals' measurements in both customary and metric units.

ONLINE CONNECTION

Direct students to the Dictionary of Units of Measurement site at www.unc.edu/~rowlett/ units. The site provides definitions of and other information about units of measurement in the customary and metric systems.

Portfolio Assessment

Sample items include:
- Vocabulary sentences from Teaching the Lesson
- Lesson 2 Review answers

Write your answers to these questions in complete sentences on a sheet of paper.

1. Why are measurements important?

2. Why is it important to use units of measurement that are the same for everyone?

3. What are some common units in the customary system of measurement?

4. What is the name of the system of measurement that scientists use?

5. Name the unit of measurement you would use to measure the length of your finger.

Answer these questions to find out how familiar you are with the customary system.

6. How many inches are in 1 foot?

7. How many feet are in 1 yard?

8. How many minutes are in 1 hour?

9. How many seconds are in 1 minute?

10. How many seconds are in 1 hour?

Technology Note

Digital measurers use sound waves to measure distance. A laser beam points at the spot from which you want to measure. At the same time, a sound wave bounces off that spot. The measurer calculates the distance the sound wave traveled. Then it displays the measurement digitally.

Workbook Activity 2

The metric system is similar to the money system used in the United States. As the figure shows, there are 10 pennies in a dime, 10 dimes in a dollar, and 10 dollars in a 10-dollar bill. You can say that the money system is based on a system of tens. Likewise, you will see that the metric system is based on a system of tens.

 =

Meter, m

The basic unit of length in the metric system; it is about 39 inches

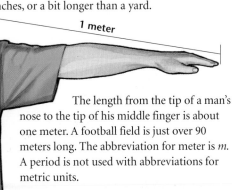

Using Meters

In the metric system, you measure length in **meters** or parts of a meter. A meter is a little more than 39 inches, or a bit longer than a yard.

1 meter

The length from the tip of a man's nose to the tip of his middle finger is about one meter. A football field is just over 90 meters long. The abbreviation for meter is *m*. A period is not used with abbreviations for metric units.

The Metric System   Chapter 1   **9**

Vocabulary

centimeter	meterstick
kilometer	millimeter
meter	

Science Background

While most people in the United States commonly use the customary system of measurement, including inches, miles, pounds, and gallons, scientists use the metric system. This system is based on such units as meters, kilometers, grams, and liters. The metric system has some advantages. Also known as the International System of Units, or SI, metric measurements are used throughout the world. Because the system is based on multiples of 10, measurements can be stated as decimals. For example, a centimeter contains 10 millimeters. A length of 14 millimeters could be written as 1.4 centimeters.

1 Warm-Up Activity

Divide the class into groups. Cut meter-length strips from poster board and give each group a strip. Ask the groups to use the strips to measure classroom objects and to record their measurements. Students should use the strips to estimate measurements less than 1 meter.

Continued on page 10

Continued from page 9

After they report their measurements, ask students how they could more accurately measure lengths shorter than a meter. Students should suggest dividing the strip into smaller units.

Teaching the Lesson

At the start of a metric unit, students often have difficulty distinguishing between the prefixes *kilo-* and *milli-*. You may find it beneficial to firmly establish the concepts of centimeter and millimeter before introducing kilometers.

Many students learn best when explaining to another person. Organize pairs of students to act as teachers and students. Have teachers explain the concept of meters, centimeters, and millimeters to the students. Teachers should use the figure and charts on pages 10 and 11 to help in the explanation. Have teachers and students switch roles and repeat the activity.

Reinforce and Extend

Did You Know?

Have students read the feature on page 10. Tell students that the speed of light is 299,792,458 meters per second. Ask them to write a fraction that shows the amount of time it takes light to travel 1 meter. ($\frac{1}{299,792,458}$ second)

LEARNING STYLES

Interpersonal/ Group Learning

Most students know the saying, "Thirty days hath September, April, June . . ." Tell students that verses such as these, called mnemonics, help people to remember things. Ask groups of students to write a mnemonic that will help them remember the metric prefixes. Students should incorporate as many prefixes as they can in their mnemonic. Ask groups to share their mnemonics with the class.

Meterstick
A common tool for measuring length in the metric system

Centimeter, cm
A metric unit of measure that is $\frac{1}{100}$ of a meter

Millimeter, mm
A metric unit of measure that is $\frac{1}{1,000}$ of a meter

 Did You Know?

The way scientists define the meter keeps changing. It used to be one ten-millionth of the distance from the North Pole to the equator. Now it is how far light travels during a small fraction of a second.

The common tool for measuring length in the metric system is the **meterstick.** It is one meter long.

The figure below shows part of a meterstick. Notice that it is divided into equal units. Each of these units is a **centimeter.** A centimeter is $\frac{1}{100}$ of a meter. You can use centimeters when the meter is too long a unit. For example, it might be difficult to measure the width of your book in meters, but you could easily use centimeters. The abbreviation for centimeter is *cm*.

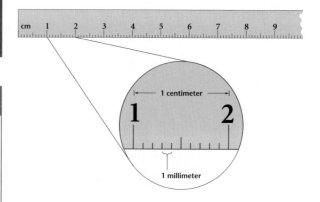

Sometimes, even the centimeter is too large a unit to measure an object. You need a smaller unit. Look at the meterstick again. Notice that each centimeter is divided into 10 smaller units. Each of these smaller units is a **millimeter.** A millimeter is $\frac{1}{1,000}$ of a meter. You would measure the width of a pencil in millimeters. Use *mm* as an abbreviation for millimeter.

LEARNING STYLES

LEP/ESL

Many students with limited English proficiency may have grown up using the metric system rather than the customary system. Provide these students with the opportunity to teach the class about the system. They can demonstrate the use of metric measuring tools and relate their own experiences with the metric system of measurement.

Using meters to describe the distance from your school to your home would likely result in a large number of units. It would be more convenient to use a unit larger than a meter. The **kilometer,** which is equal to 1,000 meters, would be more useful. The abbreviation for kilometer is *km*.

Length Equivalents	
10 millimeters	1 centimeter
1,000 millimeters	1 meter
100 centimeters	1 meter
1,000 meters	1 kilometer

Using Metric Prefixes

Once you understand how the meterstick is divided, you know how to use other units of measurement in the metric system. The prefixes in front of the word *meter* have special meanings. They are used to show how many times the meter is multiplied or divided. Just as a cent is $\frac{1}{100}$ of a dollar, a centimeter is $\frac{1}{100}$ of a meter. The prefix *centi-* means $\frac{1}{100}$. You will learn how to use the prefixes shown in the table with other units of measurement later in this chapter.

Some Metric Prefixes		
Prefix	Meaning	Unit and Its Abbreviation
kilo- (k)	$1,000 \times$	kilometer (km)
centi- (c)	$\frac{1}{100}$ (0.01)	centimeter (cm)
milli- (m)	$\frac{1}{1,000}$ (0.001)	millimeter (mm)

Lesson 3 Review Answers

1. C points to 1 mm. 2. A points to 1 cm.
3. There are 10 mm in 1 cm. 4. There are
100 mm in 10 cm. 5. The match is 40 mm
long. The match is 4 cm long.

Achievements in Science

Ask a volunteer to read aloud the
Achievements in Science feature on page
12. Direct student pairs to research
additional information about the
responsibilities and goals of the National
Institute of Standards and Technology in
an encyclopedia or at www.nist.gov/.
Encourage each pair to share their
findings with the class.

Portfolio Assessment

Sample items include:
- Measurements of room objects from
Teaching the Lesson and Reinforce and
Extend activities
- Lesson 3 Review answers

Lesson 3 REVIEW

Write your answers to these questions in complete sentences on
a sheet of paper.

1. Which letter in the figure below marks 1 millimeter?

2. Which letter shows 1 centimeter?

3. How many millimeters are there in 1 centimeter?

4. How many millimeters are there in 10 centimeters?

5. What is the measurement in millimeters of the match?
What is it in centimeters?

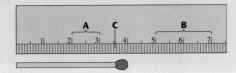

Achievements in Science

Measurement Standards

Every measurement compares an unknown quantity with a standard. A measurement
standard defines the size of a unit. People based early standards on local customs.
They sometimes used body parts to create standards. They also used objects like grains
and stones.

In the 1400s, King Edward I of England created what may have been the first uniform
standards. He ordered a measuring stick made of iron to be a master yardstick. The first
metric standards were a standard meter bar and kilogram bar. The French government
officially adopted them in 1799. The international kilogram bar and meter bar are made
of a mixture of metals.

The Bureau of Weights and Measures in France keeps standards of length and mass.
In the United States, the National Institute of Standards and Technology keeps these
same standards. All metersticks and scales are checked against these standards.

Name _____ Date _____ Period _____ | Workbook Activity
Chapter 1, Lesson 3 | 3

Adding and Subtracting Metric Units of Length

Directions Add or subtract the numbers in each problem. Then simplify your
answer. Write your answer on the line. The first one is done for you.

1. 12 centimeters 5 millimeters
    + 5 centimeters 3 millimeters   17 centimeters 8 millimeters

2. 10 meters 8 centimeters
    + 9 meters 9 centimeters

3. 22 meters 4 centimeters
    + 3 meters 5 centimeters

4. 20 meters 10 millimeters
    +   23 millimeters

5. 10 centimeters 5 millimeters
    + 22 centimeters 8 millimeters

6. 6 meters 2 centimeters
    + 4 meters

7. 23 millimeters
    + 3 millimeters

8. 11 meters 9 millimeters
    + 8 meters 6 millimeters

9. 39 meters 9 millimeters
    − 1 meter 6 millimeters

10. 20 meters 7 centimeters
    −   5 centimeters

Publishing. Permission is granted to reproduce for classroom use only.   Physical Science

Workbook Activity 3

Hands Instead of Feet

Purpose

Can you think of a measuring system that would be more useful than the metric system? In this investigation, you will create a system of measuring length and compare it to the metric system.

Procedure

1. Copy the data table on a sheet of paper.

Object	Length in Hands	Length in Centimeters

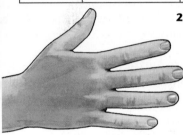

2. Measure several objects in your classroom. Your teacher will tell you which objects to measure. Each member of the class will measure the same objects.

3. Use your stretched out right hand as a measuring tool. The length of this hand from your wrist to the end of your longest finger will equal one unit of length in "hands."

4. Measure the length, in hands, of each object. Estimate to the nearest length of a hand. Record this information in the table.

SAFETY ALERT

◆ Watch for sharp edges or materials that may cause splinters.
◆ Arrange the stations so that student pairs have enough room to use metersticks without interfering with the work of other pairs.

Investigation 1-1

The Purpose portion of the stude̶ investigation begins with a ̶ draw them into the activi ̶ students to read the investig̶ ̶s and formulate their own questions before beginning the investigation. This investigation will take approximately 30 minutes to complete. Students will use these process and thinking skills: measuring, collecting, and interpreting data and comparing and drawing conclusions.

Preparation

• Select objects to be measured and carefully measure them in centimeters before the investigation begins. Choose objects that are longer than a hand's width. Include at least one object that is more than a meter long.

• You might set up measurements stations. Place two objects to be measured at each station.

• Students may use Lab Manual 2 to record their data and answer the questions.

Procedure

• Suggest students work in pairs. Student A can measure the objects and Student B can record the data. Then they switch roles and compare their data. If the measurements are different, have students remeasure.

• Have students move from station to station to measure objects. Identify the direction in which teams should move from station to station. Have students remain at each station for a specific amount of time.

• To extend the activity, have students measure some objects in uncias and/or cubits. If students do this, they will need to make an additional data table.

• As an extra challenge, have students measure objects in hands, and use uncias for distances less than 1 hand. For example, a book may be 1 hand and 3 uncias long. Tell students to determine how many uncias to a hand.

Continued on page 14

Continued from page 13

Results

The comparison of hand-based measurements should reveal variances in measurements because of the difference in hand sizes. The comparison of meterstick measurements should not vary by more than a centimeter.

Questions and Conclusions Answers

1. No, our length in hands didn't match those of the other students because the unit of measurement, our hands, varied from person to person.

2. Yes, the length in centimeters did match those of the other students because the unit of measurement was the same for everyone.

3. Yes, the metric system is more useful because the units of measurement do not vary from person to person.

Explore Further Answers

The effectiveness of the students' systems measurement depends on whether they choose a standard unit of measurement or one with a varying unit of measurement, such as a hand or cubit.

Assessment

Check students' data for accuracy of measurements. You might include the following items from this investigation in student portfolios:

• Investigation 1-1 data table

• Answers to Questions and Conclusions and Explore Further sections

5. After you have measured all the objects, compare your results with those of at least five other students.

6. Measure the objects again, using a meterstick instead of your hand. Record your measurements in centimeters.

7. Compare your results with those of other students in your class.

Questions and Conclusions

1. Did your length in hands match those of other students? Explain your answer.

2. Did your length in centimeters match those of other students? Explain your answer.

3. Do you think a system such as the metric system is more useful than one that uses units such as hands? Explain your answer.

Explore Further

Develop your own system of measurement. Determine the units you will use. Share your system with the class.

Name _____ Date _____ Period _____ | Lab Manual
Chapter 1 | 2

1-1 **Hands Instead of Feet**
Use with Investigation 1-1, pages 13–14

Purpose Can you think of a measuring system that would be more useful than the metric system? In this investigation, you will create a system of measuring length and compare it to the metric system.

Object	Length in Hands	Length in Centimeters

Questions and Conclusions

1. Did your length in hands match those of other students? Explain your answer.

2. Did your length in centimeters match those of other students? Explain your answer.

3. Do you think a system such as the metric system is more useful than one that uses units such as hands? Explain your answer.

Explore Further

Develop your own system of measurement. Determine the units you will use. Share your system with the class.

Publishing. Permission is granted to reproduce for classroom use only. | Physical Science

Lab Manual 2

You can use measurements of length to calculate other measurements. One example of a calculated measurement is **area.** Area is the amount of space the surface of an object takes up.

Notice that each side of the square in the figure below measures 1 cm. To find the area of the square, multiply the length by the width.

$$\text{area} = \text{length} \times \text{width}$$
$$= 1 \text{ cm} \times 1 \text{ cm}$$
$$= 1 \text{ cm}^2$$

EXAMPLE

When you calculate area, the units of length and width must be the same. Express the answer in square units. To do this, write a small 2 at the upper right of the unit. This is called an **exponent.** An exponent is a number that tells how many times another number is a factor. In the example above, the unit is read *square centimeter*. Square centimeter (cm^2) means centimeter $\times$ centimeter. The area of the square is 1 square centimeter (1 cm^2).

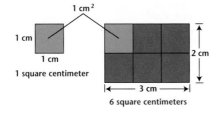

Now look at the rectangle in the figure. Its length is 3 cm. Its width is 2 cm. The figure shows that the rectangle contains 6 square centimeters.

Lesson at a Glance

Chapter 1 Lesson 4

Overview This lesson introduces the formula for finding area. Students calculate the area of a square and a rectangle.

Objectives

■ To explain and define area
■ To calculate area in metric units

Student Pages 15–19

Teacher's Resource Library

   Workbook Activity 4
   Alternative Workbook Activity 4
   Lab Manual 3

Vocabulary

area
exponent

1   Warm-Up Activity

Tell students to imagine they are going to seed their lawn. The directions on the bag of grass seed state that one bag will cover 400 m^2. They want to buy enough grass seed, but not more than they need. Ask how they can determine whether one bag will be enough.

2   Teaching the Lesson

Have students copy the lesson objectives as headings on a sheet of paper. After they read the lesson, discuss what area is and how to calculate it in metric units. Then have students record this information under the appropriate objective on their paper.

Project an overhead transparency with rectangles drawn on it. Use a transparent metric ruler to demonstrate how to measure the length and width of a rectangle. Then calculate the area of the rectangle. Repeat the demonstration several times, having students read the measurements and calculate the area.

Help students understand that area depends on the length and width of a rectangle and rectangles with different lengths and widths can have the same area. Draw on the board three sets of rectangles. Each set should have at least

two rectangles with different dimensions but equal areas. For example, a 2-cm-by-6-cm rectangle and a 3-cm-by-4-cm rectangle have the same area but different dimensions. Have students calculate the area of each rectangle.

Science Myth

Ask a volunteer to read the myth portion of the Science Myth feature on page 15. Then have another volunteer read the fact portion of the feature. Emphasize the importance of using correct unit names when identifying measurements. If you give a quiz, consider deducting points if the unit designation is missing or incorrect.

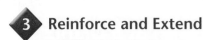

3 Reinforce and Extend

LEARNING STYLES

Auditory/Verbal

Ask pairs to suppose they work at a paint store and they have been asked to make an instructional tape for customers. On the tape, they will explain how to measure a room and to use the measurements to determine the amount of paint needed. Suggest that students write a script for their recording.

AT HOME

When houses or apartments are sold or rented, they are often described by area—how many square feet of floor space. Have students measure each room in their home, in meters. They can then add the lengths of the rooms together and the widths of the rooms together. They can use the total length and width to calculate the total area of floor space in their home.

Science in Your Life

Often students see little practical application for the science they learn. This feature offers a good opportunity to relate science context to a practical application.

Have students read the Science in Your Life feature on page 16 and answer the question. Ask a volunteer to share the answer and explain the process he or she used to calculate the answer. *(The area of the wall is 28 m². In the example, there is enough paint in the can to cover the wall.)*

Tell students to imagine they have to paint all four walls and that all the walls have the same area. Ask students how many cans of paint they will need. *(The total area of four walls would be 112 m². Students will use 3.5 cans of paint, so they will need to buy four cans.)*

You can find the area of the rectangle by using the same formula you used to find the area of the square.

> **EXAMPLE**
> area = length × width
> = 3 cm × 2 cm
> = 6 cm²

The area of the rectangle is 6 square centimeters.

What is the area of a rectangle with a length of 8.5 mm and a width of 3.3 mm?

> **EXAMPLE**
> area = length × width
> = 8.5 mm × 3.3 mm
> = 28.05 mm²

The area is 28.05 square millimeters.

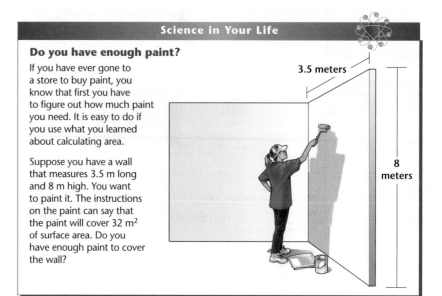

Science in Your Life

Do you have enough paint?

If you have ever gone to a store to buy paint, you know that first you have to figure out how much paint you need. It is easy to do if you use what you learned about calculating area.

Suppose you have a wall that measures 3.5 m long and 8 m high. You want to paint it. The instructions on the paint can say that the paint will cover 32 m² of surface area. Do you have enough paint to cover the wall?

3.5 meters

8 meters

16 *Chapter 1   The Metric System*

CROSS-CURRICULAR CONNECTION

Physical Education

Organize students into small groups and assign each group one of the following sports: basketball, football, and soccer. Have each group find out the dimensions of the playing field the assigned sport is played on.

With permission of the school administration, have students use tape or string to mark off the playing fields on the school grounds. Then have students calculate the area of the playing fields in metric units and order the playing fields from largest to smallest. *(football, 5,390 m²; hockey, 1,586 m²; and basketball, 435 m²)*

Lesson 4 REVIEW

Find the area for each of the rectangles in the table. Write your answers on a sheet of paper. The first one is done for you.

	Length	Width	Area (length × width)
1.	8 cm	7.2 cm	8 cm × 7.2 cm = 57.6 cm^2
2.	8 m	8 m	
3.	3.4 mm	5.2 mm	
4.	2.6 m	4.7 m	
5.	13 m	5.1 km	

▼◄▲▼◄▲▼◄▲▼◄▲▼◄▲▼◄▲▼◄▲▼◄▲▼◄▲▼◄▲▼◄▲▼◄▲▼◄▲▼◄▲▼◄▲▼◄▲▼◄▲

Science at Work

Instrument Calibration Technician

Instrument calibration technicians calibrate, or check the accuracy of, three types of instruments. The instruments make measurements, control equipment, or give information about what equipment is doing. All these instruments must be exact.

Instrument calibration technicians first test an instrument by comparing it with another instrument. They study the test results and keep a record. Instrument calibration technicians maintain and repair instruments so they stay calibrated.

Instrument calibration technicians must earn a two-year degree in electronics technology.

They must be able to handle details and must have strong fine-motor skills. They also must understand electronics.

The Metric System   Chapter 1   **17**

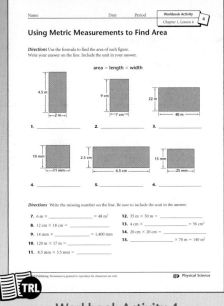

Workbook Activity 4

Lesson 4 Review Answers
1. 57.6 cm^2 2. 64 m^2 3. 17.68 mm^2
4. 12.22 m^2 5. 0.0663 km^2 or 66,300 cm^2

Science at Work

Ask volunteers to read the Science at Work feature about instrument calibration technicians on page 17.

The first two paragraphs describe the responsibilities of an instrument calibration technician. Ask students to explain why accurate instruments are important to scientists. *(Scientific findings are only as accurate as the instruments used to measure them.)*

PRONUNCIATION GUIDE

Use this list to help students pronounce difficult words in this lesson. Refer to the pronunciation key on the Chapter Planning Guide for the sounds of these symbols.

calibration (cal´ i bra´ tion)

technician (tek nish´ ən)

Portfolio Assessment

Sample items include:
• Worksheet from Teaching the Lesson
• Science in Your Life Answer
• Lesson 4 Review answers

Investigation 1-2

The Purpose portion of the student investigation begins with a question to draw them into the activity. Encourage students to read the investigation steps and formulate their own questions before beginning the investigation. This investigation will take approximately 45 minutes to complete. Students will use these process and thinking skills: measuring, collecting, and interpreting data and comparing and drawing conclusions.

Preparation

- Precut the sheets of paper so that you will have a variety of sizes to distribute to the students.
- Use light-colored construction paper, which will not tear as easily as plain white paper.
- Make sure you have paper, scissors, and a ruler for every student.
- It's a good idea to cut extra rectangles in case some get torn.
- Students may use Lab Manual 3 to record their data and answer the questions.

Procedure

- Students should do this activity individually.
- Some students might need help in understanding the words *calculate* and *grid*.
- Have students place a larger sheet of paper under the rectangle before they draw on it, so they won't mark the desk or table.
- After students mark off the four sides of the paper, they should connect all marks except those around the perimeter of the rectangle.
- For steps 6 and 7, students use their squares to make two smaller rectangles of different sizes. Make sure students use all the squares.

1-2 INVESTIGATION

Counting Squares and Calculating Area

Purpose

How is area related to square units? This investigation will show the relationship between area and the number of square units.

Materials
- safety glasses
- small sheet of paper
- ruler
- safety scissors

Procedure

1. Copy the data table on a sheet of paper.

	Length	Width	Area (length × width)	Total Number of Squares
original paper				
rectangle 1				
rectangle 2				

2. Put on your safety glasses. Obtain a small sheet of paper from your teacher. The size of your paper will be larger or smaller than your classmates' papers. Use a ruler to measure the length and width of the paper. Record these two measurements in centimeters in your table.

3. Use the following formula to calculate the area of the paper.

   $$\text{area} = \text{length} \times \text{width}$$

   Record this area. Remember that the units should be square centimeters (cm^2).

4. Use the ruler to mark off all four sides of the paper in 1-cm units. Using the ruler as a straightedge, draw straight lines to connect the marks from side to side. Now connect them from top to bottom. You will create a grid of squares similar to the one on the next page.

Lesson 4 R E V I E W

Find the area for each of the rectangles in the table. Write your answers on a sheet of paper. The first one is done for you.

	Length	Width	Area (length × width)
1.	8 cm	7.2 cm	8 cm × 7.2 cm = 57.6 cm²
2.	8 m	8 m	
3.	3.4 mm	5.2 mm	
4.	2.6 m	4.7 m	
5.	13 m	5.1 km	

Science at Work

Instrument Calibration Technician

Instrument calibration technicians calibrate, or check the accuracy of, three types of instruments. The instruments make measurements, control equipment, or give information about what equipment is doing. All these instruments must be exact.

Instrument calibration technicians first test an instrument by comparing it with another instrument. They study the test results and keep a record. Instrument calibration technicians maintain and repair instruments so they stay calibrated.

Instrument calibration technicians must earn a two-year degree in electronics technology.

They must be able to handle details and must have strong fine-motor skills. They also must understand electronics.

The Metric System   Chapter 1   **17**

Workbook Activity 4

Lesson 4 Review Answers
1. 57.6 cm² 2. 64 m² 3. 17.68 mm²
4. 12.22 m² 5. 0.0663 km² or 66,300 cm²

Science at Work

Ask volunteers to read the Science at Work feature about instrument calibration technicians on page 17.

The first two paragraphs describe the responsibilities of an instrument calibration technician. Ask students to explain why accurate instruments are important to scientists. *(Scientific findings are only as accurate as the instruments used to measure them.)*

PRONUNCIATION GUIDE

Use this list to help students pronounce difficult words in this lesson. Refer to the pronunciation key on the Chapter Planning Guide for the sounds of these symbols.

calibration (cal´ i bra´ tion)
technician (tek nish´ ən)

Portfolio Assessment

Sample items include:
• Worksheet from Teaching the Lesson
• Science in Your Life Answer
• Lesson 4 Review answers

The Metric System   Chapter 1   **17**

Investigation 1-2

The Purpose portion of the student investigation begins with a question to draw them into the activity. Encourage students to read the investigation steps and formulate their own questions before beginning the investigation. This investigation will take approximately 45 minutes to complete. Students will use these process and thinking skills: measuring, collecting, and interpreting data and comparing and drawing conclusions.

Preparation

- Precut the sheets of paper so that you will have a variety of sizes to distribute to the students.
- Use light-colored construction paper, which will not tear as easily as plain white paper.
- Make sure you have paper, scissors, and a ruler for every student.
- It's a good idea to cut extra rectangles in case some get torn.
- Students may use Lab Manual 3 to record their data and answer the questions.

Procedure

- Students should do this activity individually.
- Some students might need help in understanding the words *calculate* and *grid*.
- Have students place a larger sheet of paper under the rectangle before they draw on it, so they won't mark the desk or table.
- After students mark off the four sides of the paper, they should connect all marks except those around the perimeter of the rectangle.
- For steps 6 and 7, students use their squares to make two smaller rectangles of different sizes. Make sure students use all the squares.

1-2 INVESTIGATION

Counting Squares and Calculating Area

Purpose

How is area related to square units? This investigation will show the relationship between area and the number of square units.

Procedure

1. Copy the data table on a sheet of paper.

	Length	Width	Area (length × width)	Total Number of Squares
original paper				
rectangle 1				
rectangle 2				

2. Put on your safety glasses. Obtain a small sheet of paper from your teacher. The size of your paper will be larger or smaller than your classmates' papers. Use a ruler to measure the length and width of the paper. Record these two measurements in centimeters in your table.

3. Use the following formula to calculate the area of the paper.

$$\text{area} = \text{length} \times \text{width}$$

Record this area. Remember that the units should be square centimeters (cm^2).

4. Use the ruler to mark off all four sides of the paper in 1-cm units. Using the ruler as a straightedge, draw straight lines to connect the marks from side to side. Now connect them from top to bottom. You will create a grid of squares similar to the one on the next page.

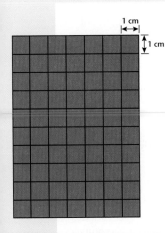

1 cm

1 cm

5. Count the squares on the paper. The area of each square is 1 square centimeter. That is because area = length × width = 1 cm × 1 cm = 1 cm². The area of the sheet of paper is the number of squares. Record that number in your table. The answer should be in square centimeters.

6. Cut the paper into squares along the lines you drew. Use all the individual squares to make two smaller rectangles of different lengths and widths. To do this, carefully place the squares next to each other in rows and columns. Make sure the squares have almost no space between them and that they do not overlap.

7. Measure the length and width of each new rectangle you create. Find the area of each one.

Questions and Conclusions

1. Does the area for the original paper in step 5 match the area calculated in step 3? Do you think it should? Explain your answer.

2. How does the sum of the areas of the two new rectangles compare to the total number of squares in the two rectangles? How does it compare to the calculated area of the original sheet of paper? Explain these results.

Explore Further

Repeat steps 1 through 5. Divide the grid in half. Use a ruler to draw a line from one corner to the opposite corner. Cut along the diagonal line. Measure the area of each triangle using the following formula.

$$\text{area} = \text{base} \times \frac{\text{height}}{2}$$

Calculate the sum of the two triangles. How does it compare to the area of the rectangle?

Results

No matter how students divide the larger rectangle, the sum of the areas of the two smaller rectangles will equal the area of the larger rectangle.

Questions and Conclusions Answers

1. Yes, the areas matched; answers will vary. (Sample answer: Area depends on length and width, not shape.)

2. The sum of the areas and the number of squares are the same. The sum of the areas and the area of the original rectangle are the same. Explanations will vary. (Sample answer: The total area was not increased or decreased, it was just arranged differently.)

Explore Further Answers

The sum of the area of the two triangles is equal to the sum of the area of the rectangle.

Assessment

Check students' work to be sure that they are using the correct formula correctly. Verify that students' results reflect the correct answer. You might include the following items from this investigation in student portfolios:

• Investigation 1-2 data table

• Questions and Conclusions and Explore Further Answers

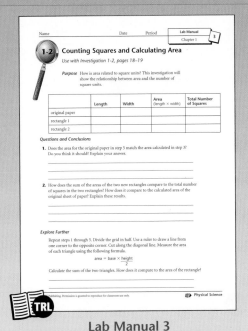

Lab Manual 3

Lesson at a Glance

Chapter 1 Lesson 5

Overview In this lesson, students calculate the volume of a box. They learn that the cubic centimeter and the liter are units of volume in the metric system. Students also convert from cubic centimeters to liters.

Objectives

- To explain what volume is
- To calculate volume in metric units
- To convert metric units of volume

Student Pages 20–23

Teacher's Resource Library

Workbook Activity 5

Alternative Workbook Activity 5

Lab Manual 4

Resource File 2

Vocabulary

cubic centimeter   milliliter
liter   volume

Warm-Up Activity

Show students 1- and 2-liter soft-drink bottles. Explain that most people around the world measure liquids in liters. Tell students that they are going to learn how liters relate to other metric units of measurement.

Teaching the Lesson

As they read, students should write two or three sentences in response to each lesson objective. Students should meet each objective before moving on to the next.

To help students visualize the quantity of 1 milliliter, fill a coffee cup and a drinking glass with water. Measure the water from the cup by using a graduated cylinder. Do the same for the glass. The glass of water may fill several cylinders. Ask students how many milliliters of orange juice they have for breakfast, or how many milliliters of water they drink in a day.

Point out to students that they may already be familiar with the term *cubic centimeter*, which is often abbreviated *cc.*

Objectives

After reading this lesson, you should be able to

- explain what volume is.
- calculate volume in metric units.
- convert metric units of volume.

Volume
The amount of space an object takes up

Cubic centimeter, cm³
A metric unit of measure that means centimeter × centimeter × centimeter

In 1975, the United States Congress passed the Metric Conversion Act. The act made the metric system the preferred system of measurement for U.S. commerce. It also directed government agencies to use the metric system.

Another calculation that you can make using metric measurements is **volume.** Volume describes the amount of space an object takes up.

Volume of a Rectangle

The small green box in the figure below measures 1 cm on each edge. You can find out how much space the box takes up—its volume—by using a simple formula.

$$\text{volume} = \text{length} \times \text{width} \times \text{height}$$
$$= 1 \text{ cm} \times 1 \text{ cm} \times 1 \text{cm}$$
$$= 1 \text{ cm}^3$$

The small 3 written to the upper right of the centimeter unit means cubic. It is read ***cubic centimeter*** or *centimeter cubed.* Cubic centimeter means centimeter × centimeter × centimeter. The volume of the small green box is 1 cubic centimeter.

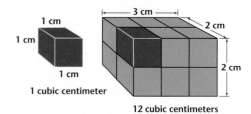

Now look at the larger box above. Its length is 3 cm. Its width is 2 cm. Its height is 2 cm. You can see that 12 small boxes will fit into the larger box. If each small box is 1 cm³, then the large box would have a volume of 12 cm³.

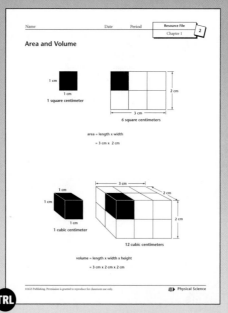

Resource File 2

You also can use the formula to find the volume of the larger box.

Liter, L
Basic unit of volume in the metric system

EXAMPLE

volume = length × width × height
= 3 cm × 2 cm × 2 cm
= 12 cm³

Volume of a Liquid

You might be familiar with another unit of volume in the metric system—the **liter.** You can see liter containers at the supermarket, especially in the soft-drink section. A liter is slightly more than a quart. The abbreviation for liter is *L*. The liter is the basic unit of volume in the metric system. It is often used to measure the volume of liquids.

As you can see in the figure, one liter of water will exactly fill a box that measures 10 cm on each side. A liter occupies the same amount of space as 1,000 cubic centimeters.

1,000 cubic centimeters = 1 liter

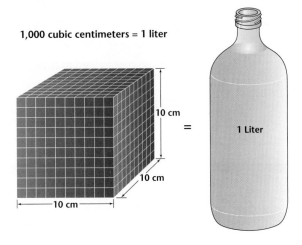

10 cm

10 cm

10 cm

=

1 Liter

The medical profession often uses cubic centimeters. For example, a typical dose of tetanus booster is 0.5 cc. Students should be aware that 1 cc is the same as 1 mL.

3 **Reinforce and Extend**

LEARNING STYLES

Visual/Spatial
Display wooden cubes measuring about 1 cubic inch. Lay the blocks side by side, and draw a line from one end to the other. Explain that this one-dimensional line represents the length of the row of blocks. Next, place three blocks along the line. Have students look down on the blocks so that they see only the flat surface. Explain that the area, or surface of the blocks, has two dimensions—length and width. Then ask students to look at the blocks from all directions. Explain that the volume of the blocks has three dimensions—length, width, and height.

GLOBAL CONNECTION

Have students contact students from other countries by Internet to find out the units in which foods, such as milk and flour, are available. Ask students to compile the information in a table. The table should identify the country, the food, and the units in which the food is available.

TEACHER ALERT

For a list of customary and metric measurement conversions, refer students to Appendix C on pages 380–381.

Science Myth

Ask a volunteer to read the myth portion of the Science Myth on page 21. Ask another volunteer to read the fact portion. Help students distinguish between the terms *accuracy* and *precision*. Point out that accuracy relates a measurement to the true value. Precision relates to how exact a measurement is made or recorded.

AT HOME

Ask students to examine containers of liquids, such as liquid soap, in their homes. Have students record the type of material in the container, as well as the amount that came in the container. The amount is usually listed in both customary and metric units.

CROSS-CURRICULAR CONNECTION

Home Economics

Have students make a list of food products in the home economics room or family kitchen whose amounts are given in milliliters and liters. Then have them order the products by their capacities from least to greatest.

Milliliter, mL
A metric unit of measure that is $\frac{1}{1,000}$ of a liter; it equals one cubic centimeter

You learned earlier in this chapter that you can use the same prefixes you used with the meter to form other units of measurement. The only prefix that is commonly used to measure volume is *milli-*. Remember that *milli-* means $\frac{1}{1,000}$. A **milliliter** is $\frac{1}{1,000}$ of a liter. The abbreviation for milliliter is *mL*. There are 1,000 milliliters in a liter. Since there are also 1,000 cubic centimeters in one liter, a milliliter is the same as one cubic centimeter.

Volume Equivalents	
1 liter (L)	1,000 cubic centimeters
1 cubic centimeter (cm³)	$\frac{1}{1,000}$ liter (0.001 L)
1 milliliter (mL)	$\frac{1}{1,000}$ liter (0.001 L)
1 milliliter (mL)	1 cubic centimeter (cm³)

Sometimes you will have to convert cubic centimeters to liters. Since one cubic centimeter is $\frac{1}{1,000}$ of a liter, you can convert by dividing by 1,000.

EXAMPLE Express 1,256 cm³ as liters.
$1,256 \div 1,000 = 1.256$ L

You can also convert liters to cubic centimeters. Simply multiply by 1,000.

EXAMPLE Express 4.3 L as cubic centimeters.
$4.3 \text{ L} \times 1,000 = 4,300 \text{ cm}^3$

You cannot measure the volume of liquids by using the formula you used to find the volume of a rectangle. In Chapter 2, you will learn how to use special equipment to find the volume of a liquid.

Lesson 5 REVIEW

Write your answers to these questions in complete sentences on a sheet of paper.

1. A box measures 8 cm by 9 cm by 12 cm. What is its volume?

2. What is the volume of a stainless-steel container with a length of 18 mm, width of 20 mm, and height of 10 mm?

3. Find the volume of a cabinet that measures 1.20 m by 5 m by 75 cm. (Hint: Convert meters to centimeters. Remember that 1 m = 100 cm.)

4. A box is 5 cm high, 4 cm wide, and 9 cm long. What is the volume in cubic centimeters? What is the volume in milliliters?

Convert each of these measurements. Write the answers on your paper.

5. 3 L = _____ mL

6. 5.5 L = _____ mL

7. 3,000 cm³ = _____ L

8. 3,700 cm³ = _____ L

9. 0.72 L = _____ mL

10. 350 mL = _____ cm³

Achievements in Science

The Metric System

The metric system is the first standardized system of measurement based on the decimal. Before the metric system, units of length, area, and weight varied from country to country. Ways of measuring were sometimes different even within a country. England had three different systems. In order to trade goods fairly, merchants and tradesmen needed a uniform system. Scientists needed a way to exchange information.

In France, the idea of the metric system first was suggested around 1670. No action was taken, however, for more than 100 years. In the 1790s, the French Academy of Sciences proposed a new system of measurement. The French revolutionary assembly adopted the metric system in 1795.

At first, the people of France had a hard time changing to a new system. For a time in the early 1800s, France went back to the old units of measure. But in 1837, the metric system became the rule in France. Soon other countries throughout the world began using the metric system.

Lesson 5 Review Answers

1. The volume of the box is 864 cm³. **2.** The volume of the container is 3,600 mm³. **3.** The volume of the cabinet is 4,500,000 cm³. **4.** The volume of the box is 180 cm³, or 180 mL. **5.** 3,000 mL **6.** 5,500 mL **7.** 3 L **8.** 3.7 L **9.** 720 mL **10.** 350 cm³

TEACHER ALERT

Some students may not realize that they must convert units to like units to solve some measurement problems. Have students compare the units in problem 3 in the Lesson Review and convert them to like units before beginning computation.

Achievements in Science

Have students read the Achievements in Science feature on page 23. Encourage them to learn more about the metric system and to make a time line showing important dates in the development of the metric system.

Portfolio Assessment

Sample items include:
• Explanations from Teaching the Lesson
• Lesson 5 Review answers

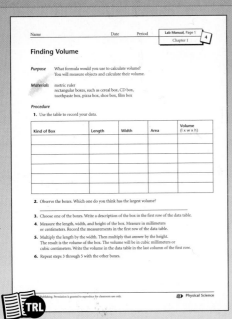

Lab Manual 4, pages 1–2

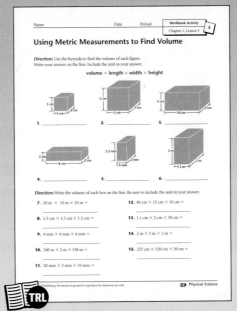

Workbook Activity 5

Lesson at a Glance

Chapter 1 Lesson 6

Overview In this lesson, students are introduced to the gram as the basic unit of mass.

Objectives

- To identify the basic unit of mass
- To convert metric units of mass

Student Pages 24–26

Teacher's Resource Library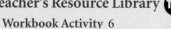

Workbook Activity 6

Alternative Workbook Activity 6

Vocabulary

centigram	kilogram
gram	milligram

 Warm-Up Activity

Set up a metric balance and find the mass of several objects on it. Have students make a record of your readings. Include objects made of wood, plastic, and metal, demonstrating that some smaller objects have more mass than some larger objects.

 Teaching the Lesson

Before students read the lesson, go over the table on page 25. Review the prefixes that students learned earlier in the chapter.

To help students conceptualize the amount of mass in a gram or kilogram, write a metric mass measurement, such as 200 grams, on the board. Ask students to suggest an object that might have that mass. For example, a human wouldn't have a mass of 200 grams, but a mouse might. The goal is to help students visualize the units, not to be exact.

Objectives

After reading this lesson, you should be able to

- identify the basic metric unit of mass.
- convert metric units of mass.

You learned earlier in this chapter that all matter has mass. Remember that mass is the amount of material an object has. But how can you measure mass?

In the metric system, the **gram** is the basic unit of mass. Look at the figure below. One gram equals the mass of one cubic centimeter of water. That is about the same mass as a large wooden match or a small paper clip. There are 454 grams in one pound. The abbreviation for gram is *g*.

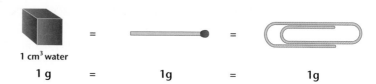

1 cm³ water

1 g   =   1g   =   1g

Gram, g

Basic unit of mass in the metric system

Mass Equivalents

Recall that the meter sometimes is too large or too small to measure the length of certain objects. The same is true for the gram. For example, a person may have a mass of 85,000 grams. That's a large number!

You can use the same prefixes you use with meters to show parts of a gram or multiples of a gram. The table on the next page shows these units of mass.

Kilogram, kg

A unit of mass in the metric system that equals 1,000 grams

Milligram, mg

A unit of mass in the metric system that is $\frac{1}{1,000}$ of a gram

Centigram, cg

A unit of mass in the metric system that is $\frac{1}{100}$ of a gram

To measure the mass of a person, you probably would use **kilograms.** One kilogram equals 1,000 grams. The abbreviation for kilogram is *kg*. However, the mass of a single hair from your head would be measured in smaller units called **milligrams.** A milligram is $\frac{1}{1,000}$ of a gram. The abbreviation for milligram is *mg*. A **centigram** is $\frac{1}{100}$ of a gram. The abbreviation for centigram is *cg*.

Mass Equivalents	
1 kilogram (kg)	1,000 g
1 centigram (cg)	$\frac{1}{100}$ g (0.01 g)
1 milligram (mg)	$\frac{1}{1,000}$ g (0.001 g)

If 1 cubic centimeter of water has a mass of 1 gram, then 1,000 cubic centimeters will have a mass of 1,000 grams, or 1 kilogram. Remember that there are 1,000 cubic centimeters in 1 liter. Therefore, as the figure below shows, 1 liter of water will have a mass of 1 kilogram.

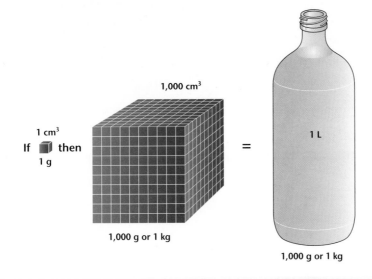

The Metric System   Chapter 1   25

---

3 Reinforce and Extend

TEACHER ALERT

Many students think that mass and weight are the same thing. Mass is the amount of matter in an object, while weight is the measure of the gravitational attraction of the object. On the space shuttle, where there is little or no gravity, a baseball would weigh nothing, but it would still have mass. However, on Earth, with a constant gravity, weight is a measure of mass.

LEARNING STYLES

Visual/Spatial

List the following words in the center of a sheet of paper: *length, area, volume,* and *mass.* Write the following units around the edges: *m, cm, mm, km, cm², m², cm³, m³, mL, g, mg,* and *kg.* Give a copy to each student. Ask students to draw a line connecting each unit to the property the unit is used to measure. For example, they would draw a line between *length* and *meter* and between *length* and *cm.*

IN THE COMMUNITY

Have students collect or copy printed material, such as maps, menus, grocery advertisements, and signs, from local businesses. Tell them to identify and underline the customary units of measures. Then have students rewrite the material substituting metric units of measurement for customary units.

CROSS-CURRICULAR CONNECTION

Language Arts

To help students relate metric units to the customary units, display a customary system/metric system conversion chart on an overhead projector. Encourage students to think of common sayings using measurements, such as "Give him an inch, he'll take a mile." Ask students to restate each saying, using the most appropriate metric units. For example, "Give him a centimeter, he'll take a kilometer."

ONLINE CONNECTION

Suggest that students visit the U.S. Metric Association's (USMA) Web site at lamar. colostate.edu/~hillger to learn about the SI metric system and the status of metric transition (metrication) in the United States.

The Metric System   Chapter 1   25

Lesson 6 Review Answers

1. 6,000 mg 2. 80 kg 3. 9,000 cg
4. 30,000 mg 5. 0.0253 kg 6. 10,000 mg
7. 5 g 8. 850 g 9. 45,000 g 10. The order
from smallest to largest is: **B** 1,203 mg,
C 0.123 kg, **A** 125 g

Portfolio Assessment

Sample items include:
• Worksheet from Visual/Spatial Learning
  Styles activity
• Lesson 6 Review answers

kilo   1,000
centi $\frac{1}{100}$
milli $\frac{1}{1000}$

Convert each of these measurements. Write the answers on a sheet of paper.

1. 6 g = _____ mg

2. 80,000 g = _____ kg

3. 90 g = _____ cg

4. 3,000 cg = _____ mg

5. 25,300 mg = _____ kg

6. 10 g = _____ mg

Write the answers to these questions on your paper.

7. Which is larger—5 g or 49 cg?

8. Which is smaller—850 g or 0.9 kg?

9. A boy weighs 45 kg. What is his weight in grams?

10. Arrange these measurements from smallest to largest.

A 125 g   **B** 1,203 mg   **C** 0.123 kg

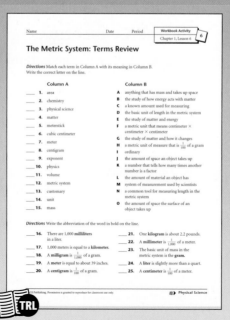

Workbook Activity 6

- Physical science is the study of matter and energy.

- Matter is anything that has mass and takes up space. Mass is the amount of material in an object.

- Measurements are important because we cannot always trust observations made with our eyes. Measurements help scientists gather exact information.

- In order for a unit of measurement to be useful, it has to be the same for everyone.

- Scientists use the metric system. The metric system is based on a system of tens.

- The meter is the basic unit of length in the metric system.

- You can measure length with a meterstick. A meterstick is divided into 100 smaller units, called centimeters. Each centimeter is divided into 10 units, called millimeters.

- You can use a system of prefixes in the metric system to show multiples or parts of a unit.

- Area is the amount of space the surface of an object takes up. The formula *length × width* is used to calculate area.

- Volume is the amount of space an object takes up. The volume of a rectangle can be calculated by using the formula *length × width × height*.

- A liter is the basic unit of volume in the metric system.

- You can convert from one unit to another in the metric system.

- The gram is the basic unit of mass in the metric system.

Science Words

area, 15	exponent, 15	matter, 2	millimeter, 10
centigram, 25	gram, 24	meter, 9	physical science, 2
centimeter, 10	kilogram, 25	meterstick, 10	physics, 3
chemistry, 3	kilometer, 11	metric system, 7	unit, 6
cubic centimeter, 20	liter, 21	milligram, 25	volume, 20
customary, 7	mass, 2	milliliter, 22	

Chapter 1 Summary

Have volunteers read aloud each Summary item on page 27. Ask volunteers to explain the meaning of each item. Direct students' attention to the Science Words box on the bottom of page 27. Have them read and review each word and its definition.

Chapter 1 Review

Use the Chapter Review to prepare students for tests and to reteach content from the chapter.

Chapter 1 Mastery Test TRL

The Teacher's Resource Library includes two parallel forms of the Chapter 1 Mastery Test. The difficulty level of the two forms is equivalent. You may wish to use one form as a pretest and the other form as a posttest.

Review Answers
Vocabulary Review

1. D 2. G 3. A 4. B 5. F 6. C 7. E

Concept Review

8. B 9. B 10. C 11. C 12. C 13. A 14. D
15. D

TEACHER ALERT

Because of limited space in this Chapter Review, not all of the vocabulary terms introduced in this chapter appear in the Vocabulary Review section. You may want to create an activity using the missing words to give students practice with all of the terms in this chapter. Here are the terms that are not covered in the section.

area

centigram

centimeter

cubic centimeter

exponent

gram

kilogram

kilometer

liter

mass

meterstick

metric system

milligram

milliliter

millimeter

volume

Vocabulary Review

Match each word in Column A with the correct definition in Column B. Write the letter of the definition on a sheet of paper.

Column A	Column B
_____ **1.** chemistry	**A** anything that has mass and takes up space
_____ **2.** unit	**B** the study of energy and matter
_____ **3.** matter	**C** ordinary
_____ **4.** physical science	**D** the study of matter and how it changes
_____ **5.** physics	**E** basic unit of length in the metric system
_____ **6.** customary	**F** the study of how energy acts with matter
_____ **7.** meter	**G** known amount used for measuring

Concept Review

Choose the answer that best completes each sentence. Write the letter of the answer on your paper.

8. Mass is the amount of _____ something has.

    A length   **B** material   **C** energy   **D** liquid

9. In the metric system, the gram is the basic unit of _____.

    A volume   **B** mass   **C** weight   **D** length

10. The longest of the following units is the _____.

    A meter   **B** centimeter **C** kilometer **D** millimeter

11. After using a meterstick to measure the length and width of a rectangle, you can find its area by _____.
    A adding the length and width
    B subtracting the shorter side from the longer side
    C multiplying the length by the width
    D dividing the longer side by the shorter side

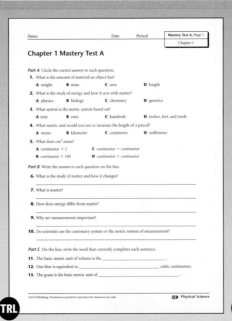

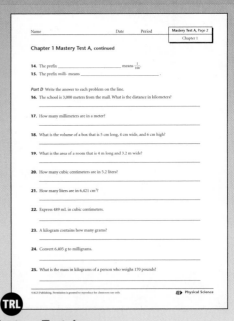

Chapter 1 Mastery Test A

12. The measurement _____ describes the area of a solid object.
   A 25 mm   **B** 25 cm   **C** 25 cm²   **D** 25 cm³

13. The amount of space an object takes up is its _____.
   A volume   **B** area   **C** mass   **D** length

14. The basic unit of volume is _____.
   A quart   **C** liter
   B cubic centimeter   **D** A and C

15. If 1 cubic centimeter of water has a mass of 1 gram, then a liter of water has a mass of _____ gram(s).
   A 1   **B** 10   **C** 100   **D** 1,000

Critical Thinking

Write the answer to each of these questions on your paper.

16. Some ancient civilizations used units of measure based on the length of certain seeds. What kinds of problems might you expect with such a system?

17. How is the relationship between units in the money system in the United States similar to the metric system?

18. For each of the following objects, tell which unit of measurement you would use:
   A length of an ant   **C** volume of a large jug of milk
   B mass of a postage stamp   **D** mass of a truck

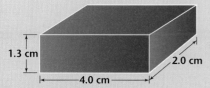

19. Calculate the volume of the rectangular object shown in the figure.

20. If one candle weighs 2.5 g, how many candles are in a 1-kg box of candles?

1.3 cm   2.0 cm   4.0 cm

Test-Taking Tip   Drawing pictures and diagrams is one way to help you understand and solve problems.

Chapter 1 Mastery Test B

Review Answers
Critical Thinking

16. All seeds aren't the same length, so there will be no uniform unit. **17.** Both systems are based on tens, and each unit is related to the other units by a multiple of ten. **18. A** mm, **B** mg, **C** L, **D** kg **19.** 10.4 cm³ **20.** 400

ALTERNATIVE ASSESSMENT

Alternative Assessment items correlate to the student Goals for Learning at the beginning of this chapter.

- Ask students to provide a written explanation of matter and energy.

- Have students give real-life examples that illustrate how and why measurement is important.

- Have students make word webs showing the relationships between the metric prefixes *kilo-, centi-* and *milli-* and the metric units of measurement.

- Provide students with metric rulers. Have them measure in centimeters a piece of paper, their science textbook, and their desk. Ask students to record their answers and then read their figures to the class. Then ask them to convert their findings to other metric units. *(kilometer, millimeter)*

- Provide students with several rectangles and have them calculate the area of each, using the correct unit.

- Distribute wooden cubes of various sizes. Have students calculate the volume of each cube in cm³.

- Display a 2-liter soft-drink bottle and a 355 mL soft-drink can and have students calculate the mass of each, using appropriate units.

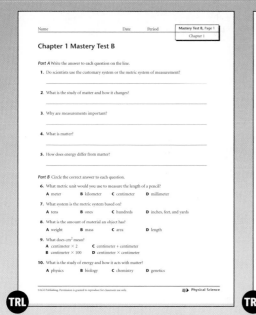

Planning Guide
The Properties of Matter

	Student Pages	Student Text Lesson Vocabulary	Lesson Review
Lesson 1 What Are Some Properties of Matter?	32–36	✔	✔
Lesson 2 Mass Is Different from Weight	37–39	✔	✔
Lesson 3 Measuring the Mass of a Liquid	40–42	✔	✔
Lesson 4 Measuring the Volume of a Liquid	43–45	✔	✔
Lesson 5 Measuring the Volume of Solid Objects	46–48	✔	✔
Lesson 6 What Is Density?	49–54	✔	✔

Chapter Activities

Student Text
Science Center

Teacher's Resource Library
Community Connection 2:
   Measuring Mass and Volume at a
   Veterinary Hospital

Assessment Options

Student Text
Chapter 2 Review

Teacher's Resource Library
Chapter 2 Mastery Tests A and B

	Student Text Features								Teaching Strategies						Learning Styles						Teacher's Resource Library				
	Achievements in Science	Science at Work	Science in Your Life	Investigation	Science Myth	Note	Technology Note	Did You Know	Science Integration	Science Journal	Cross-Curricular Connection	Online Connection	Teacher Alert	Applications (Home, Career, Community, Global, Environment)	Auditory/Verbal	Body/Kinesthetic	Interpersonal/Group Learning	Logical/Mathematical	Visual/Spatial	LEP/ESL	Workbook Activities	Alternative Workbook Activities	Lab Manual	Resource File	Self-Study Guide
		34	35			✔	✔			33	34			33, 34		33					7	7	5		✔
					38					38	38, 39							38		38	8	8	6		✔
	41						✔						40	41			41				9	9		3	✔
											44			44					44		10	10			✔
		48									47			47	47				47		11	11	7		✔
	52		53		50, 51	✔	✔	51	50, 51	51	51	52	50	50, 51							12	12	8	4	✔

Pronunciation Key

a	hat	e	let	ī	ice	ô	order	ú	put	sh	she	ə { a in about
ā	age	ē	equal	o	hot	oi	oil	ü	rule	th	thin	e in taken
ä	far	ėr	term	ō	open	ou	out	ch	child	ᵺ	then	i in pencil
â	care	i	it	ȯ	saw	u	cup	ng	long	zh	measure	o in lemon / u in circus

Alternative Workbook Activities

The Teacher's Resource Library (TRL) contains a set of lower-level worksheets called Alternative Workbook Activities. These worksheets cover the same content as the regular Workbook Activities but are written at a second-grade reading level.

Skill Track Software

Use the Skill Track Software for Physical Science for additional reinforcement of this chapter. The software program allows students using AGS textbooks to be assessed for mastery of each chapter and lesson of the textbook. Students access the software on an individual basis and are assessed with multiple-choice items.

Skill Track Software for Physical Science

Teacher's Resource Library TRL

Workbook Activities 7–12

Alternative Workbook Activities 7–12

Lab Manual 5–8

Community Connection 2

Resource File 3–4

Chapter 2 Self-Study Guide

Chapter 2 Mastery Tests A and B

(Answer Keys for the Teacher's Resource Library begin on page 402 of the Teacher's Edition. The Materials List for the Lab Manual activities begins on page 419.)

Science Center

Display a number of different objects such as salt, flour, two rocks of different sizes and compositions, a glass of water, a container with rubbing alcohol, and so on. Have students work in small groups to write phrases that describe each object. As groups share their lists, encourage students to think of other qualities that could be listed to identify each object more exactly. Then ask them to compare the salt and flour, the rocks, and the water and the alcohol, pointing out ways they are alike and different. Post the lists with the objects. As students go through the chapter, have them add more distinguishing properties to the lists, such as smell, feel, volume, and density.

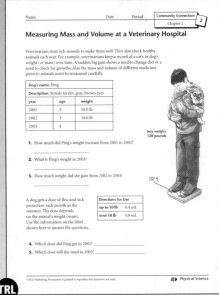

Community Connection 2

Chapter 2

The Properties of Matter

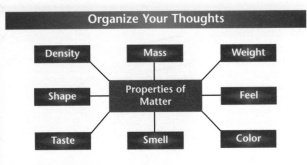

Look at the snow under the trees and on the tree branches in the photograph. Notice the patches of ice in the stream. Both snow and ice are forms of water. So is the substance in the stream. What words would you use to describe these forms of water? You might say that snow and ice are frozen water. You might say that the water in the stream is liquid. In Chapter 2, you will learn ways to describe the properties of matter. You will also learn how to measure various substances.

Organize Your Thoughts

Density

Mass

Weight

Shape

Properties of Matter

Feel

Taste

Smell

Color

Goals for Learning

◆ To describe various objects by listing their properties

◆ To measure the mass of different objects

◆ To measure the volume of a liquid, using a graduated cylinder

◆ To measure the volume of an object, using the displacement of water method

◆ To calculate density

31

Have students describe what they see in the photo on page 30. When they identify water, ice, and snow, point out that all three of these substances are made of water. Begin by making a class list of words or phrases that describe water. Then complete a list for ice and snow. When the lists are complete, tell students that they have listed the properties of each substance. Explain that they will learn more about properties of matter in the chapter.

Point out the Organize Your Thoughts chart showing kinds of properties of matter. Ask students how they can identify the properties. *(by observing and by using measuring equipment)* Have students read the Goals for Learning. Based on what they already know about properties of matter, help them formulate questions about what they do not know or what they want to know more about. For example, students might ask: "How are mass and weight related?" Such questions will set a purpose for reading the chapter. Have students write their questions so that they can refer to them as they study the chapter.

Notes and Technology Notes

Ask volunteers to read the notes that appear in the margins throughout the chapter. Then discuss them with the class.

TEACHER'S RESOURCE

The AGS Teaching Strategies in Science Transparencies may be used with this chapter. The transparencies add an interactive dimension to expand and enhance the *Physical Science* program content.

CAREER INTEREST INVENTORY

The AGS Harrington-O'Shea Career Decision-Making System-Revised (CDM) may be used with this chapter. Students can use the CDM to explore their interests and identify careers. The CDM defines career areas that are indicated by students' responses on the inventory.

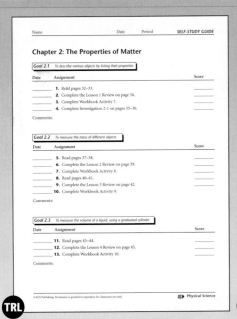

Lesson at a Glance

Chapter 2 Lesson 1

Overview In this lesson, students learn that each substance has its own set of properties. Students learn how to describe objects by their properties.

Objectives

- To explain what a property is
- To list some properties of common objects

Student Pages 32–36

Teacher's Resource Library **TRL**

Workbook Activity 7

Alternative Workbook Activity 7

Lab Manual 5

Vocabulary

property

Science Background

Although two substances might share some of the same properties, no two substances have an identical set of properties. For this reason, scientists can use properties to identify unknown substances. Physical properties include, for example, melting point, freezing point, color, odor, density, hardness, and ability to conduct heat and electricity. By contrast, chemical properties are characteristics that describe how a substance reacts chemically with other substances.

 Warm-Up Activity

Provide each student with a small stone and an index card. Be sure stones differ from each other in certain respects. Have students write a description of the stone on the card and then write a 2-digit number on their stone. They should not write the number on the index card or tell it to anyone. Collect all the stones in a container. Have students exchange cards with a partner. Pass the container of stones around the room and have each student try to find his or her partner's stone based on the description.

Objectives

After reading this lesson, you should be able to

- explain what a property is.
- list some properties of common objects.

Property
A characteristic that helps identify an object

 Matter has many properties. One property of matter is the temperature at which something melts. Another property of matter is how it dissolves. How well something conducts electricity is also a property of matter.

If someone asked you to describe sugar, what would you say? You might say "It is a solid made of small, individual pieces." Each part of that description tells a **property** of sugar. A property is a characteristic that helps identify an object. The above description identifies two properties of sugar.

- It is a solid.
- It is made of small individual pieces.

This description of sugar is correct. But it isn't enough to accurately identify sugar. As you can see in the photo, sand has the same properties. The description could be made more useful by adding other properties. For example, you might add color and taste. Your description of sugar becomes, "It is a white solid made of small, individual pieces that have a sweet taste." Sand could be described as "a tan solid made of small, individual pieces that have no taste."

Sugar and sand have some of the same properties.

Scientists group the properties of matter into two categories. Properties that describe how one kind of matter reacts with another are called chemical properties. All other properties are called physical properties.

Technology Note

Electronic noses have sensors that "sniff" different odors. Scientists use them in many ways. Electronic noses can detect the freshness of fish and identify chemical spills. They can even detect some illnesses, such as pneumonia. Scientists have also used electronic noses to measure air quality on the space shuttle.

Some Common Properties

The photo on this page shows some of the more common properties that you might use to describe matter. Scientists prefer to use some properties more than others. For example, scientists often use mass. The reason is because mass can be measured easily. If someone asked you to describe a rock you saw, you might say it was big. But how big is big? And would someone else think the same rock was big? By using specific measurements of mass, everyone can agree on the measurement. For example, everyone can find the mass of the rock and agree on its mass. Another property that can be measured easily is volume (length, width, and height).

Color: **yellowish-red**
Shape: **almost round**
Volume: **about 20 mL**
Feel: **fuzzy, soft**

Size: **similar to a baseball**
Mass: **about 0.023 kg**
Taste: **sweet**
Smell: **pleasant, sweet**

Which of these properties are easy to measure?

Some properties, such as color, cannot be measured as easily. Because of this, descriptions based on color can be misunderstood. For example, how would you describe the color of the fruit in the photo above? One person might describe the color as "pink," while another would call it "yellowish-red." When describing properties, it is important to be as exact as you can. Use measurements whenever possible.

Have partners determine if the right stones have been chosen by checking the number on the stone. Discuss why exact descriptions are important.

 2 Teaching the Lesson

Read the boxed information in the margin aloud with students. Point out that melting point and boiling point are unique to a substance. For example, ice melts at 0°C (32°F) and water boils at 100°C (212°F). Help students name some chemical properties (for example flammability). Point out that chemical properties cause a substance to change.

Distribute small pieces of aluminum foil, wax paper, construction paper, and writing paper to teams of two to four students. Tell teams to record the properties of each material, noting color, texture, and any other properties they observe. Have team members report their findings to the class. Ask students to note ways the materials are different and alike.

Tell students that they are going to determine the properties of texture, taste, and odor of some foods. **Safety Alert: Check for food allergies before students participate in this activity.** Peel and cut up small pieces of potatoes, apples, onions, and turnips. Blindfold volunteers and ask them to pinch their noses shut so that they can't smell the foods. Have students chew each food and record its properties of taste and texture. Then have them smell each food and record its odor. Ask students to identify the foods based on their observations.

 3 Reinforce and Extend

LEARNING STYLES

 Body/Kinesthetic
Obtain small swatches of different types of fabrics. Assign partners and explain that one student is to give the other student pieces of material and record the findings. Have students shut their eyes and determine the properties of texture and odor. Then have them open their eyes to determine shininess and color.

SCIENCE JOURNAL

Have students write a narrative of at least 50 words about an imaginary trip through a place of their choice. Their narrative should emphasize what they see, hear, smell, and feel as they move through the location.

AT HOME

Have students observe two solids such as baking soda and salt at home. Ask them to write at least three physical properties and one chemical property of each solid. You may want to suggest that students combine equal amounts of each solid with a little vinegar in separate containers and observe the results.

Lesson 1 Review Answers

1. A not a good description; not exact or specific. **B** a good but incomplete description; uses specific measurement **C** not a good description; not specific; could be a number of things **2.** Answers might include spherical or leather covered **3.** Yes; answers might include stitched or hard. **4.** Answers will vary, but students should use as much detail as possible. **5.** Classmates should name the properties that helped them identify the object.

Science at Work

Ask volunteers to read the Science at Work feature about perfumers on page 34.

The last paragraph states that a perfumer needs to be able to recognize and remember smells, understand chemistry, and be creative. Ask students to suggest other skills that a perfumer might need to have. *(be organized, be able to keep track of details, be able to tolerate a variety of smells)*

Encourage students who may be interested in this kind of work to research the profession to learn more about it.

CAREER CONNECTION

Invite a lab technician or hospital worker into the classroom to explain to students how identifying properties of substances is important to his or her job.

CROSS-CURRICULAR CONNECTION

Home Economics
Have a baker or home economics teacher explain properties of different kinds of flour (such as cake flour, all-purpose flour, whole wheat flour, rye flour) and identify the different properties of baked goods made using each type of flour.

Portfolio Assessment

Sample items include:
• Index card with description from Warm-Up Activity
• Lesson 1 Review answers

Write your answers to these questions on a sheet of paper.

1. For each of the following statements, tell whether it is a good description. Explain your answer.
   A It is a large, colorful box.
   B The rock has a mass of 25 kilograms.
   C The solid that formed was dark, shiny, and lumpy.

2. A baseball has several properties. Write one property that a baseball has.

3. Could the property you wrote for question 2 also be a property for another object? If yes, write a second property that a baseball has.

4. Choose an object. Write a detailed description of the object.

5. Read your description to the class. Can classmates identify the object from your description?

▼◀▲▼◀▲▼◀▲▼◀▲▼◀▲▼◀▲▼◀▲▼◀▲▼◀▲▼◀▲▼◀▲▼◀▲▼◀▲▼◀▲▼◀▲▼

Science at Work

Perfumer

Perfumers create formulas for fragrances and other scented products such as soaps and candles. Perfumers also set quality and production standards for perfumes. Each batch of a product must have exactly the same properties as earlier batches. Perfumers evaluate the smell, color, strength, and other properties of fragrances.

There are two different ways to become a perfumer. Some perfumers earn a four-year degree in chemistry. Other perfumers receive on-the-job training. They usually work for five years as an assistant to an experienced perfumer.

Perfumers must recognize and remember smells, must understand chemistry, and must be creative.

Properties of Objects

Directions Look at the objects below. On the lines, write properties that describe each object. Estimate each object's size, mass, and volume. Use the chart to help you choose units of measure.

	Volume of a Liquid	Volume of a Solid	Mass
Measured in	mL (milliliters)	cm³ (cubic centimeters)	g (grams)
	L (liters)	m³ (cubic meters)	kg (kilograms)
Examples	individual carton of milk is 237 mL	textbook is 1,500 cm³	textbook is 1 kg
	water bottle is 500 mL		

		Object 1	Object 2	Object 3
Shape	A	___	___	___
Feel	B	___	___	___
Size	C	___	___	___
Mass	D	___	___	___
Volume	E	___	___	___

Physical Science

Workbook Activity 7

INVESTIGATION

Materials

◆ bag with 5 objects
◆ balance
◆ hand lens
◆ metric ruler

Identifying Properties

Purpose

Why is it important to provide a clear description of an object? In this investigation, you will learn to write clear descriptions of objects.

Procedure

1. Copy the data table on a sheet of paper.

Object Number	Properties
1	
2	
3	
4	
5	

2. Obtain a bag from your teacher. You will find five objects in your bag.

3. Study the five objects in your bag carefully. On another sheet of paper, make a list of the objects in your bag. Number the objects from 1 to 5.

4. Now describe each object by writing as many of its properties as you can. Write the information in your table. Be sure to describe each object clearly and completely. Do not tell what the object is or what it is used for.

The Properties of Matter   Chapter 2   35

Investigation 2-1

The Purpose portion of the student investigation begins with a question to draw them into the activity. Encourage students to read the investigation steps and formulate their own questions before beginning the investigation. This investigation will take approximately 20 minutes to complete. Students will use these process and thinking skills: observing, collecting and interpreting data, comparing, collecting information, communicating, and describing.

Preparation

* Vary the objects in the bags as much as possible, for example, by using different coins. Include one regularly shaped object so that students can calculate volume, using the formula $v = l \times w \times h$. Students will learn more about this formula in Lesson 5. Avoid using objects that may crumble or break apart when handled.

* Be sure that the mass of any object does not exceed the capacity of the balance.

* Hand lenses, metric rulers, and balances are useful but not essential for completing this activity successfully.

* Students may use Lab Manual 5 to record their data and answer the questions.

Procedure

* This investigation is best completed by students working in pairs.

* Have students try identifying a few objects the day before the investigation. This will help them understand the necessity for accurate descriptions of an object's properties.

* Some students will not know how to use a balance. They can complete the activity without measuring mass. Alternatively, use Resource File 3, which discusses using a balance, before doing the investigation.

* Remind students to make observations by noting how objects feel, smell, and sound, in addition to how they look. Tell students they will not observe taste in this investigation.

Continued on page 36

Continued from page 35

SAFETY ALERT

◆ Remind students to keep their hands out of their mouths and eyes while handling objects and to wash their hands when they have completed the activity.

◆ Tell students not to taste any object used in this investigation.

Results

Students should find that the more detailed and exact their descriptions are, the easier it is for classmates to identify the objects.

Questions and Conclusions Answers

1. Answers will vary.

2. Answers will vary.

3. Answers will vary.

4. Possible answer: I could have included more details and exact measurements.

Explore Further Answers

Groupings and descriptions will vary. However, students should recognize that no one grouping is correct. Students most likely will have to be more specific with their list of properties than in the first part of the investigation because the items in a group probably are more similar than the original five items in the bag.

Assessment

Check data tables to be sure that students are making detailed descriptions. Check to see that students record what they hear, feel, and smell. You might include the following items from this investigation in student portfolios:

• Investigation 2-1 data table

• Answers to Questions and Conclusions and Explore Further sections

5. When you have completed your descriptions, give your table to a classmate. Ask your classmate to read your descriptions and identify the objects.

Questions and Conclusions

1. How many objects did your classmate identify correctly?

2. Which objects did your classmate identify?

3. Which objects did your classmate identify incorrectly?

4. What could you have done to make your descriptions more useful?

Explore Further

Work with five other students. Combine the objects from the bags of everyone in your group. Place objects with similar properties in a group. Identify the properties that describe all the objects in each group. Then list the property of each object in a group that makes it different from all the other objects. Elect someone in your group to share the list with the class.

36 *Chapter 2   The Properties of Matter*

Lab Manual 5

36 *Chapter 2   The Properties of Matter*

Objectives

After reading this lesson, you should be able to

◆ explain the difference between mass and weight.

◆ identify instruments that can be used to measure mass and weight.

Weight

The measure of how hard gravity pulls on an object

Newton

The metric unit of weight

You know from Chapter 1 that all matter has mass. Mass is a property of matter that you can measure. For example, the mass of the man in the figure is 65 kg. But what is the man's weight? Are mass and weight the same?

Mass and Weight

Mass and *weight* are often used to mean the same thing. However, scientists have different meanings for these two words. Mass measures how much matter is in an object. **Weight** is a measure of how hard gravity pulls on an object. The force of gravity depends on the mass of an object. Objects with a large mass will have a strong pull of gravity.

You may have seen a scale like the one shown here at the grocery store or supermarket. You can use a scale like this to measure the weight of produce such as grapes or tomatoes.

Scientists use the **newton** when describing weight. A mass of 1 kg has a metric weight of 9.8 newtons. You will find more information about the newton in Chapter 8.

---

2 Teaching the Lesson

Have students write the four vocabulary words on a sheet of paper, skipping several lines between each word. Ask them to write a meaning for each word before they read the lesson. Explain that they may predict the meaning if the word is unfamiliar. After reading, have them evaluate and revise the meanings.

Divide the class into groups of two to four students. Each group will construct a balance using three pencils of equal length and a ruler. Place two pencils parallel to each other and tape them together. Stand the third pencil on top of the other two and tape the three together. Have students balance a ruler on the point of the top pencil to make a

simple balance. They can use their balance to measure the mass of small objects, using paper clips as the standard masses. Have students record the mass of several small objects and present their findings to the class.

To show their understanding of the relationship between weight and gravity, ask students to choose a planet (other than Earth) from the table on page 39. Have students construct a table showing the weight of a 2,000-lb car, a 200-lb refrigerator, and a 14-lb bowling ball both on Earth and on the planet they selected. Suggest that students use calculators. You might have to explain ratio to students before they can complete the calculations.

Lesson at a Glance

Chapter 2 Lesson 2

Overview This lesson teaches students about the difference between mass and weight. Students learn that a balance is used to measure mass.

Objectives

■ To explain the difference between mass and weight

■ To identify instruments that can be used to measure mass and weight

Student Pages 37–39

Teacher's Resource Library

Workbook Activity 8

Alternative Workbook Activity 8

Lab Manual 6

Vocabulary

balance	**standard mass**
newton	**weight**

Science Background

It is important to remember that mass and weight are not the same. Weight is a measure of the pull of gravity on an object. On Earth, your weight is a direct measure of the planet's force pulling you toward its center. But the pull of gravity between objects weakens as the distance between the centers of the objects increases. At a high altitude—for example, at the top of a mountain—an object weighs less than it does at sea level. When an object is sent into space, it is said to be weightless. However, the mass of an object (the amount of matter it contains) always remains the same.

1 Warm-Up Activity

Ask students how it would be possible for a 200-pound person to suddenly weigh 99 pounds and still have his or her pants fit. The answer, of course, is to move to a planet like Mars, where the pull of gravity is less than that on Earth.

3 Reinforce and Extend

This astronaut weighs less on the moon than on Earth.

The mass of an object never changes under normal conditions. But the weight of an object can change when it is moved to some other place. For example, the pull of gravity on the moon is less than the pull of Earth's gravity. So when the astronaut in the photograph went to the moon, he weighed less on the moon than he did on Earth. But his mass did not change.

Measuring Solid Mass

Recall from Chapter 1 that in the metric system, mass is measured in units called grams. The mass of a small paper clip is about 1 g. How many grams do you think a large paper clip might be? How could you find out?

You can use an instrument called a **balance** to measure mass. There are many different kinds of balances. But the simplest kind often looks like the one in the figure below. When you use this kind of balance, you find the mass of an object by balancing it with objects of known masses.

A **standard mass** is a small object that is used with a balance to determine mass. The object is usually a brass cylinder with the mass stamped on it. Look at the standard masses in the figure. Most people use standard masses when they use a balance. You can place standard masses on the pan opposite the object to be measured until the two pans are balanced. The mass of the object is equal to the total of the standard masses.

> **Balance**
> An instrument used to measure mass
>
> **Standard mass**
> A small object that is used with a balance to determine mass

> **Did You Know?**
>
> Deimos, a moon of Mars, has very low mass. This makes its gravity much less than the Earth's gravity. On Deimos, you would weigh very little. You could jump off the surface on a pogo stick.

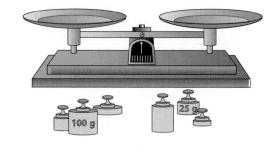

Lesson 2 REVIEW

The table below lists some planets of the solar system. It also tells each planet's force of gravity compared to the earth's. Copy the chart on a sheet of paper. Then calculate the weight of a 100-pound person on each of the planets. The first two items are done for you. Write your answers in your chart.

	Planet	Force of Gravity Compared to Earth	Weight on Earth	Weight on this Planet	Method
1.	Earth	1.00	100 lbs	100 lbs	1.00 x 100
2.	Jupiter	2.54	100 lbs	254 lbs	2.54 x 100
3.	Mars	0.379	100 lbs		
4.	Saturn	1.07	100 lbs		
5.	Mercury	0.378	100 lbs		
6.	Venus	0.894	100 lbs		

Write your answers to these questions in complete sentences on your paper.

7. How does mass differ from weight?

8. Are you measuring mass or weight when you use a grocery scale?

9. Why would you weigh less on the moon than on Earth?

10. What is the weight in newtons of a 5 kg mass?

CROSS-CURRICULAR CONNECTION

Language Arts

Have students refer to the table of planets on page 39 and use degrees of comparison to write sentences naming planets with the following characteristics:

- the planet with the *greatest* force of gravity
- the planet with the *smallest* force of gravity
- two planets on which they would weigh *less* than they do on Earth
- two planets on which they would weigh *more* than they do on Earth
- a planet with a force of gravity *larger* than Earth's but *smaller* than Jupiter's

Portfolio Assessment

Sample items include:
- Vocabulary definitions from Teaching the Lesson
- Language Arts Cross-Curricular Connection activity
- Lesson 2 Review answers

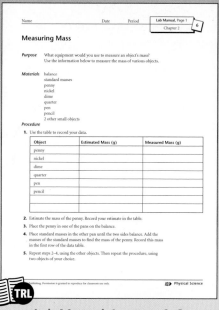

Lab Manual 6, pages 1–2

Workbook Activity 8

Lesson at a Glance

Chapter 2 Lesson 3

Overview In this lesson, students learn how to use a balance to measure the mass of a liquid.

Objectives

- To explain how to find the mass of a liquid

Student Pages 40–42

Teacher's Resource Library

Workbook Activity 9

Alternative Workbook Activity 9

Resource File 3

 Warm-Up Activity

Display a beaker of water and ask students how they could find the mass of just the water. Accept all logical answers.

 Teaching the Lesson

Have students write the steps in the procedure for measuring the weight of a boy and a dog as described on page 40 and the mass of a liquid as described on page 41.

Divide the class into small groups and give each group four containers. Use clean tin cans, soft-drink bottles, and plastic food containers. Have them measure the mass of each container and record the data. Place an equal amount of water in each container. Have students follow the instructions on page 41 to calculate the mass of water in each container and record this data.

TEACHER ALERT

 Many students are confused by the ounce unit. This is because ounce is used to measure both mass and liquid volume. The avoirdupois ounce is a mass unit measuring 16 ounces to a pound. The troy ounce, used to measure the mass of gold, is 12 ounces to a pound. The liquid ounce is 32 ounces to a quart. Usually, mass ounces are prefixed by the words *net weight* or *gross weight*. Fluid ounces are often designated as *fluid ounces*.

Lesson 3 Measuring the Mass of a Liquid

After reading this lesson, you should be able to

◆ explain how to find the mass of a liquid.

Technology Note

Most electronic scales have a load cell. A load cell changes force or weight into an electrical signal. An indicator reads the signal. The indicator shows how much an object weighs. Scales in grocery stores have load cells. So do scales used to weigh large trucks on highways.

You can find the mass of a solid by using a balance. But how do you find the mass of a liquid? A balance is made to hold solids, not liquids.

To help answer the question, think about the following example. Suppose a boy uses a scale to find his weight. The scale shows that he weighs 100 pounds. Then the boy picks up his dog and weighs himself again while holding the dog. The scale now reads 120 pounds. Why? It is because the scale is measuring the weight of both the boy and the dog.

The boy knows that his weight is 100 pounds. He knows that his and the dog's weight together is 120 pounds. Now he can easily find the weight of the dog.

120 pounds	–	100 pounds	=	20 pounds
(weight of boy and dog)	–	(weight of boy)	=	(weight of dog)

120 lbs   100 lbs

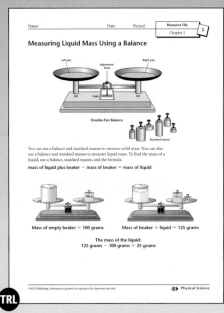

Name _____ Date _____ Period _____ | Resource File 3 | Chapter 2

Measuring Liquid Mass Using a Balance

Double-Pan Balance

Standard masses

You can use a balance and standard masses to measure solid mass. You can also use a balance and standard masses to measure liquid mass. To find the mass of a liquid, use a balance, standard masses, and the formula.

mass of liquid plus beaker – mass of beaker = mass of liquid

Mass of empty beaker = 100 grams   Mass of beaker + liquid = 125 grams

The mass of the liquid:
125 grams – 100 grams = 25 grams

Physical Science

Resource File 3

Measuring Liquid Mass

You can use a similar procedure to find the mass of a liquid.

1. Measure the mass of an empty container, such as a beaker.

2. Pour the liquid you want to measure into the beaker.

3. Measure the mass of the liquid plus the beaker.

4. Subtract the mass of the empty beaker from the mass of the beaker plus liquid. The answer will be the mass of the liquid.

mass of liquid = mass of liquid plus beaker – mass of beaker

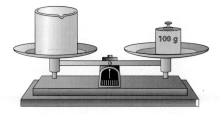 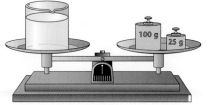

Mass of empty beaker = 100 g   **Mass of beaker plus liquid = 125 g**

The mass of the liquid is 125 g – 100 g = 25 g

Achievements in Science

Balances

The first scales were used more than 4,500 years ago in ancient Egypt. The oldest kind of scale is the balance.

The first balance was the equal-arm balance. Egyptians made the equal-arm balance around 2,500 B.C. An equal-arm balance has a bar with a pan hanging from each end. The bar is held up at the center by a piece of metal or other hard material. The object whose mass is being measured is put in one pan. Standard masses are placed in the other pan until the two pans balance. A pointer shows that the pans are balanced.

About 2,500 years later, the Romans invented the steelyard balance. A steelyard balance has a bar with arms that are not the same length. The shorter arm has a pan or hook to hold the object that is being measured. A small standard mass is moved along the longer arm until it balances. Markings on the arm show the object's weight.

LEARNING STYLES

Interpersonal/ Group Learning

For this activity, each student group will need a balance, a can of fruit or vegetables, a separate container, and a strainer. **Safety Alert: Open the cans and remove the lids.** Have each small group measure the contents of a can of fruit or vegetables to learn the mass of its liquid and solid parts. Have them find the mass of the entire container and then pour the contents through a strainer, collecting the liquid in another container and the solids in the strainer. The group members can then work together to determine the mass of the liquid, solid, and original container.

AT HOME

Have students read the labels of liquid and semiliquid food items and list the types of units used for measuring each food's mass. Ask them to group the foods to show which use liquid measuring units (*milliliters, quarts, fluid ounces*) and which use net weight units (*grams, pounds, avoirdupois ounces*).

Achievements in Science

Have students take turns reading aloud the Achievements in Science feature about balances on page 41.

Invite volunteers to sketch each balance described in the feature and explain its parts, using the text information. Once they have sketched the balances, have students find pictures of the balances in a reference book to compare with their drawings. Discuss which of the balances students think would be more accurate and easier to use.

If possible, display a triple beam balance and demonstrate its use. Ask students which of the historic balances it most resembles and why. (*steelyard balance*)

Lesson 3 Review Answers

1. The mass of the liquid is 35 g. **2.** The mass of the liquid is 38 g. **3.** The mass of the beaker plus the liquid is 110 g. **4.** The mass of the liquid is 35 g. **5.** The mass of the liquid is 100 g.

Portfolio Assessment

Sample items include:
• Procedure steps from Teaching the Lesson
• Illustrations from Achievements in Science teaching suggestions
• Lesson 3 Review answers

Write your answers to these questions in complete sentences on your paper.

1. A container has a mass of 150 g. What is the mass of a liquid if the container plus the liquid has a mass of 185 g?

2. A container has a mass of 125 g. When a liquid is added, the mass becomes 163 g. What is the mass of the liquid?

3. Suppose the mass of a certain liquid is 35 g. You place it in a beaker that has a mass of 75 g. What is the mass of the beaker plus the liquid?

4. A beaker has a mass of 100 g. Liquid is poured into the beaker. The mass of the liquid and the beaker is 135 g. What is the mass of the liquid?

5. Using this information, find the mass of the liquid:
   mass of liquid and beaker = 250 g
   mass of beaker = 150 g
   mass of liquid = _____

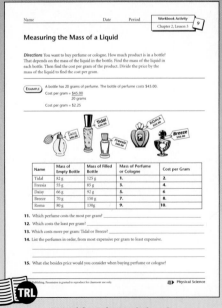

Workbook Activity 9

Objectives

After reading this lesson, you should be able to

◆ explain how to use a graduated cylinder to measure the volume of a liquid.

Graduated cylinder

A round glass or plastic cylinder used to measure the volume of liquids

Meniscus

The curved surface of a liquid

In Chapter 1, you learned that the unit of volume in the metric system is the liter. Usually, the liter is too large a unit to use in a laboratory, so scientists often use the milliliter. Remember that 1 milliliter has the same volume as 1 cubic centimeter. Liquid volumes are sometimes measured in cubic centimeters rather than milliliters.

To measure the volume of a liquid, you can use a **graduated cylinder**. Graduated cylinders come in many different sizes. The largest ones usually hold 1 L of a liquid. More common sizes hold 100 mL, 50 mL, or 10 mL. You can see two sizes of graduated cylinders in the figure on page 44.

Measuring with a Graduated Cylinder

To measure the volume of a liquid, follow this procedure.

1. Pour the liquid into the graduated cylinder.

2. Position yourself so that your eye is level with the top of the liquid. You can see the correct position in the figure below.

3. Read the volume from the scale that is on the outside of the cylinder. The top of the liquid usually is curved. This curve is called a **meniscus.** You can see the meniscus in the figure to the right. Read the scale on the bottom of the curve as shown. The volume of this liquid is 16 mL.

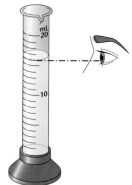

Lesson at a Glance

Chapter 2 Lesson 4

Overview This lesson guides students through the process of using a graduated cylinder to measure the volume of a liquid. It also explains how to read a scale.

Objectives

■ To explain how to use a graduated cylinder to measure the volume of a liquid

Student Pages 43–45

Teacher's Resource Library 🆃🆁🅻

Workbook Activity 10

Alternative Workbook Activity 10

Vocabulary

graduated cylinder
meniscus

Science Background

The surface of a liquid in a graduated cylinder is curved because of surface tension. Molecules of a substance are attracted to each other. Molecules of a liquid on the surface have molecules below and to their sides pulling on them. The constant pull on surface molecules causes the liquid to act as if a thin, elastic film covered its surface. Surface tension causes drops of a liquid to take a spherical shape. In the graduated cylinder, it causes the liquid surface to curve slightly. Point out to students that finding the base of the curve in the meniscus is important in order to get an accurate reading of volume.

1 Warm-Up Activity

Display three containers of similar size, each containing an equal amount of water. Have students observe the containers and tell which has the most water and which has the least. Discuss how students could confirm their observations.

2 Teaching the Lesson

Review with students how to find cubic centimeters by multiplying length, width, and height. Display a cube to model how this measurement is the same as volume in milliliters, since both show how much space a substance takes up.

Have students fold a sheet of paper in half vertically. As they read the lesson, they should write the steps in the procedure for measuring with a graduated cylinder on the left side. On the right side, they should make a drawing to illustrate each step. Have them repeat this process as they read the section about how to read a scale.

Provide practice in reading scales and illustrate the accuracy of the graduated cylinder with this activity. Give pairs of students a graduated cylinder and a measuring cup with one-quarter, one-half, and three-quarter levels. First, have partners fill the cup to the one-quarter mark. Then have them pour the water into the cylinder and record the measure. Pairs repeat the procedure for a half measure and a three-quarter measure of water. Have partners compare the measurements between the cup and the graduated cylinder. Those made with the graduated cylinder should be several milliliters more precise.

3 Reinforce and Extend

TEACHER ALERT

Point out to students that they can also find the volume represented by two long lines on a graduated cylinder by counting by twos between the 10 mL and 20 mL lines. Explain that, should a cylinder have one line between the 10 and 20 mL markings, they would count by fives.

LEARNING STYLES

Visual/Spatial
Draw several graduated cylinders on the board. Shade in some amount of water in each cylinder. Have students make the reading and record the amount of water in cm³ and mL.

Cylinder A   Cylinder B

If you look carefully at the two graduated cylinders to the left, you will see that they are marked differently. Notice that Cylinder A on the left can hold 20 mL of a liquid. Cylinder B on the right can hold 40 mL. The number of spaces between the numbers on the cylinders is also different.

Reading a Scale

In order to measure the volume of a liquid in a graduated cylinder, you need to know what the spaces between each line represent. In other words, you must be able to read the scale. It is easy to do if you follow this procedure.

1. Subtract the numbers on any two long lines that are next to each other. In the figure below, the two long lines are labeled *20* and *10*. When you subtract these numbers (20 mL – 10 mL) you get 10 mL.

2. Count the number of spaces between the two long lines. In the figure, you can see 5 spaces between the two long lines.

3. Divide the number you got in Step 1 by the number you counted in Step 2. This will tell you how much of an increase each line represents from the line below. In the figure below, each space equals 2 mL.

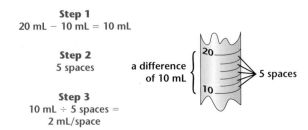

Step 1
20 mL – 10 mL = 10 mL

Step 2
5 spaces

Step 3
10 mL ÷ 5 spaces =
2 mL/space

CROSS-CURRICULAR CONNECTION

Math
Have students work together to measure the volume and mass of a sample of water. Each team should have a small container and a graduated cylinder with water in it. Have students figure out a way to find the mass of the water after they measure its volume. (*Hint:* They will use the method learned in Lesson 3 and transfer water into the small container.) Students should find that their two numbers are close, since 1 mL of water has a mass of 1 g.

Lesson 4   R E V I E W

Write your answers to these questions on a sheet of paper.

Read the volume of liquid in each cylinder. Write the volumes for A and B on the lines.

1. Cylinder A: _____

2. Cylinder B: _____

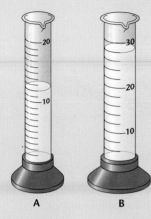

A   B

Draw the three cylinders shown here on your paper. Shade each one to show these volumes:

3. Cylinder C: 26 mL

4. Cylinder D: 13 mL

5. Cylinder E: 8 mL

C   D   E

Lesson 4 Review Answers

1. 12 mL (cm³) 2. 28 mL (cm³) 3–5. The shaded part of the cylinders should reflect the volumes indicated.

Portfolio Assessment

Sample items include:
- Explanation of procedure and illustrations from Teaching the Lesson
- Lesson 4 Review answers

Workbook Activity 10

Name _____ Date _____ Period _____ | Workbook Activity **10** | Chapter 2, Lesson 4

Measuring the Volume of Liquid

Directions Use the terms in the box to complete each sentence. Write your answer on the line. You will use some terms more than once.

bottom	laboratory	scale
cubic centimeter	level	spaces
divide	meniscus	subtract
graduated cylinder	milliliters	volume

1. Liquid volume is measured in cubic centimeters or _____.

2. In the _____, scientists use milliliters to measure the volume of liquid.

3. The largest _____ usually holds one liter of liquid.

4. One milliliter has the same volume as one _____.

5. You read the volume of a liquid by looking at the _____ on a graduated cylinder.

Procedure A: Measure with a Graduated Cylinder

6. Pour liquid into a _____.

7. Place yourself so that your eyes are _____ with the top of liquid.

8. Look at the _____, the curved surface of the liquid.

9. Find the _____ of the curve of the liquid.

10. Read the _____ on the outside of the cylinder at this point.

Procedure B: Read the Scale on a Graduated Cylinder

11. The volume of a liquid is measured in _____.

12. Find out how many mL the _____ on the scale stand for.

13. Now _____ the numbers on any two long lines next to each other.

14. Count the spaces between the long lines and _____ this number into the answer from step 13.

15. This will give you the _____ represented by each line.

TRL   Physical Science

Lesson at a Glance

Chapter 2 Lesson 5

Overview In this lesson, students use the formula v = l × w × h to find the volume of regularly shaped solids and learn to use displacement of water to measure the volume of irregularly shaped solids.

Objectives

- To measure the volume of regularly shaped solids
- To measure the volume of irregularly shaped solids

Student Pages 46–48

Teacher's Resource Library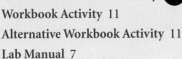

Workbook Activity 11

Alternative Workbook Activity 11

Lab Manual 7

Vocabulary

displacement of water

1 Warm-Up Activity

Show students one or more regularly shaped and irregularly shaped objects. Ask which object has the largest volume. Invite students to tell how they predicted volume. Have students tell how they would find the exact volume of each object. List their suggestions on the board. After reading the lesson, revisit the list and help students decide which suggestions are workable.

2 Teaching the Lesson

Have students read the lesson subheads and write a question about what they think they will learn in each section, for example: "How can I find the volume of regular and irregular shapes?" As they find the answers to their questions during reading, students should write them on their papers.

Ask students to identify the four objects in the illustration on page 46 and tell which ones are regular in shape and which are irregular. Display an example of a sphere and a cylinder, such as a globe and a tin can. Ask students to describe each shape and tell why they think it is considered a regular shape.

Objectives

After reading this lesson, you should be able to

- measure the volume of regularly shaped solids.
- measure the volume of irregularly shaped solids.

Displacement of water

Method of measuring the volume of an irregularly shaped object

The volume of solid objects cannot be measured using a graduated cylinder. However, you can measure the volume of solids in two different ways, depending on the shape of the solid.

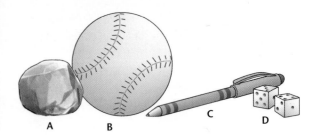

A   B   C   D

Regular and Irregular Shapes

You can describe some solids as having a regular shape. Objects B and D in the figure above have a regular shape. When a solid has a regular shape, you can find the volume by using a formula. You have already learned the formula for finding the volume of objects that have a rectangular shape.

$$\text{volume} = \text{length} \times \text{width} \times \text{height}$$

Some solids have regular shapes other than rectangular. Examples are spheres and cylinders. You can use different formulas for finding the volumes of objects with these shapes.

Objects A and C in the figure have irregular shapes. You cannot use a formula to find the volume of a solid with an irregular shape. Instead, you can use the **displacement of water** method to find the volume of irregularly shaped objects.

Using Displacement of Water

If a glass is partially filled with water and you place an object in the glass, the level of the water will rise. In fact, the water level will rise by an amount equal to the volume of the object that was placed in the glass. To accurately measure the volume, use a graduated cylinder. The object must be completely under the water.

To measure the volume of a small, solid object using the displacement of water method, follow the procedure below. Remember to cover the object completely with water.

1. Pour water into a graduated cylinder. Record the volume of the water. (Figure A)

$$volume = 10 \ cm^3$$

2. Place the object in the cylinder. The water level will then rise. Record this new volume. (Figure B)

$$volume = 16 \ cm^3$$

3. Subtract the volume of the water from the volume of the water and the object. The difference will be the volume of the object.

$$16 \ cm^3 - 10 \ cm^3 = 6 \ cm^3$$

The volume of the object is 6 cm³.

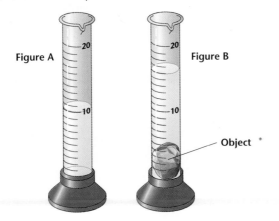

Figure A   Figure B

Object

To demonstrate displacement of water, fill a glass with water. Hold up an ice cube and ask students to predict what will happen if you put the ice cube in the glass. Add the ice to the water. Explain that the water that overflows has been displaced, or moved to another place, by the ice cube.

Have students use the steps in the procedure on page 47 to measure the volume of an irregularly shaped object. Review proper method for reading the volume of liquid in a graduated cylinder. Have students record the volume before and after the object is added to the cylinder and show their calculations on their papers.

3 Reinforce and Extend

LEARNING STYLES

Visual/Spatial

Students will benefit from repeated performance of the measuring activities described in the lesson. Provide a number of containers with water and small objects for which students should find the volume by displacement, using a graduated cylinder and the procedure described in the lesson. Remind students that the graduated cylinder must contain enough water to completely cover the object when it is added.

CROSS-CURRICULAR CONNECTION

Art/Drama

Have students in a small group collaborate to write a skit in which two people solve a problem by using what they know about volume and displacement of water. For example, the skit might show how two people monitor the erosion of a statue by demonstrating how the statue's volume has decreased.

LEARNING STYLES

Auditory/Verbal

Ask each student to choose a partner, and have one partner direct the other in how to determine the volume of an irregularly shaped object. The worker should carry out oral directions exactly and ask questions when a direction is unclear. Have students switch roles and give oral directions for determining the volume of a regularly shaped object.

GLOBAL CONNECTION

Have students read about glaciers and icebergs and locate places on a globe where glaciers are found. Ask students to draw a diagram showing how an iceberg displaces water in the ocean. Challenge them to explain the effects global warming could have on the volume of the oceans and therefore coastlines of nations.

Lesson 5 Review Answers

1. The volume of the object is 100 cm³.
2. The volume of the stone remains the same; it causes the level of water in the graduated cylinder to rise from 35 to 42 mL. **3.** The volume of the stone is 7 mL.
4. The blue marble has the greater volume. **5.** You would use the displacement of water method to find the volume of a pencil.

Science in Your Life

Have volunteers read aloud the Science in Your Life feature on page 48. Ask students to look at the illustration and describe the aquarium's dimensions. Then have them predict how they might find out how much water the tank holds, or its volume. Explain that volume of a regular-shaped solid is found by multiplying its length, width, and height. Students can find the volume of the tank by using the formula:

$v = l \times w \times h$

50 cm × 30 cm × 30 cm = 45,000 cm³

Since 45,000 cm³ is more than 40,000 cm³, the tank will accommodate all 10 fish.

Have students calculate whether an aquarium that is 30 cm wide, 45 cm long, and 25 cm high would be large enough for the fish. *(No, it would hold 33,750 cm³, which is less than the 40,000 cm³ needed.)*

Portfolio Assessment

Sample items include:
• Questions and answers from Teaching the Lesson
• Lesson 5 Review answers
• Science in Your Life answer

Write your answers to these questions in complete sentences on your paper.

1. What is the volume of an object 10 cm long, 5 cm wide, and 2 cm high?

2. A stone is placed in a graduated cylinder, which has been filled to the 35-mL mark. The level rises to 42 mL. What happens to the volume of the stone?

3. What is the volume of the stone in question 2?

4. A red marble is placed in a graduated cylinder, which has been filled to the 25-mL mark. The level rises to 41 mL. A blue marble is placed in another graduated cylinder, which has been filled to the 25-mL mark. The level rises to 52 mL. Which marble has the greater volume?

5. Explain how you would find the volume of a pencil.

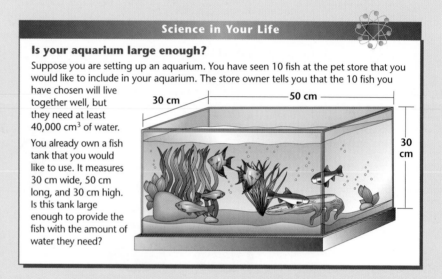

Science in Your Life

Is your aquarium large enough?

Suppose you are setting up an aquarium. You have seen 10 fish at the pet store that you would like to include in your aquarium. The store owner tells you that the 10 fish you have chosen will live together well, but they need at least 40,000 cm³ of water.

You already own a fish tank that you would like to use. It measures 30 cm wide, 50 cm long, and 30 cm high. Is this tank large enough to provide the fish with the amount of water they need?

30 cm | 50 cm | 30 cm

48 *Chapter 2 The Properties of Matter*

Name ___ Date ___ Period ___ | Lab Manual, Page 1 | 7
Chapter 2

Measuring Volume

Purpose What equipment would you use to measure the volume of an object? Use the information below to find the volume of various objects.

Materials cap from tube of toothpaste
graduated cylinder
paper towels
cap from mouthwash bottle
penny
marble
stone
game die
metric ruler

Procedure

1. Use the table to record your data.

Object	Estimated Volume (mL)	Measured Volume (mL)
toothpaste cap		
mouthwash cap		
penny		
marble		
stone		
game die—using displacement of water		
game die—using a formula		

2. Estimate the volume in milliliters of each object in the table. Record your estimates in the table.

3. Fill the toothpaste cap with water. Then pour the water into a dry graduated cylinder.

4. Read the volume of the water from the scale on the graduated cylinder. (If you need help reading a scale, use page 44 of your text.) Record the volume of the water in the table. Use a paper towel to dry the cylinder.

5. Repeat steps 3 and 4, using the mouthwash cap.

Publishing. Permission is granted to reproduce for classroom use only. | Physical Science

Lab Manual 7, pages 1–2

Name ___ Date ___ Period ___ | Workbook Activity | 11
Chapter 2, Lesson 5

Comparing and Contrasting Objects

Directions When you compare things or ideas, you tell how they are alike. When you contrast them, you tell how they are different. Compare and contrast each pair of words.

How They Are Alike	How They Are Different
1. length—volume:	
2. cube—sphere:	
3. regular shapes—irregular shapes:	
4. balance—graduated cylinder:	
5. liquid mass—liquid volume:	

Directions Tell how you would measure the volume of each item. Write formula or displacement of water method on the line.

6. a cement block ___
7. a stone ___
8. a golf ball ___
9. a refrigerator box ___
10. a game die ___

Publishing. Permission is granted to reproduce for classroom use only. | Physical Science

Workbook Activity 11

Objectives

After reading this lesson, you should be able to

◆ explain and define density.

◆ calculate density.

◆ explain how to use density to identify a substance.

Density

A measure of how tightly the matter of a substance is packed into a given volume

Buoyancy makes objects seem lighter under water. The force of the water that is displaced or spilled out is the buoyant force. The buoyant force pushes in the opposite direction of the force of gravity.

You probably have heard the riddle, "Which weighs more—a pound of feathers or a pound of lead?" The answer is that they weigh the same—one pound. A pound of lead would be a small cube. A pound of feathers would be much larger.

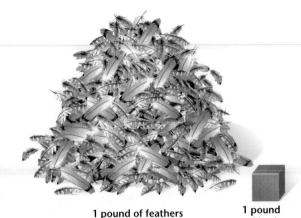

1 pound of feathers

1 pound of lead

But what if you made 1-cm cubes from both materials? Would they be equally heavy? No, the lead cube would be much heavier. The reason is that lead has more matter packed in the cube than the feathers. The lead has a higher **density**. Density is a measure of how tightly the matter of a substance is packed into a given volume.

Calculating Density

If you know the volume and mass of a substance, you can find its density. You just have to use the following formula.

$$\text{density} = \frac{\text{mass}}{\text{volume}} \left(\frac{m}{v}\right)$$

The Properties of Matter Chapter 2 **49**

Draw several 3D blocks on the board. Write in their dimensions and draw a crude balance showing the mass in grams of each. Have students solve the problems and share results. Emphasize the need to use the correct units of density. Then provide several blocks of wood and metal. Have students find the volume of each block in cm³ and the mass in grams. They can then follow the example on page 50 to solve for density.

 3 **Reinforce and Extend**

Suppose you know the mass of an object is 30 g and its volume is 15 cm³. What is the object's density?

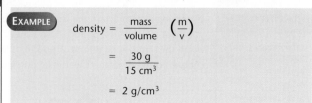

EXAMPLE
$$\text{density} = \frac{\text{mass}}{\text{volume}} \quad \left(\frac{m}{v}\right)$$
$$= \frac{30 \text{ g}}{15 \text{ cm}^3}$$
$$= 2 \text{ g/cm}^3$$

Density = 2 g/cm³. A mass of 2 grams of this object has a volume of 1 cubic centimeter.

Density Is a Property

The density of a particular substance is always the same. It does not matter how large or what shape the piece of the substance is. As the figure shows, the density of lead is always 11.3 g/cm³.

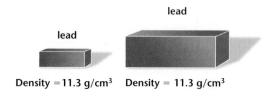

lead

lead

Density =11.3 g/cm³   Density = 11.3 g/cm³

Material	Density (g/cm³)
gold	19.3
mercury	13.6
lead	11.3
silver	10.5
aluminum	2.7
rubber	1.1
water	1.0
cork	0.24
air	0.0013

The lead block on the right has more mass. It also has a larger volume. But the density of both blocks is the same.

Look at the different kinds of material and their densities in the table. You can use density to identify a material.

Suppose you have a small piece of metal and you want to find out what it is. You can measure its mass and volume, and then use the formula to find its density.

Suppose you measure the mass of the metal on a balance. Its mass is 8 g. Then you use a graduated cylinder to find the volume of the metal. The volume is 3 cm^3. Using the formula, you find the density of the metal is 2.7 g/cm^3. Now look at the table on page 50. What metal do you have?

Sink or Float

Matter that has a greater density than water will sink in water. Matter with a density that is less than water will float.

Look at the glass of water. It holds an ice cube and a silver ball. You know from the table on page 50 that the density of silver is 10.5 g/cm^3. That density is greater than the density of water, which is 1.0 g/cm^3.

But what about the ice cube? It floats on the water. What does that tell you about the density of ice compared to water? It tells you that ice has a lower density than liquid water. Ice expands, increasing the volume. Since density is mass divided by volume, the density becomes less because the denominator is bigger. The mass stays the same.

Technology Note

Have you ever seen a liquid motion lamp? A liquid motion lamp contains two kinds of matter. One is a liquid. The other is a "blob" that has a different density from the liquid. When the lamp is on, the density of the blob decreases and the blob rises. When the blob cools, it sinks.

Lesson 6 Review Answers

1. Density is a measure of how tightly the matter of a substance is packed into a given volume. **2.** A 1 cm³ cube of lead would have more matter. **3.** Its density is 19.3 g/cm³. **4.** The density of each half of the metal bar would be 19.3 g/cm³. **5.** It would float because its density is less than that of water.

Achievements in Science

Ask for a volunteer to read aloud the Achievements in Science feature on page 52. Draw a time line on the board to illustrate how long ago Archimedes' discovery occurred. Ask a volunteer to explain how the principle stated in paragraph 1 of the feature is used in the method described on page 47.

Have pairs of students research and share their findings on other achievements of Archimedes.

ONLINE CONNECTION

Suggest that students visit www.stcms.si.edu, the National Science Resources Center Web site developed by the Smithsonian Institution. The Science and Technology Concepts for Middle Schools site provides information and links to sites that discuss and apply what students have learned about the properties of matter, including density.

Portfolio Assessment

Sample items include:
• Drawings from Teaching the Lesson
• Lesson 6 Review answers

Lesson 6   R E V I E W

Write your answers to these questions in complete sentences on your paper.

1. What is density?

2. Which would have more matter—a 1-cm cube of lead or a 1-cm cube of rubber?

3. Suppose you have a metal bar. Its mass is 57.9 g and its volume is 3 cm³. What is its density?

4. If you cut the metal bar from question 3 in half, what would the density of each half be?

5. If you put a piece of cork in a container of water, would it sink or float? Why? (Hint: Use the table on page 50 to answer the question.)

Achievements in Science

Archimedes' Principle of Displacement

Archimedes was a Greek inventor and mathematician who lived from about 287 to 212 B.C. He is best known for his discovery of the displacement of an object in water. Here is Archimedes' principle: Any object in water displaces, or spills out, the same amount of water as the object's volume.

As the story goes, Archimedes made his discovery while getting into the bathtub. He noticed that as he got into the tub, the water began overflowing. The more he lowered himself into the water, the more the water overflowed the tub. He looked at the amount of water that overflowed. He realized that the amount of his body that was in the water was the same. He was so excited about his discovery, he cried out "Eureka!" or "I have found it!" Archimedes had discovered the principle of displacement.

Archimedes' principle applies both to objects that are under water and objects that float. The principle explains why steel ships float and why helium-filled balloons rise.

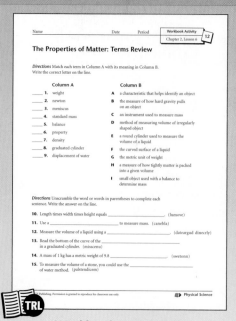

Workbook Activity 12

2-2 INVESTIGATION

Materials

- safety glasses
- 2 graduated cylinders
- balance
- cooking oil
- water

Finding Density

Purpose

Do you think cooking oil and water have the same density? In this investigation, you will calculate and compare the densities of cooking oil and water.

Procedure

1. Copy the data table on a sheet of paper.

Measurements	Cylinder with Water	Cylinder with Cooking Oil
A mass of empty cylinder		
B mass of cylinder and liquid		
C mass of liquid (B–A)		
D volume of liquid		
E density (E = $\frac{C}{D}$)		

2. Put on your safety glasses.

3. Obtain two identical graduated cylinders. Use a balance to find the mass of each cylinder. Record the masses on line A of your table.

The Properties of Matter   Chapter 2   **53**

SAFETY ALERT

- ◆ Make sure students wear their safety glasses during the investigation.
- ◆ Use plastic graduated cylinders.
- ◆ Keep paper towels handy so that all spills can be cleaned up immediately.

The Purpose portion of the student investigation begins with a question to draw them into the activity. Encourage students to read the investigation steps and formulate their own questions before beginning the investigation. This investigation will take approximately 45 minutes to complete. Students will use these process and thinking skills: predicting; measuring, collecting, and interpreting data; and comparing and drawing conclusions

Preparation

- • Use any type of cooking oil for this activity. The amount of oil and water needed will depend on the size of the graduated cylinder you give students to use.

- • You may wish to provide the oil and water for each group in individual paper cups.

- • Students may use Lab Manual 8 to record their data and answer the questions.

Procedure

- • Students should work cooperatively in groups of four to complete the activity. Student A pours the water into the graduated cylinder. Student B measures the mass of the water and cylinder. Student C pours oil into the graduated cylinder. Student D measures the mass of the oil and cylinder.

- • Have students predict which liquid—the water or the oil—will have the greater density.

- • Be sure students understand that they are to use the same volume of each liquid. Review the method for reading a graduated cylinder to be sure students understand the concept.

- • Tell students to make careful measurements. Small errors in measurements can result in large errors in calculating density.

Continued on page 54

Continued from page 53

Results

Regardless of the size of the sample students use, the density of water will be 1.0 g/cm³. The density of oil can vary depending on the type of oil used, but it will be less than that of water.

Questions and Conclusions Answers

1. The water has greater density.
2. The cooking oil will float on top.

Explore Further Answers

The corn syrup will form another layer on the bottom of the cylinder because its density is greater.

Assessment

Observe students to be sure they are measuring correctly. Also check that students have used the density formula correctly. You might include the following items from this investigation in student portfolios:

• Investigation 2-2 data table

• Answers to Questions and Conclusions and Explore Further sections

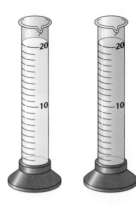

4. Fill one graduated cylinder with water and the other with cooking oil. Fill each one to the same level. You now have equal volumes of water and oil. Record this volume on line D of your data table.

5. Find the mass of the cylinder and the water. Record your data on line B.

6. Subtract the mass of the graduated cylinder from the mass of the graduated cylinder and water (line B – line A). The answer tells you the mass of the water. Write the mass on line C.

7. Repeat steps 5 and 6, using your data for the cooking oil.

8. Use the equation for density to find the densities of the water and the cooking oil.

$$density = \frac{mass}{volume}$$

Questions and Conclusions

1. Which substance—the water or the cooking oil—has the greater density?

2. Liquids with lesser densities will float on liquids with greater densities. If you pour cooking oil and water together, which liquid will float on top?

Explore Further

Corn syrup has a density of 1.3 g/cm³. If you pour corn syrup into a cylinder of cooking oil and water, what will happen?

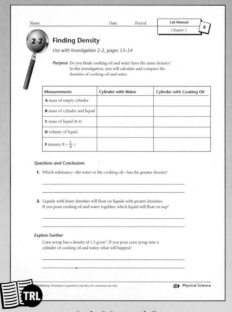

Lab Manual 8

- Mass measures how much matter is in an object.

- Weight can change when moving from one place to another, but mass generally stays the same.

- Properties are used to describe an object.

- Mass, volume, and density are important properties of matter.

- Mass is measured using a balance. A common unit of mass is the gram.

- Volume of liquids is measured by using a graduated cylinder.

- When measuring the mass of liquids, first measure the mass of an empty beaker. Then pour the liquid into the beaker and measure the mass again. Subtract these two figures to find the mass of the liquid.

- The volume of regularly shaped objects can be found by using formulas.

- The volume of irregularly shaped objects is measured by using the displacement of water method.

- Density is a property of matter that tells how tightly the matter of a substance is packed into a given volume.

- Density can be used to identify substances.

- Liquids that are less dense than water will float on water. Liquids that are more dense will sink.

Science Words		
balance, 38	graduated cylinder, 43	property, 32
density, 49	meniscus, 43	standard mass, 38
displacement of water, 46	newton, 37	weight, 37

Chapter 2 Summary

Have volunteers read aloud each Summary item on page 55. Ask volunteers to explain the meaning of each item. Direct students' attention to the Science Words box on the bottom of page 55. Have them read and review each word and its definition.

Chapter 2 Review

Use the Chapter Review to prepare students for tests and to reteach content from the chapter.

Chapter 2 Mastery Test

The Teacher's Resource Library includes two parallel forms of the Chapter 2 Mastery Test. The difficulty level of the two forms is equivalent. You may wish to use one form as a pretest and the other form as a posttest.

Review Answers
Vocabulary Review

1. volume 2. meniscus 3. standard mass 4. weight 5. property 6. displacement of water

Concept Review

7. D 8. A 9. A 10. C

TEACHER ALERT

Because of limited space in this Chapter Review, not all of the vocabulary terms introduced in this chapter appear in the Vocabulary Review section. You may want to create an activity using the missing words to give students practice with all of the terms in this chapter. Here are the terms that are not covered in the section.

balance

density

newton

Word Bank

displacement of water
graduated cylinder
meniscus
property
standard mass
weight

Vocabulary Review

Choose a word or words from the Word Bank that best complete each sentence. Write the answers on a sheet of paper.

1. You measure volume with a _____.

2. The _____ is the curved surface of a liquid.

3. You use a _____ with a balance to determine mass.

4. The measure of how hard gravity pulls on something is _____.

5. A characteristic that helps identify an object is a _____.

6. The _____ method is used to measure the volume of irregularly shaped objects.

Concept Review

Choose the answer that best completes each sentence. Write the letter of the answer on your paper.

7. The mass of an object can change if _____.

   A the object is moved to a different height

   B the object is put under water

   C the object is moved to place where the gravity is different

   D none of the above

8. A balance can measure the mass of _____.

   A solids   **C** solids and liquids

   B liquids   **D** only very heavy things

9. If you place a marble in a half-filled glass of water, the water level will _____.

   A rise   **C** stay the same

   B fall   **D** overflow

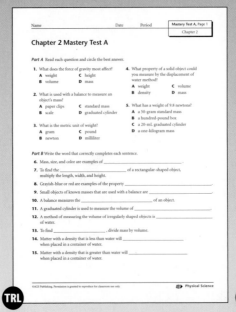

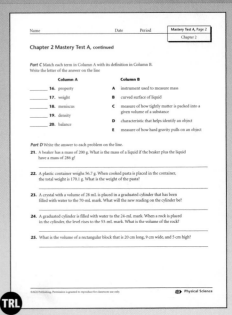

Chapter 2 Mastery Test A

10. To find the density of a substance, you must know

_____.

    A what it is made of   **C** its mass and volume

    B how much it weighs   **D** its length and width

Critical Thinking

Write the answer to each of these questions on your paper.

11. Why is the following statement *not* a good one for a scientist to use in a report? "The material was made of small, colorful pieces."

12. Explain how to find the mass of a liquid.

13. How would you measure the volume of each of the objects shown here?

14. Cork has a density of 0.24 g/cm³ and water has a density of 1.0 g/cm³. If you put a piece of cork in water, will it sink or float? Explain your answer.

15. Suppose a scientist has two solid substances that look alike. How could the scientist use density to see if the substances are the same?

Test-Taking Tip

When studying for a test, use a marker to highlight important facts and terms in your notes. For a final review, read over highlighted areas.

The Properties of Matter   Chapter 2   **57**

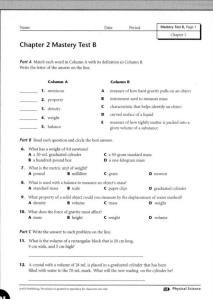

Chapter 2 Mastery Test B

Review Answers
Critical Thinking

11. The information is not specific or exact enough; it does not include measurements. **12.** Measure the mass of a graduated cylinder. Add the liquid to the cylinder and measure mass again. Subtract the cylinder's mass from the mass of the cylinder and liquid to get the liquid mass. **13.** Cube: Multiply width by length by height in cm. This is also the number of mL, since 1 mL = 1 cm³. Glass of water: Pour the liquid into a graduated cylinder and read the scale. Rock: Use the displacement of water method. Pour water into a graduated cylinder and read its volume. Add the rock and read the scale again. Subtract water volume from total volume of water and rock. **14.** The cork will float because it is less dense than water. **15.** The scientist would measure each object's volume and mass and then calculate its density (mass/volume). If the densities are identical, the objects are the same substance.

ALTERNATIVE ASSESSMENT

Alternative Assessment items correlate to the student Goals for Learning at the beginning of this chapter.

- Provide students with three objects and have them describe the properties of each object.

- Have students use a balance and a container to find the mass of a solid and a liquid. Ask students to explain the steps in the procedure they use.

- Provide each pair of students with a graduated cylinder and a small container of liquid. Have students demonstrate how to read a graduated cylinder to measure the liquid's volume.

- Have students use their graduated cylinder and the liquid they already measured to determine the volume of a small stone by the displacement of water method.

- Place equal amounts of two liquids into two graduated cylinders. Make a balance available. Have students find the mass and volume of the two liquids, determine their densities, and then explain which would rise to the top if the two were poured together.

The Properties of Matter   Chapter 2   **57**

Chapter

3

Planning Guide

The Structure of Matter

		Student Text Lesson		
		Student Pages	Vocabulary	Lesson Review
Lesson 1	What Are Molecules?	60–64	✔	✔
Lesson 2	What Are Elements?	65–69	✔	✔
Lesson 3	What Are Compounds?	70–74	✔	✔
Lesson 4	How Do Scientists Know What Atoms Are Like?	75–81	✔	✔
Lesson 5	Identifying Elements	82–86	✔	✔

Chapter Activities

Student Text

Science Center

Teacher's Resource Library

Community Connection 3: Cooking with Compounds

Assessment Options

Student Text

Chapter 3 Review

Teacher's Resource Library

Chapter 3 Mastery Tests A and B

	Student Text Features								Teaching Strategies						Learning Styles						Teacher's Resource Library				
	Achievements in Science	Science at Work	Science in Your Life	Investigation	Science Myth	Note	Technology Note	Did You Know	Science Integration	Science Journal	Cross-Curricular Connection	Online Connection	Teacher Alert	Applications (Home, Career, Community, Global, Environment)	Auditory/Verbal	Body/Kinesthetic	Interpersonal/Group Learning	Logical/Mathematical	Visual/Spatial	LEP/ESL	Workbook Activities	Alternative Workbook Activities	Lab Manual	Resource File	Self-Study Guide
				62			✔				63		61			63	62				13	13		5	✔
	69		68		67	✔		66, 67		67	67		66	66, 68							14	14	9		✔
		72		73		✔			71	71	71		71		71						15	15	10		✔
	79			80	76	✔				78	77		76				77	78		78	16	16	11	6	✔
						✔	✔	82, 83	85	85	84	83		83					84		17	17	12	7	✔

Pronunciation Key

a	hat	e	let	ī	ice	ô	order	ü	put	sh	she	
ā	age	ē	equal	o	hot	oi	oil	ü	rule	th	thin	
ä	far	ėr	term	ō	open	ou	out	ch	child	ŦH	then	
â	care	i	it	ȯ	saw	u	cup	ng	long	zh	measure	

ə = a in about, e in taken, i in pencil, o in lemon, u in circus

Alternative Workbook Activities

The Teacher's Resource Library (TRL) contains a set of lower-level worksheets called Alternative Workbook Activities. These worksheets cover the same content as the regular Workbook Activities but are written at a second-grade reading level.

Skill Track Software

Use the Skill Track Software for Physical Science for additional reinforcement of this chapter. The software program allows students using AGS textbooks to be assessed for mastery of each chapter and lesson of the textbook. Students access the software on an individual basis and are assessed with multiple-choice items.

Chapter at a Glance

Chapter 3:
The Structure of Matter
pages 58–89

Lessons

**Skill Track Software
for Physical Science**

Teacher's Resource Library **TRL**

Workbook Activities 13–17

Alternative Workbook Activities
13–17

Lab Manual 9–12

Community Connection 3

Resource File 5–7

Chapter 3 Self-Study Guide

Chapter 3 Mastery Tests A and B

(Answer Keys for the Teacher's
Resource Library begin on page 402
of the Teacher's Edition. The
Materials List for the Lab Manual
activities begins on page 419.)

Science Center

In the Science Center, place various sizes
of cardboard circle patterns. Also provide
plain and colored paper, glue, and
scissors. Have students trace the patterns,
cut out the circles, and glue them to make
models that show atomic structures.

Students should make models for an
element or of a gas, liquid, or solid.
Encourage students to label the structures
in their models. Display the models and
refer to them throughout the chapter.

Community Connection 3

Chapter

3 The Structure of Matter

The snowflake in the photograph looks like one large ice crystal. In fact, a snowflake is made up of thousands of small particles of matter called molecules. Each molecule is made of even smaller parts called atoms. In Chapter 3, you will learn more about the particles that make up matter—molecules, atoms, elements, and compounds.

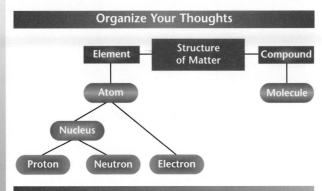

Organize Your Thoughts

Element — Structure of Matter — Compound

Atom

Molecule

Nucleus

Proton   Neutron   Electron

Goals for Learning

◆ To explain molecules, elements, and compounds

◆ To tell how scientists use models

◆ To describe the parts of an atom

◆ To explain the meaning of atomic number and mass number

◆ To calculate the number of protons, electrons, and neutrons in an element using its atomic number and mass number

59

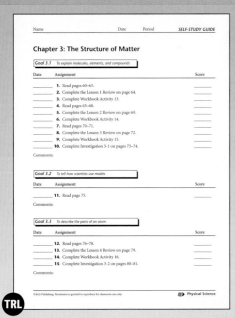

Name _____ Date ____ Period ____   SELF-STUDY GUIDE

Chapter 3: The Structure of Matter

Goal 3.1   To explain molecules, elements, and compounds

Date   Assignment   Score

_____ **1.** Read pages 60–63.
_____ **2.** Complete the Lesson 1 Review on page 64.
_____ **3.** Complete Workbook Activity 13.
_____ **4.** Read pages 65–68.
_____ **5.** Complete the Lesson 2 Review on page 69.
_____ **6.** Complete Workbook Activity 14.
_____ **7.** Read pages 70–71.
_____ **8.** Complete the Lesson 3 Review on page 72.
_____ **9.** Complete Workbook Activity 15.
_____ **10.** Complete Investigation 3-1 on pages 73–74.
Comments:

Goal 3.2   To tell how scientists use models

Date   Assignment   Score

_____ **11.** Read page 75.
Comments:

Goal 3.3   To describe the parts of an atom

Date   Assignment   Score

_____ **12.** Read pages 76–78.
_____ **13.** Complete the Lesson 4 Review on page 79.
_____ **14.** Complete Workbook Activity 16.
_____ **15.** Complete Investigation 3-2 on pages 80–81.
Comments:

©AGS Publishing. Permission is granted to reproduce for classroom use only.   ⬛▶ Physical Science

Name _____ Date ____ Period ____   SELF-STUDY GUIDE

Chapter 3: The Structure of Matter, continued

Goal 3.4   To explain the meaning of atomic number and mass number

Date   Assignment   Score

_____ **16.** Read pages 82–84.
Comments:

Goal 3.5   To calculate the number of protons, electrons, and neutrons in an element using its atomic number and mass number

Date   Assignment   Score

_____ **17.** Read page 85.
_____ **18.** Complete the Lesson 5 Review on page 86.
_____ **19.** Complete Workbook Activity 17.
_____ **20.** Read the Chapter 3 Summary on page 87.
_____ **21.** Complete the Chapter 3 Review on pages 88–89.
Comments:

Student's Signature _____ Date _____
Instructor's Signature _____ Date _____

©AGS Publishing. Permission is granted to reproduce for classroom use only.   ⬛▶ Physical Science

Chapter 3 Self-Study Guide

Introducing the Chapter

Have students examine the crystal of snow in the photo on page 58. Ask them to describe the snow crystal. Explain that all snow crystals have six sides but the details of their structure differ. Tell students that the snow crystals are like the tiniest parts of matter. Each kind of matter has its own structure.

Ask students what they know about the structures of matter. Encourage them to write what they know in the first column of a three-column chart. Ask them to write questions they have about the structure of matter in the second column of the chart. As they read the Student Text, they can use the third column of the chart to write answers to their questions. Have students examine the Organize Your Thoughts chart on page 59. Encourage them to copy and expand the chart. They can then use it to quickly review information.

Notes and Technology Notes

Ask volunteers to read the notes that appear in the margins throughout the chapter. Then discuss them with the class.

TEACHER'S RESOURCE

The AGS Teaching Strategies in Science Transparencies may be used with this chapter. The transparencies add an interactive dimension to expand and enhance the *Physical Science* program content.

CAREER INTEREST INVENTORY

The AGS Harrington-O'Shea Career Decision-Making System-Revised (CDM) may be used with this chapter. Students can use the CDM to explore their interests and identify careers. The CDM defines career areas that are indicated by students' responses on the inventory.

Lesson at a Glance

Chapter 3 Lesson 1

Overview This lesson introduces some properties of molecules. Students learn how molecules behave in each of the three common states of matter—solid, liquid, and gas.

Objectives

- To describe the size of molecules
- To explain what a molecule is
- To explain how molecules move in each of the three states of matter
- To describe what plasma is

Student Pages 60–64

Teacher's Resource Library **TRL**

Workbook Activity 13

Alternative Workbook Activity 13

Resource File 5

Vocabulary

atom	plasma
gas	solid
liquid	state of matter
molecule	

Science Background

Atoms are extremely small. In fact, about a half-million atoms would fit across the thickness of a human hair. The atoms of different elements do not vary greatly in size. An atom of uranium, one of the largest atoms, is only about three times larger than one of hydrogen, which is the smallest atom. However, different atoms do vary considerably in mass. A uranium atom is about 238 times heavier than an atom of hydrogen.

Lesson 1 — What Are Molecules?

Molecule

The smallest particle of a substance that has the same properties as the substance

How would you describe the sugar shown in the figure below? You might mention that sugar is a material made of matter. You might tell about its properties, such as its color, taste, or texture. Now think about how you might describe a single grain of sugar. You probably would say that it is very small. But how small is the smallest piece of sugar?

Size of Molecules

Each grain of sugar is made of even smaller particles that are too tiny for you to see. These tiny particles are called **molecules.** Molecules are the smallest particles of a substance that still have the properties of that substance. Each molecule of sugar has exactly the same properties. How small can molecules be? Molecules of some substances are so small that billions of them could be placed side by side on a line one centimeter long.

Describing Molecules

Look at the water spraying out of the fountain in the photo. Imagine dividing one drop of this water into smaller and smaller drops. The smallest drop you could make that still had the properties of water would be one molecule of water.

This fountain contains billions of molecules of water.

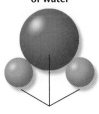

Molecule of water

Atoms

In general, all water molecules are alike. A water molecule from the fountain is the same as a water molecule in a raindrop, in a lake, or in the water you drink. The figure on the left shows a molecule of water. You can see that each water molecule has three parts—one large part and two smaller parts.

If you divided a water molecule into its three parts, it would no longer be a molecule of water. The parts would no longer have the properties of water. When a water molecule is divided into its separate parts, each individual part is called an **atom.** An atom is a building block of matter. A water molecule has three atoms. Each kind of atom has its own properties. All matter is made of atoms.

The Structure of Matter Chapter 3 **61**

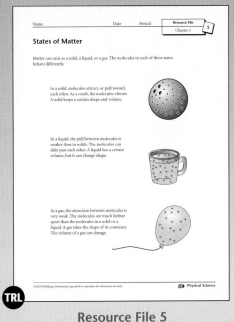

Name _____ Date _____ Period _____ | Resource File
Chapter 3 | 5

States of Matter

Matter can exist as a solid, a liquid, or a gas. The molecules in each of these states behave differently.

In a solid, molecules attract, or pull toward, each other. As a result, the molecules vibrate. A solid keeps a certain shape and volume.

In a liquid, the pull between molecules is weaker than in solids. The molecules can slide past each other. A liquid has a certain volume, but it can change shape.

In a gas, the attraction between molecules is very weak. The molecules are much farther apart than the molecules in a solid or a liquid. A gas takes the shape of its container. The volume of a gas can change.

©AGS Publishing. Permission is granted to reproduce for classroom use only. | ▶ Physical Science

TRL

Resource File 5

Place a closed container of perfume or other liquid with a strong odor in front of the class. Remove the lid and ask students to raise their hand when they smell the liquid. (Students closer to the container of liquid will probably raise their hands first.) Ask students why they think they are able to smell the liquid. Lead students to realize that the liquid is made of particles that escape from the container. As the particles spread around the room, students are able to smell them.

② **Teaching the Lesson**

Before beginning this lesson, ask students to scan the lesson, looking for unfamiliar words. Have students work in pairs or small groups to define the words on paper.

Have students describe the properties of a sheet of paper. (*Some properties of paper include shape, color, and texture.*) Then instruct students to tear the sheet of paper in half. Ask if each half has the same properties as the whole sheet of paper. (*The important properties remain the same.*) Ask whether each half is still paper. (*yes*) Instruct students to continue tearing the halves into smaller and smaller pieces until they are too small to tear. Ask whether the properties are the same. (*yes*) Ask whether the pieces are paper. (*yes*) Ask students how small they would have to tear the paper before it was no longer paper. (*until it was smaller than a molecule*) Compare the tiny pieces of paper to the molecules of a substance.

③ **Reinforce and Extend**

TEACHER ALERT

Many students think that molecules are always made up of a single kind of atom. Use the figure of a water molecule on page 61 to dispel this idea.

Ask a volunteer to read the myth portion (first sentence) of the Science Myth feature on page 62. Ask students to define *mass* and tell why people might mistakenly believe this myth. Discuss that because we often cannot see gases, people might believe they have no mass. Then have another volunteer read the fact portion of the feature.

LEARNING STYLES

Interpersonal/ Group Learning

Instruct students to hold tightly onto both hands of a partner and try to move around. Compare this behavior to that of the molecules in a solid—they do not move easily. Next, tell students to hold only one hand of their partner and try to move around. Compare this behavior to that of the molecules in a liquid, which can move about more easily than the ones in a solid. Finally, have students place their hands near their partners without touching. Have students move around. Explain that molecules in a gas can easily move.

Solid

A form of matter that has a definite shape and volume

Liquid

A form of matter that has a definite volume but no definite shape

Science Myth

Gases do not have mass.

Fact: A gas is one of the four states of matter. All matter has mass, even if we cannot see the matter.

States of Matter

You can describe matter by telling about its properties. For example, you might tell about its mass or density. The form that matter has is another one of its properties.

There are three forms of matter in the photo below. Can you find them? The boats and rocks are **solids.** A solid is a form of matter that has a definite shape and volume. The molecules in a solid attract, or pull toward, each other. In a solid, molecules vibrate, which means that they move back and forth quickly, but stay close together. For this reason, a solid keeps a certain shape and volume.

How many solids, liquids, and gases do you see?

The water in the picture is a **liquid.** A liquid is a form of matter that has a definite volume but no definite shape. The pull between the molecules is weaker in liquids than it is in solids. The molecules can slide past each other. A liquid can change its shape because its molecules can move around easily.

Gas

A form of matter that has no definite shape or volume

State of matter

The form that matter has—solid, liquid, or gas

Plasma

A very hot gas made of particles that have an electric charge

Suppose you had a liter of water in a container. If you poured the liter of water into a container that had a different shape, the water would still take up one liter of space. But its shape would be different. The water would take the shape of the new container.

Notice the shape of the helium balloon in the photo on page 62. Helium is a **gas** that fills the balloon. Gas is a form of matter that has no definite shape or volume. The molecules of a gas are much farther apart than they are in a liquid or a solid. The attraction between the molecules in a gas is very weak. A gas takes the same shape as its container because its molecules move around freely. The gas molecules will always fill a container completely. A container of water can be half full, but a container of a gas will always be completely full. The volume of a gas can change.

Solid   Liquid   Gas

These forms of matter—solid, liquid, and gas—are called the **states of matter.** The figure illustrates how the molecules move in each of these three states of matter.

Plasma

Matter can exist in a fourth state of matter called **plasma.** Plasma is a very hot gas made of particles that have an electric charge. The particles of plasma shake violently at very high temperatures. Plasma is very rare on Earth. But all stars, including the sun, are balls of plasma. Scientists estimate that 90 percent of all matter in the universe is plasma.

LEARNING STYLES

Body/Kinesthetic

Ask students to wave their hands in the air. Then have them imagine waving their hands under water and in sand. Discuss in which substance it would be easiest to wave their hands. *(in air)* Ask why they think this is so. *(Molecules in air, gases, are not as tightly connected as in water, a liquid, or sand, a solid. This allows for easy movement.)*

CROSS-CURRICULAR CONNECTION

Art

Suggest that students draw a picture containing at least one solid, liquid, and gas. Have them draw the molecules as they would be arranged in each state of matter.

Lesson 1 Review Answers

1. No, one tiny grain of sugar is made up of many sugar molecules. A single molecule is too small to be seen. **2.** A molecule of water has three parts—one large atom and two small atoms. **3.** In a solid, the molecules pull toward each other and vibrate. In a liquid, the molecules slide past each other, moving around easily. In a gas, the molecules are the farthest apart and move around freely. **4.** Plasma is a very hot gas made of particles that have an electric charge. **5.** Molecules are close together in solids. **6.** Solids have a definite shape and volume. **7.** Liquids have no definite shape, but do have a definite volume. **8.** Liquids take the shape of the container. **9.** Most plasma is in stars. **10.** The attraction between molecules is weakest in gases.

Portfolio Assessment

Sample items include:
- Words and definitions from Teaching the Lesson
- Lesson 1 Review answers

Lesson 1 REVIEW

Write your answers to these questions in complete sentences on a sheet of paper.

1. Can you see a single molecule of sugar? Explain your answer.

2. What parts make up a molecule of water?

3. Describe how molecules move in each of the three states of matter.

4. What is plasma?

5. In which form of matter are the molecules close together?

6. Which form of matter has a definite shape and volume?

7. Which form of matter has no definite shape, but has a definite volume?

8. Which form of matter takes the shape of its container?

9. Where is most plasma located?

10. In which state of matter is the attraction between molecules weakest?

Technology Note

The scanning electron microscope, or SEM, uses electron beams to look at very small items. The SEM makes a sharply detailed, 3–D picture. An SEM picture can show an item up to 200,000 times bigger than it is. The item is magnified so much that you can see molecules.

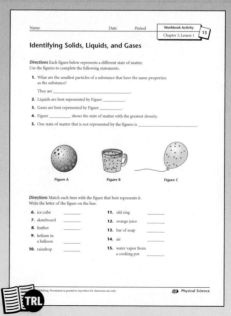

Workbook Activity 13

The Structure of Matter Chapter 3 **65**

Objectives

After reading this lesson, you should be able to

◆ explain what an element is.

◆ explain what a natural element is.

◆ give examples of natural elements.

Element

Matter that has only one kind of atom

In Lesson 1, you learned that atoms are very tiny. In fact, they are one of the smallest particles that make up matter. Remember the balloon that was filled with helium? A balloon as small as a softball would hold many billions of atoms of helium.

One Kind of Atom

Most of the matter you see around you is made up of many different kinds of atoms. However, some matter has only one kind of atom. Matter that is made of only one kind of atom is called an **element.** All atoms of the same element are alike. For example, all atoms of oxygen are the same. The atoms of oxygen are different from the atoms of all other elements.

The foil you might use to wrap a sandwich is made of atoms of the element aluminum. Gold, silver, and copper are other elements that are used to make jewelry and other common items.

The Structure of Matter Chapter 3 **65**

Lesson at a Glance

Chapter 3 Lesson 2

Overview In this lesson, students learn that an element is matter made of only one kind of atom. They learn about some uses of natural elements.

Objectives

■ To explain what an element is

■ To explain what a natural element is

■ To give examples of natural elements

Student Pages 65–69

Teacher's Resource Library **TRL**

Workbook Activity 14

Alternative Workbook Activity 14

Lab Manual 9

Vocabulary

element
natural element

Science Background

The International Union of Pure and Applied Chemistry was founded in 1911. Today the organization is considered the authority on standardizing names and symbols of the elements. Although it recognizes 109 elements, it is still investigating the discovery of elements 110 and above.

1 Warm-Up Activity

Show items made of the elements gold (jewelry), silver (jewelry), aluminum (foil), copper (wire), and lead (pipe). Ask students to describe the properties of each item and to tell how the items are alike. Help students understand that one way in which the items are alike is that each item is made of only one kind of atom.

2 Teaching the Lesson

Tell students to copy onto a sheet of paper the two vocabulary words from the lesson, leaving space after each word to write several sentences. As they read the lesson, have students copy two sentences that contain each vocabulary word.

Continued on page 66

Continued from page 65

When they have finished reading, ask them to write a new sentence for each vocabulary word.

Tell students that some elements are commonly found as solids, while others are found as liquids or gases. Mercury, for example, is the only metallic element found at normal temperatures in nature as a liquid. The other metallic elements naturally occur as solids. Oxygen, a gas, is found in the air we breathe.

Point out to students that the matter with which they come in contact every day is made of elements. Some matter, such as oxygen, is made of only one element. Other matter, such as water, is made of several elements.

 3 Reinforce and Extend

TEACHER ALERT

Some students may not understand the relationship between atoms and elements. Some students may think that atoms and elements are two different things. Make sure students understand that every atom is an element. Also, make certain they understand that the hydrogen and oxygen atoms in the water molecule shown on page 67 are the same kinds of atoms that make up the elements hydrogen and oxygen.

Did You Know?

Ask a volunteer to read the feature on page 66. Explain that in addition to the lead in pencils, carbon is part of a wide variety of common items, such as sugar, wood, gasoline, coal, and diamonds.

GLOBAL CONNECTION

 Have students find out where elements such as gold, silver, copper, lead, and zinc are mined in the United States. Help them locate these areas on a U.S. map. Then have students research to find out where else in the world these metals are mined. Help students find the countries on a world map.

Natural element
An element found in nature

 Did You Know?

Look at the tip of your pencil. It is made of a soft, black material that is a form of the element carbon. The small pencil point has billions of carbon atoms.

Scientists have discovered elements 110, 111, 112, 114, and 116. The International Union of Pure and Applied Chemistry —the authority on standardizing element names and symbols—is investigating elements 110 and above.

Natural Elements

Scientists know of about 109 different kinds of elements. Of these elements, 92 are called **natural elements.** Natural elements are those that are found in nature. For example, oxygen is an element that you get from the air you breathe. Your body is made of atoms of many different elements. Atoms of the element calcium help keep your bones and teeth strong.

Not all elements are natural elements. Scientists are able to produce a few elements in specialized laboratories. Some of the elements that scientists produce last only a short time—a fraction of a second—before they change into other elements.

The table lists some natural elements and tells what they can be used for. Can you think of other uses for some of these elements?

Some Natural Elements	
Name	Element Is Used or Found in These Items
copper	coins, frying pans, electrical wire
silver	jewelry, photography
carbon	pencils, charcoal, diamonds
helium	balloons, airships
nitrogen	air that we breathe, fertilizers
chlorine	bleach, table salt
aluminum	airplanes, cookware, soft-drink cans
neon	"neon" signs
gold	jewelry, seawater, dentistry
mercury	thermometers, drugs, pesticides
iron	steel, eating utensils

Did You Know?

Have students read the feature on page 67. Explain that silicon is a hard gray element. It is only found in compounds with other elements, often oxygen. Silicon and oxygen form glass and cement as well as sand.

Did You Know?

Living things are made up mainly of four elements. These are carbon, hydrogen, oxygen, and nitrogen. Ninety percent of the universe's atoms are hydrogen. Seventy percent of the earth's crust is oxygen and silicon.

Elements in Water

You have learned that a molecule of water is made of three parts like those in the figure below. These parts are elements. The large part of the molecule, shown in blue, is an atom of the element oxygen. The two small parts, shown in green, are atoms of the element hydrogen. The atoms of the element oxygen are different from the atoms of the element hydrogen.

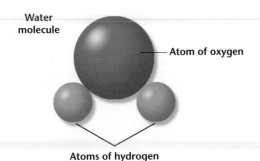

Water molecule

— Atom of oxygen

Atoms of hydrogen

Science Myth

The properties of a material's atoms are the same as the properties of the material.

Fact: Gold atoms are not shiny. Silver atoms are not silver in color. If we could see them, we would find that all individual atoms look about the same. The differences are not noticeable until billions of atoms are together.

Science Myth

Have one student read aloud the myth on page 67 and a second student read the fact. Students might be surprised to learn that a Greek philosopher, Democritus, and his followers hypothesized some of these basic facts about atoms over 2,000 years ago. They theorized about the existence of the atom, the smallest piece of matter. They thought that all atoms were made of the same material and that they were capable of joining together.

CROSS-CURRICULAR CONNECTION

 Home Economics

Most cookware is made of copper, aluminum, or stainless steel. Have students find out what properties of these elements or compounds make them useful for cooking. Also have them interview a cook, homemaker, or home economics teacher about the kind of cookware he or she prefers and why.

SCIENCE JOURNAL

Have students choose an element from the lists on pages 66 and 68. Ask them to write one or two paragraphs telling what they think the world might be like without that element.

The Food Guide Pyramid might be helpful to students as they plan a daily menu. A copy of this pyramid can be found on many cereal boxes and other food containers as well as in reference books. You can also obtain a copy of the food pyramid from the U. S. Department of Agriculture. Some researchers have suggested changes in the Food Guide Pyramid in recent years. They think that fats such as olive oil deserve a lower *(eat more)* position in the pyramid. Breads and refined starches should be higher *(eat less)* in the pyramid. They also think that nuts and beans may be better than fish and eggs as sources of protein, and that red meat consumption should be minimal. Encourage students who may interested to research the pyramid and find out the process for making changes to it.

CAREER CONNECTION

Dietitians work for hospitals, schools, and other organizations such as retirement homes. Their job is to create nutritious menus and to advise individuals on a healthy diet. They must know about nutrition requirements for people in a variety of circumstances and the foods that provide the nutrition. These requirements include the minerals on the chart on page 68 and the foods in which they are found. Invite a dietitian to class to discuss this career.

AT HOME

Have students check packaged foods, such as cereal, bread, cheese, milk, and snack foods, at home for the amounts of the natural elements in each. Explain that the nutritional facts on food packages usually include the percentages of the daily requirements of elements that are provided by the food. Students can find the best source for each element and tell how much of the element it provides.

How are elements important to health?

Your body needs many natural elements in order to stay healthy and work properly. There are two groups of elements in your body. The major elements are the elements your body needs in large amounts. Your body needs trace elements in smaller amounts. Your body cannot produce any of these elements. You must get them from food.

The table below lists some of the major elements and tells how they are important for your health. The table also lists some foods that contain these elements. Write a menu for a day. Include healthful foods in your menu that provide a variety of natural elements.

Element	Purpose in the Body	Food That Contains the Element
calcium	builds and maintains teeth and bones; helps blood clot; helps nerves and muscles work properly	cheese, milk, dark green vegetables, sardines, legumes
phosphorus	keeps teeth and bones healthy; helps release energy from the food you eat	meat, poultry, fish, eggs, legumes, milk products
magnesium	aids breaking down of foods; controls body fluids	green vegetables, grains, nuts, beans, yeast
sodium	controls the amount of water in body; helps nerves work properly	most foods, table salt
potassium	controls the fluids in cells; helps nerves work properly	oranges, bananas, meats, bran, potatoes, dried beans
iron	helps move oxygen in the blood and in other cells	liver, red meats, dark green vegetables, shellfish, whole-grain cereals
zinc	helps move carbon dioxide in the body; helps in healing wounds	meats, shellfish, whole grains, milk, legumes

Write your answers to these questions in complete sentences on a sheet of paper.

1. What is an element?

2. What is a natural element?

3. Give three examples of natural elements.

4. Table salt is made up of one sodium atom and one chlorine atom. Is table salt an element? Explain your answer.

5. Name two elements that we need to build and maintain bones in our body.

Achievements in Science

Quarks

A fundamental particle is a particle that is not made up of anything else. An electron is a fundamental particle. Protons and neutrons are made of subnuclear particles called quarks.

There are six types of quarks. Scientists usually discuss them as pairs. The up and down quarks are the first and lightest pair. The strange and charm quarks are the second pair. The last pair is made up of the bottom and top quarks. The existence of the top quark was hypothesized for 20 years before scientists discovered it in 1995. It is the most massive quark and was the last to be discovered.

Quarks are different from protons and electrons. Protons and electrons have a charge that is always a whole number. Quarks have a fractional charge. Protons and neutrons are made of up quarks and down quarks. All of the everyday matter in our world is made of electrons, up quarks, and down quarks. The other quarks usually are found only in particle accelerators.

Lesson 2 Review Answers

1. An element is matter that is made of only one kind of atom. 2. A natural element is one that occurs in nature. 3. Answers will vary, but may include calcium, phosphorus, magnesium, sodium, potassium, iron, and zinc. 4. Table salt is not an element because it is made up of two different kinds of atoms. An element is matter that is made up of only one kind of atom. 5. Calcium and phosphorus help build and maintain bones.

Achievements in Science

Have students take turns reading aloud the Achievements in Science feature on page 69. Explain that two American physicists, Murray Gell-Mann and George Zweig, first theorized the existence of quarks in 1964. The existence of quarks was confirmed through particle accelerator experiments in 1971. Scientists now know that quarks are at least 1,000 times smaller than protons. Have students work in pairs to research information about recent quark findings in popular scientific journals.

Portfolio Assessment

Sample items include:
• Words and definitions from Teaching the Lesson
• Lesson 2 Review answers

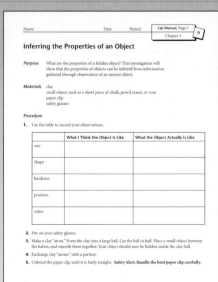

Lab Manual 9, pages 1–2

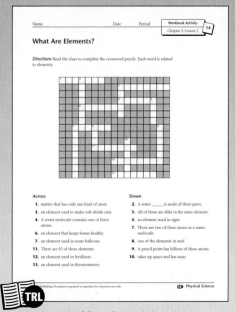

Workbook Activity 14

Lesson at a Glance

Chapter 3 Lesson 3

Overview In this lesson, students learn that a compound consists of atoms from two or more different elements. They learn about some common compounds.

Objectives

- To explain what a compound is
- To give examples of compounds

Student Pages 70–74

Teacher's Resource Library

Workbook Activity 15

Alternative Workbook Activity 15

Lab Manual 10

Vocabulary

compound

▶1 Warm-Up Activity

Show students a piece of rusted iron. Work with them to make a list of properties of the rusted part of the iron and the unrusted part. When the list is complete, ask students whether the two substances are the same. They should indicate that since the properties are different, the substances are different. Tell students that, although the substances are different, they both have some of the same kind of atoms—iron atoms. Further explain that the rusted part of the iron has oxygen atoms combined with the iron atoms.

▶2 Teaching the Lesson

Before reading, have students copy the figure of a molecule of water without its labels on page 70. Tell them to write any questions they have about the diagram. As students read, they should write information that answers their questions. After reading, have students share their questions and answers with the class.

Write the following words on the board: *atom, molecule, compound*. Review the definition of each word. Then have students label the names of the atoms *(hydrogen and oxygen)*, molecule *(water)*, and compound *(water)* on their diagrams.

Objectives

After reading this lesson, you should be able to

- ◆ explain what a compound is.
- ◆ give examples of compounds.

Compound

A substance that is formed when atoms of two or more elements join together

All the substances in the figure are different from the elements you learned about in Lesson 2. The substances in the figure are each made of two or more different kinds of atoms. When two or more atoms of different elements join together, the substance that forms is called a **compound.** A compound has properties that are different from the properties of the elements that form the compound.

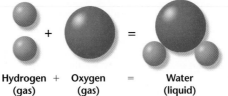

Hydrogen + Oxygen = Water
(gas)   (gas)   (liquid)

Think again about a molecule of water. The drawing shows that an atom of oxygen combines with two atoms of hydrogen to form a molecule of the compound water. Water is different from the elements that form it. Water is a liquid. Both oxygen and hydrogen are gases. You will learn more about breaking down the compound water into its elements when you do the Investigation on pages 73 and 74.

In 1661, Robert Boyle defined an *element* as a material made of only one part. A century later, Antoine Lavoisier defined a *compound*. He defined it as material made of two or more elements.

Another compound that probably is familiar to you is table salt. The chemical name of salt is sodium chloride. It is formed when the element sodium is combined with the element chlorine. Sodium chloride is very different from each of the elements it contains. Sodium is a solid. You might be surprised to learn that chlorine is a poisonous gas. However, when chlorine is combined with sodium to form sodium chloride, chlorine no longer has its poisonous property. Remember that a compound can have completely different properties from the elements that form it.

Most kinds of matter on Earth are compounds. In fact, there are more than 10 million known compounds. The table lists some common compounds and tells the elements that make up each compound.

Some Common Compounds		
Name	Elements in this Compound	How/Where It Is Used
table salt	sodium, chlorine	cooking
water	hydrogen, oxygen	drinking
sugar	carbon, hydrogen, oxygen	cooking
baking soda	sodium, hydrogen, carbon, oxygen	baking
Epsom salts	magnesium, sulfur, oxygen	medicine

You might wonder if you can tell by looking at a substance whether it is an element or a compound. An unknown substance must be tested in a laboratory to determine whether it is an element or a compound.

The Structure of Matter   Chapter 3   **71**

Ask students what elements are in the compound sugar *(carbon, hydrogen, oxygen)*. They can find the information in the table on page 71. Encourage students to describe the properties of these elements. (Most will say that hydrogen and oxygen are gases. If necessary, refer them back to Did You Know? on page 66, where carbon is described as a soft, black material.) Then ask them to describe the properties of sugar. *(sweet, granular, white)* Discuss how the properties of sugar are different from those of the elements that make it.

3 Reinforce and Extend

TEACHER ALERT

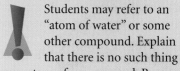

Students may refer to an "atom of water" or some other compound. Explain that there is no such thing as an atom of a compound. Be sure that students understand that water (and all other compounds) is made up of molecules. These molecules are, in turn, made up of atoms.

LEARNING STYLES

Auditory/Verbal

Ask students to look at the table on page 71. Have them complete this statement for each compound in the table: I know that *(name of compound)* is a compound because it is made of more than one kind of atom. These atoms are *(names of elements)*.

CROSS-CURRICULAR CONNECTION

Drama

Have students act out what happens when two hydrogen atoms and one oxygen atom combine to make the compound water. Encourage students to think of a creative way to show how the properties of water are different from those of hydrogen and oxygen.

SCIENCE INTEGRATION

Earth Science

Tell students that in nature the compound water is commonly found in each of the three states of matter—solid, liquid, and gas. Ask students to suggest examples. *(glaciers and snow, lakes and clouds, water vapor)* Point out that we cannot actually see water vapor. Clouds are formed when vapor condenses into droplets. Students can draw pictures of the states of water as they are found in nature.

SCIENCE JOURNAL

Have students write a paragraph that begins with the following sentence: I wonder what it would be like to be a molecule of water.

The Structure of Matter   Chapter 3   **71**

Lesson 3 Review Answers

1. A compound is a substance that forms when two or more elements join together.
2. Table salt, water, sugar, baking soda, and Epsom salts are examples of compounds.
3. The gas is a compound because it is made up of atoms of two different elements joined together. **4.** Two common compounds that contain sodium are table salt and baking soda. **5.** Four compounds that contain oxygen are water, sugar, baking soda, and Epsom salts.

Science at Work

Have students take turns reading the Science at Work text aloud. Make sure students know that a particle accelerator is an electrical device that speeds up atomic particles such as electrons and protons, enabling scientists to study the nucleus of an atom and change the atom of one element into another. Have students work in small groups to find information about particle accelerators, such as their history, the types of accelerators, and other uses for accelerators.

Portfolio Assessment

Sample items include:
• Diagram of a compound from Teaching the Lesson
• Lesson 3 Review answers

Write your answers to these questions in complete sentences on a sheet of paper.

1. Explain what a compound is.

2. Give two examples of compounds.

3. Suppose you test a gas in the laboratory. You learn that the gas is made up of carbon atoms and oxygen atoms. Is the gas a compound? Explain your answer.

4. Name two common compounds that contain sodium.

5. Name four compounds that contain oxygen.

Science at Work

Accelerator Technician

Accelerator technicians help build, maintain, repair, and operate particle accelerators and related equipment. They are responsible for recording meter readings. Accelerator technicians also keep track of parts and move heavy equipment.

Accelerator technicians need vocational training to learn to make and maintain electrical or mechanical equipment.

Accelerator technicians must be able to follow instructions and keep records. They must be able to use hand tools and electronic instruments. Accelerator technicians also must know how to measure and calculate dimensions, area, volume, and weight.

72   *Chapter 3   The Structure of Matter*

Name _____ **Date** _____ **Period** _____   Workbook Activity
Chapter 3, Lesson 3   **15**

What Are Compounds?

Directions Use the terms in the box to complete each sentence.

carbon
compound
gases
hydrogen
laboratory
liquids
salt
sodium
sugar
water

1. A _____ is formed when two or more atoms of different elements join together.

2. The compound formed from two atoms of hydrogen and one atom of oxygen is _____.

3. Oxygen and hydrogen are _____, but when combined they form a _____.

4. A compound used for cooking made from sodium and chlorine is _____.

5. Baking soda is a compound made of _____ _____, and oxygen.

6. To find out if a substance is an element or a compound, test it in a _____.

7. A compound used for cooking made of carbon, hydrogen, and oxygen is _____

Directions When you compare and contrast things, you tell how they are alike and how they are different. Answer these questions by comparing and/or contrasting.

8. How are an element and a compound alike and different?

9. How are water and hydrogen different?

10. How are sugar and baking soda alike?

Publishing. Permission is granted to reproduce for classroom use only.   ▶ **Physical Science**

Breaking Down Water

Materials
- safety glasses
- beaker or wide-mouth jar
- water (distilled water preferred)
- two 50-cm long pieces of copper wire (about 3 cm of insulation removed at ends)
- one 15-cm long piece of copper wire (about 3 cm of insulation removed at ends)
- 2 six-volt batteries
- 1 teaspoon table salt
- stirring rod
- salt water
- 2 test tubes

Purpose

How can you tell that water is a compound? This investigation will show that water is made from two different substances and is therefore a compound.

Procedure

1. Copy the data table on a sheet of paper.

Setup	After 10 Minutes
wire connected to positive (+) terminal	
wire connected to negative (−) terminal	

2. Put on your safety glasses.

3. Fill a 500 mL beaker with water.

4. Attach the end of one long copper wire to the negative (−) terminal of one battery, as shown on the next page. Attach the end of the other long copper wire to the positive (+) terminal of the second battery. **Safety Alert: The ends of the wires are sharp. Handle them carefully.**

5. Use the short copper wire to connect the positive (+) terminal of the first battery to the negative (−) terminal of the second battery.

6. Put one end of each longer wire in the beaker so that the ends are about 4 cm to 5 cm apart, as shown.

SAFETY ALERT
- Make sure students wear their safety glasses.
- Make sure students handle the sharp ends of the wires carefully and keep the wires away from their faces.
- Provide paper towels that can be used to clean up spills immediately.

Investigation 3-1

The Purpose portion of the student investigation begins with a question to draw them into the activity. Encourage students to read the investigation steps and formulate their own questions before beginning the investigation. This investigation will take approximately 45 minutes to complete. Students will use these process and thinking skills: observing, collecting, recording, and interpreting data and comparing.

Preparation
- Use sandpaper or scissors to remove 3 cm of insulation from the ends of the wires.
- A plastic straw can be substituted for the stirring rod.
- Have extra batteries on hand to replace any batteries that do not work.
- Students may use Lab Manual 10 to record their data and answer the questions.

Procedure
- You can have students work in groups of three. Assign one student to gather equipment. All students should observe the ends of the wires, record results, answer questions, and clean up when finished. Student A sprinkles the salt into the water and stirs. Student B attaches the long wires to the batteries and places them in the water. Student C attaches the short wire to the two batteries.
- Be sure students are aware of the locations of the positive (+) and negative (−) terminals on the batteries.
- If bubbles do not form at the ends of the wires, check the connections between the wires and the batteries. Also check that the battery works.
- Hold a sheet of dark paper behind the beaker to observe the bubbles more easily.
- Electrolysis is the process by which water is broken down into hydrogen and oxygen. The battery produces an electric current that provides the energy to break the water molecule apart.

Continued on page 74

Continued from page 73

- The table salt is added to the water so that the electric current travels through the water more easily.

Results

Bubbles of gas will form in the water at the ends of each wire. These bubbles are made of hydrogen gas (formed at the wire connected to the negative terminal) and oxygen gas (formed at the wire connected to the positive terminal). The electric current that travels through the water from one wire to the other breaks the water molecule down into the hydrogen and oxygen atoms that make up the water molecule.

Questions and Conclusions Answers

1. The wire connected to the negative terminal had more bubbles.

2. Students' answers should include descriptions of the gas bubbles that appeared.

3. The bubbles at the end of the wires tell us that water is a compound because these bubbles indicate that water is made of more than one kind of atom—oxygen and hydrogen.

Explore Further Answers

Bubbles form inside the test tubes. The gases that form force liquid out of each test tube.

Assessment

Check students' answers to question 3. Be sure that they understand that the hydrogen and oxygen gases are an indication that water is made of more than one kind of atom and is, therefore, a compound. You might include the following items from this investigation in student portfolios:

- Investigation 3-1 data table
- Answers to Questions and Conclusions and Explore Further sections

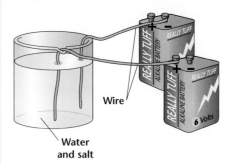

7. Sprinkle a few grains of salt into the water. Stir with the stirring rod until the salt dissolves. Observe the ends of the wires in the water. Continue adding a few grains of salt to the water. Stir until the salt dissolves. When small bubbles appear at the wire ends, stop adding salt.

8. Observe the ends of both wires in the water for about 10 minutes. Record your observations in the table.

Questions and Conclusions

1. Which of the wires had more bubbles around it? Identify the wire by telling whether it was connected to the positive (+) terminal or the negative (−) terminal.

2. Describe what you observed at the end of each wire after 10 minutes.

3. The gas you observe comes from the water. The electricity from the batteries breaks down the water into hydrogen gas and oxygen gas. How does this production of gases show that water is a compound?

Explore Further

Bend the two wires in the beaker upward. Fill two test tubes with salt water. Hold your thumb over the top of one test tube and turn it upside down. Put the test tube in the water and remove your thumb. Place the test tube over a wire. Repeat with the other test tube. What happens in each of the test tubes?

74 *Chapter 3 The Structure of Matter*

Lab Manual 10

74 *Chapter 3 The Structure of Matter*

Objectives

After reading this lesson, you should be able to

◆ describe what a model is and explain how scientists use it.

◆ explain how models of the atom have changed.

◆ describe the electron cloud model.

Model

A picture, an idea, or an object that is built to explain how something else looks or works

Since atoms are too small to be seen with the eyes alone, people have wondered for a long time what atoms look like. In fact, scientists have been studying atoms since the 1800s. But if scientists can't see an atom, how do they know what atoms look like?

Using Models

Sometimes scientists can tell what things look like by studying how they act. For example, have you ever seen wind? What does it look like? You might say that wind is leaves blowing or your hair getting messed up. If you say that you are describing what wind does, not what it looks like. You use the effects of wind to describe it. You know that wind is there because of its effects even though you can't see it. You use evidence.

Scientists use the same kind of evidence to study things they can't see, such as atoms. Scientists study how atoms act and then decide what an atom must look like. Scientists make **models.**

You have probably seen models of cars or airplanes or buildings. In science, a model is an idea, a picture, or an object that is built to explain how something else looks or works. The model may not look exactly like the object it is built to describe, but it helps people understand the way the object acts.

The Structure of Matter   Chapter 3   75

Overview This lesson introduces students to scientific models. They learn how models of the atom have changed as new evidence is gathered and find out what the current model of the atom is.

Objectives

■ To describe what a model is and explain how scientists use it

■ To explain how models of the atom have changed

■ To describe the electron cloud model

Student Pages 75–81

Teacher's Resource Library

Workbook Activity 16

Alternative Workbook Activity 16

Lab Manual 11

Resource File 6

Vocabulary

electron
model
neutron
nucleus
proton

Science Background

The word *atom* comes from the Greek word *atomos,* meaning "indivisible." In the fifth century B.C., it was proposed that all matter was composed of tiny particles called atoms. According to this proposal, these atoms could not be broken down further. Since then many models of the atom have been suggested. Two important models are those of Niels Bohr and Erwin Schrödinger. The current model of the atom is called the electron cloud model. This model is based on the idea that we do not know the exact location or the velocity of any given electron. The model uses the idea of "probability clouds" to indicate the approximate position of an electron. This model is more complicated than the concentric shell model commonly used.

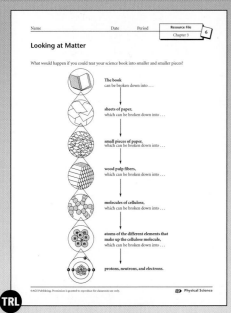

1 Warm-Up Activity

Display several different types of models. They may be simple, such as a model car or airplane, or more complex, such as a human body or a human heart. Also display a one-dimensional model such as a map. Have students explain what each model helps them understand and how it does so.

2 Teaching the Lesson

Tell students that models are important to scientists because models help them make predictions. For example, scientists can use the model of an atom to predict how a particular substance will act when it is combined with other substances.

Tell students the plus (+) symbol for protons means that they have a positive electric charge. The minus (−) symbol for electrons means that they have a negative electric charge. Neutrons have no electric charge. Direct students' attention to Figures A, B, and C shown on pages 76 and 77. Have students draw models of these atoms, using the plus and minus symbols for the protons and electrons. Have students use an *n* for the neutrons. Suggest that students draw circles around the symbols to make them more noticeable.

3 Reinforce and Extend

TEACHER ALERT

Many students may think that a model must be a 3D object, such as a model car or airplane, or must be larger than the actual object. Help them see that pictures and ideas can also be used to explain how something looks or works. Point out that the pictures in this lesson showing the arrangements of protons, neutrons, and electrons in atoms are models. They are also examples of models that are much larger than the actual atoms.

Science Myth

Ask a volunteer to read the myth portion (first sentence) of the Science Myth feature on page 76. Then have another volunteer read the fact portion of the feature. About 99.9 percent of an atom's mass is concentrated in the nucleus. If an atom were the size of a basketball, the nucleus would be invisible. If the nucleus were enlarged to the size of a softball, the nearest electron would be located about 0.8 km (0.5 mile) away.

Nucleus

The central part of an atom

Proton

A tiny particle in the nucleus of an atom

Electron

A tiny particle of an atom that moves around the nucleus

Science Myth

An atom is solid.

Fact: Atoms are mostly empty space. Imagine an atom the size of a football field. What would you put in the center to model the size of the nucleus? A grapefruit? A grape? The nucleus would be the size of one grape seed. Between the seed and the outside diameter of the field would be emptiness.

Models of Atoms

Scientists use models of atoms to show how atoms look and act without having to actually see them. Many scientists have developed models of atoms. The first model was developed over 2,000 years ago. But as scientists gather new information about atoms, they change their models.

In the early 1900s, a scientist developed a model of an atom like those shown at the bottom of the page. Although scientists know more about atoms today, this kind of model is still useful for describing atoms.

Find the center of each atom. This central part of an atom is called a **nucleus.** The nucleus of an atom contains small particles called **protons.** Protons are labeled with the letter *p*. Another symbol for a proton is a plus (+) sign. Protons have a positive charge. Look for the letter *e* in the figures below. This letter stands for **electrons.** Electrons are particles in an atom that move around the outside of the protons. The mass of an electron is much less than the mass of a proton. Another symbol for an electron is a minus (−) sign. Electrons have a negative charge. The protons and electrons of an atom stay together because they attract each other.

Notice that the numbers of protons and electrons in the models are different. Figure A shows a model of an atom of hydrogen. You can see that hydrogen has one proton and one electron. Figure B shows an atom of helium, a gas that is often used to fill balloons. How many protons and electrons does helium have?

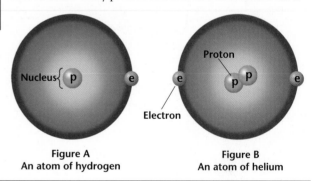

Figure A
An atom of hydrogen

Figure B
An atom of helium

Neutron

A tiny particle in the nucleus of an atom that is similar to a proton in size

In 1827, Robert Brown found the first sign that atoms exist. While studying pollen under a microscope, he noticed that particles were always moving. This *Brownian* motion comes from the movement of atoms and molecules.

In 1932, scientists had evidence that the nucleus of an atom had another kind of particle. This particle is called a **neutron**. It is similar to a proton in size. Because of the new evidence, scientists changed the model of the atom. In Figure C, an atom of boron shows how the model changed. Find the neutrons, labeled with the letter *n*.

You can see in Figure C that the electrons seem to be on certain paths around the nucleus of the atom. Scientists thought that electrons moved in different layers around protons, sometimes jumping from one layer to another.

Today scientists use another model of atoms. You can see this new model—the electron cloud model—in Figure D. The dark center area represents the nucleus. However, you can't see different layers of electrons like you see in the models in figures A, B, and C. The electron cloud model was developed because of evidence that electrons behave in more complicated ways than scientists previously thought. Because of this new evidence, scientists are not sure how electrons move around the nucleus. As scientists continue to learn more about atoms, perhaps the model will change again.

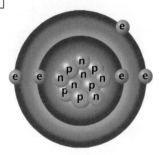

Figure C
An atom of boron

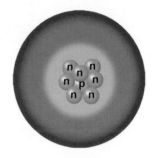

Figure D
Electron cloud model of an atom

In an electrically neutral atom, the number of protons equals the number of electrons. When an atom gains electrons or loses electrons, the charge becomes unbalanced.

You have looked at models showing the number of protons and electrons in the atoms of a few different elements. The table below lists some other elements and tells the numbers of protons and electrons in each. Find the number of protons in the element carbon. How many electrons does carbon have? Compare the numbers of protons and electrons in nitrogen. How many of each does it have? Now look at the numbers of protons and electrons in each of the elements listed. What do you notice? The number of protons in an atom is equal to the number of electrons in the atom.

$$\text{Number of protons in an atom} = \text{Number of electrons in an atom}$$

Number of Protons and Electrons for Some Elements		
Element	Number of Protons	Number of Electrons
hydrogen	1	1
helium	2	2
lithium	3	3
beryllium	4	4
boron	5	5
carbon	6	6
nitrogen	7	7
oxygen	8	8
fluorine	9	9
neon	10	10

Lesson 4 REVIEW

Write your answers to these questions in complete sentences on a sheet of paper.

1. If scientists cannot see atoms, how do they know what they look like?

2. How do scientists use models?

3. How many protons are in the element shown in the figure?

4. How many electrons are in the element?

5. What is the name of the element? (Hint: Use the table on page 78.)

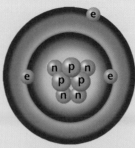

Achievements in Science

The History of the Atom Model

Democritus, a Greek philosopher, first used the term atom around 400 B.C. In 1803, English schoolteacher John Dalton showed that materials were made of atoms. Ideas about the atom have continued to change. Scientists, at different times in history, have thought about what an atom looks like. In recent years, scientists have done experiments to prove information about atoms.

Over the years, scientists discovered that atoms were made of smaller parts. They also created models for the atom. In the late 1800s, English physicist J. J. Thompson discovered the electron. He also suggested the "plum pudding" model of the atom. He imagined the electrons scattered inside an atom like bits of plum in plum pudding. Fourteen years later New Zealand physicist Ernest Rutherford disproved the plum pudding model. He showed that atoms have a nucleus in the center with electrons on the outside.

Later, Danish scientist Niels Bohr offered his planetary model of the atom. It was based on speculation that seemed to be supported by experiments. Later, however, mathematical calculations led to the electron cloud model.

The Structure of Matter Chapter 3   **79**

Lesson 4 Review Answers

Lesson 4 Review Answers

1. Scientists decide what atoms look like based on how the atoms act. **2.** Scientists use models to explain how things look or act. **3.** The element has three protons. **4.** The element has three electrons. **5.** The element is lithium.

Achievements in Science

Have students take turns reading the Achievements in Science feature on page 79 aloud. Ask volunteers to draw diagrams of the "plum pudding" model and the planetary model of the atom on the board. Have students discuss how they differ from the electron cloud model that is accepted today.

PRONUNCIATION GUIDE

Use the pronunciation shown here to help students pronounce a difficult word in this lesson. Refer to the pronunciation key on the Chapter Planning Guide for the sounds of the symbols.

beryllium (bə ril´ ē əm)

Portfolio Assessment

Sample items include:
- Models of atoms from Teaching the Lesson
- Lesson 4 Review answers

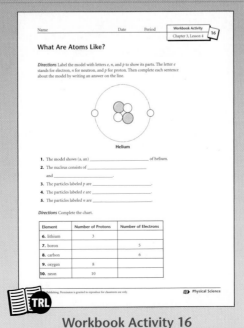

Workbook Activity 16

The Structure of Matter Chapter 3   **79**

Investigation 3-2

The Purpose portion of the student investigation begins with a question to draw them into the activity. Encourage students to read the investigation steps and formulate their own questions before beginning the investigation. This investigation will take approximately 25 minutes to complete. Students will use these process and thinking skills: observing; measuring/using numbers; making and using models, and describing.

Preparation

• Students may use Lab Manual 11 to record their data and answer the questions.

Procedure

• Organize students in working groups of three. Assign one student to gather materials. Student A can make the protons. Student B can make the neutrons. Student C can make the electrons. All students can help assemble the final model, record results, answer questions, and clean up when finished.

• Have the class decide which colors to use for protons, neutrons, and electrons.

• Tell students to refer to the chart on page 84 for the correct number of neutrons for their atoms.

• You might have students rub their hands in cornstarch before rolling the clay to prevent it from sticking to their hands.

• Have students decide on the exact number of each kind of particle they need. Then they can divide the clay into the appropriate number of small pieces.

• Suggest students roll the balls of clay on a flat surface to make them more spherical.

• Remind students that the electrons should be smaller than the protons and neutrons.

SAFETY ALERT

◆ Advise students to handle craft sticks carefully.
◆ Make sure all students are wearing their safety glasses.

Materials

◆ safety glasses
◆ 3 different colored pieces of modeling clay
◆ craft sticks
◆ metric ruler

Making Models of Atoms

Purpose

What three things must every atom have? You will make a model of an atom of a particular element in this investigation.

Procedure

1. Copy the data table on a sheet of paper.

Name of Element:	
Picture of Element:	

2. Put on your safety glasses.

3. Choose an element from the table on page 78. Find the numbers of protons, neutrons, and electrons in your element.

4. Place three different colors of modeling clay on your desk. Choose one color of clay for protons. Pull off a small piece of clay for each of the protons in your element. Roll each piece into a ball about 1 cm in diameter.

5. Use another color of clay for neutrons. Make clay balls the same size as the protons. Be sure to make the same number of balls as there are neutrons in your element.

6. With the third color of clay, make smaller clay balls to represent electrons. Make the same number of balls as the protons you made.

7. Press the protons and neutrons together gently to make the nucleus of your model atom.

8. Gently put the craft sticks into the nucleus of your model. Put the same number of sticks as there are electrons in your element.

9. Place the clay electrons on the ends of the craft sticks.

10. Write the name of the element in your table. Then draw a picture of your model.

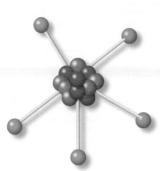

Questions and Conclusions

1. What is the name of your element?

2. How many protons are in the nucleus?

3. How many neutrons does it have?

4. How many electrons does your element have?

5. Write at least four things that your model shows about atoms.

Explore Further

Work with other students who have made models of different atoms. Find the mass number of each atom. The mass number is a number equal to the sum of the number of protons and neutrons in an atom. (You will learn more about mass number in the next lesson.) Put the atoms in order from lowest to highest mass number. What happens to the number of protons and neutrons as mass number increases?

Results

Student models should show the same number of protons and electrons as indicated in the table on page 78 of the text. The correct number of neutrons for each atom can be found on page 84 of the text.

Questions and Conclusions Answers

1. Answers will vary, depending on the element selected.

2. Answers will vary. Refer to the chart on page 78 for the correct number.

3. Answers will vary. Refer to the chart on page 84 for the correct number.

4. Answers will vary. Refer to the chart on page 78 for the correct number.

5. It shows that (A) the nucleus is made of protons and neutrons, (B) electrons surround the nucleus, (C) the number of electrons equals the number of protons, and (D) electrons are smaller than protons and neutrons.

Explore Further Answers

The number of both protons and neutrons increases as the mass number increases.

Assessment

Check student models for the correct number and placement of electrons, neutrons, and protons. You might include the following items from this investigation in student portfolios:

• Investigation 3-2 data table

• Answers to Questions and Conclusions and Explore Further sections

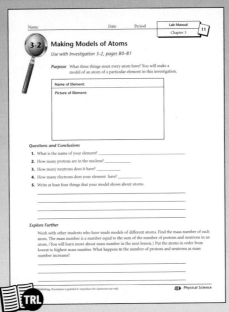

Lab Manual 11

Chapter 3 Lesson 5

Overview In this lesson, students further explore the structure of an atom. They learn about atomic number and mass number.

Objectives

- To explain what the atomic number of an element is
- To explain how the mass number of an element is determined

Student Pages 82–86

Teacher's Resource Library (TRL)

Workbook Activity 17

Alternative Workbook Activity 17

Lab Manual 12

Resource File 7

Vocabulary

atomic number
mass number

1 Warm-Up Activity

Display several library books that show their call numbers on the spine. Ask students how these numbers are used. Discuss how the numbers enable people to find books on the library shelf. A book's number also gives certain information about the book. For example, if the Dewey decimal number is 636, the book is about cats. If the number is 781, the book is about music. Tell students that in much the same way scientists use numbers to give information about elements.

2 Teaching the Lesson

As students read the lesson, have them write down what they want to remember and why they want to remember it. For example: "I want to remember what an atomic number tells me about an atom. Then I can figure out how many protons are in the nucleus of an atom."

Be sure that students see how an element's atomic number differs from its mass number. Ask students which number has to do with the number of protons in an atom. *(atomic number)*

Objectives

After reading this lesson, you should be able to

- explain what the atomic number of an element is
- explain how the mass number of an element is determined

Atomic number

A number equal to the number of protons in the nucleus of an atom

Did You Know?

All atoms are recycled. You constantly breathe atoms in and out of your body. Some atoms stay in your body for a while. Then they move on to become part of someone or something else.

Because more than 100 elements are known, scientists need a way to identify them. One way scientists can identify elements is by knowing their **atomic numbers.**

Atomic Number

The table below shows the same 10 elements listed in the table on page 78. However, a column labeled Atomic Number has been added to the table. The atomic number of an element tells the number of protons in each atom of the element.

Some Elements and Their Atomic Numbers			
Element	Atomic Number	Number of Protons	Number of Electrons
hydrogen	1	1	1
helium	2	2	2
lithium	3	3	3
beryllium	4	4	4
boron	5	5	5
carbon	6	6	6
nitrogen	7	7	7
oxygen	8	8	8
fluorine	9	9	9
neon	10	10	10

Notice that each element has a different number of protons, and therefore a different atomic number. For example, the element hydrogen has one proton. Its atomic number is also one. According to the table, how many protons does boron have? What is the atomic number of boron? For all the elements, the atomic number of the element is equal to the number of protons it has.

Atomic number = Number of protons

82 Chapter 3 The Structure of Matter

Which has to do with the total number of protons and neutrons? *(mass number)*

Tell students that an element can be referred to by its name, its symbol, or its atomic number. No two elements have the same atomic number.

Remind students that a neutral atom has equal numbers of electrons and protons. But the number of neutrons may be different. Because neutrons have no charge, the different number only affects the mass of the atom, not its neutral charge.

Did You Know?

Ask a volunteer to read the feature on page 82. Ask students what kinds of atoms they inhale *(oxygen)* and what kinds of atoms they exhale *(carbon dioxide)*. Point out that plants use the carbon dioxide atoms exhaled by other living organisms.

The Mass of an Element

You learned in Chapter 1 that mass is the amount of matter in an object. Protons and neutrons have a greater mass than electrons have. In fact, the mass of a proton or a neutron is about 1,800 times the mass of an electron. Yet protons and neutrons are still so small that it would not be possible to measure their mass on a balance scale. Instead, scientists tell about the mass of an element by using its **mass number.** The mass number of an element is equal to the sum of the numbers of protons and neutrons in an atom of the element.

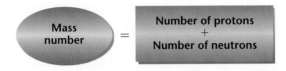

$$\text{Mass number} = \text{Number of protons} + \text{Number of neutrons}$$

The figure shows an atom of beryllium. You can see that it has 4 protons and 5 neutrons. The atomic number of beryllium is 4, the same as the number of protons. To determine the mass number of beryllium, add the number of protons, 4, and the number of neutrons, 5. The mass number of beryllium is 9 (4 + 5 = 9).

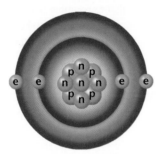

An atom of beryllium

The Structure of Matter   *Chapter 3*   **83**

3 Reinforce and Extend

Did You Know?

Have students read the feature on page 83. According to astronomers, the composition of almost all stars is the same. Hydrogen and helium combined make up to 99 percent of a star's mass. Hydrogen alone makes up 60 percent to 80 percent. The remainder of the star's mass consists of elements such as oxygen, neon, carbon, and nitrogen.

IN THE COMMUNITY

A linear accelerator is a special kind of particle accelerator that produces X-rays. Linear accelerators are used for certain kinds of medical X-rays such as those used for radiation treatment of cancer. Have students find out more about the medical uses of these kinds of accelerators. They may be able to interview a radiologist or X-ray technician who can explain how these X-ray machines work.

ONLINE CONNECTION

Students can visit the educational Web sites of Fermilab at www-ed. fnal.gov and Berkeley Lab at www.lbl.gov/abc to find out more about particle accelerators and up-to-date research on the atom.

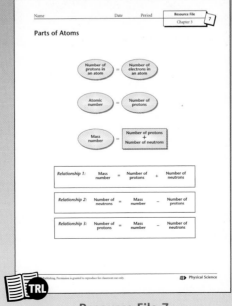

Resource File 7

You have learned about protons, neutrons, and electrons. You also have learned about atomic numbers and mass numbers of elements. The table below gives a summary of information for the first 10 elements.

The First 10 Elements					
Element	Atomic Number	Mass Number	Number of Protons	Number of Electrons	Number of Neutrons
hydrogen	1	1	1	1	0
helium	2	4	2	2	2
lithium	3	7	3	3	4
beryllium	4	9	4	4	5
boron	5	11	5	5	6
carbon	6	12	6	6	6
nitrogen	7	14	7	7	7
oxygen	8	16	8	8	8
fluorine	9	19	9	9	10
neon	10	20	10	10	10

Remember that you can use information you know about an element to determine other information. For example, look at this figure of an atom of sodium. Find the numbers of protons and neutrons. How many protons are in the nucleus? You know that the number of electrons in an element is equal to its number of protons. How many electrons does sodium have? You also know that the atomic number of an element is equal to the number of protons it has. What is the atomic number of the element sodium?

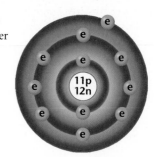

An atom of sodium

Antimatter particles can be made in laboratories. Some antimatter particles are antielectrons and antiprotons. Antiprotons and protons are exactly the same, except their charges are opposite. This is also true for antielectrons and electrons.

Technology Note

Particle accelerators make protons or electrons move very fast and collide with targets. These collisions create new types of particles. Accelerators let physicists see what's inside particles. You have a particle accelerator at home. A TV works like a particle accelerator, only on a much smaller scale.

The box below shows the relationships between the mass number of an element and the numbers of protons and neutrons it has. Notice that Relationship 1 explains how to find the mass number of an element. Simply add the number of protons and neutrons it has in its nucleus.

Relationship 1:	Mass number	=	Number of protons	+	Number of neutrons
Relationship 2:	Number of neutrons	=	Mass number	−	Number of protons
Relationship 3:	Number of protons	=	Mass number	−	Number of neutrons

Suppose you know the mass number of an element and the number of protons it has. Can you determine the number of neutrons it has? Find Relationship 2 in the box. This relationship explains how you can use the information you know to find the number of neutrons in the nucleus of an atom.

Finally, suppose you know the mass number of an element and its number of neutrons. For example, the element aluminum has a mass number of 27. You can see in the figure that aluminum has 14 neutrons in its nucleus. You can use Relationship 3 to determine the number of protons it has. How many protons are in the nucleus of the element aluminum?

An atom of aluminum

Technology

Have interested students research some of the current techniques for viewing atoms. One of these is the scanning tunneling microscope. This instrument produces pictures of the arrangement of electrons on the surface of solid objects. The scanning tunneling microscope enables scientists to see even the bonds between atoms.

SCIENCE JOURNAL

Have students write the definitions for *atomic number* and *mass number*. Then have them explain how they would use each number to get information about an element.

Lesson 5 Review Answers

1. The element has 33 protons. 2. The element's atomic number is 26. 3. It has 6 neutrons. 4. sodium—11 protons, 11 electrons; aluminum—atomic number 13, 13 protons; chlorine—atomic number 17, 17 electrons; calcium—atomic number 20, 20 protons 5. silver—atomic number 47, 47 electrons, 61 neutrons; silicon—atomic number 14, mass number 28, 14 protons; calcium—20 protons, 20 electrons, 20 neutrons; iodine—53 protons, 53 electrons, 74 neutrons; chlorine—mass number 35, 17 protons, 17 electrons; sulfur—atomic number 16, 16 protons, 16 neutrons; potassium—atomic number 19, 19 electrons, 20 neutrons

Portfolio Assessment

Sample items include:

- Statements of goals from Teaching the Lesson
- Lesson 5 Review answers

Write your answers to these questions in complete sentences on a sheet of paper.

1. An element has an atomic number of 33. How many protons does it have?

2. An element has 26 protons. What is its atomic number?

3. An element has 6 protons and a mass number of 12. How many neutrons does it have?

4. Copy the table on your paper. Then fill in the missing numbers.

Element	Atomic Number	Number of Protons	Number of Electrons
sodium	11		
aluminum			13
chlorine		17	
calcium			20

5. Copy the table on your paper. Then fill in the missing numbers. You can refer to the three relationships on page 85 for help. The first one is done for you.

Element	Atomic Number	Mass Number	Number of Protons	Number of Electrons	Number of Neutrons
carbon	6	12	6	6	6
silver		108	47		
silicon				14	14
calcium	20	40			
iodine	53	127			
chlorine	17				18
sulfur		32	16		
potassium		39	19		

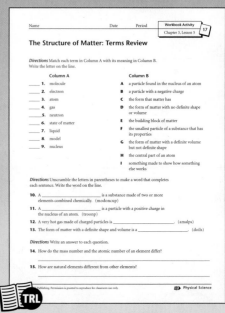

- A molecule is the smallest particle of a substance that still has the same properties of the substance.

- An atom is the basic building block of matter.

- Scientists use models to explain things they cannot see.

- Molecules move in different ways in each of the three states of matter—solids, liquids, and gases.

- An element is matter that is made of only one kind of atom. There are 92 natural elements, which are found in nature.

- A compound is formed from two or more atoms of different elements. A compound has properties that are different from the elements that form the compound.

- An atom is made of protons, neutrons, and electrons.

- The number of protons in an atom is equal to the number of electrons.

- The atomic number of an element is equal to the number of protons in its nucleus.

- The mass number of an element is equal to the number of protons plus the number of neutrons.

Science Words

atom, 61	liquid, 62	nucleus, 76
atomic number, 82	mass number, 83	plasma, 63
compound, 70	model, 75	proton, 76
electron, 76	molecule, 60	solid, 62
element, 65	natural element, 66	state of matter, 63
gas, 63	neutron, 77	

Chapter 3 Summary

Have volunteers read aloud each Summary item on page 87. Ask volunteers to explain the meaning of each item. Direct students' attention to the Science Words box on the bottom of page 87. Have them read and review each word and its definition.

Chapter 3 Review

Use the Chapter Review to prepare students for tests and to reteach content from the chapter.

Chapter 3 Mastery Test

The Teacher's Resource Library includes two parallel forms of the Chapter 3 Mastery Test. The difficulty level of the two forms is equivalent. You may wish to use one form as a pretest and the other form as a posttest.

Review Answers
Vocabulary Review

1. molecule 2. liquid 3. gas 4. solid
5. plasma 6. element 7. atom 8. nucleus
9. natural element 10. compound

Concept Review

11. A 12. C 13. D 14. B 15. D 16. B 17. C

TEACHER ALERT

Because of limited space in this Chapter Review, not all of the vocabulary terms introduced in this chapter appear in the Vocabulary Review section. You may want to create an activity using the missing words to give students practice with all of the terms in this chapter. Here are the terms that are not covered in the section.

atomic number

electron

mass number

model

neutron

proton

state of matter

Chapter 3   R E V I E W

Vocabulary Review

Choose a word or words from the Word Bank that best complete each sentence. Write the answers on a sheet of paper.

Word Bank
atom
compound
element
gas
liquid
molecule
natural element
nucleus
plasma
solid

1. A(n) _____ is the smallest particle of a substance that can still have the properties of the substance.

2. A form of matter with definite volume but no definite shape is a(n) _____.

3. A form of matter with no definite shape or volume is a(n) _____.

4. A form of matter with definite shape and volume is a _____.

5. A very hot gas made of particles with an electric charge is _____.

6. Matter that has only one kind of atom is a(n) _____.

7. The _____ is the building block of matter.

8. A(n) _____ is the central part of an atom.

9. A(n) _____ is found in nature.

10. A(n) _____ is a substance that is formed when atoms of two or more elements join together.

Concept Review

Choose the answer that best completes each sentence. Write the letter of the answer on your paper.

11. The states of matter are _____.
    A solid, liquid, gas, and plasma
    B elements and natural elements
    C atom, molecule, and compound
    D electrons, protons, and neutrons

12. Models of atoms help describe their _____, although they cannot be seen.
    A mass   C appearance and actions
    B state of matter   D volume

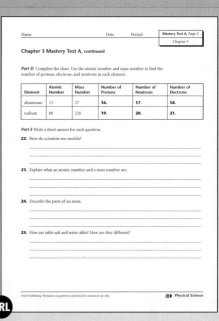

Chapter 3 Mastery Test A

13. The particles of _____ shake violently at very high temperatures.
  A solid **B** liquid **C** gas **D** plasma

14. Of the following, _____ is not a compound.
  A water **C** sodium chloride
  B oxygen **D** magnesium oxide

15. The particles in an atom are _____.
  A compounds **C** molecules
  B natural elements **D** electrons, protons, and neutrons

16. An element's atomic number is the same as the number of _____ it has.
  A electrons **B** protons **C** neutrons **D** nuclei

17. If an element has 4 protons and 5 neutrons, its mass number is _____.
  A 1 **B** 4 **C** 9 **D** 20

Critical Thinking

Write the answer to each of these questions on your paper.

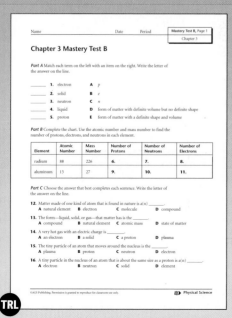

18. How is the movement of a molecule's particles different when it is a solid, a gas, and a liquid?

19. Does the figure at the right show a molecule or an atom? Explain your answer.

20. Look at the figure at the left. Then answer these questions. How many protons and neutrons does the atom have? How many electrons? What is the element's atomic number? What is the mass number?

| Test-Taking Tip | To remember facts and definitions more easily, write them down on index cards. Practice with a partner using the flash cards. |

The Structure of Matter Chapter 3 **89**

Chapter 3 Mastery Test B

Review Answers
Critical Thinking

18. In a solid, molecules vibrate back and forth but stay close together. In a liquid, the molecules are weaker and can slide past each other. In a gas, molecules are very weak and move around freely.
19. The figure shows a molecule because it is made up of two different kinds of elements. **20.** The atom has 6 protons and 6 neutrons. It has 6 electrons. The element's atomic number is 6. Its mass number is 12.

ALTERNATIVE ASSESSMENT

Alternative Assessment items correlate to the student Goals for Learning at the beginning of this chapter.

- Ask students to explain how the following are alike and different: atoms and molecules, elements and compounds.

- Have students draw a model of a lithium atom, using the charts on pages 78 and 84 to find the correct number of protons, electrons, and neutrons.

- Distribute copies of a model of an atom such as Figure C on page 77. Have students provide a written identification and definition of each part of the atom.

- Tell students that the atomic number of fluorine is 9. Its mass number is 19. Have them explain what each number means.

- Give students the atomic number *(7)* and mass number *(14)* of the element nitrogen. Have students calculate the number of protons *(7)*, electrons *(7)*, and neutrons *(7)* in the element.

The Structure of Matter Chapter 3 **89**

Chapter

4

Planning Guide
Classifying Elements

	Student Text Lesson		
	Student Pages	Vocabulary	Lesson Review
Lesson 1 What Are Symbols?	92–96	✔	✔
Lesson 2 Using the Periodic Table	97–105	✔	✔
Lesson 3 Metals, Nonmetals, and Noble Gases	106–112	✔	✔

Chapter Activities

Student Text
Science Center

Teacher's Resource Library
Community Connection 4: Metals, Nonmetals, and Nobel Gases in the Community

Assessment Options

Student Text
Chapter 4 Review

Teacher's Resource Library
Chapter 4 Mastery Tests A and B

Student Text Features								Teaching Strategies						Learning Styles						Teacher's Resource Library				
Achievements in Science	Science at Work	Science in Your Life	Investigation	Science Myth	Note	Technology Note	Did You Know	Science Integration	Science Journal	Cross-Curricular Connection	Online Connection	Teacher Alert	Applications (Home, Career, Community, Global, Environment)	Auditory/Verbal	Body/Kinesthetic	Interpersonal/Group Learning	Logical/Mathematical	Visual/Spatial	LEP/ESL	Workbook Activities	Alternative Workbook Activities	Lab Manual	Resource File	Self-Study Guide
	94	95					93			94			93				93	93		18	18	13		✔
105					✔	✔	104	98, 102	99, 101, 103	102, 103	101	99	100, 102	104	100	100	101, 103	99	99	19	19	14	8	✔
109	110	111	107, 108		✔	✔	106	109				107	108, 110		108			109		20	20	15, 16	9	✔

Pronunciation Key

a	hat	e	let	ī	ice	ô	order	ú	put	sh	she			
ā	age	ē	equal	o	hot	oi	oil	ü	rule	th	thin			
ä	far	ėr	term	ō	open	ou	out	ch	child	ŦH	then			
â	care	i	it	ȯ	saw	u	cup	ng	long	zh	measure			

ə { a in about, e in taken, i in pencil, o in lemon, u in circus }

Alternative Workbook Activities

The Teacher's Resource Library (TRL) contains a set of lower-level worksheets called Alternative Workbook Activities. These worksheets cover the same content as the regular Workbook Activities but are written at a second-grade reading level.

Skill Track Software

Use the Skill Track Software for Physical Science for additional reinforcement of this chapter. The software program allows students using AGS textbooks to be assessed for mastery of each chapter and lesson of the textbook. Students access the software on an individual basis and are assessed with multiple-choice items.

Chapter at a Glance

Chapter 4: Classifying Elements
pages 90–115

Skill Track Software for Physical Science

Teacher's Resource Library

Workbook Activities 18–20

Alternative Workbook Activities 18–20

Lab Manual 13–16

Community Connection 4

Resource File 8–9

Chapter 4 Self-Study Guide

Chapter 4 Mastery Tests A and B

(Answer Keys for the Teacher's Resource Library begin on page 402 of the Teacher's Edition. The Materials List for the Lab Manual activities begins on page 419.)

Science Center

Provide poster board and colored markers. Assign small groups of students an element or a family of elements to research. Basic information on elements can be found in dictionaries and encyclopedias. You might ask the school librarian for books containing information on the elements or visit the library as a class. Have the group make a poster for their element or family of elements, including information about properties, uses, and discovery.

Community Connection 4

Chapter 4

Classifying Elements

Y ou might recognize the substance in the photograph as crystals of native gold. When gold is mined, it looks like these crystals. Gold has many uses. We use gold in spacecrafts and satellites, in medical research and treatment, and in electronics. We can find it in computers, telephones, and home appliances. Why is gold so useful? Gold carries heat and electricity very well. It is shiny, and its shape can be changed. These are the properties of an element that is a metal. In Chapter 4, you will learn what an element is and how elements are classified.

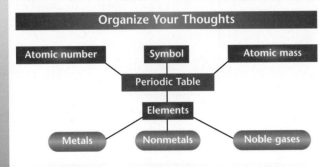

Organize Your Thoughts

Atomic number — Symbol — Atomic mass

Periodic Table

Elements

Metals — Nonmetals — Noble gases

Goals for Learning

- ◆ To identify the symbols used to represent different elements
- ◆ To explain how elements are organized in the periodic table
- ◆ To describe the kinds of information in the periodic table
- ◆ To classify elements as metals, nonmetals, or noble gases

91

Introducing the Chapter

Have students describe what they see in the photo on page 90. Encourage them to share what they know about the element gold and its uses. Then ask a volunteer to read aloud the introductory paragraph on page 91.

Review with students the meaning of the word *element*. Explain that scientists have discovered about 109 elements and analyzed their properties. This analysis has allowed them to organize all the known elements into a table that gives a lot of information about each element. It also groups them according to their similarities. Display a periodic table and have students point out squares for elements they already know something about. Read aloud the Goals for Learning. Ask students to write a question for each goal and to write the answers to their questions as they find them in the chapter.

Notes and Technology Notes

Ask volunteers to read the notes that appear in the margins throughout the chapter. Then discuss them with the class.

Name _____ Date _____ Period _____ SELF-STUDY GUIDE

Chapter 4: Classifying Elements

Goal 4.1   To identify the symbols used to represent different elements

Date	Assignment	Score
_____	**1.** Read pages 92–93.	_____
_____	**2.** Complete the Lesson 1 Review on page 94.	_____
_____	**3.** Complete Workbook Activity 18.	_____
_____	**4.** Complete Investigation 4-1 on pages 95–96.	_____

Comments:

Goal 4.2   To explain how elements are organized in the periodic table

Date	Assignment	Score
_____	**5.** Read page 97–98.	_____

Comments:

Goal 4.3   To describe the kinds of information in the periodic table

Date	Assignment	Score
_____	**6.** Read pages 99–104.	_____
_____	**7.** Complete the Lesson 2 Review on page 105.	_____
_____	**8.** Complete Workbook Activity 19.	_____

Comments:

©AGS Publishing. Permission is granted to reproduce for classroom use only.   ■▶ Physical Science

---

Name _____ Date _____ Period _____ SELF-STUDY GUIDE

Chapter 4: Classifying Elements, continued

Goal 4.4   To classify elements as metals, nonmetals, or noble gases

Date	Assignment	Score
_____	**9.** Read pages 106–109.	_____
_____	**10.** Complete the Lesson 3 Review on page 110.	_____
_____	**11.** Complete Workbook Activity 20.	_____
_____	**12.** Complete Investigation 4-2 on pages 111–112.	_____
_____	**13.** Read the Chapter 4 Summary on page 113.	_____
_____	**14.** Complete the Chapter 4 Review on pages 114–115.	_____

Comments:

Student's Signature _____ Date _____

Instructor's Signature _____ Date _____

©AGS Publishing. Permission is granted to reproduce for classroom use only.   ■▶ Physical Science

Chapter 4 Self-Study Guide

Chapter 4 Lesson 1

Overview In this lesson students learn how to identify and write element symbols.

Objectives

■ To explain what a symbol is

■ To explain how element symbols are alike and different

■ To identify symbols for common elements

Student Pages 92–96

Teacher's Resource Library

Workbook Activity 18

Alternative Workbook Activity 18

Lab Manual 13

Vocabulary

symbol

Science Background

Latin has been a useful language for scientists, allowing naming of animals and substances that can be understood and agreed upon around the world. Often, scientists use the Latin name of an element in creating its symbol. The Latin name for gold is *aurum;* the symbol for gold is Au. Likewise, the symbols for silver (Ag), iron (Fe), and mercury (Hg) are derived from the Latin names for these elements: *argentum, ferrum,* and *hydrargyrum.* Potassium (K), discovered in 1807, takes its name from the Latin word *kalium,* meaning "alkali." It is one of the alkali metals grouped in the first column of the periodic table.

 Warm-Up Activity

Ask for volunteers to explain what an abbreviation is *(shortened form of a word or phrase used to represent the complete form)* and name some common abbreviations (such as those for units of measure, organizations, titles, and degrees). List these on the board; then ask students to explain what each represents. Explain that the abbreviation is a symbol for the word.

Objectives

After reading this lesson, you should be able to

◆ explain what a symbol is.

◆ explain how element symbols are alike and different.

◆ identify symbols for common elements.

Symbol

One or two letters that represent the name of an element

Think about addressing an envelope for a letter you write to a friend. You probably use an abbreviation to indicate the state to which the letter should be delivered. What is the abbreviation for your state?

Element Symbols

Scientists also use abbreviations to represent each of the 92 natural elements. The abbreviations for elements are called **symbols.** The tables on this page and page 93 list some symbols for elements. All these symbols are alike in the following ways.

◆ All of the symbols have either one or two letters.

◆ The first letter of each symbol is a capital letter.

◆ If the symbol has a second letter, the second letter is a lowercase letter.

◆ No period appears at the end of a symbol.

Table 1	
Element Name	Element Symbol
hydrogen	H
boron	B
carbon	C
nitrogen	N
oxygen	O
fluorine	F
phosphorus	P
sulfur	S
iodine	I
uranium	U

Table 2	
Element Name	Element Symbol
helium	He
lithium	Li
neon	Ne
aluminum	Al
silicon	Si
argon	Ar
calcium	Ca
cobalt	Co
bromine	Br
barium	Ba
radium	Ra

Notice that the symbols in Table 1 on page 92 use only the first letter of the element name. Look at the symbols in Table 2. This group of symbols uses the first two letters of the element name. The symbols in Table 3 also use two letters. The first letter is the first letter of the element name. The second letter is another letter from the element name.

How do the symbols in Table 4 differ from the other symbols? Most of these symbols come from the Latin names for the elements. For example, the symbol for iron is Fe, which comes from the Latin word *ferrum*, meaning "iron."

In recent years, scientists have made new elements in the laboratory. Some of these elements have symbols with three letters. You can see the symbols for these elements in the table on pages 100 and 101.

Table 3	
Element Name	Element Symbol
magnesium	Mg
chlorine	Cl
chromium	Cr
manganese	Mn
plutonium	Pu
zinc	Zn
strontium	Sr
platinum	Pt

Table 4	
Element Name	Element Symbol
sodium	Na
potassium	K
iron	Fe
silver	Ag
tin	Sn
tungsten	W
gold	Au
mercury	Hg
lead	Pb
antimony	Sb
copper	Cu

Have students work in small groups to make a set of symbols for the following objects: a pen, a pencil, a book, a desk. Stress that the symbols should be simple and easy to understand and reproduce. Each symbol should refer to only one item.

 Teaching the Lesson

Read the lesson objectives with students and help them recast each objective as a question. Have them write the questions on paper, leaving space after each. As they read the lesson, they can write a sentence to answer each question.

Use these questions to explore the lesson:

- Why do some elements use the first letter of the element name as a symbol? *(It is simple and obvious.)*

- Why are some elements symbolized by more than one letter? *(Some elements begin with the same letter—carbon, calcium, copper. To be useful, each symbol must represent only one element.)*

 Reinforce and Extend

Did You Know?

Have a volunteer read the feature on page 93 aloud. Discuss reasons why using Latin names might be helpful in the international recognition of a name. Invite students to tell why it is important for all scientists to use the same symbols for elements.

Lesson 1 Review Answers

1. All symbols have either one or two letters. The first letter of each symbol is capitalized. **2A** He **B** Ag **C** C **D** Cl **E** Ca **3A** mercury **B** neon **C** manganese **D** oxygen **E** phosphorus **4.** Abbreviations and symbols stand for specific words. They both use letters to represent the actual words. Symbols do not have periods, and most abbreviations do not include punctuation either. **5.** The symbol for iron, Fe, comes from the Latin word *ferrum*, meaning iron.

Science at Work

Ask volunteers to read the Science at Work feature on page 94.

Explain that assayers work in a lab, testing rock samples gathered from possible mining sites. The assayer determines the exact mineral content of a sample. Specific properties of elements allow the assayer to separate valuable metals from other elements in the sample. Discuss why it is important for an assayer to have the ability to concentrate on detail.

Assayers may work for mining companies or for the government. Some specialize in testing and analyzing precious metals. They may work for the U.S. Mint. A college degree in chemistry is valuable preparation for becoming an assayer.

CROSS-CURRICULAR CONNECTION

Language Arts
Some students may wish to do library research on elements that are found in your state. Have them take notes and present a brief report on how the element is mined and refined and what it is used for.

Portfolio Assessment

Sample items include:
- Questions written from objectives and sentence answers from Teaching the Lesson
- Symbols created by groups in Warm-Up Activity
- Lesson 1 Review answers

Write your answers to these questions in complete sentences on a sheet of paper.

1. How are all of the element symbols alike?

2. Write the symbol for each of the following elements.
   A helium **B** silver **C** carbon **D** chlorine **E** calcium

3. Write the element name for each of the following symbols.
   A Hg **B** Ne **C** Mn **D** O **E** P

4. How are abbreviations and symbols alike?

5. Why is Fe the symbol for iron?

▼◄▲▼◄▲▼◄▲▼◄▲▼◄▲▼◄▲▼◄▲▼◄▲▼◄▲▼◄▲▼◄▲▼◄▲▼◄▲▼◄▲▼◄▲▼

Science at Work

Assayer

Assayers are laboratory technicians who analyze samples of precious metals. Assayers collect and analyze rocks and separate metals from them. Using chemical processes or experiments, an assayer collects information about these metals. This information includes how much and what kind of metals are in the samples.

An assayer must complete a two- to three-year technical program or earn a four-year degree in science.

An assayer must be interested in precious metals and be able to keep track of details. An assayer also must be able to work in a laboratory or at a mine site. Good math, decision-making, and communication skills are very important in an assayer's work.

PRONUNCIATION GUIDE

Use the pronunciation shown here to help students pronounce a difficult word in this lesson. Refer to the pronunciation key on the Chapter Planning Guide for the sounds of the symbols.

assayer (ə sā´ ər)

Name	Date	Period	**Workbook Activity** 18
			Chapter 4, Lesson 1

Words from Chemical Symbols

Directions Read the clue in Column A. You can find the answer from the elements in Column B. In Column C, write the symbols for the elements in Column B. The word you form should be the correct answer for the clue. The first one is done for you.

	A	**B**	**C**
1.	A farm animal	cobalt-tungsten	CoW
2.	A musical group	barium-neodymium	
3.	The opposite of *lose*	tungsten-iodine-nitrogen	
4.	A building material	bromine-iodine-carbon-potassium	
5.	Found on a door	potassium-nitrogen-oxygen-boron	
6.	Used to write on a blackboard	carbon-hydrogen-aluminum-potassium	
7.	A dog's sound	boron-argon-potassium	
8.	It's 150 million km away	sulfur-uranium-nitrogen	
9.	A source of energy	cobalt-aluminum	
10.	A funny person	chlorine-oxygen-tungsten-nitrogen	
11.	Used in hockey	plutonium-carbon-potassium	
12.	Something to run in	radium-cerium	
13.	A form of money	cobalt-iodine-nitrogen	
14.	Show of affection	potassium-iodine-sulfur-sulfur	
15.	Another word for *ill*	silicon-carbon-potassium	
16.	An infant	barium-boron-yttrium	
17.	A narrow street	lanthanum-neon	
18.	To make better	helium-aluminum	
19.	King of the beasts	lithium-oxygen-nitrogen	
20.	A form of precipitation	radium-iodine-nitrogen	

Publishing. Permission is granted to reproduce for classroom use only

📖 TRL · ▶️ Physical Science

4-1 INVESTIGATION

Finding Iron in Your Cereal

Purpose

Do you think that iron-fortified cereal contains real bits of iron? In this investigation, you will observe bits of iron in an iron-fortified cereal.

Procedure

1. Copy the data table on a sheet of paper.

Procedure Step	Observations
7	
8	
9	

2. Put on your safety glasses.

3. Place about a handful of iron-fortified cereal into the sandwich bag and seal the bag. Crush the cereal into a fine powder.

4. Place the cereal in the beaker. Add just enough water to cover the cereal.

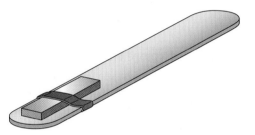

Materials
- safety glasses
- iron-fortified cereal (flakes)
- self-sealing sandwich bag
- 250-mL beaker
- warm water
- rubber band
- bar magnet
- craft stick
- white paper
- hand lens

SAFETY ALERT

◆ Be sure water is not hot enough to cause burns. If possible, use plastic beakers or containers.
◆ Remind students not to put the cereal into their mouths.
◆ Provide paper towels so that students can clean up spills immediately.

Investigation 4-1

The Purpose portion of the student investigation begins with a question to draw them into the activity. Encourage students to read the investigation steps and formulate their own questions before beginning the investigation. The investigation will take approximately 30 minutes to complete. Students will use these process and thinking skills: collecting, recording, and interpreting data; inferring; predicting; and communicating.

Preparation

- Be sure to use a cereal that says "iron fortified" on the package.

- Large plastic or paper cups could be used in place of the beaker. Containers should be large enough to hold the cereal and water without spilling.

- If craft sticks are not available, use pencils.

- If hand lenses are not available, students should still be able to see the iron pieces on the magnet if they observe carefully.

- Students may use Lab Manual 13 to record their data and answer the questions.

Procedure

- Assign groups of four to complete this investigation.

- Assign one student to gather materials. All students should observe the mixture with the hand lens, record results, and clean up when finished. Other steps in the procedure may be divided among the students.

- Have students read the ingredients on the cereal box. Have them predict which ingredient or ingredients will cling to a magnet.

- To make the iron pieces easier to see, have students stroke the magnet in one direction.

Continued on page 96

Continued from page 95

Results

Students should observe small pieces of iron clinging to the end of the magnet.

Questions and Conclusions Answers

1. pieces of a grayish material
2. pieces of a grayish material
3. yes
4. iron

Explore Further Answers

The human body requires iron in its red blood cells and red muscles to carry oxygen and see that the cells use it properly. Almost 100 percent of the iron in the human body is used up daily, so the iron needs to be replenished. Foods such as beef, pork, raisins, spinach, and apricots are rich in iron.

Assessment

Check students' answers to be sure that they understand that the material attracted by the magnet is iron. You might include the following items from this investigation in student portfolios:

• Investigation 4-1 data table
• Answers to Questions and Conclusions and Explore Further sections

5. Use the rubber band to attach the bar magnet to the craft stick.

6. Use the magnet end of the stick to stir the cereal-water mixture for about 3 minutes. Allow the magnet to stay in the mixture for about 10 minutes. Then stir again.

7. Remove the stick and the magnet from the mixture and hold them over a sheet of white paper.

8. Use a hand lens to look at the end of the magnet. Write your observations in the data table.

9. Wipe the end of the magnet on the white paper. Use a hand lens to look at any bits that are on the paper. Write your observations in the data table.

10. Use the magnet to try to pick up bits from the paper. Record your observations.

Questions and Conclusions

1. What did you observe on the end of the magnet?

2. What did you observe on the white paper?

3. Were the bits on the white paper attracted to the magnet?

4. What element from the cereal did you see?

Explore Further

Why might iron be added to cereal? Use an encyclopedia or other reference source to find out.

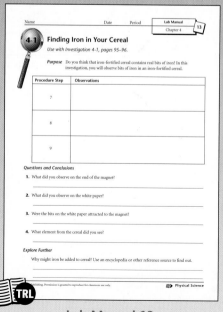

Lab Manual 13

Objectives

After reading this lesson, you should be able to

◆ explain how elements are arranged in the periodic table.

◆ explain the information contained in each box in the periodic table.

◆ explain what an isotope is.

◆ explain how elements in the periodic table are grouped in columns.

Periodic table

An arrangement of elements by increasing atomic number

Remember that the atomic number of an element tells you the number of protons in its nucleus.

For many years, scientists noticed that some elements were similar to others. In the mid-1800s, a Russian scientist named Dmitri Mendeleev designed the first chart that showed some of the similarities among the elements.

How Elements Are Arranged

Mendeleev began by making cards for each element known at that time. Then he organized the elements in order of increasing mass. He placed hydrogen, the lightest element, first. Mendeleev then used the cards to construct a table with rows and columns that organized the elements according to their properties. The cards formed the first **periodic table.**

Mendeleev left blank spaces in his table where he thought an element should fit—even for elements that he didn't know existed. When these elements were later discovered, his unknown elements were found to be in the correct spaces in the table.

The form of Mendeleev's table changed over the years as scientists learned more about atoms. Scientists found that an element's properties are related more closely to its atomic number than to its mass. The periodic table used today is an orderly arrangement of all known elements. The elements are arranged according to their atomic number.

Look at the periodic table shown on pages 100 and 101. Notice that elements are arranged from left to right in rows by increasing atomic number. The two separate rows at the bottom of the page are too long to fit into the drawing. Arrows show where the rows belong.

Chapter 4 Lesson 2

Overview Students explore the periodic table. They learn how elements are arranged and how to use information from the table. Students also learn what an isotope is.

Objectives

■ To explain how elements are arranged in the periodic table

■ To explain the information contained in each box in the periodic table

■ To explain what an isotope is

■ To explain how elements in the periodic table are grouped in columns

Student Pages 97–105

Teacher's Resource Library

Workbook Activity 19

Alternative Workbook Activity 19

Lab Manual 14

Resource File 8

Vocabulary

atomic mass	isotope
deuterium	periodic table
family	tritium

Science Background

The elements in each row of the periodic table are arranged from left to right by increasing atomic number, or the number of protons in their atoms. Elements in each column share similar, but not identical, properties. For example, the elements in the first column, the alkali metals, are all silver-white shiny metals that react violently with water. They also have low melting and boiling points.

The periodic table's organization allows you to get a great deal of information about an element at a glance: its symbol, the number of protons (and therefore electrons) in each atom, and its atomic mass. An element's placement also tells you whether it is a metal, a nonmetal, or a gas, and what other elements have similar properties.

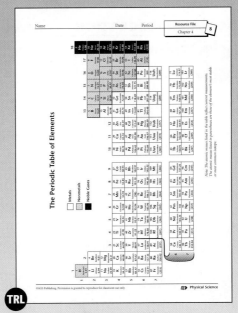

Resource File 8

Warm-Up Activity

Display a calendar and ask students to explain how it is organized and how to read it. Days of the month follow in numerical order from left to right. Ask: What is found in each row? *(the days in one week)* What do the numbers in one column represent? *(the dates in the month that fall on the same day of the week)*

Review the meanings of the terms *atom, atomic number, mass, mass number, proton, nucleus, electron,* and *neutron* with students, using diagrams on the board.

Teaching the Lesson

Before students read the lesson, have them look at the periodic table on pages 100–101. Work with students to make a K-W-L table on the board. In the first column, list what they already know about the table. In the second column, write questions students would like to answer as they read. Keep the information posted. As you discuss the lesson, write answers to the questions as they are discovered. Have students copy the table onto their own papers.

Be sure that students studying the periodic table understand that a row runs across and a column runs down. Have students explain how the calendar from the warm-up activity and the periodic table are alike. *(Days and elements are arranged in rows from left to right by increasing numbers. Dates for the same day and elements with similar properties are lined up in columns.)* Clarify that the first two elements, hydrogen and helium, do make up a row, although there is a large gap between them. Have students name these elements and find their atomic numbers. Then have them identify the atomic numbers of the elements in each row.

PRONUNCIATION GUIDE

Use the pronunciation shown here to help students pronounce a difficult word in this lesson. Refer to the pronunciation key on the Chapter Planning Guide for the sounds of the symbols.

Dmitri Mendeleev (də mē´ trē men dl ā´ ef)

A silicon chip is a piece of almost pure silicon (Si). It is usually about $\frac{1}{2}$ mm thick and less than 1 cm by 1 cm. It holds hundreds of thousands of tiny electronic circuits. Silicon chips have many uses. You find them in computers, calculators, cameras, cars, and other items.

Information in the Periodic Table

You can use the periodic table on pages 100 and 101 to learn more about the elements. Each box in the periodic table contains information about one element. The figure below shows the box from the periodic table for the element hydrogen. The symbol for hydrogen, H, is shown in the center of the box. Below the symbol, you can see the name of the element hydrogen.

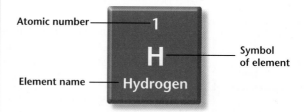

You already learned that the atomic number for hydrogen is 1. Find the atomic number in the box. You can see that the atomic number is shown above the symbol for the element.

The position of an element in the periodic table can tell you many properties of the element. The properties of elements change gradually as you move from left to right across the rows of the table. The properties change because the number of electrons that an atom of an element has increases as you move from left to right. Electrons move around the nucleus of an atom. The number of electrons that surround the nucleus of an atom determines the element's properties. Later in this chapter, you will learn how to determine some properties of an element from its position in the periodic table.

SCIENCE INTEGRATION

 Technology

Have a volunteer read aloud the Technology Note on page 98. Display a magnified picture of a computer chip, available through online encyclopedias. Explain that the chips may be one of two kinds: microprocessors that carry out instructions of computer programs, or memory chips, which hold programs. Have students brainstorm a list of items at home that they think contain silicon chips. *(video games, digital watches, microwave ovens, some telephones)*

Isotopes

Isotope

One of a group of atoms of an element with the same number of protons and electrons but different numbers of neutrons

Deuterium

An isotope of hydrogen that has one proton and one neutron

Tritium

An isotope of hydrogen that has one proton and two neutrons

Remember that all atoms of one element have the same atomic number. The atomic number tells the number of protons in the nucleus. However, different atoms of one element may have different masses. The reason for this is that almost every element can be found in slightly different forms. These forms are called **isotopes.** An isotope has the same number of protons and electrons as the original element, but has a different number of neutrons in the nucleus.

The figures below show three isotopes of hydrogen. The first figure shows the most common isotope of hydrogen (H-1). This isotope has one proton and no neutrons. The second figure shows **deuterium** (H-2). Deuterium is an isotope of hydrogen that has one proton and one neutron. The third figure shows **tritium** (H-3). Tritium is an isotope of hydrogen that has one proton and two neutrons. Tritium does not occur naturally on Earth. It is made in a laboratory. Remember that each isotope of hydrogen has the same number of protons and therefore the same atomic number. The labels H-1, H-2, and H-3 refer to the atomic mass of the hydrogen isotopes.

Isotopes have many uses. Scientists use isotopes to follow the path of certain substances in living things. Radioactive isotopes emit particles or rays that can be used to find problems with organs in the human body. Another use of isotopes is to find cracks in underground plumbing pipes.

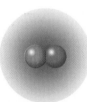
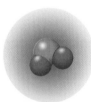

Hydrogen (H-1)
One proton

Deuterium (H-2)
One proton and
one neutron

Tritium (H-3)
One proton and
two neutrons

3 **Reinforce and Extend**

LEARNING STYLES

Visual/Spatial

Review with students the structure of the atom, labeling its parts. Have students draw diagrams of each hydrogen isotope. Suggest that they use different colors for protons and neutrons. Have them explain why there are different numbers of particles in the nucleus of each isotope.

TEACHER ALERT

Some students may think that the isotopes of an element are separate elements. Make sure they understand that the isotopes are actually different forms of the same element. Because isotopes have the same number of electrons (and therefore, the same number of protons), they have the same properties as the element.

LEARNING STYLES

LEP/ESL

Students who are learning English will benefit from making their own boxes for common elements. Assign student pairs elements for which examples can be displayed, such as calcium, copper, silver, and iron. Label examples with the element name. Have partners create periodic table boxes for their elements and label each item. As they place the boxes with the examples, have them say the element names. Also ask them to point out the symbol and atomic number of the elements and explain the meaning of each.

SCIENCE JOURNAL

Have students write a paragraph telling how they think silicon chips, at the heart of computers, changed life for the better.

LEARNING STYLES

Body/Kinesthetic

Assign each student an element from the periodic table. Have the student make a label containing all the information from the periodic table about the element and highlight or circle the atomic number. Have students discuss and figure out where in the periodic table their elements belong. Then have them place themselves in order by rows and columns. To check their placement, students can read the information on their column neighbors. For example, calcium should be in a row between potassium and scandium and in the column between magnesium and strontium.

AT HOME

Ask students to look in their kitchens and bathrooms to find products that contain different common elements, such as sulfur, oxygen, carbon, nitrogen, iodine, aluminum, and calcium. Have them tell how the element is used in the product and whether they think it is combined with other elements. Poll students to identify which elements were found most frequently.

LEARNING STYLES

Interpersonal/ Group Learning

Explain that only three of the elements on the periodic table occur naturally as liquids: mercury, gallium, and bromine. Only 11 occur as gases: hydrogen, helium, nitrogen, oxygen, fluorine, chlorine, neon, argon, krypton, xenon, and radon. Give small groups a copy of the periodic table and have them highlight the gases and liquids in different colors. Then have them discuss how each of these groupings would differ in its properties.

The Periodic Table

Legend:
- Metals
- Nonmetals
- Noble gases

		3	4	5	6	7	8	9
1 1 **H** Hydrogen 1.01								
2 3 **Li** Lithium 6.94	4 **Be** Beryllium 9.01							
3 11 **Na** Sodium 22.99	12 **Mg** Magnesium 24.31							
4 19 **K** Potassium 39.10	20 **Ca** Calcium 40.08	21 **Sc** Scandium 44.96	22 **Ti** Titanium 47.90	23 **V** Vanadium 50.94	24 **Cr** Chromium 52.00	25 **Mn** Manganese 54.94	26 **Fe** Iron 55.85	27 **Co** Cobalt 58.93
5 37 **Rb** Rubidium 85.47	38 **Sr** Strontium 87.62	39 **Y** Yttrium 88.91	40 **Zr** Zirconium 91.22	41 **Nb** Niobium 92.91	42 **Mo** Molybdenum 95.94	43 **Tc** Technetium (98)	44 **Ru** Ruthenium 101.10	45 **Rh** Rhodium 102.91
6 55 **Cs** Cesium 132.91	56 **Ba** Barium 137.33	57 **La** Lanthanum 138.91	72 **Hf** Hafnium 178.50	73 **Ta** Tantalum 180.95	74 **W** Tungsten 183.90	75 **Re** Rhenium 186.21	76 **Os** Osmium 190.20	77 **Ir** Iridium 192.22
7 87 **Fr** Francium (223)	88 **Ra** Radium 226.02	89 **Ac** Actinium (227)	104 **Rf** Rutherfordium (261)	105 **Db** Dubnium (262)	106 **Sg** Seaborgium (263)	107 **Bh** Bohrium (264)	108 **Hs** Hassium (265)	109 **Mt** Meitnerium (268)

	58 **Ce** Cerium 140.12	59 **Pr** Praseodymium 140.91	60 **Nd** Neodymium 144.24	61 **Pm** Promethium 145	62 **Sm** Samarium 150.40	63 **Eu** Europium 151.96	64 **Gd** Gadolinium 157.25
6							
7	90 **Th** Thorium 232.04	91 **Pa** Protactinium (231)	92 **U** Uranium (238)	93 **Np** Neptunium (237)	94 **Pu** Plutonium (244)	95 **Am** Americium (243)	96 **Cm** Curium (247)

# of Elements

						18
						2 **He** Helium 4.00

	13	14	15	16	17	
	5 **B** Boron 10.81	6 **C** Carbon 12.01	7 **N** Nitrogen 14.01	8 **O** Oxygen 16.00	9 **F** Fluorine 19.00	10 **Ne** Neon 20.18
	13 **Al** Aluminum 26.98	14 **Si** Silicon 28.09	15 **P** Phosphorus 30.97	16 **S** Sulfur 32.07	17 **Cl** Chlorine 35.45	18 **Ar** Argon 39.95

10	11	12						
28 **Ni** Nickel 58.70	29 **Cu** Copper 63.55	30 **Zn** Zinc 65.39	31 **Ga** Gallium 69.72	32 **Ge** Germanium 72.59	33 **As** Arsenic 74.92	34 **Se** Selenium 78.96	35 **Br** Bromine 79.90	36 **Kr** Krypton 83.80
46 **Pd** Palladium 106.42	47 **Ag** Silver 107.90	48 **Cd** Cadmium 112.41	49 **In** Indium 114.82	50 **Sn** Tin 118.69	51 **Sb** Antimony 121.75	52 **Te** Tellurium 127.60	53 **I** Iodine 126.90	54 **Xe** Xenon 131.30
78 **Pt** Platinum 195.09	79 **Au** Gold 196.97	80 **Hg** Mercury 200.59	81 **Tl** Thallium 204.40	82 **Pb** Lead 207.20	83 **Bi** Bismuth 208.98	84 **Po** Polonium 209	85 **At** Astatine (210)	86 **Rn** Radon (222)
110 **Uun** Ununnilium (269)	111 **Uuu** Unununium (272)	112 **Uub** Ununbium (277)		114 **Uuq** Ununquadium (289)		116 **Uuh** Ununhexium (289)		

65 **Tb** Terbium 158.93	66 **Dy** Dysprosium 162.50	67 **Ho** Holmium 164.93	68 **Er** Erbium 167.26	69 **Tm** Thulium 168.93	70 **Yb** Ytterbium 173.04	71 **Lu** Lutetium 174.97
97 **Bk** Berkelium (247)	98 **Cf** Californium (249)	99 **Es** Einsteinium (254)	100 **Fm** Fermium (257)	101 **Md** Mendelevium (258)	102 **No** Nobelium (259)	103 **Lr** Lawrencium (260)

Note: *The atomic masses listed in the table reflect current measurements.*
The atomic masses listed in parentheses are those of the element's most stable or most common isotope.

Health

Explain that humans need to take in certain elements to maintain good health. Pass around an empty vitamin bottle. Have students record the elements listed on the bottle. Help them calculate the recommended daily allowance of each element. (The label should list how much of each element is contained in one tablet, along with the percentage it constitutes of the RDA.) Interested students could research why each element is important and what foods contain each element.

GLOBAL CONNECTION

Ask pairs of students to choose three elements from the periodic table. Have them research information about the leading producers of the element and the uses of the element. Suggest that students prepare a world map showing the leading producers of those elements and a list of the uses for each element.

SCIENCE INTEGRATION

Earth Science

Explain that the isotope C-14, or carbon-14, is widely used to determine the age of rocks and fossils. Have a volunteer read about radioactive dating techniques and prepare a diagram showing how it is done. Other students might learn about specific finds that have been dated in this way.

Atomic mass

The average mass of all the isotopes of a particular element

Sometimes an atom's nucleus is unstable. Radioactivity results from the decay of an atom with an unstable nucleus. A radioactive atom sends out small particles and gamma rays. Isotopes that are radioactive are called radioisotopes.

Atomic Mass

An element's mass number is the sum of its numbers of protons and neutrons. The sum of the numbers of protons and neutrons is different for hydrogen, deuterium, and tritium. Therefore, each isotope of hydrogen has a different mass number. What is the mass number of each isotope?

Isotopes of most elements do not have names and are identified by their atomic mass. For example, carbon has three isotopes. The most common isotope has a mass number of 12 because it has 6 protons and 6 neutrons. This isotope is called carbon-12. Another isotope of carbon is carbon-13, which has 6 protons and 7 neutrons. Carbon-14 has 6 protons and 8 neutrons.

Look at the box for hydrogen shown below. How does it differ from the box shown on page 98? An additional number appears at the bottom of the box. Notice that the number is not a whole number. This number is the element's **atomic mass,** the average mass for all the isotopes of the element. The average mass is determined by the masses of an element's isotopes and by the amount of each isotope found in nature.

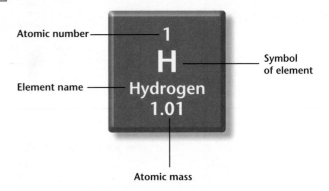

CROSS-CURRICULAR CONNECTION

Mathematics

Provide students with the following atomic mass and atomic number data for isotopes:

Element	Atomic Number	Atomic Mass	Mass Number of Isotope
helium	2	4	6
potassium	19	39.1	40
carbon	6	12.01	14

Have pairs of students determine how many more neutrons than protons each isotope has. (*Hint: Added mass of the isotope is due to extra neutrons. Atomic number shows the number of electrons and the number of protons in an atom of the element. Atomic mass is the average mass of all isotopes of the element, weighted according to the amount of each isotope found in nature.*)

Family

A group of elements with similar properties, arranged together in a column of the periodic table

Columns in the Periodic Table

Look at the periodic table shown on pages 100 and 101. The elements in the periodic table are arranged across in order of increasing atomic numbers. You can also read the periodic table another way—in columns from top to bottom.

Elements that are together in a column are said to be in the same **family.** These elements have similar properties. In other words, elements in the same family usually react with other kinds of matter in the same way.

Part of the first column from the periodic table is shown on this page. It shows the elements lithium, sodium, and potassium. Now find these three elements in the first column, or Group 1 column, of the periodic table on pages 100 and 101. The elements in Group 1, with the exception of hydrogen, are solids at room temperature. They are soft, shiny, and silvery. These elements react strongly when combined with water, exploding and releasing large amounts of heat.

Now look at the elements in Group 2, or column 2, of the periodic table. The elements in this family are found in minerals in the earth. Magnesium and calcium are the most common elements in this group.

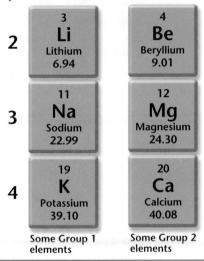

	Some Group 1 elements	Some Group 2 elements
2	3 Li Lithium 6.94	4 Be Beryllium 9.01
3	11 Na Sodium 22.99	12 Mg Magnesium 24.30
4	19 K Potassium 39.10	20 Ca Calcium 40.08

Classifying Elements   Chapter 4   **103**

CROSS-CURRICULAR CONNECTION

Social Studies

Ask students to read about the work of scientists Henri Becquerel and Pierre and Marie Curie. Have them report to the class how these scientists contributed to our understanding of radioactive elements. Lead a discussion about how radioactivity is used in science and medicine.

LEARNING STYLES

Logical/Mathematical

Have students with strong math skills demonstrate how to find the atomic mass of an invented element Zi, with isotopes Zi-21, Zi-22, and Zi-23, when Zi-22 accounts for 75 percent of all Zi found on earth, Zi-21 accounts for 10 percent, and Zi-23 accounts for 15 percent. They may first explain how to find the average of a set of numbers. *(atomic mass of Zi = 22.05)*

SCIENCE JOURNAL

Have students write a short story of what they think it would be like to discover a new element. What would they name it? Who would they tell?

Have a volunteer read aloud the text in the feature on page 104. Ask students to find rhodium on the periodic table and name the other members in its family *(cobalt, iridium, meitnerium)*. Explain that rhodium is a hard, white metal that occurs in platinum ores. It is combined in alloys with platinum.

LEARNING STYLES

Auditory/Verbal

On index cards, write the names of elements you have discussed or students have read about in the chapter, one per index card. Have students draw cards from the pile. Each student should point out the element's location on the periodic table and tell what they know about it based on the information in the box.

 Did You Know?

Rhodium is one of the rarest natural elements. Only 3 tons are mined each year. In contrast, 1,700 tons of gold are mined each year.

Look for other families in the periodic table. Fluorine and chlorine—both in Group 17—are poisonous gases. Helium, neon, and argon—elements in Group 18—are all gases that do not usually combine with any other kinds of matter. You will read more about this group of elements in Lesson 3.

As you read the rest of this chapter, continue to refer to the periodic table on pages 100 and 101. You will learn how the periodic table can give you even more information about different elements.

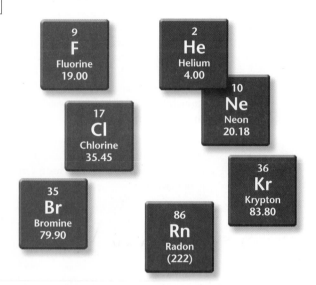

Lesson 2 REVIEW

Write your answers to these questions in complete sentences on a sheet of paper.

1. How are the elements arranged in the periodic table?

2. Draw the box from the periodic table for hydrogen. Include the symbol for hydrogen as well as its atomic number and atomic mass. Write an explanation of each piece of information in the box.

3. Write a paragraph explaining how elements are grouped in columns in the periodic table.

4. How do elements in the same family usually react?

5. List one family of elements in the periodic table.

Achievements in Science

Bronze, an Ancient Alloy

Bronze is the oldest known alloy. People learned to make bronze in about 3500 B.C. The bronze that they made at that time contained copper (Cu) and arsenic (As). Gradually, tin (Sn) replaced arsenic in the alloy. Historians are not sure how people learned to smelt copper with arsenic to make bronze. Some believe that it may have been an accidental discovery.

Bronze played an important role in the lives of early people. Indeed, the period between the Stone Age and Iron Age is called the Bronze Age. People of that time used bronze to make many different items. At first, they used it mainly to make weapons and cutting tools. Later, they also made bowls, cups, and vases from bronze.

Bronze is very hard. It is harder and stronger than any other alloy except steel. It does not rust or wear away. We still use bronze today. You can find it in doorknobs and drawer handles. It is in engine parts and bearings. Many bells also are made from bronze.

Lesson 2 Review Answers

1. Elements are arranged from left to right according to atomic number.
2. The symbol for hydrogen (H) is the abbreviation of its name. Hydrogen's atomic number (1) stands for the number of protons in the element's nucleus. Its atomic mass (1.01) is the average mass for all isotopes of hydrogen.
3. Sample answer: Elements with similar properties appear in columns in the periodic table. Elements in the same column are in the same family of elements. This means that they have some similar properties. **4.** Elements that are members of the same family react in the same way with other types of matter.
5. Answers will vary. Sample answer: Beryllium, magnesium, calcium, strontium, barium, and radium are members of one family.

Achievements in Science

Have students take turns reading aloud the Achievements in Science feature on page 105. Make a time line on the board to illustrate how long ago humans learned to make bronze. Have students find the elements used to make ancient bronze and those now used in the periodic table. Display several bronze items for students to observe. Suggest that interested students read further about the Bronze Age and report a list of ways in which civilization advanced because of this invention.

Portfolio Assessment

Sample items include:
• K-W-L charts from Teaching the Lesson
• Lesson 2 Review answers

Lab Manual 14, pages 1–2

Workbook Activity 19

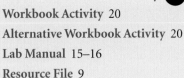

Chapter 4 Lesson 3

Overview In this lesson, students learn the properties of metals and nonmetals. They also find out what noble gases are.

Objectives

- To describe the properties of metals
- To explain what nonmetals are
- To explain what noble gases are

Student Pages 106–112

Teacher's Resource Library TRL

Workbook Activity 20

Alternative Workbook Activity 20

Lab Manual 15–16

Resource File 9

Vocabulary

alloy	noble gas
inert	nonmetal
metal	

Science Background

Eleven elements occur naturally as gases. Six of these elements, including helium and neon, are called the noble gases. These six are listed in the last column of the periodic table, Group 18. All of the noble gases are found, in small amounts, in the atmosphere. These gases are colorless and very inactive—that is they do not combine chemically with other elements under ordinary conditions. Oxygen, on the other hand, combines with many other elements. For example, oxygen and hydrogen combine to form water.

 Warm-Up Activity

Have students look around the room and name as many objects as they can that contain metal. (*Answers might include metallic parts of desks, light fixtures, writing utensils, and clothing.*) Then have them list things that are made of elements that are not metals. (*Answers might include fabrics, paper, plastics of all kinds, and gases in the air.*)

Objectives

After reading this lesson, you should be able to
- describe the properties of metals.
- explain what nonmetals are.
- explain what noble gases are.

Metal

One of a group of elements that is usually solid at room temperature, often shiny, and carries heat and electricity well

 Did You Know?

Mercury (Hg) is very poisonous and can cause illness and even death. Until the 1900s, hat makers used mercury when working with felt. This caused mercury poisoning, which was called "mad hatter's disease."

You have learned about some ways the periodic table provides information about elements. An element's position in the table also indicates whether the element is a metal, a nonmetal, or a noble gas. As you read this lesson, you will find out about each of these three groups.

Metals

Look again at the periodic table on pages 100 and 101. Find the zigzag line near the right side of the chart. Find the elements shown in the green boxes to the left of the zigzag line. These elements are **metals,** a group of elements that share certain properties.

Properties of Metals

- Most metals are solid at room temperature. Mercury is the only liquid metal.
- Most metals can be polished to look shiny.
- The shape of a metal can be changed. For example, aluminum can be pounded into a thin foil without breaking. Copper is often stretched into very thin wires.
- Electricity and heat travel well through metals.

These items illustrate the properties of metals.

 Teaching the Lesson

Have students divide a sheet of paper into three columns. Have them label the columns with the headings *Metals, Nonmetals, Noble Gases.* As students read the lesson, they can list the characteristics of each group in the proper column.

Help students understand that alloys of metals are produced to make a more usable substance. Explain that gold, for example, is very soft. Ask: Why is gold mixed with copper to make jewelry? (*The alloy is harder and will retain its shape better.*)

Display a helium balloon and discuss the properties of helium with students. (*Next to hydrogen, helium is the lightest gas. It is colorless and odorless and will not burn.*) Invite volunteers to explain why these properties make it useful for inflating balloons and airships.

Did You Know?

Have students read aloud the feature on page 106. Explain that mercury poisoning occurs over time. Students would not be poisoned by a single contact with this element. Point out that mercury is used in thermometers and in vapor form in fluorescent lights.

Alloy

A mixture of two or more metals

Nonmetal

One of a group of elements with properties unlike those of metals

Carbon, a nonmetal, plays a central role in the chemistry of living organisms.

Science Myth

All metals can rust.

Fact: The only pure metal that rusts is iron (Fe), the most important metal used in industry. However, most of the metals we use are alloys. Alloys that contain iron are called ferrous alloys. The ferrous alloys that are used most are steels. These alloys can rust because they contain iron.

Notice that hydrogen is the only element on the left side of the periodic table that is not considered a metal. As you can see, about 80 percent of all the elements are metals.

Alloys

Heat can be used to change metals into liquids. Melted metals can be combined with other metals. The mixture is cooled until it hardens. In this way an **alloy,** or mixture of metals, is formed. Alloys have a combination of the properties of the different metals. The table on this page lists some common alloys, the metals that can be combined to form them, and some of their uses.

Metal Alloys		
Alloy	Made from	Used for
alnico	aluminum (Al), nickel (Ni), cobalt (Co), iron (Fe), copper (Cu)	magnets
brass	copper (Cu), zinc (Zn)	plumbing fixtures, musical instruments, artwork
bronze	copper (Cu), tin (Sn)	coins, artwork
pewter	copper (Cu), lead (Pb), antimony (Sb), tin (Sn)	trays, pitchers, vases
solder	lead (Pb), tin (Sn)	electrical connections, plumbing connections
stainless steel	iron (Fe), chromium (Cr), nickel (Ni)	eating utensils, kitchen equipment, surgical equipment

Nonmetals

Look again at the periodic table on pages 100 and 101. Find the elements in blue boxes on the right side of the table. These elements are called **nonmetals**. They do not have the properties of metals.

Most nonmetals are solids or gases at room temperature. Sulfur and carbon are examples of solid nonmetals. You probably know about some of the nonmetal elements that are gases, such as oxygen and nitrogen.

③ Reinforce and Extend

TEACHER ALERT

Some students may think that in order to be a metal, an element must be shiny. Explain that elements such as sodium and calcium are not shiny but are considered metals because of their other properties.

Science Myth

Have a student read the myth portion (first sentence) of the Science Myth on page 107. Ask other students to read the fact portion. Point out that nickel or chromium are added to the alloy steel (made from iron and carbon) to make stainless steel. Unlike regular steel, stainless steel is very resistant to rusting.

PRONUNCIATION GUIDE

Use the pronunciation shown here to help students pronounce a difficult word in this lesson. Refer to the pronunciation key on the Chapter Planning Guide for the sounds of the symbols.

ferrous (fer´ əs)

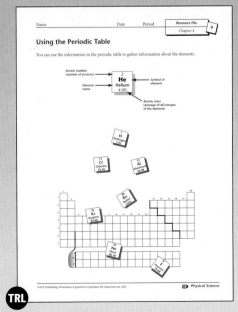

Resource File 9

Read aloud the first sentence in the Science Myth on page 108 and have students predict whether it is true or false. Ask a volunteer to read the fact section of the feature. Explain that heat results from the motion of molecules or atoms of a substance whereas electric current is caused by a flow of electrons from one place to another.

LEARNING STYLES

Body/Kinesthetic

Assign students partners and have the partners design and carry out an experiment to determine which metals conduct heat best. Assist students as necessary in planning steps in their investigation. Ask them to collect and organize their data and then draw a conclusion to report to the class.

IN THE ENVIRONMENT

Many elements are metals that people use to make products they need. These metals are obtained by mining. Mining can destroy wildlife habitats. Refining the metals can result in air pollution. Ask pairs of students to choose a metal and investigate how it is mined and refined. Encourage them to identify harm to the environment caused by the mining and production. Ask them to identify ways people are trying to protect the environment even as they mine metals and produce products.

IN THE COMMUNITY

Refer students to the list of metal alloys in the table on page 107. Have them identify and list places in their community where they have seen products made from these alloys. For example, artwork in a museum, musical instruments at a concert, and surgical equipment at a hospital.

Bromine is the only nonmetal that is a liquid at room temperature.

Science Myth

If an element can carry heat, it also can conduct electricity.

Fact: Carbon (C) in the form of a diamond is a good conductor of heat. Like other nonmetals, a diamond is a very poor conductor of electricity.

Notice on the pie chart below that these two gases make up most of the air. Bromine is the only nonmetal that is liquid at room temperature.

Many metals look somewhat similar. Nonmetals, however, can look very different from one another. For example, oxygen is a colorless gas, while sulfur is a yellow solid.

You can see that nonmetals do not have many properties in common. In fact, the only thing that many nonmetals have in common is that they are not metals. Nonmetals are not shiny. They cannot be pounded into thin sheets or stretched into wires. Except for some forms of carbon and silicon, nonmetals do not carry electricity or heat well. You will learn more about some nonmetals from the Science in Your Life feature on page 110.

Gases in air

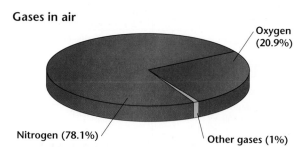

Oxygen (20.9%)

Nitrogen (78.1%)

Other gases (1%)

A few elements have some properties of both metals and nonmetals. These elements include silicon, germanium, boron, arsenic, antimony, tellurium, and polonium. You can find these elements in the periodic table next to the zigzag line that separates metals from nonmetals.

When some of these elements are combined with other materials, their ability to carry electricity is increased. This ability makes elements such as silicon useful for electronic devices like computers.

Noble Gases

Noble gas

One of a group of elements made up of gases that do not combine with other materials under ordinary conditions

Inert

Inactive; lacking the power to move

The six elements listed in the last column of the periodic table are called the **noble gases**. These gases are **inert**, or inactive. They do not react or combine with any other elements under ordinary conditions. Look at Group 18 in the periodic table on pages 100 and 101 to find the names of all the noble gases.

Neon is one noble gas that may be familiar to you. Neon is a gas used for lights such as those in the sign shown in the photo. The neon is sealed in tubes. When electricity passes through the gas, neon gives off colored light.

Technology Note

Except for radon (Rn), all the noble gases are used in lighting. These gases are usually colorless. When an electrical charge passes through them, they glow.

Neon gas makes this sign glow.

Achievements in Science

Helium

Helium (He), a noble gas, is one of the most common elements in the universe. Only hydrogen (H) is more common. Stars are made mostly of helium and hydrogen. Yet helium is very rare on earth.

Helium was first discovered on the sun. Pierre Janssen of France found evidence of helium while studying a solar eclipse in 1868. Helium's name comes from the Greek word *helios,* which means sun.

Chemists discovered helium on earth in 1895. Sir William Ramsay, Nils Langlet, and Per Theodor Cleve found helium in a mineral.

In 1905, Hamilton P. Cady and David E. McFarland made an important discovery about helium. They found that it could be taken out of natural gas wells. Their discovery led to greater use of helium in industry. Helium is largely used in welding. We also use helium to fill different kinds of balloons.

Classifying Elements Chapter 4 **109**

Achievements in Science

Invite volunteers to read aloud the information about helium in the Achievements in Science feature on page 109. Explain that most of the noble gases were not discovered until late in the nineteenth century because they are both rare and inert. Ask several students to read further about helium and report on its uses and properties.

LEARNING STYLES

Visual/Spatial

Reproduce the periodic table from Resource File 8 and distribute copies to students. Have them highlight the zigzag line dividing metals and nonmetals. Then have them use colored pencils or markers to code elements as metals, nonmetals, and noble gases.

SCIENCE INTEGRATION

Technology

Have a volunteer read aloud the Technology Note on page 109. Point out that radon is radioactive. Radon gas coming from the ground and entering water supplies and homes can cause health problems. Assign different noble elements to interested students to research. Have them report on how the element is used in industry or science. (For example, argon and helium are used in arc welding, where they provide a chemically inactive atmosphere in which metals like aluminum can be heated to melting without reacting chemically. Xenon is used in flash lamps and bubble chambers that are used by physicists to study nuclear particles. Most fluorescent lamps are filled with krypton and argon.)

Classifying Elements Chapter 4 **109**

Lesson 3 Review Answers

1. Metals are generally solid at room temperature, often shiny, and carry heat and electricity well. **2.** Nonmetals are usually a solid or gas at room temperature, are not shiny, and do not conduct heat or electricity well. Examples are carbon, chlorine, fluorine, iodine, nitrogen, oxygen, and sulfur. **3.** Nonmetals are all alike in that they are not metals. **4.** A nobel gas is a gas that does not combine with other elements under ordinary conditions **5.** Sample answer: Three metal alloys and a use for each one include alnico, used for magnets; brass, used for plumbing fixtures; stainless steel, used for eating utensils and kitchen equipment.

Science in Your Life

Have students take turns reading aloud the Science in Your Life feature on page 110. Discuss the table with students. Ask them to identify objects under the heading "Some Uses" that they have observed at home. Have students locate examples of how different elements are used. Suggest that they copy label information and report on what they learned.

CAREER CONNECTION

 Invite a metal worker, plumber, or jeweler to speak to the class about the handling of metals and the making of alloys. He or she can explain to the class why an understanding of the properties of different metals is important to his or her work.

Portfolio Assessment

Sample items include:
• Three-column table from Teaching the Lesson
• Lesson 3 Review answers

Write your answers to these questions in complete sentences on a sheet of paper.

1. Describe the properties of metals.

2. Explain what a nonmetal is and give some examples of nonmetals.

3. What one thing do nonmetals have in common?

4. Explain what a noble gas is.

5. List three metal alloys and one use for each one.

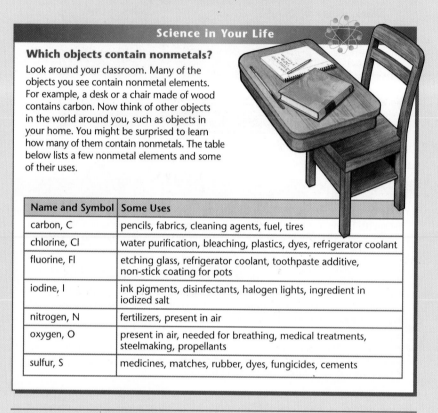

Science in Your Life

Which objects contain nonmetals?

Look around your classroom. Many of the objects you see contain nonmetal elements. For example, a desk or a chair made of wood contains carbon. Now think of other objects in the world around you, such as objects in your home. You might be surprised to learn how many of them contain nonmetals. The table below lists a few nonmetal elements and some of their uses.

Name and Symbol	Some Uses
carbon, C	pencils, fabrics, cleaning agents, fuel, tires
chlorine, Cl	water purification, bleaching, plastics, dyes, refrigerator coolant
fluorine, Fl	etching glass, refrigerator coolant, toothpaste additive, non-stick coating for pots
iodine, I	ink pigments, disinfectants, halogen lights, ingredient in iodized salt
nitrogen, N	fertilizers, present in air
oxygen, O	present in air, needed for breathing, medical treatments, steelmaking, propellants
sulfur, S	medicines, matches, rubber, dyes, fungicides, cements

---

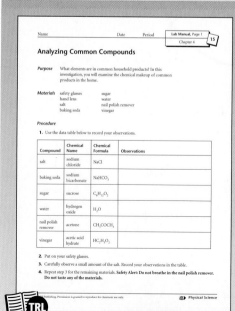

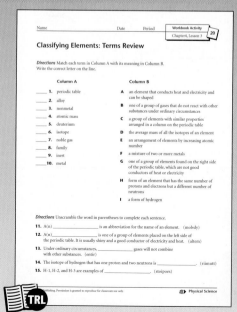

Electricity and Metals

Purpose

Do copper wire, sulfur, and aluminum all conduct electricity? In this investigation, you will identify materials that conduct electricity.

Procedure

1. Copy the data table on a sheet of paper.

Materials	Observations
copper wires	
sulfur	
aluminum	
graphite (pencil lead)	

2. Put on your safety glasses.

3. Use sandpaper to remove 3 cm of the insulated coating from each end of the copper wires. **Safety Alert: The ends of the wire can be sharp. Handle them carefully.**

4. Make a loop at the ends of each wire.

5. Using electrical tape, fasten a loop from one wire to the flat end of the battery.

6. Fasten the other loop of the wire to the lightbulb socket.

7. Tape a loop from the second wire to the other end of the battery.

Materials

- safety glasses
- sandpaper
- 3 pieces of copper wire, each 0.25 m long
- electrical tape
- 1.5-volt D-cell battery
- standard bulb in socket
- sample of sulfur
- piece of aluminum foil, about 5 cm long
- lead pencil

Investigation 4-2

The Purpose portion of the student investigation begins with a question to draw them into the activity. Encourage students to read the investigation steps and formulate their own questions before beginning the investigation. The investigation will take approximately 45 minutes to complete. Students will use these process and thinking skills: observing; collecting, recording, and interpreting data; inferring; describing objects and phenomena; and drawing conclusions.

Preparation

- Sulfur is used in this activity because it is the most affordable and available nonmetal. It can be purchased through a scientific supply house. (See list on page 420.)

- You may wish to remove the insulating coating from the wires yourself before students begin the investigation.

- Check batteries and lightbulbs before class to be sure they are working. Have extra batteries available.

- Students may use Lab Manual 16 to record their data and answer the questions.

Procedure

- Students should work cooperatively in groups of three to complete the activity. All students should record observations, answer questions, and clean up. Assign one student to gather materials and remove the insulation from the wire (if you do not strip it yourself) and make a loop. A second student can fasten the wires to the light socket and the battery. The third student can test the materials with the wires.

- In step 9, if the lightbulb doesn't light, have students make sure that the ends of the wires are firmly taped to the battery. Also they should make sure that the wires are securely attached to the bulb holder.

- Have students make sure that both ends of the unattached wires are actually touching the sulfur sample and aluminum.

Continued on page 112

Continued from page 111

- Explain to students that sulfur is an element found in abundance in nature, especially near volcanoes. It is used in the production of matches, fireworks, and dyes. It is also found in many medicines.

SAFETY ALERT

◆ Warn students to handle the wires carefully. The ends may be sharp.

Results

The bulb will light when the copper wires are touched together and when the wires are touched to the aluminum foil. The bulb does not light when the wires are attached to the sulfur.

Questions and Conclusions Answers

1. The bulb lit.

2. The bulb lit with the aluminum but did not light with the sulfur.

3. Copper and aluminum can conduct electricity. Sulfur cannot.

4. Aluminum and copper must be metals because they conduct electricity.

Explore Further Answers

The bulb lights up. Graphite (pencil lead) can conduct electricity. Most nonmetals are not good conductors of electricity. Graphite conducts electricity but is not shiny and cannot be pounded into thin sheets. It is probably one of the few nonmetals that are good conductors of electricity.

Assessment

Check student data tables to verify results. Students' answers should show an understanding that the ability to conduct electricity is a property of metals. You might include the following samples from this investigation in student portfolios:

- Investigation 4-2 data table

- Answers to Questions and Conclusions and Explore Further sections

8. Fasten a loop of the third wire to the other side of the lightbulb socket. Your circuit should look like the one in the diagram.

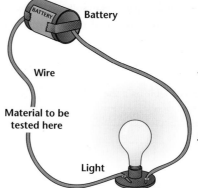

9. Hold the two unattached loops of copper wire together. Record your observations in the table.

10. Hold the sample of sulfur between the two unattached loops of wire. Record your observations.

11. Repeat step 10 with the sample of aluminum.

Questions and Conclusions

1. What happened to the lightbulb when you held the copper wires together?

2. What happened to the lightbulb when you held the samples of sulfur and aluminum between the wires?

3. What did you observe about the ability of copper, sulfur, and aluminum to conduct electricity?

4. Which materials do you think are metals? Explain your answer.

Explore Further

Pick up the pencil and hold it so the pencil lead is between the two unattached loops of wire. What happens? Can the pencil lead conduct electricity? Record your observations. Is the lead in the pencil a metal? Explain your answer.

Name _____ Date _____ Period _____   **Lab Manual** 16
Chapter 4

4-2 **Electricity and Metals**
Use with Investigation 4-2, pages 111–112

Purpose Do copper wire, sulfur, and aluminum all conduct electricity? In this investigation, you will identify materials that conduct electricity.

Materials	Observations
copper wires	
sulfur	
aluminum	
graphite (pencil lead)	

Questions and Conclusions

1. What happened to the lightbulb when you held the copper wires together?

2. What happened to the lightbulb when you held the samples of sulfur and aluminum between the wires?

3. What did you observe about the ability of copper, sulfur, and aluminum to conduct electricity?

4. Which materials do you think are metals? Explain your answer.

Explore Further

Pick up the pencil and hold it so the pencil lead is between the two unattached loops of wire. What happens? Can the pencil lead conduct electricity? Record your observations. Is the lead in the pencil a metal? Explain your answer.

Publishing. Permission is granted to reproduce for classroom use only.   ▶ Physical Science

Lab Manual 16

- Each element has a symbol, an abbreviation for its name.

- All known elements are arranged in the periodic table in order of increasing atomic number.

- Information contained in the periodic table about an element includes its name, its symbol, its atomic number, and its atomic mass.

- Almost every element has isotopes, which are different forms of the same element.

- An isotope of an element has the same numbers of protons and electrons as the original element; however, an isotope has a different number of neutrons.

- The atomic mass of an element is an average mass of the various isotopes of the element that exist in nature.

- Elements that have similar properties and are together in a column of the periodic table are in the same family.

- Elements are classified as metals, nonmetals, or noble gases.

- Most metals are solids at room temperature and can be polished. The shape of a metal can be changed. Electricity and heat travel well through metals.

- Metals can be melted and mixed with other metals to form alloys.

- Nonmetals have properties that are different from those of metals. Most nonmetals are solids or gases at room temperature. Most nonmetals have the opposite properties of metals.

- Noble gases are called inert because they do not ordinarily react or combine with other elements.

Chapter 4 Summary

Have volunteers read aloud each Summary item on page 113. Ask volunteers to explain the meaning of each item. Direct students' attention to the Science Words box on the bottom of page 113. Have them read and review each term and its definition.

Science Words		
alloy, 107	inert, 109	nonmetal, 107
atomic mass, 102	isotope, 99	periodic table, 97
deuterium, 99	metal, 106	symbol, 92
family, 103	noble gas, 109	tritium, 99

Chapter 4 Review

Use the Chapter Review to prepare students for tests and to reteach content from the chapter.

Chapter 4 Mastery Test

The Teacher's Resource Library includes two parallel forms of the Chapter 4 Mastery Test. The difficulty level of the two forms is equivalent. You may wish to use one form as a pretest and the other form as a posttest.

Review Answers

Vocabulary Review

1. atomic mass 2. periodic table 3. inert
4. metal 5. noble gas 6. alloy 7. isotope

Concept Review

8. Al 9. Cl 10. Au 11. K 12. Na 13. Ne

TEACHER ALERT

Because of limited space in this Chapter Review, not all of the vocabulary terms introduced in this chapter appear in the Vocabulary Review section. You may want to create an activity using the missing words to give students practice with all of the terms in this chapter. Here are the terms that are not covered in the section.

deuterium   nonmetal
family   symbol
noble gas   tritium

Vocabulary Review

Choose the word or words from the Word Bank that best complete each sentence. Write the answer on a sheet of paper.

1. The average mass of all of an element's isotopes is its _____.

2. The _____ is an arrangement of the elements by increasing atomic number.

3. Gases that are _____ do not react or combine with other elements under ordinary conditions.

4. An element that is usually solid at room temperature, often shiny, and carries heat well is a(n) _____.

5. A(n) _____ does not combine with other materials under ordinary conditions.

6. A mixture of two or more metals is a(n) _____.

7. A(n) _____ has the same number of protons and electrons but a different number of neutrons.

Concept Review

Match each element in Column A with the correct symbol in Column B. Write the symbol on your paper.

Column A	Column B
_____ 8. aluminum	**A** K
_____ 9. chlorine	**B** Ne
_____ 10. gold	**C** Al
_____ 11. potassium	**D** Na
_____ 12. sodium	**E** Cl
_____ 13. neon	**F** Au

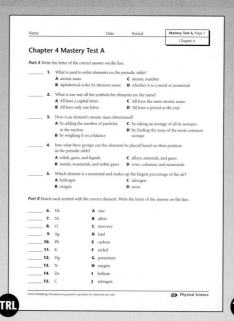

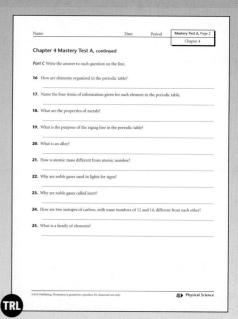

Chapter 4 Mastery Test A

Choose the answer that best completes each sentence. Write the letter of the answer on your paper.

14. _____ is an isotope of hydrogen.

A deuterium   **C** tritium

B uranium   **D** both A and C

15. Different atoms of one element may have a different

_____.

A atomic number   **C** electron

B mass number   **D** symbol

16. Elements are classified in the periodic table as _____.

A natural and synthetic

B toxic and nontoxic

C metals, nonmetals, and noble gases

D isotopes and alloys

Critical Thinking

Write the answer to each of these questions. Use the figure from the periodic table to answer questions 17 to 19.

17. What is the name of the element?

18. What is the element's symbol?

19. What is the element's atomic number? What is its atomic mass?

20. Carbon's atomic number is 6. How are two carbon atoms with mass numbers of 12 and 14 different from each other? What are these atoms called?

 Try to answer all questions as completely as possible. When asked to explain your answer, do so in complete sentences.

Classifying Elements   *Chapter 4*   **115**

20
Ca
Calcium
40.08

Review Answers

14. D **15.** B **16.** C

Critical Thinking

17. Calcium is the name of the element.

18. Ca is the symbol for calcium.

19. The atomic number of calcium is 20. The atomic mass of calcium is 40.08.

20. Carbon 12 has 6 electrons in orbit around its nucleus. It has 6 protons and 6 neutrons in its nucleus, giving it the mass number of 12. Carbon-14 has 6 electrons, 6 protons, and 8 neutrons, giving it the mass number of 14. They are different because they have different numbers of neutrons. These atoms are called isotopes.

ALTERNATIVE ASSESSMENT

Alternative Assessment items correlate to the student Goals for Learning at the beginning of this chapter.

■ Name an element, and have students write the element's abbreviation on paper, or have them find the element on a periodic chart and identify its abbreviation.

■ Have students select squares on the periodic table. For each element, have them tell what each word, symbol, and number mean. Encourage students to explain how to "read" the table.

■ Ask students to explain the organization of the periodic table as they point to features that illustrate its organization. Remind them to point to several families and explain the meaning of the term *family.*

■ Provide students with a copy of the periodic table. Have them find elements as you name them and tell whether each one is a metal, a nonmetal, or a noble gas.

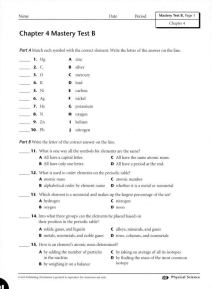

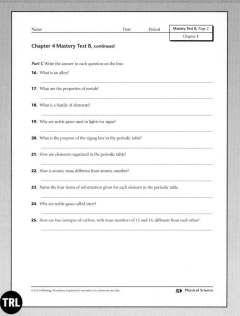

Chapter 4 Mastery Test B

Chapter

5

Planning Guide

Compounds

	Student Text Lesson		
	Student Pages	Vocabulary	Lesson Review
Lesson 1 What Are Some Characteristics of Compounds?	118–122	✔	✔
Lesson 2 How Compounds Are Formed	123–128	✔	✔
Lesson 3 Chemical Formulas	129–133	✔	✔
Lesson 4 How Compounds Are Named	134–137	✔	✔
Lesson 5 Acids and Bases	138–144	✔	✔

Chapter Activities

Student Text
Science Center
Teacher's Resource Library
Community Connection 5: Chemistry in
  Action: Fire Extinguishers

Assessment Options

Student Text
Chapter 5 Review
Teacher's Resource Library
Chapter 5 Mastery Tests A and B

	Student Text Features							Teaching Strategies						Learning Styles						Teacher's Resource Library				
Achievements in Science	Science at Work	Science in Your Life	Investigation	Science Myth	Note	Technology Note	Did You Know	Science Integration	Science Journal	Cross-Curricular Connection	Online Connection	Teacher Alert	Applications (Home, Career, Community, Global, Environment)	Auditory/Verbal	Body/Kinesthetic	Interpersonal/Group Learning	Logical/Mathematical	Visual/Spatial	LEP/ESL	Workbook Activities	Alternative Workbook Activities	Lab Manual	Resource File	Self-Study Guide
120			121		✔		119	119		119						120		120		21	21	17, 18	10	✔
	128		127		✔			127	124	126, 128	125	126	127		127		125			22	22		11	✔
							130			131, 132	130		131					132	131	23	23			✔
									137	136			135, 136	135						24	24			✔
142		141	143			✔	139	139		140	141	138, 140	139, 141						139	25	25	19, 20		✔

Pronunciation Key

a	hat	e	let	ī	ice	ô	order	ù	put	sh	she
ā	age	ē	equal	o	hot	oi	oil	ü	rule	th	thin
ä	far	ėr	term	ō	open	ou	out	ch	child	ᴴH	then
â	care	i	it	ȯ	saw	u	cup	ng	long	zh	measure

ə { a in about, e in taken, i in pencil, o in lemon, u in circus }

Alternative Workbook Activities

The Teacher's Resource Library (TRL) contains a set of lower-level worksheets called Alternative Workbook Activities. These worksheets cover the same content as the regular Workbook Activities but are written at a second-grade reading level.

Skill Track Software

Use the Skill Track Software for Physical Science for additional reinforcement of this chapter. The software program allows students using AGS textbooks to be assessed for mastery of each chapter and lesson of the textbook. Students access the software on an individual basis and are assessed with multiple-choice items.

Chapter at a Glance

Chapter 5: Compounds
pages 116–147

Lessons

Science Center

Put the title "Compounds in the News" in large letters at the top of a display. Tell each student to find an article about chemical compounds in a magazine, in a newspaper, or on the Internet. Students can put the articles on the display with a date attached. For each article, students should write a sentence or two summarizing the content.

Community Connection 5

5 Compounds

O n April 15, 1912, the *RMS Titanic* sank to the bottom
of the North Atlantic Ocean after hitting an iceberg.
In the photograph, you can see the prow of the ship
lying on the ocean floor. Underwater for more than 90 years, the
surface of the *Titanic* has been altered by iron-oxidizing bacteria,
or rust. A chemical change is taking place. Notice the "rusticles"
that have formed on the prow. Rust covers the shipwreck, and it
is slowly wearing away the ship's metal structure.

In Chapter 5, you will learn about chemical and physical changes,
and how different elements combine to form compounds. You
also will learn how compounds are classified.

Organize Your Thoughts

Formulas

Compounds — Elements — Atoms

Acids   Bases   Energy levels

Goals for Learning

◆ To describe compounds
◆ To explain how compounds are formed
◆ To tell what the information in a formula means
◆ To explain how compounds are named
◆ To classify some compounds as acids or bases

117

Introducing the Chapter

Read the paragraphs on page 117 with
students. Lead a discussion, encouraging
students to tell what they know about
the *Titanic.*

Organize teams of two or three students.
Ask each team to draw three columns on
a large sheet of paper. The columns
should be labeled *Vocabulary Words,*
Definition Before Reading, and *Definition*
After Reading. Before reading the chapter,
have students write the definition for the
vocabulary terms they know. When they
complete the lesson, students can correct
their definitions and include any that
they didn't know before the lesson began.

Notes and Technology Notes

Ask volunteers to read the notes that
appear in the margins throughout the
chapter. Then discuss them with the class.

TEACHER'S RESOURCE

The AGS Teaching Strategies in
Science Transparencies may be used
with this chapter. The transparencies
add an interactive dimension to
expand and enhance the *Physical*
Science program content.

CAREER INTEREST INVENTORY

The AGS Harrington-O'Shea Career
Decision-Making System-Revised
(CDM) may be used with this
chapter. Students can use the CDM
to explore their interests and identify
careers. The CDM defines career
areas that are indicated by students'
responses on the inventory.

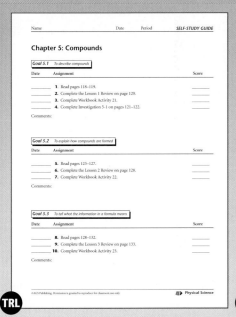

Chapter 5 Self-Study Guide

Lesson at a Glance

Chapter 5 Lesson 1

Overview This lesson develops the concept of chemical compounds. Students are introduced to physical and chemical changes, and they learn characteristics of chemical changes.

Objectives

- To describe a chemical change
- To describe some characteristics of compounds

Student Pages 118–122

Teacher's Resource Library TRL

Workbook Activity 21

Alternative Workbook Activity 21

Lab Manual 17–18

Resource File 10

Vocabulary

chemical change   physical change

Science Background

Students can best understand chemical change by contrasting it with physical change. One important kind of physical change is change of state. Under conditions normally found in nature, matter exists in three states: solid, liquid, and gas. All matter is made up of tiny particles—atoms and molecules. These particles are in constant motion. The amount of energy they possess determines state of matter. In the solid state, particles have relatively low energy levels and move about fairly slowly. The particle motion is not great enough for particles to pull apart, so matter retains a definite, "solid" form. In the liquid state, particles vibrate more energetically. They slip and slide over each other, and the rigid shape of the solid breaks down, or melts. In the gas state, particles vibrate so energetically that they fly off in all directions. A gas has no shape at all; it fills any closed container.

1 Warm-Up Activity

Tear a sheet of paper in half. Ask students if the properties of the two new pieces are different from the original piece. *(no)* Ask if the two pieces you are holding are still paper. *(yes)* Next, tear off a piece of paper from one of the halves.

Objectives

After reading this lesson, you should be able to

- describe a chemical change.
- describe some characteristics of compounds.

Only about 90 different elements combine in various ways to form the millions of different compounds you see around you. Do these millions of compounds have any common characteristics? How do these compounds form?

Compounds and Chemical Changes

You learned in Chapter 3 that two or more elements combine to form a compound. For example, hydrogen gas combines with oxygen gas to form the liquid compound water. Water has properties that are different from the elements that form it.

Chemical change
A change that produces one or more new substances with new chemical properties

When atoms of elements combine to form a compound, a **chemical change** takes place. A chemical change produces one or more new substances with new chemical properties. A chemical change takes place when hydrogen and oxygen combine to form water.

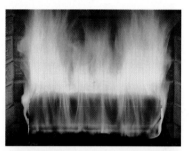

How can you tell when a chemical change has happened? There are several possible signs. Bubbles sometimes appear. A solid may form. Temperature or color may change, or light or energy may be produced.

The photos illustrate a chemical change. As the wood burns, it changes to gases and ash. The ash is a soft, gray powder that cannot burn. Wood and ash are different substances and have different properties.

A chemical change takes place when wood burns.

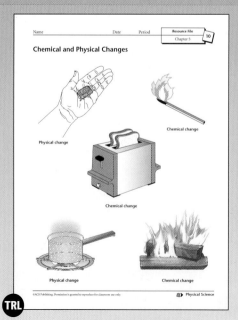

Name _____ Date _____ Period _____   Resource File
                                              10
                                              Chapter 5

Chemical and Physical Changes

Physical change

Chemical change

Chemical change

Physical change   Chemical change

©AGS Publishing. Permission is granted to reproduce for classroom use only.   Physical Science

Resource File 10

Physical change

A change in which the appearance (physical properties) of a substance changes but its chemical properties stay the same

Did You Know?

Over the years, the Statue of Liberty has changed from a reddish color to a dull green. A chemical change has taken place. The copper in the statue has combined with oxygen in the air to form a new substance—copper oxide. Copper oxide makes the statue green.

Now think about taking a similar piece of wood and chopping it into tiny pieces. Does a chemical change take place when this happens? Ask yourself if the pieces of wood have properties that are different from the original piece of wood. In this case, they do not. Each small piece is still wood. The pieces just have different sizes and shapes. Changes like this are called **physical changes.** In a physical change, the appearance (physical properties) of a substance changes but its chemical properties stay the same. In a physical change, no new substances are formed.

Characteristics of Compounds

Although there are millions of compounds, they all share some basic characteristics. Any particular compound always contains the same elements. For example, the elements that make up water—hydrogen and oxygen—are always the same. The water can be from a faucet, a river, or a puddle in the road.

Another characteristic of compounds is that the atoms in a particular compound always combine in the same numbers. A molecule of water always contains two hydrogen atoms and one oxygen atom. If you change the molecule by adding another oxygen atom, the compound is no longer water. It becomes hydrogen peroxide, the clear liquid that people can use to clean cuts and other skin wounds. Water and hydrogen peroxide are different substances with different properties.

Compounds   Chapter 5   **119**

Using forceps, hold the paper over a beaker or other heat-proof container. Light the paper with a match or lighter. **Safety Alert: Be sure to have a fire extinguisher nearby when you perform this demonstration. Make sure the ash is cool before students begin observing the ash.** Allow students to observe the ash that forms. Point out that the properties of the ash are different from properties of the paper before it burned. A new substance was formed.

▶ 2 Teaching the Lesson

Tell students to choose the most important sentence from each paragraph in Lesson 1 and write it down. The sentence they choose should tell the main idea of the paragraph. All of the sentences together can serve as an outline and study aid.

Students will probably readily recognize changes such as chopping, cutting, or pulverizing as physical changes. They may be less likely to recognize changes of state as physical changes. Examples of changes of state include water freezing into ice; ice melting into water; and water boiling into steam (water vapor). Point out that the chemical makeup of water remains the same in all three states: it consists of one oxygen and two hydrogen atoms bonded together.

Make sure students understand that the test of a chemical change is the production of a new substance. Remind students about the demonstration in which paper was burned (suggested Warm-Up Activity). Ask how they know that a chemical change took place. *(The paper was changed into a new substance—ash.)*

▶ 3 Reinforce and Extend

Did You Know?

Students may have seen TV shows about antique collecting. Ask if they have heard collectors use the word *patina*. Tell them that a patina is a change in color that occurs on the surface of a metal over time because of a chemical reaction with substances in the air. Remark that the process is similar to that described in the feature on page 119, and that a patina usually is an oxide of a metal such as copper or bronze.

SCIENCE INTEGRATION

Biology

Tell students that many chemical changes occur in the human body. One familiar example is digestion of food. The body's digestive system changes food into forms the body can use. Have interested students research information about the chemical changes that take place in the digestive system and share their findings with the class.

CROSS-CURRICULAR CONNECTION

Home Economics

Ask students to list some of the foods prepared in their homes during the last week. Then ask them to determine whether the prepared foods were the result of a chemical change or a physical change. Remind students that in a chemical change, a new substance is formed. For example, a tossed salad would be a physical change; baked bread would be the result of a chemical change.

Compounds   Chapter 5   **119**

Lesson 1 Review Answers

1. physical; no new substance formed
2. chemical; new substance—rust formed
3. physical; no new substance formed
4. chemical; new substance—cooked cake
5. physical; no new substance formed

Achievements in Science

Have students read the Achievements in Science feature on page 120. Make sure they understand that *synthetic* means "human-made." Ask students to think of other synthetic products they use in daily life.

LEARNING STYLES

Interpersonal/ Group Learning

Organize the class into groups of two to four students. Tell the groups to list at least 10 physical changes and at least 10 chemical changes. When all the groups have finished their lists, have students write one or more of the examples on the board to share with the class.

LEARNING STYLES

Visual/Spatial

Prompt students to choose a physical change and a chemical change discussed in the lesson. Have them draw a diagram illustrating each change. Ask students to share their art with the class.

Portfolio Assessment

Sample items include:
• Lesson outline assembled from topic sentences
• Lists of chemical/physical changes
• Lesson 1 Review answers

PRONUNCIATION GUIDE

Use this list to help students pronounce the difficult words in this lesson. Refer to the pronunciation key on the Chapter Planning Guide for the sounds of these symbols.

synthetic (sin thet´ ik)

quinine (kwī´ nīn)

mauveine (mō´ vin)

Copy the table on a sheet of paper. Identify each change as a chemical change or a physical change. Tell how you know which kind of change it is. (Remember, a chemical change produces new substances with new chemical properties.)

Change	Chemical or physical?	How do you know?
1. melting ice cream		
2. rusting a nail		
3. chopping onions		
4. baking a cake		
5. coloring hair		

Achievements in Science

Synthetic Dye

Before the 1850s, most dyes were made from vegetables or animals. It took 12,000 shellfish to make 1.5 g of a rare, expensive purple dye. First made in 1600 B.C., this dye—Tyrian purple—became the color of royalty. Because purple dyes were so expensive, only the rich had them.

In 1856, 18-year-old student William Perkin was trying to make artificial quinine, a malaria medication. He combined oxygen and aniline, a compound made from coal tar. The result was not quinine but aniline purple, an intense purple substance. Perkin mixed the substance with alcohol and found it turned silk a beautiful purple color. Named *mauveine,* this solution was the first synthetic, or manmade, dye.

Perkin and his father started a factory to make the dye commercially. Perkin developed the processes for the production and use of the new dye. This was the beginning of the synthetic dye industry. Mauveine made purple clothing available to everyone—not just royalty.

Name _____ Date _____ Period _____ | Workbook Activity **21** Chapter 5, Lesson 1

Physical and Chemical Changes

Directions Read each change listed in items 1 through 15. Write each change in the table. If it is a physical change, write the change in the left column. If it is a chemical change, write the change in the right column.

Physical Change	Chemical Change

1. scrambling eggs in a bowl
2. a silver spoon tarnishing
3. a puddle drying up
4. chopping onions
5. a copper roof turning green
6. water drops forming on the outside of a glass
7. bread baking
8. paper burning
9. picking tomatoes from a plant
10. mixing baking soda and vinegar
11. snow falling
12. painting a room
13. car-exhaust fumes mixing with water
14. adding a drink powder to water
15. bike spokes rusting

Directions How are physical changes and chemical changes different? Write your answer below.

_____

_____

Publishing. Permission is granted to reproduce for classroom use only.   Physical Science

TRL

Workbook Activity 21

5-1 INVESTIGATION

Observing a Chemical Change

Materials
- safety glasses
- 2 small jars with lids
- distilled water
- washing soda
- 2 plastic spoons
- Epsom salts
- clock
- soft-drink bottle
- vinegar
- baking soda
- balloon

Purpose

Look at the descriptions of the three changes listed in the data table. Can you predict which will be a physical change and which will be a chemical change? In this investigation, you will observe physical and chemical changes.

Procedure

1. Copy the data table on a sheet of paper.

Change	Appearance
washing soda in water	
Epsom salts in water	
washing soda and Epsom salts in water	

2. Put on your safety glasses.

3. Fill each jar about halfway with distilled water.

4. Add a spoonful of washing soda to one jar. Place the lid on the jar and shake for about 30 seconds. Record your observations in the table.

Investigation 5-1

The Purpose portion of the student investigation begins with a question to draw them into the activity. Encourage students to read the investigation steps and formulate their own questions before beginning the investigation. The investigation will take approximately 35 minutes to complete. Students will use these process and thinking skills: observing, collecting, and interpreting data; collecting information; and drawing conclusions.

Preparation

- Purchase Epsom salts and distilled water at a grocery store or pharmacy if necessary.
- Purchase washing soda at a grocery store; look in the laundry detergent section.
- Gather empty baby food jars or other small jars.
- Students may use Lab Manual 17 to record their data and answer the questions.

Procedure

- Suggest students work in groups of four. Assign the following division of labor: student A pours water into the jars; student B adds the washing soda to one jar and shakes; student C adds the Epsom salts to the other jar and shakes; and student D pours the contents of the two jars together. All students should make and record observations, record data, answer questions, and clean up.
- Point out that washing soda is also called sodium carbonate (Na_2CO_3) and that Epsom salts are also known as magnesium sulfate ($MgSO_4$).

Continued on page 122

SAFETY ALERT

- Remind students to keep their hands away from their mouths and eyes while working with the powders and to wash their hands when finished.
- Be sure students have safety glasses on at all times. With a pH of about 12, washing soda is caustic. Have clean water available in case students get this substance into their eyes.
- Keep paper towels on hand so that spills can be wiped up immediately.

Continued from page 121

Results

Washing soda and Epsom salts will dissolve in the water and, depending on the amount of powder added, form clear liquids. When the two jars are mixed together, a white solid precipitates out of the solution. This white solid, called a precipitate, is a new substance.

Questions and Conclusions Answers

1. The powder dissolved in the water.
2. The crystals dissolved in the water.
3. A white substance formed.
4. Physical change; the substance only changed its appearance. No new substance was formed.
5. Chemical change; a new substance was formed.

Explore Further Answers

The balloon blows up, indicating that a gas has formed. A chemical change takes place because a new substance—the gas—formed.

Assessment

Check students' answers to the questions to be sure they understand that the formation of the white solid indicates that a chemical change took place. You might include the following items from this investigation in student portfolios:

• Investigation 5-1 data table

• Answers to Questions and Conclusions and Explore Further sections

5. Use a clean spoon to add a spoonful of Epsom salts to the second jar. Place the lid on the jar and shake for about 30 seconds. Record your observations.

6. Carefully pour the contents of one jar into the other jar. Observe for 5 minutes. Record the results.

Questions and Conclusions

1. What happened when you added the washing soda to water?

2. What happened when you added the Epsom salts to water?

3. What did you observe when you mixed the contents of the jars together in step 6?

4. Did a chemical change or a physical change take place in steps 4 and 5? Explain your answer.

5. Did a chemical change or a physical change take place in step 6? Explain your answer.

Explore Further

Place a small amount of vinegar in a soft-drink bottle. Add a small amount of baking soda. Immediately cover the mouth of the bottle with a balloon. What do you observe happening? Does a chemical change take place? Explain your answer.

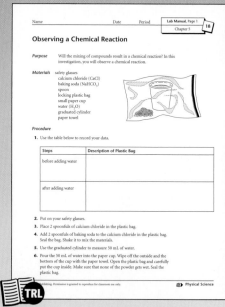

Lab Manual 17   Lab Manual 18, pages 1–2

Lesson 2 How Compounds Are Formed

Objectives

After reading this lesson, you should be able to

◆ describe how electrons in an atom are arranged.

◆ explain how electrons fill the energy levels.

◆ explain how atoms combine to form compounds.

◆ explain how ions form chemical bonds.

Energy level

One of the spaces around the nucleus of an atom in which an electron moves

You now know that compounds form when chemical changes occur. But how do the atoms of elements combine to form compounds? Electrons play an important part when elements combine. Reviewing the structure of an atom can help you understand how this happens.

Arrangement of Electrons in an Atom

Electrons in an atom move around the nucleus. Each electron moves in its own space a certain distance from the nucleus. This space is called the **energy level.** Within each energy level, electrons may move in all directions.

Compare the figure of the onion with the model of the atom below. Each energy level of an atom is somewhat like a layer of an onion. Notice that each energy level is labeled with a letter. Level K is closest to the nucleus and is the smallest. Electrons in the outer energy levels have the most effect on the properties of an element.

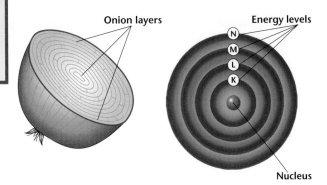

Onion layers

Energy levels

N M L K

Nucleus

Compounds *Chapter 5* **123**

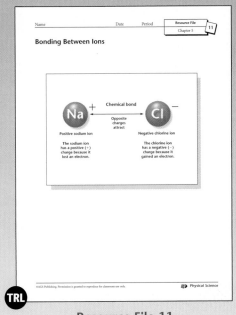

Name   Date   Period   Resource File
                                                    Chapter 5   11

Bonding Between Ions

Na +   Chemical bond   Cl −

Positive sodium ion   Opposite   Negative chlorine ion
                       charges
                       attract

The sodium ion   The chlorine ion
has a positive (+)   has a negative (−)
charge because it   charge because it
lost an electron.   gained an electron.

©AGS Publishing. Permission is granted to reproduce for classroom use only.   Physical Science

TRL

Resource File 11

Lesson at a Glance

Chapter 5 Lesson 2

Overview In this lesson, students learn how electrons are arranged in an atom and how this arrangement affects the way atoms combine to form compounds. Ions are introduced.

Objectives

■ To describe how electrons in an atom are arranged

■ To explain how electrons fill the energy levels

■ To explain how atoms combine to form compounds

■ To explain how ions form chemical bonds

Student Pages 123–128

Teacher's Resource Library

  Workbook Activity 22

  Alternative Workbook Activity 22

  Resource File 11

Vocabulary

**chemical bond   ion
energy level**

Science Background

The basic parts of an atom are the nucleus and the electrons. The nucleus, the central core that possesses most of the atom's mass, contains protons and neutrons. Each proton possesses a positive charge. Each neutron is neutral, possessing no charge. Whirling around this nucleus are one or more electrons. Though an electron has only a tiny fraction of the mass of a proton, it does have a negative charge exactly opposite the positive charge of a proton. In a stable atom the number of protons equals the number of electrons, and the overall positive and negative charges are in balance.

1 Warm-Up Activity

Place an electric fan in front of the class. Turn on the fan and ask students to describe what they see. Lead students to make observations about the "fuzzy" disc that the propeller produces.

Continued on page 124

Compounds *Chapter 5* **123**

Continued from page 123

Ask students if they can tell at any given moment exactly where the propeller is. *(no)* Compare the propeller to an electron whizzing around the nucleus of an atom.

2 Teaching the Lesson

Have students write down any questions they have about the diagrams in the lesson. As they read the lesson, have students record answers to their own questions. If any questions remain unanswered, encourage students to discuss these questions with the class.

Students may ask, "Why are there 2 electrons in the K level, 8 in the L level," and so on. Tell them that the numbers of electrons in the various energy levels are arbitrary: "they are just that way." Remark that physicists, or scientists who study matter and energy, have determined the numbers through many years of scientific analysis and experimentation. Point out that scientists have given these four levels the names of consecutive letters of the alphabet to aid in remembering their order.

3 Reinforce and Extend

SCIENCE JOURNAL

Have students review the diagrams on pages 124–125. Ask them to write one or two paragraphs telling what they think it would be like to be an electron whirling around in one of the energy levels.

Each energy level can hold only a certain number of electrons. Look at the models of the hydrogen and helium atoms in the figure below. The one electron in a hydrogen atom moves around in the first level, called level K. The two electrons in helium also move at level K. Two electrons are the limit for level K.

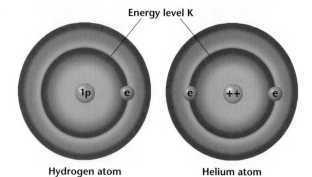

Energy level K

Hydrogen atom   Helium atom

The table shows the number of electrons each energy level can hold. Notice that the levels farther from the nucleus can hold more electrons than the levels closer to the nucleus.

An atom has seven energy levels. They are named K, L, M, N, O, P, and Q. Scientists theorize that energy level O can hold 50 electrons, level P can hold 72, and level Q can hold 98.

Energy Levels in an Atom	
Name	Number of Electrons When Filled
K	2
L	8
M	18
N	32

How Electrons Fill Energy Levels

The electrons fill the energy levels in order. Level K is the level closest to the nucleus. It is filled first. Then the second level, level L, is filled. This goes on until all the electrons are in place. For example, the element magnesium has 12 electrons. Notice in the figure that two of these electrons fill level K. Eight more electrons fill level L. The remaining two electrons are in energy level M.

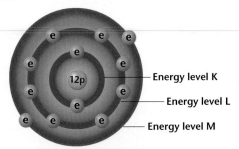

Energy level K
Energy level L
Energy level M

Magnesium atom

Different elements will have electrons in different numbers of levels. Helium has fewer electrons than magnesium. Helium has only two electrons. Its electrons are only in level K. But elements with more electrons fill more levels. For example, chlorine has 17 electrons. Look at the figure below.

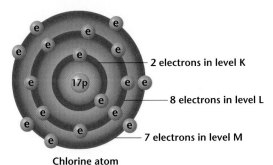

2 electrons in level K
8 electrons in level L
7 electrons in level M

Chlorine atom

Level M will not be full because it can hold more than 7 electrons. Level M can hold as many as 18 electrons.

LEARNING STYLES

Logical/Mathematical

Present the following strategy for remembering electron maximum numbers in energy levels K through N. First, students must memorize 2 for K level and 8 for L level. Then they subtract these numbers: $8 - 2 = 6$. So there is a difference of 6 between the first two levels. Next note that the difference between adjacent levels increases by 4 each time as it progresses toward the outer level, N. To determine electron numbers for levels M and N, students merely add the base difference plus the increase each time. Share the following diagram with students to make these number relationships clear.

K	2		$2 + 6 = 8$
		6	
L	8		$8 + 10 = 18$
		10	
M	18		$18 + 14 = 32$
		14	
N	32		

Differences increase by 4.

ONLINE CONNECTION

Direct students to particleadventure.org/particleadventure/. This is a kid-oriented site maintained by the Particle Data Group of Lawrence Berkeley National Laboratory. The site explains how scientific understanding of the fundamental particles of the universe, including atoms and subatomic particles, has changed from the time of Democritus in ancient Greece to today.

TEACHER ALERT

Make sure students understand how and why atoms with partially filled outer energy levels tend to acquire or give up electrons to become stable. Use lithium and fluorine in the following demonstration to assess and reteach after presenting the section, "How Atoms Combine." This example is parallel to the Student Text example featuring sodium and chlorine: sodium and lithium are chemically similar; chlorine and fluorine are similar. Show that lithium has one electron in its outer level, so it tends to give up one electron. And fluorine has 7 electrons in its outer level, so it tends to take on one electron. Make sure students understand that atoms "want to" have completed outer energy levels; that is, 2 electrons in level K and 8 electrons in level L. Ask students what they think might happen if a lithium atom and a fluorine atom come together. (*They will join to form a new compound, lithium fluoride.*)

CROSS-CURRICULAR CONNECTION

Language Arts

Point out that the words *atom*, *electron*, and *ion* all have come into English from ancient Greek. Ancient Greek thinkers, such as Democritus (460–370 B.C.), pondered the fundamental properties of matter. Our word *atom* comes from the Greek *atomos*, which meant "cannot be cut up." Democritus thought that the atom was the smallest possible particle in nature and that it could not be subdivided. From the Greek *elektron*, we get our word *electron*. In ancient Greek, *elektron* named amber, a natural substance that produces a static electrical charge when rubbed. From the Greek verb *ienai*, "to go," we get our word *ion*. Scientists chose the Greek verb because ions carry a positive or negative charge and thus tend to move, or "go," toward oppositely charged particles.

Valence electrons are electrons in the outer energy layer, or valence shell, of an atom. These electrons are the only electrons that can combine with other electrons.

In an electrically neutral atom, the number of protons equals the number of electrons. When an atom gains or loses electrons, the charge is unbalanced.

How Atoms Combine

You learned that compounds form when the atoms of elements combine. Exactly how do the atoms of different elements join together? When atoms form compounds, they share, lend, or borrow electrons that are in their outer energy level.

An atom has a tendency to fill its outer energy level. An atom becomes more stable when its outermost energy level is filled. An atom shares, lends, or borrows electrons to fill its outer energy level.

Look at the model of the sodium atom in the figure below. Sodium has 11 electrons. Notice that only one of its electrons is in the outer energy level. Sodium tends to lose one electron to another atom to become stable. By losing an electron, the outer level—level L—will have 8 electrons. It will have the most electrons it can hold. On the other hand, the chlorine atom on page 125 has 7 electrons in its outer energy level—level M. Level M can hold 18 electrons. The chlorine will become more stable if it gains or borrows one electron.

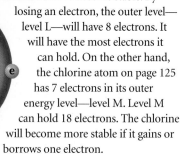

Sodium atom

Attraction Between Atoms

Table salt is a familiar compound made from one sodium atom and one chlorine atom. The figure on page 127 shows how the sodium atom lends its electron to the chlorine atom.

Keep in mind that when sodium loses an electron, the number of protons in the nucleus remains the same. As a result, the atom has more protons than electrons. Protons have a positive charge. Electrons have a negative charge. When an atom has equal numbers of electrons and protons, the atom has no charge. But when an atom has more protons than electrons, it has a positive (+) charge.

Sodium gives an electron to chlorine to form the compound sodium chloride. The chlorine atom now has more electrons than protons. When an atom has more electrons than protons, it has a negative (−) charge.

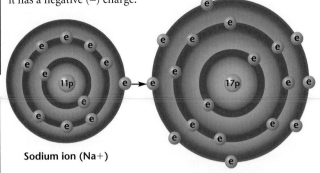

Sodium ion (Na+)

Chloride ion (Cl−)

Ionic compounds, such as sodium chloride, form a crystal shape. The shape of the crystal is based on the arrangement of the ions that are in it. Sodium chloride forms a cube-shaped crystal.

Look at the figure shown here. How has the chlorine changed? An atom that has either a positive or a negative charge is called an **ion.** In the sodium chloride example, the chlorine becomes a negative ion. The sodium becomes a positive ion. Positive ions and negative ions strongly attract each other. The figure below shows this attraction between ions. The attractive force between atoms is called a **chemical bond.** The chemical bond between ions holds the atoms together when they form a compound. For example, a chemical bond keeps sodium and chlorine ions together when they combine to form table salt.

Chemical bond

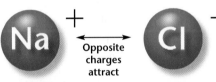

Positive sodium ion

The sodium ion has a positive (+) charge because it lost an electron.

Opposite charges attract

Negative chlorine ion

The chlorine ion has a negative (−) charge because it gained an electron.

Science Myth

All chemical bonds form in the same way.

Fact: There are two main types of chemical bonds. A covalent bond forms when two atoms share a pair of electrons. Each atom gives one electron to the electron pair. An ionic bond forms when an atom loses an electron and another atom gains the electron.

*Compounds   Chapter 5   **127***

IN THE ENVIRONMENT

One of the world's major challenges today is finding enough fresh water. In many places, the world's ground water as well as much cropland is becoming more and more salty, a process called salinization. One reason for salinization is that people are using some water sources too heavily. For example, people in the southwestern United States take so much water out of the Colorado River that the remaining water becomes more and more saline—that is, concentrated with dissolved salt. Another reason is that farmers use irrigation to water crops in many dry regions. Most water contains a little salt in acceptable amounts. As water from the same source is used over and over again on cropland, the salt in it stays in the land and becomes more and more concentrated. Eventually, the land may become unusable for farming. Still another reason is that water polluted by sewage and agricultural runoff may be returning to groundwater sources.

Lesson 2 Review Answers

1. Electrons are arranged around the nucleus of an atom in several energy levels that are rather like the multiple layers of an onion. **2.** Electrons fill the energy levels of an atom from the innermost layer, Level K, to the outermost, Level N. **3.** The atom would tend to lose electrons; Level M can hold 18 electrons, so if it has only 3 electrons, it is more likely to give up 3 rather than take on 15 more to become stable. **4.** An atom with a single electron in its outer energy level may give it up; at the same time, a nearby atom with an outer level lacking one electron may grab onto the free electron. In the process, the first atom becomes a positively charged ion, and the second, a negatively charged ion. The opposite charges cause the ions to bond together, forming a new compound. **5.** Level M can hold 18 electrons.

Science at Work

Ask students to name their favorite article of clothing and describe its color. Ask if students know what the fabric in the clothing is. *(Answers might include cotton, wool, silk, or a synthetic such as polyester.)* Ask if students have any idea what color the original materials were. Point out that most fabrics are dyed to provide colors consumers find pleasing or interesting. Point out that people who work with color in the fabric industry must have special training to do their jobs. Have students read the box feature describing the job of the textile dye technologist.

CROSS-CURRICULAR CONNECTION

Health
Have interested students research how the human body uses sodium, potassium, and chlorine ions for nerve communications.

Portfolio Assessment

Sample items include:
- Questions and answers about the lesson's diagrams
- Lesson 2 Review answers

Write your answers to these questions in complete sentences on a sheet of paper.

1. How are electrons arranged around the nucleus of an atom?

2. In what order do electrons fill energy levels?

3. Would an atom with 3 electrons in level M tend to gain or lose electrons? Explain your answer. (Hint: Use the chart on page 124.)

4. How do atoms of different elements combine?

5. How many electrons can level M hold?

▼◀▲▼◀▲▼◀▲▼◀▲▼◀▲▼◀▲▼◀▲▼◀▲▼◀▲▼◀▲▼◀▲▼

Science at Work

Textile Dye Technologist

Textile dye technologists create and test formulas for different colors of dyes for different fabrics. They have the responsibility of deciding which dye and dyeing process to use. They mix dyes, check the dyeing process at each stage, and take  samples for testing. Textile dye technologists also make sure the machinery used in dyeing fabrics works correctly.

Textile dye technologists must complete a two-year college program in textile dye or textile engineering technology. They also must have two years of on-the-job training.

Textile dye technologists have excellent color perception and a solid understanding of the principles of chemistry.

Name	Date	Period	**Workbook Activity**
			Chapter 5, Lesson 2 **22**

Energy Levels

Directions Write your answers on the lines.

1. How many electrons does the K level of an atom hold?
2. How many electrons does the L level of an atom hold?
3. How many electrons does the M level of an atom hold?
4. How many electrons does the N level of an atom hold?
5. What is the total number of electrons the four levels will hold?
6. A hydrogen atom has 1 electron. In which level is it?
7. A magnesium atom has 12 electrons. To what level are its electrons found?
8. A zinc atom has 30 electrons. To what level are its electrons found?
9. A nitrogen atom has 7 electrons. To what level are its electrons found?
10. A sulfur atom has 16 electrons. To what level are its electrons found?
11. A lithium atom has 3 electrons. To what level are its electrons found?
12. An iron atom has 26 electrons. To what level are its electrons found?
13. A mercury atom has 80 electrons. To what level are its electrons found?
14. A zirconium atom has 40 electrons. To what level are its electrons found?
15. A californium atom has 98 electrons. To what level are its electrons found?

Directions Draw a magnesium atom. Show its energy levels and electrons.

Publishing. Permission is granted to reproduce for classroom use only.   ◗ **Physical Science**

Workbook Activity 22

Objectives

After reading this lesson, you should be able to

◆ explain how to write a chemical formula.

◆ interpret a chemical formula.

◆ explain what a radical is.

◆ give examples of radicals.

Chemical formula

Tells the kinds of atoms and how many of each kind are in a compound

Suppose you want to describe a particular beverage such as the one in the figure. You might tell about its recipe. Notice that the recipe lists all the ingredients. It also tells the amount of each ingredient in the drink.

Banana-Strawberry Slush

Recipe

1 cup sliced bananas
1 cup fresh sliced strawberries
4 mint leaves
1 cup skim milk
1/4 cup crushed ice cubes

Mix all of the ingredients in a blender until slushy. Serve immediately.

You can describe a compound by using the same kind of information you use in a recipe. You can tell what elements form the compound. You can also tell the amount of each element in the compound.

Formulas for Compounds

Scientists use the symbols for the elements to write a **chemical formula** for each compound. A chemical formula tells what kinds of atoms are in a compound and how many atoms of each kind are present. You know that sodium and chlorine combine to form table salt. The symbol for sodium is Na. The symbol for chlorine is Cl. The chemical formula for table salt is NaCl. The formula shows that sodium and chlorine combine to form table salt.

for acronyms they are familiar with. Discuss the usefulness of acronyms and other abbreviations. Tell students that scientists use abbreviations to describe compounds.

 Teaching the Lesson

Have students preview the lesson. Tell them to write the lesson subheads on a sheet of paper, prefixing the phrase "What are . . ." to each subhead to make a question. As students read, have them write answers to their questions.

Remind students that all compounds are formed of elements. Every element has a standard symbol, and those symbols are listed in the periodic table of elements.

Remind students that the symbols for elements do not necessarily match the English name for the element. Offer the example of lead (from the Science Background) as an example. Also remind students that some symbols for elements consist of two letters, a capital and lowercase letter, while others consist of only one capital letter.

Suggest that students refer to the periodic table (pages 100–101) to identify element names as they study about compounds formed from the elements. Make sure that in each example in the lesson, students can identify the elements making up compounds.

Continued on page 130

Chapter 5 Lesson 3

Overview This lesson introduces students to chemical formulas. Students learn to write and interpret formulas. They also learn what a radical is.

Objectives

■ To explain how to write a chemical formula

■ To interpret a chemical formula

■ To explain what a radical is

■ To give examples of radicals

Student Pages 129–133

Teacher's Resource Library

   Workbook Activity 23

   Alternative Workbook Activity 23

Vocabulary

chemical formula
radicals
subscript

Science Background

Almost all substances in the universe are formed out of the naturally occurring elements. These elements are listed in the periodic table of the elements. Also listed in the table, in the higher number ranges, are elements that have been artificially created by scientists. For the purpose of learning traditional chemistry—that is, how compounds form in nature—these latter elements can be disregarded. Every element has a unique one- or two-letter abbreviation. For example element 8 in the periodic table is oxygen, or O; element 82 is the metal lead, or Pb. The periodic table lists elements by these abbreviations, which are universally recognized, unlike many common names (for example, the metal known as *lead* in English is named *le plomb* in French).

1 **Warm-Up Activity**

Write the following acronyms on the board: NASA *(National Aeronautics and Space Administration),* NFL *(National Football League),* and NBA *(National Basketball Association).* Ask student what each acronym means. Then ask students

Continued from page 129

Refer students to the opening paragraph of the lesson. Ask students what would happen if they were using a recipe but used twice the amount of a particular ingredient. Lead students to understand that the final product would be something other than what they expected. Likewise, if a formula is written incorrectly, the compound it describes will be a different substance than the intended one.

3 Reinforce and Extend

TEACHER ALERT

Make sure students understand that the proper subscript is important in writing a formula. When a subscript changes, the compound changes. For example, H_2O is the formula for water, but H_2O_2 is the formula for hydrogen peroxide. Both contain hydrogen and oxygen but in different amounts. Discuss the properties of each compound.

Did You Know?

Ask a volunteer to read the feature on page 130 to the class. If you or students have jewelry made with cubic zirconium, display it for the class. Tell students that diamonds are made up almost entirely of carbon. Cubic zirconium is made of zirconium and oxygen and is softer than diamonds. Ask students to compare and contrast cubic zirconium with diamonds. Have them discuss reasons why someone would choose to wear cubic zirconium jewelry rather than diamond jewelry.

130 *Chapter 5 Compounds*

Subscript

A number in a formula that tells the number of atoms of an element in a compound

 Did You Know?

Cubic zirconia (ZrO_2) is an imitation diamond made from a manmade compound. It is an oxide of zirconium. Each zirconium atom has eight oxygen atoms around it. Each oxygen atom connects to four zirconium atoms.

Scientists use a number called a **subscript** to indicate the number of atoms of an element in a compound. For example, the formula for water is H_2O. The number 2 tells that a water molecule contains two atoms of hydrogen. You can see that the subscript number 2 is smaller than the H and written slightly below the letter.

Notice that no subscript is written after the O. If no subscript number is given after the symbol of an element, the compound has only one atom of that element. The formula H_2O shows that one molecule of water contains three atoms—two of hydrogen and one of oxygen.

Look at the tables to learn the chemical formulas for some other compounds. Read carefully to find out what each formula shows about the compound it represents.

CH₄			
Symbol	Element	Subscript	Number of Atoms
C	carbon	none	1
H	hydrogen	4	+4
			5 Total atoms

C₁₂H₂₂O₁₁			
Symbol	Element	Subscript	Number of Atoms
C	carbon	12	12
H	hydrogen	22	22
O	oxygen	11	+11
			45 Total atoms

130 *Chapter 5 Compounds*

Compounds Containing Radicals

Radicals
A group of two or more atoms that acts like one atom

The formulas for some compounds contain groups of two or more atoms that act as if they were one atom. These groups of atoms are called **radicals.** They form compounds by combining with other atoms. During a chemical reaction, the atoms in a radical stay together.

Household lye is one common substance with a formula that contains a radical. This strong chemical is used to clean drains. The formula for lye is NaOH. The OH is an example of a radical. It contains one atom of oxygen and one atom of hydrogen. The chemical name for this radical is the hydroxyl radical. Other examples of radicals and their names are listed in the table.

Some Common Radicals	
Radical	**Name**
SO_4	sulfate
ClO_3	chlorate
NO_3	nitrate
CO_3	carbonate
PO_4	phosphate
OH	hydroxide

Compounds containing more than one radical are written with the radical in parentheses. A subscript outside of the parentheses tells how many units of the radical are in one molecule of the compound. For example, in the formula $Ba(OH)_2$, the Ba atom combines with two OH radicals as shown in the figure.

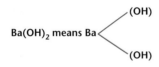

$Ba(OH)_2$ means Ba
- (OH)
- (OH)

LEARNING STYLES

Visual/Spatial

On the board, copy the chart "Some Common Radicals" on page 131. Assemble 14 index cards. Write names of the elements represented on the chart on 7 of the cards: sulfur (S), chlorine (Cl), nitrogen (N), carbon (C), phosphorus (P), oxygen (O), and hydrogen (H). On the remaining 7 cards, write names of other elements. Instruct participating students to draw a card from the deck. Have each student say whether the element on the card is represented in the chart of radicals. If it is, have the student identify the radical (or radicals) on the chart, write the name of his or her element on the board, and draw a line connecting that name to the appropriate radical. When all the constituent elements have been identified, review the chart, naming each radical and identifying its components.

CROSS-CURRICULAR CONNECTION

Math

Ask students if they recall factoring in their math classes. Then ask if the calculation in the chart on page 132 reminds them of factoring. Write the following expression on the board: 3(2 + 7). Solve the expression by
(A) multiplying 3 × 2 *(6)*;
(B) multiplying 3 × 7 *(21)*;
(C) adding the two intermediate results together: 6 + 21 = 27. Ask students if they remember the distributive property in math. That rule states that numbers within parentheses can be multiplied by the same factor. Point out that you used the distributive property to solve the expression. Ask how the distributive property is used in the chart on page 132. *(You multiply the number of atoms of each element within the radical by the subscript outside the parentheses.)*

Here is another example. In $Al(OH)_3$, the Al atom combines with three OH radicals.

When formulas contain radicals with subscripts, the subscripts multiply the number of atoms inside the parentheses. Study the table below. The compound $Ba(NO_3)_2$ is barium nitrate. The nitrate radical is made up of one nitrogen atom and three oxygen atoms. But in barium nitrate, the barium atom combines with *two* nitrate radicals. You can see from the table that the compound has a total of two nitrogen atoms and six oxygen atoms.

$Ba(NO_3)_2$				
Symbol	Element	Subscript	Radical Subscript	Number of Atoms
Ba	barium	none	not in a radical	1
N	nitrogen	none	2	2 (2 × 1)
O	oxygen	3	2	+6 (2 × 3)
				9 Total atoms

Fireworks contain the compound barium nitrate.

Lesson 3   REVIEW

Copy the table on a sheet of paper. Fill in the missing information. Use the periodic table on pages 100 and 101 if you need help naming the elements. The first one is done for you.

Compound	Symbols	Elements	Subscripts	Number of Each Kind of Atom
1. $NaHCO_3$	Na	sodium	none	1
	H	hydrogen	none	1
	C	carbon	none	1
	O	oxygen	3	3
2. $K_2Cr_2O_7$				
3. H_2SO_4				
4. $KClO_3$				
5. HCl				

Write the answers to these questions in complete sentences on your paper. Use the periodic table on pages 100 and 101 if you need help.

6. What does a formula tell about a compound?

7. Write a formula for a compound that contains one atom of aluminum and three atoms of chlorine.

Complete the table for the compound $Al_2(SO_4)_3$. Copy the table on your paper.

$Al_2(SO_4)_3$				
Symbol	Element	Subscript	Radical Subscript	Number of Atoms
8. Al				
9. S				
10. O				+ _____ Total atoms

Lesson 3 Review Answers

1. (Given) **2.** $K_2Cr_2O_7$: K, potassium, 2, 2; Cr, chromium, 2, 2; O, oxygen, 7, 7 **3.** H_2SO_4: H, hydrogen, 2, 2; S, sulfur, none, 1; O, oxygen, 4, 4 **4.** $KClO_3$: K, potassium, none, 1; Cl, chlorine, none, 1; O, oxygen, 3, 3 **5.** HCl: H, hydrogen, none, 1; Cl, chlorine, none, 1 **6.** A formula tells what kind of atoms are in a compound and how many atoms of each type are present. **7.** $AlCl_3$ **8.** Al, aluminum, 2, not in a radical, 2 **9.** S, sulfur, none, 3, 3 **10.** O, oxygen, 4, 3, 12 Total atoms 17

Portfolio Assessment

Sample items include:
• Questions and answers based on previewing the lesson subheads
• Lesson 3 Review answers

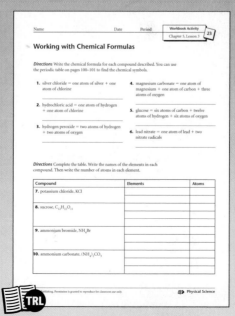

Workbook Activity 23

Compounds   Chapter 5   **133**

Chapter 5 Lesson 4

Overview Students learn how chemical compounds are named.

Objectives

■ To explain how compounds containing two elements are named

■ To explain how compounds containing more than two elements are named

Student Pages 134–137

Teacher's Resource Library  **TRL**

Workbook Activity 24

Alternative Workbook Activity 24

Vocabulary

binary compound

 1 Warm-Up Activity

Again use the analogy of using a recipe to make a food. Prompt students to imagine they will submit a recipe for a favorite dish to a publisher for inclusion in a new cookbook. Suppose the recipe calls for whole wheat flour, baking powder, and butter, among other ingredients. Tell students to pretend they carelessly write the names of these ingredients as flour, baking soda, and butter. Ask what might happen when cookbook users try to make the dish. *(The dish will probably be a failure.)* Say that naming chemical compounds improperly can also have disastrous effects and that students will learn rules for naming them in this lesson.

 2 Teaching the Lesson

Explain to students that learning to name compounds is important to understanding other aspects of chemistry. Just as learning the alphabet helped students learn to read, learning to write and name formulas helps them understand the language of chemistry.

After reading the lesson, have students construct a simple table that states the rules for naming compounds.

How would you identify yourself to a new acquaintance? You most likely would give your complete name, your first name and your last name. A compound also has a complete name, including a first and last name.

Compounds Containing Two Elements

A compound that contains two elements is called a **binary compound.** The name of a binary compound is a combination of the names of the two elements that form the compound. The number of atoms in the compound is not considered when naming a compound. The following two rules are used to name compounds containing two elements.

◆ The first name of a compound is the same as the name of the first element in the compound's formula.

◆ The second name of a compound is the name of the second element in the compound's formula with the ending changed to *-ide*. The table shows how names of some elements are written when they are the second elements in a formula.

Objectives

After reading this lesson, you should be able to

◆ explain how compounds containing two elements are named.

◆ explain how compounds containing more than two elements are named.

Binary compound

A compound that contains two elements

Naming Binary Compounds	
Element	**Element's Name in a Compound**
chlorine (Cl)	chlor**ide**
iodine (I)	iod**ide**
fluorine (F)	fluor**ide**
bromine (Br)	brom**ide**
oxygen (O)	ox**ide**
sulfur (S)	sulf**ide**

You can see how looking at the formula for a compound can help you determine the compound's name. The formula NaCl contains symbols for the elements sodium and chlorine. The first name of the compound is the name of the first element, sodium. We change chlorine to chloride to form the second name of the compound. NaCl is sodium chloride.

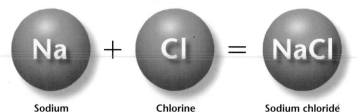

| Sodium | Chlorine | Sodium chloride |

Another example is the formula BaO. The first part of the compound's name is the name of the first element, barium. The second element is oxygen. We change its name to oxide. The compound name is barium oxide.

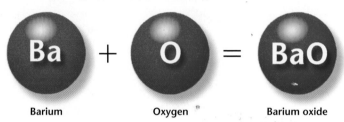

| Barium | Oxygen | Barium oxide |

Compounds with More Than Two Elements

A compound that contains more than two elements usually has a radical in its formula. The first name of such a compound is the name of the first element in the formula. The second name of the compound varies according to the radical the formula contains. Review the names for some common radicals in the table on page 131. The subscript numbers in a formula with radicals do not affect the name of the compound.

The table should include a rule for naming binary compounds and a rule for naming compounds with more than two elements. Have students include an example for each rule.

3 Reinforce and Extend

LEARNING STYLES

Auditory/Verbal

In large letters, write the symbol names of the six elements in the chart on page 134: *Cl, I, Fl, Br, O,* and *S.* Use a pointer to point to the names, one at a time. Cue a volunteer to say the name, either (1) as it appears as a lone element or (2) as it appears in the name of a binary compound. Have other participants evaluate each pronunciation and correct it if necessary. Mix up the versions as you proceed to make the activity more challenging.

IN THE COMMUNITY

In the 1940s and 1950s, communities started adding tiny amounts of sodium fluoride to their water supplies. Dental research had shown that the chemical could greatly reduce tooth decay, especially in children. However, some citizens of these communities worried that the chemical could have harmful side effects in some people. Have students find out if their community fluoridates the water supply. Suggest that students contact the director of the community's water department, who can provide a list of the chemicals in the water and their amounts. Have students ask which chemicals are added and which are naturally in the water. They should then investigate why certain chemicals are added to the water.

To find the name of the compound with the formula $Al(OH)_3$, use the name of the first element—aluminum. Then add the name of the OH radical—hydroxide. The name of the compound is aluminum hydroxide.

Identifying radicals accurately is important. The seashells shown on this page contain the compound $CaCO_3$, calcium carbonate. The radical carbonate, CO_3, is listed in the table on page 131. The formula for the compound CO_2 looks similar. However, note that CO_2 has a different subscript—a 2 instead of a 3. In fact, it is the formula for a completely different compound. CO_2 is carbon dioxide, a gas in the air.

Seashells contain calcium carbonate, a compound with the formula $CaCO_3$.

Lesson 4 REVIEW

Write the names of these binary compounds on a sheet of paper. Use the periodic table on pages 100 and 101 to find the element name for each symbol.

1. $CaBr_2$ 6. BaI_2

2. $AlCl_3$ 7. CaF_2

3. AgI 8. HCl

4. MgO 9. MgS

5. $CaCl_2$ 10. $NaBr$

Write the names of these compounds on your paper. Refer to the periodic table if you need help.

11. $Al_2(SO_4)_3$

12. $Ba(OH)_2$

13. $Al(NO_3)_3$

14. K_2CO_3

15. $ZnSO_4$

Compounds   Chapter 5   **137**

SCIENCE JOURNAL

Have students write a short story about two scientists who are trying to communicate about a particular project. Unfortunately, they keep using the wrong names for compounds. What happens?

Portfolio Assessment

Sample items include:
• Table of rules for naming compounds from Teaching the Lesson
• Lesson 4 Review answers

Name _____ Date _____ Period _____ **Workbook Activity** 24
Chapter 5, Lesson 4

Matching Chemical Formulas with Chemical Names

Directions Compounds have a chemical formula and a chemical name. Draw a line to match each formula in the left column with the correct name in the right column. You can use the periodic table on pages 100–101 to help you with this activity.

Column 1	Column 2
1. NaF	beryllium oxide
2. $MgCl_2$	potassium iodide
3. AgBr	silver chloride
4. LiOH	sodium fluoride
5. KCl	silver sulfide
6. LiF	beryllium chloride
7. BeO	lithium chloride
8. KI	gallium arsenide
9. $BeCl_2$	strontium chlorate
10. $FeCO_3$	lithium hydroxide
11. Ag_2S	magnesium chloride
12. $Sr(ClO_3)_2$	silver bromide
13. LiCl	iron carbonate
14. GaAs	potassium chloride
15. AgCl	lithium fluoride

Publishing. Permission is granted to reproduce for classroom use only.   **Physical Science**

Workbook Activity 24

Lesson at a Glance

Chapter 5 Lesson 5

Overview Students learn the properties of acids and bases and how to test for each.

Objectives

- To describe the properties of acids
- To describe the properties of bases
- To explain how to test for acids and bases

Student Pages 138–144

Teacher's Resource Library

Workbook Activity 25

Alternative Workbook Activity 25

Lab Manual 19–20

Vocabulary

acid   indicator
base   pH

 Warm-Up Activity

Ask students what would happen if they took a big bite of a juicy lemon. (*Students will probably say they'd pucker up or make a face.*) Ask why the lemon would cause such a reaction. (*The lemon is sour.*) Say that the sour taste is one property of a family of chemicals called acids. Prompt students to think of some other familiar acids—things that taste sour. (*Sample answers: vinegar, green apple, lime juice, grapefruit juice*) Point out that some acids are very strong and poisonous to people. Now ask whether students have ever tasted unscented soap by accident. Ask how it tasted. (*bitter*) Say that a bitter taste is one property of a family of chemicals called bases. Remark that bases are, in a chemical sense, the opposite of acids. Tell students they will learn more about the properties of acids and bases in this lesson.

 Teaching the Lesson

Before students read the lesson, have them make graphic organizers—one for acids and another for bases.

Students should include any information they know about these two topics. At the end of the lesson, have students correct or add information to their organizers.

As the lesson proceeds, verify that students know the chemical components of acids and bases: acids contain H; bases contain the OH radical. Make sure students include these items in their graphic organizers.

Lesson 5   Acids and Bases

Objectives

After reading this lesson, you should be able to

- describe the properties of acids.
- describe the properties of bases.
- explain how to test for acids and bases.

Acid

A compound that reacts with metals to produce hydrogen

Imagine biting into a lemon. How would it taste? You probably would describe its taste as sour. Then think about a time when you accidentally got soap in your mouth while washing. How did it taste? Soap has a bitter taste. These contrasting tastes, sour and bitter, help illustrate the differences between two groups of substances—acids and bases.

Properties of Acids

What gives a lemon its sour taste? A lemon contains a substance called an **acid.** All acids have the following characteristics.

- They taste sour.
- They contain hydrogen.
- They react with metals to produce hydrogen.

Weak acids, such as the citric acid in a lemon, give food a sour, sharp flavor. Vinegar is another familiar substance that contains an acid called acetic acid. The table lists some common acids and tells where they are found.

You can see from the table that you can eat some acids. But other acids are poisonous. Some acids can burn your skin. In fact, even touching a strong acid for a moment can cause a severe burn. That is why it is wise to never taste or touch an unknown substance.

Common Acids		
Name of Acid	Formula	Where It Is Found
acetic acid	$HC_2H_3O_2$	vinegar
boric acid	H_3BO_3	eyewashes
carbonic acid	H_2CO_3	rain water, soft drinks
hydrochloric acid	HCl	gastric juice in stomach
citric acid	$H_3C_6H_5O_7$	citrus fruits (oranges, lemons, etc.)
sulfuric acid	H_2SO_4	batteries, acid rain, volcanic smoke

 TEACHER ALERT

Sour taste is a way students can identify familiar, weak acids such as lemon juice, but stress that they should never taste any substance in the classroom or science lab without permission. Point out that many acids and bases are poisonous.

Properties of Bases

Base

A compound that contains the hydroxyl (OH) radical

Indicator

A substance that changes color when in an acid or a base

Why does soap have such a bitter taste? Soap belongs to a group of compounds called **bases.** All bases have the following characteristics.

◆ They taste bitter.
◆ They contain the OH radical.
◆ They feel slippery.

Many common bases are weak, so weak that you can eat them! For example, magnesium hydroxide is a weak base that is used in some medicines. However, strong bases, such as sodium hydroxide, or lye, can cause severe burns. Many bases can be poisonous. The table below lists some common bases and tells where they are found.

Did You Know?

You need an acid when you bake a cake. Recipes that use baking soda always have an ingredient that is an acid. It might be lemon juice or buttermilk, or even honey or molasses.

Common Bases		
Name of Base	Formula	Where It Is Found
aluminum hydroxide	$Al(OH)_3$	deodorants, antacids, water purification
magnesium hydroxide	$Mg(OH)_2$	laxatives, antacids
potassium hydroxide	KOH	soap, glass
sodium hydroxide	NaOH	drain cleaner, soap making
calcium hydroxide	$Ca(OH)_2$	mortar

Testing Acids and Bases

Tasting or feeling a substance to determine if it is an acid or a base usually is not safe. But there is a way to make this determination by using another characteristic of both acids and bases. You can find out how they react to **indicators.** Indicators change color to identify acids or bases. Litmus is a common indicator used in the laboratory. Litmus turns from blue to red in acids. It turns from red to blue in bases. You will use an indicator in Investigation 5-2.

Compounds Chapter 5 **139**

3 Reinforce and Extend

Did You Know?

Have students read the text in the feature on page 139. Point out that baking soda is a base. Ask students why they think cake recipes bring together an acid and a base. Prompt students to speculate what might happen when an acid and base are mixed together. If necessary, say that mixing the acid and base causes a chemical reaction that produces lots of bubbles. The bubbles slowly rise through the cake batter, causing the cake to rise as it bakes.

LEARNING STYLES

LEP/ESL

Make sure students are familiar with the names for the common examples used in the lesson. Suggest that students draw pictures of some of the simpler, more familiar examples. For acids, they might draw a lemon; for bases, they might draw a bar of soap.

GLOBAL CONNECTION

Point out that many of the world's cuisines use sour tastes to accent food flavors. Cooks incorporate various sour-tasting acids, such as citrus juices or vinegar, in foods. Often, a sour flavor is played off against a sweet one. Point out that in the German language, *sauer* (pronounced ZOW uhr) means "acid" or "sour," and as students will note, sounds almost the same as the English word. Ask if students have eaten German foods that use sour accents and include the German word *sauer* in their names. (*sauerkraut, sauerbraten*) Point out that sauerkraut means "sour cabbage" and sauerbraten means "sour meat roast." Prompt students to think of examples of sour flavor accents in other cuisines.

SCIENCE INTEGRATION

Biology

Tell students that litmus is made from an organism called a lichen. In fact, the name *litmus* is an old Norse word meaning "dye moss." A lichen is an unusual example of a symbiotic organism—that is, a compound organism made of two different species that live together in an interdependent way. The two species in lichens are algae and fungi. Algae have chlorophyll and make their own food, which they share with the fungal part of the lichen. The fungi absorb water from vapor in the air and supply the organism's water needs. Lichens are found throughout the world, but they thrive especially in the harsh conditions of arctic regions. In those regions, caribou feed on lichens.

Home Economics

Point out that an important part of managing a home is storing potentially harmful materials conveniently, yet safely. Identify household cleaners—such as ammonia, white vinegar, dishwasher soap, toilet bowl cleaner, and glass cleaner—that are used in the home. Explain that such substances could be harmful. Challenge students to make a plan for storing cleaning supplies in a way that will be convenient to adults but safely out of young children's reach.

TEACHER ALERT

To help students remember that a strong acid has low pH and a strong base has high pH, write the following row on the board: *A 0 1 2 3 4 5 6 7 8 9 10 11 12 13 14 B*. Explain that the letter *A* stands for acid and the letter *B* stands for base. The range of pH numbers between acids and bases is shown between the two letters. The closer the pH gets to *A*, the lower the number and the stronger the acid. The closer the pH gets to *B*, the higher the number and the stronger the base. A substance with a pH of 7 is neutral—neither an acid nor a base. Students can use a simple memory device for the pH scale as follows: *A* stands for acid and *B* stands for base. *A* is lower than *B* in the alphabet, so acids are at the lower end of the scale, and bases are at the higher end.

---

pH
A number that tells whether a substance is an acid or a base

Some indicators tell you the **pH** of a substance. The pH is a number that tells whether the substance is an acid or a base. Acids have a pH from 0 to 7. Bases have a pH from 7 to 14. Some substances are neither acids nor bases. These substances are said to be neutral. They have a pH of 7. You can see the pH of some common substances in the chart on this page.

You can use indicators to tell how strong an acid or a base is. The lower the pH number of an acid, the stronger the acid is. For example, your stomach produces acid that is very strong. Its pH is 1. Milk is only slightly acidic. Its pH is 6.9. The higher the pH of a base, the stronger the base. Lye has a pH around 13. It is a strong base. Liquid soaps are much weaker bases.

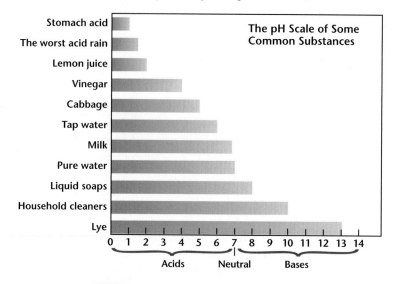

Technology Note

A pH meter is an instrument that shows the strength of an acid or base. A pH meter measures and compares the electric charge of the ions in a sample. Then the meter changes this information into a pH number. Scientists use a pH meter to test water.

CROSS-CURRICULAR CONNECTION

Health

One acid that is important to human health is citric acid, which is found in citrus fruits, such as oranges, and in other foods. Citric acid helps the digestive system break down carbohydrates and fats.

Carbohydrates include starchy foods such as bread, potatoes, and pasta. Fats come from animal fat such as fatty meat or butter and from vegetable fats such as oil in peanut butter. Survey students to see how many have some citrus fruit every day. (Tell them to include orange juice.) Have interested students make a poster showing the importance of citrus fruits in a healthy diet.

Science in Your Life

What is acid rain?

Imagine visiting a beautiful lake such as the one in the photo. You can't wait to get in the water to swim. Maybe you have been thinking about the fish you will catch there. But suppose the water is not safe for swimming. Suppose no fish or plants live in the lake. You wonder what has happened. Perhaps the water is polluted.

One cause of water pollution is acid rain, which is also called acid deposition. Acid deposition does not harm only water. It harms plants and animals, and affects buildings, bridges, and statues. Acid rain also damages human health.

Acid deposition starts when cars, factories, or power plants burn coal, gas, or oil. This produces gases in the air. The gases combine with water, oxygen, and other substances to form harmful acids.

There are two ways these acids reach the earth. When rain, snow, or cloud water carries acids to the earth, wet deposition occurs. When acidic gases or particles fall on plants, land, water, or buildings, dry deposition occurs. Rain can wash dry deposits off trees and plants, making the rain even more acidic. When the wind blows, acids in the air can travel long distances.

People first noticed the effects of acid rain in the 1960s. They noticed that fish in some lakes in Europe and North America were dying. Next, they noticed that some forests showed signs of damage.

Reducing acid deposition starts with reducing pollutants given off by cars, factories, and power plants. Since 1990, the levels of these pollutants in the air have decreased, but not enough. Governments, industries, scientists, and individuals continue to work to solve the problem of acid rain.

Science in Your Life

Ask students to recall the properties of acids they learned in Lesson 5. (Students may repeat the bullet list on page 138.) The acid in acid rain includes sulfuric acid and nitric acid, both of which are poisonous to living things. Have students read the Science in Your Life feature on page 141.

Confirm that the acid in acid rain contains hydrogen and that its ability to react with metals and stone causes damage to structures such as buildings, bridges, and statues.

Ask students where they think acid rain would fit on the pH scale. (*It would fit on the acid end of the scale, somewhere below 7.*)

Prompt students to think about a natural setting they enjoy visiting or would like to visit, a place that has forests and lakes. Have them write a descriptive paragraph about the place. Then have them write a paragraph describing what it might be like in 50 years if acid rain continues. In class, discuss ideas for helping to slow or halt acid rain. The discussion should focus on ways individuals can practice conservation so as to reduce the emission of pollutants.

ONLINE CONNECTION

Direct students to www.ec.gc.ca/acidrain/kids.html for a "kids corner" about acid rain and the pH scale. The site is maintained by Canada's Ministry of the Environment.

IN THE ENVIRONMENT

Refer students to Appendix A on pages 372–377 for information about alternative energy sources. Have students choose a fossil fuel and gather information about where the fuel is found and how it is accessed. Ask them to explore the impact that accessing the fuel has on the environment and whether fuel companies must do any remediation work after removing the fuel from the ground.

Lesson 5 Review Answers

1. acid 2. base 3. acid 4. base 5. base
6. base 7. base 8. acid 9. acid 10. acid

Achievements in Science

Have students read the Achievements in Science feature on page 142. To check comprehension, ask the following questions:

- What is a polymer? *(a giant molecule made of thousands of smaller molecules chemically bonded together in a long chain)*
- What natural fiber inspired Wallace Carothers to create a useful synthetic fiber? *(silk)*
- What atoms make up the repeating polymer chain in nylon? *(carbon, hydrogen, and oxygen atoms)*

PRONUNCIATION GUIDE

Use this list to help students pronounce the difficult words in this lesson. Refer to the pronunciation key on the Chapter Planning Guide for the sounds of these symbols.

polymer (pol´ ə mər)

hexamethylenediamine
(hek sə´ me thə lēn di ə mēn)

Portfolio Assessment

Sample items include:
- Graphic organizers for acids and bases
- Student plans for safe storage of cleaning supplies
- Lesson 5 Review answers

Lesson 5   REVIEW

Write on your paper whether each of the following is a property of an acid or a base.

1. Tastes sour
2. Is slippery
3. Has a pH of 3
4. Has a pH of 11
5. Contains the OH radical
6. Tastes bitter
7. Turns litmus from red to blue
8. Contains hydrogen
9. Turns litmus from blue to red
10. Reacts with a metal to produce hydrogen

Achievements in Science

Nylon

In the late 1920s, Wallace H. Carothers began experimenting with polymers. Polymers are giant molecules made of thousands of smaller molecules. The small molecules are identical to each other and are chemically bonded to each other. The chemically bonded molecules form a chain. Carothers had studied silk, a natural polymer. He understood that the new fiber needed to have the same properties as silk. Carothers began making polymers that were longer than any that had ever been made before.

In 1935, Carothers combined hexamethylenediamine and adipic acid to make a new fiber. This fiber, which chemists called Fiber 66, was stronger and more elastic than silk. Fiber 66 became known as nylon. Nylon is a synthetic, or manmade, polymer. Each molecule has a polymer chain of repeating molecules made of carbon, hydrogen, and oxygen atoms.

The production of nylon began in 1938. The first products made from nylon—toothbrushes—were introduced in 1939. Nylon stockings also appeared on the market in 1939. Today carpets, clothes, parachutes, tires, and thread are among the many products made of nylon.

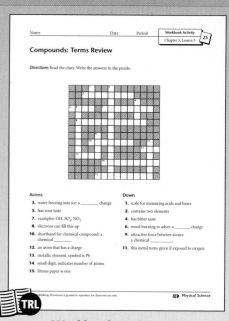

Lab Manual 19, pages 1–2

Workbook Activity 25

INVESTIGATION

5-2

Identifying Acids and Bases

Materials

- safety glasses
- marker
- 8 small paper cups
- spoon
- aspirin tablet
- baking soda
- white vinegar
- lemon juice
- weak ammonia solution
- soap
- soft drink
- milk of magnesia
- red-cabbage juice
- graduated cylinder
- litmus paper

Purpose

Read the substances listed in the data table. Can you identify which substances are acids and which are bases? In this investigation, you will use an indicator to test for acids and bases.

Procedure

1. Copy the data table on a sheet of paper.

Substance	Color After Cabbage Juice Is Added	Acid or Base
baking soda		base
vinegar		acid
lemon juice		
weak ammonia		
aspirin		
soap		
soft drink		
milk of magnesia		

2. Put on your safety glasses.

3. Use a marker to label each cup with the name of one substance from the table. Use these labels: baking soda (base), vinegar (acid), lemon juice, weak ammonia solution, aspirin, soap, soft drink, and milk of magnesia.

4. Add a small amount of each substance to the cup labeled with its name. Use a spoon to crush the aspirin tablet before adding it to the cup.

Compounds   Chapter 5   **143**

SAFETY ALERT

- Remind students to keep their safety glasses on at all times and to keep their hands away from their mouths and eyes while working with the substances.
- Remind students that they are not to taste any of the solutions.
- Tell students not to inhale vapors from the ammonia.
- Provide sufficient ventilation. The ammonia and cabbage juice have strong odors.
- Have students wash their hands with soap and water when finished.
- Keep paper towels on hand so that spills can be wiped up immediately.

The Purpose portion of the student investigation begins with a question to draw them into the activity. Encourage students to read the investigation steps and formulate their own questions before beginning the investigation. This investigation will take approximately 45 minutes to complete. Students will use these process and thinking skills: observing, collecting, and interpreting data; collecting information; and drawing conclusions.

Preparation

- Prepare the cabbage juice a day ahead of time. To make about 500 mL of cabbage juice, slice a small head of red cabbage. Place the sliced cabbage into a pan and cover it with water. Bring the water to a boil and then turn down the heat and cover the pan. Allow the mixture to simmer about 20 minutes. Turn off the heat and allow the contents to cool. Pour the contents through a sieve, keeping the cabbage juice.

- You can use either fresh, frozen, or bottled lemon juice. One lemon will yield about 25–30 mL juice.

- Dilute the ammonia, using about 10 parts water to 1 part cleaning ammonia.

- Use any kind of liquid soap. You can dilute the soap, using 5 parts water to 1 part soap.

- Use a clear soft drink, such as a lemon-lime flavor. Be sure it's not flat.

- Students may use Lab Manual 20 to record their data and answer the questions.

Procedure

- Check that all students have put on their safety glasses.

- Suggest students work in groups of four. Assign the following division of labor: students A and B label the cups; students C and D collect the samples; student A crushes the aspirin and adds it to the cup; student B adds cabbage juice to the baking soda; student C adds cabbage juice to the vinegar; and student D adds cabbage juice to the remaining cups. All students should make and record observations, record data, answer questions, and clean up.

Continued on page 144

Compounds   Chapter 5   **143**

Continued from page 143

- Be sure students understand that when cabbage juice is added to any acid, the resulting liquid will turn a color similar to that produced when cabbage juice is added to vinegar. Make sure students properly record the information for vinegar.

- By the same token, make sure students properly record the color of the cabbage juice when added to the baking soda and use this information to check for bases in other substances.

Results

The baking soda, ammonia, soap, and milk of magnesia are basic and will turn the cabbage juice blue or green. The vinegar, lemon juice, aspirin, and soft drink are acidic and will turn the cabbage juice red.

Questions and Conclusions Answers

1. Vinegar, lemon juice, aspirin, and the soft drink are acids.

2. Baking soda, ammonia, soap, and milk of magnesia are bases.

3. Yes, some bases have a higher pH than others. The color is deeper in solutions than have bases with higher pH.

Explore Further Answers

To organize and interpret the data, students should add the following columns to the right of the existing columns in their data charts: column 4, headed *Litmus Color;* column 5, headed *Acid or Base.* Have students match the color of the litmus paper with the scale that accompanies long-range litmus paper. Students will be able to read the pH of each substance. If the litmus tests produce any discrepancies, have students retest with the litmus paper. If the second testing repeats the discrepancy, have students speculate about the reasons for the discrepancy. *(Students may note that the litmus paper test is probably more exact than the cabbage juice test. Or they may guess that they could have made a mistake in the original investigation.)* Ask students what they learned from the retesting experience. *(Sometimes to obtain accurate, reliable data, you have to test several times to determine if the results repeat.)*

5. The cabbage juice will be the acid-base indicator. Record the color of the cabbage juice in the data table.

6. Use the graduated cylinder to measure 20 mL of cabbage juice. Add the cabbage juice to the cup labeled baking soda (base). Stir. Notice the color of the liquid in the cup. Record this color in the data table. Baking soda is a base. Any substance that changes to a color similar to the liquid in the baking soda cup after you add cabbage juice is a base.

7. Add 20 mL of cabbage juice to the vinegar (acid) cup. Record the results in the data table. Vinegar is an acid. Any substance that changes to a color similar to the liquid in the vinegar cup after you add cabbage juice is an acid.

8. Add 20 mL of cabbage juice to each of the remaining cups and stir. Determine whether each cup contains an acid or a base. Record your results.

Questions and Conclusions

1. Which of the substances are acids?

2. Which of the substances are bases?

3. Are some bases stronger than others? Explain your answer.

Explore Further

Use a piece of long-range litmus paper to test each substance. Record your results. How do your results compare with your previous results for each substance?

Assessment

Check data tables to be sure that students have recorded the correct observations for the vinegar and baking soda. *(The vinegar liquid should be red; the baking soda liquid should be blue or green.)* Also check answers to the questions to be sure students have identified the acids and bases correctly. You might include the following items from this investigation in student portfolios:

- Investigation 5-2 data table

- Answers to Questions and Conclusions and Explore Further sections

| Name | | Date | Period | **Lab Manual** Chapter 5 | 20 |

5-2 **Identifying Acids and Bases**

Use with Investigation 5-2, pages 143–144.

Purpose Read the substances listed in the data table. Can you identify which substances are acids and which are bases? In this investigation, you will use an indicator to test for acids and bases.

Substance	Color After Cabbage Juice Is Added	Acid or Base
baking soda		base
vinegar		acid
lemon juice		
weak ammonia		
aspirin		
soap		
soft drink		
milk of magnesia		

Questions and Conclusions

1. Which of the substances are acids?

2. Which of the substances are bases?

3. Are some bases stronger than others? Explain your answer.

Explore Further

Use a piece of long-range litmus paper to test each substance. Record your results. How do your results compare with your previous results for each substance?

Publishing. Permission is granted to reproduce for classroom use only. ◆ **Physical Science**

Lab Manual 20

Chapter 5 SUMMARY

- A compound forms when two or more elements combine. A chemical change takes place when elements combine to form a compound. In a chemical change, new substances with new chemical properties are formed.

- A physical change is a change in which the appearance (physical properties) of a substance changes but its chemical properties stay the same.

- Molecules of the same compound always contain the same elements. The atoms in the molecules of the same compound always combine in the same numbers.

- An electron moves in a certain energy level around the nucleus of an atom. Each energy level can hold only a certain number of electrons. Electrons fill the energy levels in order.

- Different elements have electrons in different numbers of levels. Atoms share, borrow, or lend electrons to other atoms in order to form compounds.

- An atom that has a charge is called an ion. Ions with opposite charges attract each other.

- A chemical formula is used to show what kinds of atoms and how many atoms of each kind are in a compound.

- A radical is a group of elements that behaves as if it were one element.

- In naming a compound, use the name of the first element and the name of the second element with the ending changed to -ide.

- Acids are compounds that contain hydrogen, react with metals to form hydrogen, and have a sour taste.

- Bases are slippery compounds that contain the hydroxyl radical, and have a bitter taste.

- Indicators can be used to identify acids and bases.

Science Words		
acid, 138	chemical formula, 129	pH, 140
base, 139	energy level, 123	physical change, 119
binary compound, 134	indicator, 139	radicals, 131
chemical bond, 127	ion, 127	subscript, 130
chemical change, 118		

Chapter 5 Summary

Have volunteers read aloud each Summary item on page 145. Ask volunteers to explain the meaning of each item. Direct students' attention to the Science Words box on the bottom of page 145. Have them read and review each term and its definition.

Chapter 5 Review

Use the Chapter Review to prepare students for tests and to reteach content from the chapter.

Chapter 5 Mastery Test TRL

The Teacher's Resource Library includes two parallel forms of the Chapter 5 Mastery Test. The difficulty level of the two forms is equivalent. You may wish to use one form as a pretest and the other form as a posttest.

Review Answers

Vocabulary Review

1. indicator **2.** physical change **3.** pH **4.** acid **5.** base **6.** ion **7.** chemical formula **8.** chemical change **9.** subscript **10.** chemical bond **11.** radicals

Concept Review

12. B **13.** A **14.** C **15.** D

Review Answers

Critical Thinking

16. Particular compounds always contain the same elements, and their atoms always combine in the same numbers. The name of binary compounds combines the name of the two elements, with the first name being the first name in the compound's formula and the second name being the second element in the formula with the ending changed to *-ide.* In compounds with more than two elements, the first name is the name of the first element in the formula and the second name varies according to the radical the formula contains. **17.** A physical change is a change in appearance but not in the chemical makeup of the substance. A chemical change produces one or more new substances that have new chemical properties. **18.** Energy levels are the leveled spaces in which electrons move around the nucleus of an atom. Electrons fill energy levels in a set order.

Teacher Alert

Because of limited space, not all of the vocabulary terms appear in the Vocabulary Review section. These terms are not covered in the section.

binary compound   energy level

Chapter 5 REVIEW

Word Bank
- acid
- base
- chemical bond
- chemical change
- chemical formula
- indicator
- ion
- pH
- physical change
- radicals
- subscript

Vocabulary Review

Choose the word or words from the Word Bank that best complete each sentence. Write the answers on a sheet of paper.

1. A(n) ____________ changes color in an acid or a base.

2. In a(n) ____________, a substance's appearance changes but its chemical properties do not.

3. A(n) ____________ tells whether a substance is an acid or a base.

4. A(n) ____________ reacts with metals to produce hydrogen.

5. A compound that contains the hydroxyl (OH) radical is a ____________.

6. A(n) ____________ is an atom that has either a positive or a negative charge.

7. A(n) ____________ tells the kinds of atoms and how many are in a compound.

8. A(n) ____________ produces one or more new substances with new chemical properties.

9. A(n) ____________ tells the number of atoms of an element in a compound.

10. A(n) ____________ is the attractive force that holds atoms together.

11. A group of two or more atoms that act like one atom are ____________.

Concept Review

Choose the best answer to each question. Write the letter of the answer on your paper.

12. Which of the following is *not* a physical change?
- **A** painting a wall
- **B** developing film
- **C** boiling water
- **D** shredding cheese

Name   Date   Period   **Mastery Test A, Page 1** Chapter 5

Chapter 5 Mastery Test A

Part A Read each sentence. Write the letter of the correct answer on the line.

____ **1.** Which of the following would result in a chemical change?
A boiling water **B** burning wood **C** tearing paper **D** melting wax

____ **2.** Hydrogen's one electron is found in the ________ energy level.
A K **B** L **C** M **D** N

____ **3.** A group of two or more atoms that act like one atom are called ________.
A electron **B** subscript **C** radicals **D** binary compound

____ **4.** Which of the following compounds has 5 atoms?
A $Ca(OH)_3$ **B** CH_4 **C** NaCl **D** H_2O

____ **5.** A sodium ion has a positive charge because it has ________.
A more electrons than protons **B** no electrons **C** the same number of electrons and protons **D** more protons than electrons

Part B Classify each of the following as an acid or a base. Write *A* on the line if it is an acid. Write *B* on the line if it is a base.

________ **6.** H_3BO_3
________ **7.** HCl
________ **8.** pH 13
________ **9.** $Ca(OH)_2$
________ **10.** $Mg(OH)_2$
________ **11.** H_2SO_4
________ **12.** NaOH
________ **13.** KOH
________ **14.** slippery
________ **15.** H_2CO_3
________ **16.** tastes sour
________ **17.** $HC_2H_3O_2$
________ **18.** OH radical
________ **19.** $Al(OH)_3$
________ **20.** red litmus

©AGS Publishing. Permission is granted to reproduce for classroom use only.   Physical Science

TRL

Name   Date   Period   **Mastery Test A, Page 2** Chapter 5

Chapter 5 Mastery Test A, continued

Part C Write a short answer for each question.

21. Describe compounds.

22. Explain how compounds are formed.

23. What does the information in a chemical formula mean?

24. Tell how the compound CaCl, which has two elements, is named.

25. How are compounds with more than two elements named?

©AGS Publishing. Permission is granted to reproduce for classroom use only.   Physical Science

TRL

Chapter 5 Mastery Test A

13. Where do compounds with more than one radical appear in a chemical formula?
   A in parentheses   C at the beginning
   B at the end   D as a subscript

14. Which of the following does not describe an acid?
   A tastes sour   C feels slippery
   B contains hydrogen   D turns litmus from blue to red

15. Which of the following substances is not a base?
   A household cleaner, which has a pH of 10
   B lye, which has a pH of 13
   C liquid soap, which has a pH of 8
   D lemon juice, which has a pH of 2

Critical Thinking

Write the answer to each of these questions on your paper.

16. Describe the characteristics of compounds and explain how compounds are named.

17. Explain the difference between a chemical change and a physical change.

18. Describe the energy levels in an atom. Explain how electrons fill energy levels and what happens to electrons when atoms form compounds.

19. Look at the figure of the compound calcium fluoride. Explain what the figure shows.

20. When you digest food, your body changes the food into nutrients. The nutrients are carried through your bloodstream to your body cells. What type(s) of changes happen to the food in your mouth and your stomach?

Calcium fluoride

Compounds   Chapter 5   147

The level closest to the nucleus is filled first. The level farthest from the nucleus is filled last. When atoms form compounds, they share, lend, or borrow electrons from their outermost energy level. 19. The calcium gives up two electrons—one to each fluorine atom to form the chemical compound calcium fluoride. 20. A physical change takes place in the mouth and stomach as food is broken down into smaller pieces. A chemical change also takes place in the mouth and stomach and the small intestine with the action of enzymes and hydrochloric acid.

ALTERNATIVE ASSESSMENT

Alternative Assessment items correlate to the student Goals for Learning at the beginning of this chapter.

■ Ask students to write a description of hydrogen peroxide as a compound.

■ Have students give a demonstration of the bonding of Na and Cl ions. Have them use plastic foam balls to represent the ions. Encourage them to use a black marker to label the ions and their electrical charges.

■ Have students choose a formula with at least one subscript. Prompt them to illustrate the formula using manipulatives, such as coins, to represent the various atoms.

■ Write element names on identical slips of paper. Use names from the first column in the chart on page 134. Have participants draw the slips. Tell each student to write the name (1) as it would appear as the first half of a compound name; and (2) as it would appear as the second half. Have students trade slips and continue the activity.

■ Present the following scenario: "You are given two unknown substances and are told that either one could be a base or an acid. You can touch the substances but are strictly prohibited from tasting them. In addition to the substances, you receive a lump of metal." Ask students to write a paragraph explaining how they could test the substances to determine if they are acids or bases.

Chapter 5 Mastery Test B

Compounds   Chapter 5   147

Chapter

6

Planning Guide

How Matter Changes

		Student Pages	Vocabulary	Lesson Review
Lesson 1	What Is a Reaction?	150–154	✔	✔
Lesson 2	Using Chemical Equations to Show Reactions	155–159	✔	✔
Lesson 3	Synthesis and Decomposition Reactions	160–163	✔	✔
Lesson 4	Single- and Double-Replacement Reactions	164–168	✔	✔

Chapter Activities

Student Text
Science Center

Teacher's Resource Library
Community Connection 6: Chemical
   Reactions in Photography

Assessment Options

Student Text
Chapter 6 Review

Teacher's Resource Library
Chapter 6 Mastery Tests A and B

	Student Text Features								Teaching Strategies						Learning Styles						Teacher's Resource Library				
	Achievements in Science	Science at Work	Science in Your Life	Investigation	Science Myth	Note	Technology Note	Did You Know	Science Integration	Science Journal	Cross-Curricular Connection	Online Connection	Teacher Alert	Applications (Home, Career, Community, Global, Environment)	Auditory/Verbal	Body/Kinesthetic	Interpersonal/Group Learning	Logical/Mathematical	Visual/Spatial	LEP/ESL	Workbook Activities	Alternative Workbook Activities	Lab Manual	Resource File	Self-Study Guide
			152	153	150				151		153			151			152			151	26	26	21, 22		✔
	159					✔	✔	157		158	157	158	156	158		157			156		27	27		12	✔
		163				✔	✔	162	162					161			162	162			28	28	23		✔
	166		167	165				164		165	166			165	165						29	29	24	13	✔

Pronunciation Key

a	hat	e	let	ī	ice	ô	order	ù	put	sh	she	ə { a in about
ā	age	ē	equal	o	hot	oi	oil	ü	rule	th	thin	e in taken
ä	far	ėr	term	ō	open	ou	out	ch	child	ŦH	then	i in pencil
â	care	i	it	ȯ	saw	u	cup	ng	long	zh	measure	o in lemon
												u in circus

Alternative Workbook Activities

The Teacher's Resource Library (TRL) contains a set of lower-level worksheets called Alternative Workbook Activities. These worksheets cover the same content as the regular Workbook Activities but are written at a second-grade reading level.

Skill Track Software

Use the Skill Track Software for Physical Science for additional reinforcement of this chapter. The software program allows students using AGS textbooks to be assessed for mastery of each chapter and lesson of the textbook. Students access the software on an individual basis and are assessed with multiple-choice items.

Chapter 6:
How Matter Changes
pages 148–171

Lessons

**Skill Track Software
for Physical Science**

Teacher's Resource Library TRL

Workbook Activities 26–29

Alternative Workbook Activities
26–29

Lab Manual 21–24

Community Connection 6

Resource File 12–13

Chapter 6 Self-Study Guide

Chapter 6 Mastery Tests A and B

Chapters 1–6 Midterm Mastery Test

(Answer Keys for the Teacher's
Resource Library begin on page 402
of the Teacher's Edition. The
Materials List for the Lab Manual
activities begins on page 419.)

Science Center

Allocate classroom space for a visual
display titled "Chemical Reactions." Have
students collect and exhibit examples of
chemical reactions throughout their
study of Chapter 6. The examples might
include formulas, models, pictures,
drawings, and actual products resulting
from chemical reactions. With each
example they display, students should
provide an index card with information
that describes the reaction or product.

Community Connection 6

Chapter

6 How Matter Changes

When cool, autumn weather arrives, the leaves on many trees change color. Leaves, like the ones in the photograph, turn from green to brilliant red, yellow, and orange. What is happening in the leaves to cause this dramatic change? Different types of chemical reactions are taking place. Some compounds are breaking down. New compounds are forming. In Chapter 6, you will learn about different types of chemical reactions. You also will learn how to read the equations scientists use to describe chemical reactions.

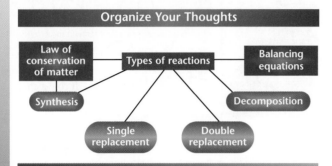

Organize Your Thoughts

Law of conservation of matter — Types of reactions — Balancing equations

Synthesis

Single replacement

Double replacement

Decomposition

Goals for Learning

◆ To explain what a reaction is

◆ To describe what occurs when something dissolves

◆ To state the law of conservation of matter

◆ To interpret and write balanced chemical equations

◆ To name and explain the four main types of chemical reactions

149

Introducing the Chapter

Have students describe what they see in the photo on page 148. Encourage them to share what they know about color of leaves and why leaves of some plants change colors in the autumn. Then read aloud the introductory paragraph on page 149. Point out that the green pigment in the leaves is broken down through chemical reactions. This reveals the other colors in the leaves.

List the following terms from the chapter on the board: *chemical reaction, mixture,* and *solution*. Ask students to tell what they know about the terms. Record their comments on the board. Help them identify how mixtures and solutions are alike and different. Provide examples, such as *I made a mixture of raisins and nuts for a snack. This is a solution of table salt and water.* Ask students whether the example of a mixture and a solution are also examples of chemical reactions. Tell them they will find out the answer to that question as they read about changes in matter.

Notes and Technology Notes

Ask volunteers to read the notes that appear in the margins throughout the chapter. Then discuss them with the class.

TEACHER'S RESOURCE

The AGS Teaching Strategies in Science Transparencies may be used with this chapter. The transparencies add an interactive dimension to expand and enhance the *Physical Science* program content.

CAREER INTEREST INVENTORY

The AGS Harrington-O'Shea Career Decision-Making System-Revised (CDM) may be used with this chapter. Students can use the CDM to explore their interests and identify careers. The CDM defines career areas that are indicated by students' responses on the inventory.

Name _____ Date _____ Period _____ *SELF-STUDY GUIDE*

Chapter 6: How Matter Changes

Goal 6.1 *To explain what a reaction is*

Date	Assignment	Score
	1. Read page 150.	

Comments:

Goal 6.2 *To describe what occurs when something dissolves*

Date	Assignment	Score
	2. Read page 151.	
	3. Complete the Lesson 1 Review on page 152.	
	4. Complete Workbook Activity 26.	
	5. Complete Investigation 6-1 on pages 153–154.	

Comments:

Goal 6.3 *To state the law of conservation of matter*

Date	Assignment	Score
	7. Read pages 155–156.	

Comments:

Goal 6.4 *To interpret and write balanced chemical equations*

Date	Assignment	Score
	9. Read pages 157–158.	
	10. Complete the Lesson 2 Review on page 159.	
	11. Complete Workbook Activity 27.	

Comments:

©AGS Publishing. Permission is granted to reproduce for classroom use only.　　　 ● Physical Science

---

Name _____ Date _____ Period _____ *SELF-STUDY GUIDE*

Chapter 6: How Matter Changes, continued

Goal 6.5 *To name and explain the four main types of chemical reactions*

Date	Assignment	Score
	12. Read pages 160–162.	
	13. Complete the Lesson 3 Review on page 163.	
	14. Complete Workbook Activity 28.	
	15. Read pages 164–165.	
	16. Complete the Lesson 4 Review on page 166.	
	17. Complete Workbook Activity 29.	
	18. Complete Investigation 6-2 on pages 167–168.	
	19. Read the Chapter 6 Summary on page 169.	
	20. Complete the Chapter 6 Review on pages 170–171.	

Comments:

Student's Signature _____ Date _____

Instructor's Signature _____ Date _____

©AGS Publishing. Permission is granted to reproduce for classroom use only.　　　 ● Physical Science

TRL   TRL

Chapter 6 Self-Study Guide

Lesson at a Glance

Chapter 6 Lesson 1

Overview This lesson introduces chemical reactions and solutions.

Objectives

- To explain a reaction
- To explain the difference between solutions, solutes, and solvents

Student Pages 150–154

Teacher's Resource Library **TRL**

Workbook Activity 26

Alternative Workbook Activity 26

Lab Manual 21–22

Vocabulary

chemical reaction	solute
dissolve	solution
mixture	solvent

Science Background

Any material can be classified as either a pure substance or a mixture. A pure substance is either an element or a compound. A mixture is made up of two or more substances that can be separated by physical means. The substances in mixtures are not chemically combined. The vast majority of materials on Earth are mixtures. Because mixtures can be combined in any proportion, the number of different mixtures is almost infinite. Examples of mixtures include most fabrics, soil, perfumes, dental fillings, and salad dressing.

Many mixtures vary in composition from sample to sample. Two samples of soil will not have the same proportion of materials. Mixtures with a composition that varies from one sample to another are called heterogeneous mixtures. Some mixtures do not differ from sample to sample. Their proportions remain the same. These kinds of mixtures are called homogeneous mixtures. Examples of homogeneous mixtures are soft drinks, tea, and glass. Solutions are homogeneous mixtures.

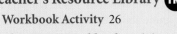 **Warm-Up Activity**

Produce a simple chemical reaction in front of the class. Drop a small piece of chalk or some eggshells into a container of vinegar. Have students describe what they

observe. Tell students that they just observed a chemical reaction. (Vinegar is a solution containing acetic acid. The acetic acids react with the calcium carbonate in the eggshells or chalk to produce carbon dioxide gas. The carbon dioxide forms the bubbles that students observe.)

PRONUNCIATION GUIDE

Use the pronunciation shown here to help students pronounce a difficult word in this lesson. Refer to the pronunciation key on the Chapter Planning Guide for the sounds of the symbols.

alchemist (al´ kə mist)

Objectives

After reading this lesson, you should be able to

- explain a reaction.
- explain the difference between solutions, solutes, and solvents.

Chemical reaction

A chemical change in which elements are combined or rearranged

Mixture

A combination of substances in which no reaction takes place

Science Myth

Air and oxygen are the same thing.

Fact: Air is a mixture of a number of substances. Oxygen makes up only 21 percent of air. Air contains mostly nitrogen. Water vapor and a very small amount of other gases are also part of air.

Hundreds of years ago, early scientists known as alchemists tried to change different materials into gold. Imagine being able to change iron or lead into solid gold!

Alchemists were early scientists who tried to turn other materials into gold.

Unfortunately for the alchemists, they never succeeded. Today, scientists know that chemically changing one element into another is not possible. But during a chemical change, elements can be combined to form compounds. The elements in compounds can be rearranged to form new compounds. When elements combine or rearrange, they are said to react. The process is called a **chemical reaction.** For some reactions, it is necessary to heat the substances. And some substances must be mixed with water for a chemical reaction to take place.

Substances do not always react when combined. Many elements and compounds can be mixed together and nothing at all happens. A **mixture** is formed when substances are combined and no reaction takes place. When you stir sugar and cinnamon together, you form a mixture.

150 Chapter 6   How Matter Changes

Science Myth

Ask a volunteer to read the myth portion (first sentence) of the Science Myth feature on page 150. Then have another volunteer read the fact portion of the feature. Air is made up not only of gases but also of solid particles. These are called aerosols and come from sources such as plant pollen, fires, and car exhaust. Aerosols gradually fall to earth or get washed away by precipitation.

Dissolving

Many reactions take place only when the substances have been dissolved in other liquids. To **dissolve** means to break up substances into individual atoms or molecules. An example of dissolving occurs when sugar is placed in water. The sugar mixes with the water and seems to disappear. But the sugar is still there. The pieces of the sugar have been broken down into tiny particles—molecules.

When a substance is thoroughly dissolved in another, the result is a mixture called a **solution.** The substance that dissolves is called the **solute.** When you dissolve sugar in water, the solute is sugar. A substance that is capable of dissolving one or more other substances is a **solvent.** In the sugar-water solution, water is the solvent. Can you think of other examples of solutions, solutes, and solvents?

Types of Solutions		
Substance (solute)	Dissolved in (solvent)	Examples
liquid	liquid	alcohol in water
	gas	water vapor in air
	solid	ether in rubber
gas	liquid	club soda in water (CO_2 in water)
	gas	air (nitrogen, oxygen, other gases)
	solid	hydrogen in palladium
solid	liquid	salt in water
	gas	iodine vapor in air
	solid	brass (copper and zinc)

A solution does not always have to be a solid dissolved in a liquid. Solutions can also be formed by dissolving substances in solids and gases. The table above gives some examples of solutions.

2 Teaching the Lesson

Write the vocabulary terms on the board. As students read the lesson, have them make a concept map showing the relationship among the terms. Students might add other terms as needed.

Reinforce the idea that when mixtures are formed, no chemical reaction takes place.

Demonstrate the solubility of sugar in water. Have students fill a clean paper cup half-full of water. Tell them to add small amounts of sugar, while stirring with a straw, until no more sugar will dissolve. Instruct students to taste some of the liquid from the top of the cup. **Safety Alert: Check health records to ensure that students can consume sugar before allowing them to taste the solution.** Then have students pour out most of the liquid. Have them taste the liquid again. Did students notice any difference between the two samples they tasted? Explain that students made a solution of sugar (solute) and water (solvent). Point out that in a solution, the particles of both substances are evenly distributed. For this reason, the sugar water should taste the same at the top of the sample and at the bottom.

Students may have difficulty identifying the solvent and solute in a solution. Tell them that the substance that seems to change or disappear is the solute. For example, when most substances are dissolved in water, they seem to disappear. These substances are solutes. Water is the solvent.

3 Reinforce and Extend

SCIENCE INTEGRATION

Technology

Refer students to Appendix A on pages 372–377 for information about alternative energy sources. Specifically, draw their attention to the Energy from Hydrogen Fuel section on page 376. A fuel cell generates electricity through a chemical reaction. Encourage students to find out more about fuel cells, how they work, and their impact on the environment.

AT HOME

Have students compile a list of five mixtures and five solutions found in their homes. Have students compile their lists into a class list. They might classify the examples into categories such as foods, cleaning substances, and clothing. Discuss the abundance and variety of mixtures and solutions found in the home.

LEARNING STYLES

LEP/ESL

Use a hands-on activity to reinforce lesson vocabulary. Provide students with the following materials: paper cup, water, sugar, sand, plastic spoon, and sand. Tell students to form a mixture (any combination of materials except sugar and water). Then have students make a solution (water and sugar). Have students identify the solvent and solute in their solution. *(solvent—water; solute—sugar)*

Lesson 1 Review Answers

1. The alchemists were trying to produce gold. No, they didn't succeed. **2.** The scientists can heat the substances or mix the substances with water. **3.** Salt is the solute, and water is the solvent. **4.** A chemical reaction is a chemical change in which elements are combined or rearranged. **5.** A mixture is a combination of substances, but no reaction takes place. A chemical reaction is a chemical change in which elements are combined or rearranged.

Science in Your Life

Have students take turns reading the feature aloud. Have anyone who has had a perm share the experience or invite a hairdresser to speak to the class about the process. Point out that hair straightening is a similar procedure. Have interested students find out how a chemical hair straightener works. Students might also want to research the science behind hair highlighting.

LEARNING STYLES

Interpersonal/ Group Learning

One common solution is salt water. The world has huge supplies of salt water in the oceans but many parts of the world often have a shortage of freshwater. For many years, people have worked on efficient ways to take the salt out of the solution so that people can drink seawater. Small desalination (salt-removing) plants are used in places such as the naval base in Guantanamo Bay, Cuba. The country of Kuwait has a larger desalination plant. Organize students into groups of two or three. Have the student groups hypothesize one or more ways to remove salt from water and experiment with these ways. Then have them research currently used methods and compare them to the results of their own work. Ask each group to share its findings with the class.

Portfolio Assessment

Sample items include:
• Concept map from Teaching the Lesson
• Lesson 1 Review answers

Write your answers to these questions in complete sentences on a sheet of paper.

1. What metal were the alchemists trying to produce? Did they succeed?

2. What are two things a scientist can do to cause some substances that are mixed together to react?

3. Suppose you dissolve salt in water. Name the solvent and the solute.

4. What is a chemical reaction?

5. How is a mixture different from a chemical reaction?

Science in Your Life

How does a permanent wave work?

To understand how a permanent wave works, you need to understand something about hair's biochemistry. Like almost everything in your body, hair is mostly protein. The proteins in hair—called keratin—are long chains of the amino acid cystine. Cystine is made of carbon, hydrogen, oxygen, nitrogen, and sulfur atoms.

In cystine, sulfur atoms can form a disulfide bond. Wherever this bond occurs in the protein chain, hair bends. All hair has some disulfide bonds. Many disulfide bonds in a protein chain make hair curly.

Permanent waves can be added to hair that doesn't have many disulfide bonds. Two chemical reactions take place to make straight hair curly. First, we need to break the existing disulfide bonds in hair. A chemical called a reducing agent breaks the disulfide bonds. This is the first chemical reaction. Next, we use curlers to give the hair a new shape. Then another chemical —a neutralizer—uses oxidation to make new disulfide bonds. This is the second chemical reaction. The longer the neutralizer is left on the hair, the curlier the hair will be when the curlers are removed, and the neutralizer is rinsed away. Now the protein in the hair has many new disulfide bonds—and lots of curls.

Lab Manual 21, pages 1–2

Workbook Activity 26

6-1 INVESTIGATION

Separating a Mixture

Investigation 6-1

Materials

- safety glasses
- spoon
- 2 g sand
- 2 g table salt (sodium chloride, NaCl)
- sheet of paper
- stirring rod
- graduated cylinder
- 200 mL water
- 2 beakers
- circular piece of filter paper or paper towel
- funnel

Purpose

Look at the materials listed in the data table. Can you predict which material will be the solvent? Which material will be the solute? In this investigation, you will separate a mixture through dissolving.

Procedure

1. Copy the data table on a sheet of paper.

Materials	Observations
salt	
sand	
mixture of salt and sand	
solution of salt, sand, and water	
filter paper	
sides of beaker	

2. Put on your safety glasses. Place about one spoonful of sand and one spoonful of salt in separate piles on a sheet of paper. Observe the appearance of the salt and the sand. Record your observations in the data table.

3. Use the stirring rod to thoroughly mix the salt with the sand. Describe the resulting mixture.

4. Using a graduated cylinder, measure 200 mL of water. Pour the water into a beaker.

5. Put the salt-sand mixture in the beaker with the water.

6. Stir the solution with the stirring rod. Observe the liquid in the beaker. Record your observations.

The Purpose portion of the student investigation begins with a question to draw them into the activity. Encourage students to read the investigation steps and formulate their own questions before beginning the investigation. The investigation will take approximately 30 minutes to complete. Students will use these process and thinking skills: observing; collecting, recording, and interpreting data; inferring; predicting; and communicating.

Preparation

- Use washed sand. It can be purchased at building-supply stores and nurseries. One cup per class will be enough.

- If you use paper towels for the filter, cut one five-inch circle per group. Coffee filters will also work.

- Plastic spoons or straws can be used in place of stirring rods.

- Plastic jars or cups can be used in place of the beakers.

- You can make funnels from plastic bottles if none are available. Cut the top off plastic bottles and use the inverted top as a funnel.

- You might provide hand lenses for observing the dry sand and salt.

- Students may use Lab Manual 22 to record their data and answer the questions.

Procedure

- You can have students work in groups of four. Student A places the sand and salt on the paper and, after all members of the group have observed the mixtures, pours them into the beaker of water. Student B measures the water and pours it into the beaker. Student C folds the filter paper and places it inside the funnel. Student D pours the liquid through the funnel.

- Do not use more than one teaspoon of salt, or some of it won't dissolve.

- Tell students to pour the liquid into the funnel slowly, or some may overflow into the beaker.

- To speed up evaporation, place the beaker with the solution in the sunlight or in a drying oven.

Continued on page 154

CROSS-CURRICULAR CONNECTION

Home Economics

Many of the foods students eat are mixtures. Challenge students to write recipes for mixtures of nutritious foods. Salads, soups, casseroles, sandwiches, and beverages make good mixtures. Compile student recipes into a class cookbook.

SAFETY ALERT

- Make sure students wear their safety glasses.
- Have paper towels ready for cleaning up spills.
- Caution students to avoid tasting the salt residue.

Continued from page 153

- Make sure students fold the filter paper correctly, or it will not filter properly.

- Students might have difficulty recognizing the crystals that form in the beaker as salt. To help with this task, have students recall what was originally mixed together. *(sand, salt, water)* Discuss what they think happened to each substance. Lead them to recognize that the substance in the beaker is salt.

Results

Depending on the type of sand, students should see the salt as crystals and the sand as very small pebbles. The salt will dissolve in the water, but the sand will not. Pouring the liquid through the filter only stops the sand. The salt solution passes through. The water will evaporate in several days, and the salt will crystallize in the beaker.

Questions and Conclusions Answers

1. The salt dissolved in the water, forming a solution.

2. The sand didn't dissolve. You can still see all the sand you added.

3. The salt was in the solution in the second beaker. It appeared later in the second beaker.

4. Sand remained on the filter paper.

5. Salt formed in the beaker.

6. Water is the solvent. Salt is the solute.

Explore Further Answers

Some students might suggest pouring the mixture into water to dissolve the sugar and then filtering out the iron filings. Other students might suggest using a magnet to pull out the iron filings.

Assessment

Check students' work to be sure they are making accurate and detailed observations. Check answers to the questions, particularly question 6, to make certain that students can identify the solvent and solute. You might include the following items from this investigation in student portfolios:

- Investigation 6-1 data table

- Answers to Questions and Conclusions and Explore Further sections

Fold paper in half

Fold again in half

Open into cone shape

Fit into funnel

7. Follow the steps shown in the figure. Fold the filter paper and put it in the funnel.

8. Hold the funnel over a second beaker. Slowly pour the solution from the first beaker into the funnel. Allow the second beaker to catch the liquid as it passes through the funnel.

9. Observe the filter paper. Record your observations.

10. Let the second beaker and its contents sit in a warm place for several days.

11. After all the liquid has evaporated, observe the sides of the beaker. Record your observations.

Questions and Conclusions

1. In steps 5 and 6, what happened to the salt when you added water to the mixture?

2. In step 6, did the sand dissolve? How do you know?

3. In step 9, where was the salt after you poured the solution into the second beaker? How do you know?

4. In step 9, which material remained on the filter paper?

5. In step 11, what substance formed in the beaker?

6. What is the solvent in this investigation? What is the solute?

Explore Further

Suppose you had a mixture of iron filings and sugar. How would you separate it? Write the procedure you would use.

Name _____ Date _____ Period _____ **Lab Manual** Chapter 6 **22**

6-1 **Separating a Mixture**
Use with Investigation 6-1, pages 153–154.

Purpose Look at the materials in the data table. Can you predict which material will be the solvent? Which material will be the solute? In this investigation, you will separate a mixture through dissolving.

Materials	Observations
salt	
sand	
mixture of salt and sand	
solution of salt, sand, and water	
filter paper	
sides of beaker	

Questions and Conclusions

1. In steps 5 and 6, what happened to the salt when you added water to the mixture?

2. In step 6, did the sand dissolve? How do you know?

3. In step 9, where was the salt after you poured the solution into the second beaker? How do you know?

4. In step 9, which material remained on the filter paper?

5. In step 11, what substance formed in the beaker?

6. What is the solvent in this investigation? What is the solute?

Explore Further

Suppose you had a mixture of iron filings and sugar. How would you separate it? Write the procedure you would use on another sheet of paper.

©AGS Publishing. Permission is granted to reproduce for classroom use only. **Physical Science**

Lab Manual 22

Objectives

After reading this lesson, you should be able to

◆ explain how a chemical equation describes a chemical reaction.

◆ balance chemical equations.

Chemical equation

A statement that uses symbols, formulas, and numbers to stand for a chemical reaction

Reactant

A substance that is altered in a chemical reaction

Product

A substance that is formed in a chemical reaction

You know that chemical symbols and formulas can be used to represent substances. You can also use these symbols to describe reactions. A **chemical equation** is a statement that uses symbols, chemical formulas, and numbers to stand for a chemical reaction. Look at the simple chemical equation below. The symbols and formulas describe the chemicals that are involved. Below the equation, you can see the description in words.

$$\text{Reactants} \qquad\qquad \text{Products}$$
$$\textbf{HCl} + \textbf{NaOH} \quad\longrightarrow\quad \textbf{NaCl} + \textbf{H}_2\textbf{O}$$

hydrogen chloride plus sodium hydroxide yields sodium chloride plus water

Notice that the arrow symbol ($\longrightarrow$) stands for "yields" or "makes." The chemicals on the left side of the arrow are called **reactants.** They are the substances that are reacting together. A reactant is a substance that is altered in a chemical reaction. The chemicals on the right side of the arrow are called **products.** A product is a substance that is formed in a chemical reaction. The product forms from the reactants. In the above example, HCl and NaOH are the reactants. The products are NaCl and H$_2$O.

Technology Note

Rubber used for most purposes is vulcanized. Before vulcanization, rubber products became soft in hot weather. In cold weather, they were brittle. Even at room temperature, rubber stuck to everything it touched and could not hold its shape. Vulcanized rubber is treated with sulfur and then heated. This chemical reaction produces rubber that is hard, strong, and elastic.

How Matter Changes   Chapter 6 **155**

Lesson at a Glance

Chapter 6 Lesson 2

Overview In this lesson, students learn how chemical equations describe a chemical reaction. In addition, students learn the basics of balancing chemical reactions, using coefficients.

Objectives

■ To explain how a chemical equation describes a chemical reaction

■ To balance chemical equations

Student Pages 155–159

Teacher's Resource Library (TRL)

Workbook Activity 27

Alternative Workbook Activity 27

Resource File 12

Vocabulary

balance
chemical equation
coefficient
law of conservation of matter
product
reactant

Science Background

During a chemical reaction, one or more substances are changed into one or more different substances. The atoms that make up a substance are rearranged. Chemical bonds are broken, and new bonds between atoms are formed. No new atoms are created.

Only the outer electrons of atoms, called valence electrons, take part in the bonding process during a chemical reaction. During chemical bonding, atoms either share or transfer electrons from one atom to another. Electrons are shared or transferred so that the resulting atoms have the same number of valence electrons as the nearest noble gas.

1 Warm-Up Activity

Write the following equation on the board: One house yields three bedrooms plus a garage. Have students make up symbols and rewrite the equation, using their symbols.

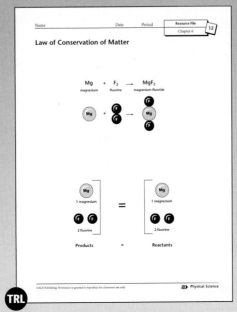

Resource File 12

How Matter Changes   Chapter 6 **155**

2 Teaching the Lesson

While reading this lesson, have students write one topic sentence for each paragraph. Discuss the sentences with students when they have finished reading the lesson.

Point out to students that in a chemical equation the arrow always points to the products. The use of models can help students visualize what is happening during chemical reactions. Have students copy the chemical reaction shown on page 156. Have them draw the models as shown below the reaction. Ask students to make similar models for the reactions in the table on page 159.

3 Reinforce and Extend

TEACHER ALERT

Students often confuse subscripts with coefficients. First, review the use of subscripts as discussed in Chapter 5. As an example, write on the board a chemical formula, such as H_2O. Have students identify the subscript in the formula and explain what it does. Then remind students that a coefficient refers to the symbol or radical that comes immediately after it. Enclose the H_2O example in parentheses. Write a coefficient before the parentheses—$2(H_2O)$. Tell students that the coefficient in the chemical formula is similar to a coefficient in a math problem that is multiplied by everything within the parentheses. But with science formulas, no parentheses are used.

LEARNING STYLES

Visual/Spatial

Provide students with wood toothpicks and small polystyrene balls. Ask them to use these materials to make models showing the chemical reaction illustrated in the diagram on page 156.

Law of conservation of matter

Matter cannot be created or destroyed in chemical and common physical changes

A chemical equation shows the rearrangement of atoms that happens after a chemical change.

Law of Conservation of Matter

The reactants present *before* a reaction can be quite different from the products present after the reaction. But the kinds of atoms do not change during the reaction. Different substances are formed, but the same atoms are there. The atoms are just rearranged. In the reaction below, magnesium and fluorine (the reactants) combine to form a new compound called magnesium fluoride. Notice how the atoms rearrange themselves.

$$Mg + F_2 \longrightarrow MgF_2$$

magnesium + fluorine → magnesium fluoride

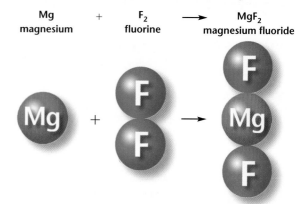

The same numbers and kinds of atoms are present before and after a reaction. Mass does not change during the reaction. The mass of the reactants equals the mass of the products. This fact illustrates the **law of conservation of matter.** The law states that matter cannot be created or destroyed in chemical and common physical changes. This law is sometimes called the law of conservation of mass.

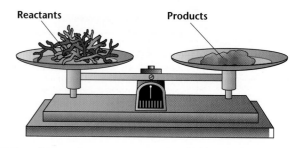

Reactants   Products

Balancing Equations

To satisfy the law of conservation of matter, a chemical equation must show the same number of each kind of atom on both sides of the equation. Scientists say that the equation must be **balanced.** To balance an equation means to keep the same number of each kind of atom on both sides of the equation.

Look at the following equation. It shows that hydrogen plus oxygen makes water.

$$H_2 + O_2 \longrightarrow H_2O$$

In a balanced equation, a coefficient of 1 usually is not written.

This equation is not balanced. Two oxygen atoms are shown on the left side of the equation. Only 1 oxygen atom is shown on the right. The left side of the equation has a total of 4 atoms, but the right side has only 3 atoms.

$$H_2 + O_2 \longrightarrow H_2O$$

$H_2 + O_2$	H_2O
H 2 atoms	H 2 atoms
O 2 atoms	O 1 atom
Total of 4 atoms	Total of 3 atoms

You can see that there are 4 atoms in the reactants and only 3 in the products. The law of conservation of matter says that atoms do not disappear in chemical reactions. You cannot change the formulas for the reactants or products.

To balance the equation, you can place numbers before the formulas. A number that is placed before a formula in a chemical equation is called a **coefficient.** A coefficient shows how many molecules or atoms are involved in the chemical reaction. For example, look at $2H_2O$. The 2 before H_2O means 2 water molecules.

You can change coefficients by changing the numbers of atoms. By writing $2H_2O$, you are saying that 4 atoms of hydrogen and 2 atoms of oxygen are in the products. If you write $3H_2O$, you are saying that 6 atoms of hydrogen and 3 atoms of oxygen are in the products.

Did You Know?

A pile of oily rags can ignite without coming in contact with a spark or a flame. Spontaneous combustion happens when chemical reactions in a substance create heat that cannot escape. The heat starts the reaction.

By placing a 2 in front of the H_2O, you have made the number of oxygen atoms equal on both sides of the equation. But the number of hydrogen atoms is not equal.

$$H_2 + O_2 \longrightarrow 2H_2O$$

H 2 atoms	H 4 atoms (2×2)
O 2 atoms	O 2 atoms (1×2)
Total of 4 atoms	Total of 6 atoms

You can see that there are 2 hydrogen atoms in the reactants. There are 4 hydrogen atoms in the product. Therefore, you need 2 more hydrogen atoms in the reactants. Again you can change the number of atoms by using a coefficient. You can balance the equation like this.

$$2H_2 + O_2 \longrightarrow 2H_2O$$

H 4 atoms	H 4 atoms
O 2 atoms	O 2 atoms
Total of 6 atoms	Total of 6 atoms

The equation is now balanced. Look at the figure below. The coefficients show that there are 2 molecules each of hydrogen and water. Since the oxygen has no coefficient, it means that there is 1 molecule. The equation tells you that whenever hydrogen and oxygen combine to form water, 2 molecules of hydrogen will combine with 1 molecule of oxygen to produce 2 molecules of water. The number of each kind of atom is the same before and after the reaction.

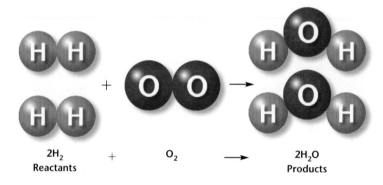

Lesson 2 REVIEW

1. Copy the table on a sheet of paper. Then complete the table. The first one is done for you.

Reaction	Reactants	Products
A Fe + S → FeS	Fe, S	FeS
B H_2SO_4 + Zn → $ZnSO_4$ + H_2		
C Mg + S → MgS		
D $AgNO_3$ + NaCl → $NaNO_3$ + AgCl		

2. Write the following chemical equations in words.

   A Mg + S ⟶ MgS   **B** Ba + S ⟶ BaS

Study the following equation. Then write your answers to the questions.

$$2Na + Cl_2 \longrightarrow 2NaCl$$

3. What are the reactants?

4. What is the product?

5. Is the equation balanced? Explain your answer.

Achievements in Science

Inexpensive Aluminum Processing

Aluminum is a light metal that carries electricity well and does not rust. It is the third most common element in the earth's crust. However, we cannot find aluminum in its pure form in nature. We must mine aluminum oxide from rocks, and that can be costly.

Scientists discovered a way to get larger amounts of aluminum oxide from rocks in the mid-1800s. The cost of aluminum dropped from $1,200 per kilogram in 1852 to $40 in 1859. Still, aluminum was too costly to be used a lot. It was so costly that, until the late1800s, aluminum was a semiprecious metal.

In 1885, chemists Charles Hall and Paul Heroult were 22 years old. The two chemists separately discovered an inexpensive way to process aluminum. The Hall-Heroult process involves dissolving aluminum oxide. It uses electricity to create a decomposition reaction that leaves pure aluminum precipitates. By 1909, the price of aluminum was $0.60 per kilogram. The Hall-Heroult process is still the only method for processing aluminum.

Lesson 2 Review Answers

1. A reactants: Fe, S; product: FeS **B** reactants: H_2SO_4, Zn; products: $ZnSO_4$, H_2 **C** reactants: Mg, S; product: MgS **D** reactants: $AgNO_3$, NaCl; products: $NaNO_3$, AgCl **2. A** magnesium plus sulfur yields magnesium sulfide. **B** barium plus sulfur yields barium sulfide. **3.** Na and Cl_2. **4.** NaCl **5.** Yes, the equation is balanced. For each kind of atom, the number of atoms is the same on the left and on the right side of the equation.

Achievements in Science

Have students take turns reading aloud the Achievements in Science feature on page 159. Explain that a *precipitate* is a solid that forms and settles out of a solution, usually sinking to the bottom. Students will learn more about precipitates in Lesson 4. Point out that aluminum is usually mixed with other elements to form aluminum alloys. Aluminum alloys are used in foil, wire, cans, cookware, and many parts of buildings such as gutters and roofs. Have students find out and report on the smelting process by which aluminum is separated from aluminum oxide.

PRONUNCIATION GUIDE

Use this list to help students pronounce the difficult words in this lesson. Refer to the pronunciation key on the Chapter Planning Guide for the sounds of these symbols.

decomposition (dē kom pə zish´ an)

semiprecious (sem´ i presh´ əs)

precipitate (pri sip´ ə tāt)

Portfolio Assessment

Sample items include:
• Equations from Warm-Up
• Topic sentences from Teaching the Lesson
• Lesson 2 Review answers

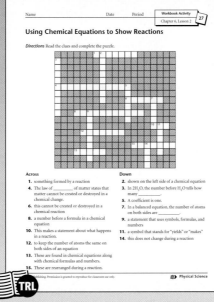

Workbook Activity 27

Lesson at a Glance

Chapter 6 Lesson 3

Overview In this lesson, students learn how to identify and predict synthesis and decomposition reactions.

Objectives

- To identify synthesis reactions
- To identify decomposition reactions

Student Pages 160–163

Teacher's Resource Library **TRL**

Workbook Activity 28

Alternative Workbook Activity 28

Lab Manual 23

Vocabulary

synthesis reaction
decomposition reaction

Science Background

During synthesis reactions, two or more elements combine to form a compound. There are two goals of synthetic chemistry. The first is to produce more of the chemicals already present in nature. The second goal of synthetic chemistry is to produce compounds not found naturally. Steel and plastics are examples of compounds formed during synthesis reactions but not found in nature.

During a decomposition reaction, a compound is broken down into two or more simpler substances. Ever since early humans discovered fire, decomposition reactions have been an important part of life. Combustion is one form of decomposition.

1 Warm-Up Activity

Write the following two reactions on the board: hamburger → amino acids + fatty acids; iron + oxygen gas → rust. Have students read the reactions. Then ask them to identify the reactants and the products in each reaction. *(reactants— hamburger, iron, and oxygen gas; products—amino acids, fatty acids, and rust)* Ask students how the reactions differ. Lead them to realize that in the first reaction, a single substance is broken down into two new substances; in the

---

Objectives

After reading this lesson, you should be able to

◆ identify synthesis reactions.

◆ identify decomposition reactions.

Synthesis reaction

A reaction in which elements combine to form a compound

Millions of different chemical reactions are possible. Even chemists cannot learn all of them. How can you make sense out of all those possibilities? It turns out that most reactions can be grouped into four major types. You will learn about two of these types of reactions in this lesson.

Synthesis Reactions

The first type of reaction is called a **synthesis reaction.** The word *synthesis* means "to combine parts." In a synthesis reaction, two or more elements combine to form a compound. An example of a synthesis reaction is combining iron and sulfur. Iron is a metal used in making steel. Sulfur is a yellow nonmetal that is used in making some medicines. You can see these two elements in the figures below.

Iron

Sulfur

Suppose you mix iron (in the form of slivers called filings) with sulfur powder. No reaction takes place. The combination of iron and sulfur is an example of a mixture. A mixture is formed when substances are simply stirred together and no new substance is formed.

Combustion is the chemical reaction that occurs when oxygen quickly combines with another substance. Combustion usually is a synthesis reaction and always produces heat and light.

In a mixture, the properties of the substances remain separate. In fact, you could separate the iron and sulfur in the mixture by using a magnet. The iron is attracted to a magnet, but the sulfur is not. The mixture is separated quite easily. The magnet pulls the iron away from the sulfur.

Now suppose you heat the iron and sulfur mixture. A reaction will occur. A new compound called iron sulfide (FeS) will form. The two elements have formed a compound. Therefore, the reaction is a synthesis. Iron sulfide has properties different from those of either iron or sulfur. When a magnet is placed near the iron sulfide, the compound will not be attracted to it.

Notice in the photo that the color of iron sulfide is gray-black. The yellow color of sulfur and the silvery color of iron are gone. The properties have changed because a new substance has formed.

The balanced chemical equation for this synthesis reaction appears below the three photos.

You can use a magnet to separate an iron and sulfur mixture.

Fe	+	S	$\longrightarrow$	FeS
Iron	plus	sulfur	yields	iron sulfide
(grey solid)		(yellow solid)		(grey-black solid)

How Matter Changes   Chapter 6   **161**

second reaction, two substances combine to form a single new substance.

2 Teaching the Lesson

Before students read the lesson, have them copy the two lesson vocabulary terms onto a sheet of paper. Tell students to leave room below each term to draw a diagram. As they read the lesson, have students make simple labeled diagrams that illustrate each type of reaction.

Discuss the meaning of the words *synthesis* and *decomposition* (*synthesis:* combining of parts into a whole; *decomposition:* separating a substance into what it is made of). Ask students to give everyday examples of decomposition and synthesis. For example, the building of a house or an office building would be a type of synthesis. The disassembly of a bicycle wheel for cleaning would be a type of decomposition.

Tell students that the reactants in a synthesis reaction can be two compounds joining to form a more complex compound or an element combining with a compound to form a different, more complex compound.

Explain to students that a synthesis reaction can usually be recognized by the formation of a single product. A decomposition reaction can be recognized by the presence of one reactant that produces two or more products.

Have students identify any synthesis or decomposition reactions in the Lesson 2 Review on page 159. *(There are no decomposition reactions and four synthesis reactions: 1A, 1C, 2A, and 2B.)*

3 Reinforce and Extend

GLOBAL CONNECTION

Iron is one of earth's most common and useful metals. Countries around the globe mine iron ore. Suggest that students identify 10 leading iron-mining countries. Ask them to prepare a graph that compares the amount of iron ore mined by the countries and a map locating the countries. Display their graphs and maps in the classroom.

IN THE ENVIRONMENT

Acid rain results from a synthesis reaction. Acid is produced when water vapor in the air reacts with sulfur dioxide or nitrogen oxides released into the air. Sulfur dioxide and nitrogen oxides are by-products of the burning of fossil fuels. Have students research information about acid rain. They should answer the following questions: What is acid rain? What causes it? What can acid rain do to the environment? How can acid rain be reduced?

Interpersonal/Group Learning

Rusting, an example of a synthesis reaction, can be a problem for car owners. Particularly in the presence of moisture, oxygen in the air combines with a metal often to produce a metal oxide, which appears as rust. Suggest that students work together to develop and perform an investigation to observe the production of rust. They might use steel wool and water in their investigation. **Safety Alert: Remind students to handle the steel wool carefully.** Ask students to prepare a brief written report outlining their investigation and noting the type of reaction that produces rust. Make sure they include the chemical equation for rust production in their report.

Did You Know?

Ask a volunteer to read the feature on page 162. Cast iron contains between 2 percent and 4 percent carbon and between 1 percent and 3 percent silicon. Point out that silicone, a compound made of silicon, carbon, and oxygen, is used to coat frying pans and baking pans. Suggest that interested students experiment with the help of an adult to compare the cooking qualities of a cast iron skillet and a skillet coated with a silicone product. Which cooks better? Which has better nonstick properties?

SCIENCE INTEGRATION

Biology

Many organisms act as decomposers. These organisms include bacteria and fungi. The decomposers play an important role in nature. Without them, dead animals and plants would accumulate on Earth. Decomposers allow the chemical compounds that are a part of every organism to be returned to the earth where they can be recycled. Have students research this role of decomposers.

Decomposition reaction

A reaction in which a compound breaks down into two or more simple substances

Did You Know?

A chemical reaction gives a cast iron frying pan a "seasoned" or slick surface. When you heat oil in the pan at high temperatures, a decomposition reaction occurs. Large carbon molecules decompose into small carbon molecules.

Decomposition Reactions

Sometimes in a chemical reaction a compound breaks down into two or more simple substances. This type of reaction is called a **decomposition reaction.** For example, sugar is a compound you are familiar with. Its formula is $C_6H_{12}O_6$. When you heat sugar, it breaks down into carbon (C) and water (H_2O). Carbon is a black solid. Water is a compound made of hydrogen and oxygen. The carbon and the water contain the same atoms that were in the sugar. The equation for the reaction is shown here.

$$C_6H_{12}O_6 \longrightarrow 6C + 6H_2O$$

| sugar (white solid) | carbon (black solid) | water (colorless liquid) |

Another example of a decomposition reaction occurs when the compound mercuric oxide is heated. The chemical equation for the reaction is shown here. The upward arrow ($\uparrow$) after the O_2 indicates that oxygen is a gas that is given off.

$$2HgO \longrightarrow 2Hg + O_2\uparrow$$

| mercuric oxide | mercury | oxygen |

Technology Note

Stainless steel is an alloy whose mass contains at least 12 percent chromium. Chromium gives stainless steel its resistance to rust and other types of corrosive chemical reactions. Knives, pots and pans, tableware, and sinks are among the household items that use stainless steel. Many automobile, airplane, and train parts also are made of stainless steel.

Logical/Mathematical

Write the following equations on the board. Have students identify each as a synthesis or decomposition reaction. $H_2F_2 \rightarrow H_2 + F_2$ *(decomposition);* $2NaCl \rightarrow 2Na + Cl_2$ *(decomposition);* $2SO_2 + O_2 \rightarrow 2SO_3$ *(synthesis);* $H_2O + CO_2 \rightarrow H_2CO_3$ *(synthesis)*

Lesson 3 REVIEW

Copy the following equations on a sheet of paper. Then tell if each is a synthesis reaction or a decomposition reaction.

1. $2MgO \longrightarrow 2Mg + O_2\uparrow$

2. $2Hg + O_2 \longrightarrow 2HgO$

3. $C + O_2 \longrightarrow CO_2$

4. $BaCl_2 \longrightarrow Ba + Cl_2$

5. $2H_2O \longrightarrow 2H_2 + O_2$

Write the products of the following synthesis reactions.

6. $2Na + Cl_2 \longrightarrow$ _____

7. $Mg + Cl_2 \longrightarrow$ _____

8. $CO + O_2 \longrightarrow$ _____

Complete the following decomposition reactions.

9. $CaCO_3 \longrightarrow$ _____ $+ CO_2$

10. $2FeO \longrightarrow$ _____ $+ O_2$

Science at Work

Food Technologist

Food technologists study the nature of foods. They experiment with new ingredients and new ways to use ingredients. Food technologists develop ways to process and to improve the quality of foods. They also test samples to make sure foods meet food laws and standards. Most often, food technologists work in a laboratory, often set up like a kitchen.

Most food technologists have a four-year degree in food science, biochemistry, or chemistry. To do research, an advanced degree is required.

Food technologists are creative. They have curiosity and good instincts about food. They also must be able to carry out tests and to work well under pressure.

Lesson 3 Review Answers

1. decomposition 2. synthesis 3. synthesis
4. decomposition 5. decomposition
6. $2NaCl$ 7. $MgCl_2$ 8. CO_3 9. CaO 10. $2Fe$

Science at Work

Have students take turns reading the Science at Work text aloud. Point out that food technologists work on projects such as producing less fattening cooking oils or more natural-tasting sugar substitutes. They also conduct studies such as analyzing the nutritional content of foods. Have students think about the kinds of foods or ingredients they would like to invent or other food topics they would like to explore as food technologists.

Portfolio Assessment

Sample items include:
• Diagrams of reactions from Teaching the Lesson
• Lesson 3 Review answers

Lab Manual 23, pages 1–2 | **Workbook Activity 28** | *How Matter Changes* Chapter 6 **163**

Lesson at a Glance

Chapter 6 Lesson 4

Overview This lesson introduces students to single-replacement and double-replacement reactions.

Objectives

- To identify single-replacement reactions
- To identify double-replacement reactions

Student Pages 164–168

Teacher's Resource Library

Workbook Activity 29

Alternative Workbook Activity 29

Lab Manual 24

Resource File 13

Vocabulary

double-replacement reaction
precipitate
single-replacement reaction

 Warm-Up Activity

Place a copper wire in a solution of silver nitrate. Allow the materials to stand for about one hour. Have students record observations every 15 minutes. They will notice that the solution turns blue and a silver material accumulates on the wire. Ask students to suggest explanations for what has happened. Accept all reasonable explanations. *(A single-replacement reaction takes place. The copper in the wire replaces the silver in the silver nitrate solution, forming silver and copper nitrate, which is blue.)*

 Teaching the Lesson

Before reading, have students write the names of the two types of reactions from this lesson on a sheet of paper, leaving space below each type for a diagram. As students read, have them make simple, labeled diagrams of each reaction type.

Tell students that a single-replacement reaction can be recognized by the presence of an element and a compound on both sides of the equation. A double-replacement reaction can be recognized

by the presence of two compounds on each side of the equation.

Students should tape labels on the pennies to represent atoms. Students can make models of chemical reactions. Assign groups of students several reactions from the Lesson 4 Review on page 166. Give the groups pennies, masking tape, and colored markers. Have groups represent each kind of atom in the reaction with a penny that is identified by a piece of tape with a dot of a particular color. By moving the pennies around, students can simulate reactions.

 Lesson 4 Single- and Double-Replacement Reactions

You now know about two kinds of reactions—synthesis reactions and decomposition reactions. Two other kinds of reactions are common.

Single-Replacement Reactions

Look at the photo below. It shows a container of a silver nitrate solution and a copper wire. Notice what happens when the copper wire is placed in the solution of silver nitrate. Silver metal forms on the wire. A chemical reaction has taken place. The equation for the reaction is shown here.

$$Cu + 2AgNO_3 \longrightarrow 2Ag + Cu(NO_3)_2$$

Notice that copper (Cu) has replaced the silver (Ag) in the silver nitrate. A new compound, copper nitrate—$Cu(NO_3)_2$—is formed. The silver is set free. That is the kind of change that occurs in a **single-replacement reaction.** A single-replacement reaction is a reaction in which one element replaces another in a compound.

Objectives

After reading this lesson, you should be able to

- identify single-replacement reactions.
- identify double-replacement reactions.

Single-replacement reaction

A reaction in which one element replaces another in a compound

Did You Know?

The same chemical reaction that causes rust also creates fireworks. Oxidation produces both, but it occurs at a different rate in each reaction. When an item rusts, oxidation moves very slowly. In fireworks, oxidation occurs almost instantly.

In this single-replacement reaction, the copper replaces the silver.

164 *Chapter 6 How Matter Changes*

Did You Know?

Ask a volunteer to read the feature on page 164 aloud. The oxidation in fireworks is an exothermic reaction; that means heat is released. Have students explain why this makes fireworks dangerous. Point out that heat is also released—in very small amounts— in rusting.

Double-replacement reaction

A reaction in which the elements in two compounds are exchanged

Precipitate

A solid that is formed and usually sinks to the bottom of a solution

Science Myth

When two reactants are brought together, a chemical reaction automatically starts.

Fact: Most chemical reactions need energy to start. That energy is called activation energy. A catalyst lowers the activation energy that is needed to start the reaction. A catalyst is a substance that enables a chemical reaction to occur faster or under different conditions than is otherwise possible. Catalysts speed up reactions, but are not changed by them. Some substances, called inhibitors, slow down reactions.

Double-Replacement Reactions

The fourth kind of chemical reaction is the **double-replacement reaction.** In this kind of reaction, the elements in two compounds are exchanged.

An example of a double-replacement reaction is the reaction between sodium chloride (NaCl) and silver nitrate ($AgNO_3$). Look at the equation for the reaction shown here.

$$NaCl + AgNO_3 \longrightarrow NaNO_3 + AgCl \downarrow$$

Sodium chloride plus silver nitrate has formed two new compounds—sodium nitrate ($NaNO_3$) and silver chloride (AgCl). The elements in the two compounds have exchanged places. That is what makes the reaction a double replacement.

The downward-pointing arrow (↓) after the AgCl means that this substance is a solid that forms and settles out of the solution. A solid formed in this way is called a **precipitate.** A precipitate usually sinks to the bottom of a solution.

The table below summarizes the four kinds of chemical reactions.

Four Kinds of Reactions	
Type	**General Form**
Synthesis	$A + B \longrightarrow AB$
Decomposition	$AB \longrightarrow A + B$
Single replacement	$A + BC \longrightarrow B + AC$
Double replacement	$AB + CD \longrightarrow AD + CB$

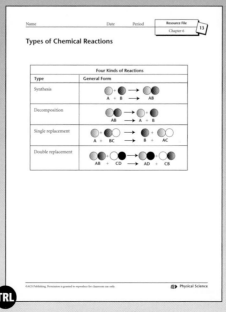

LEARNING STYLES

 Auditory/Verbal

Write the following equation on the board:

Explain that in the equation the square replaces the triangle in the "compound." Stress the word *replaces* and have students suggest definitions for the word. Tell students that the equation is an example of a single-replacement reaction. Point out the use of the words *single* and *replace.* Ask what *single* means. Then have students suggest meanings for *single-replacement reaction.* Follow a similar procedure for double-replacement reactions.

Science Myth

Ask a volunteer to read the myth portion (first sentence) of the Science Myth feature. Then have another volunteer read the fact portion of the feature. One example of the use of a catalyst is the catalytic converter in a car. It speeds up the change that turns harmful products of a car engine to harmless ones.

SCIENCE JOURNAL

 Have students describe some chemical reactions that occur in everyday life. Have them tell what kind of reaction each is.

IN THE COMMUNITY

The precipitates of lead compounds usually have colors. For example, lead iodide is bright yellow. These lead compounds were used in the production of paint for many years. Today most paints are lead-free, and laws prohibit the use of lead-based paints in households. Have students find out why. (*The lead in lead-based paint can cause brain damage if it is ingested.*)

Lesson 4 Review Answers

1. double replacement 2. synthesis
3. decomposition 4. single replacement
5. single replacement 6. $2NaCl + Br_2$;
single replacement 7. $ZnCl_2 + H_2$; single
replacement 8. KBr; double replacement
9. $BaSO_4 + 2NaCl$; double replacement
10. $AgBr + NaNO_3$; double replacement

Achievements in Science

Have students take turns reading the
feature on page 166 aloud. Explain that
one by-product of chlorination is
chloroform. It is formed in small
amounts when drinking water is
chlorinated. Scientists have found that
high doses of chloroform can cause
cancer in laboratory rats. The EPA now
limits the amount of chloroform that
can be present in drinking water.

CROSS-CURRICULAR CONNECTION

Health

Some common
stomachache remedies
contain magnesium carbonate. A
stomachache can be caused by excess
hydrochloric acid, which is naturally
present in the stomach to aid
digestion. Magnesium carbonate
creates a double-replacement
reaction in a person's stomach when
it reacts with the hydrochloric acid.
The double-replacement reaction
produces magnesium chloride
and carbonic acid. The carbonic
acid decomposes into water and
carbon dioxide.

Portfolio Assessment

Sample items include:
• Diagrams of reactions from Teaching
  the Lesson
• Lesson 4 Review answers

Lesson 4   R E V I E W

Identify each of these reactions as either synthesis,
decomposition, single replacement, or double replacement.

1. $Pb(NO_3)_2 + 2KI \longrightarrow 2KNO_3 + PbI_2$

2. $S + O_2 \longrightarrow SO_2$

3. $BaCl_2 \longrightarrow Ba + Cl_2$

4. $Cl_2 + 2NaBr \longrightarrow 2NaCl + Br_2$

5. $2Fe_2O_3 + 3C \longrightarrow 4Fe + 3CO_2$

Complete each of these reactions. Then identify the kind of
reaction (single replacement or double replacement).

6. $2NaBr + Cl_2 \longrightarrow$ _____ + _____

7. $Zn + 2HCl \longrightarrow$ _____ + _____

8. $KOH + HBr \longrightarrow$ _____ + HOH

9. $BaCl_2 + Na_2SO_4 \longrightarrow$ _____ + _____

10. $AgNO_3 + NaBr \longrightarrow$ _____ + _____

Achievements in Science

Chlorination

In 1774, Carl Wilhelm Scheele first made chlorine by combining an acid with a
compound. English chemist Sir Humphry Davy determined that chlorine was an element
in 1810. Chlorine gas reacts with water to break down and kill harmful bacteria-carrying
diseases. The process of using chlorine to disinfect water is chlorination.

In the mid-1800s, cities began using chlorination to disinfect water. One of the first
known uses was in 1850. A water supply pump in London was disinfected with chlorine
after an outbreak of cholera. Later in the century, chlorine was used to sterilize water
after a typhoid fever outbreak. In 1908, chlorination began in New Jersey, and it quickly
spread throughout the United States. From 1900 to 1960, chlorination cut cases of
typhoid fever dramatically in the United States.

Chlorination also is used to kill bacteria in swimming pools. There is debate about the
safety of some of the other products of chlorination. But chlorination continues to be
the main way water is disinfected throughout the world.

Workbook Activity 29

INVESTIGATION

Observing Different Kinds of Reactions

Materials

- safety glasses
- small piece of steel wool
- tongs
- Bunsen burner
- test-tube rack
- 4 test tubes
- hydrogen peroxide solution (H_2O_2)
- manganese dioxide (MnO_2)
- match
- wooden splint
- copper sulfate solution ($CuSO_4$)
- iron nail
- sodium carbonate solution (Na_2CO_3)
- calcium chloride solution ($CaCl_2$)

Purpose

Can you predict the outcome of each reaction described on pages 167 and 168? In this investigation, you will study the four main types of chemical reactions.

Procedure

1. Copy the data table on a sheet of paper.

Reaction	Observations
1	
2	
3	
4	

2. Put on your safety glasses.

Reaction 1

3. Pick up a small piece of steel wool with a pair of tongs. Use the tongs to touch the steel wool to the flame of the Bunsen burner. **Safety alert: Be careful not to burn yourself. If you have long hair, be sure it is pulled back.** Record what happens.

Reaction 2

4. Fill a test tube to the halfway point with hydrogen peroxide (H_2O_2) solution. Add a tiny piece of manganese dioxide (MnO_2). The manganese dioxide will simply speed up the reaction. It is a catalyst. It is not a reactant itself. Observe what happens over the next few minutes.

How Matter Changes Chapter 6 **167**

SAFETY ALERT

- ◆ Make sure that students with long hair tie it back before working around the Bunsen burner.
- ◆ Several of these chemicals are poisonous. Make sure that students rinse off any spills on their skin, clothing, or desk.
- ◆ Caution students to use the tongs to handle the steel wool only and to be careful when handling the wooden splint so that they do not get splinters.

Investigation 6-2

The Purpose portion of the student investigation begins with a question to draw them into the activity. Encourage students to read the investigation steps and formulate their own questions before beginning the investigation. The investigation will take approximately 45 minutes to complete. Students will use these process and thinking skills: observing, describing, and interpreting data; describing; and classifying.

Preparation

- You will need about 30 minutes before class to create the solutions. Use about 10 g of solute for each 100 mL of water. Label each storage container with the name and chemical formula of the solution.
- Steel wool may be purchased at the food or hardware store. Do not use the kind that contains soap.
- The hydrogen peroxide (3 percent) used in this activity is the same kind that you can purchase in a drug or food store.
- You can make test-tube racks from empty milk cartons. Lay a carton on its side and cut holes in it large enough to hold the test tubes.
- Make sure you use uncoated nails. Wipe off any oils.
- Large fireplace matches may be used instead of wooden splints. Light the matches, blow them out, and break them into smaller pieces before giving them to students.
- Sodium bicarbonate is baking soda. It can be purchased at food stores.
- Manganese dioxide, copper sulfate, and calcium chloride can be purchased from a science materials supplier.
- Students may use Lab Manual 24 to record their data and answer the questions.

Procedure

- You can have students work in groups of four. Assign one student to gather materials. All students can make and record observations and answer questions. Each student is responsible for one of the four reactions.

Continued on page 168

Continued from page 167

- Each student gathers all necessary materials for his or her reaction, does the reaction while other group members watch, and cleans up.
- Manganese dioxide (MnO_2) is a catalyst for the decomposition of hydrogen peroxide (H_2O_2) and is not a part of the reaction. If MnO_2 is not available, shine a bright light on the H_2O_2. The reaction will take longer using the light.
- Tell students that in Reaction 2 oxygen gas causes a smoldering splint to ignite.

Results

Reaction 1: The steel wool caught fire and kept on burning after removal from the flame.

Reaction 2: Bubbles of gas appeared in the liquid and rose to the top. The glowing splint began to flame again.

Reaction 3: A reddish coating appeared on the nail, and the blue solution became lighter in color.

Reaction 4: A milky or cloudy precipitate was formed and remained partly suspended. By process of elimination of elements found in the reactants, the other product must have been sodium chloride (NaCl). NaCl is table salt.

Questions and Conclusions Answers

1. synthesis **2.** decomposition **3.** single replacement **4.** double replacement

Explore Further Answers

Reaction 1: downward arrow. Reaction 2: upward arrow. Reaction 3: downward arrow. Reaction 4: downward arrow.

Assessment

Check students' data tables to be sure that they recorded their observations correctly. You might include the following items from this investigation in student portfolios:

- Investigation 6-2 data table
- Answers to Questions and Conclusions and Explore Further sections

5. Once the reaction is occurring quickly, use a match to light a wooden splint. **Safety alert: Be careful not to burn yourself. Pull back long hair.** Blow out the splint and immediately insert it into the test tube so that the glowing end is slightly above the liquid level. Record what happens.

Reaction 3

6. Fill a test tube to the halfway point with copper sulfate ($CuSO_4$) solution. Gently place an iron nail into the test tube. Record what happens.

Reaction 4

7. Add sodium carbonate (Na_2CO_3) solution to a test tube until it is one-third full.

8. Add calcium chloride ($CaCl_2$) solution to another test tube until it is one-third full.

9. Pour the contents of the second test tube into the first. Record what happens.

Questions and Conclusions

Copy the data table on your paper and complete it.

Reaction	Equation	Type of Reaction
1	$4Fe + 3O_2 \longrightarrow 2Fe_2O_3$	
2	$2H_2O_2 \longrightarrow 2H_2O + O_2$	
3	$Fe + CuSO_4 \longrightarrow FeSO_4 + Cu$	
4	$Na_2CO_3 + CaCl_2 \longrightarrow 2NaCl + CaCO_3$	

Explore Further

Remember, the chemicals on the right side of the arrow are the products. In which of the above equations on the product (right) side, would you put an upward arrow? In which would you put a downward arrow?

Name _____ Date _____ Period _____ | Lab Manual 24 Chapter 6

6-2 **Observing Different Kinds of Reactions**
Use with Investigation 6-2, pages 167–168.

Purpose Can you predict the outcome of each reaction described on pages 167 and 168? In this investigation, you will study the four main types of chemical reactions.

Reaction	Observations
1	
2	
3	
4	

Questions and Conclusions
Complete the following table.

Reaction	Equation	Type of reaction
1	$4Fe + 3O_2 \rightarrow 2Fe_2O_3$	
2	$2H_2O_2 \rightarrow 2H_2O + O_2$	
3	$Fe + CuSO_4 \rightarrow FeSO_4 + Cu$	
4	$Na_2CO_3 + CaCl_2 \rightarrow 2NaCl + CaCO_3$	

Explore Further
Remember, the chemicals on the right side of the arrow are the products. In which of the above equations on the product (right) side, would you put an upward arrow? In which would you put a downward arrow?

_____

Publishing. Permission is granted to reproduce for classroom use only. | ■▶ Physical Science

- A chemical reaction involves a change of substances into other substances.

- Reactions can be represented by chemical equations, which should be balanced for atoms.

- The law of conservation of matter states that matter cannot be created or destroyed in chemical and common physical changes.

- A combination of materials in which no reaction takes place is called a mixture.

- The four main types of chemical reactions are synthesis (A + B → AB), decomposition (AB → A + B), single replacement (A + BC → B + AC), and double replacement (AB + CD → AD + CB).

- In a synthesis reaction, elements combine to form a compound.

- In a decomposition reaction, a compound breaks down into simpler substances.

- In a single-replacement reaction, one element replaces another in a compound.

- In a double-replacement reaction, elements in two compounds are exchanged.

Chapter 6 Summary

Have volunteers read aloud each Summary item on page 169. Ask volunteers to explain the meaning of each item. Direct students' attention to the Science Words box on the bottom of page 169. Have them read and review each term and its definition.

Science Words

balance, 157	double-replacement reaction, 165	reactant, 155
chemical equation, 155	law of conservation of matter, 156	single-replacement reaction, 164
chemical reaction, 150	mixture, 150	solute, 151
coefficient, 157	precipitate, 165	solution, 151
decomposition reaction, 162	product, 155	solvent, 151
dissolve, 151		synthesis reaction, 160

Chapter 6 Review

Use the Chapter Review to prepare students for tests and to reteach content from the chapter.

Chapter 6 Mastery Test

The Teacher's Resource Library includes two parallel forms of the Chapter 6 Mastery Test. The difficulty level of the two forms is equivalent. You may wish to use one form as a pretest and the other form as a posttest.

Chapters 1–6
Midterm Mastery Test

The Teacher's Resource Library includes the Midterm Mastery Test. This test is pictured on page 399 of this Teacher's Edition. The Midterm Mastery Test assesses the major learning objectives for Chapters 1–6.

Review Answers
Vocabulary Review

1. chemical reaction 2. solution
3. coefficient 4. chemical equation
5. reactant 6. product 7. precipitate
8. solvent 9. solute 10. mixture
11. law of conservation of matter

Concept Review

12. A (decomposition) 13. B (double replacement) 14. C (single replacement)
15. D (synthesis) 16. C (single replacement)

TEACHER ALERT

Because of limited space in this Chapter Review, not all of the vocabulary terms introduced in this chapter appear in the Vocabulary Review section. You may want to create an activity using the missing words to give students practice with all of the terms in this chapter. Here are the terms that are not covered in the section.

balance
decomposition reaction
dissolve
double-replacement reaction
single-replacement reaction
synthesis reaction

Word Bank
chemical equation
chemical reaction
coefficient
law of
   conservation
   of matter
mixture
precipitate
product
reactant
solute
solution
solvent

Vocabulary Review

Choose the word or words from the Word Bank that best complete each sentence. Write the answer on a sheet of paper.

1. A chemical change in which elements are combined or rearranged is a _____.

2. A mixture in which one substance is dissolved in another is a _____.

3. A number placed before a formula in a chemical equation is a _____.

4. A statement that uses symbols, formulas, and numbers to stand for a chemical reaction is a _____.

5. A substance that is altered in a chemical reaction is a _____.

6. A substance that is formed in a chemical reaction is a _____.

7. A _____ is a solid that is formed in a chemical reaction; it usually sinks to the bottom of the solution.

8. A _____ dissolves one or more other substances.

9. A _____ is dissolved in a solution.

10. When substances are combined and no reaction occurs, a _____ is formed.

11. The _____ states that matter cannot be created or destroyed in chemical and common physical changes.

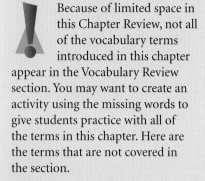

Chapter 6 Mastery Test A

Concept Review

Match the equation in Column A with the kind of reaction it represents in Column B. Write the name of the reaction on your paper. You will use one answer twice.

Column A

12. $2SO_3 \longrightarrow 2SO_2 + O_2$

13. $AgNO_3 + NaI \longrightarrow AgI + NaNO_3$

14. $Zn + SnCl_2 \longrightarrow ZnCl_2 + Sn$

15. $C + O_2 \longrightarrow CO_2$

16. $C + H_2O \longrightarrow CO + H_2$

Column B

A decomposition

B double replacement

C single replacement

D synthesis

Critical Thinking

Write the answer to each of these questions on your paper.

17. Explain what happens in a chemical reaction and what can cause it.

18. Describe what happens when a solute and a solvent are combined.

19. Balance the following equation by adding coefficients: $Al + O_2 \longrightarrow Al_2O_3$. Then identify the reactant(s) and the product(s).

20. Explain what is happening in the photo.

 **Test-Taking Tip** When you review your notes to prepare for a test, use a marker to highlight key words and example problems.

---

17. In a chemical reaction, elements combine or rearrange. A chemical reaction can happen when substances are heated or when they are mixed with water. **18.** Combining a solute and a solvent results in a mixture in which the solvent causes the solute to dissolve.

19. $4Al + 3O_2 \rightarrow 2Al_2O_3$; reactants: Al and O_2; product: Al_2O_3 **20.** A chemical reaction takes place forming a precipitate as the two liquids are mixed. The clear solution is silver nitrate, the yellow solution is sodium chromate, and the red precipitate is silver chromate.

ALTERNATIVE ASSESSMENT

Alternative Assessment items correlate to the student Goals for Learning at the beginning of this chapter.

- Have students define a chemical reaction and give an example of one. Then have them tell how a reaction differs from a mixture.

- Have students put a teaspoon of sugar in water and stir it. Have them describe what takes place and identify the solute and solvent.

- Have students write the law of conservation of matter. Then have them explain how it applies to the following equation: $2H_2 + O_2 \rightarrow 2H_2O$.

- Have students tell whether the following chemical equation is balanced and explain why or why not: $4Fe + 3O \rightarrow 2Fe_2O_3$. (*It is balanced. The number of atoms of each element is the same on both sides of the equation.*)

- Cut out large paper circles of four different colors. You will need two circles of each color. You will also need two index cards with a plus sign written on each, one index card with an arrow written on it, and four index cards with the name of one type of chemical reaction on each. Have students choose one of the index cards that identifies a type of reaction and then use the other materials to illustrate the reaction.

Name _____ Date _____ Period ___ | **Mastery Test B, Page 1**
Chapter 6

Chapter 6 Mastery Test B

Part A Identify the reactants and products in the following chemical equations.

Reaction	Reactants	Products
1. $BaCl_2 + Na_2SO_4 \rightarrow BaSO_4 + 2NaCl$		
2. $Mg + Cl_2 \rightarrow MgCl_2$		
3. $H_2SO_4 + Zn \rightarrow ZnSO_4 + H_2$		
4. $Ca + O_2 \rightarrow CaO$		
5. $2NaCl \rightarrow 2Na + Cl_2$		

Part B Complete the following chemical equations and identify the type of reaction.

Type of Reaction

6. $Fe + S \rightarrow$ _____

7. $C_6H_{12}O_6 \rightarrow$ _____ $+ 6H_2O$

8. $2NaBr +$ _____ $\rightarrow Br_2 + 2NaCl$

9. $BaCl_2 \rightarrow Ba +$ _____

10. _____ $+ NaBr \rightarrow AgBr + NaNO_3$

Part C Write the letter of the correct answer on the line.

11. A combination of substances in which no reaction takes place is a _____.
A solute   B solvent   C mixture   D synthesis

12. A reaction in which a compound breaks down into two or more simple substances is a _____.
A synthesis reaction   C decomposition reaction
B solution   D single-replacement reaction

13. Substances that are changed in a chemical reaction and appear on the left side of the arrow in a chemical equation are _____.
A solutions   B mixtures   C precipitates   D reactants

14. The solid that is formed and usually sinks to the bottom of a solution is the _____.
A product   B precipitate   C reactant   D solvent

15. A substance that is formed in a chemical reaction is a _____.
A product   B reactant   C solvent   D mixture

▶ **Physical Science**

Name _____ Date _____ Period ___ | **Mastery Test B, Page 2**
Chapter 6

Chapter 6 Mastery Test B, continued

Part D Write a short answer to these questions.

16. How are solutions like other mixtures? How do they differ from other mixtures?

17. Explain each of the four types of chemical reactions.

18. What occurs when something dissolves?

19. Write the law of conservation of matter.

20. What is a reaction?

▶ **Physical Science**

Chapter 6 Mastery Test B

Chapter

7

Planning Guide

Motion

	Student Text Lesson		
	Student Pages	Vocabulary	Lesson Review
Lesson 1 What Are Motion and Speed?	174–178	✔	✔
Lesson 2 Using a Graph to Describe Motion	179–186	✔	✔
Lesson 3 Acceleration	187–191	✔	✔
Lesson 4 The Laws of Motion	192–195	✔	✔
Lesson 5 Gravity	196–200	✔	✔

Chapter Activities

Student Text
Science Center
Teacher's Resource Library
Community Connection 7: How Fast
Does It Go?

Assessment Options

Student Text
Chapter 7 Review
Teacher's Resource Library
Chapter 7 Mastery Tests A and B

172A

	Student Text Features								Teaching Strategies						Learning Styles						Teacher's Resource Library				
	Achievements in Science	Science at Work	Science in Your Life	Investigation	Science Myth	Note	Technology Note	Did You Know	Science Integration	Science Journal	Cross-Curricular Connection	Online Connection	Teacher Alert	Applications (Home, Career, Community, Global, Environment)	Auditory/Verbal	Body/Kinesthetic	Interpersonal/Group Learning	Logical/Mathematical	Visual/Spatial	LEP/ESL	Workbook Activities	Alternative Workbook Activities	Lab Manual	Resource File	Self-Study Guide
						✔			175	177	177		176	176							30	30			✔
			185			✔	✔			183	182, 183		181			182		181			31	31	25	14	✔
	191		190							189, 190	189, 190	191	188	188	189			188			32	32	26		✔
		195			193	✔	✔	192, 194	194		194			192, 194, 195		194				194	33	33	27	15	✔
	198			199	197			197		197	197							197	197		34	34	28		✔

Pronunciation Key

a	hat	e	let	ī	ice	ô	order	ù	put	sh	she
ā	age	ē	equal	o	hot	oi	oil	ü	rule	th	thin
ä	far	ėr	term	ō	open	ou	out	ch	child	ᵺ	then
â	care	i	it	ȯ	saw	u	cup	ng	long	zh	measure

ə { a in about, e in taken, i in pencil, o in lemon, u in circus }

Alternative Workbook Activities

The Teacher's Resource Library (TRL) contains a set of lower-level worksheets called Alternative Workbook Activities. These worksheets cover the same content as the regular Workbook Activities but are written at a second-grade reading level.

Skill Track Software

Use the Skill Track Software for Physical Science for additional reinforcement of this chapter. The software program allows students using AGS textbooks to be assessed for mastery of each chapter and lesson of the textbook. Students access the software on an individual basis and are assessed with multiple-choice items.

Science Center

Gather resource books showing the development of automobiles, trains, airplanes, and other transportation vehicles. Ask students to use the books to find out how manufacturers used the principles of aerodynamics to change the shapes of the vehicles. Encourage students to draw at least two pictures with labels explaining the design changes based on aerodynamic principles. Students might also investigate whether aerodynamic designs of vehicles affect the fuel use of the vehicles.

Community Connection 7

7 Motion

Do you recognize the animal in the photograph? Have you ever seen a cheetah run? Cheetahs are the fastest land mammals in the world. How fast can a cheetah run? It can cover approximately 200 meters in 7 seconds. It can accelerate from 0 to 29 meters per second in 3 seconds. But what do these numbers actually tell us about the speed of a cheetah? In Chapter 7, you will find out about the laws of motion. You will learn what motion is, how to measure it, and how scientists describe it.

Organize Your Thoughts

```
        First law          Second law          Third law
        of motion          of motion           of motion

        Stop/Start        Acceleration      Action    Reaction

    Friction   Gravity    Speed    Time
```

Goals for Learning

◆ To define and explain motion and speed

◆ To calculate speed, distance, and time

◆ To use a graph to describe motion and make predictions

◆ To calculate acceleration and deceleration

◆ To define and explain force

◆ To explain and apply Newton's three laws of motion

◆ To define and explain gravity

◆ To explain the law of universal gravitation

173

Introducing the Chapter

Have students describe what they see in the photo on page 172. Identify the animal shown as a cheetah and encourage students to draw conclusions about why a cheetah is used to represent motion. Then read the introductory paragraph. Help students conclude that the cheetah's speed is one reason why a photograph of a cheetah is used to open this chapter. Explain that speed is just one factor related to motion. Ask students to brainstorm other factors. List these on the board. Students can add to the list as they study Chapter 7.

Have students copy the Organize Your Thoughts chart on page 173. Tell them to leave room on their paper to add information to the chart. As they read, have students add examples that illustrate each term in the graphic. For example, they might use wiping their feet on a carpet as an example of friction. Discuss students' expanded graphic organizers throughout the study of Chapter 7.

Notes and Technology Notes

Ask volunteers to read the notes that appear in the margins throughout the chapter. Then discuss them with the class.

TEACHER'S RESOURCE

The AGS Teaching Strategies in Science Transparencies may be used with this chapter. The transparencies add an interactive dimension to expand and enhance the *Physical Science* program content.

CAREER INTEREST INVENTORY

The AGS Harrington-O'Shea Career Decision-Making System-Revised (CDM) may be used with this chapter. Students can use the CDM to explore their interests and identify careers. The CDM defines career areas that are indicated by students' responses on the inventory.

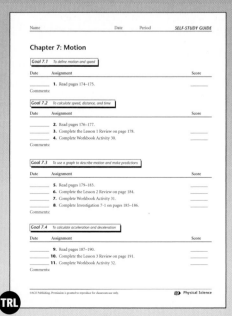

Chapter 7 Self-Study Guide

Lesson at a Glance

Chapter 7 Lesson 1

Overview In this lesson, students learn how to describe speed and motion and to calculate speed, distance, and time.

Objectives

- To define and explain motion
- To calculate elapsed time
- To explain speed and average speed
- To perform calculations involving speed

Student Pages 174–178

Teacher's Resource Library (TRL)

Workbook Activity 30

Alternative Workbook Activity 30

Vocabulary

distance
elapsed time
motion
speed

Science Background

The concepts of force and motion must be considered at the same time because neither has significance alone. Force is recognized as a push or a pull, which tends to change the motion of an object.

The action of a force on an object is a familiar experience. Most everyone recognizes the distinction between a large force and a small one. Harder to recognize is the fact that force is directional. For example, a force pushing in a northerly direction on a particular object produces no effect whatsoever in an easterly direction. The force affects the motion of the object most noticeably in the northerly direction. Moreover, the effect can be completely nullified by a force of the same magnitude pushing in a southerly direction.

Sir Isaac Newton (1642–1727) summarized the matter of force and motion in the form of three generalizations now known as the laws of motion. So far, they have withstood the test of experiment.

Objectives

After reading this lesson, you should be able to

- define and explain motion.
- calculate elapsed time.
- explain speed and average speed.
- perform calculations involving speed.

Motion
A change in position

Elapsed time
The length of time that passes from one event to another

The motion of an object is always judged with respect to another object or point.

The earth travels in space. A car carries you from place to place. You walk to the store. An amusement park ride spins you around. What do all these actions have in common? In each case, objects are changing position in space. We say they are moving. **Motion** is simply a change of position.

All change, including change in position, takes place over time. To help you understand motion, you will begin by learning how the passage of time is measured.

Elapsed Time

Suppose you have just taken an airplane trip from Miami to New York in the same time zone. Your flight began at 8:00 P.M. It ended at 11:00 P.M. How long did this trip take?

To answer this question, you calculate the **elapsed time.** Elapsed time is the amount of time that passes from one event to another. To calculate elapsed time, just subtract the time of the earlier event from the time of the later event.

In the case of the flight, subtract the departure time from the arrival time.

```
  11:00   arrival time
-  8:00   departure time
   3      hours travel time = elapsed time
```

Departure time
8:00 P.M.

Arrival time
11:00 P.M.

810 miles

Miami

New York

Speed

Speed
The rate at which the position of an object changes
Distance
The length of the path between two points

When something is moving, it is natural to wonder how fast it is going, or what its **speed** is. Speed tells how fast an object is moving. The more distance a moving object covers in a given time, the greater its speed. For example, a cheetah can travel at a speed of 100 kilometers per hour. But an ant can cover only 36 meters in an hour. The cheetah has greater speed than the ant.

Notice that speed uses two units—**distance** and time. Distance is the length of the path between two points. It is the length of the path traveled by the object in motion. You can use the following formula to find the speed of an object.

To know if something is moving, you need a reference point. A reference point is something that seems to be standing still. The motion of an object is compared to the reference point.

$$\text{average speed} = \frac{\text{distance}}{\text{time}}$$

Suppose the airplane mentioned on page 174 traveled 810 miles between the two cities. The elapsed time for the trip was 3 hours. You can use the formula to calculate the speed of the airplane. Look at the example.

EXAMPLE

$$\text{average speed} = \frac{810 \text{ miles}}{3 \text{ hours}}$$

$$\text{average speed} = \frac{270 \text{ miles}}{1 \text{ hour}}$$

The speed of the airplane is 270 miles per hour. This means that each hour the plane traveled 270 miles.

In the example, it is unlikely that the airplane traveled at a constant speed of 270 miles per hour during the entire flight. A plane starts and stops very slowly. Between the beginning and the end of the trip, the speed varies during the flight. The speed calculated is actually the average speed. The actual speed at any particular moment could be more or less than the average speed. The speed at a particular moment is called the instantaneous speed.

1 Warm-Up Activity

Provide several different wind-up toys that move in a straight path. Divide the class into groups, and give each group a toy. Have groups race their toys along a meter-length path. Groups will need stopwatches or a clock with a second hand to time how long it takes their vehicles to travel one meter. Have students record the distance and time on a sheet of paper. Later, when students have learned the formula for calculating speed, they can use their data to calculate the speed of each toy.

2 Teaching the Lesson

Before beginning instruction, ask students to scan Lesson 1, looking for unfamiliar words. Have pairs of students find the terms in the dictionary and write the definitions.

Discuss with students the meaning of the word *rate*. Inform students that rate tells how fast something is happening. The symbol for rate is a slash (/), and it is read as "per." Ask students to look for examples of rates in the lesson. Have students write the rates with the words and symbol (for example, 100 kilometers per hour—100 kilometers/hour; 36 meters per hour—36 meters/hour).

3 Reinforce and Extend

SCIENCE INTEGRATION

Biology
The opening page of the chapter shows a cheetah on the run. Students learn that the cheetah is the fastest land animal on Earth. How fast are other animals? Ask students to find out. Have each student identify 10 animals. Each should then find out how fast the animals can move. Suggest that students look in encyclopedias or other reference books to find the speed of animals. Each student then can make a list of the animals in order according to their speed from fastest to slowest.

Speed does not have to be measured in miles per hour.

Think about a race at a track meet where the distance around the track is 400 meters. Suppose a runner completes the race in 40 seconds. What was the runner's speed? Look at the example.

> **EXAMPLE**
>
> $$\text{average speed} = \frac{\text{distance}}{\text{time}}$$
>
> $$\text{average speed} = \frac{400 \text{ meters}}{40 \text{ seconds}}$$
>
> $$\text{average speed} = \frac{10 \text{ meters}}{1 \text{ second}}$$

The average speed of the runner is 10 meters per second. The runner covers an average distance of 10 meters each second.

Calculating Distance

Suppose you are taking a trip by car. You know you can travel about 50 miles an hour on the roads you will be using. You also know you can travel about 6 hours a day. You would like to know how far you can go in one day. In other words, you would like to calculate distance. Since you already know your speed and your time, you can use the formula for finding speed to calculate distance. Study the example. Notice how the hours cancel out of the equation.

> **EXAMPLE**
>
> $$\text{average speed} = \frac{\text{distance}}{\text{time}}$$
>
> $$\text{distance} = \text{speed} \times \text{time}$$
>
> $$\text{distance} = \frac{50 \text{ miles}}{1 \text{ hour}} \times 6 \text{ hours}$$
>
> $$\text{distance} = 300 \text{ miles}$$

Calculating Time

Sometimes you might want to figure out how long it will take to cover a certain distance. Suppose you have a job marking the lines on a sports field. The distance to be marked is 80 meters. You mark at a speed of 50 meters per minute. How much time will it take you to mark the whole line? The formula for speed also can be rearranged to solve for the time. Look at the example.

The answer in the first example on this page— 50 meters/minute —has a slash mark. The slash mark stands for the word *per*. The answer in this example is read as *50 meters per minute*.

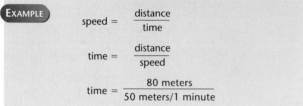

EXAMPLE

$$speed = \frac{distance}{time}$$

$$time = \frac{distance}{speed}$$

$$time = \frac{80 \text{ meters}}{50 \text{ meters}/1 \text{ minute}}$$

When you divide by a fraction, you invert the fraction and multiply.

EXAMPLE

$$time = \frac{80 \text{ meters}}{1} \times \frac{1 \text{ minute}}{50 \text{ meters}}$$

$$time = \frac{80 \text{ minutes}}{50}$$

$$time = 1.6 \text{ minutes}$$

It would take you 1.6 minutes to mark the whole line.

CROSS-CURRICULAR CONNECTION

 Math
Have students find the times of winners of three recent running races, such as a 100-meter, 400-meter, and marathon. Have them calculate the speed of each runner and compare the speeds of the runners in the three different races.

SCIENCE JOURNAL

 Have students copy the formulas for calculating speed, distance, and time in their journal. Students should provide an example of a calculation using each formula.

Lesson 1 Review Answers

1. 6 miles/hour **2.** 7.7 yd/sec **3.** 2 cm/sec
4. 190 km/hr **5.** 127.5 ft/min **6.** 120 km/hr
× 2 hr = 240 km **7.** 5 mi ÷ 16 mi/hr =
0.31 hr **8.** 500 mi/hr × 5 hr = 2,500 mi
9. 18,000 mi/hr × 4.5 hr = 81,000 mi
10. 45 mi/hr × 2 hr = 90 mi

Portfolio Assessment

Sample items include:
• Words and definitions from Teaching
  the Lesson
• Lesson 1 Review answers

Lesson 1   R E V I E W

Copy this table on a sheet of paper. Calculate the average speed
for each of the items. The first one is done for you.

	Distance Traveled	Time	Average Speed
1.	30 miles	5 hours	6 miles/hour
2.	100 yards	13 seconds	
3.	10 centimeters	5 seconds	
4.	380 kilometers	2 hours	
5.	3,825 feet	30 minutes	

Find the answer to each word problem. Write the answers
on your paper. Use one of these formulas and show your work.

$$distance = speed \times time$$

$$time = \frac{distance}{speed}$$

6. A train's average speed is 120 kilometers per hour.
Its elapsed time is 2 hours. How far did it travel?

7. A student rides her bike to school. Her school is 5 miles
from her home. She travels at an average rate of 16 miles
per hour. How much time does she need for this trip?

8. Suppose it takes a plane 5 hours to travel from
Philadelphia to San Francisco. It travels at an average speed
of 500 miles per hour. What is the approximate distance
between the two cities?

9. A rocket can travel at an average rate of 18,000 miles
per hour. How far will the rocket travel in 4.5 hours?

10. A man rode on a motorcycle for 2 hours. His average speed
was 45 miles per hour. How far did he travel?

Workbook Activity 30

Objectives

After reading this lesson, you should be able to

◆ use a graph to describe motion.

◆ make predictions about distance, using a distance-time graph.

◆ explain what is meant by varying speed.

◆ explain how to recognize varying speed on a distance-time graph.

Constant speed

Speed that does not change

Sometimes it is useful to use a graph to show motion. Suppose that a car traveled for 5 hours. The following table shows the elapsed time and the distance traveled by the car.

Time and Distance	
Elapsed Time (hours)	Distance Traveled (kilometers)
0	0
1	50
2	100
3	150
4	200
5	250

The information in the table above appears on the line graph below. The graph shows distance and time. Points have been plotted for the car. For example, the first point is the one that shows a distance of 50 km at a time of 1 hour.

Notice that the line on the graph is straight, not curved. That means that the car is traveling at a **constant speed.** Constant speed is speed that does not change. For example, observe the first point for the car on the graph. It shows that 50 kilometers are covered in 1 hour. What is the car's speed?

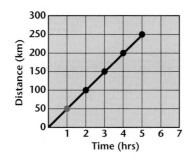

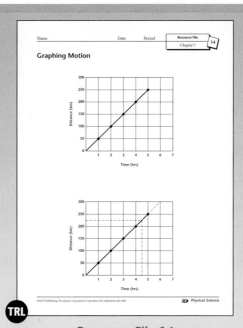

Resource File 14

Chapter 7 Lesson 2

Overview In this lesson, students learn how to interpret and use the information on graphs to solve problems about motion.

Objectives

■ To use a graph to describe motion

■ To make predictions about distance, using a distance-time graph

■ To explain what is meant by varying speed

■ To explain how to recognize varying speed on a distance-time graph

Student Pages 179–186

Teacher's Resource Library

  Workbook Activity 31

  Alternative Workbook Activity 31

  Lab Manual 25

  Resource File 14

Vocabulary

constant speed
velocity

1 Warm-Up Activity

Tell students that they are going to make a human bar graph. Place a piece of masking tape across the room near the wall. This is the horizontal axis of the graph. Write the names of shoe colors across the tape. The perpendicular wall is the vertical axis. Have all students with one shoe color, such as black, line up in a straight line, beginning at the correct spot on the horizontal axis and parallel to the vertical axis. Repeat for additional shoe colors. Determine which shoe color is most common and which is least common. (If shoe color does not vary in the classroom, choose another feature, such as pets, that varies from student to student.) Explain that bar graphs are used to describe exact data values and to compare data values.

2 Teaching the Lesson

Explain to students that when they finish reading the lesson, they should make a drawing they could use to explain part or all of the lesson's information to another person.

Students could push toy cars or other objects with wheels and calculate their average speed. Then they could graph their data.

Provide students with graph paper that has wide intervals. With graph paper, they can more easily copy the graphs on pages 180 and 181.

Briefly discuss the different kinds of graphs. Tell students that a line graph is used to show how data changes over time. It can show patterns in increases or declines. A bar graph is used to compare data. Ask students what kind of graph would be more appropriate to show the following data: distances between a city and several of its suburbs (bar graph), the improvements in fuel mileage on a particular car model over a period 5 years (line graph).

As students define terms, emphasize the difference in the meanings of the terms *speed* and *velocity*. Velocity is speed in a given direction. Ask students to describe situations in which knowing the direction given by velocity is very important. *(Students might mention that airplane pilots use velocity measurements to fly and land planes, weather forecasters must know the velocity of air masses to predict the weather, and travelers going from one city to another must know directions, as well as speed.)*

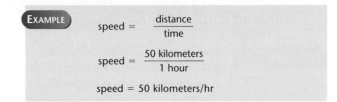

$$\text{speed} = \frac{\text{distance}}{\text{time}}$$

$$\text{speed} = \frac{50 \text{ kilometers}}{1 \text{ hour}}$$

$$\text{speed} = 50 \text{ kilometers/hr}$$

The car's speed during the first hour is 50 kilometers per hour. Likewise, the second hour, the car's speed would be 50 kilometers per hour.

EXAMPLE

$$\text{speed} = \frac{\text{distance}}{\text{time}}$$

$$\text{speed} = \frac{100 \text{ kilometers}}{2 \text{ hours}}$$

$$\text{speed} = 50 \text{ kilometers/hr}$$

If you continue to calculate the speed at each of the times, you will find that the car travels at a speed of 50 kilometers per hour each hour. The car is traveling at a constant speed.

Finding Unknown Distances

Suppose you want to know the distance traveled by the car at the end of 4.5 hours. You can use a graph to find the distances at times that are not shown. Use the method below.

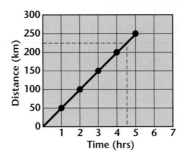

1. Copy the graph onto a sheet of paper.

2. Find the time of 4.5 hours along the time axis. This is halfway between 4 hours and 5 hours.

3. Draw a vertical (up-and-down) line from this point on the time axis up to the plotted line.

4. From the point where the vertical line touches the plotted line, draw a horizontal (side-to-side) line to the distance axis.

5. Estimate the distance on the scale. It is the point where the horizontal line touches the distance axis. The distance is about 225 kilometers.

Predicting Distances

You know from the graph how far the car travels in 5 hours. But what if you need to predict where the car will be at some later time? You can use the graph to make this kind of prediction.

For example, suppose you would like to know how far the car will travel in 6 hours. Follow these steps.

1. Copy the graph onto a sheet of paper.

2. Extend the plotted graph line as shown.

3. Draw a vertical line from the 6-hour line to the plotted line.

4. From the point where the vertical line and the extended graph line touch, draw a horizontal line to the distance axis. Then read the approximate distance. It is about 300 kilometers.

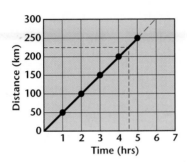

LEARNING STYLES

 Logical/Mathematical

Have students write ideas about what would cause a bicycle to have varying speeds over a certain number of minutes. Suggest factors such as riding uphill and coasting downhill. Students should draw a graph that shows the speeds and then find the average speed of the bicycle.

TEACHER ALERT

Students often forget to identify the units of distance and time when they calculate speed and distance. Help them understand that there is a large difference between units of measurement and that for their calculations to be correct, they must identify the units correctly. Check students' solutions for the identification of units.

Velocity

Velocity
The speed and direction in which an object is moving

You know quantities are velocities, not speeds, when they include information about speed and direction. These types of quantities are called vector quantities. Vector quantities have size, such as speed, and direction.

So far we have talked only about the speed of motion. But what about the direction of motion? That can be important, too. For example, you might tell someone that you drove your car north at 90 kilometers per hour. You are telling about the **velocity** of the car. Speed tells how fast an object moves. Velocity tells the speed and direction in which an object is moving.

Look at the figure below. Suppose you walk 5 kilometers in an hour in an eastward direction. Your velocity would be 5 kilometers per hour eastward.

As you walk, you pass another person traveling westward at 5 kilometers per hour. Both you and the other person have the same speed—5 kilometers per hour. However, your velocities are different because you are going in different directions.

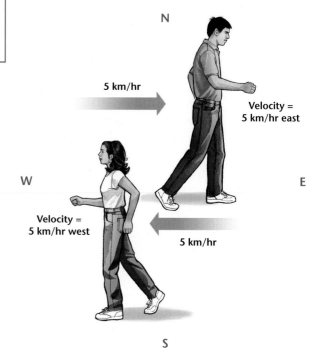

Varying Speed

Few objects move at constant velocity or speed. Look at the following graph. It shows the changes in speed as a family drove a car along a road. Notice that the plotted line in this graph is not straight. This tells you that the car's speed was not constant. But you can still use the information in the graph to find the average speed of the car. You can see that at the end of 6 hours, the car had traveled 300 kilometers. The average speed is shown in the example below.

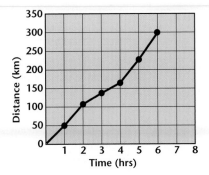

 EXAMPLE

$$speed = \frac{distance}{time}$$

$$speed = \frac{300 \text{ kilometers}}{6 \text{ hours}}$$

$$speed = 50 \text{ kilometers/hr}$$

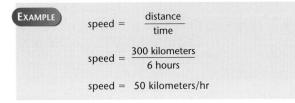

Technology Note

Speed skaters wear speed suits to help them move faster in competition. A speed suit covers a skater's body like a second skin. Speed suits are made of different fabrics so different body parts have less air resistance. By reducing air resistance, skaters subtract critical fractions of seconds from their race times. The time saved can be the difference between winning and losing.

Social Studies

Have pairs of students choose a vacation spot they would like to visit on a road trip. Ask them to use a road map to plot their route. Then they should determine the distance, and the driving time based on traveling an average speed of 55 miles per hour. Suggest that students identify places of interest along their route and sites they will visit when they arrive at their destination. Have students prepare a poster with pictures and route information.

SCIENCE JOURNAL

Ask students to write a short story telling about a car that could only travel at constant speed.

Lesson 2 Review Answers

1. Students' graphs should show distances increasing by 100 kilometers every hour. 2. The straight line shows that the speed is constant. 3. **A** 30 km **B** 450 km **C** 700 km **D** 1,000 km 4. If the plotted line is straight, the speed is constant. If the plotted line is not straight, the speed varies. 5. The plotted line on this graph should not be straight because the speed varies and is not constant.

Portfolio Assessment

Sample items include:
• Graphs from Teaching the Lesson
• Lesson 2 Review answers

Lesson 2   R E V I E W

1. Use the data in the table to make a line graph.

Elapsed Time (hours)	Distance Traveled (kilometers)
0	0
1	100
2	200
3	300
4	400
5	500

2. What does the line graph you drew tell about the data?

3. Use your graph to find the distance traveled for each of these times.
   A 3 hours   **B** 4.5 hours   **C** 7 hours   **D** 10 hours

4. How you can tell whether speed is constant or varying by looking at a graph of distance versus time? Explain your answer.

5. Use the data in the table to make a line graph of distance versus time.

Elapsed Time (minutes)	Distance Traveled (meters)
0	0
1	200
2	340
3	580
4	760
5	900

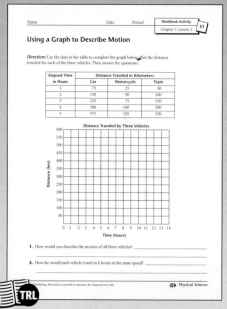

Workbook Activity 31

7-1 INVESTIGATION

Finding Speed

Investigation 7-1

The Purpose portion of the student investigation begins with a question to draw them into the activity. Encourage students to read the investigation steps and formulate their own questions before beginning the investigation. The investigation will take approximately 30 minutes to complete. Students will use these process and thinking skills: measuring; using numbers; collecting, recording, and interpreting data; communicating; observing; describing; and making inferences.

Purpose

What formula would you use to calculate speed using distance and time? In this investigation, you will calculate speed by measuring distance and time and use a graph to show motion.

Procedure

1. Copy the data table on a sheet of paper.

Length (meters)	Time (seconds)	Speed (distance/time)

2. Put on your safety glasses.

3. Work on a large table, as directed by your teacher. At one end of the table, place one end of the meterstick on the edge of a book. The ruler's groove should be on top. Refer to the figure on page 186.

4. Set a book at the other end of the table. Measure the length from the book to the edge of the ruler on the table. Record the length in your data table.

5. Set the marble at the top of the ruler's groove. Release the marble. Let it roll down the groove. Do not push it. Start the stopwatch when the marble leaves the ruler. Stop timing when the marble reaches the book at the end of the table. Record the time in your data table.

Materials

- safety glasses
- 2 books
- meterstick
- marble
- stopwatch or watch that shows seconds

Preparation

- You may wish to supply students with graph paper containing large intervals on which to draw their graphs.

- Make certain the pathway chosen as a runway for the marble is smooth and level.

- If necessary, have students practice measuring length with a meterstick and time in seconds with a stopwatch.

- Students may use Lab Manual 25 to record their data and answer the questions.

Procedure

- Have students work in pairs to complete this investigation.

- Encourage students to practice pushing the marble. This will help reduce errors.

- You might have students record the time for several trials and then use the average for their calculations.

- If individual students have difficulty making a graph, you might use their data to make a class graph.

- Have students review the graphs shown on pages 179, 180, 181, and 183 in their text.

- Suggest that students model their graph after the one shown on page 179. However, make sure students understand that on their graph the distance must be expressed in meters (m) and the time in seconds (s). Also make sure that students have properly identified the intervals along the axes.

Continued on page 186

SAFETY ALERT

- Remind students to roll the marbles.
- You might place a barrier, such as a book, so that the marble does not roll off the table or under any items if floor space is used.
- Choose a large enough area in which students can roll marbles without interfering with others.
- To avoid confusion, assign students a numerical order in which to roll marbles.

Continued from page 185

Results

Students should observe on their graphs that as the time the marble travels in seconds doubles, so too does the distance covered.

Questions and Conclusions Answers

1. Student graphs will vary but should reflect the data they collected.

2. The estimate should be half the number of recorded meters.

3. The estimate should be twice the number of recorded meters.

Explore Further Answers

The marble would roll faster. The graph would have a steep slope. It would be steeper because the marble would travel faster.

Assessment

Check students' graphs to be sure they show that as the time increases in seconds, the distance increases in meters. You might include the following items from this investigation in student portfolios:

• Investigation 7-1 data table

• Graph with distance and meters

• Answers to Questions and Conclusions and Explore Further sections

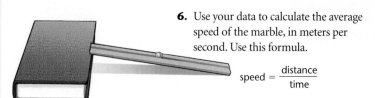

6. Use your data to calculate the average speed of the marble, in meters per second. Use this formula.

$$\text{speed} = \frac{\text{distance}}{\text{time}}$$

Questions and Conclusions

1. Make a graph with distance in meters on the vertical (up-and-down) axis. Place time in seconds on the horizontal (left-to-right) axis. Extend the axes twice as far as you need to in order to graph your data. Plot one point where 0 seconds crosses 0 meters, to show the beginning of the roll. Plot a second point, using the distance and time values you recorded. Connect the two points with a straight line.

2. Use the graph you made to estimate the distance the marble traveled after it had been moving for half the recorded time.

3. Extend the graph. Estimate the distance the marble would have gone if it had traveled for twice the recorded time.

Explore Further

What do you think would happen if you stacked another book on top of the book that is under the ruler? How would the graph for this setup look? How would this graph be different from the graph you made?

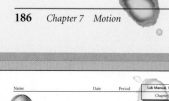

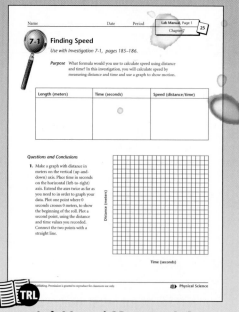

Lab Manual 25, pages 1–2

Objectives

After reading this lesson, you should be able to

◆ define and explain acceleration.

◆ perform calculations involving acceleration.

◆ define and explain deceleration.

◆ perform calculations involving deceleration.

Acceleration

The rate of change in velocity

A car stopped at a traffic light is not moving. But when the light turns green, the driver steps on the gas pedal. The car moves forward. Its speed increases. If the car moves away quickly, its velocity changes quickly. Some people might say that it has good "pickup."

Cars stopped at a stoplight accelerate as they begin to move forward.

In science, the word **acceleration**—rather than pickup—is used to describe a change in velocity. Acceleration also tells the rate at which velocity is changing. You can find the acceleration of an object by using this formula.

$$\text{acceleration} = \frac{\text{change in velocity}}{\text{change in time}}$$

A car starts from a stopped position. At the end of 5 seconds, it has a speed of 40 km/hr. Follow this method to find the car's acceleration.

1. Find the change in speed. To do so, subtract the beginning speed from the final speed.

40 km/hr	final speed
−0 km/hr	original speed
40 km/hr	change in speed

Chapter 7 Lesson 3

Overview In this lesson, students learn how to describe acceleration and deceleration and to calculate the acceleration of an object.

Objectives

- To define and explain acceleration
- To perform calculations involving acceleration
- To explain and define deceleration
- To perform calculations involving deceleration

Student Pages 187–191

Teacher's Resource Library

   Workbook Activity 32

   Alternative Workbook Activity 32

   Lab Manual 26

Vocabulary

acceleration
deceleration

 Warm-Up Activity

On the board, draw a large circle and a long straight line. Use your finger to trace along both the circle and the line. Ask students to suppose that you can move your finger at a constant rate of speed along both the circle and the line. Ask whether your speed changes on either path. *(no)* Ask whether your velocity changes on either path. *(It does on the circular path because direction is constantly changing.)* Ask students to use what they know about velocity to predict whether they accelerate when moving on either path. Encourage discussion and tell students they will find the answer in this lesson.

 Teaching the Lesson

Explain to students that velocity is a rate—speed and direction per time. Point out that acceleration is a rate of a rate. Acceleration is distance per time per time.

Have students look at the picture of the sky diver on page 188.

Continued on page 188

Continued from page 187

Ask them how they think having an open parachute causes a sky diver to decelerate. If necessary, explain that the open parachute traps air beneath it, allowing the diver to descend slowly.

 3 **Reinforce and Extend**

Deceleration
The rate of slowdown

2. Divide the change in speed by the time required to make the change, 5 seconds. The result is the acceleration.

$$\text{acceleration} = \frac{\text{change in speed}}{\text{change in time}}$$

$$\text{acceleration} = \frac{40 \text{ km}/1 \text{ hr}}{5 \text{ sec}/1}$$

$$\text{acceleration} = \frac{40 \text{ km}}{1 \text{ hr}} \times \frac{1}{5 \text{ sec}}$$

$$\text{acceleration} = 8 \text{ km/hr per sec}$$

The answer is read *8 kilometers per hour per second.* This means that the car's speed increases by 8 km per hour during every second of the acceleration.

Acceleration can also refer to a change in direction. For example, suppose a car moves at a constant speed around a curve. The car is accelerating because the direction in which it is traveling is changing.

The sky diver decelerates to land.

Deceleration

Acceleration is the rate of change in velocity. The examples of acceleration you have read about involved increases in speed. Objects can also slow down. When they slow down, they are said to decelerate. **Deceleration** is the rate of slowdown. The sky diver in the photo accelerates until the parachute opens. Then the sky diver decelerates.

Because deceleration is a form of acceleration, you can use the formula for acceleration to find deceleration. The result is a negative number instead of a positive number. A negative number is a number that is less than zero.

To understand deceleration, think about this example. A car is traveling at 20 km/hr. The driver suddenly puts on the brakes. The car comes to a complete stop 4 seconds later. You can follow this method to calculate the acceleration.

1. The original speed was 20 km/hr. The final speed is 0 km/hr. Therefore, the change in speed is calculated as follows.

0 km/hr	final speed
−20 km/hr	original speed
−20 km/hr	change in speed

2. Divide the change in speed by the change in time to obtain the acceleration.

$$\text{acceleration} = \frac{-20 \text{ km}/1 \text{ hr}}{4 \text{ sec}/1}$$

$$\text{acceleration} = \frac{-20 \text{ km}}{1 \text{ hr}} \times \frac{1}{4 \text{ sec}}$$

$$\text{acceleration} = -5 \text{ km/hr per sec}$$

The acceleration is −5 km/hour for each second. The minus (−) sign to the left of the 5 means that the number is less than zero. Therefore, this can also be expressed as a deceleration of 5 km per hour per second. The word *decelerating* already expresses the idea of negative acceleration. So, the negative sign does not have to be used if the answer is given as deceleration rather than acceleration.

SCIENCE JOURNAL

Have students copy the formula for calculating acceleration in their journal. Ask them to record examples for acceleration involving increases and decreases in speed.

LEARNING STYLES

Auditory/Verbal

Have pairs of students work together to review and understand acceleration and deceleration and how they relate to motion and speed. Have the pairs write the words *motion, speed, velocity, acceleration,* and *deceleration* on index cards. Then have them take turns choosing a card and orally defining the term. They should also give the formulas for calculating *speed, velocity, acceleration,* and *deceleration*.

CROSS-CURRICULAR CONNECTION

Language Arts

Discuss with students how some terms take on different meanings based on the context in which they are used. Point out that in everyday use, the terms *acceleration* and *deceleration* often have opposite meanings. You accelerate when you speed up and decelerate when you slow down. In scientific use, the terms are not opposites. Acceleration is any change in speed or direction. Deceleration is a form of acceleration involving a decrease in speed.

Ask volunteers to take turns reading the Science in Your Life feature on page 190. Introduce students to Newton's laws. (They will learn more about them in Lesson 4.) Lead a discussion about how they affect a pitched baseball. As stated in the first law of motion, the baseball remains at rest until the pitcher throws it; it continues moving, but not at the same speed because the forces of air resistance and gravity act on it. As stated in the second law of motion, a certain amount of force is required to give the ball acceleration. Finally, as stated in the third law of motion, if the batter makes contact with the ball, the force of the ball will be equaled by the force of the bat, making the ball travel in the opposite direction.

CROSS-CURRICULAR CONNECTION

Physical Education

Have students draw a diagram that illustrates the motion involved in a pitched baseball and a baseball that has just been hit. If the opportunity presents itself, you might have students engage in a friendly game of softball, where they can observe the forces affecting motion as they play.

SCIENCE JOURNAL

Have students write a short original story in which they describe the speed, velocity, and acceleration of an object. They could write about a ball, a balloon, a car, or another object of their choice.

When is a baseball moving fastest?

Pitchers have found ways to increase the velocity of their pitches—curveballs, fastballs, and sliders. But whatever the pitch, the ball starts slowing down when it leaves the pitcher's hand.

The pitcher puts the first force on the ball. The greatest acceleration occurs between the pitcher's windup and the release of the ball. While the ball is still in the pitcher's hand, it moves forward with increasing velocity. Once the ball is thrown, its forward velocity cannot increase. There is no longer a force acting on the ball in the direction of home plate.

Other forces are acting on the ball. Gravity pulls it toward the ground. Air resistance pushes the ball in the opposite direction of the motion. This causes the ball to decelerate. After it leaves the pitcher's hand, a baseball loses forward velocity. This loss occurs at the rate of about one kilometer per hour every 1.3 meters. By the time the ball reaches home plate, it has slowed down about 14 kilometers per hour.

Hitters depend on Newton's Laws to give them a fighting chance against a sizzling fastball.

Complete the table by finding the acceleration for each item. Some of your answers might be negative numbers. They express deceleration in terms of negative acceleration. The first one is done for you.

	Beginning Speed	Ending Speed	Elapsed Time	Acceleration
1.	40 km/hr	50 km/hr	5 sec	2 km/hr per sec
2.	20 km/sec	109 km/sec	4 sec	
3.	20 km/hr	55 km/hr	7 sec	
4.	0 m/sec	10 m/sec	10 sec	
5.	30 mm/sec	22 mm/sec	0.2 sec	
6.	20 mm/sec	22 mm/sec	0.2 sec	
7.	25 cm/sec	10 cm/sec	0.5 sec	
8.	60 km/hr	70 km/hr	2 sec	
9.	30 m/min	60 m/min	10 sec	
10.	5 cm/sec	10 cm/sec	0.5 sec	

Achievements in Science

Special Theory of Relativity

In 1905, Albert Einstein proposed his special theory of relativity. A main idea in Einstein's theory involves the speed of light. Einstein said that light always travels at the same speed and that nothing travels faster than light. The measurement of the speed of light never changes.

Einstein showed that time and space could not be considered separately. He concluded that space and time change when things move near the speed of light. Metersticks measure space; clocks measure time. At very high speeds, clocks slow down and metersticks get shorter. Measuring length and time depends on the object's speed relative to the measurer's speed. This is because measurement of the speed of light remains constant.

Einstein's conclusions shocked other physicists and still are challenging to understand. In daily life, we do not see length and time change with speed. But we also do not move at speeds close to the speed of light. Einstein's ideas have been proven mathematically and in the real world. They have changed the way scientists view the universe.

---

1. 2 km/hr per sec **2.** 22.25 km/sec per sec **3.** 5 km/hr per sec **4.** 1 m/sec per sec **5.** −40 mm/sec per sec **6.** 10 mm/sec per sec **7.** −30 cm/sec per sec **8.** 5 km/hr per sec **9.** 3 m/min per sec **10.** 10 cm/sec per sec

Achievements in Science

Have students take turns reading the Achievements in Science feature on page 191 aloud. Explain that Einstein's theory laid the groundwork for the research that resulted in atomic energy. Have groups of students find a basic explanation of the theory of relativity and summarize it.

ONLINE CONNECTION

Students may wish to learn more about Einstein and his work at www.pbs.org/wgbh/nova/einstein/genius/index.html.

Portfolio Assessment

Sample items include:
• Lesson 3 Review answers

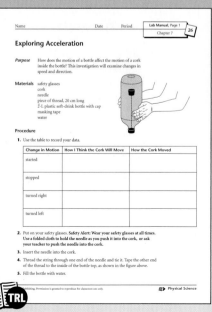

Name ___ Date ___ Period ___   Lab Manual, Page 1
Chapter 7   26

Exploring Acceleration

Purpose   How does the motion of a bottle affect the motion of a cork inside the bottle? This investigation will examine changes in speed and direction.

Materials   safety glasses
cork
needle
piece of thread, 20 cm long
2-L plastic soft-drink bottle with cap
masking tape
water

Procedure

1. Use the table to record your data.

Change in Motion	How I Think the Cork Will Move	How the Cork Moved
started		
stopped		
turned right		
turned left		

2. Put on your safety glasses. **Safety Alert: Wear your safety glasses at all times.** Use a folded cloth to hold the needle as you push it into the cork, or ask your teacher to push the needle into the cork.
3. Insert the needle into the cork.
4. Thread the string through one end of the needle and tie it. Tape the other end of the thread to the inside of the bottle top, as shown in the figure above.
5. Fill the bottle with water.

Physical Science

Lab Manual 26, pages 1–2

Name ___ Date ___ Period ___   Workbook Activity
Chapter 7, Lesson 3   32

Acceleration

EXAMPLE   To calculate acceleration, first subtract the beginning speed from the ending speed to find the change in speed. Then divide the change in speed by the time it takes to make the change.

beginning speed = 50 km/hr
ending speed = 65 km/hr → Step 1 65 km/hr − 50 km/hr = 15 km/hr
elapsed time = 5 sec
acceleration = 3 km/hr per sec

acceleration = change in speed / change in time   Step 2 3 km/hr per sec = 15 km/hr / 5 sec

Directions   Calculate the acceleration for each item. Write the answer on the line. Some answers will be negative numbers. A negative number shows deceleration.

	Beginning Speed	Ending Speed	Elapsed Time	Acceleration
1.	5 km/hr	55 km/hr	0.5 hr	
2.	0 km/hr	60 km/hr	0.2 hr	
3.	15 cm/sec	30 cm/sec	0.5 sec	
4.	120 mm/sec	250 mm/sec	20 sec	
5.	25 km/sec	10 km/sec	3 sec	
6.	105 m/min	60 m/min	9 sec	
7.	200 cm/sec	170 cm/sec	24 sec	
8.	240 km/hr	141 km/hr	33 sec	

Directions   Write the answer to each question on the line.

9. A bus was going 30 km/hr. Six seconds later, it was going 24 km/hr. What was its acceleration?

10. A bicycle was going 48 meters per minute. Five minutes earlier it was going 40 meters per minute. What was its acceleration?

Physical Science

Workbook Activity 32

Chapter 7 Lesson 4

Overview In this lesson, students learn how forces, including friction, affect a moving body. Students will also learn Newton's three laws of motion.

Objectives

- To explain what is meant by a force
- To define and explain friction
- To explain and apply the three laws of motion

Student Pages 192–195

Teacher's Resource Library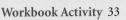

Workbook Activity 33

Alternative Workbook Activity 33

Lab Manual 27

Resource File 15

Vocabulary

force	inertia
friction	

Science Background

The First Law of Motion Every object continues at rest or in a state of uniform motion unless a force acts upon it. This law deals with a property known as inertia. Inertia is the tendency of an object to resist a change in motion. According to this law, no force is needed for an object to continue moving at a constant velocity. If an object is at rest, the object's velocity is zero. The object will remain at rest until a force acts on it.

The Second Law of Motion If a force acts upon an object, it experiences an acceleration in the direction of the force and proportional in amount to it, as well as inversely proportional to the mass of the object. In other words, for the same force, a smaller mass gets a bigger acceleration than a larger mass does. A large force will cause a greater acceleration than a small force. Because the force of gravity is dependent on the mass of an object, gravity will exert a greater force on a large mass.

Lesson 4 The Laws of Motion

Objectives

After reading this lesson, you should be able to

- explain what is meant by a force.
- define and explain friction.
- explain and apply the three laws of motion.

Force
A push or a pull

Friction
A force that opposes motion and that occurs when things slide or roll over each other

 Did You Know?

Automobile designers try to reduce air resistance from friction to make cars more efficient.

Sir Isaac Newton was a scientist who lived about 350 years ago. He studied changes in the motion of objects. From his studies, he was able to propose three laws to explain motion.

The First Law of Motion

If you wanted to move a large box that is resting on the floor, you would have to push or pull it. We call this push or pull a **force.** Whenever any object changes its velocity or accelerates, a force causes the change in motion.

> Newton's first law of motion states that if no force acts on an object at rest, it will remain at rest. The law also says that if the object is moving, it will continue moving at the same speed and in the same direction if no force acts on it.

Let's use an example to explain the second part of the law. A car on flat ground will roll to a stop if you take your foot off the gas pedal. The car slows down because an invisible force is at work. This invisible force is called **friction.** Friction is a force that opposes motion and occurs when things slide or roll over each other. Friction resists the movement of one surface past another. The rougher the surfaces are, the greater the friction.

The figure illustrates how friction helps stop a moving car. Notice the air resistance. Air resistance is a form of friction. It occurs when molecules of air touch the surface of the car.

Air resistance

Friction between road and moving tires

 Did You Know?

Ask a volunteer to read the feature on page 192. Have students name models or kinds of cars, such as sports cars and race cars, that are lower to the ground and streamlined and therefore can go faster. Have them name some car models that have much air resistance, such as minivans.

IN THE ENVIRONMENT

Point out to students that making cars sleeker and more aerodynamic not only makes them faster but enables them to use fuel more efficiently. Have students explain how this ultimately helps the environment. *(More fuel-efficient cars use less gasoline so fewer harmful emissions get into the air.)*

Inertia
The tendency of an object to resist changes in its motion

Inertia
The tendency of an object to resist changes in its motion

An object tends to resist changes in its motion. This tendency to resist changes in motion is called **inertia.** Inertia causes objects at rest to stay at rest. It also causes moving objects to continue moving.

The inertia of an object depends on its mass. The greater the mass of an object, the greater the force needed to cause a given change in its motion. For example, suppose you tried to push two rocks—a large one and a small one—across the ground. You would notice that if you apply the same push (force) to both rocks, the smaller rock will move faster after a certain amount of time. To make both rocks move at the same speed, you would have to push the large rock harder. The large rock has more mass than the small rock. Therefore, it has more inertia.

The Second Law of Motion

Newton's second law of motion says that the amount of force needed to produce a given change in the motion of an object depends on the mass of the object. The larger the mass, the more force is needed to give it a certain acceleration.

Suppose you drive a truck to a brickyard to pick up some bricks. After you load the bricks into the truck, you leave the brickyard. On the drive home, you notice that it takes longer to reach the same speed than it did when the truck was empty. What causes the difference? The truck full of bricks has more mass than the empty truck. So if you apply the same force to the truck both times (push the gas pedal the same amount), the truck with the bricks (more mass) will take longer to reach a given velocity.

Newton's second law can be written as follows.

$$\text{force} = \text{mass} \times \text{acceleration}, \text{ or } F = ma$$

A small force acting on a large mass will cause very little change in motion. A large force acting on a small mass will cause a much larger change in motion, that is, a greater acceleration.

Consequently, without air, the acceleration due to gravity at Earth's surface is 9.81 meters per second for each second. More simply, an object's speed increases by about 10 meters per second for each second it falls. When no air is present, falling objects have the same acceleration regardless of their masses.

The Third Law of Motion   Associated with every force is an equal and oppositely directed reaction force. This law does not mean that one force is a cause and the opposite force is an effect. Both forces come into existence at the same time.

Science Myth

Ask one student to read the myth portion (first sentence) of the Science Myth feature on page 193 and a second student to read the fact portion. Point out that in the case of the nonmoving book, balanced forces are being exerted. If one of the forces was stronger than the other, the book would move.

 Warm-Up Activity

Ask a volunteer to lift a book, open and close a door, and move a piece of furniture. Discuss which object required the most force to move it and whether a push or a pull action was used. Then have a volunteer stand near a wall and push on it with his or her palms. Discuss with students what is happening in terms of pushes or pulls.

 Teaching the Lesson

Have students write each lesson subhead on a sheet of paper. Encourage them to write a question about what they are to learn in each section of the lesson. For example, "The First Law of Motion" might suggest the question, What is the first law of motion? Have students write the answer to each question as they see it in the text.

Reinforce the concept of inertia. Remind students that an object with more mass has more inertia. Point out several objects in the room, and have students rank them in order of increasing inertia. Remind students that size can be deceiving. Hold up two balls—a softball and a polystyrene ball of the same size. Ask which has more inertia. *(softball)*

Continued on page 194

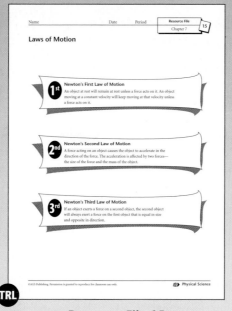

Resource File 15

Continued from page 193

Help students understand how friction is useful for vehicles. Vehicles are able to stop because the action of brakes increases friction between the tires and the road. Cars often skid on icy streets because the smooth surface of the ice lessens the friction between the tire and the road. Ask students what can be done to increase friction on an icy road. *(spread sand or some other coarse material on the road)*

 3 Reinforce and Extend

 ## IN THE COMMUNITY

Have students interview people in the community who move heavy objects every day, such as cargo loaders, furniture movers, or delivery people. Have students find out how these workers deal with the effects of mass, inertia, and friction in their jobs. For example, they use tools like dollies and hydraulic lifters. Ask students to discuss their findings in class.

LEARNING STYLES

 LEP/ESL

Ask students to draw pictures or diagrams illustrating each of the laws of motion. Encourage them to label the drawings or diagrams to help explain the law. Ask them to write a statement describing each law to accompany their pictures.

SCIENCE INTEGRATION

 Biology

Have students choose a sport to illustrate how the body uses one or more of Newton's laws of motion. *(For example, a baseball player taking off from a base, a soccer player kicking a ball, or a tennis ball connecting with a player's racket.)*

 Did You Know?

Inside a "Mexican jumping bean" is a larva that jumps upward. When the larva hits the top of the bean, its upward force exceeds the downward weight. So the entire bean jumps in the air.

 A force does not always produce a change in motion. You can push on a car and still not make it move. Why? Friction is another force acting against your push. There will be a change in motion only if there is an unbalanced, or net force.

The Third Law of Motion

Newton's third law of motion says that if an object exerts a force on a second object, the second object will always exert a force on the first object. This force will be equal to the force exerted by the first object. But the force will be in the opposite direction. This law is sometimes stated: For every action, there is an equal and opposite reaction.

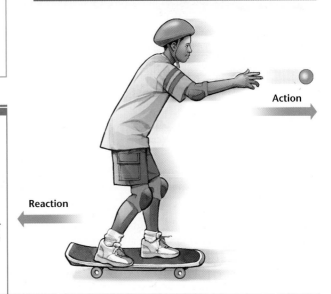

In the figure, the boy is standing on a skateboard, holding a ball in his hand. When he throws the ball forward, the boy and the skateboard move in the opposite direction from the ball. They move backward. This is an example of action and reaction. The action is throwing the ball. The reaction is the force of the ball on the boy. The boy is standing on the skateboard. Therefore, the skateboard moves backward. The action of throwing the ball causes the equal and opposite reaction of the skateboard moving backward.

194 *Chapter 7 Motion*

 ## CROSS-CURRICULAR CONNECTION

Language Arts

Explain that the word *inertia* comes from the Latin *iners,* meaning "unskilled," "idle," or "lazy." Have students use the word *inertia* in a sentence about a person. Then have them discuss how the original meaning of the Latin word is connected to the present scientific meaning.

Did You Know?

Ask a student to read the feature on page 194 aloud. If any students have access to Mexican jumping beans, have them bring them to class for a demonstration.

LEARNING STYLES

 Body/Kinesthetic

Have students create experiments that would demonstrate all three laws of motion in a bowling alley, using different sizes of bowling balls.

194 *Chapter 7 Motion*

Lesson 4 REVIEW

Write your answers to these questions in complete sentences on a sheet of paper.

1. What are Newton's three laws of motion?

2. When a marble is rolled along a floor, what force or forces cause it to slow down and stop?

3. If an object is at rest, what must happen for it to begin moving?

4. What is the reaction force when a hammer hits a nail?

5. Car A has twice the mass of car B. If the same force is used to push each car separately, how will their acceleration differ?

▼◄▲▼◄▲▼◄▲▼◄▲▼◄▲▼◄▲▼◄▲▼◄▲▼◄▲▼◄▲▼◄▲▼◄▲▼◄▲▼◄▲▼◄▲▼◄▲▼

Science at Work

Wind Tunnel Technician

Wind tunnel technicians help study the effects of wind on airplanes and other objects. In a wind tunnel, air is blown at an object and instruments record the effects. Wind tunnel technicians operate the tunnels and run the computers that collect data.

They also watch tests to be sure that they run smoothly and nothing breaks down.

Wind tunnel technicians usually have a two-year degree in a technical or engineering field. They also have engineering work experience. They often get on-the-job training as well.

Wind tunnel technicians must be observant and good with details. They must also have strong computer skills.

Motion   Chapter 7   **195**

Name   Date   Period   **Lab Manual, Page 1**
                                      Chapter 7   27

Newton's First Law of Motion

Purpose   How do forces affect objects at rest and objects in motion? In this investigation, you will observe the first law of motion.

Materials   safety glasses
              shoe box
              scissors
              tennis ball
              index card
              quarter

Procedure

1. Use the table to record your data.

Objects	Observations
tennis ball	
quarter	

2. Put on your safety glasses. **Safety Alert: Wear your safety glasses at all times.**

3. Cut one end from the side of the shoe box, as shown in the figure below. **Safety Alert: Carry the scissors with the blades pointed down. Use the scissors carefully as you cut the box.**

4. Place the shoe box on the floor with the open end pointing toward a wall. Place the tennis ball inside the box opposite the opening you made.

5. Rapidly push the box toward the wall. Then stop the box suddenly. Observe what happens to the ball. Write your observations in the data table.

Publishing. Permission is granted to reproduce for classroom use only.   **Physical Science**

Lab Manual 27, pages 1–2

Name   Date   Period   **Workbook Activity**
                                      Chapter 7, Lesson 4   33

The Laws of Motion

Directions Read the clues. Then complete the puzzle.

Across

1. force = mass × _____
3. a force that opposes motion
5. The _____ law of motion states that if no force acts on an object at rest, it will remain at rest.
7. This is a change in position.
10. The _____ law of motion describes the amount of force needed to change the motion of an object.
11. For every action, there is an equal and opposite _____.
12. One form of friction is air _____.
13. The amount of force needed to accelerate an object depends on the object's _____.

Down

2. Designers work to reduce air resistance on these.
4. a push or a pull
6. The _____ law of motion tells what happens when one object exerts a force on a second object.
8. the tendency of an object to resist changes in its motion
9. the scientist who proposed three laws to explain motion
12. If no force acts on a nonmoving object, it remains at _____.

Publishing. Permission is granted to reproduce for classroom use only.   **Physical Science**

Workbook Activity 33

Lesson 4 Review Answers

1. Law 1: If no force acts on an object at rest, it will remain at rest. If the object is moving, it will continue moving at the same speed and in the same direction if no force acts on it. Law 2: The amount of force needed to produce a given change in the motion of an object depends on the mass of the object. The larger the mass, the more force is needed to give it a certain acceleration. Law 3: For every action, there is an equal and opposite reaction. 2. Friction causes it to slow down and stop. 3. A force must act on the object for it to begin moving. 4. The reaction force is the nail hitting the hammer. 5. Car A will have half the acceleration of car B.

Science at Work

Ask volunteers to take turns reading the Science at Work feature on page 195. Have students think of additional fields, such as rocket science, the automobile industry, and the military, in which wind tunnel experiments would be conducted. Explain that most wind tunnels are smaller than the airplanes or other crafts that they test. Investigators use scaled-down models to conduct experiments. Gases can be blown into wind tunnels to duplicate certain flying conditions. Some wind tunnels can create very cold or very hot temperatures to test the performance of vehicles in various climatic conditions.

AT HOME

Have students write a brief description of three household tasks that they do frequently. Then have them discuss how the laws of motion influence each job. For example, suppose they must lift a variety of boxes and other items as they clean the garage. As described in the second law of motion, they must use greater strength to lift and move heavier objects.

Portfolio Assessment

Sample items include:
- Questions and answers from Teaching the Lesson
- Lesson 4 Review answers

Motion   Chapter 7   **195**

Chapter 7 Lesson 5

Overview In this lesson, students learn the effects gravity and air resistance have on falling objects.

Objectives

- To define and explain gravity
- To state the law of universal gravitation
- To explain how air resistance and gravity affect acceleration

Student Pages 196–200

Teacher's Resource Library

Workbook Activity 34

Alternative Workbook Activity 34

Lab Manual 28

Vocabulary

gravity
law of universal gravitation

 Warm-Up Activity

Place two small balls side by side on a desk. Gently push one ball while flicking the other. Allow both balls to roll off the desk. Ask students to describe what happened. (*The balls both started moving in a forward direction, but eventually fell downward.*)

 Teaching the Lesson

Have students use the lesson title and subheads to serve as headlines for notes they take. Encourage them to write the main idea for each paragraph in a section.

Students can experience the relationship between distance and the force of gravity by experiencing the similar effect that two opposite magnetic poles have on each other. Using magnets that they slowly pull apart, students can feel the force between them lessen. Make certain that students understand that the force between magnets is not a gravitational force.

Objectives

After reading this lesson, you should be able to

- ◆ define and explain gravity.
- ◆ state the law of universal gravitation.
- ◆ explain how air resistance and gravity affect acceleration.

Gravity

The force of attraction between any two objects that have mass

Law of universal gravitation

Gravitational force depends on the mass of the two objects involved and on the distance between them

One force with which you are probably familiar is the force of **gravity.** You might know that gravity keeps you from flying off the earth. If you are like many people, you might think of gravity as the pull exerted by Earth on other objects. But gravity is a force of attraction between any two objects that have mass.

The Law of Universal Gravitation

The gravitational force between two objects depends on the product of the masses of the two objects. Earth and the moon are two objects that have large masses. The gravitational force between them is large. Smaller objects, such as people, trees, and buildings, have much smaller gravitational forces because they have less mass. These forces are so small that they are very difficult to observe.

Mass is not the only thing that affects the pull of gravity. The distance between objects also determines how strong the force is due to gravity. The greater the distance between objects, the smaller the gravitational force is between them.

Think about an astronaut. When the astronaut is on Earth, gravity keeps him or her on the surface. The earth pulls on the astronaut. But the astronaut also pulls on the earth. The earth's gravity is strongest near the earth's surface. As the astronaut travels away from the earth in a spaceship, the pull of Earth's gravity gets weaker. But no matter how far from the earth the astronaut travels, the earth still exerts a force. In fact, Earth's gravity extends millions of kilometers into space.

The gravitational force of the sun, acting on the earth, keeps the earth in its orbit. The gravitational force prevents Earth from traveling away into space. Gravity also keeps the planets in space. And each planet exerts a gravitational force on nearby objects.

Friction between an object and liquid or gas is called drag. Sea anemones shrink their bodies to reduce the water current's drag. This keeps them from being pulled off rocks in strong currents.

Science Myth

Raindrops keep falling faster and faster until they reach the ground. **Fact:** A falling object's velocity increases but only up to terminal velocity. As velocity increases, air resistance increases. When the force of the air resistance equals the object's weight, the object's velocity no longer increases. This is called terminal velocity. If raindrops did not reach terminal velocity, they would crash through buildings.

Sir Isaac Newton, who stated the three laws of motion, put these ideas about gravity together in the **law of universal gravitation.** That law says two things. First, gravitational force depends on the product of the masses of the two objects involved. Second, the gravitational force depends on the distance between the objects.

Gravity and Acceleration

Have you ever jumped off a low diving board and then a high one? If so, you might have noticed that when you jumped from the higher board, you were moving faster when you struck the water. And you hit the water harder. That is because the force of gravity causes an object to speed up as it falls.

Gravity causes all objects to have the same acceleration as they fall. But another force—air resistance—also acts on a falling object. (Recall that air resistance is a form of friction. It is caused by molecules of air rubbing against a moving object.) Air resistance causes objects to fall at different speeds. The amount of air resistance acting on a moving object depends on the shape of the object. You can see in the figure that a sheet of paper will fall more slowly than a small stone. The reason is because the mass of the paper is spread out over a wider, thinner area than that of the stone. More molecules of air hit the surface of the paper.

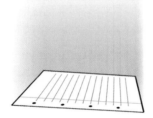

Did You Know?

Ask a student to read the feature on page 197 aloud. Have students discuss how swimmers and divers reduce drag when entering the water. (*They stretch their bodies and enter the water cleanly, hands first, instead of hitting the water with their whole body.*)

Science Myth

Ask one student to read the myth portion (first sentence) of the Science Myth feature on page 197 and a second student to read the fact portion. Explain that large raindrops are round but become flatter as they fall. Have students research the velocity of raindrops. The larger a raindrop, the faster it falls. A 0.2 inch (5 mm) diameter raindrop, which is a large drop, falls 30 feet (9 m) per second. Tiny drops, those with less than a 0.02 diameter, fall about 7 feet (2.1 m) per second.

LEARNING STYLES

Interpersonal/ Group Learning

Give pairs of students some small objects that have different masses and shapes. Tell students to rank the falling times of the objects, from slowest to fastest. Students can do this by repeated trials in which they drop two items at a time from shoulder height. (*Students should find that streamlined shapes experience the least air resistance.*)

CROSS-CURRICULAR CONNECTION

Language Arts

Tell students to imagine they are living on a planet where the force of gravity is either stronger or weaker than that on Earth. Have them write and illustrate an original story explaining what life would be like on the planet.

LEARNING STYLES

Visual/Spatial

To help students understand the concept of air resistance, give them two sheets of paper that are the same size and weight. Have them form one of the sheets into a tight ball. Then tell students to drop both sheets from the same height and to observe which reaches the floor first. (*the ball*) Explain that the sheet of paper has more area on which the air particles can hit the surface to slow it down.

SCIENCE JOURNAL

Have students write the law of universal gravitation. Have them illustrate the two parts of the law.

Lesson 5 Review Answers

1. Gravity is the force of attraction between two objects that have mass. 2. The mass of objects, the product of the masses, and the distance between objects affect the pull of gravity. 3. The moon has less gravity, so the astronaut's weight is less since weight is a factor of the pull of gravity on an object. 4. The force of gravity causes objects to speed up as they fall. It causes all objects to have the same acceleration as they fall. 5. Gravity causes an object to speed up as it falls, but other forces such as air resistance causes falling objects to slow down.

Achievements in Science

Have students take turns reading the Achievements in Science feature on page 198 aloud. Explain that Galileo's discovery became part of what is known as the law of falling bodies. Have students make a diagram that illustrates this law. The diagram should show two objects of different masses falling a certain distance in a certain time period. It should indicate the acceleration of the objects as they fall.

Portfolio Assessment

Sample items include:
• Notes from Teaching the Lesson
• Lesson 5 Review answers

Write your answers to these questions in complete sentences on a sheet of paper.

1. What is gravity?

2. What three factors affect the pull of gravity?

3. Weight is a measure of the pull of gravity on an object. Use this information to explain why an astronaut weighs less on the moon than on Earth.

4. How does gravity affect acceleration?

5. How does gravity affect deceleration?

Achievements in Science

Law of Uniformly Accelerated Motion

Aristotle believed that heavier objects fall faster than lighter ones. He believed that objects that weigh twice as much as others fall twice as fast. For about 1,000 years, scientists generally agreed with Aristotle's thinking.

In the early 1600s, Galileo conducted the first experiment that showed that Aristotle was wrong. Galileo faced challenges in constructing his experiment. He could not simply drop objects from a tall building for two reasons. First, the clocks of his time were not accurate. Second, he had no way to measure the speed when each object hit the earth.

Instead, Galileo tested Aristotle's theory by rolling objects on a slanted ramp. He determined their positions at equal time periods, using his own pulse as a clock.

Galileo's experiments showed that all objects experience constant acceleration when air resistance is not considered. No matter how much they weigh, all objects fall at a steady rate of acceleration. This type of acceleration is known as free fall. Free fall acceleration has its own symbol, g. At sea level, g equals 9.8 m/sec^2.

Name _____ Date _____ Period _____ | Workbook Activity | 34 |
Chapter 7, Lesson 5

Motion: Terms Review

Directions Match each term in Column A with its meaning in Column B.
Write the correct letter on the line.

Column A

_____ **1.** inertia

_____ **2.** acceleration

_____ **3.** friction

_____ **4.** gravity

_____ **5.** deceleration

_____ **6.** force

_____ **7.** speed

_____ **8.** elapsed time

_____ **9.** motion

Column B

A the tendency to resist change in motion

B a change in position

C the rate at which the position of an object changes

D the time that passes between one event and another

E the rate of change in velocity

F a force that opposes motion

G the force of attraction between any two objects that have mass

H the rate of slowdown

I a push or a pull

Directions Unscramble the word or words in parentheses to complete each sentence.

10. The _____ of a moving object tells the direction of motion as well as the speed. (yetlovic)

11. A _____ has no acceleration. (cannotts deeps)

12. The length of the path between two points is _____. (candetis)

13. The law of _____ states that gravity depends on mass and distance. (savenuril tatairoving)

Directions Tell how each pair is alike and different.

14. speed and velocity

_____

15. inertia and friction

_____

Publishing. Permission is granted to reproduce for classroom use only.   ▶ Physical Science

Workbook Activity 34

INVESTIGATION

Materials

◆ safety glasses
◆ string, 3 meters long
◆ 2 straws
◆ 2 chairs
◆ 2 long balloons
◆ masking tape

Newton's Third Law of Motion

Purpose

What happens when you release a balloon that is filled with air? This investigation will demonstrate action and reaction using balloons filled with air.

Procedure

Part A

1. Copy the data table on a sheet of paper.

Part A Observations	Part B Observations

2. Put on your safety glasses.

3. Thread the string through the two straws.

4. Tie the ends of the string to the backs of two chairs.

5. Blow up a balloon. Hold the end closed. Have a classmate use masking tape to attach the balloon to one of the straws, as shown in Figure A. Position the balloon near the end of the string.

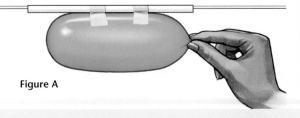

Figure A

Investigation 7-2

The Purpose portion of the student investigation begins with a question to draw them into the activity. Encourage students to read the investigation steps and formulate their own questions before beginning the investigation. The investigation will take approximately 30 minutes to complete. Students will use these process and thinking skills: observing; collecting, recording, and interpreting data; making and using models; communicating; and comparing.

Preparation

• You may wish to cut the string into 3-meter lengths yourself.

• Students may use Lab Manual 28 to record their data and answer the questions.

Procedure

• You can have students work in groups of three. Assign one student to gather equipment. Student A threads the string through the straw and attaches it to the chairs. Student B blows up the balloon, holds the end, and releases it. Student C attaches the balloon to a straw with masking tape and then attaches the ball.

• Have students review Newton's third law of motion on page 194 in their texts.

• Tell students to make sure the string is not limp but stretched out between the two chairs.

• Suggest that students have the strips of masking tape ready before they attempt to attach the blown-up balloon and the ball to a straw.

SAFETY ALERT

◆ Make certain the area in which students will conduct this investigation is large enough to accommodate all your groups.

◆ All students in the class should wear safety glasses at all times to protect their eyes from injury if a balloon should suddenly pop.

Continued on page 200

Continued from page 199

Results

Students should observe that for every force (escaping air) there is an equal and opposite reaction (movement of balloon).

Questions and Conclusions Answers

1. The escaping air moves in the opposite direction of the balloon.

2. The balloon moves in the opposite direction of the escaping air.

3. Because the balloon and air move in opposite directions and the movement of the balloon is caused by the escaping air, they demonstrate Newton's third law of motion, which states that for every action, there is an equal and opposite reaction.

4. The balloons do not move in any direction.

5. The forces are opposite horizontal forces.

Explore Further Answer

The weight would keep the balloon from moving as far or as quickly because of the added mass.

Assessment

Check students' data tables to be sure they have recorded their observations of actions and reactions correctly. You might include the following items from this investigation in student portfolios:

• Investigation 7-2 data table

• Answers to Questions and Conclusions and Explore Further sections

---

6. Release the balloon. Record your observations.

Part B

7. Tape the ends of the two straws together. Blow up the balloon again. Hold the end closed. Ask a classmate to attach the balloon to one of the straws.

8. Blow up another balloon so it has about as much air as the first balloon. Ask a classmate to attach the balloon to the other straw as shown in Figure B.

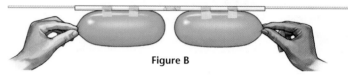

Figure B

9. Release both balloons at the same time. Record your observations.

Questions and Conclusions

1. In Part A, in what direction does the escaping air move?

2. In Part A, in what direction does the balloon move?

3. How does Part A demonstrate Newton's third law of motion?

4. In Part B, in what direction do the balloons move?

5. In Part B, describe the directions of the forces to explain what the balloons do.

Explore Further

In Part A, if you attached a weight to the balloon, how would that affect its motion?

Lab Manual 28

Chapter 7 SUMMARY

- Motion is a change in position.

- Elapsed time is the time between events. It is calculated by subtracting the time of the earlier event from the time of the later event.

- Speed is the rate at which the position of an object changes. It is equal to distance divided by time.

- The formula for speed can be rearranged for calculation of distance or time.

- Graphs of distance versus time can be used to describe motion and to make predictions about distances.

- Velocity tells about the speed and direction of a moving object.

- Objects may travel at varying speed rather than constant speed.

- Acceleration is the rate of change in velocity. Acceleration equals the change in velocity divided by the change in time.

- Deceleration is the rate of slowdown. Deceleration occurs whenever acceleration is negative. It is usually calculated as negative acceleration.

- A force is a push or a pull.

- Newton's first law of motion states that an object remains at rest or keeps moving at constant speed unless an outside force acts on it.

- Newton's second law of motion states that the amount of force needed to change the motion of an object depends on the mass of the object.

- Newton's third law of motion states that for every action there is an equal and opposite reaction.

- Gravity is a force of attraction between any two objects that have mass. According to the law of universal gravitation, the greater the masses are, the greater the force is. The greater the distance is, the less the force is.

- Gravity causes all falling objects to have the same acceleration. Air resistance acts on falling objects to slow them down.

Science Words

acceleration, 187	force, 192	law of universal
constant speed, 179	friction, 192	gravitation, 196
deceleration, 188	gravity, 196	motion, 174
distance, 175	inertia, 193	speed, 175
elapsed time, 174		velocity, 182

Chapter 7 Summary

Have volunteers read aloud each Summary item on page 201. Ask volunteers to explain the meaning of each item. Direct students' attention to the Science Words box on the bottom of page 201. Have them read and review each term and its definition.

Chapter 7 Review

Use the Chapter Review to prepare students for tests and to reteach content from the chapter.

Chapter 7 Mastery Test

The Teacher's Resource Library includes two parallel forms of the Chapter 7 Mastery Test. The difficulty level of the two forms is equivalent. You may wish to use one form as a pretest and the other form as a posttest.

Review Answers
Vocabulary Review

1. law of universal gravitation 2. motion
3. force 4. friction 5. inertia

Concept Review

6. B 7. C 8. D 9. C 10. C 11. A

Critical Thinking

12. The bicycle's speed is 4.7 miles per hour. 13. At the end of 7 hours, the train will have traveled 350 miles. The graph shows the train traveling at a constant rate of 50 miles per hour. By extending the straight line to the seventh hour, I can predict the distance the train will travel in 7 hours. 14. The empty bus has less mass and therefore less force is needed for it to accelerate. 15. A greater mass exerts a greater force of gravity.

TEACHER ALERT

Because of limited space in this Chapter Review, not all of the vocabulary terms introduced in this chapter appear in the Vocabulary Review section. You may want to create an activity using the missing words to give students practice with all of the terms in this chapter. Here are the terms that are not covered in the section.

acceleration	elapsed time
constant speed	gravity
deceleration	speed
distance	velocity

Vocabulary Review

Choose a word or words from the Word Bank that best complete each sentence. Write the answer on a sheet of paper.

Word Bank
force
friction
inertia
law of universal gravitation
motion

1. Newton put ideas about gravity together in the _____.
2. A change in position is called _____.
3. A push or pull is called _____.
4. When things slide or roll over each other, _____ occurs.
5. The tendency to resist changes in motion is called _____.

Concept Review

Choose the answer that best completes each sentence. Write the letter of the answer on your paper.

6. To find the speed of an object, you need to know _____ and time.
   A motion   **B** distance   **C** acceleration   **D** elapsed time

7. The length of time that passes from one event to another is _____.
   A average speed   **C** elapsed time
   B constant speed   **D** inertia

8. You can calculate acceleration by _____.
   A adding change in velocity and change in time
   B subtracting change in time from change in velocity
   C multiplying change in velocity and change in time
   D dividing change in velocity by change in time

9. If the result of calculating acceleration is a negative number, an object is _____.
   A speeding up   **C** decelerating
   B moving at a constant speed   **D** moving uphill

10. The formula for calculating force is _____.
    A mass + acceleration   **C** mass × acceleration
    B acceleration − mass   **D** mass ÷ acceleration

Name _____ Date _____ Period _____ | Mastery Test A, Page 1 / Chapter 7

Chapter 7 Mastery Test A

Part A Read each sentence. Write the letter of the correct answer on the line.

_____ 1. The force of attraction between any two objects that have mass is
   A motion   **B** velocity   **C** gravity   **D** friction
_____ 2. The rate at which the position of an object changes is
   A velocity   **B** acceleration   **C** speed   **D** inertia
_____ 3. A change of position is
   A motion   **B** velocity   **C** acceleration   **D** speed
_____ 4. A push or pull that causes a change in motion is
   A inertia   **B** friction   **C** speed   **D** force
_____ 5. The rate of change in velocity is
   A motion   **B** acceleration   **C** deceleration   **D** speed
_____ 6. The speed and direction in which an object is moving is
   A motion   **B** elapsed time   **C** distance   **D** velocity

Part B Write the answer to each question on the line.

7. A car traveled 330 miles in 6 hours. What was its average speed?
8. How long will it take an airplane to go 800 miles if it is traveling at an average speed of 650 miles per hour?
9. How far can a motorcycle travel at 90 kilometers per hour in 2.5 hours?
10. A truck goes from a stop to 60 km/hr in 35 seconds. What is its rate of acceleration?
11. The driver of a car traveling 60 km/hr brakes for a light and stops in 8 seconds. What is the rate of deceleration?

©AGS Publishing. Permission is granted to reproduce for classroom use only.   ▶ Physical Science

---

Name _____ Date _____ Period _____ | Mastery Test A, Page 2 / Chapter 7

Chapter 7 Mastery Test A, continued

12. Use the graph below to answer these questions.
    A How long will it take the car to go 350 kilometers?
    B How far can it travel in 7 hours?

Distance Traveled by a Car

(graph: Distance (km) vs Time (hours))

Part C Write a short answer for each question.

13. Explain Newton's first law of motion and give an example of how it works.
14. Explain Newton's second law of motion and give an example of how it works.
15. Explain Newton's third law of motion and give an example of how it works.

©AGS Publishing. Permission is granted to reproduce for classroom use only.   ▶ Physical Science

Chapter 7 Mastery Test A

11. The law that states that if no force acts on an object at rest, it will remain at rest is _____.
- **A** Newton's first law of motion
- **B** Newton's second law of motion
- **C** Newton's third law of motion
- **D** the law of universal gravitation

Critical Thinking

Write the answer to each of these questions on your paper.

12. The figure below shows the motion of a bike. Calculate the speed of the bike.

**Initial time
3:30 P.M.**

**Final time
5:00 P.M.**

◄——— 7 miles ———►

13. The graph shows distance and time for 6 hours for a train moving at a constant speed. Use the graph to predict how far the train will have traveled at the end of 7 hours. Explain how you used the graph to make your prediction.

14. Why does it take an empty bus less time than a bus filled with people to reach the same speed?

15. How does mass affect gravity?

Test-Taking Tip | When studying for a test, review any tests or quizzes you took earlier that cover the same information.

Chapter 7 Mastery Test B

Name _____ Date _____ Period _____ | **Mastery Test B,** Page 1 / Chapter 7

Chapter 7 Mastery Test B

Part A Write the answer to each question on the line.

1. How long will it take an airplane to go 800 miles if it is traveling at an average speed of 650 miles per hour?
2. How far can a motorcycle travel at 90 kilometers per hour in 2.5 hours?
3. A car traveled 330 miles in 6 hours. What was its average speed?
4. A truck goes from a stop to 60 km/hr in 35 seconds. What is its rate of acceleration?
5. The driver of a car traveling 60 km/hr brakes for a light and stops in 8 seconds. What is the rate of deceleration?
6. Use the graph below to answer these questions.
   A How long will it take the car to go 350 kilometers?
   B How far can it travel in 7 hours?

Distance Traveled by a Car

Part B Read each sentence. Write the letter of the correct answer on the line.

7. The rate at which the position of an object changes is
   A velocity   B acceleration   C speed   D inertia
8. The rate of change in velocity is
   A motion   B acceleration   C deceleration   D speed
9. The speed and direction in which an object is moving is
   A motion   B elapsed time   C distance   D velocity

©AGS Publishing. Permission is granted to reproduce for classroom use only. ■ **Physical Science**

Name _____ Date _____ Period _____ | **Mastery Test B,** Page 2 / Chapter 7

Chapter 7 Mastery Test B, continued

10. A change of position is
    A motion   B velocity   C acceleration   D speed
11. A push or pull that causes a change in motion is
    A inertia   B friction   C speed   D force
12. The force of attraction between any two objects that have mass is
    A motion   B velocity   C gravity   D friction

Part C Write a short answer for each question.

13. Explain Newton's first law of motion and give an example of how it works.

14. Explain Newton's second law of motion and give an example of how it works.

15. Explain Newton's third law of motion and give an example of how it works.

©AGS Publishing. Permission is granted to reproduce for classroom use only. ■ **Physical Science**

Chapter 7 Mastery Test B

ALTERNATIVE ASSESSMENT

Alternative Assessment items correlate to the student Goals for Learning at the beginning of this chapter.

- Have students write definitions of *motion* and *speed* and provide an example that illustrates each definition.

- Ask students to write and solve problems involving calculation of speed, distance, or time.

- Ask students to use their body or a toy car to model motion, constant speed, varying speed, and changes in velocity.

- Show students the graph on page 179. Have them explain how they would use the graph to find the distance traveled after 3.5 hours or to predict the distance traveled after 9 hours.

- Ask students to write a word problem that provides a beginning speed, ending speed, and elapsed time. Have them exchange problems with a partner and calculate the acceleration. Then repeat the activity with a problem that involves deceleration.

- Ask students to use a toy car to define and model force and tell how it relates to Newton's first law of motion.

- Provide students with an index card, several coins of different sizes, and an empty plastic glass. Place the card over the opening of the glass. Ask students to show how they could use the coins to demonstrate Newton's second law, showing that an object with more mass has more inertia. *(One by one, coins should be placed in the center of the card. The card should be pulled on to drop the coin into the glass. The largest coin should require the most force to move it.)*

- Have students use a marble and a small ball to represent Earth and the moon. Have them use them to define gravity and explain the law of universal gravitation.

Chapter

8

Planning Guide

Work and Machines

	Student Pages	Vocabulary	Lesson Review
Lesson 1 What Is Work?	206–208	✔	✔
Lesson 2 Power	209–210	✔	✔
Lesson 3 Energy	211–217	✔	✔
Lesson 4 Using Levers	218–223	✔	✔
Lesson 5 Mechanical Advantage	224–228	✔	✔
Lesson 6 Some Other Kinds of Simple Machines	229–234	✔	✔

Chapter Activities

Student Text
Science Center

Teacher's Resource Library
Community Connection 8: Machines in
the Community

Assessment Options

Student Text
Chapter 8 Review

Teacher's Resource Library
Chapter 8 Mastery Tests A and B

Student Text Features / Teaching Strategies / Learning Styles / Teacher's Resource Library

Achievements in Science	Science at Work	Science in Your Life	Investigation	Science Myth	Note	Technology Note	Did You Know	Science Integration	Science Journal	Cross-Curricular Connection	Online Connection	Teacher Alert	Applications (Home, Career, Community, Global, Environment)	Auditory/Verbal	Body/Kinesthetic	Interpersonal/Group Learning	Logical/Mathematical	Visual/Spatial	LEP/ESL	Workbook Activities	Alternative Workbook Activities	Lab Manual	Resource File	Self-Study Guide
	208				✔		207	208		207		207	207							35	35			✔
					✔											210		209		36	36			✔
		214	216	213	✔	✔		213	215	212	212	212	212, 214, 215		214				212	37	37	29		✔
223			220			✔		220		222	222	219, 222	220, 221	220		221		219		38	38		16	✔
226			227						225	225		224	225							39	39	30		✔
					✔		231	231		232		230, 233	231		232	233				40	40	31, 32	17	✔

Pronunciation Key

a hat	e let	ī ice	ô order	u̇ put	sh she	ə a in about
ā age	ē equal	o hot	oi oil	ü rule	th thin	e in taken
ä far	ėr term	ō open	ou out	ch child	ᵺ then	i in pencil
â care	i it	ȯ saw	u cup	ng long	zh measure	o in lemon
						u in circus

Alternative Workbook Activities

The Teacher's Resource Library (TRL) contains a set of lower-level worksheets called Alternative Workbook Activities. These worksheets cover the same content as the regular Workbook Activities but are written at a second-grade reading level.

Skill Track Software

Use the Skill Track Software for Physical Science for additional reinforcement of this chapter. The software program allows students using AGS textbooks to be assessed for mastery of each chapter and lesson of the textbook. Students access the software on an individual basis and are assessed with multiple-choice items.

Chapter 8:
Work and Machines
pages 204–237

Lessons

Skill Track Software for Physical Science

Teacher's Resource Library TRL

Workbook Activities 35–40

Alternative Workbook Activities 35–40

Lab Manual 29–32

Community Connection 8

Resource File 16–17

Chapter 8 Self-Study Guide

Chapter 8 Mastery Tests A and B

(Answer Keys for the Teacher's Resource Library begin on page 402 of the Teacher's Edition. The Materials List for the Lab Manual activities begins on page 419.)

Science Center

Display an assortment of simple machines, such as a pencil, manual pencil sharpener, screw-top jar lids, a claw hammer, broom, shovel, pliers, ice cube tongs, nutcracker, scissors, tweezers, fishing rod with reel, baseball bat, oars, and paper punch. As students complete the chapter, have them return to the machines several times to investigate how they perform work, what makes them useful, and how they save people effort. After reading the chapter, student volunteers can demonstrate how each machine works.

Community Connection 8

Chapter

8

Work and Machines

The falling water in a dam has a lot of mechanical energy. We can harness that mechanical energy and turn it into electrical energy. We do this through a machine called a turbine. A turbine converts the mechanical energy of the water into electrical energy. In Chapter 8, you will learn about six main forms of stored energy—mechanical, electrical, chemical, heat, nuclear, and radiant. You also will explore the nature of work and how scientists measure work. And you will learn how machines make work easier.

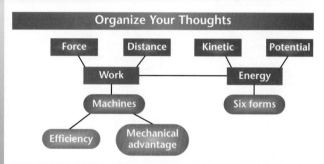

Organize Your Thoughts

Force Distance Kinetic Potential

Work Energy

Machines Six forms

Efficiency Mechanical advantage

Goals for Learning

◆ To define and explain work and power
◆ To define and explain energy
◆ To name six forms of energy
◆ To describe the classes of levers
◆ To calculate efficiency and mechanical advantage
◆ To describe six types of simple machines

205

Introducing the Chapter

Invite students to identify an activity they consider to be hard work. Explain that, no matter how tired they get, a scientist might not agree that they had done any work. Have students read the Goals for Learning and note that the first part of the chapter will provide a scientific definition of work.

Ask students to examine the photo of a dam on page 204 and tell what kind of energy it shows. Then read the introduction aloud together. Discuss the Organize Your Thoughts chart and the ways students think work, energy, and machines are related.

Have students read the Goals for Learning again. Help them write questions about what they want to find out about work, energy, and simple machines. For example, students might ask: "How do I calculate the amount of work done?" or "What is mechanical advantage?" Students can use their questions to help set a purpose for reading.

Notes and Technology Notes

Ask volunteers to read the notes that appear in the margins throughout the chapter. Then discuss them with the class.

TEACHER'S RESOURCE

The AGS Teaching Strategies in Science Transparencies may be used with this chapter. The transparencies add an interactive dimension to expand and enhance the *Physical Science* program content.

CAREER INTEREST INVENTORY

The AGS Harrington-O'Shea Career Decision-Making System-Revised (CDM) may be used with this chapter. Students can use the CDM to explore their interests and identify careers. The CDM defines career areas that are indicated by students' responses on the inventory.

Name	Date	Period	SELF-STUDY GUIDE

Chapter 8: Work and Machines

Goal 8.1	To define and explain work and power

Date	Assignment	Score
	1. Read pages 206–207.	
	3. Complete the Lesson 1 Review on page 208.	
	4. Complete Workbook Activity 35.	
	5. Read page 209.	
	6. Complete the Lesson 2 Review on page 210.	
	7. Complete Workbook Activity 36.	

Comments:

Goal 8.2	To define and explain energy

Date	Assignment	Score
	8. Read page 211.	

Comments:

Goal 8.3	To name six forms of energy

Date	Assignment	Score
	9. Read pages 212–214.	
	10. Complete the Lesson 3 Review on page 215.	
	11. Complete Workbook Activity 37.	
	12. Complete Investigation 8-1 on pages 216–217.	

Comments:

©AGS Publishing. Permission is granted to reproduce for classroom use only. ▶ Physical Science

---

Name	Date	Period	SELF-STUDY GUIDE

Chapter 8: Work and Machines, continued

Goal 8.4	To describe the classes of levers

Date	Assignment	Score
	13. Read pages 218–221.	

Comments:

Goal 8.5	To calculate efficiency and mechanical advantage

Date	Assignment	Score
	14. Read pages 221–222.	
	15. Complete the Lesson 4 Review on page 223.	
	16. Complete Workbook Activity 38.	
	17. Read pages 224–225.	
	18. Complete the Lesson 5 Review on page 226.	
	19. Complete Workbook Activity 39.	
	20. Complete Investigation 8-2 on pages 227–228.	

Comments:

Goal 8.6	To describe six types of simple machines

Date	Assignment	Score
	21. Read pages 229–233.	
	22. Complete the Lesson 6 Review on page 234.	
	23. Complete Workbook Activity 40.	
	24. Read the Chapter 8 Summary on page 235.	
	25. Complete the Chapter 8 Review on pages 236–237.	

Comments:

Student's Signature _____ Date _____

Instructor's Signature _____ Date _____

©AGS Publishing. Permission is granted to reproduce for classroom use only. ▶ Physical Science

TRL **TRL**

Chapter 8 Self-Study Guide

Lesson at a Glance

Chapter 8 Lesson 1

Overview In this lesson, students learn the scientific meaning of work and how to measure how much work is done.

Objectives

- To define and explain work
- To measure and calculate work

Student Pages 206–208

Teacher's Resource Library **TRL**

Workbook Activity 35

Alternative Workbook Activity 35

Vocabulary

joule

work

Science Background

Students will need to adjust to the specific meaning of *work* in physical science. It is not a synonym for *effort*. Movement is the key. Only when an effort force causes matter to move a measurable distance in the same direction as the force is work done. In this sense, play is work: a sled sliding downhill is doing work. Since force is measured metrically in newtons, then work (force times distance) is measured in newton-meters (*N-m*). A newton measures amount of force of the earth's gravity on an object. An object with a mass of 1 kg weighs 9.8 N. The scientific name for this type of unit is the joule. One newton-meter equals one joule (1 *N-m* = 1 *J*).

 Warm-Up Activity

Have volunteers lift a box and walk forward in clear view of their classmates. Ask observers to identify times when they think work is being done. Explain that unless movement occurs, no work is done. Have them read the lesson to learn why this is true.

Objectives

After reading this lesson, you should be able to

- ◆ define and explain work.
- ◆ measure and calculate work.

Work

What happens when an object changes its position by moving in the direction of the force that is being applied

You probably do some "work" around your home. What things do you consider work? You might think of ironing clothes, washing dishes, taking out the garbage, and sweeping the floors. In everyday language, we use the word *work* as another word for *labor*.

Scientific Meaning of Work

To scientists, however, **work** is what happens when an object changes its position by moving in the direction of the force that is being applied. Remember, a force is a push or a pull.

Suppose you struggled for an hour to lift a very heavy box, but you could not budge it. No work was done in the scientific sense, because the box did not move. If you rolled a ball down a ramp, however, work was done. The reason is the ball changed its direction due to the force of gravity.

When Sarah lifts the box, she is doing work.

Measuring Work

How can you measure work? You can start by measuring how much force is used to do the work. Spring scales, like the one shown on page 207, are used to measure force. In the metric system, force is measured in newtons. The spring scale shows that the apple is exerting a force of 1 newton.

To measure work, you must also measure the distance (in meters) through which the force acted. To find out how much work was done, use this formula.

$$work = force \times distance$$

Joule
The metric unit of work

Your answer will be in newton-meters. Scientists have a simpler name for a <u>newton-meter</u>. <u>It is called a **joule**.</u> <u>A joule is the metric unit of work.</u> When calculating work, your answer will be in joules.

Suppose a woman is pushing a bike. She uses a force of 2 newtons and pushes the bike a distance of 10 meters. How much work did she do?

 EXAMPLE

work = force × distance
work = 2 newtons × 10 meters
work = 20 newton-meters
work = 20 joules

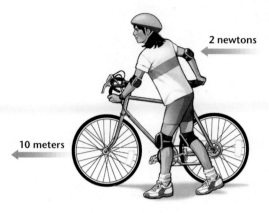

2 newtons

10 meters

 Did You Know?

Using the same mower, a shorter person can mow a lawn more easily than a taller person can. A shorter person holds the mower handle closer to the ground. This puts more force on the handle in the mowing direction.

Because force, distance, and work are always related, you can calculate any one of them if you know the other two. For example, if you know how much work was done and you know the distance, you can calculate how much force was used. Take the amount of work done and divide it by the distance.

$$force = \frac{work}{distance}$$

If you know how much work was done and how much force was needed, you can calculate the distance. Take the amount of work done and divide it by the amount of force that was used.

$$distance = \frac{work}{force}$$

Lesson 1 Review Answers

1. Work is what happens when an object changes position by moving in the direction of the applied force. 2. You need to know how much force was applied and the distance the object moved in the direction of the force. 3. The metric unit of work is the joule. 4. 8 newtons × 13 meters = 104 joules. 5. The person who picked up the kitten did more work.

Science at Work

Ask volunteers to read the Science at Work feature about machine designers on page 208. Explain that specifications are special instructions that tell exactly the materials, sizes, and other statistics needed to build or make something.

Point out that computer and mathematics skills as well as problem-solving skills and creativity are essential to succeed in this arena. Encourage students who may be interested in this kind of work to research the profession to learn more about it.

SCIENCE JOURNAL

Have students write a paragraph comparing and contrasting their ideas about what work is before and after reading this lesson.

Portfolio Assessment

Sample items include:
• Sentences about what to remember from Teaching the Lesson
• Lesson 1 Review answers

Write your answers to these questions in complete sentences on a sheet of paper.

1. What is the scientific meaning of work?

2. What must you know to find the amount of work done on an object?

3. What is the metric unit of work?

4. A man pushed a table, using a force of 8 newtons. He moved the table 13 meters. How much work did he do?

5. One person solved 40 math problems in her head. Another person picked up a kitten. Which person did more work, in the scientific sense?

Science at Work

Machine Designer

Machine designers work in teams with engineers to design and build machinery. They use computer systems to make designs, drawings, and specifications for machines and their parts. Machine designers make cost and parts estimates and project schedules. As part of their work, they also test and analyze machines and their parts.

Machine designers usually have completed a two- or three-year technical program in mechanical engineering.

Machine designers are natural inventors. They are good at sketching, drawing, mathematics, and mechanical problem solving. Machine designers must know about materials and equipment involved in designing, constructing, and operating machines.

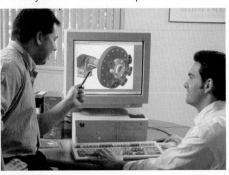

Name _____ Date _____ Period _____

Workbook Activity
Chapter 8, Lesson 1 35

What Is Work?

Directions On the line, write the word or words that best complete the sentence.

1. When work is done, an object changes its _____.

2. Work is done when a force moves an object in the _____ of the force that is applied.

3. To measure force, you must _____ the force by the distance through which it acts.

4. Work is measured in newton-meters, or _____.

5. The formula for measuring work is _____.

Directions Use the formula *work = force × distance* to find each answer. Give the answer in joules.

6. Julie rolled a 2-kg ball down a ramp 10 meters long. (Remember, 1 kg = 9.8 newtons.) How much work was done? _____

7. Kevin lifted a 10-newton box a distance of 1.5 meters. How much work did he do? _____

8. A high jumper weighing 700 newtons jumps over a bar 2.0 meters high. What work does the high jumper do? _____

9. A mountain climber who weighs 900 newtons scales a 100-meter cliff. How much work does the climber do? _____

10. A parent uses a force of 300 newtons to pull a toddler in a wagon for 400 meters. How much work did the parent do? _____

11. Pushing a lawn mower requires a force of 200 newtons. If 4,000 joules of work is performed, how far has the mower moved? _____

12. A force of 550 newtons was used to move a stone 23 meters. How much work was done? _____

13. A box was pushed 42 meters, and 13,734 joules of work was done. How much force was used? _____

14. A pitcher threw a ball of 2 newtons and did 330 joules of work. How far did she throw the ball? _____

15. A landscape worker attempted to move a 300 kg boulder for 30 minutes but was unable to budge it. How much work did the worker do? _____

Publishing. Permission is granted to reproduce for classroom use only. ▶ Physical Science

Workbook Activity 35

Objectives

After reading this lesson, you should be able to

♦ define and explain power.

♦ measure and calculate power.

Power

The amount of work a person does within a given period of time

Watt

The unit used to measure power

The watt was named for James Watt who developed the steam engine. Since a watt is a small amount of power, the kilowatt (1,000 watts) is often more convenient to use.

Imagine pushing a box 3 meters across a floor using 50 newtons of force. You would do 150 joules of work on the box. Notice that work does not take into account the amount of time it takes for you to move the box. The amount of work you do within a given period of time is called **power**. Power is the rate at which you do work. To calculate power, take the amount of work done and divide it by the amount of time it took to do the work.

$$power = \frac{work}{time}$$

Suppose you did 150 joules of work in 5 seconds. The power would be equal to 30 joules per second.

EXAMPLE
$$power = \frac{150 \text{ joules}}{5 \text{ seconds}}$$
$$power = 30 \text{ joules per second}$$

The unit for measuring power is the **watt**. A watt is 1 joule of work done in 1 second. In the example above, 30 joules of work were done in one second, so 30 watts of power were used. You will learn more about the watt in Chapter 11.

Imagine someone else pushing the box with the same force but taking 10 seconds to move it. In that case, the work that was done would still be the same—150 joules. But, the power would be different.

EXAMPLE
$$power = \frac{work}{time}$$
$$power = \frac{150 \text{ joules}}{10 \text{ seconds}}$$
$$power = 15 \text{ joules per second or 15 watts}$$

Here is another way to look at this example. If you do the same amount of work as someone else, but do it in half the time, then you have used twice as much power.

Work and Machines   Chapter 8   209

---

3 Reinforce and Extend

LEARNING STYLES

Visual/Spatial

Have a volunteer read aloud the margin note about the watt and kilowatt. Display an electric bill and show students that the electric power delivered is measured in kilowatts. Review that the metric prefix *kilo-* means thousand. Tell students

that a 1,000-watt bulb does 100 joules of work every second. The large quantities of power used need to be measured in kilowatts.

Present several other values of force, distance, and time for the box-pushing problem. Have students direct you in finding the power used in each instance.

Lesson at a Glance

Chapter 8 Lesson 2

Overview This lesson defines *power* and tells students how to measure and calculate it.

Objectives

■ To define and explain power

■ To measure and calculate power

Student Pages 209–210

Teacher's Resource Library (TRL)

Workbook Activity 36

Alternative Workbook Activity 36

Vocabulary

power   watt

Science Background

Measurement of power adds the dimension of time to work. It expresses the rate at which work is done. The number of joules of work performed per second is the power it required. One joule per second is called a watt, after James Watt. Watt determined that a strong horse could move a 750-*N* object one meter in one second. This represented power and was named horsepower. One horsepower is defined as the power of 745.56 watts. The watt is the official unit for power, but we refer to horsepower to describe the power of engines.

1 Warm-Up Activity

Have volunteers compete to see who can push a lightweight box of books a distance of 10 m fastest. Time each student with a stopwatch. Invite students to tell about how much work each student did. Challenge them to explain the difference between the work done by students with the fastest and slowest times. (*The same amount of work was done, but the rate at which the work was done differed.*)

2 Teaching the Lesson

Explain to students that they should read to discover how power differs from work and how it is measured. Have them write a definition for *power* and list the units used to express it.

Lesson 2 Review Answers

1. Power is the amount of work done in a given amount of time. **2.** Power depends on joules of work and seconds of time. **3.** 100 newtons × 10 meters/10 seconds = 100 joules/second or 100 watts **4.** 100 newtons × 10 meters/5 seconds = 200 joules/second or 200 watts **5.** When the time is shorter, the power used increases. It requires more power to do an equal amount of work in a shorter time.

LEARNING STYLES

Interpersonal/ Group Learning

Write the terms *work*, *force*, *distance*, *power*, *time*, *newton-meters*, *joule*, and *watt* on index cards. Gather students into groups of eight. Give one card to each group. Have them tell the meaning of their term and organize themselves in different ways to show how the terms are related; for example, *work* = *force* × *distance* (in *joules*), *power* = *work/time* (in *watts*).

Portfolio Assessment

Sample items include:
• Definition and units of measure from Teaching the Lesson
• Lesson 2 Review answers

Write your answers to these questions in complete sentences on a sheet of paper.

1. What is power?

2. Power depends on two quantities. What are they?

3. How much power would a person use to move a piano 10 meters in 10 seconds using a force of 100 newtons?

4. How much power would a person use to move the same piano in 5 seconds?

5. What happens to the power used when the time is shorter?

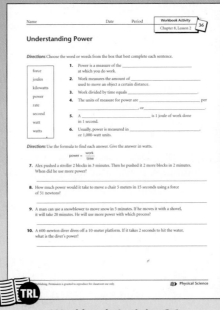

Workbook Activity 36

Objectives

After reading this lesson, you should be able to

◆ relate energy to work.

◆ explain the difference between kinetic and potential energy.

◆ explain the law of conservation of energy.

Energy
The ability to do work

Kinetic energy
Energy of motion

Potential energy
Stored energy

You can see several examples of kinetic energy around you, such as geologic faults and water falls. Can you think of other examples?

Have you ever tried to play a radio with a "dead" battery? The radio would not play because the battery had no more energy stored inside. In science, **energy** is defined as "the ability to do work." Without energy, no work can be done.

Kinetic and Potential Energy

A moving object has the energy of motion, called **kinetic energy.** When a car is moving, it can do work. It can overcome road friction and air resistance and keep going forward. The amount of kinetic energy a moving object has depends on the object's mass and speed. The greater the mass or speed, the greater the kinetic energy.

Some objects are not moving, but they have the potential to move because of their position. These objects have stored energy. This stored energy is called potential energy. A book sitting on the floor has no **potential energy.** It cannot do work. But if you set the book so that it hangs over the edge of a table, the book has stored energy. It can do work by falling to the floor. The book's potential energy changes to kinetic energy as it falls. If you place the book over the edge of a higher table, the book has more potential energy because it can fall farther. The spring of a mousetrap is another example of potential energy. It can do work as it snaps shut.

Release one end and ask what kind of energy the rubber band just displayed. *(kinetic)*

Have students look around the room to find examples potential energy. *(pencil sharpener, book on desk)* Invite volunteers to demonstrate how to change each object's potential energy into kinetic energy.

Help students identify the forms of energy shown in the photo on page 212. *(Students' answers might include: wind and blowing snow—mechanical energy; people moving—mechanical energy and heat energy; lights in the building—*

electrical energy; sound of wind—mechanical energy. Some might say the entire scene shows kinetic energy.)

Read the Technology Note on page 213 together. Display a photo of a nuclear submarine or a cutaway illustration showing its contents.

Invite volunteers to explain how energy can change forms, using the diagram of a generator on page 213. As they identify the form of energy at each stage of the production process, students can describe the nature of the energy and how it changes.

Overview This lesson describes the difference between potential and kinetic energy, lists the forms of energy, and explains the law of conservation of energy.

Objectives

■ To relate energy to work

■ To explain the difference between kinetic and potential energy

■ To explain the law of conservation of energy

Student Pages 211–217

Teacher's Resource Library

Workbook Activity 37

Alternative Workbook Activity 37

Lab Manual 29

Vocabulary

energy
generator
kinetic energy
law of conservation of energy
potential energy

1 Warm-Up Activity

Show students a flashlight, a hair dryer, and a radio. Turn the objects on one by one and discuss what kind of energy each produces. *(flashlight—light energy, hair dryer—heat energy, radio—sound energy)* Display a match and explain that it contains chemical energy. Light the match and ask students what forms they think the energy was changed to. *(light energy and heat energy)*

2 Teaching the Lesson

Have students write the subheads in the lesson after roman numerals I, II, and III on a sheet of paper. Have them leave space below each heading. As they read, students can complete their outlines by writing in the main idea of each paragraph.

Twist a large rubber band into a tight coil and hold the ends to keep it from unwinding. Display it to students in this form. Ask if the rubber band has kinetic or potential energy. *(potential)*

 **Technology Note**

Until nuclear power was developed, submarines needed to resurface regularly for air. Nuclear-powered submarines can stay underwater for many months. They can produce air and do not need oxygen to run. The U.S. Navy launched the first nuclear-powered submarine in 1954. It broke all records for underwater speed.

Joules measure both work and energy, which shows the close relationship between the two. You cannot have work without energy, or vice versa. Doing work on something adds energy to it; releasing energy is work.

The Forms of Energy

The energy you use to do work exists in six main forms. These six forms of energy can be stored. They can also produce motion. That is, each form of energy can be potential or kinetic.

Chemical energy is stored in the bonds between atoms. When substances react, they can release some of the chemical energy in the substances and warm the surroundings. For example, burning coal produces heat.

Heat energy is associated with the moving particles that make up matter. The faster the particles move, the more heat energy is present. All matter has some heat energy. You will learn more about heat in Chapter 9.

Mechanical energy is the energy in moving objects. Objects, such as a moving bicycle, wind, and a falling rock, have mechanical energy in kinetic form. Sound is a form of mechanical energy that you will learn about in Chapter 10.

Nuclear energy is energy that is stored in the nucleus, or center, of an atom. It can be released in devices such as nuclear power plants and atomic weapons.

Radiant energy is associated with light. Some energy that Earth receives from the sun is in the form of light energy. You will learn more about light in Chapter 10.

Which forms of energy can you find in this photo?

ONLINE CONNECTION

 For more information about renewable energy, visit the U.S. Department of Energy's Web site at www.energy.gov/. Select *R* from the site index. Then scroll down to *Renewable Energy* and select the name of each energy source.

Generator

A device used to convert mechanical energy to electrical energy

Science Myth

The world is running out of energy.

Fact: We cannot run out of energy, because energy is never lost. But we can run out of fuels that give us useful kinds of energy. "Energy shortages" are shortages of useful energy sources such as coal, wood, or oil. They may happen because of problems with finding, buying, or moving fuel resources.

Electrical energy is energy that causes electrons to move. Electrons are the negatively charged particles in atoms. Appliances, such as refrigerators and vacuum cleaners, use electrical energy. You will learn about electricity in Chapter 11.

Energy can be changed from one form to another. For example, at an electric power plant, chemical energy is converted to heat energy when fuel is burned. The heat energy is used to make steam. The steam turns a turbine and produces mechanical energy inside a **generator.** The generator converts mechanical energy to electrical energy by moving coils through a magnetic field. Perhaps you have a generator in your home. Or maybe you have seen one at a friend's house, or a business. Generators are commonly used as backup electrical systems in homes. They are also used to supply power to small tools and machinery.

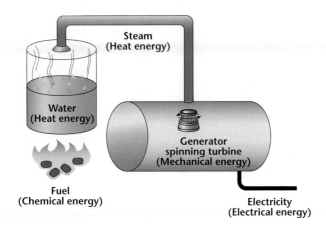

Steam (Heat energy)

Water (Heat energy)

Fuel (Chemical energy)

Generator spinning turbine (Mechanical energy)

Electricity (Electrical energy)

Have a volunteer read the first sentence of the Science Myth feature on page 213. Ask other volunteers to read the facts that follow. Ask students to name other ways people could get energy for fuels and to make electricity besides using coal, wood, or oil.

LEARNING STYLES

LEP/ESL

Have students use a dictionary to look up definitions for *chemical, heat, mechanical, nuclear, radiant,* and *electrical.* Pair students and have them discuss how the word helps them understand each form of energy. Ask them to write a sentence or draw a picture for each kind of energy, explaining how motion is involved.

SCIENCE INTEGRATION

Earth Science

Fuels that are burned to produce energy include coal, wood, natural gas, and oil. These fuels may also be used to produce electricity. Have students choose a fuel and identify how it was formed and how it is mined from the earth. Suggest that students list the advantages and disadvantages of using the fuel source they investigate.

PRONUNCIATION GUIDE

Use the pronunciation shown here to help students pronounce a difficult word in this lesson. Refer to the pronunciation key on the Chapter Planning Guide for the sounds of the symbols.

turbine (tėr´ bīn)

This feature provides students a real-life "narrative" that they can follow to observe how energy continually changes forms. Read the Science in your Life feature on page 214 together. Draw a diagram of a roller coaster on the board, making sure the hills grow progressively smaller. As students progress through the text, mark the position of the car being described in each sentence. Ask a volunteer to explain why the car has potential or kinetic energy in each position. Label the form of energy at each point marked, including heat energy.

LEARNING STYLES

Body/Kinesthetic

Have students videotape themselves throwing a ball into the air and catching it. Have them run the tape at slow speed and confirm that the ball slows on the way up until it stops, then speeds up on the way down. Pause the tape to have students point out what is happening to the amount of potential and kinetic energy in each half of the ball's arc.

GLOBAL CONNECTION

Einstein added to the law of conservation of energy by showing that matter and energy are two forms of the same thing and can be converted into one another. His theory led to the development of the atomic bomb and nuclear power plants. Have students research to find out how these two applications have affected the world community.

Law of conservation of energy
Energy cannot be created or destroyed

The Law of Conservation of Energy

Energy might change its form, but it does not disappear. You can add energy to an object or take energy away from it, but the total amount of the energy does not change. The **law of conservation of energy** states that energy cannot be created or destroyed. A book falling from a table illustrates the law of conservation of energy.

As the book falls, its potential energy decreases. The kinetic energy increases by the same amount. The total amount of energy (potential plus kinetic) stays the same. Just before the book hits the ground, its potential energy is approaching zero and all the energy has become kinetic. After the book hits the ground, the kinetic energy is changed into heat energy which causes a temperature change in the book and the ground. In this example, the energy has changed form, but the total energy remains the same.

How can energy change forms?

Have you ever ridden a roller coaster? A roller coaster is a good example of how energy can change from one form to another. When you first climb into the car at the bottom of the hill, the car has no potential energy. A chain must pull you up the first big hill. That chain changes electrical energy into potential energy. When the cars are at the top, they can fall downward. Potential energy changes to kinetic energy as the cars plunge down one hill. Kinetic energy is converted back into potential energy as the cars go up the next hill. The cars slow as they reach the top of the hill. The kinetic energy that pushed them up the hill has changed back to potential energy. That stored energy converts to kinetic energy as the cars zoom down again.

You might notice that the hills get smaller and smaller during the ride. Although energy is not actually lost, friction converts some of it to other forms of energy, such as heat energy. The heat energy warms the tracks and the air but is not useful for propelling the cars forward.

Lesson 3 REVIEW

Write your answers to these questions in complete sentences on a sheet of paper.

1. What is energy?

2. What is the difference between kinetic and potential energy?

3. Explain the law of conservation of energy.

4. Name the six forms of energy.

5. Each figure shows an example of energy changing form. List the energy changes that take place in each example.

A

B

C

Work and Machines   *Chapter 8*   **215**

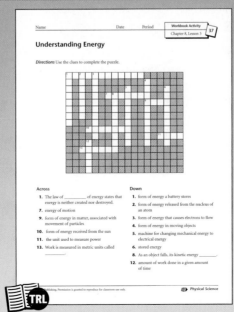

Workbook Activity 37

Lesson 3 Review Answers

1. Energy is the ability to do work.
2. Kinetic energy is energy of motion. Potential energy is stored energy.
3. The law of conservation of energy says that energy can change form but it cannot be created or destroyed. **4.** The six forms of energy are: chemical, heat, mechanical, nuclear, radiant, and electrical. **5. A** chemical energy changes to mechanical energy (sound) **B** mechanical energy changes to mechanical energy **C** chemical energy changes to heat energy and light energy

IN THE ENVIRONMENT

We are constantly being asked to conserve energy to save resources. Ask students to explain ways that their families try to save energy. As students list ways, group them under the forms of energy on the board. For example, heat energy: insulation, sweater, drapes; chemical energy: make fewer car trips, lower the thermostat; mechanical energy: wheels on garbage cans, oil gears to reduce friction; electrical energy: turn off lights, keep refrigerator closed, use less air conditioning.

SCIENCE JOURNAL

Ask students to choose one of the forms of energy described on pages 212 and 213 and write a paragraph about how that form of energy is important in their lives.

Portfolio Assessment

Sample items include:
• Outlines from Teaching the Lesson
• Lesson 3 Review answers

Work and Machines   *Chapter 8*   **215**

Investigation 8-1

The Purpose portion of the student investigation begins with a question to draw them into the activity. Encourage students to read the investigation steps and formulate their own questions before beginning the investigation. The investigation will take approximately 30 minutes to complete. Students will use these process and thinking skills: identifying and controlling variables; measuring; using numbers; collecting, recording, and interpreting data; observing; describing; and drawing conclusions.

Preparation

• Caution students not to use books that are very thick. The higher the ramp, the farther the marble will knock the cup.

• Have students work on the floor or on long tables so that the cups can move without interference from other groups.

• If necessary, have students practice measuring lengths with a ruler.

• Students may use Lab Manual 29 to record their data and answer the questions.

Procedure

• This investigation is best completed with students working in groups of three.

• Assign individual students to gather equipment, cut the window in the cup, construct the ramps, and roll the marbles. Groups measure, record results, and clean up cooperatively.

• Be sure students cut a window in the cup large enough for the large marble and the end of the ruler.

• Demonstrate how to hold and release the marbles at the top of the ramp without pushing them. Caution students to be sure to release the marbles from the same spot on the ruler each time.

• Ask students what work the marbles did in this investigation. (*They moved the cup.*)

INVESTIGATION
8-1

Mass, Height, and Energy

Purpose

Does an object's mass have an effect on its potential and kinetic energy? This investigation will demonstrate how mass affects potential and kinetic energy.

Procedure

1. Copy the data table on a sheet of paper.

Object	Distance Cup Moved
small marble	
large marble	

2. Put on your safety glasses.

3. Cut a 2.5-cm square window from the lip of the cup, as shown in Figure A.

4. Place one end of the ruler on the edge of the textbook to form a ramp, as shown in Figure B. The ruler's groove should be on top.

Figure A   Figure B

SAFETY ALERT

♦ To prevent accidents, remind students to pick up all marbles as they finish the investigation.

♦ Assign teams spaces to avoid confusion and collisions. If space is at a premium, assign teams a numerical order in which to set up their ramps and roll marbles.

5. Place the cup upside down over the other end of the ruler. The ruler should touch the back of the cup.

6. Measure the distance from the edge of the book to the back edge of the cup. Mark the base line at the back edge of the cup.

7. Set the small marble at the top of the ruler's groove. Let it roll down by itself. Do not push it.

8. Observe what happens to the cup. Measure the distance from the edge of the book to the back edge of the cup. Record this distance in the data table.

9. Reset the cup at the base line. Repeat steps 6 and 7, using the large marble. Measure and record the distance.

Questions and Conclusions

1. Which marble pushed the cup farther from the ramp?

2. What conclusion can you draw about the effect of mass on kinetic energy?

Explore Further

How does the height of the ramp affect potential energy? Repeat the investigation using ramps of different heights. Record the results in the data table.

Results

Students should observe that a marble with a larger mass has more potential energy (and thus more kinetic energy) than one with a smaller mass.

Questions and Conclusions Answers

1. The larger marble pushed the cup farther from the ramp.

2. Objects with more mass have more kinetic energy.

Explore Further Answers

A marble rolling down a higher ramp should push the cup farther than the same marble rolling down a lower ramp. Because energy is neither created nor destroyed, students should conclude that the marble on the higher ramp had greater potential energy, which resulted in greater kinetic energy.

As an alternative, students could observe and compare the indentations made by marbles dropped from varying heights into a container of wet sand or soil. Students could use a meterstick as a gauge for measuring the heights.

Assessment

Check data tables to be sure that as the mass of the marble increases, the distance the cup moves increases. You might include the following items from this investigation in student portfolios:

• Investigation 8-1 data table

• Answers to Questions and Conclusions and Explore Further sections

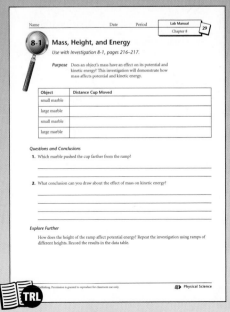

Lab Manual 29

Lesson at a Glance

Chapter 8 Lesson 4

Overview This lesson addresses the function of a lever as a simple machine. Students explore the three classes of levers and learn formulas to determine the work input, work output, and efficiency of a lever.

Objectives

- To explain what a simple machine is
- To describe how a lever works
- To distinguish among the three classes of levers
- To analyze work and efficiency for levers

Student Pages 218–223

Teacher's Resource Library (TRL)

Workbook Activity 38

Alternative Workbook Activity 38

Resource File 16

Vocabulary

efficiency	resistance force
effort force	simple machine
fulcrum	work input
lever	work output

Science Background

All simple machines do work with one movement. These simple machines serve any of three purposes: increasing speed, increasing force, or changing the direction of a force. For example, you can use a lever to help you move a large object using less force than if you tried to move it directly. Note that there is always a trade-off. In the lever example above, you can apply a smaller force to move the object if you apply it over a greater distance.

1 Warm-Up Activity

Hammer a nail into a piece of wood far enough so that it cannot be easily removed. Try to remove the nail with your hands. Then use the claw end of the hammer to remove the nail. Discuss with students why you were able to remove the nail with the hammer but not by hand. Invite students to predict why using the hammer made doing the work easier.

Objectives

After reading this lesson, you should be able to

- explain what a simple machine is.
- describe how a lever works.
- distinguish among the three classes of levers.
- analyze work and efficiency for levers.

Simple machine
A tool with few parts that makes it easier or possible to do work

Lever
A simple machine containing a bar that can turn around a fixed point

Fulcrum
A fixed point around which a lever rotates

Effort force, F_e
The force applied to a machine by the user

Resistance force, F_r
The force applied to a machine by the object to be moved

Have you ever tried to open a paint can, using only your fingers? It is hard, if not impossible, to do. With a screwdriver, you can easily pry the lid from the can. A screwdriver, used in this way, is an example of a **simple machine.** A simple machine is a tool with few parts that makes it easier or possible to do work. Simple machines change the direction or size of the force you apply. Or, they change the distance through which the force acts.

The Lever

A **lever** is a simple machine. Levers can have many shapes. In its most basic form, the lever is a bar that is free to turn around a fixed point. The fixed point is called a **fulcrum.**

In the figure below, the woman is using a lever to move a boulder. Notice that the lever changes the direction of the force the woman applies. She pushes down, but the boulder moves up. The force the woman applies to the machine is called the **effort force** (F_e).

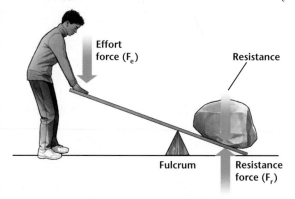

The object to be lifted is called the resistance. In this example, the boulder is the resistance. Gravity is pulling down on the boulder, so the machine must exert a force upward to lift it. The force the machine uses to move the resistance is called the **resistance force** (F_r).

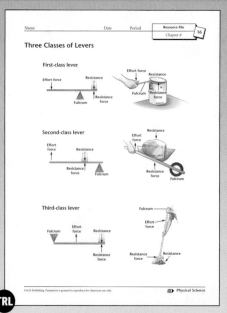

Resource File 16

The force the machine exerts is greater than the force the woman exerts. In other words, using the lever makes the woman's job easier. The lever takes the amount of force she exerts and increases that force.

The Three Classes of Levers

Levers can be grouped into three classes. The classes of levers are based on the position of the resistance force, the fulcrum, and the effort force. The figure below illustrates a first-class lever.

In a first-class lever, the fulcrum is positioned between the effort and the resistance. A first-class lever changes the direction of a force and can also increase the force.

First-class lever

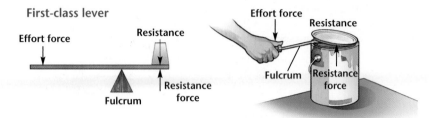

In a second-class lever, shown below, the resistance is positioned between the effort and the fulcrum. Second-class levers always increase the force applied to them. They do not change the direction of the force. Wheelbarrows, paper cutters, and most nutcrackers are examples of second-class levers.

Second-class lever

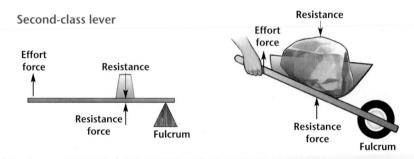

Explain to students that drawing and labeling parts of the different kinds of levers will help them understand the idea of levers and how they function. As they complete the lesson, encourage students to diagram each lever. Also suggest that they write formulas for determining lever efficiency and write a sentence explaining the meaning of each formula in their own words.

Draw three straight horizontal lines on the board with a foot of space between them. Label them "First-Class Lever," "Second-Class Lever," and "Third-Class Lever." Have volunteers draw and label the location of the fulcrum, effort force, and resistance force for each class of lever. Volunteers should also label the directions of the effort and resistance forces.

 Reinforce and Extend

TEACHER ALERT

Some students may think that levers are uncommon because of technology. In fact, they are the most common kind of simple machine. Tell students that most common tools include a lever of some kind.

LEARNING STYLES

Visual/Spatial

Have students prepare a visual display showing how levers are used. Students can search magazines for pictures of levers. Ask them to clip the pictures; label the effort force, resistance force, resistance, and fulcrum; and mount them on a display board.

Look at the third-class lever in the figure below. Notice that the effort is between the fulcrum and the resistance. Third-class levers increase the distance through which the force moves, which causes the resistance to move farther or faster. A broom is an example of a third-class lever. You use effort force on the handle between the fulcrum and the resistance force. When you move the handle of the broom a short distance, the brush end moves a greater distance.

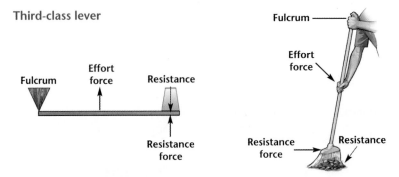

Third-class lever

Work and Efficiency for a Lever

Energy cannot be created or destroyed. Because energy is the ability to do work, work cannot be created either. No simple machine can do more work than the person using it supplies. What machines can do is increase or change the direction of the force a person exerts. Lesson 1 explained that work = force × distance. Some machines allow a person to use less force to do the same amount of work. But in return, that person must exert the force over a greater distance.

Science Myth

A machine is something that has been manufactured.

Fact: Our bodies are machines. They contain all three classes of levers. When you lift your head forward or back, you use a first-class lever. When you stand on your toes, you use a second-class lever. When you hold a weight in your hand with your arm extended, you are using a third-class lever.

In the figure below, a woman is using a lever to move a boulder. The distance the effort moves is called the effort distance (d_e). The distance the resistance moves is called the resistance distance (d_r). Notice that the effort distance is much greater than the resistance distance.

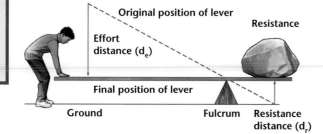

Original position of lever

Resistance

Effort
distance (d_e)

Final position of lever

Ground

Fulcrum

Resistance
distance (d_r)

Technology Note

Most appliances sold in the United States must display their energy efficiency. The label with this information is bright yellow with black lettering. It shows how much it costs to operate the appliance. Its efficiency is compared to the highest and lowest efficiency of similar appliances.

The amount of work a person puts into a machine is called the **work input.** The work input equals the person's effort force multiplied by the distance of that effort.

$$\text{work input} = F_e \times d_e$$

The amount of work actually done by the machine against the resistance is called the **work output.** The work output equals the resistance force multiplied by the distance the resistance moved.

$$\text{work output} = F_r \times d_r$$

Work output can never be greater than work input because energy cannot be created. But in reality, work output is always less than work input. No machine can do quite as much work as a person puts into it. Machines cannot destroy energy, but they change some of it to heat and other forms of energy that cannot do useful work.

The **efficiency** of a machine measures how much useful work it can do compared with how much work was put into it. You can find the efficiency of a machine by using this formula.

$$\text{efficiency} = \frac{\text{work output}}{\text{work input}} \times 100\%$$

Efficiency is written as a percent. Multiplying by 100 tells you what percent of the work input is converted to work output. All machines have efficiencies that are less than 100 percent.

Suppose a woman uses a lever to lift a crate. She applies 120 newtons of effort force. She pushes her end of the lever 1.0 meter. The machine exerts 400 newtons of resistance force. It lifts the crate 0.2 meter. What is the work input, the work output, and the efficiency of the lever?

EXAMPLE

work input = effort force (F_e) × effort distance (d_e)

work input = 120 newtons × 1.0 m

work input = 120 joules

work output = resistance force (F_r) × resistance distance (d_r)

work output = 400 newtons × 0.2 m

work output = 80 joules

$$\text{efficiency} = \frac{\text{work output}}{\text{work input}} \times 100\%$$

$$\text{efficiency} = \frac{80 \text{ joules}}{120 \text{ joules}} \times 100\%$$

$$\text{efficiency} = 66\tfrac{2}{3}\%$$

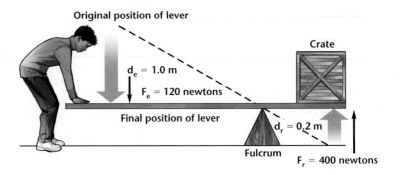

Write your answers to these questions in complete sentences on a sheet of paper.

1. Draw a first-class lever. Show the fulcrum, effort force, and resistance.

2. Draw a second-class lever. Show the fulcrum, effort force, and resistance.

3. Draw a third-class lever. Show the fulcrum, effort force, and resistance.

4. What is work input? What is work output?

5. What does efficiency tell you about a machine?

Achievements in Science

The Law of the Lever

Levers probably were used in prehistoric times. In 260 B.C., Archimedes was the first to prove mathematically how levers work. His proof is known as the law of the lever.

The law of the lever is based on three principles. The first is that equal weights at equal distances from a fulcrum balance. The second is that two weights no longer balance if something is added to one. The side with the increased weight goes down. The third principle is that two weights do not balance if something is taken from one. The side holding the weight that did not change goes down.

Here is the formula for the law of the levers: $F_1 \times l_1 = F_2 \times l_2$. F_1 is the weight of an object on one side of a fulcrum. The length from that object to the fulcrum is l_1. F_2 is the weight on the other side. The length of that object to the fulcrum is l_2.

Archimedes's proof shows that anything, no matter how heavy it is, can be lifted using a lever.

Work and Machines Chapter 8 **223**

Lesson 4 Review Answers

1. Check students' drawings. The fulcrum is between the effort and the resistance in a first-class lever. **2.** Check students' drawings. In a second-class lever, the resistance is between the effort and the fulcrum. **3.** Check students' drawings. In a third-class lever, the effort is between the fulcrum and the resistance. **4.** Work input is the work put into a machine by its user, *effort force × effort distance*. Work output is the work done by a machine against the resistance, *force distance × resistance distance*. **5.** Efficiency tells you what percent of work input is translated into useful work when a certain machine is used.

Achievements in Science

Display a balance and ask students to explain how it functions as a lever. Ask volunteers to read the Achievements in Science feature on page 223 aloud. Demonstrate each principle of the law of levers after it is read aloud. Ask questions such as "Why did this arm of the balance go down? Why did this one go up?" Be sure students understand that F1 and F2 represent the masses of objects and l1 and l2 represent the length of the effort and resistance arms (distance from the fulcrum to the effort or resistance).

Portfolio Assessment

Sample items include:
- Drawings and formula summaries from Teaching the Lesson
- Science in Your Life answer
- Lesson 4 Review answers

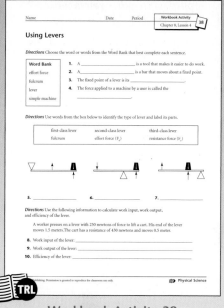

Workbook Activity 38

Chapter 8 Lesson 5

Overview In this lesson, students are introduced to the concept of mechanical advantage. They learn to calculate the mechanical advantage of simple machines in general and levers in particular.

Objectives

- To explain and calculate mechanical advantage
- To use effort arm and resistance arm to determine the mechanical advantage of a lever

Student Pages 224–228

Teacher's Resource Library (TRL)

Workbook Activity 39

Alternative Workbook Activity 39

Lab Manual 30

Vocabulary

effort arm
mechanical advantage
resistance arm

Warm-Up Activity

Display a picture of the Egyptian pyramids. Challenge students to explain how the heavy stone blocks might have been lifted into place. When levers are suggested, ask students how they think the Egyptians figured out how much effort was needed to move the blocks.

Teaching the Lesson

Have students write a question to answer about each vocabulary word in the lesson. For example, for *effort arm*, they might ask *What is an effort arm?*

Point out to students that mechanical advantage is a ratio of the force exerted by an object to the force required to move it. A machine with a mechanical advantage of 1 does not change the amount of force you have to apply. One with a mechanical advantage of 2 doubles your force, so you only have to apply half the force to move the resistance. Ask students to calculate how a machine with a mechanical advantage of 3 affects the

force applied. (*It requires you to make one-third the effort to move the resistance.*)

Draw diagrams of a second-class and third-class lever on the board. Have a volunteer measure the lengths of the effort and resistance arms with a meterstick. Then have students find the mechanical advantage of the lever, plugging the measurements into the formula $MA = effort\ arm \div resistance\ arm$.

Objectives

After reading this lesson, you should be able to

- explain and calculate mechanical advantage.
- use effort arm and resistance arm to determine the mechanical advantage of a lever.

Mechanical advantage, MA

Factor by which a machine multiplies the effort force

People often use simple machines to make tasks easier. A simple machine makes a task easier because it multiplies the force a person applies.

The number of times a machine multiplies your effort force is called the **mechanical advantage** of the machine. You can find a machine's mechanical advantage (MA) with this formula.

$$\text{mechanical advantage} = \frac{\text{resistance force}}{\text{effort force}} \quad or\ MA = \frac{F_r}{F_e}$$

Look at the figure below. Suppose a machine lifts a resistance that weighs 30 newtons when the woman applies an effort force of only 10 newtons. What is the machine's mechanical advantage?

EXAMPLE

$$MA = \frac{F_r}{F_e}$$

$$MA = \frac{30\ \text{newtons}}{10\ \text{newtons}}$$

$$MA = 3$$

The mechanical advantage is 3. The machine has multiplied the woman's effort force by 3. This makes the object easier for her to lift.

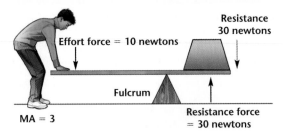

Effort force = 10 newtons
Resistance 30 newtons
Fulcrum
Resistance force = 30 newtons
MA = 3

Some machines are not used to multiply effort force. Instead, people use them to increase the distance or speed the resistance will move, or to change the direction of a force. Rather than increasing a person's effort force, the machine may even reduce it.

TEACHER ALERT

Some students may think that a machine with a greater mechanical advantage will do more work than one with a lesser mechanical advantage. Explain to students that if both machines do the same task, they each do the same amount of work, but the one with the greater mechanical advantage does the work with less of your effort force.

Effort Arm and Resistance Arm

Effort arm
The distance between the fulcrum and the effort force of a lever

Resistance arm
The distance between the fulcrum and resistance force of a lever

You can increase the mechanical advantage of a lever simply by moving the fulcrum closer to the resistance and farther from the effort force. Another way to find the mechanical advantage of a lever is to measure the **effort arm.** The effort arm is the distance between the fulcrum and the effort force of a lever. Measure the resistance force and the **resistance arm.** The resistance arm is the distance between the fulcrum and the resistance force of a lever. Now divide the effort arm by the resistance arm.

$$MA = \frac{\text{effort arm}}{\text{resistance arm}}$$

What is the mechanical advantage of the lever shown in the figure?

EXAMPLE

$$MA = \frac{\text{effort arm}}{\text{resistance arm}}$$

$$MA = \frac{2.4 \text{ m}}{0.6 \text{ m}}$$

$$MA = 4$$

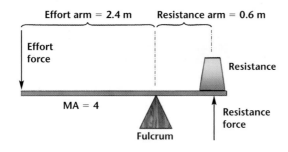

Effort arm = 2.4 m   Resistance arm = 0.6 m

Effort force

Resistance

MA = 4

Resistance force

Fulcrum

CAREER CONNECTION

Invite an auto mechanic to visit the class to describe why an understanding of how machines work is essential to the mechanic's job.

CROSS-CURRICULAR CONNECTION

Math

Have students use the formula *MA = effort arm ÷ resistance arm* to calculate which of the following levers has the greater mechanical advantage:

Lever A: effort arm, 80 cm; resistance arm, 20 cm

Lever B: effort arm, 90 cm; resistance arm, 40 cm

(Lever A: MA = 4; Lever B: MA = 2.25)

SCIENCE JOURNAL

Invite students to write a comparison of two people trying to do the same task using levers with different mechanical advantages. Their account should explain what makes the MA of the two levers differ. Point out that using a longer lever might reap a greater MA but might also be inconvenient.

Lesson 5 Review Answers

1. Mechanical advantage is the number of times by which a machine multiplies effort force. **2.** You would divide the resistance force by the effort force. **3.** You would divide the effort arm by the resistance arm. **4.** The mechanical advantage is 8. **5.** The resistance force is 40 newtons.

Achievements in Science

Have students take turns reading aloud the Achievements in Science feature on page 226. Invite volunteers to draw a diagram of how they think the gears of the calculator fit together. Ask why each wheel needed 10 teeth *(the number system is based on tens)* and each gear needed one tooth *(at the end of 10 ones, for example, the gear needed to turn the tens wheel one notch).*

Have students research the way in which odometers, utility meters, or electronic calculators work and share their findings.

Portfolio Assessment

Sample items include:
- Questions and answers from Teaching the Lesson
- Lesson 5 Review answers

Write your answers to these questions in complete sentences on a sheet of paper.

1. What is mechanical advantage?

2. How do you find the mechanical advantage of most simple machines?

3. How can you find the mechanical advantage of levers?

4. What is the mechanical advantage of a lever with an effort arm of 16 cm and a resistance arm of 2 cm?

5. A machine has a mechanical advantage of 4. Your effort force is 10 newtons. What is the resistance force?

Achievements in Science

Mechanical Calculator

Blaise Pascal was 19 when he invented his calculating machine, the Pascaline, in 1642. Others before Pascal, including Leonardo DaVinci, had put forth ideas about mechanical calculators. But Pascal's machine was the first to be built and used.

The Pascaline could add numbers automatically. It used a set of wheels linked to gears to make calculations. The wheels were arranged in a row. The first wheel represented ones, the second represented tens, the third hundreds, and so forth. Each wheel had 10 teeth. Each of the gears had one tooth. When a wheel moved 10 notches, a gear moved the next wheel one notch. The wheels and gears were in a box with windows. The windows showed the numbers on the wheels. Later inventors added keys and a crank.

People used mechanical calculators until the 1970s, when electronic calculators became available. The principles of mechanical calculators remain in use in odometers and electric and water meters. The mechanical calculator was the first in a series of inventions leading to modern computers.

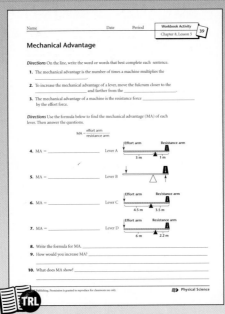

Workbook Activity 39

INVESTIGATION

8-2

Materials

◆ safety glasses
◆ spring scale
◆ 200-g weight
◆ rubber band
◆ stiff meterstick
◆ triangular wooden wedge or other fulcrum

Finding the Mechanical Advantage of a Lever

Purpose

Which fulcrum position would have a greater mechanical advantage—one at 20 cm or one at 80 cm? In this investigation, you will find the mechanical advantage of a lever.

Procedure

1. Copy the data table on a sheet of paper.

Fulcrum Position	Resistance Force	Effort Force	Resistance Arm	Effort Arm
50 cm				
80 cm				
20 cm				

2. Put on your safety glasses.

3. Use a spring scale to hold up a 200-g weight. Record the weight (the resistance force) in newtons.

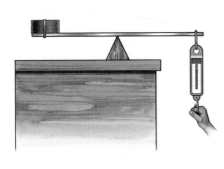

4. Using a rubber band, attach the 200-g weight to the top side of a stiff meterstick, at the 0-cm end.

5. Work at a table or desk. Place the weighted meterstick on a fulcrum so that it is positioned under the stick's 50-cm mark. The end of the stick without the weight should extend beyond the edge of the table, as shown in the diagram.

Work and Machines   Chapter 8   **227**

SAFETY ALERT

◆ Caution students not to extend the spring scale too far.
◆ Place work stations far enough apart to prevent accidents with metersticks.
◆ Make sure students wear their safety glasses.

Investigation 8-2

The Purpose portion of the student investigation begins with a question to draw them into the activity. Encourage students to read the investigation steps and formulate their own questions before beginning the investigation. The investigation will take approximately 30 minutes to complete. Students will use these process and thinking skills: making and using models; identifying and controlling variables; measuring; using numbers; collecting, recording, and interpreting data; comparing; and drawing conclusions.

Preparation

• Use a metal or other stiff meterstick to minimize bending. It should be lightweight to minimize the effect its weight has on results.

• You may wish to suggest that students add another column to their data tables to record the mechanical advantages they calculate.

• Students may use Lab Manual 30 to record their data and answer the questions.

Procedure

• Have students work in groups of three. Assign one student to gather equipment, but be sure all students record results and clean up when finished. Student roles may be assigned as follows: Student A weighs the 200-g weight, attaches it to the stick, and places the stick on the fulcrum. Student B positions the fulcrum. Student C pulls down the spring scale and reads the effort force.

• Demonstrate positioning the weight and reading the spring scale. Be sure students have attached the weight at the 0-cm end and the scale at the 100-cm end to avoid confusion about where the fulcrum should be placed.

• Masking tape can be substituted for the rubber bands to attach the weight.

• Point out that the force applied to lift the weight without the meterstick was approximately 2 newtons ($F = m \times a$; $0.2 kg \times 9.8 m/sec$ per second = about 2 newtons).

Continued on page 228

Continued from page 227

Results

Students should observe that the longer the effort arm in relationship to the resistance arm, the less force is needed to lift the weight and level the meterstick.

Questions and Conclusions Answers

1. The most effort force, around 8 newtons, should have been applied when the fulcrum was at the 80-cm mark. The least, approximately 0.5 newtons, should have been necessary at the 20-cm mark. The effort at the 50-cm mark should have been about 2 newtons.

2. MA should have been 50 cm/50 cm = 1 for the first lever, 20 cm/80 cm = 0.25 for the second lever, and 80 cm/20 cm = 4 for the third lever. However, the weight of the meterstick will affect results somewhat.

3. The setup with the fulcrum at the 20-cm mark had the greatest mechanical advantage. The setup with the fulcrum at the 80-cm mark had the least.

4. The ranking is opposite to that in question 1.

5. Moving the fulcrum closer to the resistance and farther from the effort creates greater mechanical advantage.

Explore Further Answers

The mass of the weight should not affect mechanical advantage if the effort arm and resistance arm are set up in the same way. The mechanical advantage remains the same.

Assessment

Check students' data tables to be sure they have correctly recorded their measurements of forces and lengths of arms. Verify that they have done the calculations correctly to find the mechanical advantage of each lever. You might include the following items from this investigation in student portfolios:

• Investigation 8-2 data table

• Answers to Questions and Conclusions and Explore Further sections

---

6. Use a spring scale to gently pull down on the 100-cm end of the stick until it is level at both ends. On the spring scale, read the effort force you apply to make the stick level. Record that force, in newtons, on the 50-cm line of the data table.

7. Record the length of the resistance arm (the distance from the weight to the fulcrum). Then record the effort arm (the distance from the fulcrum to the spring scale).

8. Follow the basic procedure used in steps 4 to 6 except position the fulcrum under the 80-cm mark. Record the values in the data table. Then place the fulcrum under the 20-cm mark. Repeat the basic procedure in steps 4 to 6. Record the values.

Questions and Conclusions

1. Where was the fulcrum placed when you had to apply the most force? Where was it placed when you had to apply the least force?

$$MA = \frac{\text{effort arm}}{\text{resistance arm}}$$

2. Calculate the mechanical advantage of the three levers using the formula at the left.

3. Which setup showed the greatest mechanical advantage? Which setup showed the least?

4. How do the mechanical advantages you calculated in step 3 compare to your answers to question 1?

5. Explain how the position of the fulcrum affects a lever's mechanical advantage.

Explore Further

Repeat the investigation steps, but use a weight with a different mass. Record your observations. Explain how a weight's mass affects mechanical advantage.

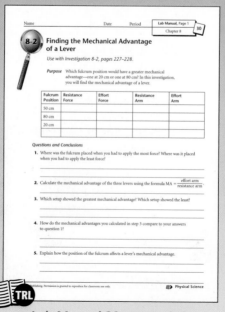

Lab Manual 30, pages 1–2

Lesson 6 Some Other Kinds of Simple Machines

Objectives

After reading this lesson, you should be able to

◆ explain how pulleys work and how to estimate their mechanical advantage.

◆ explain how inclined planes work and how to estimate their mechanical advantage.

◆ explain how screws work and relate them to inclined planes.

◆ explain how wedges work and relate them to inclined planes.

◆ explain how wheels and axles work.

Pulley

A simple machine made up of a rope, chain, or belt wrapped around a wheel

There are six types of simple machines, including the lever. In this lesson, you will learn about the other five types.

The Pulley

A **pulley** is a wheel with a rope, chain, or belt around it. The figure shows a single fixed pulley.

A single fixed pulley changes the direction of the force you apply, but it does not multiply that force. The mechanical advantage equals 1. You can use this type of pulley to lift a heavy object by pulling down instead of lifting up.

The pulley in Figure A is called a fixed pulley because it is fixed or attached at the top. The wheel is free to spin, but it cannot move up and down.

The pulley in Figure B is a movable pulley. As effort is applied to a movable pulley, the entire pulley and the object attached to it will rise. You can use this type of pulley to make a lifting job easier. Because the rope supports the pulley from two directions, you need to apply only half as much force to lift the object. Therefore, the pulley has a mechanical advantage of 2.

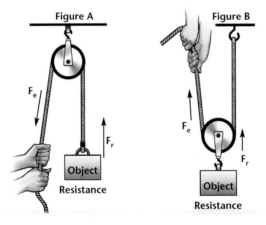

Work and Machines Chapter 8 **229**

Resource File 17

Lesson at a Glance

Chapter 8 Lesson 6

Overview This lesson explains how pulleys, inclined planes, screws, wedges, and wheels and axles work. Students will also learn how to estimate the mechanical advantage of pulleys and inclined planes.

Objectives

- To explain how pulleys work and how to estimate their mechanical advantage
- To explain how inclined planes work and how to estimate their mechanical advantage
- To explain how screws work and relate them to inclined planes
- To explain how wedges work and relate them to inclined planes
- To explain how wheels and axles work

Student Pages 229–234

Teacher's Resource Library TRL

Workbook Activity 40

Alternative Workbook Activity 40

Lab Manual 31–32

Resource File 17

Vocabulary

inclined plane   wedge
pulley   wheel and axle
screw

1 Warm-Up Activity

Ask a volunteer to draw a flagpole on the board. Ask students to explain how a flag is raised to the top. If necessary, point out that pulling down on the rope causes a wheel to turn, moving the flag upward. Explain that this system makes up a pulley, one of the simple machines they will read about.

Work and Machines Chapter 8 **229**

Before students read, review the meanings of *simple machine* and *mechanical advantage*. Read the objectives with students and have them write the name of each simple machine in the lesson on paper.

They should leave space between the names. Tell students that as they read, they should write sentences telling how each machine works and how its mechanical advantage can be found. Encourage students to draw diagrams to illustrate the simple machines.

 3 **Reinforce and Extend**

TEACHER ALERT

Point out that a movable pulley causes effort distance to be longer than resistance distance. In other words, to lift an object one meter you might have to pull down a two-meter length of rope. The reason a pulley system increases mechanical advantage is that with each pulley added, a section of rope is added. Each section of rope helps support the object.

Explain to students that mechanical advantage is an ideal rather than a real-world value. Actually, outside forces come into play. Some work output will be lost to overcoming friction.

There is a price to pay for making the object easier to lift. You must pull twice as far on the rope as the object actually moves. For example, to lift the object 1 meter, you must pull up a distance of 2 meters on the rope. The direction of the force is not reversed. To lift the object, you must pull up on the rope, not down.

Pulleys can be combined in different ways. Look at the figures below. Note the number of supporting ropes pulling up on each object. Note the mechanical advantage (MA) of each pulley system. The MA of a pulley system is usually about equal to the number of ropes that pull upward. In Figure C, two ropes pull up on the object. Mechanical advantage equals 2. In Figure D, three ropes pull up on the object. The MA of this system equals 3.

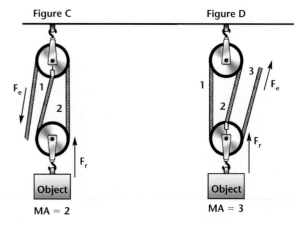

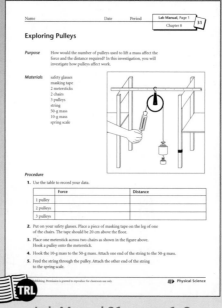

Lab Manual 31, pages 1–2

The Inclined Plane

An **inclined plane** is a simple machine made of a ramp. It has no moving parts. You use an inclined plane to lift an object.

Inclined planes, such as the one shown here in Figure E, decrease the force you need to move an object. Once again, you pay for this decrease in effort force by an increase in the distance the object has to be moved.

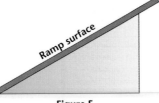

Figure E

For example, if a delivery person needs to put a box on a truck that is 1 meter from the ground, he might use an inclined plane, or ramp, to make his job easier. Rather than lifting the box 1 meter, he can push it up the ramp. It takes less force to push an object than to pick it up. However, he must move the object farther, as shown in Figure F below.

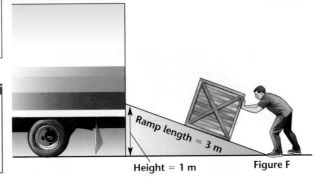

Ramp length = 3 m

Height = 1 m

Figure F

In Figure F, the mechanical advantage is 3. You divide the ramp length, 3 m, by the height, 1 m. The mechanical advantage of an inclined plane is the length of the slanted surface, divided by the vertical (up and down) height. The more gradual the slant, the greater the mechanical advantage, but the farther the object must go.

Screw
A simple machine made up of an inclined plane wrapped around a straight piece of metal

Wedge
A simple machine made up of an inclined plane or pair of inclined planes that are moved

A speedboat is a simple machine. It is a wedge. In the water, a speedboat puts force on two inclined surfaces and then pushes them apart.

The Screw

Another kind of simple machine, the **screw,** is a form of inclined plane. Think of a screw as a straight piece of metal with an inclined plane wrapped in a spiral around it. The ridges formed by this spiral are called threads.

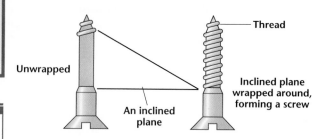

Screws make it easier to fasten objects together. The mechanical advantage of a screw depends on the distance between the threads. The smaller the distance, the more times the inclined plane is wrapped around, making the mechanical advantage greater.

The Wedge

A **wedge** is an inclined plane that moves when it is used. It is thick at one end and thinner at the other. A wedge is often made up of two inclined planes joined together. Both edges are slanted. You can use a wedge for a job like splitting wood. A force applied to the thick end is multiplied and acts at the thin end, piercing the wood. The thinner and more gradual the wedge, the greater the mechanical advantage.

A wedge is useful for splitting wood.

The Wheel and Axle

Wheel and axle — *A simple machine made up of a wheel attached to a shaft*

An automobile steering wheel and a doorknob are examples of a simple machine called a **wheel and axle.** In this simple machine, a wheel is attached to a shaft called an axle, as shown in the figure.

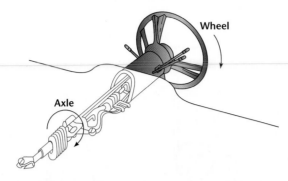

Wheel

Axle

A wheel and axle increases the twisting force you apply to the wheel. The multiplied force can then turn something else attached to the axle. The mechanical advantage of a wheel and axle depends on the size of the wheel compared to the thickness of the axle. The bigger the wheel is in comparison to the thickness of the axle, the greater the mechanical advantage.

TEACHER ALERT

It may be helpful to students to know that a wheel and axle is a lever that rotates in a circle. It consists of two wheels of different sizes. The smaller wheel is the axle; the larger wheel turns about it, moving through a greater distance than the axle. The effort force applied to the wheel is multiplied at the axle.

LEARNING STYLES

Interpersonal/ Group Learning

Have students work in a group to find pictures of real-world applications of wheel and axle. Examples might include a wheelchair, water wheel, bicycle, and gears. Challenge groups to draw a diagram showing the parts: the wheel, the axle (a smaller wheel in the center), the fulcrum (center of the axle), and the resistance arm (radius of the axle), and the effort arm (radius of wheel—distance from the center of the wheel to the edge).

Work and Machines   *Chapter 8*   **233**

Lesson 6 Review Answers

1. A fixed pulley is a simple machine consisting of a rope, chain, or belt around a wheel. **2.** A fixed pulley rotates but does not move up or down and has a MA of 1. A movable pulley is free to move up or down and increases MA by the number of wheels used. **3. A** MA = 2; **B** MA = 1 **4.** Having two ropes that pull upward on a movable pulley system doubles the mechanical advantage; MA = 2. **5.** An inclined plane is a ramp used to lift objects. **6.** You can find the MA of an inclined plane by dividing the running length of the slanted surface by the vertical height. **7.** Screws and wedges are both variations of an inclined plane. **8.** The screw with closely spaced threads will have a greater MA because its inclined plane is longer and has a more gradual slope. **9.** A thin, gradual wedge will have a greater MA because each of its inclined planes is longer, with a more gradual slope. **10.** A bus usually has a larger steering wheel because the mechanical advantage is increased to handle the larger mass of the bus.

Portfolio Assessment

Sample items include:
• Sentences and drawings from Teaching the Lesson
• Lesson 6 Review answers

234   *Chapter 8   Work and Machines*

Lesson 6   R E V I E W

Write your answers to these questions in complete sentences on a sheet of paper.

1. What is a fixed pulley?

2. What is the difference between a fixed pulley and a movable pulley?

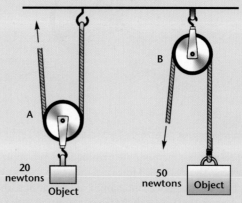

3. What is the mechanical advantage of each of the pulleys in the figure?

4. Explain the mechancial advantage of a movable pulley system that has two ropes that pull upward.

5. What is an inclined plane?

6. How can you find the mechanical advantage of an inclined plane?

7. Screws and wedges are variations of what simple machine?

8. Which will have a greater mechanical advantage: a screw with closely spaced threads or one with widely spaced threads? Explain your answer.

9. Which will have a greater mechanical advantage: a thin, gradual wedge or a thick, greatly sloping one? Explain your answer.

10. Why does a bus usually have a steering wheel that is larger than the one in a car?

234   *Chapter 8   Work and Machines*

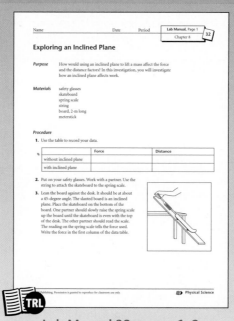

Lab Manual 32, pages 1–2

Workbook Activity 40

- Work is what happens when a force makes something move in the direction of the force.

- Power is the amount of work a person does within a given period of time.

- Energy is the ability to do work.

- Kinetic energy is energy of motion. Potential energy is stored energy.

- The six main forms of energy are chemical, heat, mechanical, nuclear, radiant, and electrical. Energy can change from one form to another.

- Energy cannot be created or destroyed.

- Simple machines make doing work easier by changing the direction or size of a force and the distance through which it acts.

- Resistance force is the force applied by a machine against a resistance. Effort force is the force applied to a machine by the person using it.

- A lever is a bar that turns around a fulcrum.

- Levers are divided into three classes, according to the relationship between the effort, fulcrum, and resistance.

- The mechanical advantage of a machine is the number of times by which the machine multiplies effort force.

- A pulley is made up of a rope, chain, or belt wrapped around a wheel.

- An inclined plane is a ramp.

- A screw and a wedge are special forms of inclined planes.

- A wheel and axle is a wheel attached to a shaft.

Science Words

efficiency, 221	joule, 207	potential energy, 211	watt, 209
effort arm, 225	kinetic energy, 211	power, 209	wedge, 232
effort force, 218	law of conservation	pulley, 229	wheel and axle, 233
energy, 211	of energy, 214	resistance arm, 225	work, 206
fulcrum, 218	lever, 218	resistance force, 218	work input, 221
generator, 213	mechanical	screw, 232	work output, 221
inclined plane, 231	advantage, 224	simple machine, 218	

Chapter 8 Summary

Have volunteers read aloud each Summary item on page 235. Ask volunteers to explain the meaning of each item. Direct students' attention to the Science Words box on the bottom of page 235. Have them read and review each term and its definition.

Chapter 8 Review

Use the Chapter Review to prepare students for tests and to reteach content from the chapter.

Chapter 8 Mastery Test

The Teacher's Resource Library includes two parallel forms of the Chapter 8 Mastery Test. The difficulty level of the two forms is equivalent. You may wish to use one form as a pretest and the other form as a posttest.

Review Answers
Vocabulary Review

1. potential energy, kinetic energy
2. energy 3. effort force 4. law of conservation of energy 5. joule

Concept Review

6. C 7. D 8. B 9. A 10. D 11. C 12. B

Critical Thinking

13. A first-class lever appears in the diagram. You can tell because the fulcrum lies between the effort force and the resistance. 14. Examples of three simple machines may include any three of these: wheel and axle, screw, wedge, inclined plane, lever, pulley. Machines multiply force or change the direction of a force to make work easier. Some machines increase the distance or speed the resistance will move.

TEACHER ALERT

Because of limited space in this Chapter Review, not all of the vocabulary terms introduced in this chapter appear in the Vocabulary Review section. You may want to create an activity using the missing words to give students practice with all of the terms in this chapter. Here are the terms that are not covered in the section.

efficiency	resistance arm
effort arm	resistance force
fulcrum	screw
generator	simple machine
inclined plane	watt
lever	wedge
mechanical advantage	wheel and axle
power	work
pulley	work input
	work output

Vocabulary Review

Choose a word or words from the Word Bank that best complete each sentence. Write the answer on a sheet of paper.

1. Stored energy is _____, and energy of motion is _____.

2. The ability to do work is _____.

3. The force applied to a machine by the user is _____.

4. The _____ states that energy cannot be created or destroyed.

5. The metric unit of work is a(n) _____.

Concept Review

Choose the answer that best completes each sentence. Write the letter of the answer on your paper.

6. Work = _____.
   - **A** force + distance
   - **B** force − distance
   - **C** force × distance
   - **D** force ÷ distance

7. Machines can be used to _____.
   - **A** multiply effort force
   - **B** increase the distance or speed the resistance will move
   - **C** change the direction of a force
   - **D** all of the above

8. A simple machine containing a bar that can turn about a fixed point is a(n) _____.
   - **A** wheel and axle
   - **B** lever
   - **C** inclined plane
   - **D** wedge

9. Work input = _____.
   - **A** $F_e \times d_e$
   - **B** $F_e \times d_r$
   - **C** $F_e \times F_r$
   - **D** $F_r \times d_r$

10. Work output = _____.
    - **A** $F_e \times d_e$
    - **B** $F_e \times d_r$
    - **C** $F_e \times F_r$
    - **D** $F_r \times d_r$

Chapter 8 Mastery Test A

Part A Write the letter of the correct answer on the line.

1. Which formula gives you the measure of how much work has been done?
   - A work input = $F_e \times d_e$
   - B efficiency = work output ÷ work input
   - C MA = effort arm ÷ resistance arm
   - D work = force × distance

2. Which term is a unit of measure for power?
   - A joule
   - B newton
   - C watt
   - D resistance

3. If you move a table 50 meters in 50 seconds using 200 newtons of force, how much power have you used?
   - A 200 watts
   - B 10,000 joules
   - C 500,000 joules
   - D 1,000 watts

4. A boulder at the top of a mountain has what kind of energy?
   - A electrical
   - B potential
   - C kinetic
   - D nuclear

5. What is meant by the law of conservation of energy?
   - A Energy used to do work may take one of six forms.
   - B As potential energy decreases, kinetic energy increases.
   - C Machines conserve energy by giving large work output for small work input.
   - D Energy may change form, but it cannot be created or destroyed.

6. What kind of lever has a fulcrum, resistance arm, and effort arm?
   - A first-class lever
   - B second-class lever
   - C third-class lever
   - D all of the above

7. A machine multiplies your effort force by 3 times. What does the number 3 represent?
   - A mechanical advantage
   - B resistance force
   - C power
   - D work

8. What kind of lever has the fulcrum between the effort and the resistance and changes the direction of a force?
   - A first-class lever
   - B second-class lever
   - C third-class lever
   - D any lever

9. Which formula expresses the work output, or the amount of work actually done by the machine?
   - A $F_e \times d_e$
   - B $F_e \times d_r$
   - C $F_r + F_e$
   - D $F_r \times l_r = F_e \times l_e$

©AGS Publishing. Permission is granted to reproduce for classroom use only.   Physical Science

---

Part B Read each description. Write the name of the simple machine it describes.

10. Rope, chain, or belt wrapped around a wheel that changes the direction of an applied force. Movable or fixed types.

11. One or two inclined planes that move when used. Thick at one end and thin at the other.

12. A wheel attached to a shaft. A doorknob is an example.

Part C Write a short answer for each question on the line.

13. What is work? _____
14. What is energy? _____
15. What is the difference between kinetic energy and potential energy?

16. List the six main forms of energy.
    A _____ C _____ E _____
    B _____ D _____ F _____

17. Write the law of conservation of energy.

Part D Write the answer to each question on the line.

18. How much work is done in moving a box 12 meters, using a force of 20 newtons?

19. What is the mechanical advantage of a simple machine if a force of 15 newtons lifts an object weighing 45 newtons?

20. A person uses a lever to lift a loaded shipping carton. The person applies 150 newtons of effort force and pushes the end of the lever 0.75 meter. The lever exerts 250 newtons of resistance force. It lifts the carton 0.4 meter.
    A What is the work input? _____
    B What is the work output? _____
    C What is the efficiency of the lever? _____

©AGS Publishing. Permission is granted to reproduce for classroom use only.   Physical Science

Chapter 8 Mastery Test A

11. To calculate the mechanical advantage of a lever you _____.

    A divide F_r by F_e
    B multiply F_r and F_e
    C divide the effort arm by the resistance arm
    D either A or C

12. Power = _____.

    A force × distance   **C** work output ÷ work input
    B work ÷ time   **D** $F_e × d_e$

Critical Thinking

Write the answer to each of these questions on your paper.

13. What class of lever is shown in the diagram below? How can you tell?

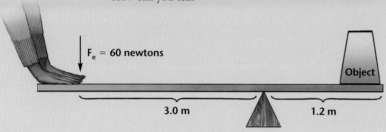

F_e = 60 newtons

Object

3.0 m   1.2 m

14. Give examples of three simple machines. Explain how simple machines make it possible or easier to do work.

15. List six main forms of energy and write a brief explanation of each one.

Test-Taking Tip Before you begin an exam, skim through the whole test to find out what is expected of you.

---

15. Electrical energy causes electrons to move. Radiant energy comes from light waves. Nuclear energy is released from the nuclei of atoms. Heat energy comes from the motion of particles in matter. Chemical energy is stored in the bonds between atoms. Mechanical energy is the energy of moving objects.

ALTERNATIVE ASSESSMENT

Alternative Assessment items correlate to the student Goals for Learning at the beginning of this chapter.

- Provide students with examples of a force moved through a set distance and have them calculate how much work has been done. Have them figure the power in each of the examples when given the amount of time each job took.

- Have students define energy and identify the six forms of energy.

- Provide students with objects and have them identify the forms of energy they contain and tell whether they have potential or kinetic energy.

- Ask students to draw or collect examples of the six simple machines.

- Have pairs of students use a meterstick, wood block, and weight to model the three classes of levers and identify the effort force, resistance, and fulcrum in each. Ask them to raise the object with a lever and explain its efficiency.

- Display a pulley system and an inclined plane. Have students use them to model work being done and explain the mechanical advantage of the machine.

- Write $MA = F_r ÷ F_e$ and $MA = $ *effort arm ÷ resistance arm* on the board. Have students explain the meaning of each factor of each equation and provide sample problems with calculations of mechanical advantage.

- Have students explain the efficiency rating of an appliance such as a refrigerator.

Chapter 8 Mastery Test B

Chapter

9

Planning Guide

Heat

	Student Pages	Student Text Lesson Vocabulary	Lesson Review
Lesson 1 What Is Heat?	240–243	✔	✔
Lesson 2 How Heat Affects Matter	244–248	✔	✔
Lesson 3 Temperature	249–255	✔	✔
Lesson 4 How to Measure Heat	256–261	✔	✔
Lesson 5 How Heat Travels	262–266	✔	✔

Chapter Activities

Student Text
Science Center
Teacher's Resource Library
Community Connection 9: Testing
  the Water

Assessment Options

Student Text
Chapter 9 Review

Teacher's Resource Library
Chapter 9 Mastery Tests A and B

	Student Text Features								Teaching Strategies						Learning Styles						Teacher's Resource Library				
Achievements in Science	Science at Work	Science in Your Life	Investigation	Science Myth	Note	Technology Note	Did You Know	Science Integration	Science Journal	Cross-Curricular Connection	Online Connection	Teacher Alert	Applications (Home, Career, Community, Global, Environment)	Auditory/Verbal	Body/Kinesthetic	Interpersonal/Group Learning	Logical/Mathematical	Visual/Spatial	LEP/ESL	Workbook Activities	Alternative Workbook Activities	Lab Manual	Resource File	Self-Study Guide
243					✔				241	242			241, 242, 243							41	41	33		✔
	246		247				244		245	245		245			245		245			42	42	34		✔
						✔	254	251, 254, 255	250	252	251		251	253		253			252	43	43		18	✔
			260	258	✔	✔	256	258		258		257					257	257		44	44	35		✔
266		265	264		✔					264	263, 265		263						264	45	45	36	19	✔

Pronunciation Key

a	hat	e	let	ī	ice	ô	order	ù	put	sh	she	a	in about
ā	age	ē	equal	o	hot	oi	oil	ü	rule	th	thin	ə { e	in taken
ä	far	ėr	term	ō	open	ou	out	ch	child	ҬH	then	i	in pencil
â	care	i	it	ȯ	saw	u	cup	ng	long	zh	measure	o	in lemon
												u	in circus

Alternative Workbook Activities

The Teacher's Resource Library (TRL) contains a set of lower-level worksheets called Alternative Workbook Activities. These worksheets cover the same content as the regular Workbook Activities but are written at a second-grade reading level.

Skill Track Software

Use the Skill Track Software for Physical Science for additional reinforcement of this chapter. The software program allows students using AGS textbooks to be assessed for mastery of each chapter and lesson of the textbook. Students access the software on an individual basis and are assessed with multiple-choice items.

Chapter 9: Heat
pages 238–269

Lessons

**Skill Track Software
for Physical Science**

Teacher's Resource Library

(Answer Keys for the Teacher's Resource Library begin on page 402 of the Teacher's Edition. The Materials List for the Lab Manual activities begins on page 419.)

Science Center

Have students cut out or draw pictures that illustrate how they use heat in everyday life. As the chapter progresses, students could add information to the display, such as whether the heat in their examples moves by convection, conduction, or radiation.

Community Connection 9

Chapter

9 Heat

Look at the flame in the photograph. What words would you use to describe the flame? You might say *fire, bright, hot, glowing,* or *heat.* In this photo, the flame is from a match. The flame is a hot gas that will burn if you touch it. It is so hot that it glows. The flame produces heat. But is fire the only way to produce heat? Are there other sources of heat? In Chapter 9, you will learn about heat energy and its sources. You also will learn ways to measure heat, how heat affects matter, and how heat travels.

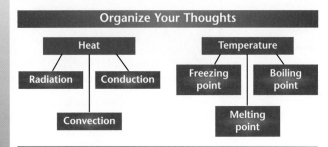

Organize Your Thoughts

Heat
- Radiation
- Conduction
- Convection

Temperature
- Freezing point
- Boiling point
- Melting point

Goals for Learning

◆ To explain how heat energy can be produced

◆ To tell how heat changes matter

◆ To explain how temperature is measured

◆ To identify the difference between temperature and heat

◆ To calculate heat gained or lost

◆ To explain how matter is heated by conduction, convection, and radiation

239

Introducing the Chapter

Ask students what they would tell a young child about the flame in the photograph. Point out that almost everyone learns that heat can burn at an early age. Then encourage students to share other things they have learned about heat. Write some topics on the board, such as "How we use heat," "Where heat comes from," "How we measure heat," "How heat affects matter," and "How heat moves from place to place." Ask each student to make one statement about heat. *(Students might mention appliances such as clothes dryers, or suggest heat sources, such as the sun or a radiator. Students might also mention thermometers used for taking people's temperatures or gauging temperatures outside.)* Write these statements under the appropriate headings. You could start each new lesson by reviewing students' statements that pertain to that lesson.

Notes and Technology Notes

Ask volunteers to read the notes that appear in the margins throughout the chapter. Then discuss them with the class.

TEACHER'S RESOURCE

The AGS Teaching Strategies in Science Transparencies may be used with this chapter. The transparencies add an interactive dimension to expand and enhance the *Physical Science* program content.

CAREER INTEREST INVENTORY

The AGS Harrington-O'Shea Career Decision-Making System-Revised (CDM) may be used with this chapter. Students can use the CDM to explore their interests and identify careers. The CDM defines career areas that are indicated by students' responses on the inventory.

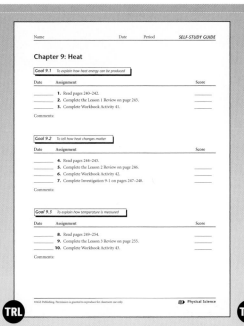

Lesson at a Glance

Chapter 9 Lesson 1

Overview This lesson introduces students to the concept that heat is caused by the motion of atoms and molecules. Students learn where heat comes from and how people use it to do work.

Objectives

- To define heat
- To explain how heat energy can do work
- To explain how heat is produced
- To describe some sources of heat

Student Pages 240–243

Teacher's Resource Library **TRL**

Workbook Activity 41

Alternative Workbook Activity 41

Lab Manual 33

Vocabulary

heat
heat source

nuclear fission
nuclear fusion

Warm-Up Activity

Ask students if they've ever gotten a rug burn when their skin rubbed against a carpet. Ask them why this type of injury is called a rug *burn*. *(They should mention that the injured area felt hot.)* Tell them that the friction of the skin against the carpet causes the skin to heat up to the point where the tissue is damaged. Tell them that this lesson will focus on heat and how it is produced.

Teaching the Lesson

Instruct students to rub their hands together for 10 seconds and to describe the sensation. *(Students should notice that their hands get warmer as they rub them together.)* Ask students to wet their hands and then rub them again for 10 seconds. Ask them to explain why their hands did not get as warm the second time. *(The friction is reduced by the water.)* Ask what would happen if students coated their hands with butter and tried rubbing them together. *(The butter would reduce the friction even more than the water did.)*

240 *Chapter 9 Heat*

Objectives

After reading this lesson, you should be able to

- define heat.
- explain how heat energy can do work.
- explain how heat is produced.
- describe some sources of heat.

Heat

A form of energy resulting from the motion of particles in matter

What happens when you hold an ice cube in your hand? Your hand is warmer than the ice cube. The warmth from your hand causes the ice cube to melt. **Heat** causes the ice to melt. Heat is a form of energy that results from the motion of particles in matter. Heat energy flows from a warmer object to a cooler object.

Heat from your hand will cause an ice cube to melt.

You learned in Chapter 8 that heat is a form of energy. Energy can do work. Therefore, heat can do work. Machines can change heat energy into useful mechanical energy. For example, a steam engine uses the heat energy contained in steam to move the parts of the engine. An automobile engine also uses heat energy. Burning fuel produces hot gases that make the engine work.

Sources of Heat

Heat source
A place from which heat energy comes

What produces heat energy? Remember that all matter is made up of atoms and molecules. These tiny particles are always moving. The random motion and vibrations of particles in matter is a measure of the heat energy. The faster the particles move, the more heat energy they have.

Imagine going outside on a summer day. You feel heat from the sun. The sun is the earth's most important **heat source.** A heat source is a place from which heat energy comes. Nuclear reactions in the sun are the source of the heat energy that warms you.

You might recall from Chapter 8 that energy comes in different forms. Other forms of energy can be changed into heat energy. For example, hold your hands together and rub them rapidly. Your hands will begin to feel warm. Friction between your hands is a form of mechanical energy—the energy of motion—that produces heat.

Rubbing your hands together produces heat.

Point out that people who work with machines use lubricants such as grease to reduce friction between moving parts, thus lessening the amount of mechanical energy that changes to heat energy.

Ask students to make a list of appliances that change electrical energy into heat energy. *(Examples might include electric blankets, electric stoves, irons, hair dryers, microwave or toaster ovens, space heaters, heating pads, and curling irons.)*

 3 Reinforce and Extend

IN THE COMMUNITY

Ask students to find out what heat sources are used to heat homes and other buildings in the community. For example, in some sunny regions, solar heating might be common, while other regions might rely on electricity generated by burning coal or on natural gas for heating.

SCIENCE JOURNAL

Point out to students that heat sources such as electricity and nuclear power plants are new developments in human history. Explain that throughout history, people have kept warm by burning wood, warming beds with containers of hot coals, or building houses that took advantage of the sun's heat. Encourage students to imagine that they were born in a different century and then write a paragraph about what heat sources they might have had and how they might have used those heat sources.

Nuclear fission

The reaction that occurs when the nucleus of an atom splits and energy is released as heat and light

Nuclear fusion

The reaction that occurs when atoms are joined together and energy is released

Fusion is the process responsible for the energy of the sun and other stars.

Sometimes the heat produced by mechanical energy can cause harmful effects. For example, the oil well drills used to drill through rock produce a lot of heat. Workers must cool the drills with water to keep them from melting.

Another source of heat is chemical energy. When substances react chemically with each other, they sometimes release heat. For example, when natural gas and other fuels burn, they produce heat.

Electricity is also a heat source. Look at the toaster below. When energy from an electric current passes through the wires of the toaster, the wires become hot. This energy can toast bread. What other appliances can you name that change electricity into heat energy?

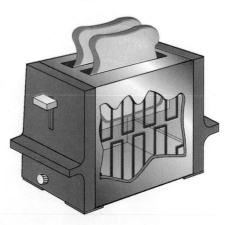

Nuclear energy is another form of energy. It is energy stored in the nucleus of an atom. When the nucleus of an atom is split, the nucleus becomes smaller nuclei. Energy is released as heat and light. This reaction is called **nuclear fission.** Nuclear energy is also released when atoms are joined together. When two nuclei are combined, they form a larger nucleus. This reaction is called **nuclear fusion.** Stars shine because their atoms release nuclear energy. Nuclear energy produces the sun's heat and light.

Lesson 1 REVIEW

Write your answers to these questions in complete sentences on a sheet of paper.

1. What is heat?

2. What produces heat energy?

3. Give an example of how another form of energy can be changed into heat energy.

4. Does heat energy flow from a warm object to a cooler object or from a cool object to a warmer one?

5. What form of energy produces the sun's heat?

Achievements in Science

Steam Engine

The first steam engine, invented by the Greeks before 300 A.D., was used as a toy. Later steam engines had more practical uses. In 1698, Thomas Savery invented a steam-powered pump to drain water from mines. In 1765, Thomas Newcomen designed a more efficient steam engine pump. James Watt's steam engine, invented in 1763, was the first to do more than pumping. Watt's steam engine could make something turn. Watt's improvements led to machines that could do work that had once been done by hand.

Steam engines use heated water to operate. Most steam engines have a furnace that burns fuel, which produces heat energy. All have a boiler in which heat energy changes water to steam. The pressure from the expanding steam pushes on the engine parts to make them move.

Some early uses of steam engines were in steam locomotives and steamships. Today we continue to use steam engines to convert heat into mechanical work. Steam engines are at work in most electric power plants and all nuclear power plants.

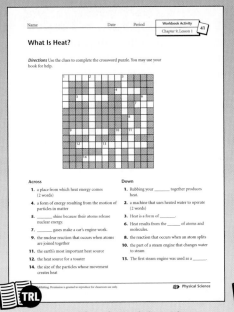

Workbook Activity 41

Lab Manual 33, pages 1–2

---

1. Heat is a form of energy that results from the motion of particles in matter. Heat flows from a warmer object to a cooler object. **2.** The motion of atoms and molecules in matter produces heat energy. **3.** Answers will vary. Possible answer: Rubbing your hands together is mechanical energy that results in friction, which produces heat. **4.** Heat energy flows from a warm object to a cooler object. **5.** Nuclear energy produces the sun's heat.

Achievements in Science

Have students form small groups to read the Achievements in Science feature on page 243. Then challenge each group to create a simple diagram of a practical steam engine. Their design should indicate the heat source, boiler, and use to which the expanding steam is put. Invite groups to draw their diagrams on the board and explain their engine's function to the class.

IN THE ENVIRONMENT

Remind students that Earth itself is a heat source. Introduce the term *geothermal* and help students use etymology to define the term. (Point out that *geo-* comes from the Greek word meaning "earth," and *thermal* has as its root the Greek word for "heat.") Students can read about geothermal energy in Appendix A on page 374. Then ask students to find Iceland on a world map or globe. Tell students that this small island country has many volcanoes, geysers, and hot springs and the people of Iceland have taken advantage of these energy sources. Have students find out about the use of geothermal power in Iceland and report their findings to the class. Students might visit the Web site iga.igg.cnr.it/iceland.php for data on geothermal power in Iceland.

Portfolio Assessment

Sample items include:
- Lists from Teaching the Lesson
- Diagram from Achievements in Science activity
- Lesson 1 Review answers

Lesson at a Glance

Chapter 9 Lesson 2

Overview This lesson explains how heat can make matter change from one state to another. Students learn that most matter expands when it is heated and contracts when it loses heat.

Objectives

- To describe how heat affects solids
- To describe how heat affects liquids
- To describe how matter expands and contracts

Student Pages 244–248

Teacher's Resource Library 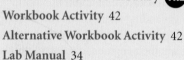 **TRL**

Workbook Activity 42

Alternative Workbook Activity 42

Lab Manual 34

Vocabulary

condensation	evaporate
contract	expand

Science Background

Most matter follows the same path as it gets hotter. It changes from a solid to a liquid and then to a gas. Some matter under certain circumstances will go directly from a solid to a gas. This is called sublimation. As an example, if you were to·hang clothes outside to dry and the temperature dropped below 0°C, the water in the clothing would freeze. If the wind was blowing, the ice would turn directly to a vapor, and the clothes would eventually dry.

1 Warm-Up Activity

Pass around a thick, unlit candle. Ask students whether the object is a solid, a liquid, or a gas. *(a solid)* Light the candle. Allow students to observe as some of the wax melts to form a pool around the flame. Carefully pour a little out onto a plate. As you pour, ask what state the wax is in now. *(liquid)* Call students' attention to the wax in the plate as it cools and hardens back into a solid. Point out that as it loses heat, the wax becomes solid

---

Objectives

After reading this lesson, you should be able to

- describe how heat affects solids.
- describe how heat affects liquids.
- describe how matter expands and contracts.

Evaporate

To change from a liquid to a gas

Condensation

To change from a gas to a liquid

 Did You Know?

There is no air inside the bubbles of boiling water. The bubbles of boiling water are made up of water vapor, also called steam.

Matter exists in different states. In a gas, the particles (molecules) are generally very far apart. They move freely. In a liquid, the particles are close together, but are still able to move freely. In a solid, the particles are close together and are not able to move past each other. They are constrained to specific positions in the solid. Heat can cause particles to move faster and move farther apart. Heat can change matter from one state to another.

Changing from a Liquid to a Gas

You might have noticed that if you boil water for a period of time, the amount of water gradually decreases. What happens to the water? Heat makes the water molecules move faster. As the molecules move faster, they bump into each other more often and push each other apart. As a result, the water **evaporates,** or changes from a liquid to a gas.

Heat rises

Changing from a Gas to a Liquid

If you have ever seen frost form on a window inside your home, you have seen an example of **condensation.** The temperature outside is cooler than the temperature inside your home. Condensation occurs when water vapor in the air returns to its original liquid state. This happens when the air cools and the temperature of the air drops. The molecules in the air move at a slower speed. Cold air cannot hold as much water vapor as warm air. Some of the water vapor condenses to form tiny drops of liquid water. Water drops that appear on a mirror after you have taken a hot shower are another example of condensation.

244 *Chapter 9 Heat*

---

again. Tell students that they are going to learn how heat affects matter.

2 Teaching the Lesson

Boil some water in front of the class. As the water warms, ask students to suggest why bubbles form on the bottom of the pan. *(That's the hottest part of the pan. The water boils there first, creating pockets of gas.)* Stir the water until the bubbles disperse. Ask: Where did the bubbles go? *(They rose to the top and dispersed, as a gas, into the air.)* If you have time, let enough water boil off to make a visible difference in the water level. Ask: What process did this activity just demonstrate? *(evaporation)*

Did You Know?

Have students read the feature on page 244. Point out that the mist rising from boiling water, commonly referred to as steam, actually consists of water droplets that have condensed as the temperature cools.

Changing from a Solid to a Liquid

What happens to an ice cube (a solid) when it is left in a warm room? It melts. But why does it melt? Heat speeds up the vibrational motion of the molecules in the ice cube. This motion disrupts the structure of the ice crystal. The molecules are free to move around relative to each other. The solid ice cube changes to liquid water.

Expanding and Contracting Matter

Heat causes particles in matter to push farther apart. Then the matter **expands,** or becomes larger in size. It fills up more space. The figure shows a joint in a metal bridge. Summer heat makes the material in the bridge expand. What might happen if the bridge did not have an expansion joint?

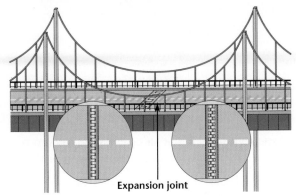

Expansion joint

Bridge in summer   **Bridge in winter**

Solids, liquids, and gases do not expand equally. In most cases, liquids expand more than solids. Gases usually expand the most.

Sometimes, matter loses heat. Particles in matter move more slowly and stay closer together as they lose heat. The matter **contracts,** or becomes smaller. It takes up less space. In the figure, notice the joint in the bridge in winter. The material in the bridge contracts in cold weather. Water is a material that behaves differently. Cooled water contracts until it reaches 4°C. Below this temperature, water expands until it freezes at 0°C.

Lesson 2 Review Answers

1. An ice cube melts when it is heated, changing from a solid to a liquid. **2.** Heat from the sun causes the water molecules in the puddle to move faster. The molecules bump into each other and push each other apart. The water changes from a liquid to a gas. **3.** Heat causes matter to expand. As matter loses heat, its particles move more slowly and stay closer together, causing the matter to contract. **4.** Heat makes the water molecules move faster, causing them to push each other apart. As a result, the water evaporates, or changes from a liquid to a gas. **5.** Yes, fog consists of tiny drops of liquid water. It can form in cool air, which cannot hold as much water vapor as warm air.

Science at Work

Ask a volunteer to read aloud the Science at Work feature on page 246. Suggest to students that HVAC technicians sometimes have to deal with critical situations. Invite students to come up with emergencies that an HVAC technician might encounter. *(heating failure during the winter; ventilation repair for underground engineering projects; air conditioning failure for products that require a cool or temperature-controlled environment such as food or computers)*

Portfolio Assessment

Sample items include:
• Observations from Body/Kinesthetic Learning Styles activity
• Conclusion from Cross-Curricular Connection
• Lesson 2 Review answers

Write your answers to these questions in complete sentences on a sheet of paper.

1. What happens to an ice cube when it is heated?
2. What happens when water in a puddle evaporates?
3. How does heat affect the amount of space matter fills?
4. Why does the amount of water decrease when it boils?
5. Is fog an example of condensation? Explain your answer.

▼◄▲▼◄▲▼◄▲▼◄▲▼◄▲▼◄▲▼◄▲▼◄▲▼◄▲▼◄▲▼◄▲▼◄▲▼◄▲▼◄▲▼◄▲▼◄▲▼

Science at Work

Heating, Ventilation, and Air Conditioning (HVAC)) Technician

HVAC technicians install, maintain, and repair heating, ventilation, and air conditioning systems. They work in both homes and businesses. They also recharge systems with refrigerants or cooling gases, such as Freon. Their other responsibilities include testing, troubleshooting, and adjusting systems to make sure they work properly.

HVAC technicians receive on-the-job training or they complete an apprenticeship program.

HVAC technicians must work well with their hands and have good vision and hand-eye coordination. They also must be patient and be able to work effectively under stressful conditions.

246   *Chapter 9   Heat*

Name _____ Date _____ Period _____ | **Workbook Activity** 42
Chapter 9, Lesson 2

How Heat Affects Matter

Directions Choose the word from the Word Bank that best completes each sentence. You will use one word twice.

Word Bank			
evaporates	condensation	expands	contracts

1. Matter generally _____ when you heat it.
2. Water _____ when you boil it.
3. That frost on your window is an example of _____.
4. Water _____ when it becomes ice.
5. When particles in matter move more slowly, the matter usually _____

Directions Each sentence tells about a process that is occurring. Write the letter of the process that is occurring on the line.

A liquid to solid   **B** liquid to gas   **C** solid to liquid   **D** gas to liquid

_____ **6.** A can of a soft drink in the freezer bursts.
_____ **7.** The bathroom walls are covered with water after your shower.
_____ **8.** The water in the teakettle is bubbling.
_____ **9.** The rain puddle is getting smaller.
_____ **10.** The ice cream is running down the cone.

Directions Complete the following sentences.

11. Cold air cannot hold as much _____ as warm air.
12. Molecules in a _____ move more freely than in a liquid.
13. Bubbles in boiling water are made up of water _____.
14. In the _____ months, a metal bridge is likely to expand.
15. One familiar material that does not contract when it gets colder is _____.

Publishing. Permission is granted to reproduce for classroom use only.   Physical Science

Workbook Activity 42

Materials

◆ safety glasses
◆ balloon
◆ flask
◆ masking tape or electrical tape
◆ 2 buckets
◆ cold water
◆ warm water
◆ paper towels

Observing and Comparing Expansion and Contraction

Purpose

What happens when a gas expands and contracts? In this investigation, you will observe and compare expansion and contraction of gases.

Procedure

1. Copy the data table on a sheet of paper.

Environment	Changes in balloon
In warm water	
In cold water	
At room temperature	

2. Put on your safety glasses.

3. Carefully stretch the opening of the balloon over the opening of the flask. Use tape to seal the balloon to the flask.

SAFETY ALERT

◆ Be sure students wear safety glasses.
◆ Be sure the water temperature is not hot enough to cause burns.
◆ Use a heat-resistant flask so that the rapid temperature change from hot to cold doesn't cause the flask to break.

The Purpose portion of the student investigation begins with a question to draw them into the activity. Encourage students to read the investigation steps and formulate their own questions before beginning the investigation. The investigation will take approximately 30 minutes to complete. Students will use these process and thinking skills: observing, collecting, recording, and interpreting data; inferring; and drawing conclusions.

Preparation

• Be sure the balloons are large enough so that the opening of the balloon fits over the mouth of the flask.

• Bring plenty of extra balloons. They are easily broken as students set up this activity.

• For best results, flask size should be 500–1,000 mL.

• Large plastic storage containers could be used instead of flasks.

• Students may use Lab Manual 34 to record their data and answer the questions.

Procedure

• Students should work in cooperative groups of three. Assign one student to gather equipment. All students should record results, answer questions, and clean up when finished.

• Fill the buckets full enough to submerge most of the flask, but not so full that the buckets overflow when the flasks are immersed.

• If possible, you may want to keep the buckets in the sink during this activity to avoid spills.

• Before students attach the balloon to the flask, have them blow the balloon up once and release the air. This will make the balloon more flexible, and students will get better results.

• Rubberized electrician's tape will make a better seal than masking tape and will be less affected by contact with water.

• Use ice in the cold water to make the test more dramatic.

Continued on page 248

Continued from page 247

- Be sure the flask is kept in the warm water long enough for all the air in the flask to become warm. About 5 to 10 minutes should be sufficient. It will take longer for larger flasks.

- If the balloon doesn't inflate in the warm water, have students check the balloon-to-flask connection to be sure the seal is tight.

Results

The balloon should slowly inflate as the flask heats in the warm water. The balloon should slowly collapse as the flask chills in the cold water.

Questions and Conclusions Answers

1. The balloon began to inflate.

2. The balloon deflated.

3. The air in the bottle expanded when it was heated, and the air moved into the balloon. When it was cooled, the air in the bottle contracted and the air in the balloon was pulled back into the flask.

Explore Further Answers

In a colder room a helium-filled balloon would diminish in size. In a warmer room it would expand.

Assessment

Check to be sure students are getting the expected results in both parts of the activity. Check students' answers to be sure they have explained their results. You might include the following items from this investigation in student portfolios:

- Investigation 9-1 data table

- Answers to Questions and Conclusions and Explore Further sections

4. Fill one bucket with cold water.

5. Fill the other bucket with hot water. **Safety Alert: Do not use water hot enough to cause a burn.** Place the flask in the bucket of hot water. Keep the flask in the water until the flask becomes hot.

6. Observe the balloon. Record any changes you see in the data table.

7. Remove the flask from the bucket of hot water. Place the flask in the bucket of cold water. Keep the flask in the cold water until the flask becomes cold. Record any changes to the balloon.

8. Take the flask out of the water and dry it. Watch the balloon as the flask returns to room temperature. Record any changes to the balloon.

Questions and Conclusions

1. What happened to the balloon when the flask was heated?

2. What happened to the balloon as the flask cooled?

3. What caused the changes you observed in the balloon?

Explore Further

Explain what would happen to a helium-filled balloon if it was moved to a colder room. Explain what would happen to the balloon if it was moved to a warmer room.

Name _____ Date _____ Period _____ | Lab Manual | 34
Chapter 9

9-1 Observing and Comparing Expansion and Contraction of Gases

Use with Investigation 9-1, pages 247–248.

Purpose What happens when a gas expands and contracts? In this investigation, you will observe and compare expansion and contraction of gases.

Environment	Changes in Balloon
in warm water	
in cold water	
at room temperature	

Questions and Conclusions

1. What happened to the balloon when the flask was heated?

2. What happened to the balloon as the flask cooled?

3. What caused the changes you observed in the balloon?

Explore Further

Explain what would happen to a helium-filled balloon if it was moved to a colder room. Explain what would happen to the balloon if it was moved to a warmer room.

Publishing. Permission is granted to reproduce for classroom use only.   ▶ Physical Science

Lab Manual 34

Objectives

After reading this lesson, you should be able to

◆ explain how temperature is measured.

◆ compare and contrast temperature scales.

◆ describe freezing point, melting point, and boiling point.

Temperature

A measure of how fast an object's particles are moving

Heat energy from Maria's hand heats the water and melts the ice cubes.

What happens when you put your hand in a bowl of cool water? Heat energy from your hand flows into the water and makes the water warmer.

The more your hand heats the water, the faster the water particles move. **Temperature** is a measure of how fast an object's particles are moving. The higher the temperature, the faster an object's particles move.

Touching an object does not always give an accurate measurement of the object's temperature.

For example, suppose you place your hand in cold water. Heat energy from your hand moves to the water and your hand becomes cooler. Now move that same hand out of the cold water and into a container of lukewarm water. The water will feel hotter than it actually is because your hand is cool.

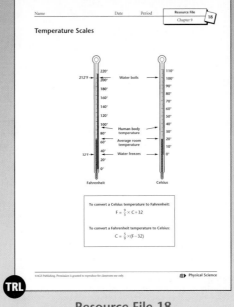
Lesson at a Glance

Chapter 9 Lesson 3

Overview This lesson explores how and why temperature is measured. Students learn about freezing points, melting points, and boiling points, as well as the Fahrenheit and Celsius scales.

Objectives

■ To explain how temperature is measured

■ To compare and contrast temperature scales

■ To describe freezing point, melting point, and boiling point

Student Pages 249–255

Teacher's Resource Library

Workbook Activity 43

Alternative Workbook Activity 43

Resource File 18

Vocabulary

boiling point	**freezing point**
Celsius scale	**melting point**
degree	**temperature**
Fahrenheit scale	**thermometer**

Science Background

Every substance has its own boiling point, the temperature at which it changes from a liquid to a gas. The boiling point of water is usually said to be 212°F (100°C). In reality, the boiling point varies. The boiling point is affected by atmospheric conditions and altitude. People who live at higher altitudes, for example, would find that water boils at a slightly lower temperature.

1 Warm-Up Activity

Ask students to suggest words that describe hot and cold weather, such as *nippy* and *broiling*. Ask them whether these words are a precise way to describe temperature. *(no)* Ask them whether they think the word *chilly* would mean the same thing to someone from Texas as it would to someone from Alaska. *(probably not)* Tell students that they will be learning about how scientists measure temperature.

2 Teaching the Lesson

Set out three large containers of water—one at room temperature, one with very cold water, and one with very warm water. Do not tell students how the containers differ. Have half the students place a hand in the cold water for about 30 seconds and then into the room temperature water. Have the other half place a hand in the warm water and then into the room temperature water. Ask each group how water in the second container felt. *(The first group should describe it as warm; the second should describe it as cool.)* Point out that the body is a poor indicator of temperature.

Boil some water. Place a heavy-duty thermometer in the water. Allow students to watch as the liquid in the thermometer rises and stops. In addition to seeing how a thermometer works, they can also see that the boiling point of a substance is indeed predictable. (See Science Background for information on why the result might not be exactly 100° C.)

A liquid cannot get hotter than its boiling point. If you heated a pot of water on the stove until it boiled and then turned the flame beneath it even higher, the temperature of the water in the pan would not climb beyond 212°F.

3 Reinforce and Extend

SCIENCE JOURNAL

Explain to students the difference between objective and subjective methods of describing temperatures. *(The objective method uses a thermometer; the subjective method is based upon personal judgment.)* Have students describe situations in which each of these methods can be helpful means of gauging temperature.

Thermometers

Thermometer
A device that measures temperature

You often cannot rely on your sense of touch to accurately tell temperature. So how can you measure temperature accurately? A **thermometer** is a device we use to measure temperature. Two different kinds of thermometers are shown below.

The thermometer in the figure at the right is a glass tube with a small amount of liquid inside. The liquid is usually mercury or alcohol. As the thermometer measures higher temperatures, heat causes the particles of liquid to expand, or move farther apart. As the liquid expands, it moves up the tube. The more heat that passes to the liquid, the more the liquid will expand and the higher it moves in the tube. When the liquid stops expanding, it stops beside a number on the tube. This number tells the temperature of the substance touching the bulb of the thermometer.

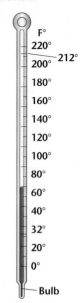

Look at the electronic thermometer in the photo below. Many doctors and medical workers use this kind of thermometer to take people's temperatures. It measures temperatures very quickly.

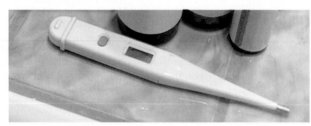

Digital (electronic) thermometers measure temperatures quickly.

Temperature Scales

Two common scales are used to measure temperature. People in the United States usually use the **Fahrenheit scale.** Fahrenheit is abbreviated as *F.* People in many other countries use the **Celsius scale.** The abbreviation for Celsius is *C.* Scientists use the Celsius scale.

Look at the thermometers on this page to compare the Fahrenheit scale with the Celsius scale. Find the equally spaced units on each scale. For both temperature scales, temperature is measured in units called **degrees.** The symbol for degree is °. The temperature shown on the Fahrenheit scale is 68 degrees Fahrenheit. It is written as 68°F. The same temperature in the Celsius scale is 20 degrees Celsius. It is written as 20°C.

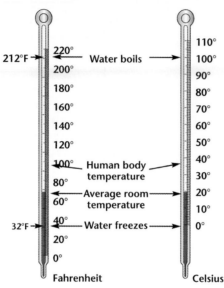

We write any temperature below zero degrees with a minus (–) sign. For example, a temperature of 10 degrees below zero on the Celsius scale is written as –10°C. The table on the next page shows how we write temperatures on the Fahrenheit scale and the Celsius scale.

Temperature Conversion

If you know the temperature of a substance on one scale, you can convert to an equal temperature on the other scale. The table shows how temperatures convert from one scale to the other.

Temperature Conversion Table			
°C	°F	°C	°F
100	212	45	113
95	203	40	104
90	194	35	95
85	185	30	86
80	176	25	77
75	167	20	68
70	158	15	59
65	149	10	50
60	140	5	41
55	131	0	32
50	122		

If you need a conversion that is not listed in the table, you can use a formula to figure it out. You can use this formula to convert a Celsius temperature to Fahrenheit.

$F = \frac{9}{5} \times C + 32$ or $F = 1.8 \times C + 32$ (the fraction $\frac{9}{5}$ is equal to 1.8)

Suppose you want to convert 22° Celsius to Fahrenheit.

EXAMPLE

$F = 1.8 \times C + 32$
$F = 1.8 \times 22 + 32$
$F = 1.8 \times 22 = 39.6 + 32$
$F = 71.6°$ or $F = 72°$

We usually round the decimal portion of the number to the nearest whole number. So, you would round 71.6 to 72.

Use this formula to convert a Fahrenheit temperature to Celsius.

$$C = \frac{5}{9} \times (F - 32)$$

Suppose you want to convert 48° Fahrenheit to Celsius.

EXAMPLE

$$C = \frac{5}{9} \times (F - 32)$$

$$C = \frac{5}{9} \times (48 - 32)$$

$$C = \frac{5 \times 16}{9} = \frac{80}{9}$$

$$C = 8.8° \ or \ C = 9°$$

Notice that $\frac{80}{9}$ is 80 ÷ 9 or 8.8888. Round the decimal portion of the number to the nearest whole number to get 9.

Freezing point

The temperature at which a liquid changes to a solid

Melting point

The temperature at which a solid changes to a liquid

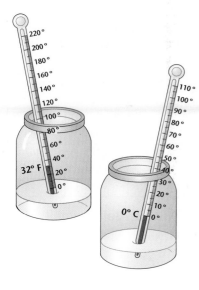

Freezing Point

What happens when you place a container of water in the freezer? The water gradually changes to ice. Suppose you recorded the temperature of the water every five minutes. You would notice that as time passed, the temperature would decrease. As the temperature of the water decreases, the water loses heat. Eventually the liquid water becomes solid.

The temperature at which a liquid changes to a solid is called its **freezing point.** The figure shows the freezing point of water. On the Celsius scale, the temperature at which water freezes is 0°. On the Fahrenheit scale, the temperature at which water freezes is 32°.

Melting Point

The temperature at which a solid changes to a liquid is called its **melting point.** The melting point of a substance is the same as its freezing point. The term *melting point* is used when a substance is being heated. When ice is heated, it changes to a liquid at a temperature of 0°C. Therefore, the melting point of ice is 0°C.

SCIENCE INTEGRATION

Technology

Knowledge of the melting point of metals, for instance, is particularly important to artists or engineers working in elements or alloys. Draw students' attention to the chart on Student Text page 254. Then ask them to research the properties of silver, lead, gold, copper, tin, tungsten, and mercury. Have them create a chart for these metals, indicating melting/freezing point temperatures in both Fahrenheit and Celsius. Some students might also investigate industries that use melted metals and how and why the metals are melted.

Boiling point

The temperature at which a substance changes from a liquid to a gas under normal atmospheric pressure

Boiling Point

The **boiling point** of a substance is the temperature at which it changes from a liquid to a gas under normal atmospheric pressure. You can see in the figure that the temperature at which water boils is 100° on the Celsius scale. On the Fahrenheit scale, the boiling point is read as 212°.

Every substance has its own freezing and boiling points. Scientists use the freezing and boiling points of substances to help identify unknown substances. You can see the freezing and boiling points of a few substances in the table.

The Freezing and Boiling Points of Some Substances				
Substance	Freezing/Melting Point		Boiling Point	
	°F	°C	°F	°C
water	32	0	212	100
aluminum	1,220	660	4,473	2,467
iron	1,762	961	4,014	2,212
alcohol	−202	−130	173	78

Changing Freezing Point and Boiling Point

You can change the freezing point and the boiling point of a substance by mixing substances together. For example, if you add alcohol to water, the freezing point of the mixture will be lower than the freezing point of water alone. Antifreeze contains alcohol. Adding antifreeze to an automobile radiator lowers the freezing point of the water in the radiator. This keeps the water from freezing and prevents engine damage. The antifreeze also has a higher boiling point than water. Antifreeze boils more slowly than water in hot weather.

Certain compounds of sodium and calcium are used on icy roads and walkways in winter. These compounds lower the freezing point of water and change the ice back to a liquid.

Lesson 3 REVIEW

Write your answers to these questions in complete sentences on a sheet of paper.

1. How does the motion of molecules affect temperature?

2. Explain how a liquid thermometer works.

3. Write the following temperatures:

    A thirty-four degrees Fahrenheit

    B sixty-six degrees Celsius

    C four degrees below zero on the Fahrenheit scale

    D one hundred ten degrees on the Celsius scale

4. What is meant by the freezing point of a substance?

5. What is meant by the melting point of a substance?

6. What is meant by the boiling point of a substance?

7. How can the freezing point of a substance be changed?

8. Change 35° Fahrenheit to Celsius.

9. Change 18° Celsius to Fahrenheit.

10. Which temperature is hotter, 23° Celsius or 65° Fahrenheit?

Technology Note

A pop-up timer shows when a turkey is cooked. The timer has an outer case. This case contains a plastic stem within a piece of soft metal and a spring. The soft metal is solid at room temperature. When it reaches its melting point, the metal releases the stem. The spring makes the stem pop up.

Lesson 3 Review Answers

1. The faster the molecules in an object move, the higher the temperature of the object. **2.** When the liquid in a thermometer is heated, it expands, rising up the thermometer. The number it stops beside shows the temperature of the substance touching the bulb of the thermometer. **3. A** 34°F **B** 66°C **C** −4°F **D** 110°C **4.** A substance's freezing point is the temperature at which the substance changes from a liquid to a solid. **5.** A substance's melting point is the temperature at which it changes from a solid to a liquid. **6.** The boiling point is the temperature at which a substance changes from a liquid to a gas. **7.** You can change a substance's freezing point by mixing in a substance with a different freezing point. **8.** 1.67°C **9.** 64.4°F **10.** 23°C. It is equal to 73.4°F.

SCIENCE INTEGRATION

Technology

Ask students what information about cooking a person designing a pop-up turkey timer would need to know in order to create a useful device. (*The designer would have to know the temperature at which the meat would be fully cooked in order to find a metal that melted at that temperature.*)

Portfolio Assessment

Sample items include:
- Data from Global Connection
- Temperature chart from Science Integration activity
- Lesson 3 Review answers

Workbook Activity 43

Chapter 9 Lesson 4

Overview In this lesson, students learn that heat, measured in calories, depends on both temperature and mass. Students also learn how heat gain and loss is calculated.

Objectives

- To explain how temperature and heat differ
- To explain how heat is measured
- To calculate heat gain and loss

Student Pages 256–261

Teacher's Resource Library **TRL**

Workbook Activity 44

Alternative Workbook Activity 44

Lab Manual 35

Vocabulary

calorie

Science Background

In everyday life, if we want to find out how hot something is, we usually just take the temperature. We use a thermometer, and we measure the *intensity* of the heat. However, heat and temperature are not the same thing. Temperature measures only intensity, or how fast the particles in an object are moving. The faster the particles are moving, the hotter the object is. But the actual amount of heat in an object depends not only on its temperature, but also on how much mass the object has. For example, if a cup of water and a large tub of water are both 50°C, the larger vessel will contain more heat.

1 Warm-Up Activity

Tell students to imagine that they are going to heat their homes with solar heat. They will do this by placing a tank of water in their home so that it soaks up heat from the sun during the day and gives off heat at night. Give them a choice of a tank the size of a book or a tank the size of a classroom wall. Ask them which would give off the most heat if the temperature of the water was the same in both tanks. *(the larger one)* Ask why they answered as they did. *(They may arrive at*

Objectives

After reading this lesson, you should be able to

- explain how temperature and heat differ.
- explain how heat is measured.
- calculate heat gain and loss.

Did You Know?

When temperatures fall, bridges become covered with ice before roads do. Bridges have more surface exposed to the air than roads. Because of this, they lose heat energy more quickly. This makes them freeze faster.

Suppose you fill a tub with warm water. Then you fill a cup with water from the tub. The temperature of the water in each container would be the same. However, the water in the tub would give off more heat than the water in the cup. The amount of heat given off depends on the mass of the water, the surface area, and the temperature of the air.

Temperature and Heat

Temperature and heat are different. Temperature is a measure of how fast the molecules in a substance are moving. The higher the temperature, the greater the atomic or molecular motion. Heat depends on the temperature of a substance and the amount of matter, or mass, the substance has.

As the temperature of an object increases, the amount of heat in the object also increases. If two objects of different mass are at the same temperature, the object with the greater mass will give off more heat. The temperature of the lighted candle in the figure is the same as the temperature of the bonfire. The bonfire contains more mass than the candle. Therefore, the bonfire gives off more heat.

the correct answer intuitively, without knowing that heat is related to mass.) Tell students that they will be learning how heat and mass are related.

2 Teaching the Lesson

This is a good time to remind students that heat flows from a warmer object to a cooler object. When discussing the rate at which a substance cools, students might mistakenly believe that coldness is somehow getting into the warm object and cooling it down. Be sure they understand that the object is cooling because heat is moving out of it.

Did You Know?

Have students read the feature on page 256. Display pictures of a roadway and a bridge. Have students note that air moves both over and under the bridge whereas air only moves *above* roadways. Point out that the ground under the road serves as an insulator.

Calorie

A unit of heat; the amount of heat needed to raise the temperature of 1 g of water by 1°C

Specific heat is the amount of heat needed to raise the temperature of 1 g of any substance by 1°C. Different things have different specific heat. Only 0.1 calorie makes 1g of iron 1°C warmer.

Other units that measure heat energy are joules and British thermal units (BTUs). One joule equals 0.239 calories. One BTU equals 251.996 calories. Calories also measure food energy. One food calorie equals 1,000 heat energy calories.

Measuring Heat

You know that temperature is measured in units called degrees. Scientists measure heat in units of energy called **calories**. A calorie is the amount of heat needed to raise the temperature of 1 gram of water by 1 degree Celsius.

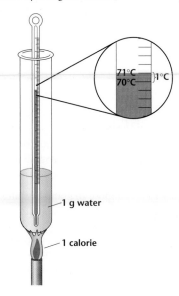

— 1 g water

— 1 calorie

You can use a formula to find out the amount of heat (calories) you would need to change the temperature of a substance.

Heat (calories) = change in temperature (°C) × mass (grams)

How many calories of heat are needed to raise the temperature of 1 gram of water by 3 degrees C?

EXAMPLE
Heat = change in temperature × mass
Heat = 3°C × 1 g
Heat = 3 calories

3 Reinforce and Extend

TEACHER ALERT

Students may think that the calories they are reading about in this lesson are the same as the Calories listed on food packaging. Although both units measure heat energy, a Calorie shown on a food box is actually a *kilocalorie*, equal to 1,000 of the calories discussed in this lesson. (A capital C distinguishes the larger unit from the smaller unit.) When you eat an apple that has 150 Calories, it is equal to 150,000 calories (150 × 1,000).

LEARNING STYLES

Visual/Spatial
Have students draw a picture or diagram that shows how heat, temperature, and mass are related. Tell them to be sure to include labels and a caption explaining the drawing.

LEARNING STYLES

Logical/Mathematical
Have students make a careful note of the food they consume on a given day and the food Calorie value for each item. (They can find Calorie values on food packaging, on the Internet, or in books on nutrition or dieting.) Ask them to bring their records to class. Have them form small groups and calculate the average of their daily Calorie intake. List the figure from each group on the board.

Have a volunteer read the myth portion (first sentence) of the Science Myth and another volunteer read the fact portion on page 258. Make sure they understand the apparent contradiction: It would seem natural that adding heat to a substance would increase its temperature. Point out that a similar phenomenon occurs when an ice cube melts. Even when a flame is applied to it, the temperature of melting ice or snow remains at near 0°C until all the ice has disappeared. Like the steam, the melting ice contains latent, or hidden, energy.

SCIENCE INTEGRATION

Earth Science

Explain to students that water warms and cools more slowly than land does. Have them investigate the year-round temperatures of two U.S. cities located at about the same latitude, one of which is on the coast, and one of which is far inland. *(for example, San Francisco and St. Louis)* Students should notice that coastal areas usually experience milder temperatures, while inland areas usually experience more extreme temperature variations. The ocean acts to some extent as a giant heating and cooling device.

CROSS-CURRICULAR CONNECTION

Physical Education

Encourage students to discover how and why the human body heats up and cools down. Suggest that they research answers to the following questions:

• How does the body adjust to temperature change?

• How does physical exercise affect the body?

• What is the best way to avoid becoming too hot or cold?

Have students form groups and pool their information. Invite groups to share their conclusions with the class.

Science Myth

Water at 100°C has the same heat energy as steam at 100°C.

Fact: Steam has more heat energy. It takes heat energy to change water from a liquid to a gas. The energy that is used to change states is latent, or hidden, energy. It is hidden because the temperature does not increase when water changes to steam.

When matter changes from one state to another, the temperature remains the same. What changes is the distance between the particles that compose the matter. The temperature may change only after a change in state.

You can use the same formula to calculate the following problem.

How many calories of heat are needed to raise the temperature of 6 grams of water from 5°C to 15°C?

> **EXAMPLE** First, calculate the temperature change.
> Change in temperature = 15°C − 5°C
> Change in temperature = 10°C
>
> Then calculate the heat.
> Heat = change in temperature × mass
> Heat = 10°C × 6 g
> Heat = 60 calories

Cooling

Heat can also be lost or given off by a substance when it is cooling. We place a minus sign (−) in front of the answer to indicate that the water is being cooled.

Suppose 20 grams of water are cooled from 20°C to 8°C. How much heat is given off?

> **EXAMPLE** First, calculate the change in temperature.
> Change in temperature = 20°C − 8°C
> Change in temperature = 12°C
>
> Then, calculate the calories.
> Heat = change in temperature × mass
> Heat = 12°C × 20 g
> Heat = 240 calories

The answer is expressed as −240 calories to show that heat is given off.

The above examples are for water. In order to calculate heat lost or gained by other substances, you would use the same formula. However, different substances require different amounts of heat to raise their temperatures by 1°. That amount is called the specific heat.

Lesson 4   R E V I E W

Write your answers to these questions in complete sentences on a sheet of paper.

1. If two objects that have the same temperature have a different mass, which object gives off the most heat?

2. Suppose 25 grams of water are heated to from 0°C to 5°C. How many calories are needed?

3. Suppose 15 grams of water are heated from 12°C to 22°C. How many calories are needed?

4. If 20 grams of water are heated to from 0°C to 1°C, how much heat is added?

5. Suppose 35 grams of water are cooled from 15°C to 10°C. How much heat is given off?

6. Suppose 88 grams of water are cooled from 22°C to 16°C. How much heat is given off?

7. Suppose 16 grams of water are cooled from 13°C to 1°C. How much heat is given off?

8. Suppose 10 calories of heat are added to 10 grams of water. The temperature of the water will increase by how much?

9. Suppose 100 calories of heat are added to 10 grams of water. The temperature of the water will increase by how much?

10. Suppose 50 calories of heat are added to 10 grams of water at 10°C. What will the final temperature be?

Technology Note

Pressure cookers cook food quickly by raising the boiling temperature of water. We can make water boil at a higher temperature by putting it under pressure. When the tightly sealed pot is heated, steam pressure builds up inside. The more pressure, the higher the temperature, and the faster food cooks.

Heat   Chapter 9 **259**

Lesson 4 Review Answers

1. The object with the greater mass gives off the most heat. **2.** 125 calories **3.** 150 calories **4.** 20 calories **5.** −175 calories **6.** −528 calories **7.** −192 calories **8.** 1°C **9.** 10°C **10.** 15°C

Portfolio Assessment

Sample items include:
• Picture or diagram from Visual/Spatial Learning Styles activity
• Data from Calorie intake record
• Lesson 4 Review answers

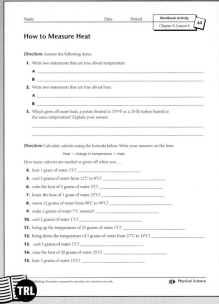

Workbook Activity 44

Investigation 9-2

The Purpose portion of the student investigation begins with a question to draw them into the activity. Encourage students to read the investigation steps and formulate their own questions before beginning the investigation. The investigation will take approximately 30 minutes to complete. Students will use these process and thinking skills: observing; collecting, recording, and interpreting data; making inferences; and drawing conclusions.

Preparation

• The thermometers should be about a foot long, to make reading them easier.

• Use plastic jars if possible.

• Students may use Lab Manual 35 to record their data and answer the questions.

Procedure

• This activity is best done by students working in pairs.

• Review with students how to read the thermometer. As they read the temperature, students should have their eyes level with the liquid in the thermometer.

• The more water that is used in the container, the slower the temperature will drop. For this reason, there should be a dramatic difference in the size of the two jars and the amount of water in each.

• The water for each pair of jars should be obtained at the same time so that they start at the same temperature.

• Some of the groups could try a variation of this investigation. Have them wrap their containers with various materials. For example, they could wrap both containers with towels or aluminum foil. Both containers must be wrapped the same way in the same material. All the groups could then compare their readings. The wrapped jars should lose heat more slowly than the plain jars. You could use the results of this variation as a jumping off point for the discussion of insulation in Lesson 5.

9-2 INVESTIGATION

Materials
- safety glasses
- large jar
- hot tap water
- small jar
- 2 Celsius thermometers
- clock or watch
- ice water

Measuring the Rate of Heat Loss

Purpose
Do different amounts of water cool at different rates? In this investigation, you will measure the cooling rates of different amounts of water.

Procedure

1. Copy the data table on a sheet of paper. Extend the length of the table to fit 15 minutes.

Time	Temperature (°C)	
	Large Jar	Small Jar
0 minutes		
1 minute		
2 minutes		
3 minutes		
4 minutes		
5 minutes		

2. Put on your safety glasses.

3. Fill the large jar with hot tap water. **Safety Alert: Do not use water hot enough to cause a burn.**

4. Fill the small jar about halfway with hot tap water.

5. Place the jars next to each other on a flat surface.

6. Place a thermometer in each jar, as shown in the figure on page 261. Immediately read the temperature on each thermometer. Record the temperatures in the section of your data table marked *0 minutes*.

SAFETY ALERT

◆ Make sure students wear their safety glasses.

◆ Be sure that the water is not hot enough to cause burns.

◆ Handle thermometers with care. If possible, get alcohol thermometers, which are safer than ones that contain mercury. If mercury thermometers are broken, the mercury must be cleaned up immediately with special equipment. Don't let students handle mercury—it gives off a poisonous vapor.

7. Leave the thermometers in the jars. Use the clock or watch to keep track of the time. Record the temperature of each water sample every minute for 15 minutes.

Questions and Conclusions

1. What was the temperature of the water in each jar the first time you measured it? After 8 minutes? After 15 minutes?

2. How did the amount of water in the jar affect how fast the temperature of the water dropped?

3. What happened to the heat from the water as the water cooled?

Explore Further

Repeat the activity, using a jar of ice water. Then answer these questions.

1. How did the temperature of the water change after 8 minutes? After 15 minutes?

2. Explain the change of temperature that occurred in the ice water.

Because the smaller container has less water and therefore less mass, it also has less heat. It should lose its heat faster than the larger container.

Questions and Conclusions Answers

1. At the start, the water in both containers should be the same temperature. After 8 minutes, the water in the smaller container should be slightly cooler. After 15 minutes, the temperature difference should be greater, with the water in the smaller container being cooler.

2. The smaller container, with less water, lost heat more quickly than the larger container.

3. Heat from the water flowed into the container and then into the air surrounding the container.

Explore Further Answers

1. After 8 minutes, the temperature of the water has increased. After 15 minutes, the temperature has increased even more.

2. Heat flows from a warmer object to a cooler object. The heat flowed from the air to the container and then to the water.

Assessment

Check that students are reading the thermometer correctly. Use the answers to the questions to verify that they understand their results. You might include the following items from this investigation in student portfolios.

- Investigation 9-2 data table
- Answers to Questions and Conclusions and Explore Further sections

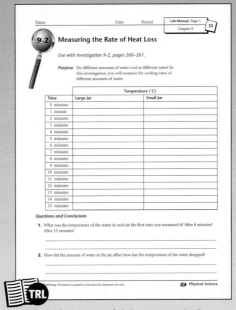

Lab Manual 35, pages 1–2

Lesson at a Glance

Chapter 9 Lesson 5

Overview This lesson describes how heat travels by radiation, conduction, and convection. Students also explore how certain materials aid or hinder the flow of heat.

Objectives

- To explain how matter is heated by radiation
- To explain how matter is heated by conduction
- To explain how matter is heated by convection

Student Pages 262–266

Teacher's Resource Library **TRL**

Workbook Activity 45

Alternative Workbook Activity 45

Lab Manual 36

Resource File 19

Vocabulary

conduction   insulator
conductor   radiation
convection   vacuum

 Warm-Up Activity

Ask students to suggest ways that people keep their homes warm in cold weather. They might mention turning on a radiator or building a fire in a fireplace. Guide them to consider insulation methods such as closing windows or sealing them with plastic. Tell students that they are going to learn how heat moves from one place to another.

 Teaching the Lesson

Tell students that as they read, they are to draw a diagram of each of the ways heat travels—by radiation, conduction, and convection.

Ask students if they dress differently for different seasons. Guide them to understand that a sweater or parka serves as an insulator to keep body heat from escaping. Point out that these garments contain pockets of air, a good insulator.

Lesson 5 How Heat Travels

Objectives

After reading this lesson, you should be able to

- explain how matter is heated by radiation.
- explain how matter is heated by conduction.
- explain how matter is heated by convection.

Vacuum
Space that contains no matter

Radiation
The movement of energy through a vacuum

Radiant energy from the sun is transferred into chemical energy through photosynthesis. Photosynthesis is the process by which plants use sunlight to make food.

Think about different ways you can travel, or move, from one place to another. You might walk or run. You might ride a bicycle. You might travel in a car, bus, train, boat, or airplane. Energy also has different ways of moving from warm matter to cool matter.

Radiation

The sun is a very long distance from Earth—150 million kilometers, in fact. Yet the sun heats Earth. How does the sun's energy travel the long distance from its surface to Earth? It must travel through a **vacuum.** A vacuum is a space that has no matter. Energy from the sun reaches us by **radiation.** Radiation is the movement of energy through a vacuum. Radiation can carry energy across space where there is no matter. The energy can heat matter.

Heat from sources other than the sun can also travel by radiation. You can see this illustrated in the figure. Heat energy from the fire moves into the room by radiation and then heats the air.

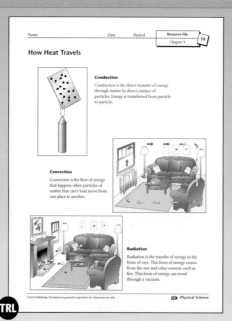

Resource File 19

Conduction

Conduction

The movement of heat energy from one molecule to the next

Conductor

Material through which heat travels easily

Insulator

Material that does not conduct heat well

You probably know that if you hold a strip of metal in a flame it will get hot. Why does this happen? The metal gets hot because of **conduction.** Conduction is the movement of heat energy from one molecule to the next. Heat travels by conduction when molecules bump into each other.

Look at the strip of copper in the figure. Heat from the flame makes the copper particles (atoms) near the flame move faster. As the particles move faster, they hit other particles. These particles then bump into the particles farther up on the strip of copper. They transfer energy. As a result, the slower particles move faster. Eventually, all the particles in the copper are moving fast. In other words, the entire piece of copper becomes hot.

Energy moves easily through some kinds of matter. A substance that allows heat energy to flow through it easily is called a **conductor.** Most metals, such as copper, silver, gold, aluminum, and tin, are good conductors.

A material that does not conduct heat well is called an **insulator.** Energy does not move easily through insulators. Insulators are used in the walls of homes to keep heat out in summer and cold out in winter. Some good insulators are glass, wood, sand, soil, Styrofoam, and air.

You can use heated water and basil flakes to demonstrate how convection currents move. Before class, fill a clear heat-resistant container with water, stir in a teaspoon of dried basil flakes, and boil the mixture, so that the flakes become saturated and sink to the bottom. In class, heat the water but do not bring it to a boil. As students observe, point out that the flakes rise and fall, carried by convection currents.

 3 **Reinforce and Extend**

ONLINE CONNECTION

 Point out that good insulators are especially important in the extreme temperatures of outer space. Encourage students to find out about NASA's research in this area by having them visit www.nasa.gov. They should type in *insulation* and click on *start search.* Invite students to print out and share findings from this site that interest them.

CAREER CONNECTION

Invite a general contractor to speak to the class about heat insulation in modern buildings. Ask the contractor to display samples of wall and ceiling insulation for students to inspect. Encourage students to discuss with their guest the importance of insulators in the building trade.

Ask students to read the myth portion (first sentence) and the fact portion of the Science Myth feature on page 264. Point out to students the difference between the following statements:

1. Heat makes things rise.
2. Hot liquids and gases rise.

The first statement is misleading because heat can travel in any direction—down a wire by conduction or across a room by radiation, for example. Statement 2 is true in one sense: hot liquids and gases *do* rise because they are displaced by cooler substances. An equally true version of this statement would be, *Cool liquids and gases sink.*

CROSS-CURRICULAR CONNECTION

Drama

Have students form small groups. Ask them to devise three silent skits, each demonstrating one of the three ways heat travels: radiation, conduction, and convection. Invite groups to perform their skits for the class. Challenge members of the audience to guess the method each skit represents.

LEARNING STYLES

LEP/ESL

Have students orally explain convection with the aid of the figure on page 264. Have partners study the figure and explain to each other, in their own words, the process it illustrates. Invite pairs to reproduce the figure on the board and to explain the concept of convection to their classmates.

Convection
Flow of energy that occurs when a warm liquid or gas rises

Science Myth

Heat makes things rise.

Fact: Cool air falls underneath warm air because warm air is less dense than cool air. Warm air is less dense because its particles are farther apart. Any denser liquid or gas will fall underneath a less dense liquid or gas. This change in density of a liquid or gas causes convection currents.

Convection

Convection is a method of heat movement that happens when the particles of a gas or a liquid rise. As they rise, they carry heat.

Find the heater in the figure. First, conduction heats the air touching the heater. Then the warm air rises. Cool air moves in to take its place. The heater warms the cool air and it rises. The warm air cools as it moves through the room. Then it flows back to the heater and is warmed again. The arrows show how heat energy flows up and around the room. Convection keeps the air moving.

Convection also happens in liquids. Suppose a pot of cold water is placed on the stove. Heat is conducted from the hot burner to the pot and then to the water at the very bottom of the pot. Then convection heats the rest of the water. The warm water rises and the cooler water sinks.

How do different heating systems work?

How can you control the temperature of your home? The chart describes some types of heating systems. People use these types of heating systems to keep their homes at a comfortable temperature.

Heating Systems		
Type of System	Description	How Heat Travels
Hot water	A furnace heats the water. A pump circulates the water through pipes to a radiator in each room.	Convection and radiation circulate heat throughout the room.
Steam	A boiler sends steam to pipes. Steam forces the heat through the pipes to radiators in each room.	Radiation and convection circulate heat throughout the room.
Forced air	Air is heated by a furnace. It is then pumped into rooms through vents at the floor of each room.	Forced convection circulates heat throughout the room.
Passive solar	The sun's rays pass through a large door or window. They heat up a large tile or rock wall. Heat radiates into the room from the wall and sets up convection currents.	Radiation and convection distribute heat.
Radiant electric	Electric current heats up wires in baseboards, walls, and/or ceilings.	Heat radiates from these specific places.

1. Which heating systems heat a home by convection?
2. Which heating systems provide radiant heat?
3. Which type of heating system would be more efficient in a hot, sunny climate? Explain your answer.
4. Which types of heating systems would be more efficient in a cold climate? Explain your answer.

Have volunteers take turns reading the Science in Your Life feature on page 265. Discuss with students the need to stay warm and the methods people have used to protect themselves from cold climates. After students have read the chart on page 265, encourage them to share their experiences of home-heating systems.

1. Hot water, steam, forced air, and passive solar systems heat a home by convection. **2.** Hot water, steam, passive solar, and radiant electric systems provide radiant heat. **3.** A passive solar system because more energy from the sun is available throughout the year. **4.** Hot water, steam, forced air or radiant electric because cold climates require systems that can heat an entire house when natural heat is unavailable.

ONLINE CONNECTION

Encourage students to learn more about heat energy by having them visit the U.S. Navy's energy Web site at energy.navy.mil/ awareness and click on *energy awareness/tools.* From there they can choose *Puzzlers* or *Tools* to find puzzles, cartoons, energy tips, and motivational quotes.

Lesson 5 Review Answers

1. The sun's heat travels to the earth by radiation through a vacuum. **2.** Heat moves from one molecule to the next. **3.** Conduction heats the air near the heater. By convection, the warm air rises and cool air moves in to take its place. The warm air cools as it moves through the room. It flows back to the heater and is warmed again. **4.** A vacuum is space that contains no matter. **5.** Heat energy can flow through a conductor easily. Energy can't move easily through an insulator.

Achievements in Science

Ask volunteers to read aloud the Achievements in Science feature on page 266. Discuss with students the purpose of temperature scales. Lead them to understand that the accuracy and consistency of the measurements—not the specific number values—are what make a scale valuable. Point out that the Celsius scale is not in as widespread use in the United States as it is in the rest of the world. Discuss with students why they think this might be the case and what problems it could create.

Portfolio Assessment

Sample items include:
• Diagrams from Teaching the Lesson
• Lesson 5 Review answers

Lesson 5 REVIEW

Write your answers to these questions in complete sentences on a sheet of paper.

1. How does the sun's heat travel to the earth?

2. How does heat move by conduction?

3. Explain how convection heats a room.

4. What is a vacuum?

5. Explain the difference between a conductor and an insulator.

Achievements in Science

Temperature Scales

For 2,000 years, people have used temperature scales. But people used different kinds of scales for different purposes. Only in the 1600s did scientists develop temperature scales like those we use today.

The Fahrenheit temperature scale was introduced in 1724. This scale began at 0°, the freezing point of an ice, water, and salt mixture. It ended at 98°, the normal body temperature. Water's freezing point was 32°. Scientists later adjusted Fahrenheit's scale, making the highest point 212°, water's boiling point.

The Celsius temperature scale was introduced in 1742. It made zero the boiling point of water and 100 the melting point of ice. The scale was divided into 100 units called degrees centigrade. Later scientists changed "centigrade" to "Celsius." They also made 0° the freezing point of water and 100° the boiling point.

The Kelvin temperature scale, introduced in 1848, is based on the Celsius scale. On the Kelvin, zero is the temperature at which the movement of all atoms stops.

Name _____ Date _____ Period _____   Lab Manual, Page 1 / 36 / Chapter 9

Exploring Heat Absorption

Purpose How would using an inclined plane to lift a mass affect the force and the distance factors? In this investigation, you will investigate how an inclined plane affects work.

Materials safety glasses / water / 2 empty frozen juice cans / black cardboard / black construction paper / white cardboard / white construction paper / 2 thermometers / scissors / sunlight or 2 lamps with 100-watt bulbs / tape

Procedure

1. Use the table below to record your data.

Time	Black Can	White Can
beginning		
3 minutes		
6 minutes		
9 minutes		
12 minutes		
15 minutes		
18 minutes		
21 minutes		

2. Put on your safety glasses. **Safety Alert: Avoid contact with the light sources, which may be hot.** Cover one of the cans with black paper, as shown in the figure on the next page. Cover the other can with white paper.

3. Fill both of the cans with water.

4. Cut a square of black paper large enough to cover the top of the black can. Carefully poke a hole in the middle of the square. Insert a thermometer through the hole. Place the square over the top of the black can. The bottom of the thermometer should be in the center of the can.

Publishing. Permission is granted to reproduce for classroom use only.   ▶ Physical Science

Lab Manual 36, pages 1–2

Name _____ Date _____ Period _____   Workbook Activity / 45 / Chapter 9, Lesson 5

Heat: Terms Review

Directions Match each term in Column A with its meaning in Column B. Write the correct letter on the line.

	Column A		Column B
___ 1.	calorie	A	to change from a liquid to a gas
___ 2.	temperature	B	a form of energy resulting from the motion of particles in matter
___ 3.	degree	C	temperature at which a solid changes into a liquid
___ 4.	Fahrenheit scale	D	the reaction occurring when the nucleus of an atom splits
___ 5.	evaporate	E	a measure of how fast an object's particles are moving
___ 6.	melting point	F	a device that measures temperature
___ 7.	nuclear fission	G	the temperature scale in which water freezes at 0°
___ 8.	freezing point	H	the temperature at which a substance changes to a gas
___ 9.	Celsius scale	I	a unit of measurement on a temperature scale
___ 10.	nuclear fusion	J	the reaction occurring when atoms are joined together
___ 11.	thermometer	K	the temperature scale commonly used in the United States
___ 12.	boiling point	L	the amount of heat needed to raise the temperature of 1 g of water 1°C
___ 13.	contract	M	the temperature at which a liquid changes to a solid
___ 14.	heat	N	to become smaller in size

Directions Unscramble the word in parentheses to complete each sentence.

15. The flow of heat energy through matter by molecules bumping into each other is _____. (noitcudonc)

16. Copper is an excellent _____ of heat energy. (rotnocduc)

17. Energy from the sun reaches us by _____. (idiotrana)

18. Warm liquids rise as a result of _____. (nevoncocit)

19. A _____ is space without matter. (camuvu)

20. A material that does not warm up or cool down quickly is called an _____. (sularotin)

Publishing. Permission is granted to reproduce for classroom use only.   ▶ Physical Science

Workbook Activity 45

- Heat is a form of energy. It results from the motion of the particles in matter. Heat energy flows from a warmer object to a cooler object.

- Mechanical, solar, electrical, chemical, and nuclear energy are sources of heat.

- Heat can cause matter to change from one state to another.

- Generally, heat (a rise in temperature) causes matter to expand; loss of heat (a drop in temperature) causes matter to contract.

- Temperature measures how fast particles are moving.

- The Fahrenheit and Celsius scales are used to measure temperature.

- The freezing point, the melting point, and the boiling point are important temperatures for all substances.

- Heat is measured in calories.

- Heat depends on the temperature and the mass of an object.

- The number of calories gained or lost by water equals the change in Celsius temperature multiplied by the mass.

- Heat travels by radiation, conduction, and convection.

Science Words

boiling point, 254	contract, 245	freezing point, 253	nuclear fusion, 242
calorie, 257	convection, 264	heat, 240	radiation, 262
Celsius scale, 251	degree, 251	heat source, 241	temperature, 249
condensation, 244	evaporate, 244	insulator, 263	thermometer, 250
conduction, 263	expand, 245	melting point, 253	vacuum, 262
conductor, 263	Fahrenheit scale, 251	nuclear fission, 242	

Chapter 9 Summary

Have volunteers read aloud each Summary item on page 267. Ask volunteers to explain the meaning of each item. Direct students' attention to the Science Words box on the bottom of page 267. Have them read and review each term and its definition.

Chapter 9 Review

Use the Chapter Review to prepare students for tests and to reteach content from the chapter.

Chapter 9 Mastery Test

The Teacher's Resource Library includes two parallel forms of the Chapter 9 Mastery Test. The difficulty level of the two forms is equivalent. You may wish to use one form as a pretest and the other form as a posttest.

Review Answers
Vocabulary Review

1. thermometer 2. temperature
3. convection 4. conduction 5. Celsius scale 6. evaporate

Concept Review

7. D 8. D 9. B 10. A 11. D 12. C 13. B

TEACHER ALERT

Because of limited space in this Chapter Review, not all of the vocabulary terms introduced in this chapter appear in the Vocabulary Review section. You may want to create an activity using the missing words to give students practice with all of the terms in this chapter. Here are the terms that are not covered in the section.

boiling point	heat
calorie	heat source
condensation	insulator
conductor	melting point
contract	nuclear fission
degree	nuclear fusion
expand	radiation
Fahrenheit scale	vacuum
freezing point	

Word Bank

Celsius scale
conduction
convection
evaporate
temperature
thermometer

Vocabulary Review

Choose a word or words from the Word Bank that best complete each sentence. Write the answer on a sheet of paper.

1. A device that measures temperature is a(n) _____.

2. A measure of how fast an object's particles are moving is _____.

3. The flow of energy that occurs when a warm liquid or gas rises is _____.

4. The movement of heat energy from one molecule to the next is _____.

5. The temperature scale in which water freezes at 0° and boils at 100° is the _____ .

6. To change from a liquid to a gas is to _____.

Concept Review

Choose the answer that best completes each sentence. Write the letter of the answer on your paper.

7. Heat energy can be produced by _____ energy.
  A nuclear   **C** chemical
  B electrical   **D** all of the above

8. When frozen water melts and then evaporates, heat energy has caused the water molecules to _____.
  A move closer together   **C** move farther apart
  B move faster   **D** both B and C

9. The melting point of a substance is the same as its _____.
  A boiling point   **C** both A and B
  B freezing point   **D** none of the above

10. As the temperature of an object increases, the amount of heat in the object _____.
  A increases   **C** stays the same
  B decreases   **D** makes the mass increase

Chapter 9 Mastery Test A

Part A Choose the answer that best completes the statement or question. Write the letter of the answer on the line next to the number.

____ **1.** When a substance changes from a liquid to a gas, it is said to ____.
  A condense   C boil
  B expand   D evaporate

____ **2.** Which of the following best defines a calorie?
  A a unit of heat   C 1 gram of water
  B a unit of measurement on a   D a place from which heat energy comes
    temperature scale

____ **3.** Heat can travel through space by means of ____.
  A contraction   C convection
  B radiation   D condensation

____ **4.** Under normal circumstances, water boils at ____.
  A 100°F   C 212°C
  B 212°F   D 200°C

____ **5.** Metal bridges are built with expansion joints because in the summer ____.
  A the hot metal evaporates   C the metal in the bridge may increase in size
  B metal contracts in the sun D some metals can reach melting point

____ **6.** What happens at the melting point?
  A Solid substances change to water.   C A solid changes to a liquid.
  B The temperature rises above 32°F   D Most liquids change to ice.

Part B Write the answer to each problem on the line.

7. How much heat is added when 22 grams of water are heated from 10°C to 15°C?

8. How much heat is given off when 10 grams of water are cooled from 50°C to 40°C?

9. How much heat is given off when 23 grams of water are cooled from 80°C to 37°C?

10. How much heat is added when 11 grams of water are heated from 5°C to 100°C?

Chapter 9 Mastery Test A, continued

Part C Write a short answer to each question.

11. How can heat be produced?

12. Explain how heat can change matter.

13. Explain how a thermometer placed in warm milk or ice water measures temperature.

14. How is temperature different from heat?

15. Describe how radiation, conduction, and convection can heat matter.

Chapter 9 Mastery Test A

11. The freezing point or boiling point of a substance can be changed by _____.

   A reducing the substance's mass

   B increasing the substance's mass

   C heating or cooling the substance

   D mixing the substance with another substance

12. The amount of heat needed to raise the temperature of 1 gram of water by 6°C is _____.

   A 1 calorie   **B** 3 calories   **C** 6 calories   **D** 12 calories

13. A material that keeps heat out of a house in summer and cold out in winter _____.

   A is a good conductor   **C** has a low freezing point

   B is a good insulator   **D** has a high boiling point

Critical Thinking

Write the answer to each of these questions on your paper.

14. Why does ice cream melt faster in a dish that is room temperature than in a dish that has been in the freezer?

   15. The objects shown in the figure to the left have the same temperature. Do they give off the same amount of heat? Explain your answer.

Test-Taking Tip Studying together in small groups and asking questions of one another is one way to review material for tests.

14. The ice cream melts faster in a dish that is room temperature because heat energy flows from a warmer object to a cooler object. The heat energy from the dish flows to the ice cream. **15.** No, the larger container has more surface area and so it gives off more heat than the cup.

ALTERNATIVE ASSESSMENT

Alternative Assessment items correlate to the student Goals for Learning at the beginning of this chapter.

- Have students write "The Journal of a Water Molecule," explaining in the first person what happens when water in a pan is heated to boiling.

- Invite students to narrate anecdotes from their own lives that illustrate how matter changes in extreme heat and cold.

- Have students form teams and test each other on information from the newspaper weather page. One team should give national temperatures in Fahrenheit; the receiving team should convert these figures to Celsius. Teams should then switch roles, with the receiving team converting temperatures from Celsius to Fahrenheit.

- Have students identify objects that have the same temperature but different heat and discuss the distinction between temperature and heat.

- Ask pairs of students to compose problems that require calculating heat gain or loss in changing water temperature. Have them exchange questions with other pairs and answer the questions.

- Ask students to make a table with three columns labeling them *Conduction, Convection,* and *Radiation.* Have students fill in the columns with examples of these processes that they have experienced or observed in the last week.

Name _____ Date _____ Period _____   **Mastery Test B, Page 1**
                                              Chapter 9

Chapter 9 Mastery Test B

Part A Write the answer to each problem on the line.

1. How much heat is given off when 10 grams of water are cooled from 50°C to 40°C? _____

2. How much heat is added when 22 grams of water are heated from 10°C to 15°C? _____

3. How much heat is added when 11 grams of water are heated from 5°C to 100°C? _____

4. How much heat is given off when 23 grams of water are cooled from 80°C to 37°C? _____

Part B Choose the answer that best completes the statement or question. Write the letter of the answer on the line next to the number.

_____ **5.** Which of the following best defines a calorie?

   A a unit of heat   **C** 1 gram of water
   B a unit of measurement on   **D** a place from which heat energy comes
        a temperature scale

_____ **6.** When a substance changes from a liquid to a gas, it is said to _____.

   A condense   **C** boil
   B expand   **D** evaporate

_____ **7.** Metal bridges are built with expansion joints because in the summer _____.

   A the hot metal evaporates   **C** the metal in the bridge may increase in size
   B metal contracts in the sun   **D** some metals can reach melting point

_____ **8.** Heat can travel through space by means of _____.

   A contraction   **C** convection
   B radiation   **D** condensation

_____ **9.** What happens at the melting point?

   A Solid substances change to water.   **C** A solid changes to a liquid.
   B The temperature rises above 32°F.   **D** Most liquids change to ice.

_____ **10.** Under normal circumstances, water boils at _____.

   A 100°F   **C** 212°C
   B 212°F   **D** 200°C

©AGS Publishing. Permission is granted to reproduce for classroom use only.   ● **Physical Science**

Name _____ Date _____ Period _____   **Mastery Test B, Page 2**
                                              Chapter 9

Chapter 9 Mastery Test B, continued

Part C Write a short answer to each question.

11. Explain how heat can change matter.
_____
_____

12. Describe how radiation, conduction, and convection can heat matter.
_____
_____
_____
_____

13. How can heat be produced?
_____
_____

14. How is temperature different from heat?
_____
_____

15. Explain how a thermometer placed in warm milk or ice water measures temperature.
_____
_____
_____
_____
_____

©AGS Publishing. Permission is granted to reproduce for classroom use only.   ● **Physical Science**

TRL   **TRL**

Chapter 9 Mastery Test B

Planning Guide

Sound and Light

	Student Pages	Vocabulary	Lesson Review
Student Text Lesson			
Lesson 1 What Is Sound?	272–274	✔	✔
Lesson 2 Different Sounds	275–279	✔	✔
Lesson 3 How Sound Travels	280–288	✔	✔
Lesson 4 What Is Light?	289–293	✔	✔
Lesson 5 How Light Is Reflected	294–300	✔	✔
Lesson 6 Bending Light	301–304	✔	✔

Chapter Activities

Student Text
Science Center

Teacher's Resource Library
Community Connection 10: Using
Sound and Light

Assessment Options

Student Text
Chapter 10 Review

Teacher's Resource Library
Chapter 10 Mastery Tests A and B

Achievements in Science	Science at Work	Science in Your Life	Investigation	Science Myth	Note	Technology Note	Did You Know	Science Integration	Science Journal	Cross-Curricular Connection	Online Connection	Teacher Alert	Applications (Home, Career, Community, Global, Environment)	Auditory/Verbal	Body/Kinesthetic	Interpersonal/Group Learning	Logical/Mathematical	Visual/Spatial	LEP/ESL	Workbook Activities	Alternative Workbook Activities	Lab Manual	Resource File	Self-Study Guide
									273	273			273		273			273		46	46	37	20	✔
279				277	✔		278			276, 277		275	277, 278				276			47	47			✔
		287		285	✔	✔	284			282	283	281	281	285	283	282			284	48	48	38		✔
293		292			✔		290		291	292		290	290, 292					291	291	49	49			✔
				299		✔		295	296	296		295	295, 297		295			295		50	50	39, 40	21	✔
	304						302		303	302	303	301	302				303	302		51	51			✔

Pronunciation Key

a	hat	e	let	ī	ice	ô	order	u̇	put	sh	she
ā	age	ē	equal	o	hot	oi	oil	ü	rule	th	thin
ä	far	ėr	term	ō	open	ou	out	ch	child	ᵀH	then
â	care	i	it	ȯ	saw	u	cup	ng	long	zh	measure

ə { a in about / e in taken / i in pencil / o in lemon / u in circus }

Alternative Workbook Activities

The Teacher's Resource Library (TRL) contains a set of lower-level worksheets called Alternative Workbook Activities. These worksheets cover the same content as the regular Workbook Activities but are written at a second-grade reading level.

Skill Track Software

Use the Skill Track Software for Physical Science for additional reinforcement of this chapter. The software program allows students using AGS textbooks to be assessed for mastery of each chapter and lesson of the textbook. Students access the software on an individual basis and are assessed with multiple-choice items.

Chapter at a Glance

Chapter 10:
Sound and Light
pages 270–307

Lessons

Skill Track Software
for Physical Science

Teacher's Resource Library TRL

Workbook Activities 46–51

Alternative Workbook Activities
46–51

Lab Manual 37–40

Community Connection 10

Resource File 20–21

Chapter 10 Self-Study Guide

Chapter 10 Mastery Tests A and B

(Answer Keys for the Teacher's
Resource Library begin on page 402
of the Teacher's Edition. The
Materials List for the Lab Manual
activities begins on page 419.)

Science Center

Some reference books provide directions
for making musical instruments from
simple materials. For example, stringed
instruments can be made from rubber
bands and boxes. Flutes can be made from
plastic straws. Provide several references
and some simple materials, such as rubber
bands, cardboard tubes, empty boxes,
glass bottles, and straws, from which
students might construct their own
instruments. You might also provide art
materials for students to decorate their
instruments. At the end of the chapter,
you might have a "class orchestra" play
a tune.

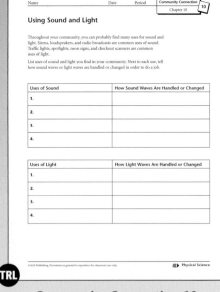

Chapter

10 Sound and Light

Almost everyone enjoys watching a fireworks display like the one in the photograph. Fireworks help us celebrate special holidays and events. What happens when you view fireworks? First, you see an explosion of bright, colorful light. Then, you hear the explosion's crashing boom or sharp whistle. Why do you see the light before you hear the sound? In Chapter 10, you will learn how sound is produced and how light travels. You also will discover how sound and light are alike and how they are different.

Organize Your Thoughts

```
Vibrating matter                          Photons

     Sound  ──── Waves ────  Light

Intensity   Reflected    Reflected   Refracted

Frequency   Echo         Mirror      Lens
```

Goals for Learning

◆ To explain how sound is produced
◆ To describe intensity and volume of sound
◆ To tell how sound travels
◆ To describe the nature of light
◆ To explain reflection of light
◆ To explain refraction of light

271

Introducing the Chapter

Discuss the photo on page 270. Ask students what two senses are involved in watching fireworks. Ask them why they think such explosions appear as light in the night sky. Read the introductory paragraph together. Write the word *sound* on the board. Together brainstorm words or phrases that relate to sound. If vocabulary terms from the chapter relate to students' ideas, write them on the board in a different color. Then invite students to suggest ways to arrange the words into a concept map. For example, they might use organizing phrases such as *what sound is, how sound travels,* and *uses of sound.* Before starting Lesson 4, repeat this procedure for light.

Refer students to the Organize Your Thoughts chart showing properties of sound and light. Have students point out any similarities it shows between sound and light. Have students read the Goals for Learning. Ask them to use these goals to create questions they want to answer as they read the chapter.

Notes and Technology Notes

Ask volunteers to read the notes that appear in the margins throughout the chapter. Then discuss them with the class.

TEACHER'S RESOURCE

The AGS Teaching Strategies in Science Transparencies may be used with this chapter. The transparencies add an interactive dimension to expand and enhance the *Physical Science* program content.

CAREER INTEREST INVENTORY

The AGS Harrington-O'Shea Career Decision-Making System-Revised (CDM) may be used with this chapter. Students can use the CDM to explore their interests and identify careers. The CDM defines career areas that are indicated by students' responses on the inventory.

TRL

Name ___ Date ___ Period ___ **SELF-STUDY GUIDE**

Chapter 10: Sound and Light

Goal 10.1 To explain how sound is produced

Date	Assignment	Score
___	**1.** Read pages 272–273.	___
___	**2.** Complete the Lesson 1 Review on page 274.	___
___	**3.** Complete Workbook Activity 46.	___

Comments:

Goal 10.2 To describe intensity and volume of sound

Date	Assignment	Score
___	**4.** Read pages 275–278.	___
___	**5.** Complete the Lesson 2 Review on page 279.	___
___	**6.** Complete Workbook Activity 47.	___

Comments:

Goal 10.3 To tell how sound travels

Date	Assignment	Score
___	**7.** Read pages 280–285.	___
___	**8.** Complete the Lesson 3 Review on page 286.	___
___	**9.** Complete Workbook Activity 48.	___
___	**10.** Complete Investigation 10-1 on pages 287–288.	___

Comments:

©AGS Publishing. Permission is granted to reproduce for classroom use only. ▶ Physical Science

---

TRL

Name ___ Date ___ Period ___ **SELF-STUDY GUIDE**

Chapter 10: Sound and Light, continued

Goal 10.4 To describe the nature of light

Date	Assignment	Score
___	**11.** Read pages 289–292.	___
___	**12.** Complete the Lesson 4 Review on page 293.	___
___	**13.** Complete Workbook Activity 49.	___

Comments:

Goal 10.5 To explain reflection of light

Date	Assignment	Score
___	**14.** Read pages 294–297.	___
___	**15.** Complete the Lesson 5 Review on page 298.	___
___	**16.** Complete Workbook Activity 50.	___
___	**17.** Complete Investigation 10-2 on pages 299–300.	___

Comments:

Goal 10.6 To explain refraction of light

Date	Assignment	Score
___	**18.** Read pages 301–303.	___
___	**19.** Complete the Lesson 6 Review on page 304.	___
___	**20.** Complete Workbook Activity 51.	___
___	**21.** Read the Chapter 10 Summary on page 305.	___
___	**22.** Complete the Chapter 10 Review on pages 306–307.	___

Comments:

Student's Signature ___ Date ___

Instructor's Signature ___ Date ___

©AGS Publishing. Permission is granted to reproduce for classroom use only. ▶ Physical Science

---

Chapter 10 Self-Study Guide

Lesson at a Glance

Chapter 10 Lesson 1

Overview This lesson introduces sound. Students learn how sound is produced.

Objectives

- To explain what sound is
- To explain how sound is produced
- To explain how sound energy moves in waves

Student Pages 272–274

Teacher's Resource Library **TRL**

Workbook Activity 46

Alternative Workbook Activity 46

Lab Manual 37

Resource File 20

....

Vocabulary

sound wave
vibrate

....

Science Background

A wave is a disturbance that transfers energy through matter or space. It is important to note that the particles of matter do not move along with the wave. The motion of the wave is actually the motion of energy passing through space or matter. All waves have three characteristics: amplitude, wavelength, and frequency.

Sound waves travel through a medium—usually air. They are called longitudinal waves. This means that the molecules of air carrying the sound along vibrate back and forth parallel to the direction of wave travel.

1 Warm-Up Activity

Display a tuning fork and a container of water. Tap the fork against the heel of your hand and ask students to listen for the sound produced. Ask students what produced the sound. *(the tuning fork)* Tap the fork again and place its prongs into a shallow container of water. If possible, place a clear container of water on an overhead projector. Have students observe what happens and explain why the water moved. *(The tuning fork is vibrating.)*

Objectives

After reading this lesson, you should be able to

- explain what sound is.
- explain how sound is produced.
- explain how sound energy moves in waves.

Vibrate

To move rapidly back and forth

You hear many kinds of sounds every minute of every day. But do you know what sound is? Sound is a form of energy. Scientists who study sound also study human hearing and the effect of sound on different objects.

How Sound Is Produced

All the sounds you hear are made when matter **vibrates.** To vibrate means to move quickly back and forth. Look at the figure of the bells. When the clapper hits the bell, energy from the clapper causes the bell to vibrate. When the bell vibrates, it moves back and forth. The bell pushes the air around it. You can see in the figure that as the bell vibrates to the right, it pushes together the air particles to the right of the bell. When it vibrates back to the left, the air particles to the right of the bell move apart. Those particles to the left of the bell are squeezed together. As the bell continues to vibrate, the air particles on each side are squeezed together and spread apart many times.

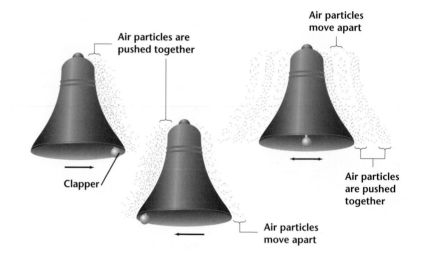

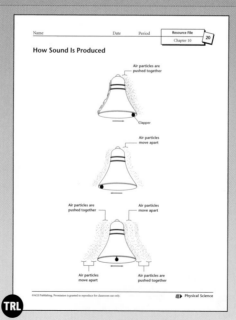

Resource File 20

How Sound Travels

Sound wave

A wave produced by vibrations

The movement of the air molecules around a vibrating object is a **sound wave.** You cannot see a sound wave. Sound waves move out from the vibrating object in all directions. As the sound waves travel farther from the object, they become weaker. The figures of the wire spring show how sound energy travels in waves. In Figure A, the wire is pinched together at one end. In Figure B, the "wave" moves across the spring.

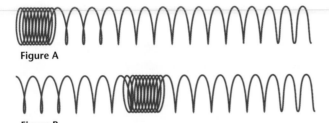

Figure A

Figure B

Some things make sounds even though you cannot see them vibrate. For example, if you strike a tuning fork, you will not see it vibrate. But you will hear the sound it makes. You can see evidence of sound waves by placing the end of a tuning fork that has been struck into a small container filled with water. You will notice water splashing out of the container. The vibrations of the tuning fork cause the water to move about.

When a tuning fork vibrates, it produces sound waves.

CROSS-CURRICULAR CONNECTION

Music

Have students who play musical instruments bring them into class on a specific day. Ask each musician to demonstrate how sound is produced in the instrument.

AT HOME

You may want to have students search for speakers in stereos, radios, or CD players at home. They can experiment with ways to demonstrate that vibrations from the speakers carry the sound.

Teaching the Lesson

Before students read the lesson, have them copy the two vocabulary terms and their definitions. After reading, ask volunteers to demonstrate each term.

Students can experience sound vibration in their own bodies. Tell students to place their fingertips on their neck at the location of their voice box. As students hum or say "aaahhh," they can feel their vocal chords vibrate.

If possible, display a speaker in which the baffle (part that vibrates) is visible. Play some music that has a lot of low notes. Have students watch the baffle and place their hands close to the speaker. Ask students to describe what they observed. *(vibration, air pressure)* Explain that the speaker moves particles of air allowing us to hear the sound produced.

 3 **Reinforce and Extend**

LEARNING STYLES

Body/Kinesthetic

Hang a table tennis ball from a ring stand or by some other support. Have students strike a tuning fork with a hand and touch it to the ball. Ask them to write an explanation for why the ball bounces away. *(The vibration causes the ball to move; it also causes sound.)*

SCIENCE JOURNAL

Have students write a list of words that describe sound.

LEARNING STYLES

Visual/Spatial

Have two students stretch a long, coiled spring between them. Strike one end of the spring with a stick or rolled up newspaper. Have students observe how the wave travels back and forth. Strike twice in quick succession. Have students notice how the waves travel together and then interfere with one another after they bounce back.

Lesson 1 Review Answers

1. Matter vibrates and causes air particles to move; the sound travels through the air in waves. **2.** It moves in waves similar to the way a wire spring moves. **3.** A sound wave is the movement of molecules around a vibrating object. **4.** Vibrate means to move quickly back and forth. **5.** The sound waves become weaker.

Portfolio Assessment

Sample items include:
- Terms and definitions from Teaching the Lesson
- Lesson 1 Review answers

Lesson 1   R E V I E W

Write your answers to these questions in complete sentences on a sheet of paper.

1. How is sound produced?

2. How does sound travel?

3. What is a sound wave?

4. What word means "to move quickly back and forth"?

5. What happens to the strength of sound waves as they travel farther from the vibrating object?

Name _____ Date _____ Period _____ | Lab Manual, Page 1
Chapter 10   37

Making Musical Sounds

Purpose   What causes sounds to be higher or lower in pitch? In this investigation, you will produce the notes of the musical scale.

Materials   8 empty 16-oz glass bottles
masking tape
water
graduated cylinder

Procedure

1. Use the table below to record your data.

Bottle	Amount of Water (mL)	What the Sound Is Like
1	none	
2	93	
3	151	
4	215	
5	277	
6	315	
7	348	
8	374	

2. Label each bottle with a number from 1 to 8.

3. Put no water in bottle 1. In bottle 2, put 93 mL of water.

4. Blow across the opening of the bottle to produce a musical sound. Write a description of this sound in the data table.

5. Add 151 mL of water to bottle 3. Blow across the opening to produce a musical sound. How does this sound compare with the sound produced by bottle 2? Record your observations in the data table.

6. Fill the remaining bottles with the amount of water shown in the table.

7. Blow across the opening of each bottle to produce a tone of the musical scale. Each bottle will produce a different note of the scale. You may need to practice to obtain good results.

TRL   Physical Science

Lab Manual 37, pages 1–2

Name _____ Date _____ Period _____ | Workbook Activity
Chapter 10, Lesson 1   46

What Is Sound?

Directions Choose the term from the box that completes each sentence.

1. For a sound to occur, matter must _____ or move back and forth.

2. Vibration of an object causes _____ to compress and expand many times.

3. Air moves out in all directions from a vibrating object as a _____

4. You may not see these waves, but you can hear the resulting _____

5. Sounds grow fainter over distance because the sound waves become _____ the farther they travel from the vibrating object.

| molecules |
| sound wave |
| sounds |
| vibrate |
| weather |

Directions Look at the figures below. Write a sentence or two that explains how the movement of the wire spring is like sound waves.

_____
_____
_____

Directions Write the answer to the question on the lines.

You toss a stone into water, and ripples spread out from where it hits. How are these ripples like sound waves?

_____
_____

TRL   Physical Science

Workbook Activity 46

Objectives

After reading this lesson, you should be able to

◆ explain intensity and volume of sound.

◆ explain how the frequency of a sound wave affects its pitch.

Intensity
The strength of a sound

Decibel
A unit that measures the intensity of sound

Amplitude is how far particles move from a wave's midpoint to its highest or lowest point. A high amplitude means high energy. The more energy a sound wave has, the more intense the sound.

How would you describe the sounds around you? You might point out that some sounds are loud or soft. You might also describe some sounds as high or low.

Loud and Soft Sounds

You might barely be able to hear the sounds of rustling leaves. The noise made by a jet, however, might make you want to cover your ears. The strength of a sound is known as its **intensity.** A sound wave that carries a lot of energy has a high intensity. A sound wave that carries less energy has a lower intensity.

Scientists measure the intensity of sounds in units called **decibels.** The sound of rustling leaves would be measured at about 20 decibels. The roar of a jet engine would be approximately 135 decibels. You can see the decibel levels of some common sounds below.

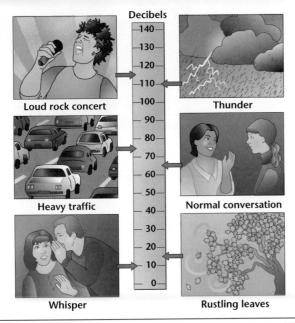

Decibels
- 140
- 130
- 120
- 110
- 100 — Loud rock concert
- 90
- 80
- 70
- 60
- 50
- 40 — Heavy traffic
- 30
- 20
- 10
- 0

Thunder
Normal conversation
Whisper
Rustling leaves

TEACHER ALERT

Be sure students understand the difference between intensity and loudness. Intensity determines loudness—the greater the intensity of a sound, the louder it is to the ear. But intensity is an objective measure of the amplitude of sound waves; it depends on the amount of energy a sound wave carries. Loudness is the impact of intensity on the ear; it depends on the listener.

Lesson at a Glance

Chapter 10 Lesson 2

Overview In this lesson, students explore the characteristics that make sounds differ. They learn about intensity, frequency, and the units used to measure each.

Objectives

■ To explain what intensity and volume of sound are

■ To explain how the frequency of a sound wave affects its pitch

Student Pages 275–279

Teacher's Resource Library

Workbook Activity 47

Alternative Workbook Activity 47

Vocabulary

cycle	intensity
decibel	pitch
frequency	volume
Hertz	

Science Background

Two characteristics of sound are intensity and pitch. Intensity is the amount of energy in a wave. It is determined by the amplitude, or vertical height, of the wave. It determines loudness of a sound—or the way in which the ear perceives intensity. Intensity is measured in decibels. Sounds with intensities greater than 90 decibels can actually cause pain in human beings. Pitch describes how high or low a sound is. It depends on the frequency of sound waves, or how fast the molecules of a medium vibrate. It is a function of the rate of vibration, or the number of vibrations per second. Frequency is measured in Hertz: one Hertz = one wave per second. A soprano's high note may have a frequency of 1,000 Hz; a bass's low note may have a frequency of 70 Hz. The human ear can hear sounds ranging from 20 Hz to 20,000 Hz.

1 Warm-Up Activity

Place a 30-cm plastic ruler over the edge of a desk with about 20 cm extending past the desk. With one hand, press the end of the ruler against the desk.

Continued on page 276

Continued from page 275

With the other hand, quickly strike the free end of the ruler to make it vibrate. Have students listen carefully to the sound it makes. Repeat the procedure several times, each time shortening the portion of the ruler that extends past the desk. Invite students to tell how the sound changes. *(It becomes higher.)*

 2 Teaching the Lesson

Have students copy the vocabulary terms for the lesson on a sheet of paper, leaving several lines between terms. As they read, students can use their own words to write a definition for each term.

Have students make a table titled *The Sounds I Heard,* with these column headings: *Very High, High, Medium, Low,* and *Very Low.* Ask students to complete the chart by identifying 20 different sounds they hear over a 24-hour period. Tell students to record the source of each sound and the time they heard it. Invite volunteers to share their completed lists and tell how they chose the column for each.

 3 Reinforce and Extend

Volume
The loudness or softness of a sound

The point at which a wave is at its highest is called its crest. A wave's lowest point is its trough. The distance between one wave crest and the next crest is called the wavelength.

Your hearing interprets the intensity of a sound as loud or soft. The loudness or softness of a sound is the **volume** of the sound. The more intense a sound, the higher its volume seems.

In some cases, loud sounds can help keep you safe. For example, the siren on a fire truck is loud enough to be heard above other sounds.

Loud sounds can also be harmful. Listening to loud music or other loud sounds for a long period of time can damage your hearing. Sounds above 90 decibels can cause pain to your ears. Sounds above 130 decibels can damage your ears.

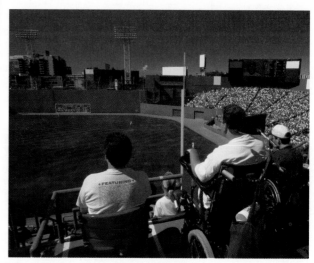

Loud sounds can cause pain, and they can damage your ears.

Science Myth

Hitting something harder changes the pitch of the sound that is produced.

Fact: Hitting something harder does not change the sound waves' frequency. The sound might be louder or last longer, but the pitch will not be different.

High and Low Sounds

How does the sound of a flute differ from the sound of a tuba? The flute has a high sound. The tuba has a low sound. We say that the flute has a higher **pitch** than the tuba. Pitch is how high or low a sound seems. Look at the sound waves in the figure below. You can see that the sound waves made by the flute are closer together than those made by the tuba. The flute produces more sound waves per second than the tuba.

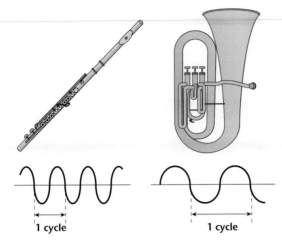

1 cycle   **1 cycle**

Frequency of a sound wave is the number of vibrations per second. If an object vibrates 5 times in each second, the resulting sound wave would have a frequency of 5 **cycles** per second. A cycle is one complete back-and-forth motion of a vibration.

We measure frequency in units called **Hertz**. One Hertz equals one cycle per second. For example, an object that has a frequency of 10 Hertz has 10 back-and-forth motions in one second. The abbreviation for Hertz is *Hz*.

Have students study the chart and graph on page 278 and pick out the animal that hears sounds with the lowest frequencies *(dog)* and highest frequencies *(bat)*. Have students predict which can hear sounds with the higher pitch—a human or a dog. *(dog)* Then ask a volunteer to read aloud the paragraph in the feature on page 278.

AT HOME

Ask students to observe a pet's behavior in response to different sounds and predict whether it hears sounds at lower and/or higher frequencies than humans can hear. Have students write the reasons for their predictions based on their observations. Then ask students to research the animal's hearing characteristics to check their predictions.

Did You Know?

Sometimes people who train dogs use special whistles. Dogs can hear the high-pitched sounds from the whistles, but people cannot hear these sounds.

Although objects can vibrate at many different rates, the human ear can hear only a certain range of frequencies. Generally, the human ear can detect sounds with frequencies ranging from 20 Hz to 20,000 Hz. The range can vary somewhat depending on a person's hearing ability.

The figures below compare the frequencies of sounds that a human can hear with those that some animals can hear.

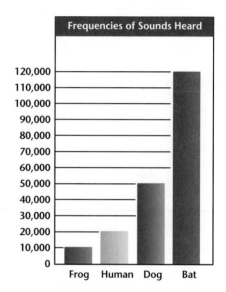

Frequencies of Sounds Heard	
Sounds Heard by	Frequencies
frog	50 to 10,000 Hz
human	20 to 20,000 Hz
dog	15 to 50,000 Hz
bat	1,000 to 120,000 Hz

Frequencies of Sounds Heard

Lesson 2 REVIEW

Write your answers to these questions in complete sentences on a sheet of paper.

1. Describe the intensity of a sound wave that carries a lot of energy.

2. How does volume relate to intensity?

3. How does the frequency of a sound wave affect pitch?

4. What unit is used to measure frequency?

5. What property of sound does a decibel measure?

Achievements in Science

The Doppler Effect

The Doppler effect, described by Christian Doppler in 1842, is an apparent change in wave frequency. The Doppler effect occurs with all types of waves: sound, light, or radio waves. This effect happens when the sound source is moving or when the observer is moving. The relative motion of the waves' source and the observer causes the frequency change.

As the wave source moves forward, the waves in the front of it get crowded. When the waves move closer together, the frequency of the waves increases. As the source of the waves moves away, the waves spread apart. These waves have a lower frequency.

Scientists use the Doppler effect in many ways. They use it to study the speed and direction of a star. They measure the change that motion causes to the frequency of the star's light. Meteorologists use Doppler radar to track storms by finding changes in wind speed or direction. Police use Doppler radar to measure a car's speed. Edwin Hubble used the Doppler effect to show that the universe is expanding.

Sound and Light   Chapter 10   **279**

Lesson 2 Review Answers

1. Its intensity is high. **2.** A person's hearing interprets intensity as high or low volume. A sound with a higher intensity will be louder than one with a lower intensity. **3.** A high frequency means more vibrations per second and a higher pitch; a low frequency means fewer vibrations per second and a lower pitch. **4.** Hertz is the unit we use to measure frequency. **5.** A decibel measures intensity.

Achievements in Science

Ask volunteers to take turns reading the Achievements in Science feature on page 279. Emphasize that as the source of a sound approaches, the length of the waves do not change but the distance they have to travel to reach you shortens. This makes the pitch of the sound seem higher. As the sound source moves away, the waves must travel a longer distance to reach you, so the pitch seems lower.

Portfolio Assessment

Sample items include:
- Vocabulary definitions from Teaching the Lesson
- Table from Teaching the Lesson
- Lesson 2 Review answers

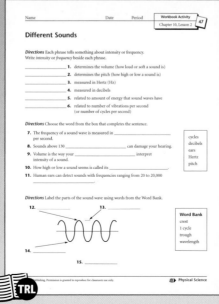

Workbook Activity 47

Sound and Light   Chapter 10   **279**

Lesson at a Glance

Chapter 10 Lesson 3

Overview This lesson explains how sound travels through matter and compares the speed of sound through various types of matter. Students also learn about sound reflection, sonar, and ultrasound.

Objectives

- To explain how sound travels through matter
- To compare the speed of sound in solids, liquids, and gases
- To explain how sound can be reflected
- To explain how sound waves are used to measure distances under water

Student Pages 280–288

Teacher's Resource Library **TRL**

Workbook Activity 48

Alternative Workbook Activity 48

Lab Manual 38

Vocabulary

echo   sonar
reflect   ultrasound

Warm-Up Activity

Review the meanings of *vibrate, molecule, solid, liquid,* and *gas.*

Place four marbles in a row on the stage of an overhead projector so that they are touching. Keep them in line with rulers on each side. Roll a fifth marble at the head marble in the line. The middle marbles probably will not move much, but the marble at the opposite end of the line will move forward. Explain that energy is transferred from one marble to another down the line.

Teaching the Lesson

Preview the lesson with students, having them look at photos and diagrams. Have them write down any questions they have about these visuals. As they read, students can answer their questions. After students complete the lesson, discuss any questions for which they did not find answers.

Objectives

After reading this lesson, you should be able to

◆ explain how sound travels through matter.

◆ compare the speed of sound in solids, liquids, and gases.

◆ explain how sound can be reflected.

◆ explain how sound waves are used to measure distances under water.

Suppose you wake up to the roar of a jet plane. It is high in the air. How does the noise from the jet reach you in your home?

Sound Moves Through Matter

Heat energy can move through empty space. Sound energy cannot travel through empty space. In outer space, there are no molecules of matter. You can only hear sound when it travels through matter. Therefore, no sounds can travel through outer space. Sound, however, can travel through air.

Sound travels through all matter in a similar way. Sound waves travel through matter by causing the particles in matter to vibrate. When a particle begins to vibrate, it bumps into another particle. Then that particle bumps into another particle, and so on.

The dominoes in the photo help illustrate how sound travels through matter. As each domino falls, it strikes the next domino, causing it to fall over. Each of the dominoes travels only a short distance. But the effect of one domino's motion can travel a large distance.

The motion of falling dominoes shows how sound travels through matter.

The Speed of Sound

If you put the dominoes closer together, they fall down in less time. In the same way, sound waves travel more quickly through substances with molecules that are closer together.

Chapter 3 described molecules in solids, liquids, and gases. Molecules of matter in solids are closest together. For this reason, sound moves fastest through solids.

Molecules in liquids are farther apart than those in solids. Sound travels more slowly through liquids. Molecules of gases are the farthest apart. Sounds move slowest through gases.

The speed of sound in air depends on the temperature of the air. Higher temperatures cause molecules of air to move faster. As a result, sound travels more quickly. The speed of sound through air is about 346 meters per second (or 700 miles per hour) at a temperature of 25 degrees Celsius. The graph below lists the speed of sound through some different materials.

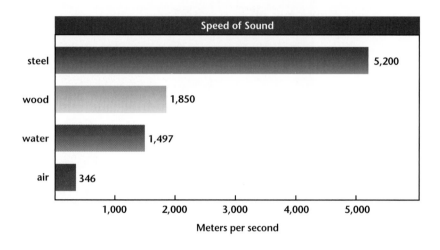

Speed of Sound

steel	5,200
wood	1,850
water	1,497
air	346

Meters per second

Sound and Light   Chapter 10   **281**

Call attention to the dominoes in the photo on page 280. Be sure students understand that the molecules of a medium, such as air, do not move far. They bounce into the molecules "next-door," and then those molecules bounce into others, sending the sound wave energy along. Students should be able to see that the energy is what passes through to the end.

Call attention to the graph on page 281. Emphasize that sound waves can travel only through matter. The closer the particles of matter are packed together, the faster sound will travel. Solids have more molecules per unit of volume. They tend to be more elastic, or to move only a small distance and bounce back into their regular position more quickly than do molecules in liquids. So solids transmit sound better than liquids, and liquids transmit sound better than gases.

3 Reinforce and Extend

TEACHER ALERT

You may want to point out to students that solids with more massive molecules transmit sound slower because they have more inertia. These molecules require more energy to begin moving and do not move as quickly as less massive molecules. Therefore, the speed of sound in the denser solids such as lead and gold is much less than in less dense solids such as steel and aluminum.

TEACHER ALERT

"Breaking the sound barrier" has nothing to do with the sound the airplane is making. A more descriptive phrase might be "breaking the pressure barrier." Any object passing through the air starts to compress the air in front of its leading edge. As long as air can move away from the leading edge of the object, there is little pressure built up.

Once the plane approaches the maximum speed at which the air can move, pressure starts to build up quickly. As the plane's speed continues to increase, air cannot move out of the way fast enough, and pressure is built up to a point where a pressure wave forms. Once this pressure wave hits the ground, a loud clap is heard. At high altitudes, the sound is barely noticeable; at low altitudes, it can break windows.

CAREER CONNECTION

Ask the manager or an employee of an electronics or stereo store to talk to students about what makes a good listening room. Ask the manager about the placement of speakers in the room and why placement makes a difference. Have the visitor relate the movement of sound through different materials to his or her discussion.

Sound travels quickly, but light travels even faster. Because light travels faster than sound, you will see a flash of lightning before you hear the thunder. You can use the speeds of sound and light to figure out how far away a storm is. Follow these steps to calculate the distance of a storm.

1. When you see a flash of lightning, count the number of seconds until you hear the thunder.

2. Divide the number of seconds by 3 seconds per kilometer. The answer tells you how many kilometers away the storm is. (For example, if it takes 3 seconds for you to hear the thunder, the flash of lightning is about 1 kilometer away.)

Suppose you see a flash of lightning. You find that it takes 6 seconds until you hear the thunder. How far away is the storm?

$$\text{distance of storm} = \frac{6 \text{ sec}}{3 \text{ sec/km}}$$

$$\text{distance of storm} = 2 \text{ km}$$

Sound travels quickly, but light travels even faster.

How Sound Bounces

Reflect

To bounce back

Echo

A sound that is reflected to its source

Suppose a radio is playing in the next room. You may hear music from the radio because some of the sound travels through the solid wall. However, some of the sound might not travel through the wall. The matter in the wall might absorb, or trap, some of the sound. For this reason, the sound of the music might seem softer to you than to a person standing next to the radio.

Other sound waves from the radio might be **reflected.** That is, the sound might bounce back from the wall. The figure of the ball bouncing against the wall illustrates how sound can be reflected. Sound that bounces back from an object is an **echo.** Echoes can be heard best when sound bounces from hard, smooth surfaces.

You have probably heard echoes at one time or another. Did you ever call out someone's name in a large, empty room? If so, you might have heard an echo of your voice even after you stopped speaking.

Have groups of students use their bodies to demonstrate how sound travels. One group, representing a solid, stands close together. One student passes sound energy to a second student by touching the second student's hand. The second student touches a third student, and so on. Two other groups represent a liquid and a gas by standing farther apart, accordingly. Have the groups repeat the procedure. Have students determine in which group the sound traveled fastest. *(the solid)*

ONLINE CONNECTION

 The Physics Classroom site can connect students to lessons explaining the nature of sound waves, sound properties and their perception, and behavior of sound waves. Visit www.glenbrook.k12.il.us/gbssci/ phys/Class/sound/soundtoc.html.

Have a volunteer read the feature on page 284. Discuss what sort of device could be installed inside the cane (*battery-operated transducer, like a ship's sonar instrument in miniature*). Invite students to predict how the person could "translate" the sounds bounced back to tell how far away an object is. (*Pitch of the sounds would change as object grew closer.*)

LEARNING STYLES

LEP/ESL

Students who are learning English may not be familiar with acronyms, words formed from the initial letters of a phrase. Write *sonar* on the board. Below it, write *sound navigation and ranging*. Read and explain the meanings of each word in the phrase. Then have students find and circle the letters that were used to form *sonar*.

Sonar
A method of using sound to measure distances under water

Did You Know?

A cane developed for sightless people sends out sound waves. The sound waves reflect off obstacles and return to a sensor that the person wears. The sensor gives off sounds to indicate the distances to obstacles.

Measuring Distances with Sound Waves

Scientists can use **sonar** to find objects below the surface of water. Sonar is a method that uses sound to measure distances under water. People can use sonar to locate schools of fish, to explore shipwrecks, and to find other underwater objects.

Scientists can use sonar to find out exactly how deep water is at a particular location. The figure illustrates how sonar works. Instruments on the ship send out sound waves. The sound waves are reflected by the ocean bottom back to the surface of the water.

Scientists can measure the time it takes for the sound to reach the bottom of the ocean and return to the surface. Because scientists know how fast sound travels through water, they can tell how far the sound travels. Scientists can use sonar to measure very deep parts of the ocean. They can also use sonar to map the ocean floor.

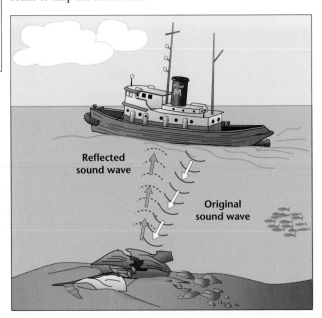

Reflected sound wave

Original sound wave

Ultrasound

A technique that uses sound waves to study organs inside the human body

"Seeing" Inside the Body with Sound

Scientists also use sound waves, called **ultrasound,** to "see" inside the human body. Ultrasound waves are sound waves that humans cannot hear. When these waves are beamed into the body, some are reflected back. Each part of the body reflects the waves a little differently. Ultrasound equipment picks up these reflected waves and makes a picture. By looking at the picture, doctors can tell if an organ is an unusual size or shape. Doctors can also use the picture to find tumors.

Ultrasound is commonly used to study the development of an unborn baby. Ultrasound waves are directed into the mother's body. These waves echo off the unborn baby. The picture below shows an image made by an ultrasound screen. Ultrasound waves do not hurt the mother or the baby.

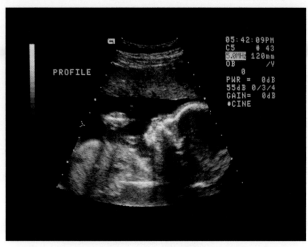

Ultrasound waves are used to make a picture of an unborn baby.

Lesson 3 Review Answers

1. They travel through matter by causing its molecules to vibrate; the motion is passed from molecule to molecule in waves resulting from a series of compressions and expansions. 2. Sound moves most quickly through solids. The molecules are closest together in solids, so they don't move far as the sound wave passes through them, and they bounce back into their original position quickly. 3. Higher temperatures cause air molecules to move faster, so sound travels more quickly. 4. Sound waves sent into the water are reflected by the ocean bottom and return to the surface. Because scientists know how fast sound travels in water, they can tell how far the sound travels.
5. Sound waves can be used to find tumors inside the body and to see the development of an unborn baby.

Portfolio Assessment

Sample items include:
- Questions and answers from Teaching the Lesson
- Lesson 3 Review answers

Lesson 3   R E V I E W

Write your answers to these questions in complete sentences on a sheet of paper.

1. How do sound waves move from place to place?

2. Does sound move most quickly through solids, liquids, or gases? Explain your answer.

3. How does air temperature affect the speed of sound?

4. Explain how sonar can be used to measure distances in the ocean.

5. List two ways that sound waves can be used for medical purposes.

Technology Note

Most speakers produce audible sound beams that spread out. Hypersonic speakers produce audible beams that stay narrow. This gives hypersonic speakers an advantage. The sound they produce is directed at a specific target or targets. We can hear sound through these speakers only if we are directly in their path. Ambulances with hypersonic sirens can be heard on the street but not in nearby houses.

Name _____ Date _____ Period _____ | **Workbook Activity** 48 | Chapter 10, Lesson 3

How Sound Travels

Directions Write the answer to each question on the line.

1. Why can't sound travel through space? _____

2. Why does sound travel fastest through solids? _____

3. What is an echo? _____

4. How are sonar and ultrasound alike? _____

Directions Use what you know about the speed of sound to answer each question.

5. Lightning flashes in the distance. Seven seconds later, you hear the thunder. How far away is the storm?

6. You yell into a canyon. You hear the echo in 3 seconds. How long did the sound of your voice travel before bouncing off a cliff?

7. A ship sends out a sonar signal. The echo is heard after 6 seconds. How long did it take for the signal to reach the ocean bottom?

Directions Put the kinds of matter in order according to sound's ability to travel through them. List the fastest speed of sound first.

8. Sound travels fastest through _____

9. Sound travels a little slower through _____

10. Sound travels even slower through _____

Kinds of Matter
water
aluminum
warm air

TRL   Physical Science

Workbook Activity 48

Inferring How Sound Waves Travel

Purpose

Can sound waves travel through matter? This investigation will demonstrate that sound waves are vibrations that travel through matter.

Procedure

1. Copy the data table on a sheet of paper.

How the Rubber Band Was Plucked	Observations

2. Put on your safety glasses.

3. Use the point of the pencil to punch a small hole in the bottom of the cup.

4. Push one end of the cut rubber band through the hole in the cup. Tie a knot in the end of the rubber band so that it cannot be pulled through the hole. The knot should be inside the cup.

5. Stretch a piece of plastic wrap tightly over the top of the cup. Use the other rubber band to hold the plastic wrap in place, as shown in the figure on the next page.

6. Hold the cup with the plastic wrap facing up. Sprinkle a few grains of salt on the plastic wrap.

Materials

- safety glasses
- pencil with sharpened point
- large plastic-foam cup
- 2 rubber bands (one cut)
- plastic food wrap
- salt
- plastic beaker
- water
- tuning fork

Sound and Light Chapter 10 **287**

SAFETY ALERT

- Make sure that students wear safety glasses throughout the activity so that salt doesn't get into their eyes or the rubber band doesn't strike their eyes.
- Caution students to be careful as they use the pencil to punch a hole in the bottom of the cup. Suggest that they turn the cup upside down on a table and hold it in position. They should increase pressure as they make the hole with the pencil.

Investigation 10-1

The Purpose portion of the student investigation begins with a question to draw them into the activity. Encourage students to read the investigation steps and formulate their own questions before beginning the investigation. This investigation will take approximately 30 minutes to complete. Students will use these process and thinking skills: observing, collecting, and interpreting data; comparing, inferring, and drawing conclusions.

Preparation

- Cut half the rubber bands so that each forms a long rubber string.
- Thick rubber bands work best.
- Cups should be at least an 8-oz size.
- Students may use Lab Manual 38 to record their data and answer the questions.

Procedure

- This investigation is best done with students working in groups of three. All students observe and record observations and clean up. One student can assemble the cup, a second can hold the cup and add the salt, and the third can pluck the rubber band.
- Advise students to use a sharp pencil point to avoid tearing the bottom of the cup and to rotate the pencil when inserting it into the bottom of the cup.
- Instruct students to tie several knots on the end of the rubber band inside the cup so that the rubber band doesn't slip out. Caution them that they cannot pull too hard on the rubber band, or it will pull through the bottom of the cup. To reinforce the bottom of the cup, students might use masking or nylon tape.
- Have students pluck the rubber band at various distances from the cup and compare the pitch.

Continued on page 288

Continued from page 287

Results

The salt grains should move around on the plastic every time the rubber band is plucked. A harder pluck results in more vigorous movement of the salt and in a higher pitch of sound.

Questions and Conclusions Answers

1. Salt grains bounced up and down.

2. Vibrations of the rubber band also caused the plastic wrap to vibrate. This in turn caused the salt to move.

3. The more force used, the more intense the sound, or the greater its volume.

4. The more force used, the more the salt moved around.

Explore Further Answers

1. The vibrating tuning fork causes waves on the surface of the water.

2. The more vigorously the tuning fork is vibrating, the more pronounced the waves on the water's surface.

Assessment

Be sure students pluck the rubber band with different intensities. Check their data tables for detailed observations. You might include the following items from this investigation in student portfolios.

• Investigation 10-1 data table

• Answers to Questions and Conclusions and Explore Further sections

7. Hold the cup while your partner slowly stretches the rubber band. Gently pluck the stretched rubber band and observe what happens to the salt. Record your observations in the data table.

8. Vary the force used to pluck the rubber band. Notice the difference in sound the rubber band makes as you vary the force.

Questions and Conclusions

1. In Step 7, what happened to the salt when you plucked the rubber band?

2. What do you think caused the salt to move? Explain your answer.

3. In Step 8, how did the force you used to pluck the rubber band affect the sound it made?

4. In Step 8, how did the force you used to pluck the rubber band affect the salt on the plastic wrap?

Explore Further

1. Use a tuning fork and a plastic beaker half-filled with water. Gently tap the tuning fork against the heel of your hand and place the tips of the fork into the beaker of water. What happens to the water?

2. Vary the force used to tap the tuning fork. Notice what happens to the water as you vary the force.

Name _____ Date _____ Period _____ | Lab Manual | 38 | Chapter 10

10-1 **Inferring How Sound Waves Travel**
Use with Investigation 10-1, pages 287–288.

Purpose Can sound waves travel through matter? This investigation will demonstrate that sound waves are vibrations that travel through matter.

How the Rubber Band Was Plucked	Observations

Questions and Conclusions

1. In Step 7, what happened to the salt when you plucked the rubber band?

2. What do you think caused the salt to move? Explain your answer.

3. In Step 8, how did the force you used to pluck the rubber band affect the sound it made?

4. In Step 8, how did the force you used to pluck the rubber band affect the salt on the plastic wrap?

Explore Further

1. Use a tuning fork and a plastic beaker half-filled with water. Gently tap the tuning fork against the heel of your hand and place the tips of the fork into the beaker of water. What happens to the water?

2. Vary the force used to tap the tuning fork. Notice what happens to the water as you vary the force.

Publishing. Permission is granted to reproduce for classroom use only. **◆)) Physical Science**

TRL

Lab Manual 38

Objectives

After reading this lesson, you should be able to

◆ define light and explain how visible light is produced.

◆ describe the nature of light.

◆ explain how light waves travel.

◆ describe the visible spectrum.

Light

A form of energy that can be seen

Photons

Small bundles of energy that make up light

You see **light** everywhere. You see objects because light is reflected from them. But what is light? Light is a form of energy that you can sometimes see. Most visible light is produced by objects that are at high temperatures. The sun is the major source of light on Earth. The sun loses energy by emitting light. The sun's energy arrives as light with a range of wavelengths, consisting of visible light, infrared, and ultraviolet radiation.

Light as a Particle

Scientists have done experiments to gather information about light. Some scientific experiments suggest that light acts like a particle. Evidence tells scientists that light is made up of bundles of energy called **photons.** Photons are like small particles. A single photon is too small to be seen.

Look at the light coming from the flashlight. Streams of photons make up each beam of light. Each photon carries a certain amount of energy.

Lesson at a Glance

Chapter 10 Lesson 4

Overview In this lesson, students explore the wave and particle properties of light. They also learn about the visible spectrum.

Objectives

■ To define light and explain how visible light is produced

■ To describe the nature of light

■ To explain how light waves travel

■ To describe the visible spectrum

Student Pages 289–293

Teacher's Resource Library **TRL**

Workbook Activity 49

Alternative Workbook Activity 49

Vocabulary

light	prism
photons	visible spectrum

Science Background

Electromagnetic waves are arranged by their wavelengths and frequencies into the electromagnetic spectrum. From long wavelength, low frequency to short wavelength, high frequency, they include radio waves, infrared rays, visible light rays, ultraviolet rays, X-rays, and gamma rays.

We detect each type of electromagnetic wave in different ways. For example, we detect light with our eyes but need special equipment to detect X-rays. However, all the electromagnetic waves share these characteristics:

• carry energy

• can travel through empty space

• can be changed into other forms of energy

 Warm-Up Activity

Set a large pan of water in bright sunlight. Place a mirror in the pan of water and lean it against an inside edge. Adjust the mirror and pan until a color band or spectrum appears on the wall. Invite students to explain what causes the color. Explain that they will learn the answer as they read this lesson.

2 Teaching the Lesson

Have students write the titles of the three sections in the lesson, leaving space after each one. As they read the lesson, they can write one or two sentences summarizing each section.

Use the acronym Roy G. Biv to help students learn the colors of the visible spectrum. The letters in this name represent the first letters of the colors in the spectrum: R = red, O = orange, Y = yellow, G = green, B = blue, I = indigo, V = violet.

Use a prism to demonstrate its ability to separate white light into its colors. Explain that when a rainbow forms, drops of water in the sky act like tiny prisms, separating sunlight into its colors.

3 Reinforce and Extend

TEACHER ALERT

Some students might think that black and white are colors. Point out that black is the absence of all color, and white is a combination of all colors.

Did You Know?

Have a volunteer read the feature on page 290. Then have students compute the distance light travels from the moon *(300,000 km/sec × 2 sec = 600,000 km)* and from the sun *(300,000 km/sec × 480 sec = 144,000,000 km)*.

IN THE ENVIRONMENT

Refer students to Appendix A on pages 372–377 for information about alternative energy sources. Ask them to read the Energy from the Sun and Energy from the Wind sections on pages 373–374. Encourage students to find out more about solar energy and its use in producing electric power. Have them use the information they find to design a solar-powered home. They could make a model, a diorama, or a blueprint drawing to illustrate their design.

Did You Know?

Light takes less than two seconds to reach the earth from the moon. Light takes about eight minutes to travel from the sun to the earth. Light from the nearest star takes more than four years to reach the earth.

Waves—including waves in water, earthquake waves, sound waves, and light waves—transfer energy when they interact with matter.

Light as a Wave

Other scientific evidence suggests that, like sound, light travels in waves. As a result of their findings, most scientists agree that light seems to have properties of both particles and waves. Scientists agree that light travels as waves in a straight line. Light is a type of electromagnetic wave. Most properties of light can be explained in terms of its wave nature.

Light waves move like water waves.

Light waves move like waves in water. However, light waves travel fastest through empty space. Light waves move more slowly as they pass through matter. In fact, light waves cannot pass through some matter at all.

Light waves travel more quickly than sound waves. Light waves travel about 300,000 kilometers per second. This is the fastest possible speed anything can travel.

Visible spectrum

The band of colors that make up white light; the colors in a rainbow

Prism

A clear piece of glass or plastic that is shaped like a triangle; it can be used to separate white light

How is color determined? Usually it is determined by which colors of light an object absorbs or reflects. A red ball is red because it absorbs all colors of the visible spectrum but red.

Colors in White Light

The light you see from the sun is white light. Did you know that white light is actually made up of many colors of light? If you have ever seen a rainbow, you have actually seen the colors that make up white light.

A rainbow contains all the colors of the visible spectrum.

The band of colors you see in a rainbow is known as the **visible spectrum.** The colors of the visible spectrum always appear in the following order: red, orange, yellow, green, blue, indigo, and violet.

You can use a **prism** like the one in the photo to see the colors in white light. A prism is a piece of glass or plastic shaped like a triangle. A prism can separate white light into the colors of the visible spectrum.

A prism shows the colors in white light.

Sound and Light   Chapter 10   **291**

LEARNING STYLES

Visual/Spatial

Have students observe the visible spectrum using a prism and record the order in which the colors are arranged. Then ask them to draw, color, and label a diagram showing the splitting of white light into its component colors.

LEARNING STYLES

LEP/ESL

Use the terms *photon* and *visible spectrum* to help students enlarge their English vocabularies. Explain that *photo-* is a Greek root meaning "light," *videre* is a Latin word meaning "to see," and *specere* is a Latin word meaning "to look" or "to look at." Pair students who are learning English with English-proficient students and have them use a dictionary to list at least five words using each of these roots. Ask them to add a definition for each word.

SCIENCE INTEGRATION

Biology

Review with students the flow of energy from the sun to plants and then to animals, which become sources of energy, or food, for people. Have students explain this flow of light as energy, using the terms *photon, particles,* and *waves.*

Have a volunteer read the first paragraph of the Science in Your Life feature on page 292. Explain that white light mixes the frequencies of all eight kinds of light, but light from a laser has only one frequency and color. It is called *coherent light*, and it travels in nearly parallel lines with very little spreading. This makes it powerful.

Ask volunteers to read the uses for lasers. You might suggest that interested students research some recent applications for laser light and explain to the class how they use light energy.

IN THE COMMUNITY

Assign four small groups of students each a different arena in the community, such as retail sales, government offices, health-care delivery, or service businesses. Have each group research the use of lasers by individuals or groups in their category. Groups can gather information and pictures for a presentation.

CROSS-CURRICULAR CONNECTION

Home Economics

Invite a home economics teacher to speak to students about primary and complementary colors. Be sure students understand the difference between light and pigments. Hold a discussion about why certain colors in the visible spectrum "go together"—that is why they are pleasing when combined.

What are lasers and how do we use them?

A laser is a device that produces a powerful beam of light. Laser light is unique. Wavelengths in ordinary white light differ from one another. They also overlap each other. Wavelengths in laser light are all the same and are in step. The crests, or tops, and the troughs, or bottoms, of the waves are lined up exactly.

Lasers have many uses. We can use lasers to find gas leaks and detect pollutants in the air. Lasers can monitor and identify air pollutants around landfills, factories, and highways. Unlike a flashlight, the concentrated light of a laser can travel miles and miles. So lasers that monitor air pollution do not have to be near the pollution's source. The table shows some other uses for lasers.

Some Other Uses for Lasers	
Communication and entertainment	• transmitting telephone and TV signals
	• producing and reading compact discs
Business	• identifying bar codes on products
	• doing sales transactions
	• making maps
	• surveying land
	• printing and scanning
Medicine	• detecting medical problems, diseases, and disorders
	• doing surgery, such as removing cataracts from eyes, removing cancerous cells, clearing blocked arteries, removing tonsils
	• treating skin conditions including removal of birthmarks
Scientific research	• collecting data from the moon
	• studying the atom
	• studying chemical reactions

Lesson 4 REVIEW

Write your answers to these questions in complete sentences on a sheet of paper.

1. What makes up a beam of light?

2. How does light travel?

3. Would light travel faster through space or through a window? Explain your answer.

4. What colors make up white light?

5. Explain what a prism does.

Achievements in Science

Electromagnetic Waves and the Electromagnetic Spectrum

In 1864, James Maxwell presented the theory that electromagnetic waves exist. He said visible light is an electromagnetic wave, and there also are invisible electromagnetic waves. In the 1880s, Heinrich Hertz proved Maxwell's theory.

Different electromagnetic waves form the electromagnetic spectrum. Waves with lower frequencies than visible light are radio waves, microwaves, and infrared rays. Waves with higher frequencies than visible light are gamma rays, X-rays, and ultraviolet rays.

Radio waves have the lowest frequencies. They carry broadcast signals. Microwaves have a higher frequency and are used to cook food. Doctors use infrared rays, whose frequencies are just below visible light, to treat skin diseases.

Gamma rays have the highest frequencies. They are used to treat cancer. The frequencies of X-rays are just below gamma rays. X-rays help diagnosis illnesses. Ultraviolet rays have frequencies just above visible light. They are used in sun lamps and fluorescent lights.

Electromagnetic waves travel at the speed of light in a vacuum. They can be reflected and refracted. Their only differences are frequency and wavelength.

Sound and Light   Chapter 10   **293**

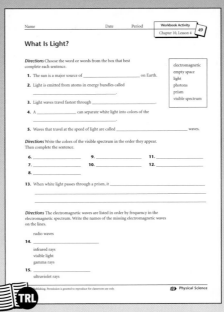

Workbook Activity 49

Lesson 4 Review Answers

1. A stream of photons, which has properties of both waves and particles, makes up a beam of light. **2.** Light travels as waves in a straight line. However, it also gives evidence of traveling in a stream as particles. **3.** Light travels faster through space. A window is matter; light travels slower through matter. **4.** The colors that make up white light are red, orange, yellow, green, blue, indigo, and violet. **5.** A prism separates white light into its component colors of the visible spectrum.

Achievements in Science

After students read the Achievements in Science feature on page 293, make a diagram on the board. Draw waves with decreasing wavelengths from left to right across the top. Add left to right arrows labeled *Wavelength*, *Frequency*, and *Photon Energy*. Add *Long* on the left end and *Short* on the right end of the wavelength arrow. Add *Low* and *High* on the left and right ends of the frequency and photon arrows. Have students direct you where to place each type of electromagnetic wave on the spectrum. Invite students to explain what the diagram shows them about each wave. Have students copy the diagram and save it for review of the chapter.

Portfolio Assessment

Sample items include:
• Sentences from Teaching the Lesson
• Science in Your Life research
• Lesson 4 Review answers

Chapter 10 Lesson 5

Overview In this lesson, students learn how light is reflected and explore the effects of three kinds of mirrors—plane, concave, and convex—on reflection.

Objectives

■ To describe how plane mirrors reflect light

■ To describe how concave and convex mirrors reflect light

Student Pages 294–300

Teacher's Resource Library **TRL**

Workbook Activity 50

Alternative Workbook Activity 50

Lab Manual 39–40

Resource File 21

Vocabulary

concave mirror	image
convex mirror	plane mirror
focal point	

 Warm-Up Activity

Provide students with mirrors. Have them look in the mirror and touch the right side of their face. What side does the mirror show them touching? *(the left side)* Tell students that they will learn how mirrors reflect images and why they reverse them.

 Teaching the Lesson

Have students copy the diagrams from the lesson. As they read, they can pause to write sentences explaining the meaning of each diagram.

Point out to students that the word *plane*, used to refer to a mirror, means "flat."

To help students remember the difference between convex and concave mirrors, point out the word *cave* in *concave*. Tell students that a con*cave* mirror curves inward like a cave.

Have students trace with their fingers the path of light rays in the lesson diagrams. Use Resource File 21 to produce a transparency. Project it and trace the path on the transparency.

Objectives

After reading this lesson, you should be able to

◆ describe how plane mirrors reflect light.

◆ describe how concave and convex mirrors reflect light.

What happens when you look into a mirror? Why can you see yourself? The answers to these questions have to do with the way light waves act.

Light Bounces

When you throw a ball to the floor, it bounces back. Light also bounces back when it hits an object. When light bounces off a surface, we say that the light is reflected. Reflection is the bouncing back of a light wave. Few objects give off their own light. We see most objects only because of the light they reflect.

The figure below illustrates how light is reflected. Like a tennis ball, light waves bounce off a surface at the same angle that they hit the surface.

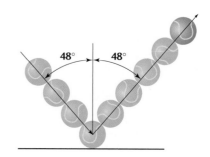

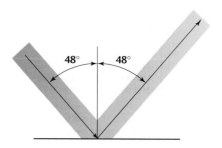

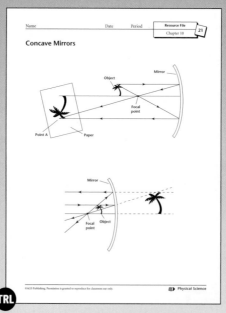

Concave Mirrors

Resource File 21

You can see an **image**, a copy or likeness, in a mirror because light waves are reflected. Study the figure. Notice how light from the cup hits the mirror and is reflected toward the observer's eye. Then the eye forms an image. The cup looks as if it is behind the mirror. The image is the same size as the original cup, but it is reversed. The handle of the cup appears on the opposite side when it is seen in the mirror. The angles at which the light reflects back causes this reversal. Follow the lines of light in the figure to see how this happens.

> **Image**
> A copy or likeness
>
> **Plane mirror**
> A flat, smooth mirror

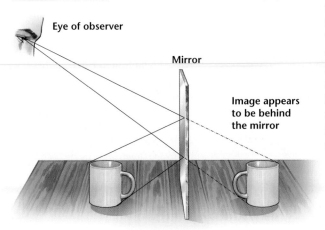

Eye of observer

Mirror

Image appears to be behind the mirror

Plane Mirrors

A mirror with a flat, smooth surface is called a **plane mirror.** The flatter the surface of the mirror, the clearer the image. Few surfaces are completely flat, including surfaces of plane mirrors. The figure below shows how light reflected from a completely flat surface differs from light that is reflected from a surface that is not flat. The small bumps in the surface on the right cause the reflected light to return at many different angles. Therefore, the image is not as clear.

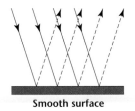

Smooth surface

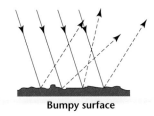

Bumpy surface

Sound and Light Chapter 10 **295**

3 Reinforce and Extend

TEACHER ALERT

As students view the figure near the top of page 295, be sure they understand that although the image of the mug appears to be behind the mirror, no image appears at that actual location.

SCIENCE INTEGRATION

Technology
Interested students could build a periscope and demonstrate its use to the class. Have the group explain how light is reflected to bring the image from above water to a viewer underwater.

LEARNING STYLES

Visual/Spatial
Have students make diagrams to explain why an object viewed through a plane mirror appears to be behind the mirror.

IN THE ENVIRONMENT

Have students investigate what is meant by "light pollution" in heavily populated areas. As a class, list and discuss the effects of being continuously subjected to artificial light or bright, reflected light for long periods of time.

LEARNING STYLES

Body/Kinesthetic
Interested students might bounce a tennis ball off a smooth surface, then off a bumpy surface to demonstrate that the angle of reflection is unpredictable or random with a bumpy surface but predictable with a smooth surface.

Sound and Light Chapter 10 **295**

CROSS-CURRICULAR CONNECTION

Home Economics

Invite an interior design professional to talk to the class. He or she can explain how mirrors are used in decorating and the effects they have on perceptions of space.

SCIENCE JOURNAL

Have students write about an experience in a carnival funhouse. They can describe mirrors that distort their appearances and explain how they think the mirrors changed light rays to do this.

Concave mirror

A mirror that curves in at the middle

Focal point

The point where reflected light rays from a concave mirror come together in front of the mirror

Concave Mirrors

Many mirrors have curved surfaces rather than flat surfaces. Look at the curved mirror in the figure. This kind of mirror is called a **concave mirror.** A concave mirror has a reflecting surface that curves inward, like the inside of a spoon. The figure shows how a concave mirror reflects parallel light rays. Notice that the light rays come together at one point, the **focal point.**

Now look at the figure below. The tree is behind the focal point of the mirror. Find the focal point of the mirror in the figure.

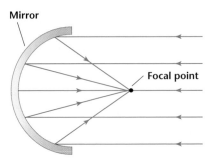

Rays of light from the tree hit the mirror's surface and are reflected back. Notice how the reflected rays pass through the focal point. If you put a piece of paper at Point A, you could see an image on it. The image would be upside down and larger.

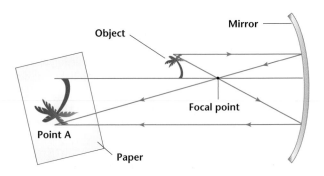

What would happen if the tree were between the concave mirror and the focal point? Look at the figure on the next page. If you follow the rays, you can see that the image of the tree would appear larger, right-side-up, and behind the mirror.

When you use a magnifying mirror to shave or apply makeup, you hold the mirror so that your face is between the focal point and the mirror.

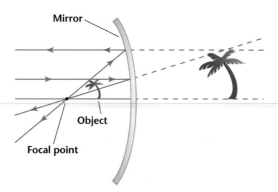

Convex Mirrors

The reflecting surface of some mirrors curves outward like the outside of a spoon. These kinds of mirrors are called **convex mirrors.** A convex mirror creates an image that looks smaller than the real object. However, you can see much more area in a convex mirror. For this reason, rearview and side-view mirrors on vehicles are often convex mirrors.

The side-view mirror on this vehicle is a convex mirror.

AT HOME

Have students find one example of a concave mirror and one example of a convex mirror in their homes or a family vehicle. *(Concave: makeup mirror, shaving mirror, spotlight, car headlights, flashlight. Convex: side-view and rearview mirrors.)* After using each mirror, students should write a paragraph summarizing its effect on the reflected image.

Lesson 5 Review Answers

1. Images reflected from a rough surface are not as clear as those from a smooth surface because the reflected light returns at many different angles from the rough surface. **2.** A concave mirror curves inward like a cave and tends to form an image that is upside down and may be larger or smaller than the reflected object. A convex mirror curves outward like the surface of a ball and forms a right-side-up image that is smaller than the reflected object. **3.** Convex mirrors reflect a much larger area and give a wider view. **4.** In a plane mirror, the object is reversed. **5.** A concave mirror curves inward.

Portfolio Assessment

Sample items include:
- Diagrams and sentences from Teaching the Lesson
- Lesson 5 Review answers

Lesson 5 R E V I E W

Write your answers to these questions in complete sentences on a sheet of paper.

1. Why are images reflected from a rough surface not as clear as those reflected from a smooth surface?

2. How does a concave mirror differ from a convex mirror?

3. Why are side-view and rearview mirrors on vehicles often convex?

4. How is the image in a plane mirror different from the object itself?

5. What type of mirror curves inward?

Technology Note

Holograms are lifelike images on film. To make holograms, designers split a laser beam. One beam goes to mirrors and through lenses and reflects off the object being photographed. The other beam goes across the first. The pattern made by their crossing goes to the film. When light shines on holograms, a 3D image appears.

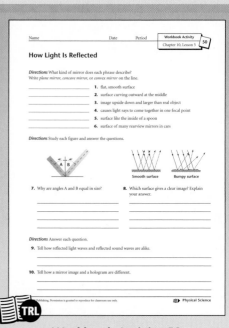

Materials

- ◆ safety glasses
- ◆ mirror
- ◆ textbook
- ◆ masking tape
- ◆ unlined white paper
- ◆ pencil
- ◆ flashlight
- ◆ comb
- ◆ protractor
- ◆ ruler
- ◆ sheet of white paper

Measuring Angles of Reflected Rays

Purpose

Does the angle of a light ray when it hits a mirror match the angle of its reflection? In this investigation, you will measure the angles at which a light ray hits and is reflected from a mirror.

Procedure

1. Copy the data table on a sheet of paper.

Trial	Angle A	Angle B
1		
2		
3		

2. Put on your safety glasses.

3. Look at the figure. Using masking tape, tape the mirror to the book, as shown.

4. Place the book on its edge on a sheet of paper. Draw a line along the bottom of the mirror.

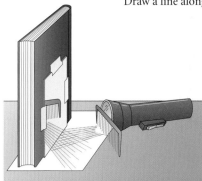

5. Turn on the flashlight. Hold the comb in front of the flashlight. Shine the flashlight on the mirror. Move the light around until you see a pattern of light rays and reflected rays like those shown in the figure.

Investigation 10-2

The Purpose portion of the student investigation begins with a question to draw them into the activity. Encourage students to read the investigation steps and formulate their own questions before beginning the investigation. This investigation will take approximately 45 minutes to complete. Students will use these process and thinking skills: observing; measuring; collecting, recording, and interpreting data; recalling facts; comparing; and drawing conclusions.

Preparation

- Use combs that are long enough to cover more than half the flashlight lens.
- A 4" x 6" mirror works well.
- Check mirrors to be sure edges are not sharp. Cover any sharp edges with masking tape.
- Check flashlight batteries before class to make sure they work. Provide extra batteries in case they need replacement during this investigation.
- Students may need practice in using protractors to draw angles.
- Students may use Lab Manual 40 to record their data and answer the questions.

Procedure

- This investigation is best done with students working in pairs.
- If possible, darken the room when using the flashlights.
- Be sure the paper is perpendicular to the mirror so that correct angles can be calculated.

SAFETY ALERT

- ◆ Instruct students to handle the mirrors carefully to avoid breakage.
- ◆ Instruct students not to shine flashlights or reflect light in the eyes of other students.

Continued on page 300

Continued from page 299

Results

Students should observe that the angle approaching the mirror and traveling from the mirror are the same. Errors will cause the angles to differ slightly.

Questions and Conclusions Answers

1. Answers will vary, depending on how students labeled their drawings. However, they should identify the angle of the ray that approaches the mirror.

2. Answers will vary, depending on how students labeled their drawings. However, students should identify the angle of the ray that travels from the mirror.

3. The angles are the same.

Explore Further Answers

You can read the word AMBULANCE. The letters no longer appear to be backwards.

Assessment

Observe students as they measure the angles to be sure they are using the correct technique. Check answers to the questions to be sure that students record that the angles are equal. You might include the following items from this investigation in student portfolios:

• Investigation 10-2 data table

• Answers to Questions and Conclusions and Explore Further sections

6. Find a single light ray. Then find the reflected ray for that light ray. Trace both lines on the paper. The point where the two rays meet should be on the mirror line that you drew.

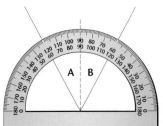

7. Remove the flashlight and turn it off. Move the book and the mirror. Lay the protractor along the mirror line. Place the center of the bottom of the protractor on the point where the rays meet. Draw a line at a right angle to the mirror line, as shown below.

8. Use the protractor to measure angles A and B. Record the measurements.

9. Repeat steps 3 to 7 two more times. Each time, draw rays with different angles.

Questions and Conclusions

1. Which angle—A or B—shows the angle at which the light traveled to the mirror?

2. Which angle shows the angle at which the light was reflected from the mirror?

3. How do angles A and B compare?

Explore Further

On a piece of paper, write the word AMBULANCE backwards as shown below.

AMBULANCE

Hold the paper up to a mirror. How are the letters reflected in the mirror?

Lab Manual 40

After reading this lesson, you should be able to

◆ explain how light is refracted.

◆ describe how concave and convex lenses refract light.

◆ explain how lenses in eyeglasses can correct vision.

Refraction

The bending of a light wave as it moves from one material to another

Lens

A curved piece of clear material that refracts light waves

Concave lens

A lens that is thin in the middle and thick at the edges

When light moves from one kind of matter to another, the light waves change speed. As a result, the direction of the light changes. The bending of a light wave as it moves from one material to another is called **refraction.**

Notice that the pencil in the photo appears to be bent. Light travels more slowly in water than it does in air. When light passes from the water to the air, the light waves change speed and change direction. As a result, the pencil seems to bend.

Lenses

A **lens** bends light by acting like the water in the container. A lens is a curved piece of glass or other clear material that refracts light waves that pass through it. Lenses are used in eyeglasses, cameras, magnifying glasses, microscopes, and telescopes. What you see through a lens depends on the kind of lens you use.

A **concave lens** curves inward. Look at Figure A. The lens is thin in the middle and thick at the edges. Light rays that pass through a concave lens are spread apart.

Refraction causes the pencil to look like it is bent.

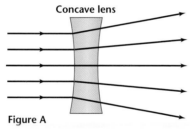

Concave lens

Figure A

---

lenses change the direction of light rays. Mirrors only reflect light rays while lenses bend them.

TEACHER ALERT

Point out to students that a concave lens bends light toward the edges—the thickest part of the lens. They make light rays diverge, or pull apart. A convex lens bends light toward the center—also the thickest part of the lens. They make light rays converge, or come together to a point.

Overview In this lesson, students explore the use of lenses to refract light. They learn how convex and concave lenses bend light to correct the focal point of light rays on the retina.

Objectives

- To explain how light is refracted
- To explain how concave and convex lenses refract light
- To explain how lenses in eyeglasses can correct vision

Student Pages 301–304

Teacher's Resource Library **TRL**

Workbook Activity 51

Alternative Workbook Activity 51

Vocabulary

concave lens	lens
convex lens	nearsighted
farsighted	refraction

---

1 Warm-Up Activity

Cover a ring attached to a stand with clear plastic wrap. Tape the wrap firmly in place and pour a small amount of water onto it. Have students observe what happens to the plastic. *(It curves.)* Then ask students to hold a hand under the ring and observe it through the water. Have students describe what they observe. *(Their hands appear larger.)*

2 Teaching the Lesson

Draw a Venn diagram on the board for comparing and contrasting convex and concave lenses. Label one oval *Convex Lens* and the other *Concave Lens.* Label the section where the two ovals intersect *Alike.* Have students copy the diagram onto their papers. As they read, have them write characteristics unique to each type of lens in the left and right sections. Have them list ways the two types of lenses are alike in the center section.

Lead a discussion comparing and contrasting mirrors and lenses. Guide students to see that both mirrors and

3 Reinforce and Extend

Did You Know?

Provide hands-on experience for students before they read the feature on page 302. Display a piece of colored cloth and ask students to examine its color. Soak the cloth in water, wringing it out and displaying it for student examination again. Ask students to suggest reasons for differences in the shade of the color. Have students examine the cloth periodically as it dries, noting the color changes. Then read the feature and compare the reasons students provided for the difference in color to the explanation in the text.

LEARNING STYLES

Visual/Spatial

Provide groups of students with a smooth-sided glass filled with water and a penlight flashlight. Dim the lights in the room. Have students shine the light through the glass at a 90-degree angle to the glass surface onto a sheet of dark construction paper. Ask students to observe where the light strikes the paper and draw a diagram showing light as it enters and leaves the glass. *(Diagrams should show the light is bent outward from the center of the glass.)*

IN THE COMMUNITY

Have students work in pairs to locate places in the community where convex or concave lenses are at work. *(for example, department store—wide angle lens cameras; newspaper—cameras with telephoto and wide-angle lenses; medical lab—microscopes using paired convex lenses)*

Convex lens
A lens that is thick in the middle and thin at the edges

Nearsighted
Able to see objects that are close up clearly

Did You Know?

Many things look darker when they are wet because less light is coming from them. The wet item reflects some light and refracts some light. This reduces the light that reaches our eyes.

When you look through a concave lens, objects appear to be smaller than they really are. Some people say the objects look "sharper." You can see this effect by looking through the glasses of someone who is nearsighted.

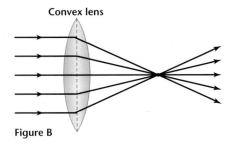

Convex lens

Figure B

A **convex lens** curves outward. Look at Figure B. The lens is thick in the middle and thin at the edges. Light rays that pass through a convex lens are refracted inward. A convex lens focuses light.

If you hold a convex lens close to your eye, the lens will magnify an image. If you hold a convex lens far from your eye and observe an object at a distance, the image appears upside down.

Lenses in Eyeglasses

The human eye has a convex lens. The lens forms an image on the retina, or the back wall of the eye. Figure C on page 303 shows a normal eye. You can see that the image formed is an upside-down image. Your brain interprets the image as right-side-up.

Figure D on page 303 shows the eye of a **nearsighted** person. People who are nearsighted can form clear images of close objects but not of distant objects. Notice that the image is formed in front of the retina instead of on it.

CROSS-CURRICULAR CONNECTION

Health

Have students research ultraviolet light rays and their harmful effects on skin and eyes. Then have them research how polarized sunglasses work. Invite students to try on different sunglasses on a sunny day and report the differences in their vision.

PRONUNCIATION GUIDE

Use the pronunciation shown here to help students pronounce a difficult word in this lesson. Refer to the pronunciation key on the Chapter Planning Guide for the sounds of the symbols.

retina (ret´ n ə)

People who are nearsighted wear glasses that have concave lenses. Figure E shows how a concave lens refracts, or bends, light before it enters the eye. As a result, a proper image is formed on the retina.

Figure F shows the eye of a **farsighted** person. A farsighted person can see objects at a distance clearly. The person has difficulty seeing objects that are close. Notice that there is not enough room for the image to be focused properly. The image is focused behind the retina.

Convex lenses are used in eyeglasses for people who are farsighted. Figure G shows how a convex lens changes the focus of the light so that the image is formed properly on the retina.

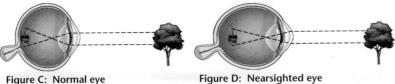

Figure C: Normal eye   Figure D: Nearsighted eye

Figure E: Nearsighted eye with concave lens

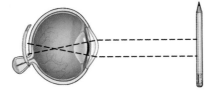

Figure F: Farsighted eye

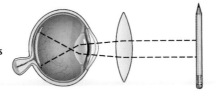

Figure G: Farsighted eye with convex lens

Lesson 6 Review Answers

1. Refraction is the bending of a light wave as it moves from one material to another. **2.** A concave lens causes rays to diverge, or spread apart. **3.** A convex lens causes rays to converge, or bend inward. **4.** A concave lens is used to refract light rays apart. Then the rays strike the lens of the eye in a position that causes the focal point to fall on the retina instead of in front of it. **5.** A convex lens converges light rays so the lens of the eye can make them focus on the retina instead of behind it.

Science at Work

Have volunteers take turns reading aloud the Science at Work feature on page 304. List *optician, ophthalmologist,* and *optometrist* on the board and explain the difference among the terms. *(An ophthalmologist is a medical doctor; an optometrist is a professional licensed to examine the eye for defects and faults of refraction and to prescribe corrective lenses. An optician is a technician who can fill the prescription written by an optometrist or ophthalmologist—order the lenses, fit the glasses, etc.)*

Discuss reasons why opticians need good people skills and an understanding of the physics of light.

Portfolio Assessment

Sample items include:
• Venn diagram from Teaching the Lesson
• Lesson 6 Review answers

Write your answers to these questions in complete sentences on a sheet of paper.

1. What is refraction?

2. How does a concave lens refract light?

3. How does a convex lens refract light?

4. How do concave lenses correct the vision of a nearsighted person?

5. How do convex lenses correct the vision of a farsighted person?

Science at Work

Optician

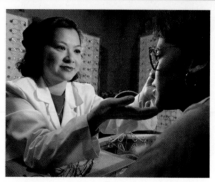

Opticians fit eyeglasses by following prescriptions written by ophthalmologists or optometrists. They also measure customers' eyes and recommend frames. Opticians write orders to laboratories for grinding and inserting lenses into frames. Some opticians grind and insert lenses themselves. Opticians make sure lenses are correctly ground and frames fit properly. Some opticians specialize in fitting contact lenses.

Most opticians complete an apprenticeship or receive on-the-job training. In some states, opticians must be licensed.

Opticians must be courteous, patient, and have good communication skills. They need to work well with their hands and be very detailed. Opticians also must take measurements accurately and have a good understanding of physics.

			Workbook Activity
Name	Date	Period	51
			Chapter 10, Lesson 6

Sound and Light: Terms Review

Directions Match each term in Column A with its meaning in Column B. Write the correct letter on the line.

	Column A		Column B
____ **1.**	photon	**A**	how high or low a sound is; determined by frequency
____ **2.**	farsighted	**B**	the bending of light as it passes through a material
____ **3.**	intensity	**C**	to bounce light or sound off a surface
____ **4.**	plane mirror	**D**	form of energy that can be seen
____ **5.**	pitch	**E**	able to see objects up close clearly
____ **6.**	nearsighted	**F**	point where reflected light rays come together
____ **7.**	refraction	**G**	a flat, smooth, dark reflecting surface
____ **8.**	light	**H**	the strength of a sound, perceived as loudness or softness
____ **9.**	reflect	**I**	tiny bundles of energy that make up light
____ **10.**	focal point	**J**	able to see objects at a distance clearly

Directions Unscramble the word or words in parentheses to complete each sentence.

11. A(n) _____ is a sound wave reflected back to its source. (hoec)

12. A(n) _____ curves inward in the middle. (venocca rimror)

13. White light can be split into the _____. (blisive crumptes)

14. In order for sound to occur, matter must _____. (tearbiv)

15. The loudness or softness of a sound is its _____. (moveul)

16. One_____ measures one back and forth movement of a vibration. (leycc)

17. A(n) _____ helps correct nearsightedness. (naveoc snel)

18. A(n) _____ curves outward at the middle. (coxven roirmr)

19. A(n) _____ is produced by vibrations. (dunso evwa)

20. A human ear cannot hear a sound with a _____ of 10 Hz. (queencryf)

Publishing. Permission is granted to reproduce for classroom use only.   ● Physical Science

Workbook Activity 51

- Sound is caused by vibrations.

- Sound travels in waves.

- The intensity of sound is measured in decibels.

- A person's hearing interprets intensity as volume.

- A pitch is how high or low a sound is.

- Sound travels at different speeds through different kinds of matter.

- An echo is a reflected sound.

- Scientists use sonar to measure distances under water.

- People see objects because light is reflected from them.

- Light is made up of bundles of energy called photons.

- Light has properties of both particles and waves.

- Light waves travel fastest through empty space.

- The visible spectrum makes up white light.

- Refraction is the bending of a light wave.

- A mirror is an object that reflects light.

- Three types of mirrors are plane, concave, and convex.

- Concave and convex lenses refract light and can correct vision.

Chapter 10 Summary

Have volunteers read aloud each Summary item on page 305. Ask volunteers to explain the meaning of each item. Direct students' attention to the Science Words box on the bottom of page 305. Have them read and review each term and its definition.

Science Words

concave lens, 301	farsighted, 303	light, 289	refraction, 301
concave mirror, 296	focal point, 296	nearsighted, 302	sonar, 284
convex lens, 302	frequency, 277	photons, 289	sound wave, 273
convex mirror, 297	Hertz, 277	pitch, 277	ultrasound, 285
cycle, 277	image, 295	plane mirror, 295	vibrate, 272
decibel, 275	intensity, 275	prism, 291	visible spectrum, 291
echo, 283	lens, 301	reflect, 283	volume, 276

Chapter 10 Review

Use the Chapter Review to prepare students for tests and to reteach content from the chapter.

Chapter 10 Mastery Test

The Teacher's Resource Library includes two parallel forms of the Chapter 10 Mastery Test. The difficulty level of the two forms is equivalent. You may wish to use one form as a pretest and the other form as a posttest.

Review Answers
Vocabulary Review

1. prism 2. image 3. sonar 4. lens
5. ultrasound 6. decibel 7. Hertz
8. convex lens

Concept Review

9. D 10. B 11. D

Critical Thinking

12. Intensity is strength of sound. Intensity is based on how much energy the sound wave carries. Volume is the way your ear interprets intensity of sound as loud or soft. Pitch is how high or low a sound seems and is determined by its frequency. Frequency is the number of vibrations per second of the sound wave.
13. An object whose echo takes 9 seconds to return is 3,114 meters away.

TEACHER ALERT

Because of limited space in this Chapter Review, not all of the vocabulary terms introduced in this chapter appear in the Vocabulary Review section. You may want to create an activity using the missing words to give students practice with all of the terms in this chapter. Here are the terms that are not covered in the section.

concave lens	nearsighted
concave mirror	photons
convex mirror	pitch
cycle	plane mirror
echo	reflect
farsighted	refraction
focal point	sound wave
frequency	vibrate
intensity	visible spectrum
light	volume

Vocabulary Review

Choose a word or words from the Word Bank that best completes each sentence. Write the answer on a sheet of paper.

1. A(n) _____ is a clear piece of glass or plastic that can be used to separate white light.

2. A(n) _____ is a copy or likeness of something.

3. We use _____ to measure distances under water.

4. A(n) _____ is a curved piece of clear material that refracts light waves.

5. A(n) _____ uses sound waves to study organs inside the human body.

6. A(n) _____ measures the intensity of sound.

7. One _____ equals one frequency cycle per second.

8. A(n) _____ is thick in the middle and thin at the edges.

Concept Review

Choose the answer that best completes each sentence. Write the letter of the answer on your paper.

9. Sounds are made when matter _____.

   A rotates

   B moves quickly back and forth

   C vibrates

   D both B and C

10. Light is made of tiny bundles of energy called _____.

   A photographs   **C** neurons

   B photons   **D** none of the above

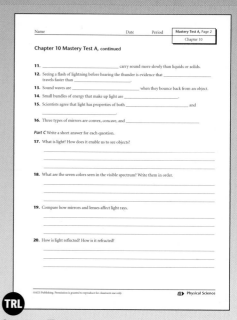

Chapter 10 Mastery Test A

11. A straw sticking out of a glass of lemonade looks bent due to _____.

   A light traveling more slowly in water than in air

   B refraction

   C light waves changing speed and direction

   D all of the above

Critical Thinking

Write the answer to each of these questions on your paper.

12. What is the difference between a sound's intensity, volume, pitch, and frequency?

13. How far away is an object whose echo takes 9 seconds to return?

14. Copy the drawing of each of these lenses. Draw lines to show how the light waves are refracted as they pass through each lens. Explain what you drew for each lens. What type of vision can each of the lenses help improve, and why?

15. Explain what is meant when something is called the mirror image of an object.

Test-Taking Tip When answering multiple-choice questions, first identify the questions you know are untrue.

14. Left drawing: Students' drawings should show parallel lines entering the concave lens and diverging as they leave it. The concave lens has rays that spread out. Concave lenses are useful for correcting nearsightedness. They cause the image to form on the retina instead of in front of it. **Right drawing:** Students' drawings should show parallel lines entering the convex lens and converging as they leave it. The light waves converge, or draw together, as a result of passing through a convex lens. Convex lenses are useful for correcting farsightedness. They cause the image to form on the retina instead of behind it. **15.** A mirror image is identical to an original image, only reversed. The term relates to things seen in a mirror because the angle of reflection of light causes the image to be seen in reverse.

ALTERNATIVE ASSESSMENT

Alternative Assessment items correlate to the student Goals for Learning at the beginning of this chapter.

■ Have students use a tuning fork to produce a sound and explain how the sound is produced. Then ask them to explain the effects of the vibration as they place the tuning fork in a glass of water.

■ Give a pair of students a slinky or wire spring and have them demonstrate how sound travels. Draw a line on the board to represent the slinky and ask the pair to draw the sound waves over it.

■ Have students compare and contrast light waves and sound waves in order to explain the nature of light. Then ask them to list one way light is like particles.

■ Ask pairs of students to use a mirror to explain how light is reflected.

■ Have pairs of students use a magnifying glass to explain how light is refracted.

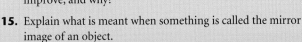

Chapter 10 Mastery Test B

Sound and Light   *Chapter 10*   **307**

Planning Guide

Electricity

	Student Text Lesson		
	Student Pages	Vocabulary	Lesson Review
Lesson 1 How Electricity Flows Through a Circuit	310–314	✔	✔
Lesson 2 Conductors and Insulators	315–319	✔	✔
Lesson 3 Some Sources of Electric Current	320–324	✔	✔
Lesson 4 Ohm's Law	325–327	✔	✔
Lesson 5 Series Circuits	328–334	✔	✔
Lesson 6 Parallel Circuits	335–339	✔	✔
Lesson 7 Measuring Electricity	340–342	✔	✔

Chapter Activities

Student Text
Science Center
Teacher's Resource Library
Community Connection 11: Electricity
  in Your Home

Assessment Options

Student Text
Chapter 11 Review
Teacher's Resource Library
Chapter 11 Mastery Tests A and B

Student Text Features								Teaching Strategies						Learning Styles						Teacher's Resource Library				
Achievements in Science	Science at Work	Science in Your Life	Investigation	Science Myth	Note	Technology Note	Did You Know	Science Integration	Science Journal	Cross-Curricular Connection	Online Connection	Teacher Alert	Applications (Home, Career, Community, Global, Environment)	Auditory/Verbal	Body/Kinesthetic	Interpersonal/Group Learning	Logical/Mathematical	Visual/Spatial	LEP/ESL	Workbook Activities	Alternative Workbook Activities	Lab Manual	Resource File	Self-Study Guide
313				310			312	313		312				313	311			312		52	52	41	22	✔
	319				✔		316	317		317, 318		318			316			317		53	53	42		✔
324				322	✔	✔	322	322	323	322			321, 323			322		323		54	54			✔
						✔				326							326	326		55	55			✔
			333							329, 331		329	330	331	330				329	56	56	43		✔
			338						336	336									336	57	57	44	23	✔
		341		342						341	342	341								58	58			✔

Pronunciation Key

a	hat	e	let	ī	ice	ô	order	u̇	put	sh	she
ā	age	ē	equal	o	hot	oi	oil	ü	rule	th	thin
ä	far	ėr	term	ō	open	ou	out	ch	child	ᴛʜ	then
â	care	i	it	ȯ	saw	u	cup	ng	long	zh	measure

ə { a in about / e in taken / i in pencil / o in lemon / u in circus }

Alternative Workbook Activities

The Teacher's Resource Library (TRL) contains a set of lower-level worksheets called Alternative Workbook Activities. These worksheets cover the same content as the regular Workbook Activities but are written at a second-grade reading level.

Skill Track Software

Use the Skill Track Software for Physical Science for additional reinforcement of this chapter. The software program allows students using AGS textbooks to be assessed for mastery of each chapter and lesson of the textbook. Students access the software on an individual basis and are assessed with multiple-choice items.

Science Center

Challenge students to create a new electric appliance. Tell students to begin by first thinking of a purpose for the appliance. Encourage them to make the purpose as original as possible. Then have students draw a design showing what the appliance will look like and how it will work. Supply boxes, cardboard, scissors, paint, rulers, glue, batteries, wires, and any other materials that you think students could use to make a 3-D model of the appliance.

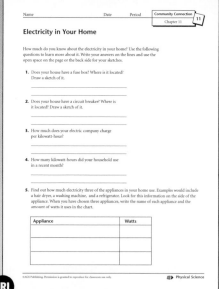

Community Connection 11

11 Electricity

The lightning in the photograph is an example of electricity—static electricity. Electricity is all around us. Every day we use electricity. It lights homes and runs appliances. It starts cars and operates traffic signals. There are even electrical signals in our bodies that make our organs work. Do you know how electricity works and where it comes from? In Chapter 11, you will learn what electricity is, how it works, and how it travels.

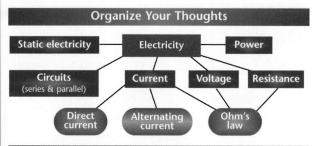

Organize Your Thoughts

Static electricity — Electricity — Power

Circuits (series & parallel) — Current — Voltage — Resistance

Direct current — Alternating current — Ohm's law

Goals for Learning

◆ To explain how electric current flows through a circuit
◆ To compare insulators and conductors
◆ To tell how resistance is useful
◆ To describe how batteries produce current
◆ To explain direct current and alternating current
◆ To apply Ohm's law
◆ To compare series and parallel circuits
◆ To describe how electricity is measured

309

Introducing the Chapter

Ask students to describe what the photo on page 308 shows. *(lightning)* Have students describe lightning they have observed. Then ask what they think lightning is. *(Accept any reasonable answers.)*

Many students may consider electricity to be quite a mysterious phenomenon. Have students create two vertical columns on a sheet of paper. Have them label the left column *Facts* and the right column *Questions*. Instruct them to write down in the left column any facts they know about electricity. In the right column, they can list any questions about electricity they would like answered. Suggest that students read the Goals for Learning for this chapter before writing down any facts and questions. When students finish writing, ask which is larger—their list of facts or questions. *(Most likely, students will determine that they have far more questions about electricity than answers.)*

Notes and Technology Notes

Ask volunteers to read the notes that appear in the margins throughout the chapter. Then discuss them with the class.

TEACHER'S RESOURCE

The AGS Teaching Strategies in Science Transparencies may be used with this chapter. The transparencies add an interactive dimension to expand and enhance the *Physical Science* program content.

CAREER INTEREST INVENTORY

The AGS Harrington-O'Shea Career Decision-Making System-Revised (CDM) may be used with this chapter. Students can use the CDM to explore their interests and identify careers. The CDM defines career areas that are indicated by students' responses on the inventory.

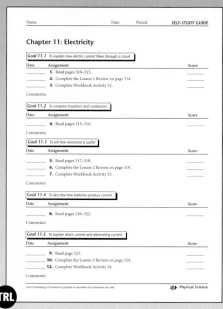

Chapter 11 Self-Study Guide

Chapter 11 Lesson 1

Overview In this lesson, students learn what static electricity is, how electricity moves through an open circuit, and how an open circuit is different from a closed circuit.

Objectives

- To explain static electricity
- To explain how electricity moves through a circuit
- To compare an open circuit to a closed circuit

Student Pages 310–314

Teacher's Resource Library (TRL)

Workbook Activity 52

Alternative Workbook Activity 52

Lab Manual 41

Resource File 22

Vocabulary

ampere	electricity
circuit	open circuit
closed circuit	schematic diagram
electric current	static electricity

Science Background

The terms *positive* and *negative* when used in connection with electricity merely indicate a distinction between two opposite types of electrical charge. A positive charge does not have more charge than a negative charge. Like charges, such as two positive charges, repel. Unlike charges attract. The amount of attraction or repulsion depends on the amount of charge on the two interacting objects and on the distance between them.

Rubbing different materials together can produce electrical charges. When two objects are rubbed together, electrons can move from one object to the other. The object that gains electrons becomes negatively charged. The object that loses electrons becomes positively charged. When an object becomes charged, it can exert a force on other objects.

Static electricity results when electric charge builds up in one place. For example, if you rub one end of a plastic comb, that end becomes charged.

Objectives

After reading this lesson, you should be able to

- explain static electricity.
- explain how electricity moves through a circuit.
- compare an open circuit to a closed circuit.

Electricity

Flow of electrons

Static electricity

Buildup of electrical charges

Science Myth

Electricity only flows through wires.

Fact: Electrons (electricity) can flow without wires. The transfer of electrons from fingers to a metal doorknob (as shown in the figure on this page) is one example of this.

In Chapter 3, you read about atoms and the particles that make them. Electrons are negatively charged particles. Under the right conditions, electrons can escape from one atom and move to another one. The atom that loses the electron becomes positively charged. The atom that has picked up the electron becomes negatively charged. In turn, this negatively charged atom can pass the electron on again. This movement, or flow, of electrons is the basis of **electricity**. Electricity is a form of energy.

Static Electricity

Have you ever gotten a shock when you touched metal after walking across a carpet? The shock was caused by a buildup of charge, called **static electricity.** Walking across the carpet caused electrons to leave the carpet and enter your body. When you touched the metal, the extra electrons jumped from your finger to the metal.

When electrons move from one place to another, energy is transferred. Lightning is a discharge of static electricity between clouds or between a cloud and Earth.

When you touch the comb and get "shocked," a transfer of electrons takes place between your finger and the comb.

1 Warm-Up Activity

Choose a volunteer with clean, long hair for this demonstration. Instruct the volunteer to run a comb through her or his hair, and then hold the comb near some small pieces of paper. The paper should be attracted to the comb. Ask the class what they think is causing this attraction to happen. *(an electric charge)*

Have one student read the myth portion (first sentence) and one student read the fact portion of the Science Myth on page 310. Many students think that wires must be present in order for electricity to flow. To dispel this notion, emphasize the example of the transfer of electrons from fingers to doorknob pictured on page 310. Invite students to give other examples of electricity that flows without wires. *(for example, lightning)*

Closed Circuits

The movement of electrons from one place to another is called **electric current.** The rate at which electrons move from one place to another can vary. Electric current is measured in **amperes.** An ampere tells how much current is moving past a point in a circuit in one second. One ampere is the flow of about 6 billion billion electrons per second! An ampere is often called an amp.

Currents from static electricity are not easy to control. But an electric current produced by a power source can be controlled and is easy to use.

When electrons travel in an electric current, they follow a path. This path is called a **circuit.** Follow the path of current in the figure below. The circuit begins at the power source. It travels through the wire to the light bulb. It lights up the bulb, and then returns to the power source.

Electrons can only follow a complete, unbroken path. You can see that the path in this circuit is unbroken. This path is called a **closed circuit.** As long as the current continues to flow in the circuit, the light will remain lit.

Electric current

Movement of electrons from one place to another

Ampere

The unit used to describe how much electric current flows through a wire

Circuit

A path for electric current

Closed circuit

A complete, unbroken path for electric current

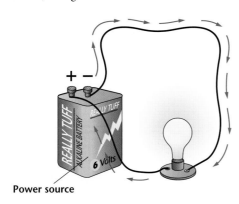

Power source

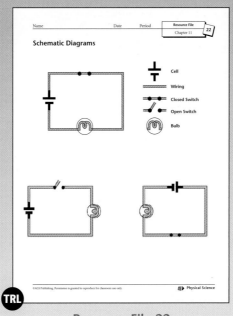

Schematic Diagrams

Cell

Wiring

Closed Switch

Open Switch

Bulb

Name   Date   Period   Resource File
Chapter 11   22

©AGS Publishing. Permission is granted to reproduce for classroom use only.   Physical Science

TRL

Resource File 22

---

2 Teaching the Lesson

Before beginning this lesson, pronounce the vocabulary words for students. Have them look for and write down the meanings of these words as they read through the lesson.

You might wish to review the structure of the atom (Chapter 3, Lesson 4) with students before they read this lesson.

Explain to students that when they walk across a carpet, electrons move from the carpet to their body because the electrons gain energy when their feet and the carpet rub together.

Have students look at the figure of the circuit on page 311. Tell them that every electric circuit has three main parts. Help students identify these parts: battery—power source; wire—connects path of electricity; lightbulb—object that uses electricity.

Encourage students to compare the flow of electricity to that of water. (*Answers should include the idea that both flow in currents.*)

3 Reinforce and Extend

LEARNING STYLES

Body/Kinesthetic

Provide bar magnets to students. Allow them to manipulate the magnets to feel the unlike poles attract and the like poles repel. Point out to students that magnetic attraction is similar to the attraction that occurs between negatively and positively charged atoms.

LEARNING STYLES

Visual/Spatial

Have a volunteer hold the top of a sheet of newspaper against a wall while you smooth out the newspaper by rubbing the entire surface several times with a wool cloth. Then have the volunteer let go of the paper. The paper will cling to the wall. Ask students for possible explanations. *(The wall and the newspaper have opposite electric charges that attract each other.)* Next, gently pry one corner of the newspaper away from the wall and then quickly release it. Ask students what they think caused the corner of the newspaper to go back against the wall.

CROSS-CURRICULAR CONNECTION

Social Studies

Have students research information about the electrical investigations Benjamin Franklin conducted. Ask them to find out how he developed the lightning rod. Encourage students to write a short paper or design a poster outlining Franklin's achievements in studying electricity.

Open circuit
An incomplete or broken path for electric current

Did You Know?

Brain cells produce electrical signals. These signals travel from cell to cell along circuit-like paths. An electroencephalograph, or EEG, measures a brain's electrical activity. This machine can show the existence of brain damage and where it is located.

Open Circuits

Suppose you have a light turned on in your room. You decide you want to turn off the light. What do you do? Most likely you turn off a switch. To turn on the light again, you turn the switch on.

How does a switch work? Look at Figure A. You can see that the wires of the circuit are connected to a switch. When the switch is closed, the electrons can flow in an unbroken path. The light stays lit.

In Figure B, the switch is open. The current cannot pass through it. The bulb does not light. This is an incomplete, or broken, path for electric current. It is called an **open circuit.**

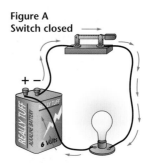

**Figure A
Switch closed**

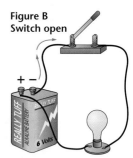

**Figure B
Switch open**

The switches you see in Figures A and B are called knife switches. The switches in your home are different from knife switches, but they work the same way. The switches in your home break the flow of electrons when they are turned off. These three images show some of the switches you might find in your home.

A lamp switch

A doorbell switch

A wall switch

Schematic
diagram

A diagram that uses
symbols to show the
parts of a circuit

Schematic Diagrams

Scientists often use drawings of circuits. To make this job easier, they have developed symbols to show different parts of a circuit. Different symbols represent wires, switches, bulbs, and power sources. You can see some of these symbols in the diagram below.

A diagram that uses such symbols to show the parts of a circuit is called a **schematic diagram.** The schematic diagram below shows a battery in a circuit with a closed switch, wiring, and a bulb.

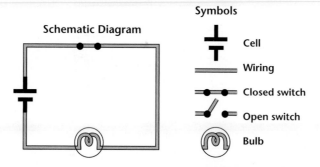

Schematic Diagram

Symbols

 Cell

Wiring

Closed switch

Open switch

Bulb

Achievements in Science

Van de Graaff Generator

In 1931, Robert Van de Graaff invented the electrostatic generator that is named after him. Van de Graaff generators produce high voltage but low currents.

The top of an electrostatic generator is a hollow metal dome. The base is a motor. The motor turns a conveyor-like belt made of insulating material. The belt carries electrons from the base to the dome. When the electrons reach the top, they gather on the dome's outside surface. As more gather, the dome's voltage increases. The result is a source with very high voltage but low current. It is so low that when someone touches the dome, no harm is done.

Van de Graaff generators can be as small as 2 inches high, producing 5,000 volts. They can be several stories high, producing millions of volts. Scientists use Van de Graaff generators to accelerate charged particles for nuclear physics experiments. Teachers use Van de Graaff generators in classroom demonstrations. You may have seen Van de Graaff generators at work in old movies. This is the machine that makes the mad scientist's hair stand on end.

Achievements in Science

Have students take turns reading aloud the Achievements in Science feature on page 313. Explain that Van de Graaff was on the staff of the Massachusetts Institute of Technology, where the first Van de Graaff generator was built in 1931. One difficulty of the generator is that it allows some charged particles to escape. To prevent this, freon or another gas under very high pressure is put in a vessel that surrounds the generator.

LEARNING STYLES

 Auditory/Verbal

Suggest that students research some people in the history of the discovery of electricity. Have them find out about the contribution each of the following people made to the knowledge and use of electricity: Thales of Miletus, Jerome Cardan, William Gilbert, Stephen Gray, Charles F. Du Fay, Luigi Galvani, Alessandro Volta, Andre Marie Ampère, Michael Faraday, and James Clerk Maxwell. Have students prepare and deliver a brief oral report on the person they research.

SCIENCE JOURNAL

Have students write one or two paragraphs telling what they know about circuits now that they didn't know before they read the lesson.

Lesson 1 Review Answers

1. Walking across a carpet causes electrons to leave the carpet and enter your body. When you touch the metal, the extra electrons jump from your hand to the metal doorknob. **2.** A is an open circuit. B is a closed circuit. **3.** Current would flow through B because it has a complete unbroken path along which electrons can travel. **4.** Circuit is the name of the path that electrons follow. **5.** An ampere is used to measure electric current.

Portfolio Assessment

Sample items include:
• Meanings of vocabulary terms from Teaching the Lesson
• Lesson 1 Review answers

Lesson 1   R E V I E W

Write your answers to these questions in complete sentences on a sheet of paper.

1. Explain what happens when you get a shock from a metal doorknob after walking across a carpet.

2. Look at the following schematic diagrams, A and B. Which of the circuits is a closed circuit? Which is an open circuit?

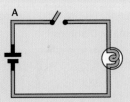
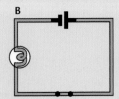

3. In which of the schematic diagrams above would current flow? Explain your answer.

4. What is the name for the path that electrons follow?

5. What unit is used to measure electric current?

Name _____ Date _____ Period _____ **Lab Manual, Page 1**
Chapter 11   **41**

Exploring Electric Charges

Purpose   What happens when you rub two different kinds of materials together? In this investigation, you will observe how an electric charge affects the way an object behaves.

Materials   safety glasses
meterstick
masking tape
2 balloons
string
wool cloth

Procedure

1. Use the table to record your data.

Steps	Objects	What I Think Will Happen	What Happened
5–6			
7–8			
9			
10–11			

2. Put on your safety glasses. Tape the meterstick to the top of your desk. Make sure it extends over the edge.

3. Blow up one of the balloons. Tie the end of the balloon shut. Attach one end of the string to the balloon. Use the other end of the string to hang the balloon from the meterstick.

4. Hold the piece of wool cloth away from the balloon.

5. What do you think will happen if you move the wool toward the balloon? Record your prediction in the data table.

6. Slowly move the wool cloth close to the balloon. Observe what happens. Write your observations in the data table.

7. Rub the balloon with the wool cloth for 30 seconds. Move the wool cloth away from the balloon. What do you think will happen if you move the cloth toward the balloon? Record your prediction in the data table.

Publishing. Permission is granted to reproduce for classroom use only.   **Physical Science**

Lab Manual 41, pages 1–2

Name _____ Date _____ Period _____ **Workbook Activity**
Chapter 11, Lesson 1   **52**

How Electricity Flows

Directions Write the correct word or words for each definition on the line. Then circle the word in the puzzle below.

1. a discharge of electricity from a cloud _____
2. a complete, unbroken path for electric current _____
3. an incomplete path for electric current _____
4. flow of electrons _____
5. Electricity is a form of _____.
6. kind of diagram that uses symbols to show parts of a circuit _____
7. unit that tells how much electric current flows through a wire _____
8. We measure electric _____ in amperes. _____
9. where an electric circuit begins _____
10. kind of electricity caused by a buildup of charge _____

```
P  B  C  C  S  D  V  I  V  U  K  R  O  U  B  E  E
T  H  P  D  A  E  S  F  D  S  T  A  T  I  C  L  L
N  A  Z  E  N  E  R  G  Y  J  I  A  U  O  Y  E  P
E  R  U  M  I  C  E  A  G  S  L  M  Z  A  Z  C  S
R  A  T  I  E  U  C  N  X  R  V  P  T  O  H  T  C
R  L  A  K  S  Q  I  P  L  F  M  E  I  T  K  R  H
U  L  Y  M  C  N  O  E  X  U  T  R  R  M  A  I  E
C  E  W  W  T  M  P  R  Y  T  N  E  V  F  H  C  M
E  L  E  H  R  P  T  E  O  I  S  K  U  S  P  I  A
P  C  G  V  E  O  P  E  N  C  I  R  C  U  I  T  T
C  I  N  R  U  R  D  N  I  G  H  E  P  N  O  Y  I
L  R  O  O  I  E  Q  T  O  O  C  B  R  N  T  F  C
I  C  L  O  S  E  D  C  I  R  C  U  I  T  H  S  O
A  F  C  P  D  X  I  O  N  S  P  N  T  S  G  P  T
R  Q  L  T  E  C  R  U  O  S  R  E  W  O  P  Y  N
C  N  T  O  R  L  D  H  W  Y  T  R  I  F  D  P  X
```

Publishing. Permission is granted to reproduce for classroom use only.   **Physical Science**

Workbook Activity 52

Objectives

After reading this lesson, you should be able to

◆ explain the difference between a conductor and an insulator.

◆ give examples of conductors and insulators.

◆ explain what resistance is.

◆ list three things that affect the resistance of a material.

◆ explain how resistance is useful.

Conductor
Material through which electricity passes easily

Insulator
Material through which electricity does not pass easily

Look at the electrical cords that carry electric current in your home. You will notice that the metal wire that carries the electricity is covered with a material. This material is often plastic. Why do you think electrical cords have this covering?

Look at the cross section of the electrical cord in the figure. The wire in the center of the electrical cord is a **conductor.** A conductor is a material through which electrons can flow easily. Electricity passes easily through the wire from a power source to the lamp.

Metals, such as copper, gold, aluminum, and silver, are good conductors. Silver is a very good conductor of the metals. But it is too expensive to use in most wires. Most electrical circuits use copper wire.

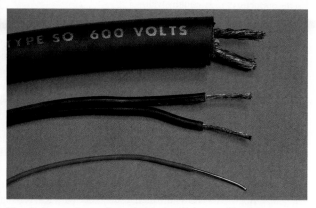

The plastic covering on these electrical cords is a good insulator.

The outer covering of the electrical cord is an **insulator.** An insulator does not conduct electricity well. The electrons in an insulator are not as free to move as the electrons in a conductor. Electricity does not pass through an insulator easily. Examples of good electrical insulators are glass, rubber, wood, and plastic.

Electricity Chapter 11 **315**

Lesson at a Glance

Chapter 11 Lesson 2

Overview In this lesson, students learn how conductors differ from insulators and about some materials that are examples of each. Students also learn about resistance—what it is, factors that affect it, and how it can be useful.

Objectives

■ To explain the difference between a conductor and an insulator

■ To give examples of conductors and insulators

■ To explain what resistance is

■ To list three things that affect the resistance of a material

■ To explain how resistance is useful

Student Pages 315–319

Teacher's Resource Library

Workbook Activity 53

Alternative Workbook Activity 53

Lab Manual 42

Vocabulary

conductor   ohm
insulator   resistance

Science Background

All substances can be ordered in a list by their ability to conduct electrical charges. Those at the top of the list are referred to as conductors and those at the bottom as insulators. In general, metals make up the conductors. Substances, such as porcelain, glass, and hard rubber, make up the insulators. The electrons in conductors are free to move from one atom to another. The insulators do not have as many moving electrons.

Warm-Up Activity

Find out what students already know about electric shocks by asking these questions: Why shouldn't you use a fork or knife in an electric toaster to remove bread that is stuck? *(You might get an electric shock. Electrons can travel easily through metal utensils.)* Why should you stay inside a building during an electrical

storm? *(Most buildings are made of materials that prevent electrons from moving through them easily, thus helping to prevent electric shocks.)*

Teaching the Lesson

Ask students to write this lesson's title and objectives on paper. Tell students that as they read this lesson, they should write sentences that meet the objectives.

If possible, provide an electric appliance, such as a toaster or small heater, so that students can use it to observe the wires as they heat up.

3 Reinforce and Extend

Did You Know?

Ask a student to read the feature on page 316 aloud. Have students point out some safety measures that the feature's facts suggest. *(For example, make sure your skin is thoroughly dry before using a hair dryer. Never use electrically powered objects such as radios or televisions near a bathtub or pool.)*

LEARNING STYLES

Body/Kinesthetic

Provide students with an electric cord or insulated wire with some of the insulation stripped away. Ask students to identify the material that is the conductor of electricity and the material that is the insulator. *(The conducting material would be encased by the insulating material.)* Ask what material the conductor is made of. *(most likely rubber or plastic)* Ask why the cord has an insulator. *(to prevent shock)*

Resistance
Measure of how easily electric current will flow through a material

Ohm
The unit used to measure resistance

Semiconductors are minerals that can be made to act like conductors and insulators. The mineral used most often in semiconductors is silicon. The microchip used in computers is an example of a semiconductor device.

Did You Know?

If your skin is wet, your chance of electrical shock is higher. The water mixed with the salt on your skin lowers your body's electrical resistance. This lets voltage pass more current through your body.

The insulator that covers the electrical cord keeps the electricity flowing in the wire. The covering prevents the current from flowing to places where it might cause fires or electrical shock. For example, if you touch a wire that is carrying an electric current, the electrons are free to travel through your body. You will get a shock. But if the wire is covered with an insulator like the one in the photo on page 315, the electricity cannot flow through your body.

When using electrical cords, be sure to check for worn insulation. If the bare wire is exposed, the cord is dangerous. You should replace or repair the cord. Electrical tapes that are good insulators can be used to repair the area where the wire is exposed.

Resistance

Not all conductors allow electricity to pass through them in the same way. Likewise, not all insulators slow down electricity equally well.

Resistance is a measure of how easy or hard it is for electric current to flow through a material. Resistance is measured in **ohms.** To understand resistance, think about two water hoses. They are the same in every way, except one has a larger hole running down the middle than the other. A pump pushes water through the two hoses equally. Through which of the hoses will more water pass in one minute?

If you answered that more water would pass through the hose with the larger opening, you are correct. The hose with the larger opening offers less resistance to the water flow than the hose with the smaller opening. In a similar way, more current flows through a substance with less resistance than through a substance with more resistance. Insulators have high resistance. Conductors have low resistance.

The resistance of a wire depends on three things.

◆ The material the wire is made of. Some materials have more resistance than others. For example, tungsten has a greater resistance than copper. Tungsten wire is used in lightbulbs.

◆ The length of the wire. The longer a wire is, the greater its resistance. Look at the two wires below. One wire is longer than the other. The longer wire has greater resistance. If you use a long extension cord to plug in a lamp, less electric current will go through the wire to the lamp.

◆ The thickness of the wire. The thinner the wire, the greater its resistance. You can see wires of two thicknesses below. The thinner wire has greater resistance than the thicker wire.

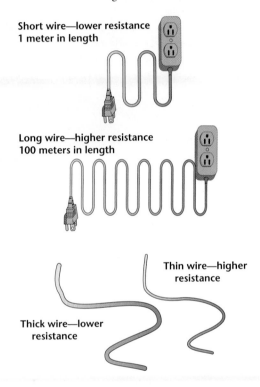

Short wire—lower resistance
1 meter in length

Long wire—higher resistance
100 meters in length

Thin wire—higher resistance

Thick wire—lower resistance

Some students may think that all the wires in appliances are made of materials that are good conductors of electricity. Make certain that students understand that many appliances are deliberately constructed to have some wires made from materials that are poor conductors. Poor conductors prevent electrons from flowing through the wires easily. This resistance causes the wires to heat up. The wires get so hot that they give off heat or light. Point out the examples of such appliances mentioned in the last paragraph of this lesson on page 318.

CROSS-CURRICULAR CONNECTION

Home Economics
Have students in small groups watch as you toast bread in a toaster. Encourage students to look inside the toaster as the bread toasts. Remind students not to touch the toaster as they make their visual observations. What evidence of resistance do they observe? Following the activity, provide spreads and have students enjoy the toast.

Resistance causes electrical energy to change into heat and light energy. Without resistance, many appliances in your home would not work.

Nichrome is a metal with a high resistance. When electricity passes through a nichrome wire, it gets hot. The wire coils in a toaster are made of nichrome. When electricity passes through the toaster, the wires get hot and toast your bread. Other appliances that use materials with high resistance include curling irons, hair dryers, and irons. Some of these appliances are shown here.

Lesson 2 REVIEW

Write your answers to these questions in complete sentences on a sheet of paper.

1. What is the difference between a conductor and an insulator?

2. Give two examples of conductors and two examples of insulators.

3. Sometimes the insulation on an electrical cord gets destroyed. Why would it be dangerous to use such a cord?

4. What are three things that affect the resistance of a wire? How is resistance useful?

5. List the appliances you have used in the last 24 hours. Put a check behind those that use materials with high resistance to produce heat and light.

▼◄▲▼◄▲▼◄▲▼◄▲▼◄▲▼◄▲▼◄▲▼◄▲▼◄▲▼◄▲▼◄▲▼◄▲▼◄▲▼◄▲▼

Science at Work

Line Installer

Line installers install electrical power, telephone, and cable TV lines. They put up poles and towers and dig trenches to carry wires and cables. They also set up service for customers and maintain and repair wires and cables. In emergencies, they have the important responsibility of restoring utility and communications services.

Most line installers complete several years of on-the-job training. Some have a two-year technical degree and have received on-the-job-training through an apprenticeship.

Line installers must have mechanical ability and a basic knowledge of algebra and trigonometry. They need stamina, strength, and coordination. They must also be comfortable working high above the ground. Good customer service skills are also important.

Electricity Chapter 11 **319**

Lesson 2 Review Answers

1. Electricity passes easily through a conductor but not easily through an insulator. **2.** Answers will vary. Sample answers include: Conductors—copper, gold, aluminum, and silver; Insulators—glass, rubber, wood, and plastic **3.** You might get shocked because you could come into contact with the wire. **4.** The material the wire is made of, its length, and its thickness affect its resistance. It is useful because it causes electrical energy to change into heat and light, so it can be used in many appliances. **5.** On students' lists of appliances, those identified as producing heat and light might include microwave oven, electric stove, television, electric dryer, and lamp.

Science at Work

Have volunteers read the Science at Work feature on page 319 aloud. Have students name some specific companies in your community for which line installers work. Also have them describe some recent emergencies during which line installers were needed. You might point out to students that in many communities the power, telephone, and cable lines are buried. Ask them to find out how the work of installers changes depending on whether the lines are above ground or buried.

Portfolio Assessment

Sample items include:
- Lesson title, objectives, and sentences from Teaching the Lesson
- Lesson 2 Review answers

Lab Manual 42, pages 1–2

Name _____ Date _____ Period _____ | Lab Manual, Page 1 | 42 | Chapter 11

Identifying Electric Conductors

Purpose What solutions are good conductors of electricity? In this investigation, you will explore how various solutions conduct electricity.

Materials safety glasses / graduated cylinder / spoon / salt / mineral oil / rubbing alcohol / dry-cell battery / 3 wires with insulation removed from the ends / 8 paper cups / baking soda / 4 drinking straws / sugar / orange juice / vinegar / lightbulb and holder / 2 nails / water

Procedure
1. Use the table to record your data.

Material	Prediction	Observations	Conductor or Nonconductor
baking soda			
salt			
sugar			
mineral oil			
orange juice			
rubbing alcohol			
vinegar			
water			
other			

2. For each of the materials in the table, predict whether it is a conductor or a nonconductor. Write your prediction in the data table.
3. Put on your safety glasses. Pour 125 mL of water into each of 4 cups.
4. Pour ½ spoonful of baking soda into one of the cups of water. Stir with a drinking straw until the baking soda dissolves.

Publishing. Permission is granted to reproduce for classroom use only. | Physical Science

---

Workbook Activity 53

Name _____ Date _____ Period _____ | Workbook Activity | 53 | Chapter 11, Lesson 2

Conductors and Insulators

Directions Complete the outline by filling in the details about conductors and insulators.

Conductors and Insulators

A. Parts of an electrical cord
1. Wire: _____
2. Covering: _____

B. Some good electrical conductors
1. _____
2. _____
3. _____
4. _____

C. Some good electrical insulators
1. _____
2. _____
3. _____
4. _____

D. Resistance
1. Definition: _____
2. Unit used to measure it: _____

E. Three things the resistance of a wire depends on
1. _____
2. _____
3. _____

Publishing. Permission is granted to reproduce for classroom use only. | Physical Science

Electricity Chapter 11 **319**

Lesson at a Glance

Chapter 11 Lesson 3

Overview In this lesson, students learn about electromotive force and how voltage is related to it. Students learn about the structure and uses of dry-cell and wet-cell batteries. Students also learn how direct current differs from alternating current.

Objectives

- To define and explain electromotive force
- To explain how voltage relates to electromotive force
- To describe the structure and use of dry-cell batteries
- To describe wet-cell batteries
- To explain the difference between direct current and alternating current

Student Pages 320–324

Teacher's Resource Library (TRL)

Workbook Activity 54

Alternative Workbook Activity 54

Vocabulary

alternating current	terminal
battery	volt
direct current	voltage
dry-cell battery	wet-cell battery
electromotive force	

Science Background

A movement of electrons through a conductor is an electric current. A continuing movement of current is needed for practical uses of electricity, such as running an appliance. A battery of some kind is one source of constant electric power. Electric current moves through some conductors better than through others. A material that is a good conductor is thought of as having low resistance. Resistance is the measure of how difficult it is to move electrons through a conductor. All materials have some resistance.

Often the movement of electrons in an electric current is referred to as the "flow of electricity." Electrons in an unconnected wire also move, but they

---

Lesson 3 Some Sources of Electric Current

Objectives

After reading this lesson, you should be able to

- define and explain electromotive force.
- explain how voltage relates to electromotive force.
- describe the structure and use of dry-cell batteries.
- describe wet-cell batteries.
- explain the difference between direct current and alternating current.

Electromotive force

The push that keeps the current (electrons) flowing in an electric circuit

Volt

The metric unit used to measure electromotive force that tells the amount of push

In order for current to move through a circuit, something has to "push" it. You might compare the flow of current to the flow of water through a hose. Something has to push the water through the hose. A water pump provides this push.

The push that keeps the current flowing in a circuit is called the **electromotive force.** Electromotive force is sometimes written as EMF. Electromotive force is measured in **volts.** A volt tells the amount of push. It also tells how much energy the electrons have. The energy that a power source gives to electrons in a circuit is called the **voltage.** When voltage is high, electrons have more energy available to do work.

Dry-Cell Batteries

Batteries are a common source of voltage. All batteries change chemical energy into electrical energy. One common type of battery is the **dry-cell battery.** This type of battery is called a dry cell because the materials inside the battery are somewhat dry or pastelike. Dry cells are used in flashlights, radios, and other small appliances. These batteries come in many sizes and shapes. D-size dry-cell batteries are used in flashlights and large radios. Smaller dry-cell batteries are used with devices that do not require much power.

Technology Note

Some batteries can be recharged. Rechargeable batteries work like regular batteries. But they can take electrical energy and store it as chemical energy for later use. Electrons flow in the opposite direction while the batteries are being recharged. The electrons keep flowing until a full charge is reached.

---

move randomly and chaotically at a speed of approximately 1,000 km/sec. The electrons do not move in one specific direction. When a power source is connected to the wire, electrons move in a single direction.

1 Warm-Up Activity

Provide several small flashlights without batteries for groups of students to examine. Then allow students to place the batteries inside a flashlight until they find the arrangement and action that cause the bulb to light. *(With the flashlight's switch turned on, the positive end of one battery must touch the bulb. The battery's negative end must touch the positive end of the second battery.)*

Batteries or other power sources do not supply electrons. The electrons in a circuit were there before the power source. Power sources move electrons that are already in the circuit. They cause electrons to flow.

The construction of most dry-cell batteries is similar to the one in the figure. Dry-cell batteries are not completely dry. They are made of a zinc container filled with black, moist manganese dioxide powder. In the center of the cell is a long rod made of carbon.

Each dry-cell battery has two **terminals,** or points, where electrons leave or enter the cell. Wires can be attached to the terminals to connect the cell to an electrical device. Larger batteries have both terminals on top.

Dry-Cell Battery

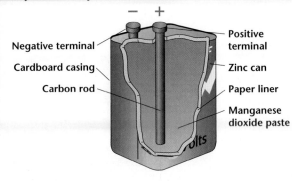

Negative terminal
Cardboard casing
Carbon rod
Positive terminal
Zinc can
Paper liner
Manganese dioxide paste

The center terminal is the positive terminal. It is attached to the carbon rod. The positive terminal is marked with a plus sign (+). The other terminal is the negative terminal. It is connected to the zinc container. The negative terminal is labeled with a minus sign (−). This terminal is negative because it has an excess of electrons. The "pressure" at the negative terminal "pumps" the electrons along the circuit to the positive terminal.

A smaller dry-cell battery has only one terminal on top. The top terminal is the positive terminal. The negative terminal is located on the bottom of the battery. You would use this kind of battery in an ordinary flashlight.

Ask students to read the feature on page 322. Explain to students that the bushmaster is a pit viper. Because the pit between its eyes and nostril senses heat, it helps the snake find prey. Scientists are uncertain about why the electric shock seems to neutralize the snake venom of the bushmaster.

Science Myth

Have one student read the myth portion (first sentence) and another read the fact portion of the Science Myth feature on page 322. If possible, display several of the batteries mentioned so students can compare their sizes.

SCIENCE INTEGRATION

Biology

Some fishes, such as the electric eel, discharge electricity. They use these discharges, between 350 and 650 volts, to sense objects under water and communicate with other eels as well as to stun prey. Encourage students to find out more about how these animals produce electricity and other facts about them, such as where they live. Some students may wish to draw a picture of an electric eel or other animal that generates electricity.

CROSS-CURRICULAR CONNECTION

Health

Ask students if they know how batteries can be used to help some parts of the body work as they should. If students offer no explanations, tell them that tiny battery-operated devices are used in some patients to help keep their hearts beating and in others to improve hearing. Interested students could research how these devices work and share their findings with the class.

Wet-cell battery
Electric power source with a liquid center

Did You Know?

The bite of the South American bushmaster snake is sometimes treated with electric shock. The snake bite victim receives a series of short shocks of about 20,000 volts. Sometimes car or outboard motors are used to deliver the voltage.

Wet-Cell Batteries

The lead storage battery that you find in most cars is an example of a wet-cell battery. A wet-cell battery is different from a dry-cell battery because it is an electric power source that is filled with a liquid. Look at the figure below. Most wet-cell batteries have a hard rubber case filled with a solution of sulfuric acid. Plates are placed inside the sulfuric acid. Often, these plates are made of lead or lead dioxide.

A chemical reaction between the acid and the plates causes a series of reactions. As the reactions happen, electrons flow from one plate to another. This produces an electric current.

Wet-Cell Battery

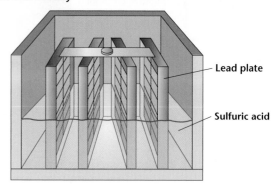

Lead plate

Sulfuric acid

Science Myth

A larger battery makes things run faster.

Fact: A battery's voltage determines how fast things run. A large battery does not necessarily have more voltage than a small battery. Nine-volt batteries are smaller than 1.5-volt D-cell batteries. A 12-volt car battery is much larger than a 9-volt battery. Yet the car battery's voltage is only slightly higher.

LEARNING STYLES

Interpersonal/ Group Learning

Explain that electric, or battery-operated, cars are one alternative to gasoline-powered cars. Pair up students and have them research the advantages and disadvantages of battery-powered cars. Then have them conclude whether these cars are a practical option for most Americans.

Direct and Alternating Current

The current in a wet-cell battery and a dry-cell battery flows in one direction. This type of current is called **direct current.** It sometimes is referred to as DC. The figure below on the left shows direct current. Notice that the arrow points one way. Direct current is not the most common kind of current.

The electricity in your home probably is **alternating current.** Alternating current is also called AC. The figure on the right shows alternating current. The arrow indicates that current moves in two directions. In alternating current, the flow of electrons changes direction regularly. Machines called generators produce alternating current. The generators that produce electricity for your home change the direction of the current about 60 times per second.

Direct current

Alternating current

LEARNING STYLES

Visual/Spatial

Instruct students to look back at the diagram that shows a closed circuit on page 311. Ask students if this diagram shows direct current or alternating current and why they think so. (*Direct current is shown because the electricity is flowing in one direction.*)

GLOBAL CONNECTION

Explain that electrical appliances used in the United States cannot be used in many places in Europe and other countries. Have students find out why and tell how to overcome this. (*The standard voltage in electrical outlets in other countries may be different. Also, while the current in the United States usually changes direction at 60 times per second, the current is different in many other countries. For example, the current in many European countries is 50 cycles per second. In addition, electrical outlets may have different configurations, for example requiring a cord with two round prongs. People who travel with dual-voltage appliances may purchase adapters so that their appliances will work in other countries.*)

SCIENCE JOURNAL

Have students write a description of a "tour through a wet- or dry-cell battery."

Lesson 3 Review Answers

1. Electromotive force is the push that keeps the current flowing in an electric circuit. 2. A water pump pushes water through a hose just as a battery pushes electrons along a wire. 3. A dry-cell battery changes chemical energy into electrical energy. 4. A wet-cell battery is filled with a liquid. A dry-cell battery contains a somewhat dry or pastelike material. 5. Direct current flows in one direction. Alternating current flows back and forth.

Achievements in Science

Have students take turns reading the Achievements in Science feature on page 324 aloud. Ask students to name several items besides those listed that work with transistors, such as calculators, battery-operated televisions, stereo speakers, microphones, and telephones. Point out that one author, Ira Flatow, called the transistor "probably the most important invention of the 20th century." Explain that the invention involved secrecy by Bell Laboratories, for whom the inventors worked, and some rivalry among the scientists themselves. Bell announced the invention excitedly in 1948, but few people, if any, immediately recognized its value. Interested students can find out more about the invention and uses of the transistor at www.PBS.org/transistor/.

Portfolio Assessment

Sample items include:
• Questions from Teaching the Lesson
• Lists of devices using AC and DC current from Teaching the Lesson
• Lesson 3 Review answers

Lesson 3 REVIEW

Write your answers to these questions in complete sentences on a sheet of paper.

1. What is electromotive force?

2. How is a battery like a water pump?

3. Explain how a dry-cell battery works.

4. How does a wet-cell battery differ from a dry-cell battery?

5. What is the difference between direct current and alternating current?

Achievements in Science

Transistor

John Bardeen, Walter H. Brattain, and William Shockley invented the transistor in 1947. All progress made in electronics since—from vacuum tubes to microprocessors—rests on that invention. Transistors control the flow of electric current in circuits. They switch current off and on and they strengthen current. Transistors are made of a semiconductor material that can conduct and insulate.

Before transistors, vacuum tubes were used in circuits. Vacuum tubes were large, used lots of energy, and created lots of heat. The first electronic computers had vacuum tubes. Transistors dramatically changed the electronics industry. Radios, computers, and hearing aids used to be big and bulky. Now they are quite small thanks to transistors. The first transistor was .5-inch high. Now millions of transistors in integrated circuits sit on silicon chips smaller than a dime.

In 1959, Jack Kilby and Robert Noyce patented the integrated circuit. An integrated circuit is a tiny chip of semiconductor material. Transistors and other electronic parts are built into it. The integrated circuit led to the development of the microprocessors that operate computers today.

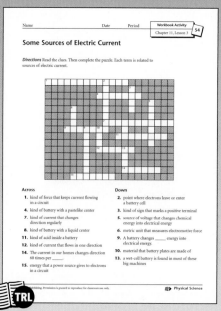

Workbook Activity 54

Lesson 4 — Ohm's Law

Objectives

After reading this lesson, you should be able to

◆ explain how current, voltage, and resistance are related.

◆ use Ohm's law to calculate current.

Ohm's law

Current equals voltage divided by resistance

In the early 1800s, Georg Ohm, a German schoolteacher, discovered that volts, amps, and ohms in an electrical circuit are all related to one another. To understand Ohm's idea, remember these things that you have learned about electricity:

◆ Power sources, such as batteries, provide the push (voltage) to the current in a circuit.

◆ The rate at which the current flows can be measured in amperes.

The flow of current can be slowed down by the resistance of the material through which the current flows. Resistance is measured in ohms.

Ohm put these relationships into a formula. This formula is known as **Ohm's law.**

$$\text{current (amperes)} = \frac{\text{electromotive force (volts)}}{\text{resistance (ohms)}}$$

The formula is more commonly written as:

$$I = \frac{V}{R}$$

Notice in the equation that the letter I is the symbol for current. The symbol for resistance is R. The law shows that as resistance increases, current tends to decrease. Using this equation, you can find the current of a circuit if you know the voltage and resistance.

Electricity Chapter 11 **325**

Lesson at a Glance

Chapter 11 Lesson 4

Overview In this lesson, students learn how current, voltage, and resistance are related and how to calculate current, using Ohm's law.

Objectives

■ To explain how current, voltage, and resistance are related

■ To use Ohm's law to calculate current

Student Pages 325–327

Teacher's Resource Library

Workbook Activity 55

Alternative Workbook Activity 55

....

Vocabulary

Ohm's law

....

 Warm-Up Activity

Show students the information panel on the back of at least two major electric appliances in the classroom, such as a television and a computer. Have students identify the amount of amperes listed on each appliance's panel.

 Teaching the Lesson

Ask students to write this lesson's title and objectives on paper. Tell them that as they read the lesson, they should write sentences that meet the objectives.

Have students recall from Chapter 4 that symbols are used to represent elements. Tell students that scientists use other symbols as well when they record information. Have students construct a table to record the symbol and unit for electromotive force, electric current, and resistance. *(electromotive force: V, volt; electric current: I, ampere; resistance: R, ohm)*

Explain to students that Ohm's law can help them find the electromotive force (EMF), the resistance, or the current in an electric circuit. Write on the board the formula that illustrates Ohm's law: $I = V \div R$.

Continued on page 326

Electricity Chapter 11 **325**

Continued from page 325

Tell students the formula can be adjusted to find resistance if they know EMF and current. Write this formula on the board: $R = V \div I$. Show how the original formula can be adjusted again to find EMF if current and resistance are known. ($V = R \times I$) Have students write the three formulas on paper. Then assign these numerical values to the symbols: I = 6, V = 12, and R = 2. Have students use the numbers appropriately in each of the formulas. *(I = V $\div$ R, 6 = 12 $\div$ 2; R = V $\div$ I, 2 = 12 $\div$ 6; V = R $\times$ I, 12 = 2 $\times$ 6)*

3 Reinforce and Extend

LEARNING STYLES

Visual/Spatial

Demonstrate resistance by setting up a circuit containing a lightbulb. You can use the closed-circuit setup pictured on page 311 as a guide. Show how the bulb's brightness changes as you use wires of different lengths or thicknesses.

CROSS-CURRICULAR CONNECTION

Social Studies

Have students research the backgrounds of Alessandro Volta and George S. Ohm, the scientists in whose honor the *volt* and *ohm* were named. Have students report important facts about each scientist. *(For example: In the late 18th century, Alessandro Volta, an Italian physicist, produced the first steady flow of electric current. During the early 19th century, German physicist George S. Ohm studied voltage, current, and resistance.)*

The diagram on this page shows an electric circuit. It has a 1.5-volt dry-cell battery and a lamp, or bulb. A lamp is a resistor. How much current is in the circuit?

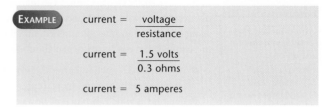

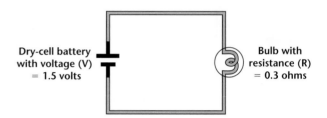

Notice that when you divide volts by ohms, your answer is in amperes.

Dry-cell battery with voltage (V) = 1.5 volts

Bulb with resistance (R) = 0.3 ohms

LEARNING STYLES

Logical/Mathematical

Students can write an original word problem about finding out how much electric current an appliance uses. Then they can exchange problems with a partner to find the answers. (Sample problem: A washing machine uses 120 volts and has 30 ohms of resistance. How much electric current does it use? 120 ÷ 30 = 40 amperes)

Lesson 4   R E V I E W

Copy the table on a sheet of paper. Then write the answers in your table.

Find the current in amperes for each circuit in the table. The first one is done for you.

	Voltage (volts)	Resistance (ohms)	Current (amperes)	$\frac{V}{R}$
1.	10	5	$\frac{10\ volts}{5\ ohms} = 2$ amperes	
2.	15	5		
3.	50	5		
4.	35	10		
5.	1.5	10		

Technology Note

Hybrid electric vehicles (HEVs) combine a gasoline-powered engine and a battery-powered electric motor. These high-tech cars switch to electric power when less power is needed. Sometimes, when more power is needed, they use energy from electricity and the engine together. An HEV's computer decides which type of energy to use and when.

Electricity   Chapter 11   **327**

Lesson 4 Review Answers

1. 10 volts/5 ohms = 2 amperes **2.** 15 volts/5 ohms = 3 amperes **3.** 50 volts/5 ohms = 10 amperes **4.** 35 volts/10 ohms = 3.5 amperes **5.** 1.5 amperes

Portfolio Assessment

Sample items include:
- Lesson title, objectives, and sentences from Teaching the Lesson
- Formulas based on Ohm's law from Teaching the Lesson
- Lesson 4 Review answers

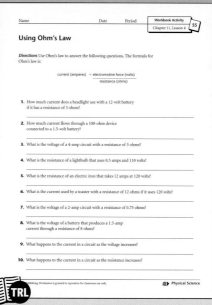

Workbook Activity 55

Lesson at a Glance

Chapter 5 Lesson 11

Overview In this lesson, students explore series circuits. Students learn how adding electrical devices or batteries to a series circuit affects its voltage, and the advantages of using fuses and circuit breakers.

Objectives

- To describe a series circuit
- To explain how adding electrical devices or batteries to a series circuit affects the voltage of the circuit
- To explain the advantage of using fuses and circuit breakers

Student Pages 328–334

Teacher's Resource Library

Workbook Activity 56

Alternative Workbook Activity 56

Lab Manual 43

Vocabulary

series circuit

1 Warm-Up Activity

Obtain a string of decorative lights that are wired in series. *(If one light goes out, all the lights go out.)* Replace one light with a burned-out bulb. Give students a replacement bulb and have them use it to find the burned-out bulb.

2 Teaching the Lesson

Explain to students that when they finish reading the lesson, they should make a drawing that explains part or all of the lesson's information to another person.

Have someone from the school's maintenance staff show students the location of the circuit-breaker box or fuse box in your school. Allow students to observe the switches or fuses but do not allow students to touch them.

Provide fuses for students to observe. If possible, some fuses should be burned out and some new. Students can use a hand lens to observe the metal piece inside each fuse.

Objectives

After reading this lesson, you should be able to

- ◆ describe a series circuit.
- ◆ explain how adding electrical devices or batteries to a series circuit affects the voltage of the circuit.
- ◆ explain the advantage of using fuses and circuit breakers.

Series circuit

A circuit in which all current (electrons) flows through a single path

Have you ever had a string of decorative lights? You might know that with some strings of lights, if one light burns out, all the remaining lights stay lit. But in other strings, all the lights will go out if one burns out. Then you have to change each bulb on the string until you find the one that is burned out. Why do these strings of lights act differently? The answer is in the way the circuit is made.

Devices in Series Circuits

Look at the circuit in the diagram. It includes a source of energy, such as a battery, and wire to carry the current. It also has different electrical devices attached to it. This kind of circuit is called a **series circuit.** In a series circuit, current (electrons) flows through only one path around the circuit.

Series Circuit

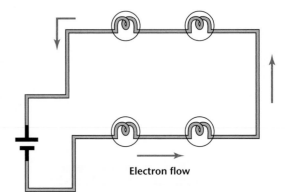

Electron flow

You can see in the circuit on page 328 that all the electrons must pass through each electrical device. In the example of the decorative lights, each light is a separate device. The electrons must pass through each lightbulb.

Series circuits have a disadvantage. If one light is unscrewed or burns out, all of the other lights will go out. That is because the circuit becomes open, and electrons cannot flow.

When electrical devices are connected in series, the current is the same throughout the circuit. That means that adding electrical devices to the series lowers the voltage through each device. Notice in the diagram below that if only one bulb is connected to a dry cell, the bulb may shine brightly. If another bulb is added in series, each of the bulbs will be dimmer than the single bulb was.

Series Circuits

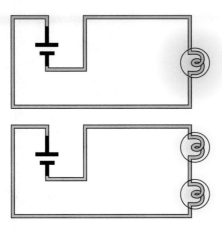

TEACHER ALERT

Many students think that bulbs, batteries, and switches are the only items that are in series circuits. Series circuits can have many other kinds of electric items in them. Have students look at the items in the series circuit shown on page 330. Point out to students that the circuit could have a bell and a motor in addition to the bulb, batteries, and switch.

LEARNING STYLES

LEP/ESL

Demonstrate a fuse. Use copper bell wire to connect three dry-cell batteries, a small lightbulb and socket, and a switch. Place two nails in a cork, about 1.25 cm apart. Cut the wire between the switch and dry cell and wrap each end around a nail. (First remove some insulation at the end of the wires.) Put a small piece of thin wire (thinner than the bell wire) between the nails and touching the copper wire. Close the switch. The thin wire will melt and the light will go out. Explain that too much heat in the circuit melted the wire and the circuit broke.

CROSS-CURRICULAR CONNECTION

 Art

Students could draw Rube Goldberg-like series circuits with many items in them. Encourage students to be as inventive as possible, but remind them that all the items in their series must operate on electric power. Post the ridiculous circuits for the class to enjoy.

Batteries in Series Circuits

Batteries in a circuit can be connected in series, too. Batteries in series increase the voltage of the circuit. To find the total voltage, add the voltages of the cells together.

In the figure of the circuit shown below, the batteries are in series. A wire connects a positive terminal to a negative terminal. A second wire connects the lamp and switch to the batteries. When batteries are connected in series, they can deliver more energy in the same amount of time. Bulbs in this kind of circuit burn brighter because the voltage is higher.

Cells in Series

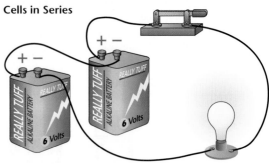

6 volts + 6 volts = 12 volts
Total voltage = 12 volts

In a flashlight, dry-cell batteries are usually connected in series. You can see in the figure below how the positive terminal of one battery touches the negative terminal (the bottom metal plate) of the next battery.

1.5 volts + 1.5 volts = 3 volts

Fuses and Circuit Breakers

Connecting electrical devices in series can be inconvenient. But there are practical uses for series circuits, too. For example, your home is probably protected by fuses or circuit breakers. Fuses and circuit breakers help prevent fires.

Look at the fuse in the drawing. Notice the piece of metal on the top of the fuse. It is designed to melt at a certain temperature. When the wires get too hot, the fuse will melt and break the circuit. When a fuse melts, it must be replaced. A circuit breaker, on the other hand, is a switchlike device that can be reset after the circuit has been repaired.

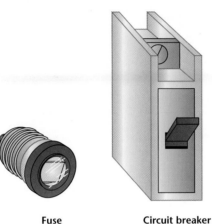

Fuse   **Circuit breaker**

Lesson 5 Review Answers

1. A series circuit is a circuit in which there is only one path for current. **2.** In a series circuit, electrons only have to flow through one path around the circuit. **3.** The bulb becomes dimmer. **4.** The voltage is increased. **5.** A fuse and a circuit breaker are both connected in a series. They both break a circuit if current becomes too high. A fuse melts and must be replaced, but a circuit breaker can be reset.

Portfolio Assessment

Sample items include:
• Drawing of lesson information from Teaching the Lesson
• Lesson 5 Review answers

Write your answers to these questions in complete sentences on a sheet of paper.

1. What is a series circuit?

2. What is one advantage of a series circuit?

3. What happens to the brightness of a bulb when more bulbs are added to the same series circuit?

4. When two cells with the same voltage are connected in series, what happens to the voltage?

5. Compare a fuse and a circuit breaker.

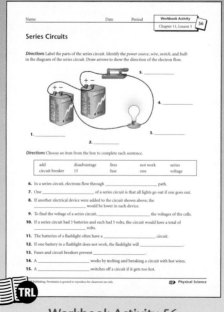

Workbook Activity 56

Constructing Series Circuits

Investigation 11-1

The Purpose portion of the student investigation begins with a question to draw them into the activity. Encourage students to read the investigation steps and formulate their own questions before beginning the investigation. This investigation will take approximately 20 minutes to complete. Students will use these process and thinking skills: identifying and controlling variables; collecting, recording, and interpreting data; predicting; recalling facts; comparing and contrasting; and explaining ideas.

Materials

- safety glasses
- two 1.5-volt dry-cell batteries
- 2 holders for batteries
- 2 flashlight bulbs
- 2 bulb sockets
- 1.5 m-long piece of common bell wire, cut into various lengths
- switch
- 1–3 additional 1.5-volt dry-cell batteries
- 1–3 additional flashlight bulbs

Purpose

How would you create a series circuit? In this investigation, you will construct and study a series circuit.

Procedure

1. Copy the data table on a sheet of paper.

Circuit	Schematic Diagram	Prediction	Observations
A			
B			
C			

2. Put on your safety glasses.

3. Draw each of the schematic diagrams shown below in the correct space in the data table. Then label each item in each diagram.

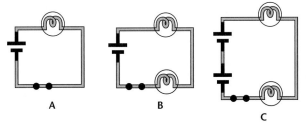

A   B   C

Electricity Chapter 11 **333**

SAFETY ALERT

- Remind students to keep their safety glasses on throughout the investigation.
- Tell students to make certain their hands are dry before working with circuits to prevent any electric shocks.
- Tell students to handle the sharp ends of the wires carefully to prevent any puncture injuries.

Preparation

- Prepare each group's allotment of bell wire by dividing it into seven lengths to be used in constructing the circuits.
- Remove the insulation from the ends of the wires. You can do this with sandpaper or scissors.
- Check batteries and bulbs before doing the activity. Provide extras in case any batteries or bulbs burn out.
- Students may use Lab Manual 43 to record their data and answer the questions.

Procedure

- This investigation is best done with students working in groups of three. Assign one student to gather equipment. All students make predictions, observe and record results, and put equipment away when finished. Student A constructs and does operations for circuit A. Student B constructs and does operations for circuit B. Student C constructs and does operations for circuit C.
- Review with students the symbols used in schematic diagrams. Suggest that they review the symbols shown on page 313. Be sure students understand the schematic diagrams in step 3 of the procedure.
- Show students how to wrap the exposed ends of the wire around the posts of the sockets, cell holders, and switches.
- If necessary, help students progress from the diagrams to the actual circuits.

Continued on page 334

Continued from page 333

- Remind students to reserve the closing of the switch for the last step in each circuit construction.

- If students' bulbs do not light when the circuit is closed, remind them to make sure that all the connections in their circuit are tight.

Results

Students should observe that brightness decreases as the number of bulbs in a series circuit increases. Students should also notice that brightness increases when the number of batteries in a series circuit increases.

Questions and Conclusions Answers

1. A dry cell, wire, bulb, and switch make up circuit A. It's a series circuit.

2. A dry cell, wire, 2 bulbs, and switch make up circuit B. It's a series circuit.

3. The bulbs in B were dimmer than in A because there were two devices using energy in a circuit with only one path for current.

4. The other bulb went out because the circuit was broken.

5. The bulbs in C shined more brightly than in B because there were two power sources in series and, therefore, voltage was doubled.

Explore Further Answers

Students should find that if they add more bulbs to the circuit, the bulbs will shine less brightly. If they add more batteries, the bulbs will shine more brightly.

Assessment

Check students' data tables to be sure they have copied the schematic diagrams correctly. Also, check that the data tables show the correct observations. You might include the following items from this investigation in student portfolios:

- Investigation 11-1 data table

- Answer to Questions and Conclusions and Explore Further sections

4. Use the materials to construct circuit A. What do you think will happen to the bulb when you close the switch? Write your prediction in the data table. Close the switch. Record how brightly the bulb shines.

5. Take apart circuit A. Construct circuit B. Predict how brightly the bulbs will shine compared to the single bulb in circuit A. Record your prediction. Close the switch. Record your observations.

6. Unscrew one of the bulbs and record what you observe.

7. Construct circuit C. Predict how brightly the bulbs will shine compared to the bulbs in circuit B. Close the switch. Record your observations.

Questions and Conclusions

1. What items make up circuit A? What kind of circuit is it?

2. What items make up circuit B? What kind of circuit is it?

3. How brightly did the bulbs in circuit B shine compared to the bulb in circuit A? Explain your answer.

4. What happened in circuit B when one of the bulbs was unscrewed? Why did that happen?

5. How brightly did the bulbs in circuit C shine compared to the bulbs in circuit B? Explain your answer.

Explore Further

What do you think would happen if you added more bulbs or more batteries to your circuit? Write your prediction on a sheet of paper. Then construct a circuit and find out. Record your observations.

334 *Chapter 11 Electricity*

Lab Manual 43, pages 1–2

The lights and appliances in your home are not wired in a series circuit. If they were, every time a bulb burned out, none of the other lights and appliances would work. Instead, most circuits in houses are **parallel circuits.** In a parallel circuit, there is more than one path for the current to follow.

Devices in Parallel Circuits

Look at the following diagram of two lamps connected in parallel. As you can see, there are two paths around this circuit. If one bulb burned out, the other bulb would stay lit. That is because there is more than one path for the electrons.

Parallel Circuit

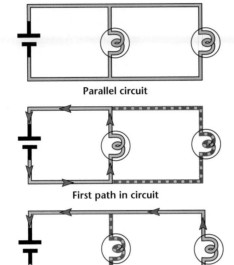

Parallel circuit

First path in circuit

Second path in circuit

Objectives

After reading this lesson, you should be able to

◆ describe a parallel circuit.

◆ explain what happens to the brightness of bulbs in a parallel circuit when more bulbs are included.

◆ explain what happens to voltage when two batteries with the same voltage are connected in parallel.

Parallel circuit

A circuit in which there is more than one path for current

Lesson at a Glance

Chapter 11 Lesson 6

Overview In this lesson, students explore parallel circuits. Students learn how including more bulbs in a parallel circuit affects the brightness of bulbs and how voltage is affected when two batteries with the same voltage are connected in parallel.

Objectives

■ To describe a parallel circuit

■ To explain what happens to the brightness of bulbs in a parallel circuit when more bulbs are included

■ To explain what happens to voltage when two batteries with the same voltage are connected in parallel

Student Pages 335–339

Teacher's Resource Library

Workbook Activity 57

Alternative Workbook Activity 57

Lab Manual 44

Resource File 23

Vocabulary

parallel circuit

---

1 Warm-Up Activity

Draw the same building on the board twice. Draw a single route to one building. Draw at least two routes to the other building. Then draw a series of *Xs* on each route to symbolize a traffic jam. Discuss with students which route they would be able to use to get to each building. Help students see that for the building with several routes, when one route is blocked, another can be used.

2 Teaching the Lesson

Have students write each subhead they find in this lesson on their paper followed by a statement about what they think they will learn in each section, based on the subhead. Then have them turn the statement into a question.

Continued on page 336

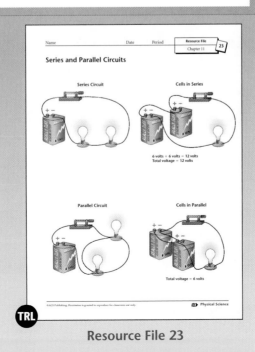

Resource File 23

Continued from page 335

For example, "Devices in Parallel Circuits" might suggest the question, What devices do parallel circuits have? Have students write the answer to each question as they come to it in their reading.

Review the definition of *parallel* with students. *("straight lines extending alongside one another, always equidistant")* Ask a volunteer to draw parallel lines on the board. Have students identify objects in their environment that are made with parallel lines. *(curbs of roads, railroad tracks, power lines, and so on)*

Be sure that students understand that in a parallel circuit, electrons have a choice of paths. Point out that more current will flow through the paths with lower resistances.

3 Reinforce and Extend

LEARNING STYLES

LEP/ESL

Draw a schematic diagram of a series circuit on the board. Use the diagram with two bulbs on page 329 for an example. Use an eraser to break the line between the two bulbs. Ask students if the bulbs will light up and why they think so. *(No, the flow of electrons along the circuit was stopped.)* Now draw a schematic diagram of a parallel circuit. Use the top diagram on page 335 for an example. Then erase part of a line leading directly to the outer bulb. Ask students to explain how the bulbs will be affected. *(The outer bulb will not light up because the flow of electrons to it was stopped; the other bulb will not be affected.)*

SCIENCE JOURNAL

Have students list some science concepts they might need to know to work as an electrician.

When we connect several bulbs in parallel, all the bulbs will remain as bright as just one bulb alone would. However, more current must be drawn from the battery to power the extra bulbs.

When more electrical devices are added to the same circuit, more current runs through the circuit. As current in a circuit increases, wires begin to heat up. If they get too hot, the wires can start a fire in the walls. The fuses you read about in Lesson 5 help prevent this problem.

Batteries in Parallel Circuits

Batteries can be connected in parallel. A parallel connection between batteries allows them to keep providing energy longer. A parallel connection does not increase the voltage.

Look at the figures below. Figure A shows a circuit with only one 6-volt battery. The circuit in Figure B has two 6-volt batteries connected in parallel. The bulb in the circuit will stay lit longer. However, it will not burn brighter than the other bulb. The total voltage is still only 6 volts. The voltage is the same for both circuits in the figure. The two bulbs burn equally bright.

Cells in Parallel

Figure A
Total voltage = 6 volts

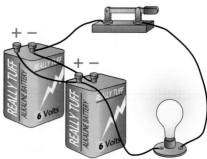

Figure B
Total voltage = 6 volts

CROSS-CURRICULAR CONNECTION

Language Arts
Students can write one or two paragraphs explaining the advantage of using parallel circuits in a home. *(Explanations might include the idea that if homes were not wired in parallel, you would have to turn all lights and appliances on in order for any of them to work. Parallel circuits allow you to use only the lights and appliances needed.)*

Lesson 6   R E V I E W

Write your answers to these questions in complete sentences.

1. How can you recognize a parallel circuit? What happens to the bulbs in a parallel circuit when one bulb burns out?

2. Determine the number of paths in each of these parallel circuits.

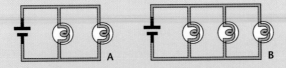

3. What happens to the brightness of bulbs in a parallel circuit when one bulb is added?

4. When two batteries with the same voltage are connected in parallel, what happens to the voltage?

5. Identify each of these circuits as either a parallel or series circuit.

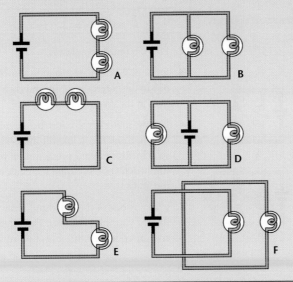

Lesson 6 Review Answers

1. A parallel circuit has more than one path for current. When the bulb burns out, the others will continue to shine. **2A** 2 **B** 3 **3.** The brightness remains the same. **4.** The voltage remains the same. **5A** series **B** parallel **C** series **D** parallel **E** series **F** parallel

Portfolio Assessment

Sample items include:
• Questions and answers from Teaching the Lesson
• Lesson 6 Review answers

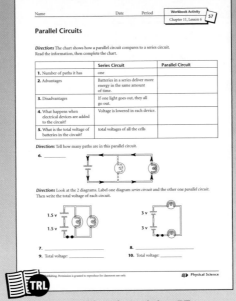

Workbook Activity 57

Investigation 11-2

The Purpose portion of the student investigation begins with a question to draw them into the activity. Encourage students to read the investigation steps and formulate their own questions before beginning the investigation. This investigation will take approximately 30 minutes to complete. Students will use these process and thinking skills: identifying and controlling variables; collecting, recording, and interpreting data; predicting; recalling facts; explaining ideas; and comparing and contrasting.

Preparation

- Prepare each group's allotment of bell wire by dividing it into nine lengths to be used in constructing the circuits.

- Remove the insulation from the ends of the wires. You can do this with sandpaper or scissors.

- Check batteries and bulbs before doing the activity. Provide extras in case any batteries or bulbs burn out.

- Students may use Lab Manual 44 to record their data and answer the questions.

Procedure

- Have students work in groups of five. Assign one student to gather equipment. All students make predictions, observe and record results, and put equipment away when finished. Student A constructs and does operations for circuit A. Student B constructs and does operations for circuit B. Student C constructs and does operations for circuit C. Student D constructs and does operations for circuit D. Student E constructs and does operations for circuit E.

- Review the symbols used in schematic diagrams with students. Suggest that they review the symbols shown on page 313.

- Show students how to wrap the exposed ends of the wire around the posts of the sockets, cell holders, and switches.

- If necessary, help students to interpret the schematic diagrams and to construct the circuits.

- Remind students to reserve the closing of the switch for the last step in each circuit construction.

11-2 INVESTIGATION

Materials

- safety glasses
- two 6-volt dry-cell batteries
- 2 holders for batteries
- 3 flashlight bulbs
- 3 bulb sockets
- 1.5 m-long piece of common bell wire, cut into various lengths
- switch

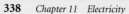

A

B

Constructing Parallel Circuits

Purpose

How do you know a circuit is a parallel circuit? In the investigation, you will construct and study parallel circuits.

Procedure

1. Copy the data table on a sheet of paper.

Circuit	Schematic Diagram	Prediction	Observations
A			
B			
C			
D			
E			

2. Put on your safety glasses.

3. Draw each schematic diagram shown here and on page 339 in the correct space in your data table. Label each item in the diagram.

4. Use the materials to construct circuit A. How brightly do you think the bulbs will shine when you close the switch? Record your prediction in your table. Close the switch and note what happens. Notice how brightly the bulbs shine.

5. Unscrew one of the bulbs and observe what happens. Record your observations. Then tighten the bulb again and unscrew the other one. Record your observations.

SAFETY ALERT

- Remind students to keep their safety glasses on throughout the investigation.
- Tell students to make certain their hands are dry before working with circuits to prevent any electric shocks.
- Tell students to handle the sharp ends of the wires carefully to prevent any puncture injuries.

C

D

E

6. Take apart circuit A. Construct circuit B. Predict how brightly the bulbs will shine compared to the bulbs in circuit A. Close the switch. Record your observations. Then unscrew different combinations of bulbs. Record your observations.

7. Construct circuit C, and close the switch. Try loosening various combinations of bulbs. Record your observations.

8. Construct circuit D. Predict how brightly the bulbs will shine compared to the bulbs in circuit A. Close the switch. Record your observations.

9. Construct circuit E. Predict how brightly the bulbs will shine compared to the bulbs in circuit D. Close the switch. Record your observations.

Questions and Conclusions

1. What items make up circuit C? What kind of circuit is it?

2. Are the cells in circuit E connected in series or in parallel?

3. How brightly did the bulbs in circuit B shine compared to the bulbs in circuit A? Why?

4. What happened in circuit C when various bulbs were unscrewed?

5. How brightly did the bulbs in circuit D shine compared to the bulbs in circuit A? Why?

6. How brightly did the bulbs in circuit E shine compared to the bulbs in circuit D? Why?

Explore Further

Which circuit—C or D—will stay lit longer? Which uses less power?

- If students' bulbs do not light when the circuit is closed, remind them to make sure that all the connections in their circuit are tight.

Results

Students should observe that electricity must have a complete circuit if it is to be used and that more than one battery connected in series will give more power than a single battery.

Questions and Conclusions Answers

1. A dry cell, wire, 3 bulbs, and switch make up circuit C. It is partly parallel, partly series circuit.

2. The cells are connected in parallel.

3. They shined equally brightly in circuit B because the parallel paths allowed the same amount of electricity to flow through each bulb in B as in A.

4. The bulb that was alone on one path shined even when one or both of the other bulbs were unscrewed because it was on a separate current path. If one of the two bulbs in series was unscrewed, the other bulb in series went out because that branch of the circuit was broken and both bulbs were on the same current path.

5. They shined equally brightly in D as in A because there were two power sources in series and, therefore, voltage was doubled.

6. They shined less brightly in E than in D because the parallel cell connection did not increase the voltage.

Explore Further Answer

Circuit D will stay lit longer because it has fewer bulbs and twice the power. Circuit C uses less power.

Assessment

Check students' data tables to be sure they have copied the schematic diagrams correctly. Also check that the recorded observations are correct. You might include the following items from this investigation in student portfolios:

- Investigation 11-2 data table
- Answers to Questions and Conclusions and Explore Further sections

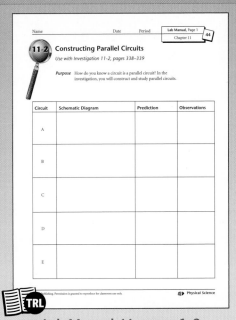

Lab Manual 44, pages 1–2

Lesson at a Glance

Chapter 11 Lesson 7

Overview In this lesson, students learn how to describe electric power and how electric power is measured.

Objectives

- To explain what electric power is
- To explain how electric power is measured

Student Pages 340–342

Teacher's Resource Library

Workbook Activity 58

Alternative Workbook Activity 58

Vocabulary

electric power
kilowatt-hour

 Warm-Up Activity

Provide a selection of lightbulbs of different sizes and shapes for students to observe. Carefully secure the necks of the bulbs to a table or desktop with masking tape. Allow students to use magnifying lenses to look at the labels on top of the lightbulbs. Have students identify the information contained in the labels. *(manufacturer, watts, and volts)*

 Teaching the Lesson

Before beginning this lesson, ask students to write each vocabulary term and its definition. Then for each term have students tell why they might like to have more information about the term.

Have a member of the school's maintenance staff show students the school's electric meter. Help students determine the reading on the meter. *(A meter has five dials. The dials, like numbers, are arranged by place value. For example, the reading might be 42,762 kwh.)*

Explain that the dials on an electric meter are read on the same day every month. Then the current month's reading is subtracted from the reading of the previous month to determine the amount of kilowatt-hours used. This amount is multiplied by the amount of money the electric company charges for each

---

Objectives

After reading this lesson, you should be able to

- explain what electric power is.
- explain how electric power is measured.

Electric power

The amount of electrical energy used in a certain amount of time

Kilowatt-hour

A unit to measure how much electric energy is used; it is 1,000 watts used in one hour

Your home has many electrical devices. Every time you turn one of them on, you use electricity. How can you measure how much electricity you use?

Electric Power

Look at the lightbulb in the photo. Notice that the top of the bulb has 100 W stamped on it. The W stands for watt. It was named for James Watt, one of the inventors of the steam engine. You may recall from Chapter 8 that the watt is the unit we use to measure power, including **electric power.** Electric power is the amount of electrical energy used in a certain amount of time. This lightbulb uses 100 watts. It uses four times as much energy each second as a 25-watt bulb.

Using Electricity

When you pay your electric bill, you are paying for the amount of electricity you use. The electric company measures the amount of electricity you use in **kilowatt-hours.** A kilowatt-hour is 1,000 watts used in one hour. A meter measures the number of kilowatt-hours you use.

The 100 W on this bulb tells how much power it uses.

Science in Your Life

How can you check your home's electrical safety?

Electricity is helpful but it also can be harmful. Knowing how electricity works can help avoid electrical shock or electrocution. Electric current flows naturally to the ground through anything that will conduct it. Electric current can flow through your body if your body is touching the ground. Grounding circuits is an important safety practice. It lets electric current take another path if an electric device is not working correctly.

The plugs of many electric devices have a third prong. The third prong lets current flow to the ground if the device is not working correctly. Some outlets have a ground-fault circuit interrupter (GFCI). Sensors in GFCI outlets quickly detect tiny changes in current flow. They protect you if you accidentally come in contact with water and an ungrounded appliance. Surge protectors help protect electronic equipment from damage.

Use this checklist to check the electrical safety of your home. Be sure a parent or guardian knows that you are checking the items listed in the checklist. Check off things that are safe and unsafe. If anything is in an unsafe condition, tell a parent or guardian.

Electrical Items	Safe	Unsafe
Check that outlets and extension cords are not overloaded.		
Make sure electric cords are not frayed or cracked.		
Check that lightbulbs are the correct wattage for fixtures.		
Check that lightbulbs fit tightly in the fixtures.		
Make sure plugs fit the outlets into which they are plugged.		
Make sure no third prongs have been removed from plugs to fit an outlet.		
Make sure halogen floor lamps and space heaters are positioned away from materials that can catch fire.		
Make sure all plugged-in appliances are placed away from water.		

Electricity   Chapter 11   **341**

In the Environment

Discuss the importance to the environment of power conservation. Explain that most power plants that provide home electricity burn fossil fuels. This causes concerns about using up nonrenewable resources and polluting the environment. Explain that some electrical appliances we use require large amounts of power, but that many appliance manufacturers have reduced these amounts. They have also begun giving consumers more information on appliances' power usage. Have students research the amounts of power common appliances need and find out which ones use especially large amounts of electricity *(for example, dishwashers, ovens, and clothes dryers)*. Have them discuss ways these appliances can be used more efficiently.

kilowatt-hour. Write the following equation on the board to show students an example of the data contained on an electric bill. 17,512 kwh (current reading) − 17,908 kwh (previous reading) = 414 kwh (consumption). 414 × \$.07 (per kwh) = \$28.98. You might like to provide an electric bill for students to examine. You might be able to get one from the school's office or from volunteers who are willing to bring one from home.

 Reinforce and Extend

IN THE COMMUNITY

Have students find out from the local electric company the rate charged per kilowatt-hour. With students, record the reading on the school's electric meter for two consecutive days. Then calculate the cost of the school's electric usage for one day. *(current day's reading − previous day's reading × rate/kwh = cost)*

Science in Your Life

Have volunteers take turns reading the Science in Your Life feature on page 341. Then discuss each safety item, having students explain why each one can be unsafe. Have students mention other electrical safety measures, such as putting plastic prongs into unused plugs in houses with small children.

CROSS-CURRICULAR CONNECTION

Math
Tell students the amount of kilowatts some appliances use per hour. *(television: 0.14; computer: 0.12; microwave oven: 1.35)* For each appliance, have students multiply to find the amount of kilowatt-hours for two, four, and six hours of usage. *(television: 0.28, 0.56, 0.85; computer: 0.24, 0.48, 0.72; microwave: 2.7, 5.4, 8.1)* Then have students determine the cost of running each appliance for six hours by multiplying this amount by the local rate charged per kilowatt-hour.

Electricity   Chapter 11   **341**

Lesson 7 Review Answers

1. The 25 W stamped on the lightbulb means it uses 25 watts each second. 2. A 75-watt bulb uses more energy. 3. A kilowatt-hour is a unit to measure how much electric energy is used. It is 1,000 watts used in one hour. 4. It is used to measure the amount of electricity used in one hour. 5. Electric power describes the amount of electrical energy used in a certain amount of time.

Science Myth

Have one student read the myth portion and another student the fact portion of the feature on page 342. Have students mention some items that use batteries, such as portable radios or CD players. Then have them tell how much the batteries for one of the items cost and estimate how many hours the batteries last. Finally, have them figure out how much it costs per hour to use this battery-operated item.

ONLINE CONNECTION

 To review what they have learned about electricity, find projects and experiments, and learn more about energy conservation, students might visit the California Energy Commission Web site at www.energyquest.ca.gov/index.html.

Portfolio Assessment

Sample items include:
• Questions and answers from Teaching the Lesson
• Checklist from Science in Your Life
• Lesson 7 Review answers

Lesson 7 R E V I E W

Write your answers to these questions in complete sentences on a sheet of paper.

1. A lightbulb has 25 W stamped on it. What does this mean?

2. Which would use more energy, a 50-watt bulb or a 75-watt bulb of the same kind?

3. What is a kilowatt-hour?

4. How is a kilowatt-hour used?

5. What term describes the amount of electrical energy used in a certain amount of time?

Science Myth

Batteries are an inexpensive source of energy.

Fact: The cost per kilowatt-hour of batteries is far higher than the cost per kilowatt-hour of household electricity. A large D-cell battery can cost 2,700 times more than your home electricity. Smaller batteries, like those in watches and cameras, can cost 10,000 to 100,000 times more. People use batteries because they are convenient.

Name _____ Date _____ Period _____

Workbook Activity
58
Chapter 11, Lesson 7

Electricity: Terms Review

Directions Match the terms in Column A with the meanings in Column B. Write the letter of the answer on the line.

Column A		Column B
____ 1.	open circuit	**A** a type of circuit having more than one path for current
____ 2.	dry-cell battery	**B** a type of electricity that flows in only one direction
____ 3.	direct current	**C** electric power source with a liquid center
____ 4.	series circuit	**D** an unbroken path for electric current
____ 5.	closed circuit	**E** amount of electrical energy used in a certain amount of time
____ 6.	wet-cell battery	**F** a type of circuit having only one path for current
____ 7.	parallel circuit	**G** electric power source with a pastelike center
____ 8.	circuit	**H** a type of electricity that continuously changes direction
____ 9.	alternating current	**I** an incomplete path for electric current
____ 10.	electric power	**J** a path for electric current
____ 11.	schematic diagram	**K** current = voltage ÷ resistance
____ 12.	electricity	**M** buildup of electrical charge
____ 13.	Ohm's law	**N** an illustration that uses symbols to show the parts of a circuit
____ 14.	electromotive force	**P** movement of electrons from one place to another
____ 15.	electric current	**Q** flow of electrons
____ 16.	static electricity	**S** push that keeps current flowing in an electric circuit

Directions Unscramble the word or words in parentheses to complete each sentence.

17. A(n) _____ is a very poor conductor. (salurtion)

18. The _____ of a battery is where electrons enter or leave. (rainmelt)

19. A(n) _____ is a device that changes chemical energy into electrical energy. (treabty)

20. Electricity passes easily through a(n) _____. (trunccodo)

Publishing. Permission is granted to reproduce for classroom use only.   **Physical Science**

Workbook Activity 58

Chapter 11 SUMMARY

- Electricity is the flow of electrons.

- Static electricity is a buildup of electric charge.

- Current, the rate of flow of electricity, is measured in amperes.

- A closed circuit is a complete, unbroken path for current. An open circuit is an incomplete or broken path for current.

- A schematic diagram uses symbols to show the parts of a circuit.

- A conductor is a material through which a current can easily pass. An insulator is a material through which a current cannot easily pass.

- Resistance is a measure of how easily electric current will flow through a material. It is measured in ohms.

- Fuses and circuit breakers prevent electrical wires from getting too hot or causing fires.

- Electromotive force is the force that keeps current flowing. It is measured in volts.

- Batteries are a common source of voltage. Two types of batteries are dry cells and wet cells.

- Two types of current are direct current and alternating current. Direct current flows in one direction. Alternating current changes direction regularly.

- According to Ohm's law, current equals voltage divided by resistance.

- In a series circuit, all current flows through a single path. In a parallel circuit, current flows in more than one path.

- Power is the rate at which work is done. It is measured in watts.

Science Words

alternating current, 323	electric power, 340	resistance, 316
ampere, 311	electricity, 310	schematic diagram, 313
battery, 321	electromotive force, 320	series circuit, 328
circuit, 311	insulator, 315	static electricity, 310
closed circuit, 311	kilowatt-hour, 340	terminal, 321
conductor, 315	ohm, 316	volt, 320
direct current, 323	Ohm's law, 325	voltage, 321
dry-cell battery, 321	open circuit, 312	wet-cell battery, 322
electric current, 311	parallel circuit, 335	

Chapter 11 Summary

Have volunteers read aloud each Summary item on page 343. Ask volunteers to explain the meaning of each item. Direct students' attention to the Science Words box on the bottom of page 343. Have them read and review each term and its definition.

Chapter 11 Review

Use the Chapter Review to prepare students for tests and to reteach content from the chapter.

Chapter 11 Mastery Test

The Teacher's Resource Library includes two parallel forms of the Chapter 11 Mastery Test. The difficulty level of the two forms is equivalent. You may wish to use one form as a pretest and the other form as a posttest.

Review Answers
Vocabulary Review

1. kilowatt-hour 2. volt 3. terminal 4. ampere 5. ohm

Concept Review

6. D 7. B 8. C 9. B 10. A 11. A 12. B

TEACHER ALERT

Because of limited space in this Chapter Review, not all of the vocabulary terms introduced in this chapter appear in the Vocabulary Review section. You may want to create an activity using the missing words to give students practice with all of the terms in this chapter. Here are the terms that are not covered in the section.

alternating current
battery
circuit
closed circuit
conductor
direct current
dry-cell battery
electric current
electric power
electricity
electromotive force
insulator
Ohm's law
open circuit
parallel circuit
resistance
schematic diagram
series circuit
static electricity
voltage
wet-cell battery

Chapter 11 R E V I E W

Word Bank
ampere
kilowatt-hour
ohm
terminal
volt

Vocabulary Review

Choose a word or words from the Word Bank that best complete each sentence. Write the answer on a sheet of paper.

1. A(n) _____ measures how much electric energy is used.

2. The metric unit used to measure electromotive force is a(n) _____.

3. Electrons leave or enter a battery through the _____.

4. We use a(n) _____ to describe how much electric current flows through a wire.

5. A(n) _____ is a unit used to measure resistance.

Concept Review

Choose the answer that best completes each sentence. Write the letter of the answer on your paper.

6. Lightning is a discharge of _____ between clouds or between a cloud and earth.

   A electric current   **C** static electricity
   B energy   **D** all of the above

7. _____ is an example of a good conductor.

   A Glass   **B** Gold   **C** Rubber   **D** Wood

8. _____ is an example of a good insulator.

   A Aluminum **B** Copper   **C** Plastic   **D** Silver

9. Of the following materials, _____ has higher resistance.

   A water   **B** rubber   **C** silver   **D** aluminum

Chapter 11 Mastery Test A

Chapter 11 Mastery Test A

Part A Read each sentence. Write the letter of the correct answer on the line.

1. The unit that measures resistance is _____.
   A an ohm   C an ampere
   B a volt   D a kilowatt-hour

2. An example of a good conductor is _____.
   A glass   C aluminum
   B plastic   D wood

3. Current that changes direction regularly is _____.
   A direct current   C electric current
   B alternating current D series circuit

4. A buildup of electrical charges is _____.
   A electricity   C static electricity
   B resistance   D electric current

5. Wet-cell batteries and dry-cell batteries produce _____.
   A resistance   C alternating current
   B static electricity D direct current

Part B Write the word that correctly completes each sentence.

6. The _____ of a wire depends on the type of material and the length and thickness of the wire.

7. All batteries produce current by changing chemical energy into _____ energy.

8. When devices are added in a _____ circuit, voltage to each device is lowered.

9. When devices are added to a _____ circuit, voltage to each device stays the same.

Chapter 11 Mastery Test A, continued

Part C Write a short answer for each question.

10. Describe how electricity flows through a circuit.

11. How are conductors and insulators different?

12. How is resistance useful?

13. What is the difference between a series circuit and a parallel circuit?

14. How is electricity measured?

15. How much current is flowing in a circuit with 36 volts and a resistance of 10 ohms?

Chapter 11 Mastery Test A

10. Wet-cell and dry-cell batteries have _____ current.

    A direct   **B** alternating   **C** series   **D** parallel

11. The formula for Ohm's law is _____.

    A $I = \dfrac{V}{R}$ **B** $V = \dfrac{I}{R}$ **C** $I = \dfrac{R}{V}$ **D** $V = \dfrac{R}{I}$

12. When cells are in _____, the voltage is the sum of the voltages of the cells.

    A parallel   **C** an open circuit

    B series   **D** a closed circuit

Critical Thinking

Write the answer to each of these questions on your paper.

13. What is the effect of resistance on electrical energy?

14. Based on the following schematic diagram, calculate the current.

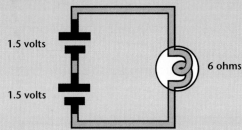

1.5 volts

1.5 volts

6 ohms

15. Explain the circuitry of a string of lights that will not light up if one of the lights is burned out.

Test-Taking Tip Take time to organize your thoughts before writing answers to short-answer tests.

---

13. Resistance causes electrical energy to change into heat and light energy. **14.** The current is 2 amperes. **15.** It is a series circuit; current flows through only one path around the circuit.

ALTERNATIVE ASSESSMENT

Alternative Assessment items correlate to the student Goals for Learning at the beginning of this chapter.

- Have students draw a schematic diagram of an open circuit and of a closed circuit.

- Give students a cross-section drawing of an electrical wire encased in insulating material. Have them label the insulator and the conductor and give examples of materials that each might be made of.

- Have students give an oral or written explanation of how resistance enables a toaster to work.

- Display a diagram of a wet-cell battery and of an alternating current. Have students explain how each produces an electric current.

- Prepare two stacks of index cards. On each card in one stack, write various voltages, ranging from 5 volts to 50 volts. On each card in the second stack, write varying resistances, ranging from 5 ohms to 10 ohms. Have students choose a card from each stack and calculate the current in amperes, using the values on the two cards they have chosen.

- Show students a drawing of a pole lamp with two bulbs attached to the pole. Ask students to draw a schematic diagram of the circuit in the lamp. (*Schematic diagrams should show a parallel circuit with each bulb having a separate path for electrons to travel on.*)

- Have students use the terms *watt* and *kilowatt-hour* in sentences.

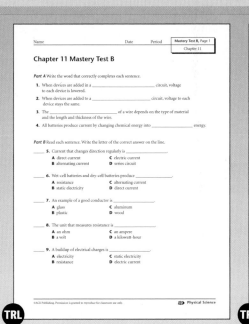

Chapter 11 Mastery Test B

Planning Guide

Magnets and Electromagnetism

		Student Text Lesson		
		Student Pages	Vocabulary	Lesson Review
Lesson 1	What Are Magnets?	348–350	✔	✔
Lesson 2	Identifying a Magnetic Field	351–355	✔	✔
Lesson 3	Identifying Magnetism	356–359		✔
Lesson 4	The Relationship Between Magnetism and Electricity	360–368	✔	✔

Chapter Activities

Student Text
Science Center

Teacher's Resource Library
Community Connection 12: Making a Map

Assessment Options

Student Text
Chapter 12 Review

Teacher's Resource Library
Chapter 12 Mastery Tests A and B

	Student Text Features								Teaching Strategies						Learning Styles						Teacher's Resource Library				
	Achievements in Science	Science at Work	Science in Your Life	Investigation	Science Myth	Note	Technology Note	Did You Know	Science Integration	Science Journal	Cross-Curricular Connection	Online Connection	Teacher Alert	Applications (Home, Career, Community, Global, Environment)	Auditory/Verbal	Body/Kinesthetic	Interpersonal/Group Learning	Logical/Mathematical	Visual/Spatial	LEP/ESL	Workbook Activities	Alternative Workbook Activities	Lab Manual	Resource File	Self-Study Guide
	350							348, 349		350	349		349	349							59	59			✔
			354	353				352		352		353	352			352			352		60	60	45, 46		✔
		359				✔			358	358	358		357		358	357	357			358	61	61		24	✔
	366		365	367	363	✔	✔			365	361, 362	364		361, 363, 364	363	362	365				62	62	47, 48	25	✔

Pronunciation Key

a	hat	e	let	ī	ice	ô	order	u̇	put	sh	she		a	in about
ā	age	ē	equal	o	hot	oi	oil	ü	rule	th	thin	ə	e	in taken
ä	far	ėr	term	ō	open	ou	out	ch	child	ᴛʜ	then		i	in pencil
â	care	i	it	ȯ	saw	u	cup	ng	long	zh	measure		o	in lemon
													u	in circus

Alternative Workbook Activities

The Teacher's Resource Library (TRL) contains a set of lower-level worksheets called Alternative Workbook Activities. These worksheets cover the same content as the regular Workbook Activities but are written at a second-grade reading level.

Skill Track Software

Use the Skill Track Software for Physical Science for additional reinforcement of this chapter. The software program allows students using AGS textbooks to be assessed for mastery of each chapter and lesson of the textbook. Students access the software on an individual basis and are assessed with multiple-choice items.

Chapter at a Glance

Chapter 12: Magnets and Electromagnetism
pages 346–371

Lessons

Skill Track Software for Physical Science

Teacher's Resource Library

(Answer Keys for the Teacher's Resource Library begin on page 402 of the Teacher's Edition. The Materials List for the Lab Manual activities begins on page 419.)

Science Center

Display disassembled motors. Allow students to handle and observe the different parts. As the chapter progresses, encourage students to label with tape the parts that are magnets or electromagnets.

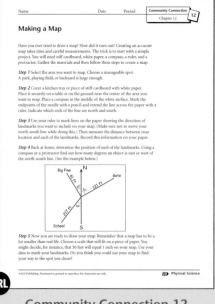

Community Connection 12

Chapter

12 Magnets and Electromagnetism

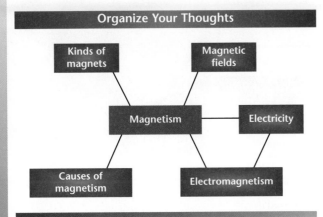

ook at the piece of lodestone in the photograph. Lodestone is a natural magnet made of the mineral magnetite. Years ago, sailors used magnetite to navigate their ships around the world. The sailors discovered that when magnetite was hung from a string it would point north or south. Do you know what causes magnetism? Can a magnet be demagnetized? Are magnets still used to navigate ships? In Chapter 12, you will learn more about magnets and how they work.

Organize Your Thoughts

```
        Kinds of              Magnetic
        magnets                fields

              Magnetism        Electricity

        Causes of            Electromagnetism
        magnetism
```

Goals for Learning

◆ To describe various kinds of magnets

◆ To explain what a magnetic field is

◆ To tell what causes magnetism

◆ To describe electromagnetism and its uses

347

Introducing the Chapter

Point out that great inventions often have very simple origins. Ask students to think about how people long ago might have discovered that a stone like the one pictured on page 346 could help them find directions. Lead them to understand that pieces of the mineral magnetite led to the development of the compass. Encourage students to share any experiences they have had with compasses and to explain their importance. Instruct them to write an explanation of how they think a compass works. Invite volunteers to discuss their explanations. Some students might be aware that compasses work because of magnetism. Use this discussion as a springboard to find out what else students know or believe about magnetism.

Notes and Technology Notes

Ask volunteers to read the notes that appear in the margins throughout the chapter. Then discuss them with the class.

TEACHER'S RESOURCE

The AGS Teaching Strategies in Science Transparencies may be used with this chapter. The transparencies add an interactive dimension to expand and enhance the *Physical Science* program content.

CAREER INTEREST INVENTORY

The AGS Harrington-O'Shea Career Decision-Making System-Revised (CDM) may be used with this chapter. Students can use the CDM to explore their interests and identify careers. The CDM defines career areas that are indicated by students' responses on the inventory.

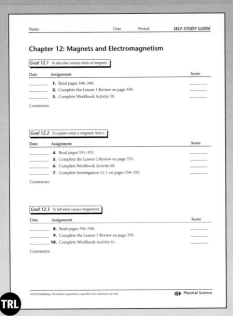

TRL Chapter 12 Self-Study Guide

Magnets/Electromagnetism Chapter 12 **347**

Lesson at a Glance

Chapter 12 Lesson 1

Overview In this lesson, students learn some common shapes of magnets, what magnetic poles are, and how the magnetic poles of a magnet affect another magnet.

Objectives

- To describe several kinds of magnets
- To explain what magnetic poles are
- To describe how magnetic poles behave

Student Pages 348–350

Teacher's Resource Library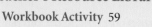

Workbook Activity 59

Alternative Workbook Activity 59

Vocabulary

attract	magnetic pole
magnet	repel

Science Background

All magnets have two poles, called north and south, usually at opposite ends of the magnet. Magnetic forces are strongest at a magnet's poles. When the like poles of two magnets are placed together—for example, two south poles—they push each other away. Unlike poles, on the other hand, attract each other. This relationship is similar to the relationship between electric charges. Opposite electric charges attract and like charges repel.

1 Warm-Up Activity

Show students a variety of magnets of different sizes and shapes. Have them identify the shapes. *(bar, doughnut, cylindrical, horseshoe)* Ask for their ideas on why magnets are made in different shapes and sizes. *(Answers should reflect the idea that shape and size depend on the purpose for which a magnet is used.)*

2 Teaching the Lesson

Ask students to write this lesson's title and objectives on paper. Tell them that as they read this lesson, they should write sentences that meet the objectives.

Lesson 1 · What Are Magnets?

Objectives

After reading this lesson, you should be able to

- describe several kinds of magnets.
- explain what magnetic poles are.
- describe how magnetic poles behave.

Magnet

An object that attracts certain kinds of metals, such as iron

 Did You Know?

The ancient Greeks knew about the magnetic properties of lodestone. Lodestone is also called magnetite. The word *magnet* comes from the name Magnesia, the Greek province where the mineral was mined.

You are probably familiar with **magnets.** Magnets attract certain kinds of metals. They pick up metal objects, such as paper clips and other things made from iron. Most of the magnets you have seen are made by people. But there are also naturally occurring magnets such as lodestone. Lodestone, one of a variety of magnetite, is made of iron oxide. It is found naturally in the earth and comes in many sizes and shapes.

Most manmade magnets come in several common shapes. These shapes include the horseshoe, bar, cylinder, and doughnut shapes. You may have seen magnets like the ones in the photo.

Magnets come in a variety of different shapes.

Allow students to experiment with a magnet to see which classroom objects the magnet attracts and which it doesn't. Then have students exchange their magnet for one of a different size or shape. Have them test the same classroom objects as before to determine if shape or size affects what objects a magnet attracts. *(Shape and size have no effect on what objects a magnet attracts.)*

Did You Know?

Have students read the feature on page 348. Students might be interested to learn that the ancient Greeks were fascinated by the lodestone's properties. The philosopher Thales (c. 624–546 B.C.), noting the way iron was drawn to the stone, believed that the magnet had a soul. There was also the legend of a Greek shepherd, who got stuck fast on a mountainside when his iron-tipped staff and iron hobnailed boots attached themselves to magnetic rocks.

Magnetic Poles

Look at the magnets in the figure. The ends of a magnet are called its **magnetic poles.** Whatever the shape, all magnets have two opposite magnetic poles. The magnetic forces are greatest at the poles. You know this because the ends of the magnet will pick up more paper clips than the center of the magnet.

The poles on a magnet are called the north pole and the south pole. On a marked magnet, the north pole is marked with an *N*. The south pole is marked with an *S*.

You cannot tell whether the end of an unmarked magnet is a north pole or a south pole simply by looking at it. But you can find out by placing the magnet close to another magnet whose poles are marked. Observe whether the poles **attract** (pull together) or **repel** (push apart). To figure out the poles of the unmarked magnet, use the following rules.

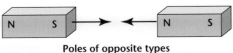

Poles of opposite types
attract each other.

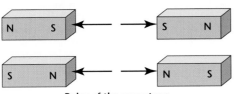

Poles of the same type
repel each other.

3 Reinforce and Extend

TEACHER ALERT

Many students think that round magnets do not have north and south poles as other magnets do. Instruct students to hold a bar magnet, with poles labeled, near a round magnet. (*In most cases, students should find that one side of a round magnet is the north side; the other side is the south side.*)

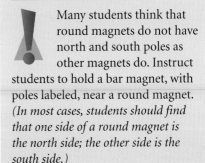

Did You Know?

Ask a volunteer to read the feature on page 349. Point out that cows can pick up nails, staples, and bits of wire with their natural food, especially when windstorms have littered their fields with debris. This can lead to a condition known as "hardware disease." A magnet, about the size of a person's thumb, will stay in the cow's stomach for at least a year.

AT HOME

Have students investigate how magnets are used in their home and list the uses. For example, to attach notes to a refrigerator door, to hold paper clips, to keep cabinet doors closed, and so on. The lists can be compiled into a class master list.

CROSS-CURRICULAR CONNECTION

Art

Students could think up and draw a new invention that makes use of magnets. For example, they might wish to mount a magnet on a fishing pole to help locate keys. Inventions can be as simple or as elaborate as students wish.

Lesson 1 Review Answers

1. Place the magnet next to a marked magnet. Because opposite poles always attract and like poles always repel, the behavior of the poles will tell you the identity of the unmarked pole.
2. They will repel. **3.** They will attract.
4. Lodestone is a naturally occurring magnet made of iron oxide. **5.** Four familiar shapes of magnets are the horseshoe, bar, cylinder, and doughnut.

Achievements in Science

Ask volunteers to read the Achievements in Science feature on page 350 aloud. Encourage students to conduct their own research into the field of MRIs. Instruct them to type the keywords *Magnetic Resonance Imaging* in an Internet search engine. (Suggest that they add the words *facts, history, kids, sports* or *x-rays* to refine their search.) Ask students to bring to school information from two or three sites that interested them. Invite them to share their findings with the class.

SCIENCE JOURNAL

Ask students to write a description about how some simple tasks would be different if there were no magnets. For example, refrigerator notes could be hung with tape, which is not reusable, and leaves a sticky residue.

Portfolio Assessment

Sample items include:
• Lesson title, objectives, and sentences from Teaching the Lesson
• Art from Cross-Curricular Connection
• Lesson 1 Review answers

Write your answers to these questions in complete sentences on a sheet of paper.

1. How can you determine the poles of an unmarked magnet?

2. If two south poles are placed close together, what will happen?

3. If a north and a south pole are placed close together, what will happen?

4. What is lodestone?

5. Name four familiar shapes of magnets.

Achievements in Science

Magnetic Resonance Imaging (MRI)
Scientists first considered using magnetic resonance to make pictures of the human body in 1946. In 1977, the first Magnetic Resonance Imaging (MRI) exam was performed on a human being. Magnetic resonance imaging uses two things to create high-quality cross-sectional images of bodies. Computer-controlled radio waves work with a powerful doughnut-shaped magnet that creates magnetic fields. The magnetic field of an MRI magnet is stronger than an industrial crane magnet.

The protons of hydrogen atoms in the body act like magnetic spinning tops. MRI aligns these hydrogen protons with its magnetic fields. MRI then uses radio waves to move the protons out of alignment temporarily. As the protons return to their original position, they release their own radio waves. These radio waves are used to create a computer image of internal body parts.

MRI shows doctors the difference between healthy and diseased tissues. It lets doctors see into bones and organs without surgery to diagnose illnesses and injuries. MRI is safer than X-rays because it has fewer possible side effects.

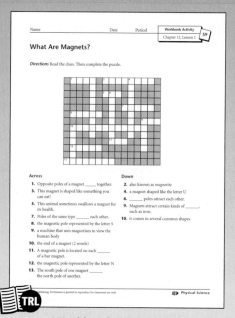

Workbook Activity 59

Lesson 2 — Identifying a Magnetic Field

Objectives

After reading this lesson, you should be able to

◆ explain what a magnetic field is.

◆ describe Earth as a magnet.

◆ explain how a magnet works.

Magnetic field

Area around a magnet in which magnetic forces can act

Lines of force

Lines that show a magnetic field

A **magnetic field** surrounds all magnets. A magnetic field is an area around a magnet in which magnetic forces can act. The magnetic forces will attract or repel other magnets.

Although you cannot see magnetic fields, you can easily see their effects. Place a bar magnet under a sheet of paper. Sprinkle iron filings on top of the paper. The filings will line up in a pattern of curving lines like those shown in the figure. These lines are called **lines of force.** They are caused by the magnetic field and they show the field. The lines of force reach around the magnet from one pole to another. The lines are closest together near the poles. That is where the field is strongest and the forces are greatest.

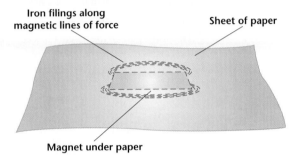

Iron filings along magnetic lines of force

Sheet of paper

Magnet under paper

You can see in the figure below how the lines of force of two magnets affect each other. Notice how they cause the poles of magnets to attract or repel each other.

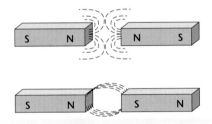

Magnets and Electromagnetism Chapter 12 **351**

Lesson at a Glance

Chapter 12 Lesson 2

Overview In this lesson, students learn about magnetic fields and lines of force. They discover that the earth acts as a magnet. They also learn how a compass works.

Objectives

■ To explain what a magnetic field is

■ To describe Earth as a magnet

■ To explain how a magnet works

Student Pages 351–355

Teacher's Resource Library

Workbook Activity 60

Alternative Workbook Activity 60

Lab Manual 45–46

Vocabulary

lines of force

magnetic field

Science Background

Earth itself is like a giant magnet. Students are sometimes amazed that a compass can work even in locations very far from Earth's poles. In fact, the magnetic field of Earth extends about 50,000 miles out into space. Like any other magnet, Earth has a north and south magnetic pole. These are not in the same place as the geographic poles. In fact, scientists have discovered that the exact locations of the magnetic poles have changed many times since Earth was formed. They can tell that this has occurred by examining the magnetism in ancient rocks.

1 Warm-Up Activity

Spread some paper clips on a table. Paper clips are made of steel, which is mostly iron, and are attracted by a magnet. Lower a bar magnet over the paper clips. Ask students where most of the paper clips stick to the magnet. *(Most of the clips stick to the magnet at its poles. The magnetic field is strongest at the poles.)*

2 Teaching the Lesson

Have students point to the compass in the middle of the figure of Earth shown on page 352. Make certain they realize that a compass needle is a magnet. Emphasize that the north pole of a compass, or any other magnet, is really a north-seeking pole.

Ask students why they think a compass might not work correctly in a large steel building or on a steel ship. Have students write their answers and review them after they have completed the lesson. *(Magnets attract steel objects. The compass needle used inside a steel building or ship would be affected by the closest steel object and not necessarily point in a northerly direction.)*

Magnets/Electromagnetism Chapter 12 **351**

3 Reinforce and Extend

TEACHER ALERT

Many students may think that magnetic fields only exist around magnets. Tell students that scientists have observed magnetic fields around the sun and most of the planets that revolve around it. Have students trace the lines representing the earth's magnetic field shown in the figure on page 352.

Did You Know?

Ask students to read the feature on page 352. Familiarize students with the fantastic beauty of the northern lights. Have them conduct an Internet search, using the keywords *northern lights* or *aurora borealis,* in combination with the words *images* or *photographs.* Ask them to print out their favorite photographs. Create a classroom art gallery of this electromagnetic phenomenon.

LEARNING STYLES

Body/Kinesthetic

Provide small groups of students with a compass. Have them use the compass to determine which classroom wall is north, east, west, and south. *(If students stand with the compass needle pointing toward the north wall, east should be to their right, west to their left, and south behind them. If the walls in your classroom are oriented northeast, northwest, southeast and southwest, instead of north, east, west, and south, you could have students identify the corners of the room rather than walls.)*

Did You Know?

Electrically charged particles from the sun continually stream toward the earth. When they reach the earth's magnetic field, some are trapped in the magnetic poles. They collide with molecules, and the collisions cause colorful displays known as the northern lights.

The Earth as a Magnet

You may be surprised to learn that Earth itself is a giant bar magnet. Like other magnets, Earth has magnetic poles. These magnetic poles are located near the geographic north and south poles.

Earth's natural magnetism allows compasses to work. The needle of a compass is a magnet, too. It has a north pole and a south pole. They are located at opposite ends of the needle.

Like magnetic poles repel each other. However, you can see in the figure that the north magnetic pole of Earth attracts the north pole of a compass. This happens because Earth's north magnetic pole is actually like the south pole of a magnet. But it is called the north magnetic pole because it is located near the geographic North Pole. Earth's south magnetic pole is really like the north pole of a magnet.

Earth's magnetic field attracts and lines up the compass needle. The north pole of the magnet in a compass is attracted to the Earth's magnetic pole. As a result, it points north.

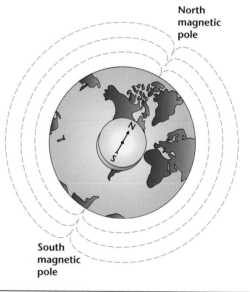

North magnetic pole

South magnetic pole

352   *Chapter 12   Magnets and Electromagnetism*

CROSS-CURRICULAR CONNECTION

Social Studies

Explain to students that historians are not sure exactly where and when the magnetic compass was invented. Point out that it may have been invented independently in different lands. Students could research and write a short report on the early use of the compass and how it aided in world exploration.

LEARNING STYLES

Visual/Spatial

Have students draw a diagram that illustrates why a compass works. The diagram should indicate that Earth is a natural magnet, with two magnetic poles. The compass needle is also magnetized. It aligns with Earth's magnetic field so that the north arrow always points toward Earth's north magnetic pole.

Write your answers to these questions in complete sentences on a sheet of paper.

1. What is a magnetic field?

2. What pattern is made by magnetic lines of force around a bar magnet?

3. How does a compass work?

4. How can you see the lines of force around a magnet?

5. Where are magnetic lines of force closest?

Science Myth

The earth's magnetic field never changes.

Fact: The earth's magnetic field changes slowly but constantly. Over time, the North and South Poles trade places. This last happened about 700,000 years ago. More than 20 flip-flops have occurred in the past five million years. The ocean floor shows evidence of these changes. Why this happens, however, continues to puzzle scientists.

Magnets and Electromagnetism   *Chapter 12*   **353**

Lesson 2 Review Answers

1. A magnetic field is an area around a magnet in which magnetic forces can act. **2.** They form a pattern of curving lines around the magnet from pole to pole. **3.** The earth's magnetic field lines up the compass needle. The north pole of the magnet in a compass points north because it is attracted to the earth's magnetic pole. The pole near the geographic North Pole is actually like the south pole of a magnet. **4.** Place the magnet under a sheet of paper and sprinkle iron filings over it. **5.** The magnetic lines of force are closest near the poles.

Science Myth

Have one student read the myth portion (the first sentence) of the Science Myth on page 353 and another read the fact portion. Lead students to understand how rocks serve as evidence for the earth's pole reversals. Point out that when volcanic rocks are still in a molten form, their magnetic mineral grains align themselves like little compasses with the earth's magnetic field. When these rocks harden, their grains are locked in place. Geologists study the magnetic orientation of volcanic rocks for evidence of pole flip-flops.

ONLINE CONNECTION

Direct students interested in learning more about the earth as a magnet to NASA's educational outreach Web site at image.gsfc.nasa.gov/poetry. They can find a wealth of accessible information, including a multimedia gallery and a useful page called *Ask the Space Scientist*.

Portfolio Assessment

Sample items include:
- Answers about a compass from Teaching the Lesson
- Report from Cross-Curricular Connection
- Lesson 2 Review answers

Name _____ Date _____ Period _____   Lab Manual, Page 1   45   Chapter 12

Exploring Magnetism

Purpose What materials can block a magnetic field? In this investigation, you will identify which materials, if any, can block a magnetic field.

Materials safety glasses   support stand
clamp   rod
bar magnet   thread
paper clip   metric ruler
sheet of paper   copper sheet
cotton fabric   aluminum foil
plastic wrap   plywood

Procedure

1. Use the table to record your data.

Material	Does it block a magnetic field?
sheet of paper	
copper sheet	
cotton fabric	
aluminum foil	
plastic wrap	
plywood	

2. Put on your safety glasses. Clamp the rod onto the support stand.
3. Place the bar magnet on the desktop some distance from the support stand, as shown in the figure.
4. Tie one end of the thread around the paper clip. Tie the other end to the rod. Make sure that the paper clip is attracted to the bar magnet. Tighten the thread to leave a 3-cm gap between the paper clip and the magnet.

Publishing. Permission is granted to reproduce for classroom use only.   Physical Science

Lab Manual 45, pages 1–2

Name _____ Date _____ Period _____   Workbook Activity   60   Chapter 12, Lesson 2

Identifying a Magnetic Field

Directions Look at the two pairs of bar magnets. The broken lines represent their lines of force. Beside the numbers 1 through 8, write the letters *N* or *S*, for north pole or south pole. (Hint: There is more than one possible solution.)

Directions Use words from the word box to complete the paragraph.

attract	Earth	field	lights	pole	sun

9. _____ is like a giant magnet. It has a north and a south magnetic **10.** _____. Like a magnet, the earth's magnetic **11.** _____ is strongest at the poles. Electrically charged particles from the **12.** _____ get trapped at the earth's poles. They collide with molecules to create the spectacular northern **13.** _____.

Directions Write your answers to the questions on the lines.

14. Explain how you could use iron filings and a piece of paper to help reveal the effect of a magnetic field.

_____

15. Why does the north pole of a compass point towards the earth's north magnetic pole?

_____

Publishing. Permission is granted to reproduce for classroom use only.   Physical Science

Workbook Activity 60

Investigation 12-1

The Purpose portion of the student investigation begins with a question to draw them into the activity. Encourage students to read the investigation steps and formulate their own questions before beginning the investigation. This investigation will take approximately 30 minutes to complete. Students will use these process and thinking skills: observing; identifying and controlling variables; collecting, recording, and interpreting data; describing; explaining ideas; drawing conclusions; and comparing.

Preparation

• Place iron filings into shaker-type containers before class.

• Students may use Lab Manual 46 to record their data and answer the questions.

Procedure

• Students should work in cooperative groups of three. Give each student one part to set up and perform. All students observe and record results and clean up when finished.

• You may wish to demonstrate the shaking technique, gently sprinkling the filings from a height of about 1 foot (about 31 cm).

• Instruct students to cover the area just above the magnet and for two or three inches on all sides of the magnet with filings.

• Suggest students tap the paper lightly several times with a pencil point to spread the filings out evenly.

• Be sure students have correctly positioned like and unlike poles for parts B and C.

• Tell students that they can easily retrieve any spilled filings by holding a magnet near them.

Observing Magnetic Lines of Force

Purpose

Do the lines of force around a bar magnet look different than the lines of force around a horseshoe magnet? In this investigation, you will observe the lines of force around two magnets.

Procedure

Part A

1. Copy the data table on a sheet of paper.

Parts	Bar Magnet	Horseshoe Magnet
Part A		
Part B		
Part C		

2. Put on your safety glasses.

3. Place one bar magnet and one horseshoe magnet on a flat surface. Cover each magnet with a sheet of paper.

4. Sprinkle some of the iron filings on each of the pieces of paper. Do not pour the filings. It is best to sprinkle them lightly from a height of about 31 cm (about 1 foot).

5. Observe the pattern of iron filings made by the lines of force. Record your observations in the data table.

6. Carefully pour the iron filings from each paper back into the cup.

Materials
◆ safety glasses
◆ 2 bar magnets
◆ 2 horseshoe magnets
◆ 2 sheets of paper
◆ cup of iron filings
◆ metal bar that attracts a magnet

SAFETY ALERT

◆ Instruct students to wear safety glasses.
◆ Caution students to be careful when working with iron filings and to keep their hands away from their face and eyes. Be sure students wash their hands after this activity.

Part B

7. Place the bar magnets end to end with like poles close together.

8. Place a sheet of paper over the magnets and sprinkle with iron filings. Record your observations.

9. Carefully pour the iron filings from the paper back into the cup.

Part C

10. Reverse the poles of one of the bar magnets so that opposite poles are close together. Cover with a sheet of paper.

11. Sprinkle the paper with iron filings. Record your observations.

12. Repeat Part B and Part C with the horseshoe magnets. Record your observations.

Questions and Conclusions

1. Describe the pattern made by the lines of force of the single bar magnet.

2. In Part B, did the poles of the bar magnets attract or repel each other? How did the lines of force show this?

3. In Part C, did the poles of the bar magnets attract or repel each other? How do you know?

4. How were the patterns on the bar magnet similar to those on the horseshoe magnet?

Explore Further

Find a metal bar that is attracted to a magnet. Repeat Parts B and C using the metal bar. Record your observations.

Magnets and Electromagnetism Chapter 12 **355**

Results

Students should find that in all three parts of this investigation, iron filings are thickest at the poles of a magnet. The iron filings show the magnetic lines of force and illustrate whether two poles are attracted to or repelled by each other.

Questions and Conclusions Answers

1. The curved lines extend from one pole to the other. The lines were closest and thickest with filings near the poles, which showed that the field was strongest there.

2. The like poles repelled each other. The lines from each of the close poles curved sharply away from the other pole.

3. The unlike poles attracted each other. The lines of force arched toward each other, forming one continuous pattern.

4. With both magnets, more filings were concentrated near the poles.

Explore Further Answers

If the metal bar replaced the iron filings: The metal bar clung to the paper and magnets. You could pick up the paper and magnets when you lifted the bar. Placing like poles together had no impact on the attraction of the bar to the magnets.

If the metal bar replaced the magnets: The filings scattered randomly without any pattern.

Assessment

Check students' data tables to be sure they indicate that iron filings came together between the unlike poles of two magnets. Students' answers to the questions should be consistent with their data sheets and should show that they understand the reasons for their results. You might include the following items from this investigation in students' portfolios:

• Investigation 12-1 data table

• Answers to Questions and Conclusions and Explore Further sections

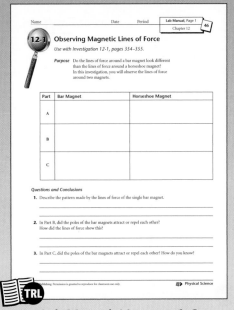

Lab Manual 46, pages 1–2

Lesson at a Glance

Chapter 12 Lesson 3

Overview In this lesson, students learn how and why certain materials can be magnetized. They will also learn how objects can be demagnetized.

Objectives

- To explain what causes magnetism
- To describe how to make a magnet
- To describe how magnetism is destroyed
- To list materials that are attracted by magnets

Student Pages 356–359

Teacher's Resource Library

Workbook Activity 61

Alternative Workbook Activity 61

Resource File 24

Science Background

Most materials are not attracted by magnets and cannot be magnetized. All materials that are attracted by magnets can also be magnetized. These materials include iron, nickel, cobalt, and steel (which is made from iron). A 5-cent coin, although called a nickel, is not attracted by magnets because it does not actually contain much nickel. You might want to keep this in mind when planning classroom demonstrations.

Materials such as iron can be magnetized because they have regions called magnetic domains. Magnetic domains are clusters of many atoms that can be thought of as tiny magnets. An object is not magnetic when its domains are randomly arranged. When the domains line up in one direction, however, the object is magnetized. You can line up the magnetic domains in an object by stroking it repeatedly in one direction with a magnet.

 Warm-Up Activity

Challenge students to find out how many paper clips a magnet will hold in a chain. Students should position a paper clip on a magnet so that one end of the clip is hanging downward.

Objectives

After reading this lesson, you should be able to

- explain what causes magnetism.
- describe how to make a magnet.
- describe how magnetism is destroyed.
- list materials that are attracted by magnets.

Scientists have observed that some atoms have north and south magnetic poles. In most substances, though, the atoms point in all different directions. As a result, the atoms cancel out each other's magnetism. So these substances are not magnetic. Materials that are not magnetic include wood, copper, plastic, rubber, gold, and glass. In addition, magnets are not attracted to these materials.

Look at Figure A. In a nonmagnetized material, the magnetic fields of atoms do not line up.

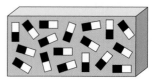

Figure A

Now look at Figure B. In a magnetized material, the magnetic fields of atoms line up.

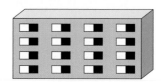

Figure B

In some substances, atoms can be made to line up so that most of them are aligned in the same direction. This arrangement causes the substance to act like a magnet. Only a few materials can be made into magnets. They include iron, nickel, and cobalt. Magnets are attracted to these materials.

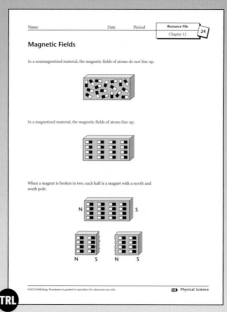

Resource File 24

Making a Magnet

One of the simplest ways to make a magnet is to take an iron wire and stroke it with a magnet. Hold one of the poles of the magnet at one end of the wire. Slowly stroke the magnet in one direction down the length of the wire. After four or five strokes, the wire will become a magnet. Figure C shows this process.

What do you think would happen if you cut the wire into two pieces? Look at Figure D. Each of the two pieces would become magnets.

Figure E shows that each piece of cut wire still contains atoms that are lined up in the same direction. When a magnet is broken in two, each half is a magnet with a north and a south pole.

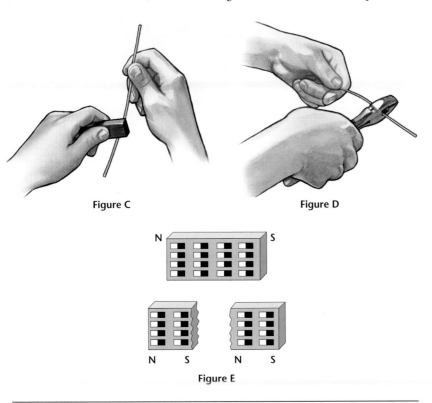

Figure C

Figure D

Figure E

They should use that end to touch a second paper clip, and continue in this manner until no more paper clips attach to the chain. Tell students that they are going to learn how an object can be made into a magnet.

2 Teaching the Lesson

Help students identify objects in the classroom that are made of wood, copper, plastic, rubber, gold, and glass. Then have students hold magnets near the objects to confirm that magnets do not attract them.

Show students a magnet and a small steel object, such as a pair of scissors. Let students observe as the magnet attracts the object. Point out that the object does not have one of the common shapes of magnets, such as a bar or horseshoe. Then ask if students think the object could be magnetized. *(yes)* Ask them why it could be magnetized. *(because it is made of steel; in steel, the atoms that make up the object can be aligned in the same direction, which causes magnetism)*

When they have finished this lesson, ask students to write a description of how they could make a magnet and then demagnetize it.

3 Reinforce and Extend

LEARNING STYLES

Logical/Mathematical

Have pairs of students use blank sheets of paper and paper clips to model the arrangements of atoms in magnetized and nonmagnetized materials. Tell them that the clips represent atoms; the paper represents the materials. Students' arrangements for magnetized material should show the clips aligned in parallel columns and rows on the paper as shown in Figure B on page 356. The double end of all the clips should be facing the same direction. For the nonmagnetized material, the clips should be arranged in a random fashion.

TEACHER ALERT

Students may believe that when a magnet is broken in half, one half will contain the north pole, and the other half will contain the south pole. Use the diagram on page 356 to emphasize that both halves of the magnet will have a north and a south pole.

LEARNING STYLES

Body/Kinesthetic

Provide wires or iron nails and bar magnets so students can try making a magnet. Have students follow the directions given on page 357. Ask them how they'll be able to tell if they made a magnet. *(Hold the wire near a steel object to see if the wire attracts it.)*

If you break a magnet in two, you will have two magnets. If you break each of those two magnets in half, you will have four magnets. Each magnet has a north and a south pole. Magnetic poles are always in pairs.

Demagnetizing a Magnet

You can break a magnet into two parts. This action will not destroy the magnet's magnetism. Both parts remain magnetic. However, it is possible to destroy magnetism or demagnetize a magnet. Have you ever tried to demagnetize a magnet?

Two common ways to demagnetize a magnet are by heating it or by striking it with a hard blow. The figure below illustrates these two ways to demagnetize a magnet. Both of these actions can cause atoms to rearrange themselves so that they are no longer facing the same direction.

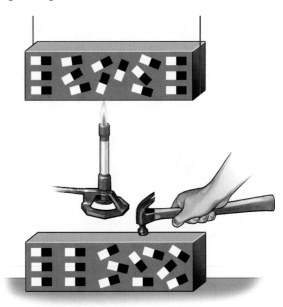

358 *Chapter 12 Magnets and Electromagnetism*

Lesson 3 REVIEW

Write your answers to these questions in complete sentences on a sheet of paper.

1. What causes magnetism?

2. What happens when you break a magnet into two pieces?

3. How can you destroy magnetism?

4. Name some materials that can be made into magnets.

5. Name some materials that are not magnetic.

▼◄▲▼◄▲▼◄▲▼◄▲▼◄▲▼◄▲▼◄▲▼◄▲▼◄▲▼◄▲▼◄▲▼◄▲▼◄▲▼◄▲▼◄▲▼
Science at Work

Appliance Service Technician

Appliance service technicians check appliances such as refrigerators, dryers, and ovens for different problems. They perform tests on different parts of appliances, including motors, heating elements, and switches. Because of differences among types of appliances, many appliance service technicians specialize.

Appliance service technicians receive training either through on-the-job experience or a post-high school technical program. Some complete an apprenticeship. Apprenticeships often combine on-the-job training and schooling and may last four to five years.

Appliance service technicians must understand the mechanical workings of machines. They must also be able to work with their hands. In addition, these technicians must enjoy solving problems and managing details.

Magnets and Electromagnetism Chapter 12 **359**

Lesson 3 Review Answers

1. The magnetic fields of atoms line up in the same direction. **2.** The magnet becomes two magnets. **3.** Heat a magnet or strike it with a hard blow. **4.** Iron, cobalt, and nickel are some materials that can be made into magnets. **5.** Sample answers: Wood, plastic, rubber, copper, gold, and glass are some materials that are not magnetic.

Science at Work

Invite a volunteer to read aloud the Science at Work feature on page 359. Then have students write one thing they believe they would like about this career and one thing they would not enjoy. Ask them to share their statements. As they do so, make a list of their pros and cons on the board.

Use this feature as a preview for the final lesson. Ask: *What does being an appliance service technician have to do with magnets?* Lead students to understand that magnetism is an essential part of the electric motor, which is at the heart of many household appliances.

Portfolio Assessment

Sample items include:
• Descriptions from Teaching the Lesson
• Lesson 3 Review answers

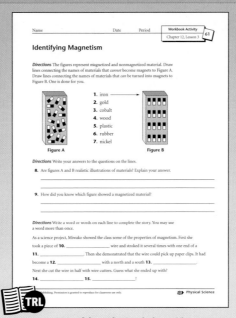

Workbook Activity 61

Magnets/Electromagnetism Chapter 12 **359**

Lesson at a Glance

Chapter 12 Lesson 4

Overview In this lesson, students explore the relationship between magnetism and electricity. They learn how electromagnets work and how they are used in everyday life.

Objectives

- To explain how magnetism and electricity are related
- To describe electromagnetism
- To list devices that use electromagnetism
- To explain how magnetism can be produced from electricity

Student Pages 360–368

Teacher's Resource Library

Workbook Activity 62

Alternative Workbook Activity 62

Lab Manual 47–48

Resource File 25

Vocabulary

electromagnet   motor
electromagnetism

Science Background

You can use electricity to produce magnetism by passing current through a wire coil. This device is called an electromagnet. One end of the coil becomes the north pole and one becomes the south pole. If you reverse the direction of the current, the north and south poles exchange places. The more turns of wire in the coil and the greater the current, the stronger the electromagnet is. Putting a piece of iron, called a core, into the center of the coil also makes a stronger electromagnet. However, the magnetic effect continues only as long as current passes through the wire. Electromagnets are used as switches in telephones, doorbells, automobiles, stereo loudspeakers, tape recorders, and many other devices because their magnetic forces can be readily switched on and off. They are an important part of motors.

Objectives

After reading this lesson, you should be able to

- explain how magnetism and electricity are related.
- describe electromagnetism.
- list devices that use electromagnetism.
- explain how magnetism can be produced from electricity.

Electromagnetism
The relationship between magnetism and electricity

Electromagnet
A temporary magnet made by passing a current through a wire wrapped around an iron core

Magnets are not the only things that can produce a magnetic field. Electricity can also produce a magnetic field. You can see this when you place a compass near a wire that is carrying electricity. The compass needle will turn until it is at right angles to the wire. The current produces a magnetic field around the wire.

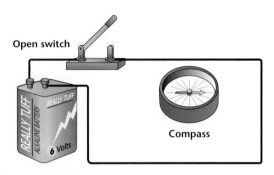
Open switch

Compass

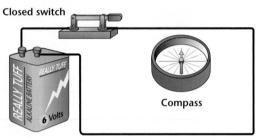
Closed switch

Compass

The relationship between magnetism and electricity is called **electromagnetism.** Moving electric charges produce magnetic forces and moving magnets produce electric forces.

Electricity can be used to make a type of magnet called an **electromagnet.** An electromagnet is a temporary magnet. It is made by passing a current through a wire wrapped around an iron core. An electromagnet is magnetic as long as an electric current is flowing.

---

360   *Chapter 12   Magnets and Electromagnetism*

 Warm-Up Activity

Use a 6-volt dry-cell battery, some bell wire, and a switch to construct a circuit like the one on page 360. With the switch open, hold the compass near the wire. Allow students to see that the compass still points to the north. Ask students to predict what will happen to the compass needle when you close the switch, allowing electricity to run through the wire. After students have made their predictions, close the switch. The compass should point toward the wire carrying the electricity.

2 Teaching the Lesson

Direct students' attention to the diagram of the electromagnet at the top of page 361. Have a volunteer read the paragraph next to the diagram. Make sure students understand that adding more turns of wire to the coil increases its magnetic field. An increased magnetic field allows the electromagnet to attract more and larger objects.

Have students work in small groups to list all the machines they can think of with motors. Compile all the examples into a master list.

Ask students to write a brief summary of information provided in the lesson.

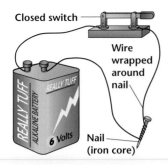

Closed switch

Wire wrapped around nail

6 Volts

Nail (iron core)

An electromagnet, like the one in the figure, can be made with a large nail, some common bell wire, and a 6-volt dry-cell battery. The nail serves as the iron core. The flow of current through the wire surrounding the core creates a magnetic field.

The strength of an electromagnet depends on a number of factors. Power sources with higher voltages make more powerful electromagnets. More turns of wire around the core will also increase the strength of a magnet.

Using Electromagnets

The magnetism that electromagnets produce is the same as the magnetism a magnet produces. An electromagnet has a magnetic field and a north and south pole. Unlike a regular magnet, an electromagnet can be switched off and on. This quality makes electromagnets very useful. Many salvage yards have electromagnets like the one in the photo.

Electromagnets can be turned on and off.

GLOBAL CONNECTION

Electromagnetism makes television possible, and you can use television to connect to people and places around the world. Through entertainment and news programs, students can learn about cultures and events other than their own. Suggest that students research information to find out how television has provided people with a global connection. For example, they might investigate where specific television programs are broadcast. They might scan through the channels and find out where specific programs are from. They might listen to the news to find out what countries are featured in news stories. Encourage discussion about the role television has played in connecting people and cultures from around the world.

CROSS-CURRICULAR CONNECTION

History

Suggest that students find out what two scientists, Michael Faraday and Christian Oersted, discovered about electricity and magnetism. Have students write a report on their findings. (*In 1820, Hans Christian Oersted accidentally discovered that electric current produces magnetism. In 1831, Michael Faraday found that magnetism produces an electric current.*)

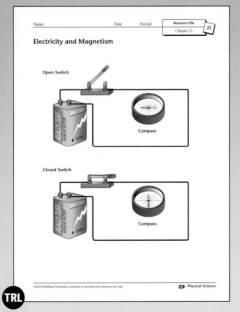

Name   Date   Period   Resource File
                                                Chapter 12   25

Electricity and Magnetism

Open Switch

6 Volts   Compass

Closed Switch

6 Volts   Compass

©AGS Publishing. Permission is granted to reproduce for classroom use only.   Physical Science

Resource File 25

Winding wire into coils makes the wire's magnetic fields stronger. Coiled wire with current flowing through it is called a solenoid. Putting an iron core inside a solenoid creates an electromagnet and even stronger magnetic fields.

When the current is turned on, the electromagnet picks up pieces of metal from piles of scrap. When the current is turned off, the electromagnet loses it magnetism. The metal pieces fall to the ground.

You may not be aware that you use electromagnets every day. Many appliances use electromagnets. Speakers, earphones, and telephones use electromagnets to change electric currents into sound waves.

Find the electromagnet in the figure below. Notice the device that provides electric current to the electromagnet. The level of electric current passing to the electromagnet from this device changes. These changes cause the strength of the electromagnet to change, too. As the strength of the electromagnet changes, the plate located in front of the electromagnet vibrates back and forth. The vibration of the plate creates sound waves.

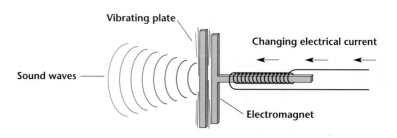

Vibrating plate

Changing electrical current

Sound waves

Electromagnet

Technology Note

Superconducting magnets are electromagnets that produce a very strong magnetic field. Their magnetic field can be 200,000 times greater than the earth's. Superconducting magnets are unique because they are made from materials that have no resistance. The lack of resistance results in greater electric current, which creates a stronger magnetic field.

Motors

Motors also make use of electromagnetism. A motor converts electrical energy to mechanical energy, which is used to do work. The figure illustrates how a motor works.

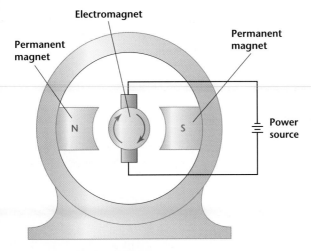

Electromagnet

Permanent magnet

Permanent magnet

N   S

Power source

A motor has three basic parts. One part is a permanent magnet that cannot move. A second part is an electromagnet that is free to turn. The electromagnet turns between the opposite poles of the permanent magnet. A third part is a device that supplies alternating electric current to magnetize the electromagnet. As you learned in Chapter 11, alternating current changes direction at a regular rate.

When current is supplied to the electromagnet, each pole of the electromagnet is attracted to the opposite pole of the permanent magnet. This attraction causes the electromagnet to turn so that its poles line up with the opposite poles of the permanent magnet. The constant switch of poles in the electromagnet of a motor causes it to turn.

Magnets and Electromagnetism   Chapter 12   **363**

IN THE ENVIRONMENT

 Discuss with students the relationship between transportation and quality of life. Lead them to understand that few environmental issues are so hotly contested as those involving how we get from place to place. Have students choose and research an environmental issue related to transportation. Topics might include clean cars, bicycles, urban design, trains vs. cars, road construction, mass transit, noise pollution, or air pollution. Suggest that combining one of these words or phrases with the word *environment* will bring up a number of Internet sources. Have students bring to class information on their topic. Invite volunteers to share their findings with classmates in small groups.

IN THE COMMUNITY

 Point out that most people take access to household electricity for granted. Challenge students to find out more about the electric supply in their own community. Have them find answers to the following questions: How is the electricity for our community generated? Where does it come from? How does it get here? Who provides it? How do we pay for it? Do we have a choice? Invite them to share their findings with the class.

ONLINE CONNECTION

 Electricity and Magnetism, a Web site administered by Kennesaw State University in Georgia, offers elementary and middle school students information on topics related to this lesson. The site address is edtech.kennesaw.edu/web/electric. html. Links from this site to other reliable sites provide access to interactive games, information, history, and quizzes.

Permanent magnets, which keep their magnetism after they are magnetized, are often made of alloys. Alnico magnets contain aluminum, nickel, iron, cobalt, and copper. Alloy magnets can lift many times their own weight.

As the direction of current changes, the electromagnet's poles reverse. As a result, the aligned poles repel each other. And the electromagnet continues to turn. The current in the electromagnet continues to reverse direction after every half turn, causing the electromagnet to continue to turn.

The spinning motion of the electromagnet in a motor can be used to do work or operate other devices. Motors operate cars, refrigerators, electric toys, hair dryers, air conditioners, and many kitchen appliances. Look at the figure below. These items are examples of devices that have motors.

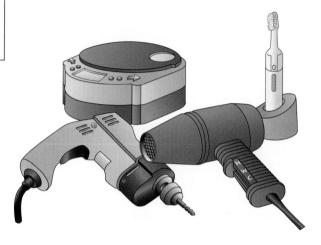

 Technology Note

Electric guitars have electromagnetic devices called magnetic pickups. Pickups are bar magnets wrapped with thousands of turns of narrow wire. When the guitar's strings are plucked, they vibrate. Their vibration produces a vibration in the magnet's magnetic field, which creates an electronic signal. An amplifier makes the signal louder. Speakers change the signal into sound waves.

364 Chapter 12 Magnets and Electromagnetism

How does magnetism move a train?

Imagine riding in a train that moves on a cushion of air instead of rolling along tracks. Such trains use electromagnetism to travel at very fast speeds. These vehicles are called maglev trains—short for "magnetic levitation." Electromagnetism is used to levitate, or lift up, the train, to move it forward, and to guide it. There is no friction with the track to slow down the train. Maglev trains actually float about 10 centimeters above the tracks.

The maglev train starts out by rolling on rubber wheels. Once the train reaches a faster speed, current is sent through the metal coils on the sides of the train. This current causes the coils to become magnetized. The track also is magnetized. The coils on the train are repelled by the electromagnets in the track. This causes the train to lift off the tracks.

The train moves forward because poles in the magnets in the tracks can be changed. The magnets in the track in front of the train have poles that are opposite to those of the train. The attraction between the train and the track ahead moves the train forward. The repulsion between the train and the track below it keeps the train levitated. By controlling the current to the tracks, a magnetic wave is created that keeps the train moving forward.

In 2002, the world's first public maglev train began running in Shanghai, China. The train reaches 415-km/h speeds along a 32-km route. The route connects Shanghai's financial area with its airport.

Magnets and Electromagnetism   *Chapter 12*   **365**

Ask volunteers to take turns reading the Science in Your Life feature on page 365. Point out that exciting new technology often fascinates the general public. Have students conduct an Internet search, using the keywords *maglev train*. Ask them to visit several Web sites and to print out material from one that they find particularly informative or interesting. Have students share their information in small groups and present their findings in a cooperative report to the class.

LEARNING STYLES

Interpersonal/ Group Learning

Challenge small groups of students to make posters explaining how a maglev train works. They can use information from the feature on page 365 as well as reference material to help them design their posters. Students' diagrams should clearly label the key elements of the technology and include brief explanatory text. Have groups present their posters to the class.

SCIENCE JOURNAL

Ask students to think of themselves as tourists in Shanghai. Have them describe their trip from the airport to the city center aboard the maglev train.

Lesson 4 Review Answers

1. Electromagnetism is the relationship between magnetism and electricity. **2.** A current is passed through a wire wrapped around an iron core. **3.** Answers will vary. Sample answers include: speakers, telephones, earphones, or devices with motors. **4.** The changing poles in a motor's electromagnet are alternately attracted and repelled by the poles of a permanent magnet, causing the motor to turn. This motion can be used to operate a device. **5.** Because the direction of the current changes, the poles reverse and north would be opposite of its present position.

Achievements in Science

Have a volunteer read aloud the Achievements in Science feature on page 366. Point out that Oersted discovered the relationship between electricity and magnetism by chance. Then write the following quotation by Louis Pasteur on the board: "Where observation is concerned, chance favors only the prepared mind." Ask students what Pasteur might have meant by the phrase "prepared mind." *(an educated, open mind)* Invite them to consider whether achievements ever happen by chance. You might extend this discussion with a second quote, one by Sir Isaac Newton: "If I have seen further it is by standing on the shoulders of giants." Ask what Newton might have meant by "giants," *(great minds who preceded him)* and challenge students to connect this observation with their own experience.

Portfolio Assessment

Sample items include:
• Lists from Teaching the Lesson
• Summaries from Teaching the Lesson
• Lesson 4 Review answers

Write your answers to these questions in complete sentences on a sheet of paper.

1. What is electromagnetism?

2. Explain how an electromagnet works.

3. Name two devices that use electromagnets.

4. Explain how a motor works.

5. What would happen to the compass needle in the figure on page 360 if the wires attached to the bottom battery were reversed?

Achievements in Science

Electromagnetism

Until the 1800s, the only magnetism known came from natural magnets like lodestone and iron. Scientists believed that magnetism and electricity were unrelated.

This belief changed in 1820 after Hans Oersted made a discovery while doing a classroom demonstration. He saw a wire with electricity running through it make a compass needle move. He discovered that every conductor carrying an electric current is surrounded by a magnetic field.

Oersted's discovery of the connection between magnetism and electricity led Andre-Marie Ampere to experiment further. He found that when current flows through coiled wire, the current acts like a magnet. Ampere's law, published in 1827, is one of the basic laws of electromagnetism. It shows the mathematical relationship between electric currents and magnetic fields.

Oersted's and Ampere's discoveries showed that two forces—electric and magnetic—are associated with electricity. Their work led to the development of the electromagnet. It also led to the prediction of the existence of electromagnetic waves.

Name _____ Date _____ Period _____ Lab Manual, Page 1
Chapter 12   47

Experimenting with a Compass

Purpose How can you make a simple compass? What materials will affect it? In this investigation, you will make a compass and observe what materials affect it.

Materials safety glasses, small piece of sponge, tray, magnetic compass, iron nail, steel paper clip, needle / bar magnet, correction fluid, water, crumpled paper ball, wooden pencil, eraser

Procedure

1. Use the table below to record your data.

Material	Does it affect the compass?
paper ball	
iron nail	
wooden pencil	
paper clip	
eraser	

2. Put on your safety glasses. Rub one end of the bar magnet along the needle. Rub it in the same direction 25 times. **Safety Alert: Handle the needle carefully to avoid poking yourself.**

3. Find an object in the classroom that is attracted to the magnet. Use this object to test the needle. The object should be attracted to the needle, too. If the needle does not attract the object, repeat step 2.

4. Slide the needle through the sponge so that it sticks out on each end. Use the correction fluid to paint one end of the needle white.

5. Fill the tray with water. Float the sponge in the water. Keep the bar magnet away from the needle. If it floats freely, one end of the needle should point toward Earth's magnetic north pole. Use a compass to check your magnet.

Publishing. Permission is granted to reproduce for classroom use only.   ● Physical Science

Lab Manual 47, pages 1–2

Name _____ Date _____ Period _____ Workbook Activity
Chapter 12, Lesson 4   62

Magnets and Electromagnetism: Terms Review

Word Bank		
alloy magnet	electromagnetism	magnetic field
amplifier	engine	magnetic poles
attract	lines of force	motor
core	maglev train	repel
electromagnet	magnet	superconducting magnets

Directions Choose a term from the Word Bank that matches each definition.

1. an object that will attract certain types of metal _____

2. areas around a magnet in which magnetic forces can act _____

3. the end of a magnet, where magnetic forces are greatest _____

4. lines that show a magnetic field _____

5. the relationship between magnetism and electricity _____

6. a device that converts electrical energy to mechanical energy _____

7. to push apart _____

8. a temporary magnet made by passing an electric current through a wire wrapped around an iron core _____

9. to pull together _____

Directions There are six terms in the Word Bank that you did not use. Use them to complete the following sentences.

10. _____ can produce magnetic fields 200,000 stronger than Earth's.

11. In a home-made electromagnet, a nail can serve as the _____

12. A(n) _____ uses fuel such as gasoline to produce mechanical energy.

13. A(n) _____ is made of a mixture of metals.

14. A(n) _____ can travel at over 300 miles per hour.

15. You can barely hear an electric guitar without a(n) _____

Publishing. Permission is granted to reproduce for classroom use only.   ● Physical Science

Workbook Activity 62

12-2 INVESTIGATION

Constructing an Electromagnet

The Purpose portion of the student investigation begins with a question to draw them into the activity. Encourage students to read the investigation steps and formulate their own questions before beginning the investigation. This investigation will take approximately 30 minutes to complete. Students will use these process and thinking skills: observing; identifying and controlling variables; collecting, recording, and interpreting data; describing; explaining ideas; comparing; and inferring.

Materials
◆ safety glasses
◆ copper wire, 0.5 m long
◆ large nail
◆ metric ruler
◆ electrical tape
◆ 1.5 volt D-cell battery
◆ paper clips
◆ iron filings
◆ sheet of paper

Purpose

Is it possible to increase an electromagnet's magnetic properties? In this investigation, you will see how to increase the magnetic properties of an electromagnet.

Procedure

1. Copy the data table on a sheet of paper.

Number of Turns of Wire Coil	Number of Paper Clips
5	
10	
15	
25	

2. Put on your safety glasses.

3. Make a small loop in both ends of the copper wire.

4. Start 10 cm from one end of the wire. Wrap the wire around the nail 5 times, as shown in the figure.

5. Using electrical tape, tape one end of the wire to one end of the battery. Tape the other end of the wire to the other end of the battery.

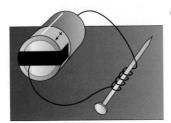

6. Hold the nail near the paper clips. Observe what happens. Record your observations in the right-hand column on the first line of the data table.

Preparation

• Check batteries before class. Have some spare batteries on hand.
• Place iron filings into shaker-type containers before class.
• Students may use Lab Manual 48 to record their data and answer the questions.

Procedure

• This activity is best done by students working in pairs.
• Remind students that the batteries will last longer if they do the procedures quickly.
• For step 7, explain to students that some paper clips might cling to the nail when they remove one end of the wire from the battery. This is because the nail retains its magnetism for a period of time after the current stops.

SAFETY ALERT

◆ Have students wear their safety glasses.
◆ Tell students to handle the sharp ends of the wires carefully to prevent any puncture injuries.
◆ Caution students not to touch both ends of the battery at the same time. A short might occur that could result in burns.

Continued on page 368

Continued from page 367

Results

Students should observe that the more times the wire is coiled around the nail, the more paper clips the electromagnet attracts.

Questions and Conclusions Answers

1. They were no longer attracted to the nail and dropped away.
2. The electromagnet picked up more paper clips with the added coils. Its strength increased.

Explore Further Answers

1. The pattern is well formed and compact.
2. Fewer filings form a less distinct and smaller pattern.
3. Adding more turns makes the magnetic force around the wire stronger.
4. The power of the electromagnet would increase.

Assessment

Check students' data tables to be sure their data reflect the idea that as the number of turns of wire increases, so does the number of attracted paper clips. You might include the following items from this investigation in student portfolios:

- Investigation 12-2 data table
- Answer to Questions and Conclusions and Explore Further sections

7. Remove one end of the wire from the battery. Wrap the wire around the nail 5 more times. You should now have a total of 10 coils. Tape the end of the wire to the battery again.

8. Hold the nail near the paper clips. Record your observations.

9. Repeat steps 7 and 8, making the coil with 15 turns of the wire. Record your observations.

10. Repeat steps 7 and 8, making the coil with 25 turns of the wire. Record your observations.

Questions and Conclusions

1. In step 7, what happened to the paper clips when you removed one end of the wire from the battery?

2. How did the number of coils in the wire affect the electromagnet?

Explore Further

1. Sprinkle iron filings on a sheet of paper. Hold the paper over the wire when the coil has 25 turns of the wire. Describe the pattern made by the iron filings.

2. Hold the paper with the iron filings over the wire coil when it has 10 turns of the wire. How does the pattern made by the iron filings compare with the pattern you saw in step 1?

3. How does the number of turns in the wire coil affect the magnetic force around the wire?

4. What would happen if you used two batteries in series?

368 *Chapter 12   Magnets and Electromagnetism*

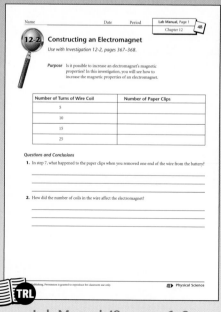

- Magnets can attract materials such as iron. Magnets may be natural, such as lodestone, or manmade.

- A magnet has a north pole and a south pole. Unlike poles of magnets attract. Like poles of magnets repel.

- A magnetic field surrounds a magnet. Magnetic lines of force extend from pole to pole.

- The earth is a magnet. It has a north magnetic pole and a south magnetic pole.

- Materials that can be magnetized and that are attracted to magnets include iron, nickel, and cobalt.

- A magnet can be made by stroking an iron wire with a magnet. Magnets can be destroyed by heat or by hard blows.

- Electromagnetism is the relationship between magnetism and electricity.

- Speakers, earphones, and telephones are devices that use electromagnets.

- Motors make use of electromagnets and permanent magnets to turn electrical energy into mechanical energy.

Chapter 12 Summary

Have volunteers read aloud each Summary item on page 369. Ask volunteers to explain the meaning of each item. Direct students' attention to the Science Words box on the bottom of page 369. Have them read and review each term and its definition.

Science Words		
attract, 349	lines of force, 351	magnetic pole, 349
electromagnet, 360	magnet, 348	motor, 363
electromagnetism, 360	magnetic field, 351	repel, 349

Chapter 12 Review

Use the Chapter Review to prepare students for tests and to reteach content from the chapter.

Chapter 12 Mastery Test

The Teacher's Resource Library includes two parallel forms of the Chapter 12 Mastery Test. The difficulty level of the two forms is equivalent. You may wish to use one form as a pretest and the other form as a posttest.

Chapters 1–12 Final Mastery Test TRL

The Teacher's Resource Library includes the Final Mastery Test. This test is pictured on pages 400–401 of this Teacher's Edition. The Final Mastery Test assesses the major learning objectives of this text, with emphasis on Chapters 7–12.

Review Answers
Vocabulary Review

1. motor 2. electromagnet 3. magnetic field 4. lines of force 5. attract 6. magnetic poles 7. electromagnetism 8. repel

Concept Review

9. B 10. D 11. D 12. B

TEACHER ALERT

One of the vocabulary terms introduced in this chapter—*magnet*—is missing from the Vocabulary Review section. You may want to create an activity that includes this word to give students practice with all of the terms in this chapter.

Chapter 12 R E V I E W

Chapter 12 Review

Vocabulary Review

Choose a word or words from the Word Bank that best complete each sentence. Write the answer on a sheet of paper.

Word Bank
- attract
- electromagnet
- electromagnetism
- lines of force
- magnetic field
- magnetic poles
- motor
- repel

1. A device that converts electrical energy to mechanical energy is a(n) _____.

2. A temporary magnet made by passing a current through wire wrapped around an iron core is a(n) _____.

3. The area around a magnet in which magnetic forces can act is the _____.

4. The lines that show a magnetic field are the _____.

5. Magnetic poles of opposite types _____ each other.

6. The opposite points or ends of a magnet where magnetic forces are greatest are the _____.

7. The relationship between magnetism and electricity is _____.

8. Magnetic poles of the same type _____ each other.

Concept Review

Choose the answer that best completes each sentence. Write the letter of the answer on your paper.

9. A magnet's lines of force are closest together near the _____.

  A fields   **B** poles   **C** center   **D** edges

10. The magnetic fields of atoms line up in _____.

  A a nonmagnetized field   **C** iron

  B a magnetized field   **D** both B and C

Chapter 12 Mastery Test A

Name _____ Date _____ Period _____ | Mastery Test A, Page 1 — Chapter 12

Chapter 12 Mastery Test A

Part A Write the letter of the best answer on the line next to the number.

_____ **1.** The earth is sometimes described as a giant _____.
  A electromagnet   **C** magnet
  B solenoid   **D** compass

_____ **2.** An electromagnet will not work without which of the following?
  A an iron nail   **C** a size D battery
  B an electric current   **D** superconducting material

_____ **3.** Which of the following techniques can demagnetize a magnet?
  A drop it in water   **C** pass it near another magnet
  B subject it to cold temperatures   **D** strike it with a hard blow

_____ **4.** Telephones use electromagnets to change _____.
  A electric currents to light waves   **C** magnetism to light waves
  B electric currents to sound waves   **D** magnetism to sound waves

_____ **5.** When the north poles of two magnets are placed together, the poles _____.
  A repel each other   **C** have no effect on each other
  B attract each other   **D** demagnetize each other

_____ **6.** Which of the following could you "fish" out of a pond with a magnet?
  A a nickel necklace   **C** a copper bracelet
  B a gold ring   **D** a plastic badge

Part B Match each term on the left with its meaning on the right. Write the letter of the correct answer on the line.

_____ **7.** motor   **A** opposite ends of a magnet
_____ **8.** attract   **B** push apart
_____ **9.** magnetic field   **C** temporary magnet
_____ **10.** repel   **D** something that attracts
_____ **11.** lines of force   **E** pull together
_____ **12.** magnetic poles   **F** converts electrical energy to mechanical energy
_____ **13.** electromagnet   **G** show a magnetic field
_____ **14.** magnet   **H** space in which magnets can act

©AGS Publishing. Permission is granted to reproduce for classroom use only.   Physical Science

---

Name _____ Date _____ Period _____ | Mastery Test A, Page 2 — Chapter 12

Chapter 12 Mastery Test A, continued

Part C Write a short answer for each question.

15. What is a magnetic field?

16. Explain what causes magnetism.

17. Explain how a compass works.

18. Explain what happens when a bar magnet is cut in half.

19. Explain how electromagnets work.

20. Describe one use of electromagnetism.

©AGS Publishing. Permission is granted to reproduce for classroom use only.   Physical Science

Chapter 12 Mastery Test A

11. A motor is made of a(n) _____.

 A alternating electric current supply

 B electromagnet

 C permanent magnet

 D all of the above

12. An electromagnet is magnetic as long as _____ is flowing through it.

 A air   **B** current   **C** heat   **D** water

Critical Thinking

Write the answer to each of these questions on your paper.

13. What is the difference between a regular magnet and an electromagnet?

14. Explain a way to make a magnet and a way to destroy a magnet.

15. Suppose a bar magnet like the one shown here was cut into three pieces. Explain what would happen to the magnet's poles.

Test-Taking Tip   Read test questions carefully to identify the questions that require more than one answer.

Review Answers
Critical Thinking

13. A regular magnet is constantly magnetized. An electromagnet can be turned off by stopping the flow of current through the coiled wire. **14.** You can make a magnet by stroking an iron wire in one direction with a magnet. You can destroy a magnet by heating it or striking it with a hard blow. **15.** Each piece would be a complete magnet with a north and a south pole. Each piece would still contain atoms lined up in the same direction.

ALTERNATIVE ASSESSMENT

Alternative Assessment items correlate to the student Goals for Learning at the beginning of this chapter.

■ Give students a small box filled with differently shaped magnets. Have students group the magnets according to shape and label the shape names.

■ Give each student a piece of blue or red paper. Tell students that they are magnetic poles and ask them to find appropriate partners. They should team up with someone who has paper of the opposite color.

■ Supply pairs of students with two rulers and several paper clips. Instruct each pair to arrange the clips around a ruler to demonstrate the magnetic field around a magnet. Then have them show how the lines of force affect each other when two magnets are pole to pole—both like and opposite.

■ Have small groups of students prepare a lesson on magnetism for younger children. Suggest they create illustrations and demonstrate how to make and destroy a magnet.

■ Invite three or four volunteers to role-play scientists with expertise in electromagnetism. Have them form a panel and field questions from the class.

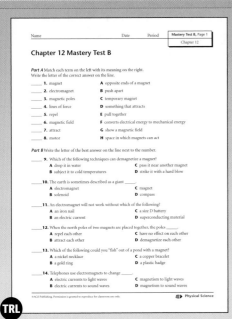

Chapter 12 Mastery Test B

Appendix A: Alternative Energy Sources

Fossil Fuels

We fly through the air in planes. We roll down highways in cars. On the coldest days, our homes are warm. Our stores are full of products to satisfy our needs and wants.

The power that runs our lives comes from fossil fuels. A fossil is the remains of ancient life. Fossil fuels formed from the remains of dead matter—animals and plants. Over millions of years, forests of plants died, fell, and became buried in the earth. Over time, the layers of ancient, dead matter changed. The carbon in the animals and plants turned into a material we now use as fuel. Fossil fuels include coal, oil, natural gas, and gasoline.

Fossil fuels power our lives and our society. In the United States, electricity comes mainly from power plants that burn coal. Industries use electricity to run machines. In our homes, we use electricity to power lightbulbs, TVs, and everything else electric. Heat and hot water for many homes come from natural gas or oil, or from fuels that come from oil.

Of course, cars and trucks run on gasoline, which is also made from oil. Powering our society with fossil fuels has made our lives more comfortable. Yet our need for fossil fuels has caused problems. Fossil fuels are a nonrenewable source of energy. That means that there is a limited supply of these fuels. At some point, fossil fuels will become scarce. Their cost will increase. And one day the supply of fossil fuels will run out. We need to find ways now to depend less and less on fossil fuels.

Fossil fuels cause pollution. The pollution comes from burning them. It is like the exhaust from a car. The pollution enters the air and causes disease. It harms the environment. One serious effect of burning fossil fuels is global warming. Carbon dioxide comes from the burning of fossil fuels. When a large amount of this gas enters the air, it warms the earth's climate. Scientists believe that warming of the climate will cause serious problems.

Renewable Energy

Many people believe that we should use renewable fuels as sources of energy. Renewable fuels never run out. They last forever.

What kinds of fuels last forever? The energy from the sun. The energy in the wind. The energy in oceans and rivers. We can use these forms of energy to power our lives. Then we will never run out of fuel. We will cut down on pollution and climate warming. Using renewable energy is not a dream for the future. It is happening right now—right here—today.

Energy from the Sun

As long as the sun keeps shining, the earth will get energy from sunlight. Energy from the sun is called solar energy. It is the energy in light. When you lie in the sun, your skin becomes hot. The heat comes from the energy in sunlight. Sunlight is a form of renewable energy we can use forever.

We use solar energy to make electricity. The electricity can power homes and businesses. Turning solar energy into electricity is called photovoltaics, or PV for short. Here's how PV works.

Flat solar panels are put near a building or on its roof. The panels face the direction that gets the most sunlight. The panels contain many PV cells. The cells are made from silicon—a material that absorbs light. When sunlight strikes the cells, some of the light energy is absorbed. The energy knocks some electrons loose in the silicon. The electrons begin to flow. The electron flow is controlled. An electric current is produced. Pieces of metal at the top and bottom of each cell make a path for electrons. The path leads the electric current away from the solar panel. The electric current flows through wires to a battery. The battery stores the electrical energy. The electrical wiring in a building is connected to the battery. All the electricity used in the building comes from the battery.

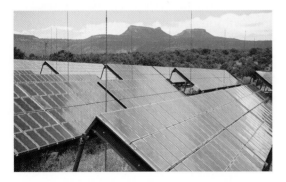

Today, PV use is 500 times greater than it was 20 years ago. And PV use is growing about 20 percent per year. Yet solar energy systems are still not perfect. PV cells do not absorb all the sunlight that strikes them, so some energy is lost. Solar energy systems also are not cheap. Still, every year, PV systems are improved. The cost of PV electricity has decreased. The amount of sunlight PV cells absorb has increased.

On a sunny day, every square meter of the earth receives 1,000 watts of energy from sunlight. Someday, when PV systems are able to use all this energy, our energy problems may be solved.

Energy from the Wind

Sunlight warms different parts of the earth differently. The North Pole gets little sunlight, so it is cold. Areas near the equator get lots of sunlight, so they are warm. The uneven warming of the earth by the sun creates the wind. As the earth turns, the wind moves, or blows. The blowing wind can be used to make electricity. This is wind energy. Because the earth's winds will blow forever, the wind is a renewable source of energy.

Wind energy is not new. Hundreds of years ago, windmills created energy. The wind turned the large fins on a windmill. As the fins spun around, they turned huge stones inside the mill. The stones ground grain into flour.

Modern windmills are tall, metal towers with spinning blades, called wind turbines. Each wind turbine has three main parts. It has blades that are turned by blowing wind. The turning blades are attached to a shaft that runs the length of the tower. The turning blades spin the shaft. The spinning shaft is connected to a generator.

A generator changes the energy from movement into electrical energy. It feeds the electricity into wires, which carry it to homes and factories.

Wind turbines are placed in areas where strong winds blow. A single house may have one small wind turbine near it to produce its electricity. The electricity produced by the wind turbine is stored in batteries. Many wind turbines may be linked together to produce electricity for an entire town. In these systems, the electricity moves from the generator to the electric company's wires. The wires carry the electricity to homes and businesses.

Studies show that 34 of the 50 United States have good wind conditions. These states could use wind to meet up to 20 percent of their electric power needs. Canada's wind conditions could produce up to 20 percent of its energy from wind, too. Alberta already produces a lot of energy from wind, and the amount is expected to increase.

Energy from Inside the Earth

Deep inside the earth, the rocks are burning hot. Beneath them it is even hotter. There, rocks melt into liquid. The earth's inner heat rises to the surface in some places. Today,

people have developed ways to use this heat to create energy. Because the inside of the earth will always be very hot, this energy is renewable. It is called geothermal energy (*geo* means earth; *thermal* means heat).

Geothermal energy is used where hot water or steam from deep inside the earth moves near the surface. These areas are called "hot spots." At hot spots, we can use geothermal energy directly. Pumps raise the hot water, and pipes carry it to buildings. The water is used to heat the space in the buildings or to heat water.

Geothermal energy may also be used indirectly to make electricity. A power plant is built near a hot spot. Wells are drilled deep into the hot spot. The wells carry hot water or steam into the power plant. There, it is used to boil more water. The boiling water makes steam. The steam turns the blades of a turbine. This energy is carried to a generator, which turns it into electricity. The electricity moves through the electric company's wires to homes and factories.

Everywhere on the earth, several miles beneath the surface, there is hot material. Scientists are improving ways of tapping the earth's inner heat. Some day, this renewable, pollution-free source of energy may be available everywhere.

Energy from Trash

We can use the leftover products that come from plants to make electricity. For example, we can use the stalks from corn or wheat to make fuel. Many leftover products from crops and lumber can fuel power plants. Because this fuel comes from living plants, it is called bioenergy (*bio* means life or living). The plant waste itself is called biomass.

People have used bioenergy for thousands of years. Burning wood in a fireplace is a form of bioenergy. That's because wood comes from trees. Bioenergy is renewable, because people will always grow crops. There will always be crop waste we can burn as fuel.

Some power plants burn biomass to heat water. The steam from the boiling water turns turbines. The turbines create electricity. In other power plants, biomass is changed into a gas. The gas is used as fuel to boil water, which turns the turbine.

Biomass can also be made into a fuel for cars and trucks. Scientists use a special process to turn biomass into fuels, such as ethanol. Car makers are designing cars that can run on these fuels. Cars that use these fuels produce far less pollution than cars that run on gas.

Bioenergy can help solve our garbage problem. Many cities are having trouble finding places to dump all their trash. There would be fewer garbage dumps if we burned some trash to make electricity.

Bioenergy is a renewable energy. But it is not a perfect solution to our energy problems. Burning biomass creates air pollution.

Energy from the Ocean

Have you ever been knocked over by a small wave while wading in the ocean? If so, you know how much power ocean water has. The motion of ocean waves can be a source of energy. So can the rise and fall of ocean tides. There are several systems that use the energy in ocean waves and tides. All of them are very new and still being developed.

In one system, ocean waves enter a funnel. The water flows into a reservoir, an area behind a dam where water is stored. When the dam opens, water flows out of the reservoir. This powers a turbine, which creates electricity. Another system uses the waves' motion to operate water pumps, which run an electric generator. There is also a system that uses the rise and fall of ocean waves. The waves compress air in a container. During high tide, large amounts of ocean water enter the container. The air in the container is under great pressure. When the high-pressure air in the container is released, it drives a turbine. This creates electricity.

Energy can also come from the rise and fall of ocean tides. A dam is built across a tidal basin. This is an area where land surrounds the sea on three sides. At high tide, ocean water is allowed to flow through the dam. The water flow turns turbines, which generate electricity. There is one serious problem with tidal energy. It damages the environment of the tidal basin and can harm animals that live there.

The oceans also contain a great deal of thermal (heat) energy. The sun heats the surface of the oceans more than it heats deep ocean water. In one day, ocean surfaces absorb solar energy equal to 250 billion barrels of oil! Deep ocean water, which gets no sunlight, is much colder than the surface.

Scientists are developing ways to use this temperature difference to create energy. The systems they are currently designing are complicated and expensive.

Energy from Rivers and Dams

Dams built across rivers also produce electricity. When the dam is open, the flowing water turns turbines, which make electricity. This is called hydroelectric power (*hydro* means water). The United States gets 7 percent of its electricity from hydroelectric power. Canada gets up to 60 percent of its electricity from hydroelectric plants built across its many rivers.

Hydroelectric power is a nonpolluting and renewable form of energy—in a way. There will always be fresh water. However, more and more people are taking water from rivers for different uses. These uses include

drinking, watering crops, and supplying industry. Some rivers are becoming smaller and weaker because of the water taken from them. Also, in many places dams built across rivers hurt the environment. The land behind the dam is "drowned." Once the dam is built, fish may not be able swim up or down the river. In northwestern states, salmon have completely disappeared from many rivers that have dams.

Energy from Hydrogen Fuel

Hydrogen is a gas that is abundant everywhere on the earth. It's in the air. It is a part of water. Because there is so much hydrogen, it is a renewable energy source. And hydrogen can produce energy without any pollution.

The most likely source of hydrogen fuel is water. Water is made up of hydrogen and oxygen. A special process separates these elements in water. The process produces oxygen gas and hydrogen gas. The hydrogen gas is changed into a liquid or solid. This hydrogen fuel is used to produce energy in a fuel cell.

Look at the diagram on page 377. Hydrogen fuel (H_2) is fed into one part of the fuel cell. It is then stripped of its electrons. The free electrons create an electric current (e). The electric current powers a lightbulb or whatever is connected to the fuel cell.

Meanwhile, oxygen (O_2) from the air enters another part of the fuel cell. The stripped hydrogen (H+) bonds with the oxygen, forming water (H_2O). So a car powered by a fuel cell has pure water leaving its tailpipe. There is no exhaust to pollute the air.

When a regular battery's power is used up,

the battery dies. A fuel cell never runs down as long as it gets hydrogen fuel.

A single fuel cell produces little electricity. To make more electricity, fuel cells come in "stacks" of many fuel cells packaged together. Stacked fuel cells are used to power cars and buses. Soon, they may provide electric power to homes and factories.

Hydrogen Fuel Cell

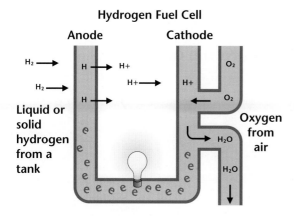

Hydrogen fuel shows great promise, but it still has problems. First, hydrogen fuel is difficult to store and distribute. Today's gas stations would have to be changed into hydrogen-fuel stations. Homes and factories would need safe ways to store solid hydrogen.

Second, producing hydrogen fuel by separating water is expensive. It is cheaper to make hydrogen fuel from oil. But that would create pollution and use nonrenewable resources. Scientists continue to look for solutions to these problems.

Energy from Atoms

Our sun gets its energy—its heat and light— from fusion. Fusion is the joining together of parts of atoms. Fusion produces enormous amounts of energy. But conditions like those on the sun are needed for fusion to occur. Fusion requires incredibly high temperatures.

In the next few decades, scientists may find ways to fuse atoms at lower temperatures. When this happens, we may be able to use fusion for energy. Fusion is a renewable form of energy because it uses hydrogen atoms. It also produces no pollution. And it produces no dangerous radiation. Using fusion to produce power is a long way off. But if the technology can be developed, fusion could provide us with renewable, clean energy.

Today's nuclear power plants produce energy by splitting atoms. This creates no air pollution. But nuclear energy has other problems. Nuclear energy is fueled by a substance we get from mines called uranium. There is only a limited amount of uranium in the earth. So it is not renewable. And uranium produces dangerous radiation, which can harm or kill living things if it escapes the power plant. Used uranium must be thrown out, even though it is radioactive and dangerous. In 1999, the United States produced nearly 41 tons of radioactive waste from nuclear power plants. However, less uranium is being mined. No new nuclear power plants have been built. The amount of energy produced from nuclear power is expected to fall. People are turning toward less harmful, renewable energy sources: the sun, wind, underground heat, biomass, water, and hydrogen fuel.

Fuel That U.S. Electric Utilities Used to Generate Electricity in 2000

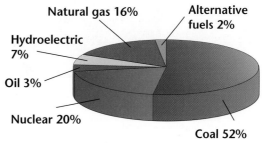

Source: U.S. Dept. of Energy Hydropower Program

Appendix B: The Periodic Table of Elements

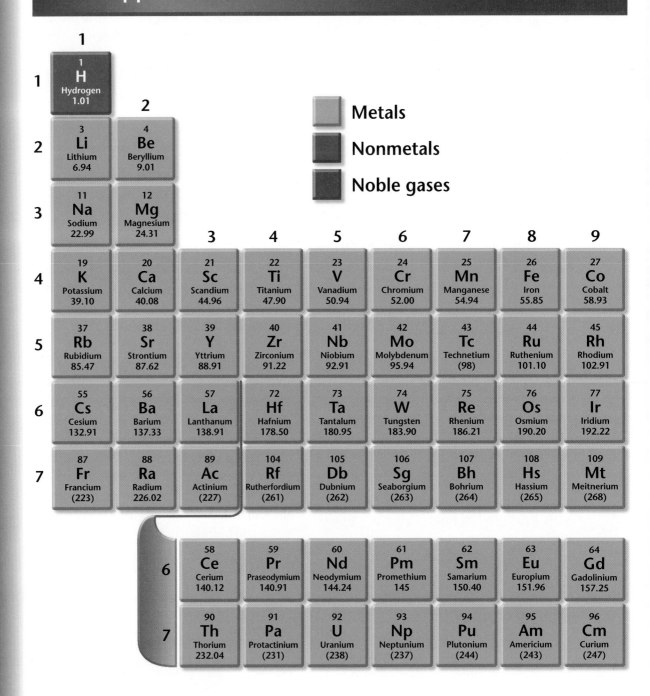

Metals

Nonmetals

Noble gases

1								
1 1 **H** Hydrogen 1.01								

1 H Hydrogen 1.01

2
3 **Li** Lithium 6.94   4 **Be** Beryllium 9.01

11 **Na** Sodium 22.99   12 **Mg** Magnesium 24.31

3 21 **Sc** Scandium 44.96

4 22 **Ti** Titanium 47.90

5 23 **V** Vanadium 50.94

6 24 **Cr** Chromium 52.00

7 25 **Mn** Manganese 54.94

8 26 **Fe** Iron 55.85

9 27 **Co** Cobalt 58.93

Period 4: 19 **K** Potassium 39.10 | 20 **Ca** Calcium 40.08

Period 5: 37 **Rb** Rubidium 85.47 | 38 **Sr** Strontium 87.62 | 39 **Y** Yttrium 88.91 | 40 **Zr** Zirconium 91.22 | 41 **Nb** Niobium 92.91 | 42 **Mo** Molybdenum 95.94 | 43 **Tc** Technetium (98) | 44 **Ru** Ruthenium 101.10 | 45 **Rh** Rhodium 102.91

Period 6: 55 **Cs** Cesium 132.91 | 56 **Ba** Barium 137.33 | 57 **La** Lanthanum 138.91 | 72 **Hf** Hafnium 178.50 | 73 **Ta** Tantalum 180.95 | 74 **W** Tungsten 183.90 | 75 **Re** Rhenium 186.21 | 76 **Os** Osmium 190.20 | 77 **Ir** Iridium 192.22

Period 7: 87 **Fr** Francium (223) | 88 **Ra** Radium 226.02 | 89 **Ac** Actinium (227) | 104 **Rf** Rutherfordium (261) | 105 **Db** Dubnium (262) | 106 **Sg** Seaborgium (263) | 107 **Bh** Bohrium (264) | 108 **Hs** Hassium (265) | 109 **Mt** Meitnerium (268)

6 58 **Ce** Cerium 140.12 | 59 **Pr** Praseodymium 140.91 | 60 **Nd** Neodymium 144.24 | 61 **Pm** Promethium 145 | 62 **Sm** Samarium 150.40 | 63 **Eu** Europium 151.96 | 64 **Gd** Gadolinium 157.25

7 90 **Th** Thorium 232.04 | 91 **Pa** Protactinium (231) | 92 **U** Uranium (238) | 93 **Np** Neptunium (237) | 94 **Pu** Plutonium (244) | 95 **Am** Americium (243) | 96 **Cm** Curium (247)

Periodic table (partial)

Group 18

| 2 | He | Helium | 4.00 |

Group 13

| 5 | B | Boron | 10.81 |
| 13 | Al | Aluminum | 26.98 |

Group 14

| 6 | C | Carbon | 12.01 |
| 14 | Si | Silicon | 28.09 |

Group 15

| 7 | N | Nitrogen | 14.01 |
| 15 | P | Phosphorus | 30.97 |

Group 16

| 8 | O | Oxygen | 16.00 |
| 16 | S | Sulfur | 32.07 |

Group 17

9	F	Fluorine	19.00
17	Cl	Chlorine	35.45
18	Ar	Argon	39.95
10	Ne	Neon	20.18

Group	10	11	12	13	14	15	16	17	18
	28 Ni Nickel 58.70	29 Cu Copper 63.55	30 Zn Zinc 65.39	31 Ga Gallium 69.72	32 Ge Germanium 72.59	33 As Arsenic 74.92	34 Se Selenium 78.96	35 Br Bromine 79.90	36 Kr Krypton 83.80
	46 Pd Palladium 106.42	47 Ag Silver 107.90	48 Cd Cadmium 112.41	49 In Indium 114.82	50 Sn Tin 118.69	51 Sb Antimony 121.75	52 Te Tellurium 127.60	53 I Iodine 126.90	54 Xe Xenon 131.30
	78 Pt Platinum 195.09	79 Au Gold 196.97	80 Hg Mercury 200.59	81 Tl Thallium 204.40	82 Pb Lead 207.20	83 Bi Bismuth 208.98	84 Po Polonium 209	85 At Astatine (210)	86 Rn Radon (222)
	110 Uun Ununnilium (269)	111 Uuu Unununium (272)	112 Uub Ununbium (277)		114 Uuq Ununquadium (289)		116 Uuh Ununhexium (289)		

65 Tb Terbium 158.93	66 Dy Dysprosium 162.50	67 Ho Holmium 164.93	68 Er Erbium 167.26	69 Tm Thulium 168.93	70 Yb Ytterbium 173.04	71 Lu Lutetium 174.97
97 Bk Berkelium (247)	98 Cf Californium (249)	99 Es Einsteinium (254)	100 Fm Fermium (257)	101 Md Mendelevium (258)	102 No Nobelium (259)	103 Lr Lawrencium (260)

Note: *The atomic masses listed in the table reflect current measurements.*
The atomic masses listed in parentheses are those of the element's most stable or most common isotope.

Appendix C: Measurement Conversion Factors

Metric Measures

Length
1,000 meters (m) = 1 kilometer (km)
100 centimeters (cm) = 1 m
10 decimeters (dm) = 1 m
1,000 millimeters (mm) = 1 m
10 cm = 1 decimeter (dm)
10 mm = 1 cm

Area
100 square millimeters (mm^2) = 1 square centimeter (cm^2)
10,000 cm^2 = 1 square meter (m^2)
10,000 m^2 = 1 hectare (ha)

Volume
1,000 cubic meters (m^3) = 1 cubic centimeter (cm^3)
1,000 cubic centimeters (cm^3) = 1 liter (L)
1 cubic centimeter (cm^3) = 1 milliliter (mL)
100 cm^3 = 1 cubic decimeter (dm^3)
1,000,000 cm^3 = 1 cubic meter (m^3)

Capacity
1,000 milliliters (mL) = 1 liter (L)
1,000 L = 1 kiloliter (kL)

Mass
100 grams (g) = 1 centigram (cg)
1,000 kilograms (kg) = 1 metric ton (t)
1,000 grams (g) = 1 kg
1,000 milligrams (mg) = 1 g

Temperature Degrees Celsius (°C)
0°C = freezing point of water
37°C = normal body temperature
100°C = boiling point of water

Time
60 seconds (sec) = 1 minute (min)
60 min = 1 hour (hr)
24 hr = 1 day

Customary Measures

Length
12 inches (in.) = 1 foot (ft)
3 ft = 1 yard (yd)
36 in. = 1 yd
5,280 ft = 1 mile (mi)
1,760 yd = 1 mi
6,076 feet = 1 nautical mile

Area
144 square inches (sq in.) = 1 square foot (sq ft)
9 sq ft = 1 square yard (sq yd)
43,560 sq ft = 1 acre (A)

Volume
1,728 cubic inches (cu in.) = 1 cubic foot (cu ft)
27 cu ft = 1 cubic yard (cu yard)

Capacity
8 fluid ounces (fl oz) = 1 cup (c)
2 c = 1 pint (pt)
2 pt = 1 quart (qt)
4 qt = 1 gallon (gal)

Weight
16 ounces (oz) = 1 pound (lb)
2,000 lb = 1 ton (T)

Temperature Degrees Fahrenheit (°F)
32°F = freezing point of water
98.6°F = normal body temperature
212°F = boiling point of water

To change	To	Multiply by	To change	To	Multiply by
centimeters	inches	0.3937	meters	feet	3.2808
centimeters	feet	0.03281	meters	miles	0.0006214
cubic feet	cubic meters	0.0283	meters	yards	1.0936
cubic meters	cubic feet	35.3145	metric tons	tons (long)	0.9842
cubic meters	cubic yards	1.3079	metric tons	tons (short)	1.1023
cubic yards	cubic meters	0.7646	miles	kilometers	1.6093
feet	meters	0.3048	miles	feet	5,280
feet	miles (nautical)	0.0001645	miles (statute)	miles (nautical)	0.8684
feet	miles (statute)	0.0001894	miles/hour	feet/minute	88
feet/second	miles/hour	0.6818	millimeters	inches	0.0394
gallons (U.S.)	liters	3.7853	ounces avdp	grams	28.3495
grams	ounces avdp	0.0353	ounces	pounds	0.0625
grams	pounds	0.002205	pecks	liters	8.8096
hours	days	0.04167	pints (dry)	liters	0.5506
inches	millimeters	25.4000	pints (liquid)	liters	0.4732
inches	centimeters	2.5400	pounds advp	kilograms	0.4536
kilograms	pounds avdp	2.2046	pounds	ounces	16
kilometers	miles	0.6214	quarts (dry)	liters	1.1012
liters	gallons (U.S.)	0.2642	quarts (liquid)	liters	0.9463
liters	pecks	0.1135	square feet	square meters	0.0929
liters	pints (dry)	1.8162	square meters	square feet	10.7639
liters	pints (liquid)	2.1134	square meters	square yards	1.1960
liters	quarts (dry)	0.9081	square yards	square meters	0.8361
liters	quarts (liquid)	1.0567	yards	meters	0.9144

Appendix D: Decimal, Percent, and Fraction Conversions

Renaming Decimals as Percents

Example   Rename 0.75 as a percent.

Solution   0.75

0.75 = 75%

Step 1   Move the decimal point two places to the right.

Step 2   Then insert a percent symbol.

Example   Rename 0.5 as a percent.

Solution   0.5 = 0.50

0.5 = 50%

Renaming Percents as Decimals

Example   Rename 80% as a decimal.

Solution   80% = 80.%

80% = 0.80

= 0.8 ◀── You can always drop zeros at the end of a decimal.

Step 1   Move the decimal point two places to the left.

Step 2   Then drop the percent symbol.

Renaming Fractions as Decimals

Example   Rename $\frac{7}{20}$ as a decimal.

Solution   **Method 1**

$\frac{7}{20} = \frac{7 \times 5}{20 \times 5} = \frac{35}{100}$

$= 0.35$

Choose a multiplier that makes the denominator a power of 10 (10, 100, 1,000, . . .)

Method 2

$$\frac{7}{20} = \quad 20 \overline{)7.00} \atop \begin{array}{r} .35 \\ \hline -6\,0 \\ \hline 1\,00 \\ -1\,00 \end{array}$$

Divide the numerator by the denominator.

Renaming Decimals as Fractions

Example   Rename 0.025 as a fraction.

Solution   First, read the decimal: "25 thousandths."

Then write the fraction and simplify.

$$0.025 = \frac{25}{1,000} = \frac{25 \div 25}{1,000 \div 25} = \frac{1}{40}$$

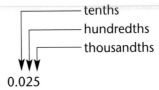

Renaming Fractions as Percents

Example   Rename $\frac{9}{25}$ as a percent.

Solution   **Method 1**

Write as an equivalent fraction with denominator 100.

$$\frac{9}{25} = \frac{9 \times 4}{25 \times 4} = \frac{36}{100} = 36\%$$

Percent means per 100.
So, 36 hundredths is 36%.

Method 2

$$\frac{9}{25} = 0.36 = 36\%$$

Step 1   Divide the numerator by the denominator.

Step 2   Rewrite the decimal as a percent.

Renaming Percents as Fractions

Example   Rename 2% as a fraction.

Solution

$$2\% = \frac{2}{100}$$ ⟵   *Percent* means *per 100.*

$$= \frac{1}{50}$$ ⟵   Simplify.

Glossary

A

Acceleration (ak sel ə rā′ shən) the rate of change in velocity (p. 187)

Acid (as′ id) a compound that reacts with metals to produce hydrogen (p. 138)

Alloy (al′ oi) a mixture of two or more metals (p. 107)

Alternating current (ȯl tər nā′ ting ker′ənt) current that changes direction regularly (p. 323)

Ampere (am′ pir) the unit used to describe how much electric current flows through a wire (p. 311)

Area (âr′ ē ə) amount of space the surface of an object takes up (p. 15)

Atom (at′ əm) the building block of matter (p. 61)

Atomic mass (ə tom′ ik mas) the average mass of all the isotopes of a particular element (p. 102)

Atomic number (ə tom′ ik num′ bər) a number equal to the number of protons in the nucleus of an atom (p. 82)

Attract (ə trakt′) to pull together (p. 349)

B

Balance (bal′ əns) an instrument used to measure mass (p. 38); to keep the number of atoms the same on both sides of the equation (p. 157)

Base (bās) a compound that contains the hydroxyl (OH) radical (p. 139)

Battery (bat′ erē) a source of voltage that changes chemical energy into electrical energy (p. 321)

Binary compound (bī′ nərē kom′ pound) a compound that contains two elements (p. 134)

Boiling point (boi ling pȯint) the temperature at which a substance changes from a liquid to a gas under normal atmospheric pressure (p. 254)

C

Calorie (kal′ ə re) a unit of heat; the amount of heat needed to raise the temperature of 1 g of water by 1°C (p. 57)

Celsius scale (sel′ sē əs skāl) the temperature scale used by scientists and by people in most countries, in which water freezes at 0° and boils at 100° (p. 251)

Centigram (cg) (sen′ tə gram) a unit of mass in the metric system that is $\frac{1}{100}$ of a gram (p. 25)

Centimeter (cm) (sen′ tə mē tər) a metric unit of measure that is $\frac{1}{100}$ of a meter (p. 10)

Chemical bond (kem′ ə kəl bond) the attractive force that holds atoms together (p. 127)

Chemical change (kem′ ə kəl chānj) a change that produces one or more new substances with new chemical properties (p. 118)

Chemical equation (kem′ ə kəl i kwā′ zhən) a statement that uses symbols, formulas, and numbers to stand for a chemical reaction (p. 155)

Chemical formula (kem′ ə kəl fôr′ myə lə) tells the kinds of atoms and how many of each kind are in a compound (p. 129)

Chemical reaction (kem′ ə kəl rē ak′ shən) a chemical change in which elements are combined or rearranged (p.150)

Chemistry (kem′ ə strē) the study of matter and how it changes (p. 3)

Circuit (ser′ kit) a path for electric current (p. 311)

Closed circuit (klōzd′ sėr′ kit) a complete, unbroken path for electric current (p. 311)

Coefficient (kō′ ə fish′ ənt) a number placed before a formula in a chemical equation (p. 157)

Compound (kom′ pound) a substance that is formed when atoms of two or more elements join together (p. 70)

Concave lens (kon kav´ lenz) a lens that is thin in the middle and thick at the edges (p. 301)

Concave mirror (kon kav´ mir´ ər) a mirror that curves in at the middle (p. 296)

Condensation (kon den sā´ shən) to change from a gas to a liquid (p. 244)

Conduction (kan duk´ shən) the movement of heat energy from one molecule to the next (p. 263)

Conductor (kan duk´ tər) material through which heat travels easily (p. 263); material through which electricity passes easily (p. 315)

Constant speed (kon´ stənt spēd) speed that does not change (p. 179)

Contract (kən trakt´) to become smaller in size (p. 245)

Convection (kən vek´ shən) flow of energy that occurs when a warm liquid or gas rises (p. 264)

Convex lens (kon veks´ lenz) a lens that is thick in the middle and thin at the edges (p. 302)

Convex mirror (kon veks´ mir´ ər) a mirror that curves outward at the middle (p. 297)

Cubic centimeter (cm³) (kyü´ bik sen´ tə mē tər) a metric unit of measure that means centimeter x centimeter x centimeter (p. 201)

Customary (kus´ tə mer´ ē) ordinary (p. 7)

Cycle (sī´ kəl) the complete back-and-forth motion of a vibration (p. 277)

D

Deceleration (dē sel´ ə rā shən) the rate of slowdown (p. 188)

Decibel (des´ ə bəl) a unit that measures the intensity of sound (p. 275)

Decomposition reaction (dē´ kom pə zish´ ən rē ak´ shən) a reaction in which a compound breaks down into two or more simple substances (p. 162)

Degree (di grē´) a unit of measurement on a temperature scale (p. 251)

Density (den´ sə tē) a measure of how tightly the matter of a substance is packed into a given volume (p. 49)

Deuterium (dü tir´ ē əm) an isotope of hydrogen that has one proton and one neutron (p. 99)

Direct current (də rekt´ kėr´ ənt) current that flows in one direction (p. 323)

Displacement of water (dis plās´ mənt ov wo´ tər) method of measuring the volume of an irregularly shaped object (p. 46)

Dissolve (di zolv´) to break apart (p. 151)

Distance (dis´ təns) the length of the path between two points (p. 175)

Double-replacement reaction (dub´ əl ri plās´ mənt rē ak´ shən) a reaction in which the elements in two compounds are exchanged (p. 165)

Dry-cell battery (drī sel bat´ ərē) electric power source with a dry or pastelike center (p. 321)

E

Echo (ek´ ō) a sound that is reflected to its source (p. 283)

Efficiency (ə fish´ ən sē) how well a machine performs (p. 221)

Effort arm (ef´ ərt ärm) the distance between the fulcrum and the effort force of a lever (p. 225)

Effort force (F$_e$) (ef´ ərt fôrs) the force applied to a machine by the user (p. 218)

Elapsed time (i´ lapsd tim) the length of time that passes from one event to another (p. 174)

Electric current (i lek´ trik kėr´ ənt) movement of electrons from one place to another (p. 311)

Electric power (i lek´ trik pou´ ər) the amount of electrical energy used in a certain amount of time (p. 340)

a	hat	e	let	ī	ice	ȯ	order	u̇	put	sh	she		a	in about
ā	age	ē	equal	o	hot	oi	oil	ü	rule	th	thin	ə	e	in taken
ä	far	ėr	term	ō	open	ou	out	ch	child	ᵺ	then		i	in pencil
â	care	i	it	ȯ	saw	u	cup	ng	long	zh	measure		o	in lemon
													u	in circus

Electricity (i lek tris´ ə tē) flow of electrons (p. 310)

Electromagnet (i lek trō mag´ nit) a temporary magnet made by passing a current through a wire wrapped around an iron core (p. 360)

Electromagnetism (i lek trō mag´ ni tism) the relationship between magnetism and electricity (p. 360)

Electromotive force (i lek trə mō´ tiv fôrs) the push that keeps the current (electrons) flowing in an electric circuit (p. 320)

Electron (i lek´ tron) a tiny particle of an atom that moves around the nucleus (p. 76)

Element (el´ ə mənt) matter that has only one kind of atom (p. 65)

Energy (en´ ər jē) the ability to do work (p. 211)

Energy level (en´ ər jē lev´ əl) one of the spaces around the nucleus of an atom in which an electron moves (p. 123)

Evaporate (i vap´ ə rat´) to change from a liquid to a gas (p. 244)

Expand (ek spand´) to become larger in size (p. 245)

Exponent (ek spō´ nənt) a number that tells how many times another number is a factor (p. 15)

F

Family (fam´ ə lē) a group of elements with similar properties, arranged together in a column of the periodic table (p. 103)

Fahrenheit scale (far´ ən hīt skāl) the temperature scale commonly used in the United States, in which water freezes at 32° and boils at 212° (p. 251)

Farsighted (fär´ sī´ tid) able to see objects at a distance clearly (p. 303)

Focal point (fō´ kəl point) the point where reflected light rays from a concave mirror come together in front of the mirror (p. 296)

Force (fôrs) a push or a pull (p. 192)

Freezing point (frēz´ ing point) the temperature at which a liquid changes to a solid (p. 253)

Frequency (frē´ kwən sē) the number of vibrations per second of a sound wave (p. 277)

Friction (frik´ shən) a force that opposes motion and that occurs when things slide or roll over each other (p. 192)

Fulcrum (ful´ krəm) a fixed point around which a lever rotates (p. 218)

G

Gas (gas) a form of matter that has no definite shape or volume (p. 63)

Generator (jen´ ə rā tər) a device used to convert mechanical energy to electrical energy (p. 213)

Graduated cylinder (graj´ ü ā tid sil´ ən dər) a round glass or plastic cylinder used to measure the volume of liquids (p. 43)

Gram (g) (gram) basic unit of mass in the metric system (p. 24)

Gravity (grav´ ə tē) the force of attraction between any two objects that have mass (p. 196)

H

Heat (hēt) a form of energy resulting from the motion of particles in matter (p. 240)

Heat source (hēt sôrs) a place from which heat energy comes (p. 241)

Hertz (Hz) (hėrts) the unit used to measure frequency of a sound; one Hertz equals one cycle per second (p. 277)

I

Image (im´ ij) a copy or likeness (p. 295)

Inclined plane (in klīnd´ plān) a simple machine made up of a ramp, used to lift an object (p. 231)

Indicator (in´ də kā tər) a substance that changes color when in an acid or a base (p. 139)

Inert (in ėrt´) inactive; lacking the power to move (p. 109)

Inertia (in ėr´ shə) the tendency of an object to resist changes in its motion (p. 193)

Insulator (in´ sə lā tər) material that does not conduct heat well (p. 263); material through which electricity does not pass easily (p. 315)

Intensity (in ten´ sə tē) the strength of a sound (p. 275)

Ion (ī′ ən) an atom that has either a positive or a negative charge (p. 127)

Isotope (ī′ sə tōp) one of a group of atoms of an element with the same number of protons and electrons but different numbers of neutrons (p. 99)

J

Joule (jül) metric unit of work (p. 207)

K

Kilowatt-hour (kil′ ə wot our′) a unit to measure how much electric energy is used; it is 1,000 watts used in one hour (p. 340)

Kinetic energy (ki net′ ik en′ ər jē) energy of motion (p. 211)

Kilogram(kg) (kil′ ə gram) a unit of mass in the metric system that equals 1,000 grams (p. 25)

Kilometer (km) (kə lom′ ə tər) a metric unit of measure that is equal to 1,000 meters (p. 11)

L

Law of conservation of energy (lò ov kon′ sər vā shən ov en′ ar jē) energy cannot be created or destroyed (p. 214)

Law of conservation of matter (lò ov kon′ sər vā shən ov mat′ ər) matter cannot be created or destroyed in chemical and common physical changes (p. 156)

Law of universal gravitation (lò ov yü nə ver′ səl grav ə tā′ shən) gravitational force depends on the mass of the two objects involved and on the distance between them (p. 196)

Lens (lenz) a curved piece of clear material that refracts light waves (p. 301)

Lever (lev′ ər) a simple machine containing a bar that can turn around a fixed point (p. 218)

Light (līt) a form of energy that can be seen (p. 289)

Lines of force (linz′ ov fôrs) lines that show a magnetic field (p. 351)

Liquid (lik′ wid) a form of matter that has a definite volume but no definite shape (p. 62)

Liter (L) (lē′ tər) basic unit of volume in the metric system (p. 21)

M

Magnet (mag′ nit) an object that attracts certain kinds of metals, such as iron (p. 348)

Magnetic field (mag net′ ik fēld) area around a magnet in which magnetic forces can act (p. 351)

Magnetic pole (mag net′ ik pōl) the end of a magnet, where magnetic forces are greatest (p. 349)

Mass (mas) the amount of material an object has (p. 2)

Mass number (mas num′ bər) a number equal to the sum of the numbers of protons and neutrons in an atom of an element (p. 83)

Matter (mat′ ər) anything that has mass and takes up space (p. 2)

Mechanical advantage (MA) (mə kan′ ə kəl ad van′ tij) factor by which a machine multiplies the effort force (p. 224)

Melting point (melt′ ing pȯint) the temperature at which a solid changes to a liquid (p. 253)

Meniscus (mə nis′ kəs) the curved surface of a liquid (p. 43)

Metal (met′ l) one of a group of elements that is usually solid at room temperature, often shiny, and carries heat and electricity well (p. 106)

Meter (m) (mē′ tər) the basic unit of length in the metric system; it is about 39 inches (p. 9)

Meterstick (mē′ tər stik) a common tool for measuring length in the metric system (p. 10)

Metric system (met′ rik sis′ təm) system of measurement used by scientists (p. 7)

Milligram (mg) (mil′ ə gram) a unit of mass in the metric system that is $\frac{1}{1,000}$ of a gram (p. 25)

Milliliter (mL) (mil′ ə lē tər) a metric unit of measure that is $\frac{1}{1,000}$ of a liter; it equals one cubic centimeter (p. 22)

Millimeter (mm) (mil′ ə mē tər) a metric unit of measure that is $\frac{1}{1,000}$ of a meter (p. 10)

Mixture (miks′ chər) a combination of substances in which no reaction takes place (p.150)

Model (mod′ l) a picture, an idea, or an object that is built to explain how something else looks or works (p. 75)

Molecule (mol′ ə kyül) the smallest particle of a substance that has the same properties as the substance (p. 60)

Motion (mō′ shən) a change in position (p. 174)

Motor (mō′ tər) a device that converts electrical energy to mechanical energy (p. 363)

N

Natural element (nach′ ər əl el′ ə mənt) an element found in nature (p. 66)

Nearsighted (nir′ sī′ tid) able to see objects that are close up clearly (p. 302)

Neutron (nü tron) a tiny particle in the nucleus of an atom that is similar to a proton in size (p. 77)

Newton (nüt′ n) the metric unit of weight (p. 37)

Noble gas (nō′ bəl gas) one of a group of elements made up of gases that do not combine with other materials under ordinary conditions (p. 109)

Nonmetal (non met′ l) one of a group of elements with properties unlike those of metals (p. 107)

Nuclear fission (nü′ klē ar fish′ ən) the reaction that occurs when the nucleus of an atom splits and energy is released as heat and light (p. 242)

Nuclear fusion (nü′ klē ar fyü′ zhan) the reaction that occurs when atoms are joined together and energy is released (p. 242)

Nucleus (nü′ klē əs) the central part of an atom (p. 76)

O

Ohm (ōm) the unit used to measure resistance (p. 316)

Ohm's law (ōmz lò) current equals voltage divided by resistance (p. 325)

Open circuit (ō′ pən ser′ kit) an incomplete or broken path for electric current (p. 312)

P

Parallel circuit (par′ ə lel ser′ kit) a circuit in which there is more than one path for current (p. 335)

Periodic table (pir ē od′ ik tā′ bəl) an arrangement of elements by increasing atomic number (p. 97)

pH (pē āch) a number that tells whether a substance is an acid or a base (p. 140)

Photons (fō′ tonz) small bundles of energy that make up light (p. 289)

Physical change (fiz′ ə kəl chānj) a change in which the appearance (physical properties) of a substance changes but its chemical properties stay the same (p. 119)

Physical science (fiz′ ə kəl sī′ əns) the study of matter and energy (p. 2)

Physics (fiz′ iks) the study of how energy acts with matter (p. 3)

Pitch (pich) how high or low a sound is (p. 277)

Plane mirror (plān mir′ ər) a flat, smooth mirror (p. 295)

Plasma (plaz′ mə) a very hot gas made of particles that have an electric charge (p. 63)

Potential energy (pə ten′ shəl en′ ər jē) stored energy (p. 211)

Power (pou′ ər) the amount of work a person does within a given period of time (p. 209)

Precipitate (pri sip′ ə tāt) a solid that is formed and usually sinks to the bottom of a solution (p. 165)

Prism (priz′ əm) a clear piece of glass or plastic that is shaped like a triangle; it can be used to separate white light (p. 291)

Product (prod´ əkt) a substance that is formed in a chemical reaction (p. 155)

Property (prop´ ər tē) a characteristic that helps identify an object (p. 32)

Proton (prō´ ton) a tiny particle in the nucleus of an atom (p. 76)

Pulley (pu̇l´ ē) a simple machine made up of a rope, chain, or belt wrapped around a wheel (p. 229)

R

Radiation (rā de ā´ shən) the movement of energy through a vacuum (p. 262)

Radicals (rad´ ə kalz) a group of two or more atoms that acts like one atom (p. 131)

Reactant (rē ak´ tənt) a substance that is altered in a chemical reaction (p. 155)

Reflect (ri flekt´) to bounce back (p. 283)

Refraction (ri frak´ shən) the bending of a light wave as it moves from one material to another (p. 301)

Repel (ri pel´) to push apart (p. 349)

Resistance (ri zis´ təns) measure of how easily electric current will flow through a material (p. 316)

Resistance arm (ri zis´ təns ärm) the distance between the fulcrum and resistance force of a lever (p. 225)

Resistance force (F_r) (ri zis´ təns fôrs) the force applied to a machine by the object to be moved (p. 218)

S

Schematic diagram (ski mat´ ik di´ ə gram) a diagram that uses symbols to show the parts of a circuit (p. 313)

Screw (skrü) a simple machine made up of an inclined plane wrapped around a straight piece of metal (p. 232)

Series circuit (sir´ ēz sėr´ kit) a circuit in which all current (electrons) flows through a single path (p. 328)

Simple machine (sim´ pəl mə shēn´) a tool with few parts that makes it easier or possible to do work (p. 218)

Single-replacement reaction (sing´ gəl ri plās´ mənt rē ak´ shən) a reaction in which one element replaces another in a compound (p. 164)

Solid (sol´ id) a form of matter that has a definite shape and volume (p. 62)

Solute (sol´ yüt) the substance that is dissolved in a solution (p. 151)

Solution (sə lü´ shən) a mixture in which one substance is dissolved in another (p. 151)

Solvent (sol´ vənt) a substance capable of dissolving one or more other substances (p. 151)

Sonar (sō´ när) a method of using sound to measure distances under water (p. 284)

Sound wave (sound wāv) a wave produced by vibrations (p. 273)

Speed (spēd) the rate at which the position of an object changes (p. 175)

Standard mass (stan´ dard mas) a small object that is used with a balance to determine mass (p. 38)

State of matter (stāt ov mat´ ər) the form that matter has—solid, liquid, or gas (p. 63)

Static electricity (stat´ ik i lek tris´ ə tē) buildup of electrical charges (p. 310)

Subscript (sub´ skript) a number in a formula that tells the number of atoms of an element in a compound (p. 130)

Symbol (sim´ bəl) one or two letters that represent the name of an element (p. 92)

Synthesis reaction (sin´ thə sis re ak´ shən) a reaction in which elements combine to form a compound (p. 160)

a	hat	e	let	ī	ice	ȯ	order	u̇	put	sh	she	ə	a	in about
ā	age	ē	equal	o	hot	oi	oil	ü	rule	th	thin		e	in taken
ä	far	ėr	term	ō	open	ou	out	ch	child	ŦH	then		i	in pencil
â	care	i	it	ȯ	saw	u	cup	ng	long	zh	measure		o	in lemon
													u	in circus

T

Temperature (tem´ pər ə char) a measure of how fast an object's particles are moving (p. 249)

Terminal (tėr´ mə nəl) points where electrons leave or enter a battery (p. 321)

Thermometer (thər mom´ ə tər) a device that measures temperature (p. 250)

Tritium (trit´ ē əm) an isotope of hydrogen that has one proton and two neutrons (p. 99)

U

Ultrasound (ul´ trə sound) a technique that uses sound waves to study organs inside the human body (p. 285)

Unit (yü´ nit) a known amount used for measuring (p. 6)

V

Vacuum (vak´ yü əm) space that contains no matter (p. 262)

Velocity (və los´ ə tē) the speed and direction in which an object is moving (p. 182)

Vibrate (vī´ brāt) to move rapidly back and forth (p. 272)

Visible spectrum (viz´ ə bəl spek´ trəm) the band of colors that make up white light; the colors in a rainbow (p. 291)

W

Volt (vōlt) the metric unit used to measure electromotive force that tells the amount of push (p. 320)

Voltage (vōl´ tij) the energy that a power source gives to electrons in a circuit (p. 321)

Volume (vol´ yəm) the amount of space an object takes up (p. 20); the loudness or softness of a sound (p. 276)

W

Watt (wät) the unit used to measure power (p. 209)

Wedge (wej) a simple machine made up of an inclined plane or pair of inclined planes that are moved (p. 232)

Weight (wāt) the measure of how hard gravity pulls on an object (p. 37)

Wet-cell battery (wet sel bat´ ərē) electric power source with a liquid center (p. 322)

Wheel and axle (wēl and ak´ səl) a simple machine made up of a wheel attached to a shaft (p. 233)

Work (wėrk) what happens when an object changes its position by moving in the direction of the force that is being applied (p. 206)

Work input (wėrk in´ put) work put into a machine by its user (p. 221)

Work output (wėrk out´ put) work done by a machine against the resistance (p. 221)

Index

centimeters, 10, 15, 20
cheetahs, 173
chemical bonds, 126–127, 152
chemical changes, 118–119,
  121–122
chemical energy defined, 212
chemical equations, 155–158
chemical formulas, 129–132
chemical properties defined, 33
chemical reactions
  equations, 155–158
  Observing Different Kinds
    of Reactions,
    Investigations, 167–168
  types of, 149–151, 160–162,
    164–165
chemistry defined, 3
chlorate, 131
chlorination, 166
chlorine, 66, 93, 104, 125
chromium, 93
circuit breakers, 331
circuits, 310–314, 328–332,
  335–336, 341
citric acid, 138
Cleve, Per Theodor, 109
closed circuits, 311
cobalt, 92, 356
coefficient defined, 157
color, determining, 291
compounds, 70–71, 119, 127,
  129–130, 134–137
concave lenses, 301–302
concave mirrors, 296–297
concentration, 140, 151
condensation defined, 244
conduction defined, 263
conductors, 263, 315–318
constant speed defined, 179
contract defined, 245
convection, 263, 264
conversion factors,
  mathematical, 382–383
convex lenses, 302–303
convex mirrors, 297
copper, 66, 93, 315, 356
cork, 50
corn syrup, 54
cows and magnets, 349

crest of sound wave, 276
cubic centimeters, 20
cubit defined, 7
customary defined, 7
cycle defined, 277

D

Dalton, John, 79, xvii
deceleration, 188–189.
  See also velocity
decibel defined, 275
decimal conversion factors,
  382–383
decomposition reactions, 162
degree defined, 251
demagnetizing magnets, 357
Democritus, 79
density, 49–50
deuterium, 99
Did You Know, 302
  Arabic system of weighing
    things, 6
  baking, 139
  brain cells and electricity, 312
  bridges freezing, 256
  carbon atoms, 66
  cooking eggs faster, 254
  copper oxide, 119
  cows and magnets, 349
  cubic zirconia, 130
  density, 51
  dog whistles, 278
  electric shock treatments, 323
  electricity and the human
    body, 316
  elements and atoms, 67
  friction, 192
  hydrogen and helium, 83
  inclined planes, 231
  light, 290
  magnetite, 348
  mass & weight, 38
  mercury, 106
  meter, definition of, 10
  metric system, use of, 11
  Mexican jumping beans, 194
  mowing the lawn, 207
  northern lights, 352
  oxidation, 164

recycled atoms, 82
rhodium, 104
sea anemones and drag, 197
sound waves and the
  blind, 284
spontaneous combustion, 157
steam, 244
symbols of elements, 93
digital measurers, 8
direct current (DC), 323
displacement of water, 46–47, 51
dissolve defined, 151
distance defined, 175
distances, 176, 180, 181
disulfide chemical bonds, 152
dog whistles, 278
Doppler effect, 279
Doppler, Christian, 279
double-replacement reactions
  defined, 165
drag defined, 197
dry deposition defined, 141
dry-cell batteries, 4, 320–321

E

Earth, 39, 352, 353
echo defined, 283
efficiency, 221
effort arm defined, 225
effort force defined, 218
Einstein, Albert, 191
elapsed time, 174
electric charge, 310–311, 312,
  330, 336
electric force, 360–364
electric guitars, 364
electricity, 108, 111–112,
  310–312, 316, 320–324,
  340–341. *See also*
  electromagnetism
Electricity and Metals,
  Investigations, 111–112
electromagnet defined, 360
electromagnetic spectrum, 293
electromagnetic waves, 293
electromagnetism, 293, 320,
  360–362, 366, 367–368.
  See also electricity
electromotive force defined, 320

electron cloud model of the atom, 77
electronic noses, 33
electronic scales, 40
electrons, 76, 126, 321
electrostatic generators, 313
elements, 65, 69, 83, 92
energy, 3, 211–215
energy efficiency, 221
energy levels, 123, 124–125
energy shortages, 213
energy sources, alternative, 372–377
energy, nonrenewable, 372
energy, renewable, 372
engines, 363
Epsom salts, 71
equal-arm balances, 41
ethanol, 375
evaporate defined, 244
expand defined, 245
experiments. *See* investigations
exponent defined, 15
eyeglasses, lenses in, 302–303
eyes, human, 302–303

F

Fahrenheit scale, 251, 252, 266
family defined, 103
farsightedness defined, 303
First Law of Motion, 192–193
Fleming, Alexander, xvii
fluorine, 78, 82, 84, 92, 104
focal point defined, 296
Food Technologist, 163
force, 192, 193
forced air heating systems, 265
fossil defined, 372
fossil fuels, 372
fraction conversion factors, 382–383
freezing point defined, 253. *See also* boiling point; melting point
frequency defined, 277
friction, 192, 193
fulcrum defined, 218
fundamental particles, 69
fuses, 331
fusion, 242, 377

G

Galileo, 198
gamma rays, 293
gas in solution, 151
gases, 62
gauge of wires, 317
generators, 213, 313
geothermal energy, 374
germanium, 108
glass, 356
global warming, 372
gold, 50, 66, 91, 93, 315, 356
graduated cylinder, 4, 43
gram (g) defined, 24
graphs, 179–183
gravity, 196, 197
ground fault circuit interrupter (GFCI), 341

H

Hall, Charles, 159
Hall-Heroult process, 159
heat, 240, 257–258
heat energy, 212, 258
heat source defined, 241
heating systems, 265
Heating, Ventilation, and Air Conditioning (HVAC) Technician, 246
helium
    atomic properties of, 78, 82, 84, 104, 124
    symbol for, 92
    uses, 66
Heroult, Paul, 159
hertz (Hz) defined, 277
Hertz, Heinrich, 293
History of the Atom Model, 79
holograms, 298
hot spots, 374
hot water heating systems, 265
household lye, 131
Hubble, Edwin, 279
hybrid electric vehicles (HEVs), 327
hydrochloric acid, 138
hydroelectric power, 376
hydrogen
    atomic properties of, 78, 82, 84, 124

fuel, 376–377
    isotopes of, 99
    symbol for, 92
hydroxide, 131
hypersonic speakers, 286

I

ice, 51. *See also* water
identifying properties, 35–36
image defined, 295
inclined plane defined, 231
indicator defined, 139
inert defined, 109
inertia defined, 193
infrared rays, 293
inhibitors, 165
Instrumentation Calibration Technician, 17
insulators, 263, 315–318
intensity defined, 275
Internet, 5
Investigations
    Breaking Down Water, 73–74
    Calculating Area, 18–19
    Constructing an Electromagnet, 367–368
    Constructing Parallel Circuits, 338–339
    Constructing Series Circuits, 333–334
    Electricity and Metals, 111–112
    Finding Density, 53–54
    Finding Iron In Your Cereal, 95–96
    Finding Speed, 185–186
    Finding the Mechanical Advantage of a Lever, 227–228
    Identifying Acids and Bases, 143–144
    Identifying Properties, 35–36
    Inferring How Sound Waves Travel, 287–288
    Mass, Height, and Energy, 216–217
    Measurement Systems, 13–14
    Measuring Angles of Reflected Rays, 299–300
    Measuring the Rate of Heat Loss, 260–261

noble gases, 109
nonmetals, 17, 107–108, 110
nonrenewable energy, 372
northern lights, 352
Notes
  amplitude, 275
  antimatter, 85
  atomic charge, 78, 126
  atomic number, 97
  balancing equations, 157
  batteries and electron
    flow, 321
  bromine, 108
  Brownian motion, 77
  buoyancy, 49
  carbon, 107
  chemical changes, 118
  chemical equations, 156
  combustion, 161
  determining color, 291
  elements and compounds, 71
  force and motion, 194
  friction, 231
  fusion, 242
  heat, measuring, 257
  ionic compounds, 127
  magnets, 364
  measurement, requirements
    of, 11
  Metric Conversion Act, 20
  motion, 174
  photosynthesis, 262
  properties of matter, 32, 33
  protium, 99
  Radioactivity, 102
  reference points, 175
  semiconductors, 316
  slash mark, in calculations, 177
  slope on a graph, 183
  solenoids, 362
  specific heat, 257
  speedboats, 232
  states of matter, 258
  technology vs. science, 3
  valence electrons, 126
  vector quantities, 182
  velocity, 182
  watts, 209
  wavelength, 276
  waves, 290

  wire thickness, 317
  work and energy, 212
Noyce, Robert, 324
nuclear energy, 212, 242, 377
nuclear fission, 242
nuclear fusion, 242, 377
nucleus defined, 76
nylon, 142

O

Observing Different Kinds of
  Reactions, Investigations,
  167–168
ocean wave energy, 375–376
Oersted, Hans, 366
ohm defined, 316
Ohm's Law, 325–326
open circuits, 312
Optician, 304
oxidation, 152, 164
oxygen, 78, 82, 84, 92

P

parallel circuits, 335–336
particle accelerators, 85
Pascal, Blaise, 226
Pascaline, 226
passive solar heating systems, 265
penicillin, xvi–xvii
percent conversion
  factors, 382–383
Periodic Table of Elements,
  97–104, 378–379
Perkin, William, 120
permanent magnets, 364
permanent waves in hair, 152
pewter, 107
pH defined, 140
phospate, 131
phosphorus, 68, 92
photons defined, 289
photosynthesis, 262
photovoltaic (PV) cells, 373
physical change defined, 119
physical science defined, 2
physics defined, 3
pitch defined, 277
plane mirrors, 295
planetary model of the atom, 79
plastic, 356

platinum, 93
plum pudding model of the
  atom, 79
plutonium, 93
polonium, 108
pop-up timers, 255
potassium, 68, 93, 103
potassium hydroxide, 139
potential energy defined, 211
power, 209
precipitate defined, 165
prefixes, metric, 11
pressure cookers, 259
prisms, 291
product defined, 155
properties of matter, 32, 33
properties of metals, 106–107
protium, 99
protons, 69, 76, 85
pulleys, 4, 229–230

Q

quarks, 69

R

radiant electric heating
  systems, 265
radiant energy defined, 212
radiation, 99, 377
radiation defined, 262
radicals, 131. See also individual
  radicals by name
radio waves, 293
radioactivity, 102
radium, 92
raindrops, 197
Ramsay, Sir William, 109
reactant defined, 155
reaction rate, 164, 165
rechargeable batteries, 320
reducing agents, 152
reference points, 175
reflect defined, 283
refraction defined, 301
renewable energy, 372
repel defined, 349
resistance, 316–318
resistance arm defined, 225
resistance force defined, 218
rhodium, 104

Photo and Illustration Credits

Midterm Mastery Test

Midterm Mastery Test

Part A Choose the best answer. Write the letter on the line.

_____ **1.** What metric unit would you use to measure the length of a pen?

    A meter   **B** kilometer   **C** centimeter   **D** millimeter

_____ **2.** If you multiply length times width, you are finding an object's _____.

    A mass   **B** volume   **C** weight   **D** area

_____ **3.** What property of matter do scientists measure in newtons?

    A shape   **B** weight   **C** volume   **D** density

_____ **4.** Water has a density of $1.0 \ g/cm^3$. Which object will float in water?

    A gold with a density of $19.3 \ g/cm^3$ **C** rubber with a density of $1.1 \ g/cm^3$

    B cork with a density of $0.24 \ g/cm^3$ **D** aluminum with a density of $2.7 \ g/cm^3$

_____ **5.** What state of matter is not common on Earth?

    A gas   **B** liquid   **C** plasma   **D** solid

_____ **6.** The sum of neutrons and protons in an element is equal to what?

    A mass number   **C** number of electrons

    B atomic number   **D** number of atoms

_____ **7.** Which element is a nonmetal and makes up the largest percentage of the air?

    A hydrogen   **B** oxygen   **C** nitrogen   **D** neon

_____ **8.** A sodium ion has a positive charge because it has _____.

    A more electrons than protons   **C** the same number of electrons and protons

    B no electrons   **D** more protons than electrons

_____ **9.** A group of two or more atoms that act like one atom are called _____.

    A electron   **B** subscript   **C** binary compound   **D** radicals

_____ **10.** A substance that is formed in a chemical reaction is a _____.

    A product   **B** reactant   **C** solvent   **D** mixture

Physical Science

Midterm Mastery Test Page 1

Midterm Mastery Test, continued

Part B Write the word or words that correctly complete each sentence.

11. Anything that has mass and takes up space is _____.

12. _____ is the area of physical science that studies energy and how it acts with matter.

13. A(n)_____ is equal to $\frac{1}{100}$ of a meter.

14. Characteristics that are used to help identify an object are called _____.

15. _____ is the measure of how tightly matter is packed into a given volume of a substance.

16. The measure of how hard _____ pulls on an object is called weight.

17. A form of matter with definite volume but no definite shape is a(n) _____.

18. Matter that has only one kind of atom is a(n) _____.

19. _____ are negatively charged particles that move around the nucleus of an atom.

20. Because hydrogen has a single proton, its _____ is equal to 1.

21. An element whose atoms do not react in nature with atoms of other elements is a(n) _____.

22. A(n) _____ takes place when atoms of elements combine to form a compound.

23. A base is a compound that contains the _____ radical.

24. The law of conservation of matter states that matter cannot be created or destroyed in _____ and common physical changes.

25. Two elements combine to form a compound in a(n) _____ reaction.

Physical Science

Midterm Mastery Test Page 2

Midterm Mastery Test, continued

Part C Match each term in Column A with an item in Column B. Write the letter of the correct answer on the line.

Column A	Column B
_____ **26.** acid	**A** the building block of matter
_____ **27.** atom	**B** tells whether a substance is an acid or a base
_____ **28.** balance	**C** form of matter with a definite shape and volume
_____ **29.** solute	**D** basic unit of volume in the metric system
_____ **30.** centi-	**E** the substance that is dissolved in a solution
_____ **31.** chemical bond	**F** chemicals on the left side of the arrow in a chemical equation
_____ **32.** coefficient	**G** matter that has only one kind of atom
_____ **33.** element	**H** instrument used to measure mass
_____ **34.** isotope	**I** compound that reacts with metals to produce hydrogen
_____ **35.** meniscus	**J** substance that can dissolve other substances
_____ **36.** pH	**K** $\frac{1}{100}$
_____ **37.** chemistry	**L** one or two letters that stand for the name of an element
_____ **38.** potassium	**M** curved surface of a liquid
_____ **39.** reactants	**N** one of a group of atoms of an element with a different number of neutrons
_____ **40.** symbol	**O** attractive force that holds atoms together
_____ **41.** liter	**P** study of matter and how it changes
_____ **42.** solid	**Q** number placed before a formula in a chemical equation
_____ **43.** solvent	**R** K

Physical Science

Midterm Mastery Test Page 3

Midterm Mastery Test, continued

Part D Write the answer to each question.

44. What is the volume of a carton that measures 12 cm long, 9 cm wide, and 12 cm high?

_____

45. What is the density of a substance that has a mass of 154.4 g and a volume of $8 \ cm^3$?

_____

46. Iodine has an atomic number of 53 and an atomic mass number of 127. How many protons, neutrons, and electrons does it have?

Protons: _____   Neutrons: _____   Electrons: _____

47. Complete the equation and identify the kind of chemical reaction. Then identify the reactants and products.

    A $2NaBr + Cl_2 \rightarrow$ _____ $+ 2NaCl$ **B** Reaction: _____

    C Reactants: _____   Products: _____

Part E Write a short answer to each question.

48. Explain what happens when atoms of elements combine to form compounds.

_____

_____

_____

49. Compare and contrast metals and nonmetals.

_____

_____

_____

50. Explain the meanings of atomic number and mass number.

_____

_____

_____

_____

Physical Science

Midterm Mastery Test Page 4

Final Mastery Test

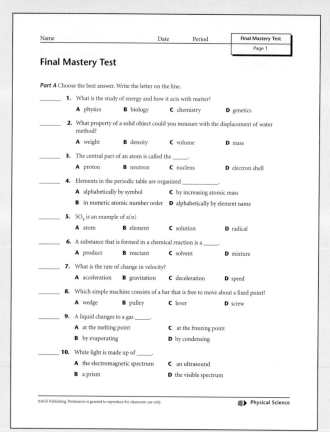

Final Mastery Test

Part A Choose the best answer. Write the letter on the line.

_____ **1.** What is the study of energy and how it acts with matter?
   A physics   B biology   C chemistry   D genetics

_____ **2.** What property of a solid object could you measure with the displacement of water method?
   A weight   B density   C volume   D mass

_____ **3.** The central part of an atom is called the _____.
   A proton   B neutron   C nucleus   D electron shell

_____ **4.** Elements in the periodic table are organized _____.
   A alphabetically by symbol   C by increasing atomic mass
   B in numeric atomic number order   D alphabetically by element name

_____ **5.** SO_4 is an example of a(n)
   A atom   B element   C solution   D radical

_____ **6.** A substance that is formed in a chemical reaction is a _____.
   A product   B reactant   C solvent   D mixture

_____ **7.** What is the rate of change in velocity?
   A acceleration   B gravitation   C deceleration   D speed

_____ **8.** Which simple machine consists of a bar that is free to move about a fixed point?
   A wedge   B pulley   C lever   D screw

_____ **9.** A liquid changes to a gas _____.
   A at the melting point   C at the freezing point
   B by evaporating   D by condensing

_____ **10.** White light is made up of _____.
   A the electromagnetic spectrum   C an ultrasound
   B a prism   D the visible spectrum

Final Mastery Test Page 1

Final Mastery Test, continued

_____ **11.** What unit is used to measure resistance of a wire?
   A volt   B ohm   C kilowatt   D ampere

_____ **12.** When the north poles of two magnets are placed together, the poles _____.
   A attract each other   C demagnetize each other
   B repel each other   D have no effect on each other

_____ **13.** Batteries produce current by changing _____ into electrical energy.
   A kinetic energy   C mechanical energy
   B heat   D chemical energy

_____ **14.** Decibels are used to measure the _____ of sound.
   A pitch   B frequency   C intensity   D reflection

_____ **15.** Which of these items is a good conductor of heat?
   A tin   B glass   C wood   D air

Part B Write the word or words that correctly complete each sentence.

16. Anything that has mass and takes up space is _____.

17. _____ is equal to mass divided by volume.

18. The _____ of an atom is equal to the number of its protons and neutrons.

19. A shiny solid that is a good conductor of heat and electricity is classified as a(n) _____.

20. A compound that reacts with metals to produce _____ is an acid.

21. _____ is one in which a compound breaks down into two or more simple substances.

22. The rate at which the position of an object changes is _____.

23. Velocity is the speed and _____ in which an object moves.

Final Mastery Test Page 2

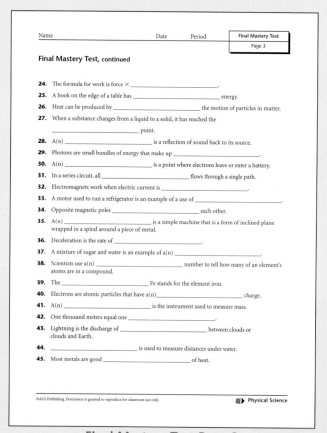

Final Mastery Test, continued

24. The formula for work is force × _____.

25. A book on the edge of a table has _____ energy.

26. Heat can be produced by _____ the motion of particles in matter.

27. When a substance changes from a liquid to a solid, it has reached the _____ point.

28. A(n) _____ is a reflection of sound back to its source.

29. Photons are small bundles of energy that make up _____.

30. A(n) _____ is a point where electrons leave or enter a battery.

31. In a series circuit, all _____ flows through a single path.

32. Electromagnets work when electric current is _____.

33. A motor used to run a refrigerator is an example of a use of _____.

34. Opposite magnetic poles _____ each other.

35. A(n) _____ is a simple machine that is a form of inclined plane wrapped in a spiral around a piece of metal.

36. Deceleration is the rate of _____.

37. A mixture of sugar and water is an example of a(n) _____.

38. Scientists use a(n) _____ number to tell how many of an element's atoms are in a compound.

39. The _____ Fe stands for the element iron.

40. Electrons are atomic particles that have a(n) _____ charge.

41. A(n) _____ is the instrument used to measure mass.

42. One thousand meters equal one _____.

43. Lightning is the discharge of _____ between clouds or clouds and Earth.

44. _____ is used to measure distances under water.

45. Most metals are good _____ of heat.

Final Mastery Test Page 3

Final Mastery Test, continued

Part C Write the answer to each question.

46. What is the volume of a box that measures 15 cm long, 20 cm wide, and 25 cm high?

_____

47. What is the density of a substance that has a mass of 38.6 g and a volume of 2 cm³?

_____

48. Aluminum has an atomic number of 13 and an atomic mass number of 27.
   A How many protons does it have? _____
   B How many neutrons does it have? _____
   C How many electrons does it have? _____

49. Complete the equation and identify the kind of chemical reaction.
   A $BaCl_2 \rightarrow Ba + $ _____   B Reaction: _____

50. Balance the equation. Then identify the reactants and products.
   $Fe + 3O_2 \rightarrow 2Fe_2O_3$ _____
   Reactants: _____   Products: _____

51. How far can a car travel at 90 kilometers per hour in 4.5 hours?

_____

52. How much work is done in moving a load 15 meters, using a force of 15 newtons?

_____

53. A person used a lever to lift a machine with 200 newtons of resistance force 0.2 meters. The person applied 150 newtons of effort force and pushed the end of the lever 0.5 meter.
   A What is the work input? _____
   B What is the work output? _____
   C What is the efficiency of the lever? _____

54. How much current is flowing in a circuit with 50 volts and a resistance of 15 ohms? _____

55. Use the formula to convert 50°F to Celsius. You may use a calculator. _____
   $$C = \frac{5}{9} \times (F - 32)$$

Final Mastery Test Page 4

Final Mastery Test

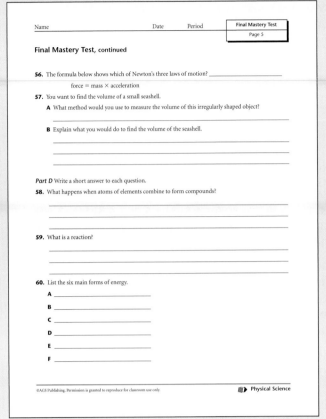

Final Mastery Test Page 5

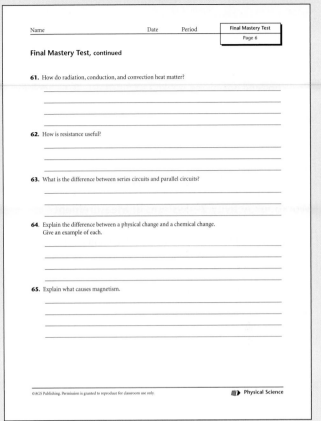

Final Mastery Test Page 6

The lists below show how items from the Midterm and Final correlate to the chapters in the student edition.

Midterm Mastery Test

Chapter 1: 1–2, 11–13, 30, 37, 41, 44

Chapter 2: 3–4, 14–16, 28, 35, 45

Chapter 3: 5–6, 17–19, 27, 33, 42, 46, 48

Chapter 4: 7, 20–21, 34, 38, 40, 49, 50

Chapter 5: 8–9, 22–23, 26, 31, 36

Chapter 6: 10, 24–25, 29, 32, 39, 43, 47

Final Mastery Test

Chapter 1: 1, 16, 42, 46

Chapter 2: 2, 17, 41, 47, 57

Chapter 3: 3, 18, 40, 48, 58

Chapter 4: 4, 19, 39

Chapter 5: 5, 20, 38, 64

Chapter 6: 6, 21, 37, 49–50, 59

Chapter 7: 7, 22–23, 36, 51, 56

Chapter 8: 8, 24–25, 35, 52–53, 60

Chapter 9: 9, 15, 26–27, 45, 55, 61

Chapter 10: 10, 14, 28–29, 44

Chapter 11: 11, 13, 30–31, 43, 54, 62–63

Chapter 12: 12, 32–34, 65

Workbook Activities

Workbook Activity 1—What Is Physical Science?
1. physics **2.** mass **3.** matter **4.** chemistry **5.** physical science **6.** energy **7.** tuning fork: A tuning fork is a tool scientists use. Predicting and organizing are skills scientists use. **8.** technology: Technology is not a physical science, but physics and chemistry are two areas of physical science. **9.** measurements: Measurements are information scientists use, whereas the balance scale and Bunsen burner are tools scientists use. **10.** matter: Matter makes up all objects; it was not developed by scientists. Scientists studying physics developed computers and microwaves.

Workbook Activity 2—Systems of Measurement
1. about 1.9 kilometers per hour **2.** 200 milligrams **3.** 10.2 centimeters **4.** 4.828 kilometers **5.** 9.460 trillion kilometers **6.** 201.2 meters **7.** 0.4536 kilogram **8.** 1.8 meters **9.** 219.5 meters **10.** 3.7853 liters **11.** 22.9 centimeters **12.** 5 meters **13.** 1.14 meters **14.** 8.8 liters **15.** 0.3048 meter

Workbook Activity 3—Adding and Subtracting Metric Units of Length
1. 17 centimeters 8 millimeters **2.** 19 meters 17 centimeters **3.** 25 meters 9 centimeters **4.** 20 meters 33 millimeters or 20 meters 3 centimeters 3 millimeters **5.** 32 centimeters 13 millimeters or 33 centimeters 3 millimeters **6.** 10 meters 2 centimeters **7.** 26 millimeters or 2 centimeters 6 millimeters **8.** 19 meters 15 millimeters or 19 meters 1 centimeter 5 millimeters **9.** 38 meters 3 millimeters **10.** 20 meters 2 centimeters

Workbook Activity 4—Using Metric Measurements to Find Area
1. 9 m^2 **2.** 63 cm^2 **3.** 880 m^2 **4.** 110 mm^2 **5.** 16.25 cm^2 **6.** 375 mm^2 **7.** 8 m **8.** 216 cm^2 **9.** 100 mm **10.** $2,040 \text{ m}^2$ **11.** 29.75 mm^2 **12.** $1,050 \text{ m}^2$ **13.** 14 cm **14.** 400 cm^2 **15.** 2 m

Workbook Activity 5—Using Metric Measurements to Find Volume
1. 27 cm^3 **2.** 125 cm^3 **3.** 300 cm^3 **4.** 48 cm^3 **5.** 7.5 mm^3 **6.** 5.2 m^3 **7.** $1,000 \text{ m}^3$ **8.** 3.375 cm^3 **9.** 64 mm^3 **10.** $72,000 \text{ m}^3$ **11.** $1,000 \text{ mm}^3$ **12.** $6,000 \text{ cm}^3$ **13.** 110 cm^3 **14.** 12 m^3 **15.** $1,687,500 \text{ cm}^3$

Workbook Activity 6—The Metric System: Terms Review
1. O **2.** G **3.** E **4.** A **5.** N **6.** F **7.** D **8.** H **9.** K **10.** B **11.** J **12.** M **13.** I **14.** C **15.** L **16.** mL **17.** km **18.** mg **19.** m **20.** cg **21.** kg **22.** mm **23.** g **24.** L **25.** cm

Workbook Activity 7—Properties of Objects
Answers may vary. Possible answers are given.

	Object 1	Object 2	Object 3
A	rectangle	cylinder	mostly like a cylinder
B	hard, smooth	hard, smooth	smooth, possibly wet
C	21.5 cm × 28 cm	18 cm long	21 cm high
D	0.25 kg	55 g	560 g
E	600 cm^3	4 cm^3	0.5 L

Workbook Activity 8—Mass and Weight
Across: **4.** gravity **7.** force **8.** Jupiter **11.** mass **12.** standard mass **15.** Venus

Down: **1.** kilogram **2.** matter **3.** balance **5.** grams **6.** weight **9.** pound **10.** less **12.** scale **13.** newton **14.** Mars

Workbook Activity 9—Measuring the Mass of a Liquid
1. 43 g **2.** $0.70/g **3.** 30 g **4.** $1.33/g **5.** 26 g **6.** $1.54/g **7.** 80 g **8.** $0.63/g **9.** 50 g **10.** $0.90/g **11.** Daisy **12.** Breeze **13.** Tidal **14.** Daisy, Freesia, Roma, Tidal, Breeze **15.** Answers will vary.

Workbook Activity 10—Measuring the Volume of Liquid
1. milliliters **2.** laboratory **3.** graduated cylinder **4.** cubic centimeter **5.** scale **6.** graduated cylinder **7.** level **8.** meniscus **9.** bottom **10.** scale **11.** milliliters **12.** spaces **13.** subtract **14.** divide **15.** volume

Workbook Activity 11—Comparing and Contrasting Objects
1. Alike: Both measure properties of matter. Different: Length is one-dimensional, measuring a surface in one direction; volume is three-dimensional and measures how much space something takes up. **2.** Alike: Both are three-dimensional solids. Different: A cube has six flat sides of equal area; a circle has a continually curved surface. **3.** Alike: Both are solids that have specific volumes. Different: A regular shape has predictable surfaces called length, width, and height that can be measured externally; an irregular shape has a surface that can be measured by using the displacement of water method. **4.** Alike: Both are instruments for measuring substances. Different: A balance measures mass in grams; a graduated cylinder measures volume in milliliters. **5.** Alike: Both describe properties of liquids. Different: Liquid mass is the pull of gravity on a liquid; liquid volume is the amount of space a liquid takes up. **6.** formula **7.** displacement of water method **8.** displacement of water method **9.** formula **10.** formula

Workbook Activity 12—The Properties of Matter: Terms Review
1. B **2.** G **3.** F **4.** I **5.** C **6.** A **7.** H **8.** E **9.** D **10.** volume **11.** balance **12.** graduated cylinder **13.** meniscus **14.** newtons **15.** displacement

Workbook Activity 13—Identifying Solids, Liquids, and Gases
1. molecules **2.** B **3.** C **4.** A **5.** plasma **6.** A **7.** A **8.** A **9.** C **10.** B **11.** A **12.** B **13.** A **14.** C **15.** C

Workbook Activity 14—What Are Elements?

Across: 1. element
3. aluminum
4. oxygen
6. calcium
7. helium
11. natural
12. nitrogen
13. mercury

Down: 2. molecule
3. atoms
5. neon
7. hydrogen
8. iron
9. carbon
10. matter

Workbook Activity 15—What Are Compounds?

1. compound **2.** water
3. gases; liquid **4.** salt
5. sodium, hydrogen, carbon
6. laboratory **7.** sugar **8.** Both
are made up of atoms. An
element has only one kind of
atom; a compound has two or
more kinds of atoms. **9.** Water
is a liquid; hydrogen is a gas.
10. Both are compounds; both
contain carbon, hydrogen, and
oxygen; both are used in foods.

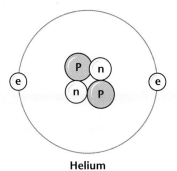

Helium

Workbook Activity 16—What Are Atoms Like?

1. atom **2.** protons, neutrons **3.** protons **4.** electrons **5.** neutrons
6. 3 **7.** 5 **8.** 6 **9.** 8 **10.** 10

Workbook Activity 17—The Structure of Matter: Terms Review

1. F **2.** B **3.** E **4.** D **5.** A **6.** C **7.** G **8.** I **9.** H **10.** compound
11. proton **12.** plasma **13.** solid **14.** The mass number equals the
sum of the number of protons and neutrons in an atom. The atomic
number equals the number of protons in an atom. **15.** Natural
elements are found in nature.

Workbook Activity 18—Words from Chemical Symbols

1. CoW **2.** BaNd **3.** WIN **4.** BrICK **5.** KNOB **6.** CHAlK **7.** BArK
8. SUN **9.** CoAl **10.** ClOWN **11.** PuCK **12.** RaCe **13.** CoIN
14. KISS **15.** SiCK **16.** BaBY **17.** LaNe **18.** HeAl **19.** LiON **20.** RaIN

Workbook Activity 19—Using the Periodic Table

Atomic numbers, by rows: Fe 26, As 33, Ne 10, Cl 17, Cr 24; Ge 32, Si
14, S 16, V 23, Mn 25; Al 13, P 15, Ti 22, Cu 29, Ga 31; K 19, Sc 21, Ni
28, Zn 30, Mg 12; Ca 20, Co 27, Se 34, Na 11, Ar 18; Every sum is 110.

Workbook Activity 20—Classifying Elements: Terms Review

1. E **2.** F **3.** G **4.** D **5.** I **6.** H **7.** B **8.** C **9.** J **10.** A **11.** symbol
12. metal **13.** inert **14.** tritium **15.** isotopes

Workbook Activity 21—Physical and Chemical Changes

1. physical change **2.** chemical change **3.** physical change **4.** physical
change **5.** chemical change **6.** physical change **7.** chemical change
8. chemical change **9.** physical change **10.** chemical change
11. physical change **12.** physical change **13.** chemical change
14. physical change **15.** chemical change In a physical change the
substance remains the same; only some of its properties change. In a
chemical change, a new substance is produced and the elements react
with one another.

Workbook Activity 22—Energy Levels

1. 2 **2.** 8 **3.** 18 **4.** 32 **5.** 60 **6.** K **7.** M **8.** N **9.** L **10.** M **11.** L
12. M **13.** O **14.** N **15.** O Drawings should show the 5 energy
levels around the nucleus with 2 electrons in the K level, 8 electrons
in the L level, and 2 electrons in the M level.

Workbook Activity 23—Working with Chemical Formulas

1. AgCl **2.** HCl **3.** H_2O_2 **4.** $MgCO_3$ **5.** $C_6H_{12}O_6$ **6.** $Pb(NO_3)_2$

Compound	Elements	Atoms
7. potassium chloride, KCl	potassium	1
	chlorine	1
8. sucrose, $C_{12}H_{22}O_{11}$	carbon	12
	hydrogen	22
	oxygen	11
9. ammonium bromide, NH_4Br	nitrogen	1
	hydrogen	4
	bromine	1
10. ammonium carbonate, $(NH_4)_2CO_3$	nitrogen	2
	hydrogen	8
	carbon	1
	oxygen	3

Workbook Activity 24—Matching Chemical Formulas with Chemical Names

1. NaF—sodium fluoride **2.** $MgCl_2$—magnesium chloride
3. AgBr—silver bromide **4.** LiOH—lithium hydroxide **5.** KCl—
potassium chloride **6.** LiF—lithium fluoride **7.** BeO—beryllium
oxide **8.** KI—potassium iodide **9.** $BeCl_2$—beryllium chloride
10. $FeCO_3$—iron carbonate **11.** Ag_2S—silver sulfide
12. $Sr(ClO_3)_2$—strontium chlorate **13.** LiCl—lithium chloride
14. GaAs—gallium arsenide **15.** AgCl—silver chloride

Workbook Activity 25—Compounds: Terms Review

Across: 3. physical
5. acid
7. radicals
8. energy level
10. formula
12. ion
13. lead
14. subscript
15. indicator

Down: 1. pH
2. binary compound
4. base
6. chemical
9. bond
11. copper

Workbook Activity 26—Reactions and Solutions

1. alchemist **2.** reaction **3.** solvent **4.** dissolve **5.** solution **6.** heat
7. mixture **8.** rearrange **9.** solute **10.** molecules **11.** A mixture is
formed when substances are combined with no chemical reaction. A
solution is a mixture in which one substance is dissolved in another.
12. A solute is the substance that is dissolved in a solution. A solvent is
the substance that dissolves other substances in a solution. **13.** In a
mixture, substances combine, but there is no chemical reaction. In a
chemical reaction, elements combine or rearrange. **14.** An example of
a gas dissolved in a liquid is club soda. **15.** An example of a solution
with a liquid solute and a solid solvent is ether in rubber.

Workbook Activity 27—Using Chemical Equations to Show Reactions

Across: 1. product **4.** conservation **6.** matter **8.** coefficient **10.** law **12.** balance **13.** symbols **15.** atoms

Down: 2. reactant **3.** molecules **5.** number **7.** equal **9.** equation **11.** arrow **14.** mass

Workbook Activity 28—Synthesis and Decomposition Reactions

1. synthesis **2.** decomposition **3.** decomposition **4.** decomposition **5.** synthesis **6.** decomposition **7.** decomposition **8.** synthesis **9.** Al, O_2 **10.** Al_2O_3 **11.** Cu, O_2 **12.** CuO **13.** 2 **14.** 2 **15.** synthesis

Workbook Activity 29—How Matter Changes: Terms Review

1. H **2.** G **3.** E **4.** F **5.** A **6.** C **7.** D **8.** B **9.** precipitate **10.** solvent **11.** solution **12.** conservation **13.** product **14.** In a single-replacement reaction, one element replaces another in a compound. In a double-replacement reaction, the elements in two compounds are exchanged. **15.** In a synthesis reaction, elements combine to form a compound. In a decomposition reaction, a compound breaks down into two or more simple substances.

Workbook Activity 30—Calculating Speed

1. 2 mm/sec **2.** 5 m/sec **3.** 20 cm/sec **4.** 10 m/sec **5.** 35 mi/hr **6.** 25 mm/sec **7.** 0.09 m/sec **8.** 0.15 mm/sec **9.** 23 yd/sec **10.** 66 km/hr **11.** 4 m/sec **12.** 94 mi/hr **13.** 4.33 hrs **14.** 2,250 mi **15.** 8 hrs

Workbook Activity 31—Using a Graph to Describe Motion

1. Each vehicle moves at a constant speed. **2.** car—450 km; motorcycle—150 km; train—300 km

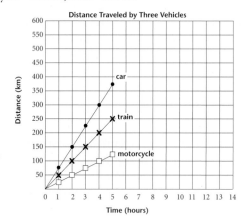

Workbook Activity 32—Acceleration

1. 100 km/hr per hr **2.** 300 km/hr per hr **3.** 30 cm/sec per sec **4.** 6.5 mm/sec per sec **5.** −5 km/sec per sec **6.** −5 m/min per sec **7.** −1.25 cm/sec per sec **8.** −3 km/hr per sec **9.** −1 km/hr per sec **10.** 1.6 m/min per min

Workbook Activity 33—The Laws of Motion

Across: 1. acceleration **3.** friction **5.** first **7.** motion **10.** second **11.** reaction **12.** resistance **13.** mass

Down: 2. automobiles **3.** force **4.** roll **6.** third **8.** inertia **9.** Newton **12.** rest

Workbook Activity 34—Motion: Terms Review

1. A **2.** E **3.** F **4.** G **5.** H **6.** I **7.** C **8.** D **9.** B **10.** velocity **11.** constant speed **12.** distance **13.** universal gravitation **14.** Both measure motion. Speed shows how fast the position of something changes while velocity shows how fast both the speed and direction change. **15.** Both keep objects from moving. Inertia is the tendency to keep bodies at rest at rest and bodies in motion in motion; friction slows down moving bodies.

Workbook Activity 35—What Is Work?

1. position **2.** direction **3.** multiply **4.** joules **5.** work = force × distance **6.** 19.6 newtons × 10 meters = 196 joules **7.** 10 newtons × 1.5 meters = 15 joules **8.** 700 newtons × 2.0 meters = 1,400 joules **9.** 900 newtons × 100 meters = 90,000 joules **10.** 300 newtons × 400 meters = 120,000 joules **11.** 4,000 joules ÷ 200 newtons = 20 meters **12.** 550 newtons × 23 meters = 12,650 joules **13.** 13,734 joules ÷ 42 meters = 327 newtons **14.** 330 joules ÷ 2 newtons = 165 meters **15.** 2,940 newtons × 0 meters = 0 joules

Workbook Activity 36—Understanding Power

1. rate **2.** force **3.** power **4.** joules, second, watts **5.** watt **6.** kilowatts **7.** Alex used more power when he covered the distance in 2 minutes. **8.** 255 joules ÷ 15 seconds = 17 watts **9.** He uses more power with the snowblower. **10.** 6,000 joules ÷ 2 seconds = 3,000 watts

Workbook Activity 37—Understanding Energy

Across: 1. conservation **7.** kinetic **9.** heat **10.** radiant **11.** watt **13.** joules

Down: 1. chemical **2.** nuclear **3.** electrical **4.** mechanical **5.** generator **6.** potential **8.** increases **12.** power

Workbook Activity 38—Using Levers

1. simple machine **2.** lever **3.** fulcrum **4.** effort force **5.** third-class lever; *pictured from left to right:* fulcrum, effort force, resistance force **6.** first-class lever; *pictured from left to right:* effort force, fulcrum, resistance force **7.** second-class lever; *pictured from left to right:* effort force, resistance force, fulcrum **8.** 250 newtons × 1.5 meters = 375 joules **9.** 430 newtons × 0.5 meter = 215 joules **10.** 215 ÷ 375 = .573 × 100 % = 57.3%

Workbook Activity 39—Mechanical Advantage

1. effort force **2.** resistance force; effort force **3.** divided **4.** MA = 3 **5.** MA = 0.66 **6.** MA = 1.2 **7.** MA = 2.73 **8.** MA = effort arm ÷ resistance arm **9.** move the fulcrum closer to the resistance **10.** the number of times a lever multiplies the effort force

Workbook Activity 40—Work and Machines: Terms Review
1. D 2. F 3. K 4. J 5. M 6. G 7. H 8. E 9. B 10. L 11. A 12. C
13. I 14. watts 15. lever 16. resistance 17. work input 18. work
output 19. mechanical advantage 20. inclined plane

Workbook Activity 41—What Is Heat?

Across: 1. heat source Down: 1. hands
4. heat 2. steam engine
5. stars 3. energy
7. hot 6. motion
9. fusion 8. fission
11. sun 10. boiler
12. electricity 13. toy
14. tiny

Workbook Activity 42—How Heat Affects Matter
1. expands 2. evaporates 3. condensation 4. expands 5. contracts
6. A 7. D 8. B 9. B 10. C 11. water 12. gas 13. vapor
14. summer 15. water

Workbook Activity 43—Temperature
1. heat 2. liquid 3. gas 4. temperature 5. thermometer 6. Fahrenheit
7. Celsius 8. melting point 9. boils 10. degree 11. freezes 12. alcohol
13. convert 14. solid 15. mercury

Workbook Activity 44—How to Measure Heat
Possible statements might include: 1. Temperature is measured in
degrees on a thermometer. Temperature measures how fast the
molecules in a substance are moving. 2. Heat is a form of energy.
Heat increases as an object's mass increases. 3. the turkey, which has
more mass than the potato 4. 1 calorie 5. –20 calories 6. 15
calories 7. –25 calories 8. 12 calories 9. 14 calories 10. –2 calories
11. 25 calories 12. –16 calories 13. –10 calories 14. 500 calories
15. 45 calories

Workbook Activity 45—Heat: Terms Review
1. L 2. E 3. I 4. K 5. A 6. C 7. D 8. M 9. G 10. J 11. F 12. H
13. N 14. B 15. conduction 16. conductor 17. radiation
18. convection 19. vacuum 20. insulator

Workbook Activity 46—What Is Sound?
1. vibrate 2. molecules 3. sound wave 4. sounds 5. weaker
Sound waves move through space like the pinched section of wire
moves across the spring. The ripples spread out from the source like
sound waves from a vibrating object.

Workbook Activity 47—Different Sounds
1. intensity 2. frequency 3. frequency 4. intensity 5. intensity
6. frequency 7. cycles 8. decibels 9. ears 10. pitch 11. Hertz
12. crest 13. wavelength 14. trough 15. 1 cycle

Workbook Activity 48—How Sound Travels
1. There is no matter in space, and sound can only travel through
matter. 2. Molecules are close together. They bump each other and
move back in place very quickly. 3. An echo is sound that is
reflected back from an object. 4. Both are ways of using reflected
sound waves to gather data about something that cannot be seen.
5. $7 \div 3 = 2\frac{1}{3}$ km 6. $1\frac{1}{2}$ seconds 7. 3 seconds 8. aluminum
9. water 10. warm air

Workbook Activity 49—What Is Light?
1. light 2. photons 3. empty space 4. prism, visible spectrum
5. electromagnetic 6. red 7. orange 8. yellow 9. green 10. blue
11. indigo 12. violet 13. is broken into a band of seven colors
called the visible spectrum 14. microwaves 15. X-rays

Workbook Activity 50—How Light Is Reflected
1. plane mirror 2. convex mirror 3. concave mirror 4. concave
mirror 5. concave mirror 6. convex mirror 7. Light is reflected
from the surface at an angle the same size as the angle with which it
strikes the surface. 8. The smooth, flat surface gives a clear image
because the light rays all leave at the same angle. 9. Both bounce off
an object or a surface. 10. Mirror images are reversed and two-
dimensional. Holograms are three-dimensional.

Workbook Activity 51—Sound and Light: Terms Review
1. I 2. J 3. H 4. G 5. A 6. E 7. B 8. D 9. C 10. F 11. echo
12. concave mirror 13. visible spectrum 14. vibrate 15. volume
16. cycle 17. concave lens 18. convex mirror 19. sound wave
20. frequency

Workbook Activity 52—How Electricity Flows
1. lightning 2. closed circuit 3. open circuit 4. electricity 5. energy
6. schematic 7. ampere 8. current 9. power source 10. static

Workbook Activity 53—Conductors and Insulators
A. 1. conductor 2. insulator; B. 1. copper 2. gold 3. aluminum
4. silver; C. 1. glass 2. rubber 3. wood 4. plastic; D. 1. measure of
how easily electric current will flow through a material 2. ohm;
E. 1. the material the wire is made of 2. the length of the wire 3. the
thickness of the wire

Workbook Activity 54—Some Sources of Electric Current

Across: 1. electromotive **4.** dry cell **7.** alternating **8.** wet cell **11.** sulfuric **12.** direct **14.** second **15.** voltage

Down: 2. terminal **3.** plus **5.** battery **6.** volt **9.** chemical **10.** lead **13.** cars

Workbook Activity 55—Using Ohm's Law

1. 4 amperes **2.** .015 amperes **3.** 12 volts **4.** 220 ohms **5.** 10 ohms **6.** 10 amperes **7.** 1.5 volts **8.** 12 volts **9.** If the resistance remains the same, the current increases. **10.** If the voltage remains the same, the current decreases.

Workbook Activity 56—Series Circuits

1. power source **2.** wire **3.** bulb **4.** wire **5.** switch Students should put arrows around the wire from the batteries to the bulb and back to the batteries. **6.** one **7.** disadvantage **8.** voltage **9.** add **10.** 15 **11.** series **12.** not work **13.** fires **14.** fuse **15.** circuit breaker

Workbook Activity 57—Parallel Circuits

1. more than one **2.** If one bulb or device goes out, the others stay lit. **3.** More current must be drawn from the power source; as current increases, wires can heat up and cause a fire. **4.** Voltage stays the same in each device. **5.** Total voltage equals the voltage of one battery. **6.** 2 **7.** parallel circuit **8.** series circuit **9.** 1.5 V **10.** 6 V

Workbook Activity 58—Electricity: Terms Review

1. I **2.** G **3.** B **4.** F **5.** D **6.** C **7.** A **8.** J **9.** H **10.** E **11.** M **12.** O **13.** K **14.** P **15.** N **16.** L **17.** insulator **18.** terminal **19.** battery **20.** conductor

Workbook Activity 59—What Are Magnets?

Across: 1. pull **3.** doughnut **5.** cow **7.** repel **8.** south **9.** MRI **10.** magnetic pole **11.** end **12.** north **13.** attracts

Down: 2. lodestone **4.** horseshoe **6.** opposite **9.** metal **10.** magnet

Workbook Activity 60—Identifying a Magnetic Field

Solution 1: 1. N **2.** S **3.** S **4.** N **5.** N **6.** S **7.** N **8.** S
Solution 2: 1. S **2.** N **3.** N **4.** S **5.** S **6.** N **7.** S **8.** N
9. Earth **10.** pole **11.** field **12.** sun **13.** lights **14.** You can sprinkle iron filings on a piece of paper. When you hold a magnet under the paper, the iron filings line up to reveal the magnetic field. **15.** Earth's north magnetic pole acts like the south pole of a magnet. It is called the north magnetic pole because it is near the geographic North Pole.

Workbook Activity 61—Identifying Magnetism

Students' lines should connect listed materials to the following figures: **1.** B **2.** A **3.** B **4.** A **5.** A **6.** A **7.** B **8.** No. Those little rectangles represent atoms, which you'd never be able to see in real life. **9.** When atoms become magnetized they line up like the rectangles in Figure B. **10.** iron **11.** magnet **12.** magnet **13.** pole **14.** Two **15.** magnets

Workbook Activity 62—Magnets and Electromagnetism: Terms Review

1. magnet **2.** magnetic field **3.** magnetic poles **4.** lines of force **5.** electromagnetism **6.** motor **7.** repel **8.** electromagnet **9.** attract **10.** superconducting magnets **11.** core **12.** engine **13.** alloy magnet **14.** maglev train **15.** amplifier

Alternative Workbook Activities

Alternative Workbook Activity 1—What Is Physical Science?

1. test tube **2.** matter **3.** chemistry **4.** energy **5.** mass **6.** physical science **7.** physics **8.** observing: Observing is a skill scientists use; a tuning fork and a battery are tools scientists use. **9.** energy: Energy is not matter; air and a potted plant are matter. **10.** technology: Technology is not a physical science; physics and chemistry are physical sciences.

Alternative Workbook Activity 2—Systems of Measurement

1. 0.3048 meters **2.** 5 meters **3.** 2.54 centimeters **4.** 10.2 centimeters **5.** 0.4536 kilograms **6.** 3.7853 liters **7.** 1.6 kilometers **8.** 1.8 meters **9.** 4.828 kilometers **10.** 200 milligrams

Alternative Workbook Activity 3—Adding and Subtracting Metric Units of Length

1. 17 centimeters 8 millimeters **2.** 25 meters 9 centimeters **3.** 20 meters 33 millimeters or 20 meters 3 centimeters 3 millimeters **4.** 10 meters 2 centimeters **5.** 26 millimeters or 2 centimeters 6 millimeters **6.** 19 meters 15 millimeters or 19 meters 1 centimeter 5 millimeters **7.** 40 meters 15 millimeters or 40 meters 1 centimeter 5 millimeters **8.** 20 meters 12 centimeters **9.** 2 meters 2 centimeters **10.** 2 meters 93 centimeters

Alternative Workbook Activity 4—Using Metric Measurements to Find Area

1. 8 m^2 **2.** 63 cm^2 **3.** 100 mm^2 **4.** 12 cm^2 **5.** 6 m **6.** 8 m **7.** 120 cm^2 **8.** 100 mm **9.** 840 m^2 **10.** 24 mm^2

Alternative Workbook Activity 5—Using Metric Measurements to Find Volume

1. 12 cm^3 **2.** 300 cm^3 **3.** 125 cm^3 **4.** 48 cm^3 **5.** 80 cm^3 **6.** 6 m^3 **7.** 1,000 m^3 **8.** 1,000 mm^3 **9.** 6,000 cm^3 **10.** 1,100 m^3

Alternative Workbook Activity 6—The Metric System: Terms Review

1. K **2.** N **3.** H **4.** B **5.** J **6.** L **7.** F **8.** D **9.** I **10.** A **11.** G **12.** M **13.** E **14.** C **15.** mL **16.** mg **17.** cm **18.** cg **19.** km **20.** kg

Alternative Workbook Activity 7—Properties of Objects
Answers may vary. Possible answers are given.

	Object 1	Object 2
A	rectangle	mostly like a cylinder
B	hard, smooth	wet
C	25 cm × 20 cm × 6 cm	21 cm high
D	1 kg	560 g
E	3,000 cm^3	0.5 L

Alternative Workbook Activity 8—Mass and Weight

Across: **1.** mass   Down: **1.** matter
    4. balance   **2.** standard mass
    7. scale   **3.** weight
    8. Mars   **5.** newtons
    9. kilogram   **6.** gravity
    10. less

Alternative Workbook Activity 9—Measuring the Mass of a Liquid

1. 25 g **2.** $1/g **3.** 55 g **4.** $0.91/g **5.** 80 g **6.** $0.50/g **7.** 50 g
8. $.0.90/g **9.** Rose **10.** Autumn

Alternative Workbook Activity 10—Measuring the Volume of Liquid

1. graduated cylinder **2.** level **3.** meniscus **4.** bottom **5.** scale
6. milliliters **7.** spaces **8.** subtract **9.** divide **10.** volume

Alternative Workbook Activity 11—Comparing and Contrasting Objects

1. Alike: Both are properties of substances that can be measured. Different: Volume is how much space a substance takes up; mass is the amount of matter in a substance. **2.** Alike: Both are forms of matter. Different: A solid is matter in an unchanging shape; a liquid is matter that can pour and takes the shape of the container that holds it. **3.** Alike: Both are solids. Different: Regular shapes have surfaces that are regular and can be measured easily; irregular shapes have unpredictable surfaces. **4.** displacement of water method **5.** formula

Alternative Workbook Activity 12—The Properties of Matter: Terms Review

1. F **2.** E **3.** B **4.** D **5.** C **6.** A **7.** graduated cylinder **8.** meniscus **9.** volume **10.** displacement

Alternative Workbook Activity 13—Identifying Solids, Liquids, and Gases

1. gas **2.** solid **3.** liquid **4.** B **5.** B **6.** C **7.** A **8.** B **9.** A **10.** C

Alternative Workbook Activity 14—What Are Elements?

Across: **1.** element   Down: **2.** molecule
    4. oxygen   **3.** atoms
    6. calcium   **5.** gold
    7. helium   **8.** iron
    10. natural   **9.** silver

Alternative Workbook Activity 15—What Are Compounds?

1. compound **2.** water **3.** carbon, hydrogen, oxygen **4.** medicine **5.** sodium chloride **6.** baking soda **7.** gas **8.** An element has only one kind of atom; a compound has two or more different kinds. **9.** Chlorine is poisonous. In sodium chloride, it is not poisonous. **10.** Both are compounds; both contain carbon, hydrogen, and oxygen; both are used in foods.

Alternative Workbook Activity 16—What Are Atoms Like?

1. protons, neutrons **2.** protons **3.** electrons **4.** neutrons **5.** two
6. 3 **7.** 5 **8.** 6 **9.** 7 **10.** 9

Alternative Workbook Activity 17—The Structure of Matter: Terms Review

1. B **2.** E **3.** D **4.** A **5.** C **6.** F **7.** G **8.** compound **9.** solid **10.** The mass number equals the sum of the number of protons and neutrons in an atom of an element. The atomic number equals the number of protons in an atom of the element.

Alternative Workbook Activity 18—Words from Chemical Symbols

1. CoW **2.** LaNe **3.** KNOB **4.** SUN **5.** ClOWN **6.** RaCe **7.** CoIN
8. SiCK **9.** BOOK **10.** LiON **11.** BiB **12.** NiNe **13.** TaSTe **14.** CoAl
15. CuB

Alternative Workbook Activity 19—Using the Periodic Table

Atomic numbers by rows: Sc 21, Al 13, Cr 24; Mg 12, Ti 22, Na 11; Mn 25, Ne 10, V 23; Down: 58, 45, 58; Across: 58, 45, 58 The pattern is 58, 45, 58.

Alternative Workbook Activity 20—Classifying Elements: Terms Review

1. C **2.** D **3.** F **4.** G **5.** B **6.** A **7.** E **8.** symbol **9.** nonmetal **10.** family

Alternative Workbook Activity 21—Physical and Chemical Changes

1. chemical change **2.** chemical change **3.** physical change
4. chemical change **5.** chemical change **6.** physical change
7. chemical change **8.** physical change **9.** chemical change
10. chemical change   In a physical change, the substance remains the same; only some of its properties change. In a chemical change, a new substance is produced, and the elements react with one another.

Alternative Workbook Activity 22—Energy Levels

1. 2 **2.** 8 **3.** 18 **4.** 32 **5.** 60 **6.** K **7.** M **8.** L **9.** O **10.** N Drawings should show the five energy levels around the nucleus with 2 electrons in the K level, 8 electrons in the L level, and 1 electron in the M level.

Alternative Workbook Activity 23—Working with Chemical Formulas

1. chlorine **2.** one atom **3.** sodium **4.** hydrogen **5.** oxygen
6. hydroxide

Compound	Elements	Atoms
7. sulfate, SO_4	sulfur	1
	oxygen	4
8. sodium chloride, NaCl	sodium	1
	chlorine	1
9. hydrogen sulfide, H_2S	hydrogen	2
	sulfur	1
10. sucrose, $C_{12}H_{22}O_{11}$	carbon	12
	hydrogen	22
	oxygen	11

Alternative Workbook Activity 24—Matching Chemical Formulas with Chemical Names

1. NaF—sodium fluoride **2.** HBr—hydrogen bromide **3.** LiOH—lithium hydroxide **4.** KCl—potassium chloride **5.** LiF—lithium fluoride **6.** BeO—beryllium oxide **7.** KI—potassium iodide **8.** AgI—silver iodide **9.** $FeCO_3$—iron carbonate **10.** Ag_2S—silver sulfide

Alternative Workbook Activity 25—Compounds: Terms Review

Across: 1. radicals **Down:** 2. acid
3. indicator 4. chemical formula
5. chemical bond 7. energy level
6. chemical change 8. pH
9. physical change
10. binary compound

Alternative Workbook Activity 26—Reactions and Solutions

1. alchemist 2. reaction 3. solvent 4. dissolve 5. solution 6. mixture
7. solute 8. A mixture is formed when substances are combined with no chemical reaction. A solution is a mixture in which one substance is dissolved in another. 9. A solute is the substance that is dissolved in a solution. A solvent is the substance that dissolves other substances in a solution. 10. In a mixture, substances combine, but there is no chemical reaction. In a chemical reaction, elements combine or rearrange.

Alternative Workbook Activity 27—Using Chemical Equations to Show Reactions

Across: 1. product **Down:** 2. reactant
4. conservation 3. coefficient
6. law 5. equation
7. matter 8. arrow
10. balance 9. equal

Alternative Workbook Activity 28—Synthesis and Decomposition Reactions

1. synthesis 2. decomposition 3. synthesis 4. decomposition
5. Al, O_2 6. Al_2O_3 7. Cu, O_2 8. CuO 9. 2 10. synthesis

Alternative Workbook Activity 29—How Matter Changes: Terms Review

1. F 2. D 3. E 4. A 5. B 6. C 7. mixture 8. precipitate 9. In a synthesis reaction, elements combine to form a compound. In a decomposition reaction, a compound breaks down into two or more simple substances. 10. In a single-replacement reaction, one element replaces another in a compound. In a double-replacement reaction, the elements in two compounds are exchanged.

Alternative Workbook Activity 30—Calculating Speed

1. 5 m/sec 2. 20 cm/sec 3. 35 mi/hr 4. 25 mm/sec 5. 23 yd/sec
6. 30 m/sec 7. 110 mi/hr 8. 22 hr 9. 2,250 mi 10. 5.5 hr

Alternative Workbook Activity 31—Using a Graph to Describe Motion

1. Each vehicle moves at a constant speed. 2. car—480 km; motorcycle—240 km

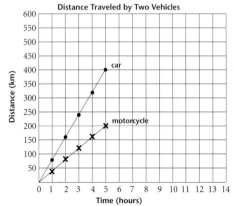

Alternative Workbook Activity 32—Acceleration

1. 100 km/hr per hr 2. −5 km/sec per sec 3. 5 m/sec per sec
4. 30 cm/sec per sec 5. −6 km/hr per sec 6. −5 m/min per sec
7. 6.5 mm/sec per sec 8. −3 km/hr per sec 9. 5 km/hr per sec
10. 1.6 m/min per min

Alternative Workbook Activity 33—The Laws of Motion

Across: 1. friction **Down:** 1. force
5. third 2. Newton
6. second 3. first
7. inertia 4. motion
9. reaction 8. rest

Alternative Workbook Activity 34—Motion: Terms Review

1. B 2. C 3. F 4. E 5. D 6. G 7. H 8. A 9. universal gravitation
10. constant speed

Alternative Workbook Activity 35—What Is Work?

1. work 2. newtons 3. multiply 4. force 5. joule 6. 10 newtons × 1.5 meters = 15 joules 7. 600 newtons × 2.0 meters = 1,200 joules 8. 900 newtons × 100 meters = 90,000 joules 9. 4,000 joules ÷ 200 newtons = 20 meters 10. 330 joules ÷ 2 newtons = 165 meters

Alternative Workbook Activity 36—Understanding Power

1. rate 2. force 3. work ÷ time 4. watt 5. kilowatt 6. He used more power when he covered the distance in 3 minutes.
7. 255 joules ÷ 15 seconds = 17 watts 8. 255 joules ÷ 10 seconds = 25.5 watts 9. 120,000 joules ÷ 10 seconds = 12,000 watts
10. 120,000 joules ÷ 12 seconds = 10,000 watts

Alternative Workbook Activity 37—Understanding Energy

Across: 1. electrical **Down:** 1. energy
3. potential 2. chemical
5. kinetic 4. mechanical
6. nuclear 7. joules
8. radiant
9. decreases

Alternative Workbook Activity 38—Using Levers

1. lever 2. resistance 3. second-class 4. effort force 5. fulcrum
6. resistance force 7. effort force 8. resistance force 9. fulcrum
10. fulcrum 11. effort force 12. resistance force 13. 200 × 1.5 = 300 joules 14. 400 × 0.5 = 200 joules 15. 200 ÷ 300 = 0.66 × 100% = 66%

Alternative Workbook Activity 39—Mechanical Advantage

1. effort arm 2. resistance arm 3. mechanical advantage 4. MA = 4
5. MA = 0.66

Alternative Workbook Activity 40—Work and Machines: Terms Review

1. D 2. I 3. G 4. E 5. F 6. B 7. H 8. A 9. J 10. C
11. conservation 12. effort force 13. work output
14. mechanical advantage 15. inclined plane

Alternative Workbook Activity 41—What Is Heat?

Across: 1. heat source **Down:** 1. hands
4. heat 2. steam engine
5. stars 3. energy
8. sun 6. motion
9. electricity 7. fission

Alternative Workbook Activity 42—How Heat Affects Matter
1. expand 2. contract 3. condensation 4. evaporate 5. expand
6. A 7. B 8. C 9. water vapor 10. vapor

Alternative Workbook Activity 43—Temperature
1. Fahrenheit 2. gas 3. temperature 4. thermometer 5. heat
6. Celsius 7. boils 8. degree 9. alcohol 10. liquid

```
P B A C T A I F I K H N A H O
D F A H R E N H E I T U A R T
D E O E N J O E T B T K U G E
N H L N D E G R E E E Y O R B
T O H E H E A T X C H A U W Z
R H E N O F S Z O N T T D H E
I T E L U G O E Q S A K O R S
A S P R O W A C B R C L Y T R
B M I A M S Z D E S C I J I X
O E M K L O T P R L X Q L A R
I I F E E U M L Y Q S U M E F
L T D H T E V E O I T I N O R
S R D H T O E G T D A D U K I
L W E G R A B B W E B O B S D
N A L C O H O L B Q R Y H O S
```

Alternative Workbook Activity 44—How to Measure Heat
Possible statements might include: 1. Temperature is something you read on a thermometer. 2. Heat is energy caused by tiny particles in motion. 3. the gallon of water because there's more water to give off heat 4. 8 calories 5. –20 calories 6. 15 calories 7. –25 calories 8. 14 calories 9. –10 calories 10. 100 calories

Alternative Workbook Activity 45—Heat: Terms Review
1. H 2. D 3. F 4. G 5. A 6. B 7. C 8. I 9. E 10. conduction
11. conductor 12. radiation 13. convection 14. vacuum 15. insulator

Alternative Workbook Activity 46—What Is Sound?
1. vibrates 2. air particles 3. sound wave 4. sounds 5. weaker
The wire is pinched together at one end. This "wave" moves across the spring. Sound waves move away from a vibrating object in the same way.

Alternative Workbook Activity 47—Different Sounds
1. intensity 2. frequency 3. frequency 4. intensity 5. intensity
6. frequency 7. frequency 8. decibels 9. volume 10. high or low

Alternative Workbook Activity 48—How Sound Travels
1. Energy moves through matter when sound is produced.
2. Molecules are close together. They bump each other and move back in place very quickly. 3. Both sonar and ultrasound use reflected sound waves to gather data about something unseen.
4. There is no matter in space, and sound can only travel through matter. 5. An echo is sound that is reflected back from an object.
6. 9 ÷ 3 = 3 km 7. 3 seconds 8. steel 9. water 10. air

Alternative Workbook Activity 49—What Is Light?
1. light 2. prism 3. photons 4. empty space 5. visible spectrum
6. orange 7. green 8. blue 9. radio waves 10. gamma rays

Alternative Workbook Activity 50—How Light Is Reflected
1. plane mirror 2. convex mirror 3. concave mirror 4. convex mirror 5. plane mirror 6. concave mirror 7. concave mirror
8. Light bounces from the surface at an angle that is the same size as the angle with which it hit. 9. The smooth, flat surface gives a clear image because the light rays all leave at the same angle. 10. Both waves bounce off an object or a surface.

Alternative Workbook Activity 51—Sound and Light: Terms Review
1. I 2. A 3. H 4. G 5. J 6. D 7. C 8. E 9. B 10. F 11. concave
12. visible spectrum 13. concave lens 14. convex mirror
15. sound wave

Alternative Workbook Activity 52—How Electricity Flows
1. lightning 2. circuit 3. static 4. ampere 5. energy

```
P B C C S D V I V U K R O U B
T H P D A E S F D S T A T I C
C A Z E N E R G Y J I A U O Y
R U M I C E A G S L M Z A Z
R A T I E U C N X R V P T O H
C L A K S Q I P L F M E I T K
U L Y M C N O E X U T R R M A
I E W W T M P R Y T N E V F H
T L E H R P T E O I S K U S P
P C G V E O T T N C I R C U I
C I N R U R D N J G H E P N O
L R O O I E Q T O O C B R N T
```

Alternative Workbook Activity 53—Conductors and Insulators
A. 1. conductor 2. insulator; B. 1. copper 2. gold
3. aluminum/silver; C. 1. glass 2. rubber 3. wood/plastic;
D. 1. measure of how easily electric current will flow through a material 2. ohm

Alternative Workbook Activity 54—Some Sources of Electric Current
Across: 1. electromotive   Down: 2. cars
5. chemical   3. terminal
6. dry cell   4. voltage
8. AC   6. direct
9. battery   7. lead

Alternative Workbook Activity 55—Using Ohm's Law
1. 4 amperes 2. .015 amperes 3. 12 volts 4. 20 ohms 5. 11 ohms

Alternative Workbook Activity 56—Series Circuits
1. power source 2. wire 3. bulb 4. wire 5. switch Students should put arrows around the wire from the batteries to the bulb and back to the batteries. 6. one 7. voltage 8. add 9. 8 volts 10. fires

Alternative Workbook Activity 57—Parallel Circuits
1. one 2. Batteries in a series deliver more energy in the same amount of time. 3. If one light goes out, all go out. 4. Voltage is lowered in each device. 5. It's the total voltages of all the cells.
6. 2 7. parallel circuit 8. series circuit 9. 1.5 V 10. 6 V

Alternative Workbook Activity 58—Electricity: Terms Review
1. I 2. G 3. B 4. F 5. D 6. C 7. A 8. J 9. H 10. E 11. K
12. insulator 13. terminal 14. battery 15. conductor

Alternative Workbook Activity 59—What Are Magnets?
Across: 1. magnetic pole   Down: 2. attract
4. north   3. lodestone
6. doughnut   5. south
7. iron   8. repel
10. magnet   9. bar

Alternative Workbook Activity 60—Identifying a Magnetic Field
1. N **2.** N **3.** S **4.** S **5.** N **6.** S **7.** Earth **8.** pole **9.** field **10.** particles

Alternative Workbook Activity 61—Identifying Magnetism
Students' lines should connect listed materials as follows: **1.** B **2.** A **3.** B **4.** A **5.** A **6.** iron **7.** magnet **8.** pole **9.** Two **10.** magnets

Alternative Workbook Activity 62—Magnets and Electromagnetism: Terms Review
1. magnetic field **2.** magnetic poles **3.** lines of force **4.** electromagnetism **5.** attract **6.** electromagnet **7.** repel **8.** magnet **9.** motor **10.** maglev train

Lab Manual

Lab Manual 1—Safety in the Classroom
1. Answers will vary, depending on the layout of the classroom. **2.** Answers will vary, depending on the type of equipment in the classroom. **Explore Further** Diagrams will vary but should show safety equipment, electrical and gas outlets, and an emergency exit.

Lab Manual 2—Hands Instead of Feet (Investigation 1-1)
1. No, our length in hands didn't match those of the other students because the unit of measurement, our hands, varied from person to person. **2.** Yes, the length in centimeters did match those of the other students because the unit of measurement was the same for everyone. **3.** Yes, metric system is more useful because the units of measurement do not vary from person to person. **Explore Further** The effectiveness of the students' systems measurement depends on whether they choose a standard unit of measurement or one with a varying unit of measurement, such as a hand or cubit.

Lab Manual 3—Counting Squares and Calculating Area (Investigation 1-2)
1. Yes, the areas matched; answers will vary. (Sample answer: Area depends on length and width, not shape.) **2.** The sum of the areas and the number of squares are the same. The sum of the areas and the area of the original rectangle are the same. Explanations will vary. (Sample answer: The total area was not increased or decreased, it was just arranged differently.) **Explore Further** The sum of the area of the two triangles is equal to the sum of the area of the rectangle.

Lab Manual 4—Finding Volume
1. Answers will vary, depending on the boxes used. **2.** Answers will vary, depending on the boxes used. **3.** Answers will vary, depending on the boxes used. **4.** Answers will vary, depending on the boxes used. **5.** Answers will vary, depending on students' predictions and activity results. **6.** Answers will vary, depending on the boxes used. **7.** Students most likely discover that predicting volume without knowing actual measurements is difficult. **Explore Further** Answers will vary, depending on the boxes used.

Lab Manual 5—Identifying Properties (Investigation 2-1)
1. Answers will vary. **2.** Answers will vary. **3.** Answers will vary. **4.** Possible answer: I could have included more details and exact measurements. **Explore Further** Groupings and descriptions will vary. However, students should recognize that no one grouping is correct. Students most likely will have to be more specific with their list of properties than in the first part of the investigation because the items in a group probably are more similar than the original five items in the bag.

Lab Manual 6—Measuring Mass
1. Answers will vary, depending on the objects used. **2.** Answers will vary, depending on the objects used. **3.** the nickel **4.** two pennies **5.** Answers will vary, depending on students' estimated masses. **Explore Further** 1,500 kilograms = 14,700 newtons; answers will vary.

Lab Manual 7—Measuring Volume
1. Answers will vary, depending on the objects used. **2.** Answers will vary, depending on the objects used. **3.** Answers will vary slightly due to errors in measurement but should be close enough for students to see the relationship. **4.** Answers will vary, depending on students' predictions. **Explore Further** Fill the cup with water. Measure one portion of the water in the cup at a time. Then add the measured volumes.

Lab Manual 8—Finding Density (Investigation 2-2)
1. The water has greater density. **2.** The cooking oil will float on top. **Explore Further** The corn syrup will form another layer on the bottom of the cylinder because its density is greater.

Lab Manual 9—Inferring the Properties of an Object
1–4. Answers will vary, depending on how well students probe the clay ball and then relate their observations to the actual object. **5.** Answers will vary. **6.** Answers will vary. **Explore Further** Answers will vary. However, students should note that they had to rely on observations made by touch. They could infer properties by comparing what they felt to the properties of known objects. The model "atom" is like a model scientists make to explore the properties of atoms that they cannot see.

Lab Manual 10—Breaking Down Water (Investigation 3-1)
1. The wire connected to the negative terminal had more bubbles. **2.** Students' answers should include descriptions of the gas bubbles that appeared. **3.** The bubbles at the end of the wires tell us that water is a compound because these bubbles indicate that water is made of more than one kind of atom—oxygen and hydrogen. **Explore Further** Bubbles form inside the test tubes. The gases that form force liquid out of each test tube.

Lab Manual 11—Making Models of Atoms (Investigation 3-2)
1. Answers will vary, depending on the element selected. **2.** Answers will vary. Refer to the chart on page 78 for the correct number. **3.** Answers will vary. Refer to the chart on page 84 for the correct number. **4.** Answers will vary. Refer to the chart on page 78 for the correct number. **5.** It shows that (A) the nucleus is made of protons and neutrons, (B) electrons surround the nucleus, (C) the number of electrons equals the number of protons, and (D) electrons are smaller than protons and neutrons. **Explore Further** The number of both protons and neutrons increases as the mass number increases.

Lab Manual 12—Exploring the Space Between Particles
1. 200 mL **2.** No, because when sand and water were added to the marbles, the volume did not increase. **3.** Answers will vary. **4.** Answers will vary. **5.** Answers will vary, depending on the answers to questions 3 and 4. **6.** The volume of space is equal to the volume calculated in question 5. **Explore Further** The investigation models the space between atoms. It enables me to note that space between particles in atoms is similar to the space between marbles in a container. Even though an atom takes up a certain amount of space, some of that space is empty.

Lab Manual 13—Finding Iron in Your Cereal (Investigation 4-1)

1. pieces of a grayish material 2. pieces of a grayish material 3. yes 4. iron **Explore Further** The human body requires iron in its red blood cells and red muscles to carry oxygen and see that the cells use it properly. Almost 100 percent of the iron in the human body is used up daily, so the iron needs to be replenished. Foods such as beef, pork, raisins, spinach, and apricots are rich in iron.

Lab Manual 14—Exploring Elements

1. Answers will vary. 2. Most students will find that some classifications worked better than others. One reason might be that a particular classification system was more exact. 3. Answers will vary, depending on students' classification systems. 4. Students might suggest breaking the system down into more levels. **Explore Further** Answers will vary.

Lab Manual 15—Analyzing Common Compounds

1. salt—sodium, chlorine; baking soda—sodium, hydrogen, carbon, oxygen; sugar—carbon, hydrogen, oxygen; water—hydrogen, oxygen; nail polish remover—carbon, hydrogen, oxygen; vinegar—hydrogen, carbon, oxygen 2. baking soda 3. baking soda, sugar, nail polish, and vinegar 4. none **Explore Further** Sugar and nail polish remover do not have the same properties. One is a white crystal and the other is a clear liquid. The elements bind to one another differently in the two substances. The number of each element differs in the substances.

Lab Manual 16—Electricity and Metals (Investigation 4-2)

1. The bulb lit. 2. The bulb lit with the aluminum but did not light with the sulfur. 3. Copper and aluminum can conduct electricity. Sulfur cannot. 4. Aluminum and copper must be metals because they conduct electricity. **Explore Further** The bulb lights up. Graphite (pencil lead) can conduct electricity. Most nonmetals are not good conductors of electricity. Graphite conducts electricity but is not shiny and cannot be pounded into thin sheets. It is probably one of the few nonmetals that are good conductors of electricity.

Lab Manual 17—Observing a Chemical Change (Investigation 5-1)

1. The powder dissolved in the water. 2. The crystals dissolved in the water. 3. A white substance formed. 4. Physical change; the substance only changed its appearance. No new substance was formed. 5. Chemical change; a new substance was formed. **Explore Further** The balloon blows up, indicating that a gas has formed. A chemical change takes place because a new substance—the gas—formed.

Lab Manual 18—Observing a Chemical Reaction

1. calcium chloride, baking soda, and water; compounds 2. A gas was present. 3. No; no new substance formed. 4. Yes, a new substance (the gas) formed. **Explore Further** The baking soda and water do not result in a chemical change when they are mixed. There is only a physical change. The calcium chloride and water do not result in a chemical change when they are mixed. There is only a physical change. Calcium chloride and baking soda must be mixed together for a chemical change to take place when water is added.

Lab Manual 19—Exploring Acidity

1. The orange juice should not affect the red litmus paper. 2. The orange juice turned the blue litmus paper red. 3. Acids have no effect on red litmus paper. 4. Acids turn blue litmus paper red. 5. Bases turn red litmus paper blue. 6. Bases have no effect on blue litmus paper. 7. Materials that are neither acids nor bases have no effect on red litmus paper. 8. Materials that are neither acids nor bases have no effect on blue litmus paper. 9. Place the litmus paper in the substance. If the paper turns red, the substance is an acid. If the litmus paper turns blue, the substance is a base. **Explore Further** Vinegar and orange juice are acids. Ammonia, soap, and liquid antacids are bases. Salt water and milk are neither acids nor antacids. Results for additional substances will vary.

Lab Manual 20—Identifying Acids and Bases (Investigation 5-2)

1. Vinegar, lemon juice, aspirin, and the soft drink are acids. 2. Baking soda, ammonia, soap, and milk of magnesia are bases. 3. Yes, some bases have a higher pH than others. The color is deeper in solutions that have bases with higher pH. **Explore Further** To organize and interpret the data, students should add the following columns to the right of existing columns in their data charts: column 4, headed *Litmus Color*; column 5, headed *Acid or Base*. Have students match the color of the litmus paper with the scale that accompanies long-range litmus paper. Students will be able to read the pH of each substance. If the litmus tests produce any discrepancies, have students retest with the litmus paper. If the second testing repeats the discrepancy, have students speculate about the reasons for the discrepancy. (*Students may note that the litmus paper test is probably more exact than the cabbage juice test. Or they may guess that they could have made a mistake in the original investigation.*) Ask students what they learned from the retesting experience. (*Sometimes to obtain accurate, reliable data, you have to test several times to determine if the results repeat.*)

Lab Manual 21—Speed of Dissolving

1. in the beaker with the crushed sugar 2. The figure shows that the crushed sugar has more sides that are in contact with the water. As a result, the sugar can dissolve more quickly. 3. Stirring increased the speed of dissolving. **Explore Further** A powdered mixture dissolves more rapidly than a cube of the mixture would.

Lab Manual 22—Separating a Mixture (Investigation 6-1)

1. The salt dissolved in the water, forming a solution. 2. The sand didn't dissolve. You can still see all the sand you added. 3. The salt was in the solution in the second beaker. It appeared later in the second beaker. 4. Sand remained on the filter paper. 5. Salt formed in the beaker. 6. Water is the solvent. Salt is the solute. **Explore Further** Some students might suggest pouring the mixture into water to dissolve the sugar and then filtering out the iron filings. Other students might suggest using a magnet to pull out the iron filings.

Lab Manual 23—Temperature and Chemical Reactions

1. A chemical reaction occurred in both flasks because a new substance, a gas, was produced. 2. The reaction happened faster in the flask with the warmer water. 3. Heat causes a chemical reaction to occur faster. **Explore Further** Heat speeds up the reaction; therefore, greater heat should make the reaction take place even quicker. The reaction in Flask C would take place more quickly than the reaction in Flask A.

Lab Manual 24—Observing Different Kinds of Reactions (Investigation 6-2)

1. synthesis **2.** decomposition **3.** single replacement **4.** double replacement **Explore Further** Reaction 1: downward arrow. Reaction 2: upward arrow. Reaction 3: downward arrow. Reaction 4: downward arrow.

Lab Manual 25—Finding Speed (Investigation 7-1)

1. Student graphs will vary but should reflect the data they collected. **2.** The estimate should be half the number of recorded meters. **3.** The estimate should be twice the number of recorded meters. **Explore Further** The marble would roll faster. The graph would have a steep slope. It would be steeper because the marble would travel faster.

Lab Manual 26—Exploring Acceleration

1. The cork stayed back. **2.** The cork continued moving forward. **3.** The cork continued moving in the original direction. **4.** The cork continued moving in the original direction. **Explore Further** The cork accelerates with each change in direction or speed. The cork moves in the opposite direction because it is reacting to the change in direction or speed.

Lab Manual 27—Newton's First Law of Motion

1. The ball didn't move until the back of the box hit it. **2.** The ball continued to move. **3.** The quarter did not move. **Explore Further** When the box was stopped in step 4, the ball continued to move forward because no force acted on it to cause it to stop. The quarter in step 7 did not move because no force acted on it to cause it to move.

Lab Manual 28—Newton's Third Law of Motion (Investigation 7-2)

1. The escaping air moves in the opposite direction of the balloon. **2.** The balloon moves in the opposite direction of the escaping air. **3.** Because the balloon and air move in opposite directions and the movement of the balloon is caused by the escaping air, they demonstrate Newton's third law of motion, which states that for every action, there is an equal and opposite reaction. **4.** The balloons do not move in any direction. **5.** The forces are opposite horizontal forces. **Explore Further** The weight would keep the balloon from moving as far or as quickly because of the added mass.

Lab Manual 29—Mass, Height, and Energy (Investigation 8-1)

1. The larger marble pushed the cup farther from the ramp. **2.** Objects with more mass have more kinetic energy. **Explore Further** A marble rolling down a higher ramp should push the cup farther than the same marble rolling down a lower ramp. Because energy is neither created nor destroyed, students should conclude that the marble on the higher ramp had greater potential energy, which resulted in greater kinetic energy.

As an alternative, students could observe and compare the indentations made by marbles dropped from varying heights into a container of wet sand or soil. Students could use a meterstick as a gauge for measuring the heights.

Lab Manual 30—Finding the Mechanical Advantage of a Lever (Investigation 8-2)

1. The most effort force, around 8 newtons, should have been applied when the fulcrum was at the 80-cm mark. The least, approximately 0.5 newtons, should have been necessary at the 20-cm mark. The effort at the 50-cm mark should have been about 2 newtons. **2.** MA should have been 50 cm ÷ 50 cm = 1 for the first lever, 20 cm ÷ 80 cm = 0.25 for the second lever, and 80 cm ÷ 20 cm = 4 for the third lever. However, the weight of the meterstick will affect results somewhat. **3.** The setup with the fulcrum at the 20-cm mark had the greatest mechanical advantage. The setup with the fulcrum at the 80-cm mark had the least. **4.** The ranking is opposite to that in question 1. **5.** Moving the fulcrum closer to the resistance and farther from the effort creates greater mechanical advantage. **Explore Further** The mass of the weight should not affect mechanical advantage if the effort arm and resistance arm are set up in the same way. The mechanical advantage remains the same.

Lab Manual 31—Exploring Pulleys

1. 60 grams **2.** 30 grams **3.** The force required to lift a mass is equal to the mass divided by the number of pulleys involved. **4.** 20 cm **5.** 60 cm **6.** To lift a mass a certain distance, you must pull for that distance times the number of pulleys involved. **Explore Further** A fixed pulley changes the direction of the effort force but does not multiply it. A movable pulley multiplies effort force but does not change its direction.

Lab Manual 32—Exploring an Inclined Plane

1. The amount of force decreased. **2.** The distance increased. **Explore Further** The smaller the angle the greater the MA and the smaller the effort force required.

Lab Manual 33—Exploring Heat and Motion of Particles

1. In each beaker, the food coloring began to spread. In Beaker A, it spread more slowly than in Beakers B or C. It spread most quickly in beaker C. **2.** Answers will depend on conclusions that students draw. Most will conclude that the water is moving. **3.** The particles move faster when they are heated. **Explore Further** The drop of food coloring broke up and spread throughout the water as the water became warm. As water heats, its particles start moving faster.

Lab Manual 34—Observing and Comparing Expansion and Contraction of Gases (Investigation 9-1)

1. The balloon began to inflate. **2.** The balloon deflated. **3.** The air in the bottle expanded when it was heated, and the air moved into the balloon. When it was cooled, the air in the bottle contracted and the air in the balloon was pulled back into the flask. **Explore Further** In a colder room a helium-filled balloon would diminish in size. In a warmer room it would expand.

Lab Manual 35—Measuring the Rate of Heat Loss (Investigation 9-2)

1. At the start, the water in both containers should be the same temperature. After 8 minutes, the water in the smaller container should be slightly cooler. After 15 minutes, the temperature difference should be greater, with the water in the smaller container being cooler. **2.** The smaller container, with less water, lost heat more quickly than the larger container. **3.** Heat from the water flowed into the container and then into the air surrounding the container. **Explore Further** **1.** After 8 minutes, the temperature of the water has increased. After 15 minutes, the temperature has increased even more. **2.** Heat flows from a warmer object to a cooler object. The heat flowed from the air to the container and then to the water.

Lab Manual 36—Exploring Heat Absorption

1. the sun or the lamp **2.** The can with the black covering absorbed more heat. **3.** Darker colors absorb more heat. **4.** The lighter clothing will not absorb as much heat as darker clothing. **Explore Further** People would stay cooler if they wore light clothing in the summer sun. This is because light clothing will not absorb as much heat as darker clothing.

Lab Manual 37—Making Musical Sounds

1. Tune A: Twinkle, Twinkle, Little Star **Tune B:** Row, Row, Row Your Boat **2.** Add more water to the bottle. **3.** Take some water out of the bottle. **Explore Further** Answers will vary, but students should connect a high pitch with a high frequency and a low pitch with a low frequency. They may suggest that a small instrument vibrates quickly and produces a high sound while a larger instrument vibrates more slowly and produces a lower sound.

Lab Manual 38—Inferring How Sound Waves Travel (Investigation 10-1)

1. Salt grains bounced up and down. **2.** Vibrations of the rubber band also caused the plastic wrap to vibrate. This in turn caused the salt to move. **3.** The more force used, the more intense the sound, or the greater its volume. **4.** The more force used, the more the salt moved around. **Explore Further 1.** The vibrating tuning fork causes waves on the surface of the water. **2.** The more vigorously the tuning fork is vibrating, the more pronounced the waves on the water's surface.

Lab Manual 39—Making a Pinhole Camera

1. The images are upside-down. **2.** A greater difference in brightness between the object viewed and the place the camera is increases the quality of the image. **3.** The image becomes less clear. **Explore Further** Answers will vary. The clarity of the images and their sizes depend on how well the materials control light that is admitted or how well they absorb light.

Lab Manual 40—Measuring Angles of Reflected Rays (Investigation 10-2)

1. Answers will vary, depending on how students labeled their drawings. However, they should identify the angle of the ray that approaches the mirror. **2.** Answers will vary, depending on how students labeled their drawings. However, students should identify the angle of the ray that travels from the mirror. **3.** The angles are the same. **Explore Further** You can read the word AMBULANCE. The letters no longer appear to be backwards.

Lab Manual 41—Exploring Electric Charges

1. No, they did not attract or repel each other. **2.** Yes, they attracted each other. **3.** The charges were opposite because the balloon and cloth attracted each other. Opposite charges attract. **4.** The charge on the balloons was the same because they repelled each other. Like charges repel. **Explore Further** Electrons were transferred, giving the balloons a negative charge and the cloth a positive charge.

Lab Manual 42—Identifying Electric Conductors

1. conductors—salt, baking soda, vinegar, orange juice; nonconductors—water, sugar, mineral oil, rubbing alcohol **2.** Answers will vary. **3.** Answers will vary, depending on the type of materials used. **Explore Further** Distilled water would not conduct electricity as well as tap water because it would not have the minerals contained in tap water that help make it a good conductor.

Lab Manual 43—Constructing Series Circuits (Investigation 11-1)

1. A dry cell, wire, bulb, and switch make up circuit A. It's a series circuit. **2.** A dry cell, wire, 2 bulbs, and switch make up circuit B. It's a series circuit. **3.** The bulbs in B were dimmer than in A because there were two devices using energy in a circuit with only one path for current. **4.** The other bulb went out because the circuit was broken. **5.** The bulbs in C shined more brightly than in B because there were two power sources in series and, therefore, voltage was doubled. **Explore Further** Students should find that if they add more bulbs to the circuit, the bulbs will shine less brightly. If they add more batteries, the bulbs will shine more brightly.

Lab Manual 44—Constructing Parallel Circuits (Investigation 11-2)

1. A dry cell, wire, 3 bulbs, and switch make up circuit C. It is partly parallel, partly series circuit. **2.** The cells are connected in parallel. **3.** They shined equally brightly in circuit B because the parallel paths allowed the same amount of electricity to flow through each bulb in B as in A. **4.** The bulb that was alone on one path shined even when one or both of the other bulbs were unscrewed because it was on a separate current path. If one of the two bulbs in series was unscrewed, the other bulb in series went out because that branch of the circuit was broken and both bulbs were on the same current path. **5.** They shined equally brightly in D as in A because there were two power sources in series and, therefore, voltage was doubled. **6.** They shined less brightly in E than in D because the parallel cell connection did not increase the voltage. **Explore Further** Circuit D will stay lit longer because it has fewer bulbs and twice the power. Circuit C uses less power.

Lab Manual 45—Exploring Magnetism

1. None **2.** Nothing blocks a magnetic field. **Explore Further** In a magnetic window cleaner, a strong magnet connects a cleaning pad outside the window to one on the inside. When a person cleans the inside of the window, the outside pad follows the movement of the magnet.

Lab Manual 46—Observing Magnetic Lines of Force (Investigation 12-1)

1. The curved lines extend from one pole to the other. The lines were closest and thickest with filings near the poles, which showed that the field was strongest there. **2.** The like poles repelled each other. The lines from each of the close poles curved sharply away from the other pole. **3.** The unlike poles attracted each other. The lines of force arched toward each other, forming one continuous pattern. **4.** With both magnets, more filings were concentrated near the poles. **Explore Further** *If the metal bar replaced the iron filings:* The metal bar clung to the paper and magnets. You could pick up the paper and magnets when you lifted the bar. Placing like poles together had no impact on the attraction of the bar to the magnets. *If the metal bar replaced the magnets:* The filings scattered randomly without any pattern.

Lab Manual 47—Experimenting with a Compass

1. The needle stopped in a north-south position. The earth's magnetic poles attracted the magnetic needle. **2.** the iron nail and the steel paper clip **3.** paper ball, wooden pencil, and eraser **Explore Further** Directions will vary depending on the place chosen by students.

Lab Manual 48—Constructing an Electromagnet (Investigation 12-2)
1. They were no longer attracted to the nail and dropped away.
2. The electromagnet picked up more paper clips with the added coils. Its strength increased. **Explore Further 1.** The pattern is well formed and compact. **2.** Fewer filings form a less distinct and smaller pattern. **3.** Adding more turns makes the magnetic force around the wire stronger. **4.** The power of the electromagnet would increase.

Community Connection

Completed activities will vary for each student. Community Connection activities are real-life activities that students complete outside the classroom. These activities give students practical learning and practice of the concepts taught in *Physical Science*. Check completed activities to see that students have followed directions, completed each step, filled in all charts and blanks, provided reasonable answers to questions, written legibly, and used appropriate science terms and proper grammar.

Self-Study Guides

Self-Study Guides outline suggested sections from the text and workbook. These assignment guides provide flexibility for individualized instruction or independent study.

Mastery Tests

Chapter 1 Mastery Test A
Part A 1. B **2.** A **3.** A **4.** C **5.** D
Part B 6. Chemistry is the study of matter and how it changes.
7. Matter is anything that has mass and takes up space. **8.** You can't hold energy or measure it with a ruler. **9.** Measurements are important because they help to gather exact information.
10. Scientists use the metric system of measurement.
Part C 11. liter **12.** 1,000 **13.** mass **14.** centi- **15.** $\frac{1}{1,000}$
Part D 16. 3 km **17.** 1,000 mm **18.** 120 cm^3 **19.** 12.8 m^2
20. 5,200 cm^3 **21.** 6.421 L **22.** 489 cm^3 **23.** 1,000 g
24. 6,405,000 mg **25.** 77.18 kg

Chapter 1 Mastery Test B
Part A 1. Scientists use the metric system of measurement.
2. Chemistry is the study of matter and how it changes.
3. Measurements are important because they help to gather exact information. **4.** Matter is anything that has mass and takes up space. **5.** You can't hold energy or measure it with a ruler.
Part B 6. C **7.** A **8.** B **9.** D **10.** A
Part C 11. 120 cm^3 **12.** 6.421 L **13.** 6,405,000 mg **14.** 3 km
15. 1,000 mm **16.** 77.18 kg **17.** 12.8 m^2 **18.** 5,200 cm^3 **19.** 489 cm^3
20. 1,000 g
Part D 21. 1,000 **22.** liter **23.** $\frac{1}{1,000}$ **24.** mass **25.** centi-

Chapter 2 Mastery Test A
Part A 1. A **2.** C **3.** B **4.** C **5.** D
Part B 6. properties **7.** volume **8.** color **9.** standard masses **10.** mass
11. liquids **12.** displacement **13.** density **14.** float **15.** sink
Part C 16. D **17.** E **18.** B **19.** C **20.** A
Part D 21. 86 g **22.** 113.4 g **23.** 98 mL **24.** 29 mL **25.** 900 cm^3

Chapter 2 Mastery Test B
Part A 1. D **2.** C **3.** E **4.** A **5.** B
Part B 6. D **7.** D **8.** A **9.** B **10.** C
Part C 11. 900 cm^3 **12.** 98 mL **13.** 86 g **14.** 29 mL **15.** 113.4 g
Part D 16. float **17.** volume **18.** sink **19.** density **20.** properties
21. liquids **22.** color **23.** mass **24.** displacement **25.** standard masses

Chapter 3 Mastery Test A
Part A 1. D **2.** B **3.** A **4.** D **5.** D
Part B 6. nucleus **7.** compound **8.** element **9.** smallest **10.** atom
Part C 11. C **12.** D **13.** B **14.** A **15.** E
Part D 16. 13 **17.** 14 **18.** 13 **19.** 88 **20.** 138 **21.** 88
Part E Answers will vary but should cover the following points:
22. Scientists use models—pictures, ideas, or objects—to explain something based on studies of how it works or acts. A model helps scientists understand how something acts even though it may not look like the object. **23.** Atomic number and mass number are ways to identify elements. Atomic number is the number of protons in the nucleus of each atom of an element. Mass number is the number of protons plus the number of neutrons in an atom of an element. **24.** Every atom has three parts. The protons, positively charged particles, and neutrons, particles with no electric charge, are in the nucleus, or central part of the atom. Electrons, negatively charged particles, move around the nucleus in unknown ways. **25.** Both table salt and water are compounds made up of two elements. Table salt is a solid made up of sodium and chlorine atoms; water is a liquid made up of hydrogen and oxygen.

Chapter 3 Mastery Test B
Part A **1.** B **2.** E **3.** C **4.** D **5.** A
Part B **6.** 88 **7.** 138 **8.** 88 **9.** 13 **10.** 14 **11.** 13
Part C **12.** A **13.** D **14.** D **15.** D **16.** B
Part D Answers will vary but should cover the following points:
17. Every atom has three parts. The protons, positively charged particles, and neutrons, particles with no electric charge, are in the nucleus, or central part of the atom. Electrons, negatively charged particles, move around the nucleus in unknown ways. **18.** Atomic number and mass number are ways to identify elements. Atomic number is the number of protons in the nucleus of each atom of an element. Mass number is the number of protons plus the number of neutrons in an atom of an element. **19.** Both table salt and water are compounds made up of two elements. Table salt is a solid made up of sodium and chlorine atoms; water is a liquid made up of hydrogen and oxygen. **20.** A model helps scientists understand how something acts even though it may not look like the object. Scientists use models—pictures, ideas, or objects—to explain something based on studies of how it works or acts.
Part E **21.** smallest **22.** element **23.** compound **24.** atom **25.** nucleus

Chapter 4 Mastery Test A
Part A **1.** C **2.** A **3.** C **4.** B **5.** C
Part B **6.** I **7.** F **8.** H **9.** B **10.** D **11.** G **12.** C **13.** J **14.** A **15.** E
Part C **16.** They are organized in order of increasing atomic number. **17.** element name, symbol, atomic number, atomic mass **18.** They are shiny, conduct heat and electricity, and can have their shape changed. **19.** It divides metals and nonmetals. **20.** An alloy is a mixture of metals that are combined when melted. **21.** Atomic number is the number of protons; atomic mass is the average of the mass numbers of all isotopes of the element. **22.** They glow when electricity passes through them. **23.** They do not react readily with other elements. **24.** C-12 has 6 neutrons; C-14 has 8 neutrons. **25.** elements in the same column of the periodic table that have similar properties

Chapter 4 Mastery Test B
Part A **1.** C **2.** E **3.** H **4.** G **5.** F **6.** B **7.** I **8.** J **9.** A **10.** D
Part B **11.** A **12.** C **13.** C **14.** B **15.** C
Part C **16.** An alloy is a mixture of metals that are combined when melted. **17.** They are shiny, conduct heat and electricity, and can have their shape changed. **18.** elements in the same column of the periodic table that have similar properties **19.** They glow when electricity passes through them. **20.** It divides metals and nonmetals. **21.** They are organized in order of increasing atomic number. **22.** Atomic number is the number of protons; atomic mass is the average of the mass numbers of all isotopes of the element. **23.** element name, symbol, atomic number, atomic mass **24.** They do not react readily with other elements. **25.** C-12 has 6 neutrons; C-14 has 8 neutrons.

Chapter 5 Mastery Test A
Part A **1.** B **2.** A **3.** C **4.** B **5.** D
Part B **6.** A **7.** A **8.** B **9.** B **10.** B **11.** A **12.** B **13.** B **14.** B **15.** A **16.** A **17.** A **18.** B **19.** B **20.** A
Part C Answers will vary but should cover the following points. **21.** A compound can be described by the names and amounts of each element that the compound contains. **22.** When atoms of elements combine to form compounds, they share, lend, or borrow electrons that are in their outermost energy level. **23.** A chemical formula tells what kinds of atoms are in a compound and how many

atoms of each kind are present. The number of atoms is indicated by a subscript. **24.** The first name of the compound is the same as the first element in the compound's formula, or calcium. The second name is the name of the second element with the ending changed to *-ide*, or chloride. The name of the compound is calcium chloride. **25.** The first name of a compound is the same as the first element in the compound's formula. The second name varies, according to the radical the formula contains.

Chapter 5 Mastery Test B
Part A **1.** A **2.** B **3.** A **4.** B **5.** A **6.** B **7.** A **8.** B **9.** A **10.** B **11.** B **12.** B **13.** B **14.** A **15.** A
Part B **16.** B **17.** D **18.** B **19.** A **20.** C
Part C Answers will vary but should cover the following points. **21.** When atoms of elements combine to form compounds, they share, lend, or borrow electrons that are in their outermost energy level. **22.** The first name of a compound is the same as the first element in the compound's formula. The second name varies, according to the radical the formula contains. **23.** A compound can be described by the names and amounts of each element that the compound contains. **24.** The first name of the compound is the same as the first element in the compound's formula, or calcium. The second name is the name of the second element with the ending changed to *-ide*, or chloride. The name of the compound is calcium chloride. **25.** A chemical formula tells what kinds of atoms are in a compound and how many atoms of each kind are present. The number of atoms is indicated by a subscript.

Chapter 6 Mastery Test A
Part A **1.** B **2.** D **3.** C **4.** A **5.** C
Part B **6.** Reactants: H_2SO_4, Zn; Products: $ZnSO_4$, H_2 **7.** Reactant: NaCl; Products: Na, Cl_2 **8.** Reactants: Ca, O_2; Product: CaO_2 **9.** Reactants: Mg, Cl_2; Product: $MgCl_2$ **10.** Reactants: $BaCl_2$, Na_2SO_4; Products: $BaSO_4$, NaCl
Part C **11.** FeS; synthesis **12.** Cl_2; decomposition **13.** 6C; decomposition **14.** Cl_2; single replacement **15.** $AgNO_3$; double replacement
Part D **16.** A reaction occurs when one substance becomes part of another substance. The substances may be heated, mixed, or dissolved for the reaction to occur. **17.** A solute breaks up, or dissolves, into individual molecules when it is placed in a solvent. **18.** Matter cannot be created or destroyed in any chemical change. **19.** Solutions like other mixtures combine different elements without a chemical reaction taking place. Unlike other mixtures, solutions have solutes that dissolve when combined with solvents. **20.** In a synthesis reaction, elements combine to form a compound. In a decomposition reaction, a compound breaks down into two or more simple compounds. In a single-replacement reaction, one element replaces another in a compound. In a double-replacement reaction, the elements in two compounds are exchanged.

Chapter 6 Mastery Test B
Part A **1.** Reactants: $BaCl_2$, Na_2SO_4; Products: $BaSO_4$, NaCl **2.** Reactants: Mg, Cl_2; Product: $MgCl_2$ **3.** Reactants: H_2SO_4, Zn; Products: $ZnSO_4$, H_2 **4.** Reactants: Ca, O_2; Product: CaO_2 **5.** Reactant: NaCl; Products: Na, Cl_2
Part B **6.** FeS; synthesis **7.** 6C; decomposition **8.** Cl_2; single replacement **9.** Cl_2; decomposition **10.** $AgNO_3$; double replacement
Part C **11.** C **12.** C **13.** D **14.** B **15.** A

Part D 16. Solutions like other mixtures combine different elements without a chemical reaction taking place. Unlike other mixtures, solutions have solutes that dissolve when combined with solvents. **17.** In a synthesis reaction, elements combine to form a compound. In a decomposition reaction, a compound breaks down into two or more simple compounds. In a single-replacement reaction, one element replaces another in a compound. In a double-replacement reaction, the elements in two compounds are exchanged. **18.** A solute breaks up, or dissolves, into individual molecules when it is placed in a solvent. **19.** Matter cannot be created or destroyed in any chemical change. **20.** A reaction occurs when one substance becomes part of another substance. The substances may be heated, mixed, or dissolved for the reaction to occur.

Chapter 7 Mastery Test A

Part A 1. C **2.** C **3.** A **4.** D **5.** B **6.** D
Part B 7. 55 mi/hr **8.** 1.23 hr **9.** 225 km **10.** 1.71 km/hr per sec **11.** 7.5 km/hr per sec **12. A** 6.5 hr **B** 375 km
Part C 13. Law 1: If no force acts on an object at rest, it will remain at rest. If the object is moving, it will continue moving at the same speed and in the same direction if no force acts on it. **14.** Law 2: The amount of force needed to produce a given change in the motion of an object depends on the mass of the object. The larger the mass, the more force is needed to give it a certain acceleration. **15.** Law 3: For every action, there is an equal and opposite reaction. Students should correctly explain each law and give reasonable examples.

Chapter 7 Mastery Test B

Part A 1. 1.23 hr **2.** 225 km **3.** 55 mi/hr **4.** 1.71 km/hr per sec **5.** 7.5 km/hr per sec **6. A** 6.5 hr **B** 375 km
Part B 7. C **8.** B **9.** D **10.** A **11.** D **12.** C
Part C 13. Law 1: If no force acts on an object at rest, it will remain at rest. If the object is moving, it will continue moving at the same speed and in the same direction if no force acts on it. **14.** Law 2: The amount of force needed to produce a given change in the motion of an object depends on the mass of the object. The larger the mass, the more force is needed to give it a certain acceleration. **15.** Law 3: For every action, there is an equal and opposite reaction. Students should correctly explain each law and give reasonable examples.

Chapter 8 Mastery Test A

Part A 1. D **2.** C **3.** A **4.** B **5.** D **6.** D **7.** A **8.** A **9.** B
Part B 10. pulley **11.** wedge **12.** wheel and axle
Part C 13. Work is moving an object in the direction of the applied force. **14.** Energy is the ability to do work. **15.** An object in motion has kinetic energy; an object at rest has potential, or stored, energy because it has the potential to move. **16.** chemical, electrical, radiant, mechanical, nuclear, heat **17.** Energy can be changed but it cannot be destroyed or created.
Part D 18. 240 joules **19.** 3 **20. A** 112.5 joules input **B** 100 joules output **C** 89%

Chapter 8 Mastery Test B

Part A 1. wheel and axle **2.** wedge **3.** pulley
Part B 4. D **5.** C **6.** D **7.** D **8.** A **9.** A **10.** A **11.** B **12.** B
Part C 13. 3 **14. A** 112.5 joules input **B** 100 joules output **C** 89% **15.** 240 joules
Part D 16. Energy can be changed but it cannot be destroyed or created. **17.** An object in motion has kinetic energy; an object at rest has potential, or stored, energy because it has the potential to move.

18. Work is moving an object in the direction of the applied force. **19.** Energy is the ability to do work. **20.** chemical, electrical, radiant, mechanical, nuclear, heat

Chapter 9 Mastery Test A

Part A 1. D **2.** A **3.** B **4.** B **5.** C **6.** C
Part B 7. 110 calories **8.** 100 calories **9.** 989 calories **10.** 1,045 calories
Part C Answers may vary, but the following points should be covered. **11.** Heat can be produced by increasing the motion of particles in matter. **12.** Heat can cause particles to move faster and farther apart. It can change matter from a liquid to a gas or a solid to a liquid or cause matter to expand. **13.** The heat of the milk causes the particles of mercury or alcohol in the thermometer to expand and move up the tube until they stop expanding. The coldness of the water causes the particles of mercury or alcohol in the thermometer to contract and move down the tube until they stop contracting. The number on the tube where the liquid stops is the temperature of the milk or water. **14.** Temperature is the measure of how fast molecules in a substance are moving. Heat depends on the temperature of the substance and the substance's mass. **15.** Radiation carries heat across space or through a vacuum, where there is no matter. Conduction carries heat when molecules bump into each other, or transfer energy. Convection moves heat when particles of a gas or liquid rise.

Chapter 9 Mastery Test B

Part A 1. 100 calories **2.** 110 calories **3.** 1,045 calories **4.** 989 calories
Part B 5. A **6.** D **7.** C **8.** B **9.** C **10.** B
Part C Answers may vary, but the following points should be covered. **11.** Heat can cause particles to move faster and farther apart. It can change matter from a liquid to a gas or a solid to a liquid or cause matter to expand. **12.** Radiation carries heat across space or through a vacuum, where there is no matter. Conduction carries heat when molecules bump into each other, or transfer energy. Convection moves heat when particles of a gas or liquid rise. **13.** Heat can be produced by increasing the motion of particles in matter. **14.** Temperature is the measure of how fast molecules in a substance are moving. Heat depends on the temperature of the substance and the substance's mass. **15.** The heat of the milk causes the particles of mercury or alcohol in the thermometer to expand and move up the tube until they stop expanding. The coldness of the water causes the particles of mercury or alcohol in the thermometer to contract and move down the tube until they stop contracting. The number on the tube where the liquid stops is the temperature of the milk or water.

Chapter 10 Mastery Test A

Part A 1. B **2.** D **3.** D **4.** D **5.** B **6.** C
Part B 7. vibrates **8.** waves **9.** matter **10.** molecules **11.** Gases **12.** light; sound **13.** reflected **14.** photons **15.** waves; particles **16.** plane
Part C 17. Light is a form of energy that can be seen. We see objects because light reflects off them. **18.** The seven colors in the visible spectrum are red, orange, yellow, green, blue, indigo, and violet. **19.** Mirrors reflect light rays at an angle that depends on the angle of approach. Lenses refract light rays at an angle that depends on the type and shape of the lens material. **20.** Light is reflected by being bounced off objects. It is refracted, or bent, when it passes through different material that changes its speed and direction.

Chapter 10 Mastery Test B

Part A 1. Gases 2. matter 3. waves 4. vibrates 5. light; sound
6. plane 7. waves; particles 8. molecules 9. photons 10. reflected
Part B 11. D 12. D 13. C 14. A 15. C 16. B
Part C 17. Mirrors reflect light rays at an angle that depends on the angle of approach. Lenses refract light rays at an angle that depends on the type and shape of the lens material. 18. Light is reflected by being bounced off objects. It is refracted, or bent, when it passes through different material that changes its speed and direction.
19. The seven colors in the visible spectrum are red, orange, yellow, green, blue, indigo, and violet. 20. Light is a form of energy that can be seen. We see objects because light reflects off them.

Chapter 11 Mastery Test A

Part A 1. A 2. C 3. B 4. C 5. D
Part B 6. resistance 7. electrical 8. series 9. parallel
Part C 10. A circuit begins at the power source. It travels through the wire to the light bulb. It lights up the bulb and then returns to the power source. 11. Conductors allow electricity to pass through easily; insulators do not allow electricity to pass through easily.
12. Resistance causes electrical energy to change into heat and light energy, so it is useful for household appliances. 13. In a series circuit, current flows through only one path around the circuit. In a parallel circuit, there is more than one path for the current to follow.
14. Electricity is measured in kilowatt-hours, which measure how much electric energy is used. 15. 3.6 amperes

Chapter 11 Mastery Test B

Part A 1. series 2. parallel 3. resistance 4. electrical
Part B 5. B 6. D 7. C 8. A 9. C
Part C 10. Electricity is measured in kilowatt-hours, which measure how much electric energy is used. 11. In a series circuit, current flows through only one path around the circuit. In a parallel circuit, there is more than one path for the current to follow. 12. A circuit begins at the power source. It travels through the wire to the light bulb. It lights up the bulb and then returns to the power source.
13. Resistance causes electrical energy to change into heat and light energy, so it is useful for household appliances. 14. 3.6 amperes
15. Conductors allow electricity to pass through easily; insulators do not allow electricity to pass through easily.

Chapter 12 Mastery Test A

Part A 1. C 2. B 3. D 4. B 5. A 6. A
Part B 7. F 8. E 9. H 10. B 11. G 12. A 13. C 14. D
Part C 15. A magnetic field is an area in which magnetic forces can attract or repel other magnets. 16. Atoms line up in some substances so that most atoms are in the same direction. This grouping causes a substance to act like a magnet. 17. The hands of the compass are attracted to Earth's magnetic pole. 18. Both halves become magnets with a north pole and a south pole. 19. Electromagnetism is using electricity to produce a temporary magnet by passing a current through a wire wrapped around an iron core. An electromagnet works as long as current flows through it. 20. Accept any description that identifies and explains the use of electromagnets. Students might note that telephones use electromagnets to change electric currents into sound waves, cranes use it to pick up scrap metal, motors use it to make appliances and vehicles work, and the maglev train uses it to travel fast above rails.

Chapter 12 Mastery Test B

Part A 1. D 2. C 3. A 4. G 5. B 6. H 7. E 8. F
Part B 9. D 10. C 11. B 12. A 13. A 14. B
Part C 15. Atoms line up in some substances so that most atoms are in the same direction. This grouping causes a substance to act like a magnet. 16. The hands of the compass are attracted to Earth's magnetic pole. 17. A magnetic field is an area in which magnetic forces can attract or repel other magnets. 18. Electromagnetism is using electricity to produce a temporary magnet by passing a current through a wire wrapped around an iron core. An electromagnet works as long as current flows through it. 19. Accept any description that identifies and explains the use of electromagnets. Students might note that telephones use electromagnets to change electric currents into sound waves, cranes use it to pick up scrap metal, motors use it to make appliances and vehicles work, and the maglev train uses it to travel fast above rails. 20. Both halves become magnets with a north pole and a south pole.

Midterm Mastery Test

Part A 1. C **2.** D **3.** B **4.** B **5.** C **6.** A **7.** C **8.** D **9.** D **10.** A

Part B 11. matter **12.** Physics **13.** centimeter **14.** properties
15. density **16.** gravity **17.** liquid **18.** element **19.** electrons
20. atomic number **21.** noble gas **22.** chemical change
23. hydroxyl (OH) **24.** chemical **25.** synthesis

Part C 26. I **27.** A **28.** H **29.** E **30.** K **31.** O **32.** Q **33.** G **34.** N
35. M **36.** B **37.** P **38.** R **39.** F **40.** L **41.** D **42.** C **43.** J

Part D 44. 1,296 cm^3 **45.** 19.3 g/cm^3 **46.** 53 p, 74 n, 53 e **47. A** Br_2
B single-replacement reaction **C** NaBr, Cl_2; Br_2, NaCl

Part E 48. When atoms of elements combine to form compounds, they share, lend, or borrow electrons that are in their outermost energy level. **49.** Both are elements. Most metals are solids that can be made shiny, can be shaped into sheets or wires, and are good conductors of electricity and heat. Most nonmetals are solids or gases, are not shiny, cannot be shaped into sheets or wires, and do not carry electricity or heat well. **50.** Atomic number and mass number are ways to identify elements. Atomic number is the number of protons in the nucleus of each atom of an element. Mass number is the number of protons plus the number of neutrons in an atom of an element.

Final Mastery Test

Part A 1. A **2.** C **3.** C **4.** B **5.** D **6.** A **7.** A **8.** C **9.** B **10.** D **11.** B
12. B **13.** D **14.** C **15.** A

Part B 16. matter **17.** Density **18.** mass number **19.** metal
20. hydrogen **21.** decomposition reaction **22.** speed
23. direction **24.** distance **25.** potential **26.** increasing **27.** freezing
28. echo **29.** light **30.** terminal **31.** electricity (or current) **32.** flowing **33.** electromagnetism **34.** attract **35.** screw **36.** slowdown
37. solution **38.** subscript **39.** symbol **40.** negative **41.** balance
42. kilometer **43.** static electricity **44.** sonar **45.** conductors

Part C 46. 7,500 cm^3 **47.** 19.3 g/cm^3 **48. A** 13 p **B** 14 n **C** 13 e
49. A Cl_2 **B** decomposition **50.** To balance the equation, add 4 to Fe to make 4Fe. Reactants: Fe, O_2; Products: Fe_2O_3 **51.** 405 km
52. 225 joules **53. A** 75 joules **B** 40 joules **C** 53.3% **54.** 3.3 amperes
55. 10°C **56.** Newton's Second Law of Motion **57. A** displacement of water method **B** Record the volume of water in a graduated cylinder. Then place the seashell in the cylinder and record the new volume. Then subtract the original volume of water from the volume containing the seashell; the difference is the volume of the seashell.

Part D 58. When atoms of elements combine to form compounds, they share, lend, or borrow electrons that are in their outermost energy level. **59.** A reaction occurs when one substance becomes part of another substance. The reaction may occur through heating, mixing, or dissolving the substances. **60.** Answers may appear in any order: chemical, heat, mechanical, nuclear, radiant, electrical. **61.** Radiation carries heat across space, or through a vacuum where there is no matter. Conduction carries heat when molecules bump into each other, or transfer energy. Convection moves heat when particles of a gas or liquid rise. **62.** Resistance causes electricity to change into heat and light, allowing many appliances to work. **63.** In series circuits, all current flows through a single path. In parallel circuits, current flows through more than one path. **64.** In a physical change, the substance remains the same, but some of its properties change. In a chemical change, a new substance is produced and the elements react with one another. An example of each is the physical change that results from tearing a sheet of paper in half, and the chemical change produced when burning a sheet of paper. **65.** Atoms line up in some substances so that most atoms are arranged in the same direction. This grouping causes a substance to act like a magnet.

Materials List for Physical Science Lab Manual

Note: The quantities of materials listed here are enough for one student. Students can do some of these activities in pairs or groups. The Lab Manual worksheets for the Investigations in the Student Edition are identified in this list.

Chapter 1

Lab Manual 1: Safety in the Classroom
meterstick, meter ruler, colored pencil

Lab Manual 2: Hands Instead of Feet
Investigation 1-1
meterstick; a variety of objects that are longer than a hand's width with at least one object that is longer than a meter

Lab Manual 3: Counting Squares and Calculating Area
Investigation 1-2
safety glasses, small sheets of construction paper in various sizes, large sheet of paper, ruler, safety scissors

Lab Manual 4: Finding Volume
metric ruler; rectangular boxes, such as cereal boxes, CD boxes, toothpaste boxes, pizza boxes, shoe boxes, or film boxes

Chapter 2

Lab Manual 5: Identifying Properties
Investigation 2-1
bag with 5 objects for each group, including one regular-shaped object; balance; hand lens; metric ruler
Choose objects that won't break or crumble.

Lab Manual 6: Measuring Mass
balance, standard masses, penny, nickel, dime, quarter, pen, pencil, 2 other small objects to be chosen by student

Lab Manual 7: Measuring Volume
cap from tube of toothpaste, graduated cylinder, paper towels, cap from mouthwash bottle, penny, marble, stone, game die, metric ruler

Lab Manual 8: Finding Density
Investigation 2-2
safety glasses, 2 plastic graduated cylinders, balance, cooking oil, water, paper cups, paper towels

Chapter 3

Lab Manual 9: Inferring the Properties of an Object
safety glasses; clay; small object, such as a short piece of chalk, pencil eraser, or coin; paper clip

Lab Manual 10: Breaking Down Water
Investigation 3-1
safety glasses; beaker or wide-mouth jar; water (distilled water preferred); two 50-cm long pieces of copper wire with about 3 cm of insulation removed at ends; one 15-cm long piece of copper wire with about 3 cm of insulation removed at ends; 2 six-volt batteries; 1 teaspoon table salt, stirring rod or plastic straw; salt water; 2 test tubes; sandpaper or scissors; paper towels
Have extra batteries available.

Lab Manual 11: Making Models of Atoms
Investigation 3-2
safety glasses, 3 different-colored pieces of modeling clay, craft sticks, metric ruler, corn starch

Lab Manual 12: Exploring the Space Between Particles
safety glasses, three 250-mL beakers, marbles, sand, water, paper towels

Chapter 4

Lab Manual 13: Finding Iron in Your Cereal
Investigation 4-1
safety glasses, iron-fortified cereal (flakes), self-sealing sandwich bag, 250-mL beaker or large plastic or paper cups, warm water, rubber band, bar magnet, craft stick or pencil, white paper, hand lens, paper towels

Lab Manual 14: Exploring Elements
encyclopedia or other reference materials, index cards

Lab Manual 15: Analyzing Common Compounds
safety glasses, hand lens, salt, baking soda, sugar, water, nail polish remover, vinegar, paper towels

Lab Manual 16: Electricity and Metals
Investigation 4-2
safety glasses; sandpaper; 3 pieces of copper wire, each 0.25 m long; electrical tape; 1.5-volt D-cell battery; standard bulb in socket; sample of sulfur; piece of aluminum foil, about 5 cm long; lead pencil
Have extra 1.5-volt D-cell batteries available.

Chapter 5

Lab Manual 17: Observing a Chemical Change
Investigation 5-1
safety glasses; 2 small jars with lids, such as baby food jars; distilled water; washing soda; 2 plastic spoons; Epsom salts; clock; soft-drink bottle; vinegar; baking soda; balloon; paper towels

Lab Manual 18: Observing a Chemical Reaction
safety glasses, calcium chloride $(CaCl)$, baking soda $(NaHCO_3)$, spoon, locking plastic bag, small paper cup, water (H_2O), graduated cylinder, paper towels

Lab Manual 19: Exploring Acidity
safety glasses, salt, spoon, drinking straw, orange juice, dish-washing liquid, red litmus paper, 6 small paper cups, water, vinegar, milk, antacid liquid, blue litmus paper, paper towels

Lab Manual 20: Identifying Acids and Bases
Investigation 5-2
safety glasses; marker; 8 small paper cups; spoon; aspirin tablet; baking soda; white vinegar; lemon juice, fresh, frozen, or bottled (one lemon yields about 25–30 mL juice); weak ammonia solution; soap (any kind of liquid soap); soft drink (clear soft drink such as lemon lime); milk of magnesia; red-cabbage juice (small head of cabbage makes about 500 mL of cabbage juice); graduated cylinder; litmus paper; paper towels

Chapter 6

Lab Manual 21: Speed of Dissolving
safety glasses, 4 beakers, water, 4 sugar cubes, metal spoon, clock with second hand, paper towels

Lab Manual 22: Separating a Mixture
Investigation 6-1
safety glasses, spoon, 2 g washed sand, 2 g table salt (sodium chloride, NaCl), sheet of paper, stirring rod or plastic spoon or straw, graduated cylinder, 200 mL water, 2 beakers, circular piece of filter paper or paper towel, funnel, hand lens, paper towels

Lab Manual 23: Temperature and Chemical Reactions
safety glasses, 2 balloons, 2 one-hole rubber stoppers, 2 flasks, 250 mL hot water, 250 mL cold water, 4 antacid tablets, clock with second hand, paper towels

Lab Manual 24: Observing Different Kinds of Reactions
Investigation 6-2
safety glasses, small piece of steel wool (the kind without soap), tongs, Bunsen burner, test-tube rack, 4 test tubes, hydrogen peroxide solution (H_2O_2), manganese dioxide (MnO_2), match, wooden splint, copper sulfate solution $(CuSO_4)$, uncoated iron nail, sodium carbonate solution (Na_2CO_3), calcium chloride solution $(CaCl_2)$, paper towels
Large fireplace matches, broken into small pieces, can be used in place of wooden splints. You can make test-tube racks from empty milk cartons.

Chapter 7

Lab Manual 25: Finding Speed
Investigation 7-1
safety glasses, 2 books, meterstick, marble, stopwatch or watch that shows seconds, graph paper that contains large intervals

Lab Manual 26: Exploring Acceleration
safety glasses; cork; needle, piece of thread, 20 cm long; 2-L plastic soft-drink bottle with cap; masking tape; water; paper towels

Lab Manual 27: Newton's First Law of Motion
safety glasses, shoe box, scissors, tennis ball, index card, quarter

Lab Manual 28: Newton's Third Law of Motion
Investigation 7-2
safety glasses; string, 3 meters long; 2 straws; 2 chairs; 2 long balloons; masking tape

Chapter 8

Lab Manual 29: Mass, Height, and Energy
Investigation 8-1
safety glasses, paper cup, grooved ruler, textbook, safety scissors, small marble, large marble

Lab Manual 30: Finding the Mechanical Advantage of a Lever
Investigation 8-2
safety glasses, spring scale, 200-g weight, rubber band or masking tape to attach the weight, stiff meterstick, triangular wooden wedge or other fulcrum

Materials List for Physical Science Lab Manual

Lab Manual 31: Exploring Pulleys
safety glasses, masking tape, 2 lightweight metal or stiff metersticks, 2 chairs, 3 pulleys, string, 50 g mass, 10 g mass, spring scale

Lab Manual 32: Exploring an Inclined Plane
safety glasses; skateboard; spring scale; string; board, 2 m long; meterstick

Chapter 9

Lab Manual 33: Exploring Heat and Motion of Particles
safety glasses, 3 beakers, room-temperature water, ice cube, hot water, dark food coloring, dropper, lock, paper towels

Lab Manual 34: Observing and Comparing Expansion and Contraction of Gases

Investigation 9-1
safety glasses, balloon with opening that fits over mouth of flask, 500–1,000 mL flask or large plastic storage container, masking tape or electrical tape, 2 buckets, cold water, warm water, paper towels, ice (optional; to add to cold water), paper towels
Have extra balloons available.

Lab Manual 35: Measuring the Rate of Heat Loss

Investigation 9-2
safety glasses; large plastic jar; hot tap water; small plastic jar; 2 Celsius alcohol thermometers, each about 1 ft long; clock or watch; ice water; cloth towels; aluminum foil; paper towels

Lab Manual 36: Exploring Heat Absorption
safety glasses; 2 empty frozen juice cans, black construction paper, white construction paper, scissors, tape, water, black cardboard, white cardboard, 2 thermometers, sunlight or 2 lamps with 100-watt bulbs, paper towels

Chapter 10

Lab Manual 37: Making Musical Sounds
8 empty 16-oz glass bottles, masking tape, water, graduated cylinder, paper towels

Lab Manual 38: Inferring How Sound Waves Travel

Investigation 10-1
safety glasses, pencil with sharpened point, 8-oz or larger plastic-foam cup, 2 thick rubber bands, plastic food wrap, salt, plastic beaker, water, tuning fork, paper towels

Lab Manual 39: Measuring Angles of Reflected Rays

Investigation 10-2
safety glasses, 4" x 6" mirror, textbook, masking tape, unlined white paper, pencil, flashlight, comb that is long enough to cover more than half the flashlight lens, protractor, ruler, sheet of white paper
Have extra flashlight batteries available.

Lab Manual 40: Making a Pinhole Camera
safety glasses, empty oatmeal box, waxed paper, rubber band, pin

Chapter 11

Lab Manual 41: Exploring Electric Charges
safety glasses, meterstick, masking tape, 2 balloons, string, wool cloth

Lab Manual 42: Identifying Electric Conductors
safety glasses, graduated cylinder, spoon, salt, mineral oil, rubbing alcohol, dry-cell battery, 3 wires with insulation removed from ends, 8 paper cups, baking soda, 4 drinking straws, sugar, orange juice, vinegar, lightbulb and holder, 2 nails, water, paper towels

Lab Manual 43: Constructing Series Circuits

Investigation 11-1
safety glasses; two 1.5-volt dry-cell batteries; 2 holders for batteries; 2 flashlight bulbs; 2 bulb sockets; 1.5 m long piece of common bell wire, cut into various lengths; switch; 1 to 3 additional 1.5-volt dry-cell batteries; 1 to 3 additional flashlight bulbs; sandpaper or scissors
Have extra batteries and bulbs available.

Lab Manual 44: Constructing Parallel Circuits

Investigation 11-2
safety glasses; two 6-volt dry-cell batteries; 2 holders for batteries; 3 flashlight bulbs; 3 bulb sockets; 1.5 m long piece of common bell wire, cut into various lengths; switch; sandpaper or scissors
Have extra batteries and bulbs available.

Chapter 12

Lab Manual 45: Exploring Magnetism
safety glasses, clamp, bar magnet, paper clip, sheet of paper, cotton fabric, plastic wrap, support stand, rod, thread, metric ruler, copper sheet, aluminum foil, plywood, paper towels

Lab Manual 46: Observing Magnetic Lines of Force

Investigation 12-1
safety glasses, 2 bar magnets, 2 horseshoe magnets, 2 sheets of paper, cup of iron filings in shaker-type container, metal bar that attracts a magnet, pencil

Lab Manual 47: Experimenting with a Compass
safety glasses, small piece of sponge, tray, magnetic compass, iron nail, steel paper clip, needle, bar magnet, correction fluid, water, crumpled paper ball, wooden pencil, eraser, paper towels

Lab Manual 48: Constructing an Electromagnet

Investigation 12-2
safety glasses; copper wire, 0.5 m long; large nail; metric ruler; electrical tape; 1.5-volt D-cell battery; paper clips; iron filings in shaker-type container; sheet of paper
Have extra batteries available.

Some Suppliers of Science Education Materials

Carolina Biological Supply Company
700 York Road
Burlington, NC 27215
800-334-5551
Fax: 800-222-7112
www.carolina.com

Fisher Science Education
4500 Turnberry Drive
Hanover Park, PA 60133
800-955-1177
Fax: 800-955-0740
www.fisheredu.com

NASCO
901 Janesville Avenue
Fort Atkinson, WI 53538
800-558-9595
Fax: 920-563-8296
www.nascofa.com

Sargent-Welch
P.O. Box 5229
Buffalo Grove, IL 60089-5229
800-727-4368
Fax: 800-676-2540
www.Sargentwelch.com

**National Science
Teachers Association (NSTA)**
1840 Wilson Blvd.
Arlington, VA 22201
703-243-7100
nsta.org
suppliers.nsta.org for supplier list

Teacher Questionnaire

Attention Teachers! As publishers of *Physical Science,*
we would like your help in making this textbook more valuable to you.
Please take a few minutes to fill out this survey. Your feedback will
help us to better serve you and your students.

1. What is your position and major area of responsibility? _____

   _____

   _____

2. Briefly describe your setting:

   ____ regular education ____ special education ____ adult basic education

   ____ community college ____ university ____ other _____

3. The enrollment in your classroom includes students with the following
   (check all that apply):

   ____ at-risk for failure ____ low reading ability ____ behavior problems

   ____ learning disabilities ____ ESL ____ other _____

4. Grade level of your students: _____

5. Racial/ethnic groups represented in your classes (check all that apply):

   ____ African-American ____ Asian ____ Caucasian ____ Hispanic

   ____ Native American ____ Other

6. School Location:

   ____ urban ____ suburban ____ rural ____ other _____

7. What reaction did your students have to the materials? (Include comments about
   the cover design, lesson format, illustrations, etc.)

   _____

   _____

   _____

8. What features in the student text helped your students the most?

   _____

   _____

9. What features in the student text helped your students the least? Please include suggestions for changing these to make the text more relevant.

    _____

    _____

10. How did you use the Teacher's Edition and support materials, and what features did you find to be the most helpful?

    _____

    _____

11. What activity from the program did your students benefit from the most? Please briefly explain.

    _____

    _____

    _____

12. Optional: Share an activity that you used to teach the materials in your classroom that enhanced the learning and motivation of your students.

    _____

    _____

    _____

Several activities will be selected to be included in future editions. Please include your name, address, and phone number so we may contact you for permission and possible payment to use the material.

Thank you!

▼ fold in thirds and tape shut at the top ▼

- -